Forest Fragmentation
in the
Southern Rocky Mountains

The frontiers have been explored and crossed. It is probably time we settled down. It is probably time we looked around us instead of looking ahead. We need to know our history in much greater depth. . . . Plunging into the future through a landscape that had no history, we did both the country and ourselves some harm along with some good. Neither the country nor the society we built out of it can be healthy until we stop the raiding and running, and learn to be quiet part of the time, and acquire the sense not of ownership but of belonging.

—WALLACE STEGNER, *Where the Bluebird Sings to the Lemonade Springs: Living and Writing in the West* (1992)

Forest Fragmentation
in the
Southern Rocky Mountains

Edited by

Richard L. Knight

Frederick W. Smith

Steven W. Buskirk

William H. Romme

William L. Baker

University Press of Colorado

Copyright © 2000 by the University Press of Colorado
International Standard Book Number 0-87081-541-5

Published by the University Press of Colorado
5589 Arapahoe Avenue, Suite 206C
Boulder, Colorado 80303

The University Press of Colorado is a cooperative publishing enterprise supported, in part, by Adams State College, Colorado State University, Fort Lewis College, Mesa State College, Metropolitan State College of Denver, University of Colorado, University of Northern Colorado, University of Southern Colorado, and Western State College of Colorado.

The paper used in this publication meets the minimum requirements of the American National Standard for Information Sciences—Permanence of Paper for Printed Library Materials. ANSI Z39.48-1984

Library of Congress Cataloging-in-Publication Data

Forest fragmentation in the southern Rocky Mountains / Richard L.
    Knight . . . [et al.].
        p.   cm.
    Includes bibliographical references.
    ISBN 0-87081-541-5 (alk. paper)
    1. Fragmented landscapes—Rocky Mountains. I. Knight, Richard L.
QH541.15.F73F65 2000
333.75'0978—dc21   99-42729
                                                                 CIP

09 08 07 06 05 04 03 02 01 00   10 9 8 7 6 5 4 3 2 1

To the women and men of natural resource agencies and organizations who work to restore land health to the Southern Rocky Mountains.

Contents

Contents

Contents

Preface

Most of what humans do fragments landscapes. The very act of being human seems inevitably to draw administrative lines across the land that often result in sharp demarcations embedded in ecosystems. Whether building roads, trails, or houses, cutting forests, or developing recreational areas, humans divide and shape the landscape into smaller pieces with configurations and edges controlled by our activities rather than those of nature. As we increasingly use public lands, these regions undergo a transition from natural areas with human-altered habitat embedded within it, to managed landscapes that contain natural habitat remnants. Because virtually everything humans do fragments landscapes, conservation of regional biota depends on the retention and management of these habitat remnants. In addition, it is incumbent for land managers to consider management actions that minimize human-caused fragmentation and that encourage landscape connectivity. Natural resource managers, therefore, are faced with the dual issues of what conservation values are associated with habitat remnants, and the broader landscapes within which these remnants are embedded.

This book is about a place, the Southern Rocky Mountains of South Dakota, Wyoming, Colorado, and New Mexico (although the latter is minimally covered in our material). The forests of the Southern Rockies have seen extensive human alterations. Many forest communities had been extensively logged at the turn of the century to support mining, railroad construction, and homestead activities. Forests of the Southern Rocky Mountains are also characterized by natural patchiness due to a variety of natural ecological processes (e.g., fires, avalanches, windstorms, disease outbreaks) and physical characteristics (i.e., slope, aspect, elevation, soil type). In addition, forest practices and policies that relate to forest inholdings, logging, mining, outdoor recreation, and fire suppression have altered these historic forests.

Because sustaining biological diversity within a region requires knowledge of regional flora and fauna and the processes that affect these communities, a synthesis of what is now known about forests and fragmentation in the Southern Rockies will contribute to natural resources management in this area. That is the purpose of this book. The contributors of our book believe that it is imperative to summarize what is known regarding fragmentation in our region. This will result in management schemes based on ideas from studies in our region and augmented from studies elsewhere. We hope that such a book will allow a better understanding of the effects of changes in spatial arrangements of plant communities on the diversity of species and natural ecological processes within these ecosystems.

Chapter authors in this book describe the current state of understanding of fragmentation and its ecological conseque ces in the Southern Rocky Mountains. They also draw upon their experience in this region to critically evaluate some of the leading ideas and theories in conservation biology and landscape ecology. Ecologists are working to develop a general theory and conceptual framework for understanding the effects of landscape heterogeneity and patch structure on wildlife population viability, movement of materials and organisms, biogeochemical cycling, and other ecological processes that operate at broad spatial and temporal scales. Authors in this book have evaluated our current state of knowledge of these topics in the context of a detailed case study of a region that has received relatively little attention to date. Therefore, we hope the book will be of interest and value to scientists, managers, students, and the general public who are concerned with these issues in the Southern Rocky Mountains.

Acknowledgments

This book would not have been possible without the farsighted-ness of Susan Gray of the USDA Forest Service. Susan believed that a synthesis of what was known regarding forest health in the Southern Rocky Mountains was necessary in order to get on with the proper stewardship of these prodigious public lands. She secured the neces-sary resources for a two-day conference at Colorado State University on this topic and encouraged us to edit the presentations in a book. Samantha J. Rayroux served as copy editor for the book. She took some-times unreadable prose and helped make it both more correct and more understandable. For her untiring work and devotion to this project we owe her a debt we cannot easily repay.

Richard L. Knight thanks the students and faculty of Colorado State University for their encouragement and support of his intellec-tual efforts over the years. By their criticism and ideas he has benefit-ted enormously. His research on Colorado forests has been funded by the Colorado Division of Wildlife, the City of Boulder Open Space Program, and the regional office of the USDA Forest Service. Frederick W. Smith thanks all those he has worked with these past decades for their inspiration and criticism. William H. Romme thanks Fort Lewis College and Harvard University, respectively, for a sabbatical leave and Bullard Fellowship during the academic year 1997–1998, which pro-vided time for thinking and working on this book. The San Juan Na-tional Forest also supported research on twentieth-century changes in the forests of southwestern Colorado, which contributed directly to some of the ideas presented in this book. Steven W. Buskirk thanks the Wyoming Game and Fish Department for its support of research on forest fragmentation issues. William L. Baker thanks the University of Wyoming for a sabbatical leave during the academic year 1997–1998 which provided time for working on this book. Finally, we are in-debted to the staff of the University Press of Colorado and, in particu-lar, to Laura Furney, who made this project her own.

Forest Fragmentation

in the

Southern Rocky Mountains

Part One

Patterns and Processes of Forest Fragmentation
in the Southern Rocky Mountains

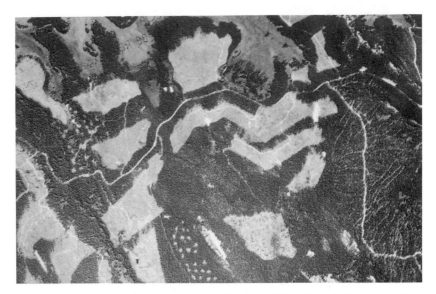

Fig. 1.1. Perforation and fragmentation of forest resulting from timber harvesting, Rock Creek, Medicine Bow National Forest, Wyoming, 1983. Shown are natural openings (top), clear-cuts, patch cuts (bottom and left), commercial thinning with skid trails (right) and logging roads. U.S. Forest Service photo.

Fig. 1.2. Invasion of herbaceous meadow by bristlecone pine, Spanish Peaks, Colorado. Photo by W. L. Baker.

1

An Overview of Forest Fragmentation in the Southern Rocky Mountains

Steven W. Buskirk, William H. Romme,
Frederick W. Smith, and Richard L. Knight

INTRODUCTION

Human-caused forest fragmentation is, to various beholders, a source of satisfaction at resources well managed, cause for grave environmental concern, or imperceptible altogether. Some see in clear-cutting (Fig. 1.1) a reasoned, cost-effective, and sustainable method of timber harvest, whereas others see resource exploitation, with profound ecological implications, run amuck. A system of roads (Fig. 1.2) with a mean density of 1.5 km/km² in some national forests (Baker and Knight, *this volume*) is viewed by some as necessary to facilitate timber harvest and motorized recreation, but by others as the mycelia of resource decay, reducing wildlife habitat values substantively and wilderness values to nil. Likewise, the construction of homes in wildland forests (Fig. 1.3) is for some the fulfillment of a personal dream, but for others the creation of multiple new resource conflicts involving wildfire, wildlife, and scenic values, where none existed before. And, the decline, through time, in numbers of nesting neotropical migrant birds is invisible to most forest users, but to others a dramatic and clear consequence of increased nest predation along forest edges created by roads (Fig. 1.2) and recreational trails (Knight, *this volume*).

The polarity and variation in acuity of views regarding how human actions affect forest-dominated landscapes (Figs. 1.1–1.5) in the Rocky Mountains is the cause of much controversy and complication in decision making. Although issues in life zones other than forests in the Rocky Mountain region provoke similar debate, forests are unique in the Southern Rocky Mountains in the controversy they spawn about

Fig. 1.3. Residential development, including a golf course, in mixed conifer forest, Middle Park, Colorado, 1998. Photo by S. W. Buskirk.

the propriety, sustainability, and consequences to biological diversity of multiple land uses.

This difference is for several reasons. First, forests are generally rare in Colorado and Wyoming, with about 19.7% of Wyoming (Merrill 1996) and 33.2% of Colorado (Colorado Gap Analysis Project, *unpublished data*) in forest and woodland cover types (Table 1.1). Second, by virtue of their large quantities of biomass relative to other community types (e.g., grassland, shrubland, and tundra) in this region, forests present special problems and opportunities. For example, short-term opportunities for timber extraction result in multi-decade effects, or constraints are put on motorized access because of the barriers presented by trees. As a correlate, discontinuities of forest cover, such as those caused by clear-cutting and fire, are, in comparison with disturbances in grasslands, more visible for a longer time to the lay person. Third, forested lands in the Southern Rockies generally occur above the elevational limit of crop agriculture and industrial development. Therefore, forested systems tend to retain the character of wildlands, whereas lands at lower elevations tend to be dominated by agricultural, industrial, and residential development. Thus, montane forests, more than lower elevation areas, tend to be forested wildlands with developed enclaves. This mix of wilderness and development at

Fig. 1.4. Ski area development, including ski runs on north-facing slopes, and business and residential buildings in a riparian zone, Copper Mountain, Colorado, 1998. Photo by S. W. Buskirk.

Fig. 1.5. A secondary forest road, Medicine Bow National Forest, Wyoming, 1997. Photo by W. L. Baker.

Table 1.1. Forested cover types (area [10³ ha] and % of total area of the state) in Colorado and Wyoming. Colorado data are unpublished, from Colorado Gap Analysis project, Wyoming data from Merrill (1996).

	Colorado		Wyoming		Total
Forest types	*area*	*%*	*area*	*%*	*area*
Spruce-fir	1,882	7.0	611	2.5	2,493
Douglas fir	433	1.6	363	1.5	796
Lodgepole pine	877	3.3	1,502	6.1	2,379
Whitebark pine	0	0.0	68	0.3	68
Limber pine woodland	1	<0.1	196	0.8	197
Ponderosa pine	1,394	5.2	663	2.7	2,057
Piñon-juniper woodland	2,507	9.3	0	0.0	2,507
Juniper woodland	468	1.7	493	2.0	961
Aspen forest	1,271	4.7	327	1.3	1,598
Burr oak woodland	0	0.0	27	0.1	27
Forest-dominated riparian	83	0.3	297	1.2	380
Other forest	54	0.1	309	1.2	363
Total Forest	8,969	33.2	4,856	19.7	13,825

times leads to fierce philosophical and policy battles about land uses that would not occur in farmlands or suburbs. Lastly, and related to their occurring at high elevations, forests in the Southern Rockies are publicly owned to a greater degree than other land types, having been passed over by homesteaders and then withdrawn from settlement, beginning with the Yellowstone Forest Reserve in 1891 (Frome 1962). For Wyoming, only 23.4% of forested lands are privately owned. Of 12 forest cover types in Wyoming, only forest-dominated riparian (75%) and ponderosa pine (64%) are predominantly private (Merrill 1996). The public ownership of forests of the Rocky Mountains results in involvement by a pluralistic public in decisions about how forests are managed.

HISTORY OF THOUGHT ABOUT FOREST FRAGMENTATION IN THE ROCKIES

Interest in human-caused discontinuities in Rocky Mountain forests has a history of over a century, and of being much influenced by events elsewhere. Some of the earliest writings about Rocky Mountain forests refer to fires set by Indians and Euro-Americans (reviewed by Gruell 1985), often in pejorative terms. On the other hand, timber harvest for human uses was regarded in a more positive light. Early mining led to clear-cutting near mine sites for cabins and mine supports, and hewn logs were used for the railroad tie industry (Fig. 1.6; Knight 1994).

The effect of forest cutting on vertebrates was generally seen positively early in this century. Leopold (1933), for example, referred mostly to Midwestern game species when he wrote, "A majority of game species are associated with an interspersion of the early and intermediate stages of plant succession." However, his view was applied more broadly. As late as the 1960s, pristine coniferous forest was considered "a biological desert, as far as most wildlife is concerned" (Allen and Sharpe 1960). Events of the next twenty years would force fundamental change in how we view the relationships among forest successional stage, timber cutting, and biodiversity.

From the Pacific Northwest we have adopted the concept and terminology (Harris 1984, Thomas et al. 1988) of old-growth forests: late successional forests with multiple tree species dominant; trees of highly variable sizes and ages, including large, old trees; large amounts of coarse woody debris; and small gaps in the canopy. Also in the Northwest we have witnessed extensive and highly controversial clear-cutting of public forests, the endangerment and possible extinction of vertebrate taxa because of timber harvest (Harris 1984), and major controversies over the effects of timber harvest on biodiversity (Lehmkuhl and Ruggiero 1991). From the tropics we have learned how forests contribute to biodiversity and how their conversion to other uses has impacted global biodiversity (Groom and Schumaker 1993). And from the southeastern United States we have discovered that some species, now endangered, have specific needs for late successional stages that are difficult or impossible to reconstruct (Simberloff 1994).

ATTRIBUTES OF ROCKY MOUNTAIN FORESTS

Rocky Mountain forests differ from those in the Pacific Northwest and elsewhere in fundamental ways that affect how we can extrapolate from those settings to here. First, Rocky Mountain forests are naturally patchy, being island remnants of late Pleistocene forests that were more widespread 20,000–10,000 years ago than today (Findley and Anderson 1956). This means that human-caused fragmentation is superimposed on existing heterogeneity, confounding the question of what is "good" or natural heterogeneity and what is "bad." Second, most Rocky Mountain forest types were, at the time of the Europeans' arrival, themselves the products of episodic disturbance, especially fire (Peet 1988). Fires were, in turn, probably strongly influenced by indigenous Americans,

Fig. 1.6. Tie hacking, one of the earliest forms of forest fragmentation caused by European humans. *Top:* A tie hacker hand hewing a tie with a broadaxe. Photo courtesy of Univ. of Wyoming, American Heritage Center, Albert Thompson Collection. *Bottom:* Ties and saw logs being driven down a river, Cheyenne National Forest. Photo courtesy of Univ. of Wyoming, American Heritage Center, William H. Wroten Collection.

who set them to signal and to improve forage for wildlife and horses. Lodgepole pine, ponderosa pine, and quaking aspen were all influenced strongly by fire, lodgepole and aspen being regarded as post-fire seral types. The open character of ponderosa pine during the period of indigenous settlement was the result of frequent low-intensity fires (Peet 1988), which limited understory plants and regeneration by ponderosas. Thus, disturbance, the primary mechanism of human-caused fragmentation, also has helped sculpt the Rocky Mountain landscapes that we value so highly. Last, timber cutting in Rocky Mountain forests takes the form of rather small clear-cuts, at times referred to as perforations (Forman 1995), in contrast to the large-patch clear-cutting in some other areas (Harris 1984). In the Northwest, for example, cutting has left islands of pristine forest in a matrix of clear-cuts that, over time, recover their forest character. Because of the relatively smaller amount of forest in our region and cutting patterns, timber harvesting in the Rocky Mountains makes a small contribution to the national wood supply, with only 5% of the nation's timber harvest coming from the Rocky Mountains in 1991, compared with 23% from Pacific Coast forests and 55% from forests of the South (Darr 1995).

What Is Fragmentation?

"Fragmentation" is a sweeping term for a host of processes related to the disruption of continuity in predominantly natural landscapes (Lord and Norton 1990). Forman (1995) uses "land conversion" for these processes collectively, of which he considers fragmentation only one. Here, we limit "fragmentation" to human-caused patterns, reserving "natural patchiness" or "natural heterogeneity" for others. Still, "fragmentation" is neither precise nor comprehensive. For example, in Rocky Mountain forests, livestock grazing and pollution of water by mine leachates are two important human-caused processes that fall outside the umbrella of what is usually considered forest fragmentation. Although, as the following chapters show, the meaning of "fragmentation" varies among observers, certain features can be stated with certainty. First, fragmentation is context-specific. The fragmentation of one cover or habitat type invariably results in the expansion and joining of another type. Thus referring to the fragmentation of a complex landscape that includes nonforest as well as forest types makes little sense without specifying what is being fragmented and, by inference, what is being joined and expanded. Customary usage is to refer to the fragmentation of late successional forest by early successional stands or to the fragmentation of forests by other land uses, such as roads. However, the reverse meaning is sometimes used, implying that late successional stands can fragment younger ones, or that nonforest types (e.g., grasslands) can be fragmented by expansion of forest (Fig. 1.5), such as has occurred in the Black Hills (Knight 1994). Such encroachment of forest into herbaceous or shrub types has been considered to be important in the decline and loss of populations of bighorn sheep in Colorado (Wakelyn 1987).

Second, fragmentation involves a reduction of total area and the interior area (the area more than some specified distance within a fragmenting feature like a clear-cut) of a cover type, but can reflect variable effects on density of edges, connectivity of forest patches, and other landscape attributes. Third, fragmentation is taken to include, and by some to require, secondary effects associated with human-caused discontinuities (e.g., roads), including behavioral disturbance of wildlife by humans and their vehicles, increased hunting pressure, increased predation by generalist vertebrates, increased nest parasitism by birds, and increased windthrow and tree death along forest edges. Some of these secondary effects are implied and intuitive, for example the use of logging roads by logging trucks. But others are far more indirect and nonintuitive, such as the use of snowmobile trails by coyotes, which gain access to high elevation forest with deep snow not ordinarily accessible to them. Coyotes are aggressive competitors with or predators of vertebrate species adapted and limited to deep snow.

In sum, the fragmentation of natural habitats by human-caused structures and disturbance is blamed for wide-ranging impacts on biodiversity (Wilcove 1987). These impacts include reductions and losses of late-successional species, increased predation on interior species, increased competition from habitat generalists, and increased mortality inflicted by humans through hunting and collisions with vehicles. Further, some forms of fragmentation result in the interruption of ecological processes, especially those involving disturbance, that allow some stand types to persist in the long term. Therefore, forest fragmentation threatens the future existence of some forest types themselves.

DIMENSIONS OF FRAGMENTATION

Although here we define forest fragmentation only broadly, we believe that at least two important dimensions of forest fragmentation can be identified (Fig. 1.7). The first of these, novelty, relates to how often a perturbation has been experienced over the evolutionary history of a forest community. The second, distinctness, relates to how different a perturbation is, in terms of structure and function, from the matrix or area around it. Examples follow of how these two dimensions can characterize fragmentation. A human-caused wildfire during cool weather might produce a site that differs moderately from the unburned forest around it, having lost much of the fine woody debris, herbs, and shrubs. However, such a fire would be very similar to perturbations with which coniferous forests in our region have evolved—specifically lightning-caused fires. By contrast, an interstate highway, with associated fencing and right-of-way management, passing through a riparian forest would differ sharply from the matrix around it and is unprecedented in the evolutionary history of Rocky Mountain forests. The impoundment of a stream and creation of a reservoir would result in an area very different from that surrounding it, but, excepting its drawdown characteristics, a reservoir may be much like a lake, a common natural feature. Representing another extreme, the

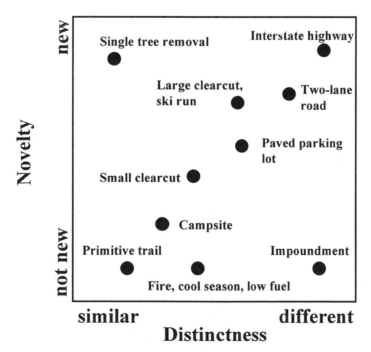

Fig. 1.7. Characterization of human-caused perturbations on two axes, distinctness and novelty. Distinctness refers to how different a perturbed site is from the structure and function of the surrounding area; novelty refers to how often a perturbation has been experienced over the evolution of Rocky Mountain forests.

selective cutting and removal of a single tree from a forest would be unusual in the history of Rocky Mountain forests, inasmuch as other natural perturbations (e.g., avalanches) would either leave the tree or remove many trees from a site. However, the structure and function of the resulting site would not differ sharply from the matrix around it. The perturbations that are the focus of public debate about forest fragmentation in the Southern Rocky Mountains and the primary focus of this book occupy the upper right quadrant of Fig. 1.7. They are new in the history of Rocky Mountain forests and are structured and function very differently from the forests around them.

Although most public discussion about forest fragmentation concerns disturbance that reduces forest area or sets back ecological succession, on balance forests in the western United States are, if anything, more extensive now than during the period of indigenous settlement (Gruell 1983, Veblen and Lorenz 1991). This is attributable to frequent disturbance by fire in Rocky Mountain forests before the twentieth century, and to the exclusion of fire, since then, by grazing, reduced ignition by humans, and more effective suppression. The effect has been to expand some forest types, particularly xerophytic types (e.g., ponderosa pine forest). Dry ponderosa pine, particularly, has increased in stem density on sites that were already in forest and encroached into grasslands and other previously nonforest vegetation types (Romme et al., *this volume*). In this case particularly, fragmentation can only be discussed in a highly context-specific way.

CONCLUSIONS

In earlier times, we tended to think of human impacts on forests in highly site-specific ways. This road will cause little harm, that clearcut leaves many surrounding trees uncut, my new log cabin will have no measurable impact upon wildlife. Today, we see that the cumulative effect of these incremental impacts has been the widespread modification of forested landscapes and forest wildlife. Some subalpine forests (Fig. 1.1) are patchworks of cuts and remnant uncut stands, with some cuts showing little regeneration. Some national forests are so intensively and thoroughly roaded that, outside statutory wilderness, virtually no place is more than a few hundred meters from the nearest road access. And homes in wildland forest settings, once a rarity, now are so locally common as to resemble subdivisions, influencing fire management policies and interfering with migration by ungulates. Clearly, we must no longer fail to see the forest of landscape-scale human impacts for the trees of single local actions.

Our increased awareness of the scale of human impacts on Rocky Mountain forests coincides with the rise of the philosophy and practice of ecosystem management. This philosophy, articulated in a progression of statements by practitioners and theorists of natural resource management (reviewed by Grumbine 1994), emphasizes multi-scale analyses of and cross-jurisdictional and science-based approaches to resource management actions. Such philosophy is ideally suited to the problem of forest fragmentation in the Southern Rockies, with its vegetative and jurisdictional mosaic, and forest-tree problem of scale in perceiving impacts.

How forests in the Southern Rocky Mountains will appear and function one hundred years from now will largely reflect the forces, processes, and management actions discussed in the following chapters. They place these topics in the light of fact and informed opinion, so that future forests will reflect the best choices that could have been made.

LITERATURE CITED

Allen, S. W., and G. W. Sharpe. 1960. *An introduction to American forestry.* McGraw-Iill, New York, New York, USA.

Darr, D. R. 1995. U.S. forest resources. Pages 214–215 *in* E. T. LaRoe, G. S. Farris, C. E. Puckett, P. D. Doran, and M. J. Mac, editors, *Our living resources: a report to the nation on the distribution, abundance, and health of U.S. plants, animals, and ecosystems.* USDI National Biological Service, Washington, D.C., USA.

Findley, J. S., and S. Anderson. 1956. Zoogeography of the montane mammals of Colorado. *Journal of Mammalogy* 37: 80-82.

Forman, R.T.T. 1995. *Land mosaics: the ecology of landscapes and regions.* Cambridge University Press, Cambridge, UK.

Frome, M. 1962. *Whose woods these are: the story of the national forests.* Doubleday, Garden City, New York, USA.

Groom, M. J., and N. Schumaker. 1993. Evaluating landscape change: patterns of worldwide deforestation and local fragmentation. Pages 24–44 *in* P. M. Kareiva, J. G. Huey, and R. B. Huey, editors, *Biotic interactions and global change.* Sinauer Associates, Sunderland, Massachusetts, USA.

Gruell, G. E. 1983. Fire and vegetative trends in the northern Rockies: interpretations from 1871–1982 photographs. USDA Forest Service, General Technical Report INT–158.

Gruell, G. E. 1985. Fire on the early western landscape: an annotated record of wildland fires 1776–1900. *Northwest Science* 59: 97–107.

Grumbine, R. E. 1994. What is ecosystem management? *Conservation Biology* 8: 27–38.

Harris, L. D. 1984. *The fragmented forest.* University of Chicago Press, Chicago, Illinois, USA.

Knight, D. H. 1994. *Mountains and plains: the ecology of Wyoming landscapes.* Yale University Press, New Haven, Connecticut, USA.

Lehmkuhl, J. F., and L. F. Ruggiero. 1991. Forest fragmentation in the pacific northwest and its potential effects on wildlife. Pages 35–46 in L. F. Ruggiero, K. B. Aubry, A. B. Carey, and M. H. Huff, coordinators, *Wildlife and vegetation of unmanaged Douglas-fir forests.* USDA Forest Service, General Technical Report PNW-285.

Leopold, A. 1933. *Game management.* Charles Scribner's Sons, New York, New York, USA.

Lord, J. M., and D. A. Norton. 1990. Scale and the spatial concept of fragmentation. *Conservation Biology* 4: 197–202.

Merrill, E. H. 1996. The Wyoming Gap Analysis project final report. Unpublished report, Wyoming Cooperative Fish and Wildlife Research Unit, University of Wyoming, Laramie, Wyoming, USA.

Peet, R. K. 1988. Forests of the Rocky Mountains. Pages 63–101 *in* M. G. Barbour and W. D. Billings, editors. *North American terrestrial vegetation.* Cambridge University Press, Cambridge, UK.

Simberloff, D. 1994. Habitat fragmentation and population extinction of birds. *Ibis* 137: S105–S111.

Thomas, J. W., L. F. Ruggiero, R. W. Mannan, J. W. Schoen, and R. A. Lancia. 1988. Management and conservation of old-growth forests in the United States. *Wildlife Society Bulletin* 16: 252–262.

Veblen, T. T., and D. C. Lorenz. 1991. *The Colorado Front Range: a century of ecological change.* University of Utah Press, Salt Lake City, Utah, USA.

Wakelyn, L. A. 1987. Changing habitat conditions on bighorn sheep ranges in Colorado. *Journal of Wildlife Management* 51: 904–912.

Wilcove, D. S. 1987. From fragmentation to extinction. *Natural Areas Journal* 7: 23–29.

2

Natural Patterns in Southern Rocky Mountain Landscapes and Their Relevance to Forest Management

Dennis H. Knight and William A. Reiners

INTRODUCTION

Human-caused fragmentation of forested landscapes is a concern of many land managers and is thought to be one of the most unnatural effects of timber harvesting, road building, campground construction, and other developments. The felling of trees is nothing new, as fires, windstorms, and tree-killing insect epidemics have done essentially the same. However, most of the wood is not removed after natural disturbances and many believe that a new kind of landscape mosaic has been created that could adversely affect important ecosystem components and processes.

Prior to extensive timber harvesting, a high level of landscape heterogeneity or patchiness was undoubtedly caused from time to time by natural disturbances that broke up continuous stands of interior forest—forests where the effects of edges on the microenvironment are difficult to detect. The minimal dimensions of "interior forest" vary with the requirements of different species, but the proportions of interior and edge habitats surely fluctuated considerably from century to century, due to natural disturbances and climate change. The abundance of some species must have fluctuated accordingly (Hansen et al. 1991). Now, however, many forested landscapes in the Southern Rocky Mountains appear to have lost large areas of interior forests due to timber harvesting and road construction (Reed et al. 1996, Tinker et al. 1998). To understand the severity of this fragmentation, the nature and causes of the spatial patterns that would have existed in the absence of extensive harvesting should be considered. Our focus will be on patchiness caused by gradual and abrupt environmental gradients; Veblen (*this volume*) addresses the effects of disturbances.

LANDSCAPE HETEROGENEITY AT DIFFERENT SCALES

Landscapes are heterogeneous in space and they change through time, even without the influences of human activity (Forman 1995, Pickett and Cadenasso 1995). At the smallest scale, spatial heterogeneity arises when different plant species occur side-by-side, each having different effects on the environment and offering tissues of different quality to herbivores and other heterotrophs. Additional small scale heterogeneity is created when a tree dies, forming an opening in a forest canopy that otherwise might have been quite uniform. The understory vegetation that develops under the canopy gap usually is different, and when the tree falls, it adds a new kind of organic substrate to the forest floor (Harmon et al. 1986, Spies et al. 1988). The belowground ecosystem may change as well if the roots of the fallen tree die. As one log on the forest floor gradually decomposes and disappears under a mat of leaves and twigs, and as new trees and branches fill the canopy gap that was created when the tree fell, new gaps and downed wood are created nearby.

Though important for some ecological processes, spatial heterogeneity at the scale of individual trees and coarse woody debris has not been of great concern to forest managers and scientists. Individual tree harvesting methods certainly do change the forest, but the coarse-grained patchiness created by clear-cutting and measured in hectares has attracted more attention. Landscapes are dynamic at this larger scale also. Consistent with the shifting mosaic hypothesis of Bormann and Likens (1979), as young forests develop into older forests, the older forests nearby may be converted by a natural disturbance to openings that usually develop into young forests. If the climate changes during the centuries required for old forest development, or if plant propagule availability changes, the next disturbance could lead to the development of a meadow, shrubland, or woodland that is quite different from the preexisting forest.

Over large areas, natural heterogeneity in Rocky Mountain landscapes at the scale of hectares is expressed by the often abrupt transitions or borders between patches of younger forests and older forests, between forests and meadows, between dense forests and open woodlands or shrubland, and between subalpine forests and the alpine zone. Landscape heterogeneity or patchiness at this scale also exists due to lakes and rivers. In general, this heterogeneity can be attributed to large scale disturbances and changes in elevation, soil conditions or topography. This chapter is about the patches created by changes in environmental conditions rather than by disturbances, though they are difficult to separate.

CLIMATIC GRADIENTS

Elevation and topography combine to create much of the heterogeneity in Southern Rocky Mountain landscapes. Elevation alone causes gradual changes, with declines in temperatures, growing season length, and precipitation regimes effecting shifts from forests dominated by ponderosa pine and Douglas-fir at lower elevations to forests dominated by lodgepole pine, Engelmann spruce, and subalpine fir above. The amount and seasonality of precipitation also change. Normally such gradual changes are not considered when discussing landscape patchiness, but when elevation zones are classified into categories, a human-imposed landscape mosaic does emerge (Fig. 2.1). Because elevation is so closely linked to climatic conditions, it provides the template on which all other causes of variation can be superimposed.

Because of the strong influence of topography, mountain landscapes are much patchier than would be predicted by elevation alone. To illustrate, the environment is cooler and more mesic in ravines and on north-facing slopes than on south slopes at the same elevation (in the northern hemisphere). Two-dimensional diagrams with topographic position on one axis and elevation on the other provide a powerful tool for predicting where different vegetation types can be found in the Southern Rocky Mountains (Romme and Knight 1981, Peet 1988, Knight 1994). However, landscape mosaics as seen from photographs and maps are not depicted by such diagrams.

LANDSCAPE PATCHINESS AT LOWER ELEVATIONS

Forests at lower elevations are dominated by ponderosa pine and Douglas-fir, with the pine tolerating warmer conditions than the Douglas-fir. Often the forests are distributed in small patches on mesic north slopes (Fig. 2.2). Limber pine and ponderosa pine can occur on south-facing slopes, but usually they form savannas or woodlands in this drier environment. More common on south slopes are foothill shrublands dominated by various combinations of big sagebrush, bitterbrush, snowberry, Saskatoon serviceberry, Rocky Mountain juniper, and mountain mahogany.

Away from mesic north slopes, the trees at lower elevations often are restricted to outcrops of rock, where the funneling of rain and

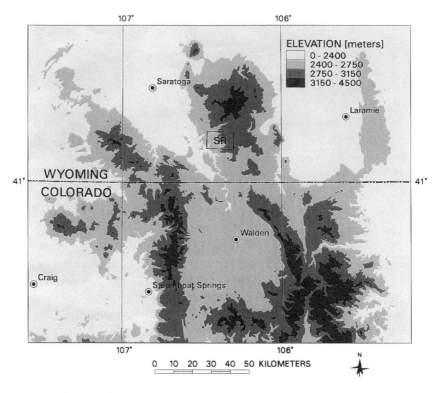

Fig. 2.1. Elevational zones in the Central Rocky Mountains of southern Wyoming and northern Colorado. The 2,400–2,750 m zone includes foothill shrublands and woodlands of ponderosa pine, Douglas-fir, and aspen at lower elevations, and forests of lodgepole pine at higher elevations. The 2,750–3,150 m zone includes forests of lodgepole pine intermingled with forests dominated by Engelmann spruce and subalpine fir. The uppermost 3,150–4,500 m zone includes higher elevation spruce-fir forests that grade into krummholz and alpine vegetation. The rectangle marked "SR" shows the location of the Savage Run Wilderness image in Figs. 2.6, 2.7, and 2.8. Elevations were derived from 3-arc-second data from the U.S. Geological Survey (1987).

melting snow into cracks provides more water than in adjacent fine-textured soils where the water is held nearer the surface and is more easily evaporated—an extreme example of the inverse texture effect (Sala et al. 1988). Additional patchiness is created by groves of aspen. Also, riparian zones with alluvial soils support patches of meadow or shrublands dominated by thinleaf alder and various species of willow or birch. Foothill forests usually will cover too little land area to

Fig. 2.2. An example of a low-elevation landscape where forests are found only on north-facing slopes. Near Hoback Junction, south of Jackson, in western Wyoming.

qualify as interior forests for wide-ranging species, but they are still important for wildlife habitat and the aesthetic quality of the foothill landscape.

LANDSCAPE PATCHINESS AT HIGHER ELEVATIONS

Forests at higher elevations occur in nearly all topographic positions. Species composition and productivity vary with aspect and other environmental variables, but the structural properties of interior forests would have been widespread prior to intensive timber harvesting, especially in areas with little relief, such as in the Medicine Bow Mountains of southern Wyoming. If the mountains are steep and heavily dissected, such as much of the Front Range in Colorado, the land area with interior forests would have been less.

While forests usually replace forests at high elevations following disturbances in the Rocky Mountains, different successional trajectories are possible, depending on various biotic and abiotic factors that characterize the site and disturbance (Stahelin 1943, Doyle 1997, Turner et al. 1997, Lynch 1998). For example, Stahelin (1943) observed that subalpine forests dominated by Engelmann spruce and subalpine fir could become young forests dominated by aspen or lodgepole pine. Doyle (1997) found that postfire tree species

Fig. 2.3. A landscape illustrating the absence of trees on fluvial soils in the valley and in the alpine zone above a narrow band of forest dominated by Engelmann spruce and subalpine fir. Cache la Poudre River, Rocky Mountain National Park, Colorado.

composition is more variable for stands dominated by Engelmann spruce, subalpine fir, or Douglas-fir than for stands dominated by lodgepole pine or aspen. Notably, high intensity fires in forests can lead to the formation of long-persisting meadows or shrublands, especially if the disturbance occurs after a period of climate change (Lynch 1998).

Abrupt forest-to-meadow transitions are common in the Southern Rocky Mountains and occur in at least three environmental situations. Perhaps the most common is on the alluvial soils of riparian zones that are wet for extended periods (Fig. 2.3). Unlike the meadow species, conifers and aspen cannot tolerate the usually saturated, anaerobic soils. Such meadows commonly occur over broad, flat areas that may have developed because of sedimentation caused by beaver dams. As stream channels shifted due to flood events, the beaver would also move, building new dams and causing sedimentation in new locations. Relatively flat riparian zones with meandering streams are among the most dynamic landscapes in the region, and they commonly interrupt the continuity of forests.

Fig. 2.4. On the left, a dry meadow without trees, with a ribbon forest and snowglade on the leeward side of the meadow to the right, and a clear-cut with a regenerating stand of trees to the right of the snowglade. Cinnabar Park, Medicine Bow Mountains, Wyoming.

Meadows also occur on sites with soils that are apparently too dry, too shallow, or too fine-textured for tree seedling establishment. Often they occur at relatively high elevations where strong winds greatly reduce the amount of snow accumulation (Fig. 2.4). This snow removal deprives the meadow of an important source of water for plant growth. Elsewhere, sedimentary strata come to the surface that contribute to the development of fine-textured soils not favorable for tree seedling establishment (Fig. 2.5). Various studies have shown edaphic differences between forests and adjacent meadows in the Rocky Mountains (Dunnewald 1930, Jackson 1957, Patten 1963, Despain 1973, Doering and Reider 1992), though such differences are not always

Fig. 2.5. A slope in the Big Horn Mountains of Wyoming that is devoid of trees because of the fine-textured soils that develop on shales in the Gros Ventre formation. The surrounding forests occur on coarse-textured soils and are dominated by lodgepole pine and aspen.

obvious (Behan 1957, Cary 1966, Miles and Singleton 1975). Forests usually occur on relatively coarse soils, though fine-textured soils do support trees where water stress is less severe.

A third cause of meadow formation in an otherwise forested landscape is unusually deep snow accumulation. Referred to as "snow glades," such openings typically are found on the lee side of dry meadows and just beyond a "ribbon" of trees that functions as a snow fence (see Fig. 2.4). Snow may accumulate to such depths downwind of the trees that the soil remains snow-covered until August and nearly saturated for the remainder of the growing season, thereby inhibiting tree seedling establishment. Near the alpine zone, numerous parallel strips of ribbon forests and snowglades may occur (Billings 1969, Buckner 1977, Knight 1994). In some areas trees form doughnut-shaped groves around a long-persisting snow-drift caused by a combination of topography and vegetation (Griggs 1938, Knight 1994).

Less conspicuous patchiness in Rocky Mountain landscapes occurs where the difference between adjacent vegetation types is primarily species composition. For example, elongated stands of Engelmann spruce and subalpine fir can be found in valley bottoms having moist environments and longer fire-return intervals (Romme and Knight 1981). Forests on adjacent slopes are typically lodgepole pine or aspen. Several forest types can be expected in a watershed, each correlated with different environmental conditions but with variable ecotones between them that provide insights on the adaptations of the dominant trees (Stohlgren and Bachand 1997, Stohlgren et al. 1998).

LANDSCAPE PATTERNS APPARENT FROM SATELLITE IMAGERY

We used Landsat Thematic Mapper (TM) imagery to examine spatial heterogeneity for a specific landscape that included the Savage Run Wilderness on the west slopes of the Medicine Bow Mountains in south-central Wyoming (Figs. 2.6, 2.7, and 2.8). The TM imagery (scene 35/31, 24 June 1991, 0900–1000 hr RDT) was subjected to a K-means unsupervised classification (MicroImages, Inc. 1996). The classification was run for all of the national forest land in the Wyoming portion of the Medicine Bow–Routt National Forest and was restricted a priori to 30 classes. Bands 3, 4, and 5 were stretched linearly, with a few percent of the data dropped at the upper and lower ends, and were colored blue, green, and red, respectively. The Resource Information System (RIS) database of the U.S. Forest Service and our own observations were used for ground truthing.

Clearly, the 3-band, K-means classification (Fig. 2.8) produces more spectral classes than are obvious to the eye on the natural color image (Fig. 2.7). The high degree of spatial variability appears to be caused by the interaction of topography and elevation (Figs. 2.6, 2.7, and 2.8). Not seen in the image we used are the impacts of disturbance events such as fires, perhaps because the vegetation has recovered sufficiently from past fires to obscure the mosaic. For reasons described previously, the forests at high elevations are more uniform than the vegetation at lower elevations. However, various combinations of tree and understory plant species can be found in the forested areas that cannot be identified by the TM imagery. For example, small but important stands of aspen are not apparent.

MANAGEMENT RECOMMENDATIONS AND RESEARCH NEEDS

As with all ecological phenomena, a complex of factors interact in determining the configuration of natural landscape mosaics. Human-caused patches, by whatever means, are now being superimposed on an already patchy landscape that has varied through time for millennia.

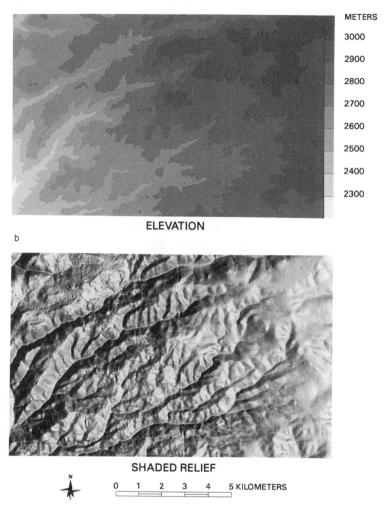

a

METERS
3000
2900
2800
2700
2600
2500
2400
2300

ELEVATION

b

SHADED RELIEF

N

0 1 2 3 4 5 KILOMETERS

Fig. 2.6. a. A portion of the Medicine Bow Mountains in Wyoming (identified as SR on Fig. 2.1), with 100-m elevational belts displayed in shades of gray. This figure was derived from 30-m DEM data (USGS 1987). The image boundary encompasses 12,500 ha ranging from 2200–3000 m elevation. The northeastern third of this area is a gently rolling upland representing a Tertiary erosion surface (Mears 1993, Blackstone 1996), while the southwestern two-thirds of this area consists of more or less parallel ridges and valleys extending westward. b. The same area showing terrain configuration. To produce this rendering of "shaded relief," the sun was set at an azimuth of 118° and an elevation of 59°, which were the values for the sun at the time the satellite data for Figs. 2.7 and 2.8 were obtained. This rendering produces shadows in realistic positions at the time the TM data were collected.

THEMATIC MAPPER (BAND 4)
0   1   2   3   4   5 KILOMETERS

Fig. 2.7. Landsat Thematic Mapper image of the area delimited in Fig. 2.6 on the west flank of the Medicine Bow Mountains and centered on the Savage Run Wilderness (large area in dark gray). Forests outside the wilderness area have been fragmented by clear-cutting. This gray-tone image was derived from TM band 4 data. Most of the darkest tones coincide with topographic shadows on north-facing slopes (see Fig. 2.6).

The proportion of the landscape in interior forests surely has fluctuated from one century to the next, and the native flora and fauna have evolved in that context. Will human-caused fragmentation make a difference to those species? Undoubtedly it will to some of them, but if their required environments are available over a large enough area, their populations probably will not decline (or increase) to an alarming level based on fragmentation alone. Significantly, however, fragmentation is occurring at a time when other characteristics of forest ecosystems are quite different because of human activity, such as the potential effects of wood removal, introduced organisms (including pathogens), nitrogen enrichment from air pollutants, and rapid climate change. Much information is not known about such relationships. To predict the cumulative effects of different human-caused changes is a difficult challenge for managers and scientists alike.

Patchiness in forested landscapes occurs at various scales and undoubtedly is an important feature for the survival of many species. Some species will depend on occasional treefalls that cause canopy

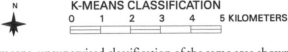

Fig. 2.8. K-means, unsupervised classification of the same area shown in Fig. 2.7. Numbered crosses are centered on examples of the gray-scaled pixels and patterned pixel aggregates that identify the following land cover types: (1) nonforested riparian zones; (2) coniferous forest on mesic, north-facing slopes dominated by Engelmann spruce, subalpine fir, and lodgepole pine; (3) coniferous forest on dry-mesic sites dominated by Engelmann spruce, subalpine fir, and lodgepole pine; (4) lodgepole pine forest on comparatively flat terrain, on broad ridgetops, or on south-facing slopes; (5) rock outcrops, exposed soil, open woodlands with limber pine or lodgepole pine, and the margins of clear-cuts; (6) post-harvest vegetation developing after clear-cutting in the 1980s (diagonal hatch marks); (7) post-harvest vegetation developing after clear-cutting done prior to the 1980s; (8) aspen (light horizontal lines across dark gray), typically in moist environments or on the margins of coniferous forests at lower elevations; (9) foothill meadows and forblands (horizontal/vertical cross-hatch); (10) foothill shrubland dominated by big sagebrush and bitterbrush (diagonal crosshatch); (11) foothill shrubland dominated by mountain mahogany; and (12) nonforested, south-facing slopes with unstable soils. (A larger color image is available from the authors.)

gaps; at a larger scale, other species may depend on the juxtaposition of meadows, wetlands, and forests of different kinds. Some patch-types shift from one part of the landscape to another, such as forest patches of different age, while others are essentially confined to specific areas, such as riparian meadows or avalanche tracks. Whether or not changes in the landscape mosaic adversely affect plant and animal species depends on how widely distributed the species of concern are and how dependent they are on a particular patch type or landscape mosaic.

Our focus for this analysis has been on physiognomic or structural patchiness, but patchiness in species composition may be just as important. Such patchiness is subtle but should not be ignored when considering the effects of management on landscape mosaics. If a species is restricted to a specific forest type, that species may be endangered by fragmentation (perforation) even if large areas of other forest types remain nearby. Also, if clear-cuts are designed to remove the entirety of a stand that originated following the same disturbance, the adverse effects on biodiversity could be more severe than if only a portion of the stand is harvested.

That physiognomic and species patchiness always existed is significant from the perspective of fragmentation because, within landscapes that have high levels of patchiness (heterogeneity) for environmental reasons, some forests may never have been classified as "interior forest," at least for some comparatively large organisms (Fig. 2.9). In such areas, many so-called "sensitive species" are already adapted to edge environments and further fragmentation by timber harvesting may have little effect on biological diversity. The effects of fragmentation also could be subtle if a forested landscape is uniform over a very large area and only a small portion of the landscape is affected by, for example, timber harvesting. Populations of interior species may decline as the area of interior forest is reduced, but that would be expected following a natural disturbance as well, and suitable habitat would still exist for much of the population. This rationale underlies recommendations for aggregated timber harvesting (Franklin 1989, Hansen et al. 1991). The most adverse effects of fragmentation may occur where landscape heterogeneity is intermediate, with comparatively small areas of interior forest. Biologists often can use existing knowledge to identify species that are most likely to be affected by further fragmentation at the scale commonly caused by human activity, but additional research is necessary before the hypothesized relationships in Fig. 2.9 can be quantified and used as a guideline for management decisions.

Decisions to further fragment a forest by timber harvesting also should consider the potential for additional fragmentation by natural disturbances beyond human control, such as fires or windstorms. Tracts of interior, old-growth forest are becoming increasingly rare in Rocky Mountain landscapes, hence the present-day concern about further fragmentation. Using existing knowledge about natural disturbance regimes in conjunction with information on current landscape patterns,

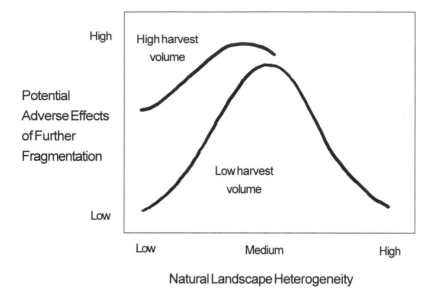

High

High harvest
volume

Potential
Adverse Effects
of Further
Fragmentation

Low harvest
volume

Low

Low   Medium   High

Natural Landscape Heterogeneity

Fig. 2.9. Hypothetical relationships between the potential adverse effects of further fragmentation, such as by clear-cutting, and the natural heterogeneity (patchiness) of a landscape. Landscapes with an intermediate level of natural heterogeneity may be most susceptible to further fragmentation, unless the amount of land area affected by timber harvesting is high, in which case a larger proportion of a homogeneous landscape would be affected. Quantification of the axes will require additional research on the species and ecological processes of greatest concern.

scientists should be able to predict where naturally caused fragmentation is most likely to aggravate problems created by human-caused fragmentation.

In sum, we suggest three management guidelines. First, considering the heterogeneity created by both natural and human-caused factors, and the apparently increasing amounts of forest edge in some parts of the Southern Rocky Mountains, managers should place high value on the homogeneous tracts of interior forests that remain. Second, managers and scientists should work together in identifying those ecosystems that will be changed most adversely by landscape fragmentation in the future, whether human-caused or not. And third, current harvesting practices should be done in a way that maintains the biological diversity and soils now existing after centuries of ecosystem development, thereby conserving the potential for restoration and continued wood production in the future.

ACKNOWLEDGMENTS

The authors thank Steven E. Williams for assistance in using the Resource Information System of the Medicine Bow–Routt National Forest; Robert C. Thurston for preparation of the GIS and remote sensing imagery; and William H. Romme, Thomas J. Stohlgren, and an anonymous reviewer for helpful comments on an earlier draft of the manuscript.

LITERATURE CITED

Behan, M. J. 1957. The vegetation and ecology of Dry Park in the Medicine Bow Mountains. M.S. thesis, University of Wyoming, Laramie, Wyoming, USA.

Billings, W. D. 1969. Vegetational pattern near alpine timberline as affected by fire-snowdrift interactions. *Vegetation* 19: 192–207.

Blackstone, D. L., Jr. 1996. Structural geology of the Laramie Mountains, southeastern Wyoming and northeastern Colorado. Wyoming State Geological Survey Report of Investigation No. 51, Laramie, Wyoming, USA.

Bormann, H. L., and G. Likens. 1979. Catastrophic disturbance and the steady state in northern hardwood forests. *American Scientist* 67: 660–669.

Buckner, D. L. 1977. Ribbon forest development and maintenance in the central Rocky Mountains of Colorado. Ph.D. dissertation, University of Colorado, Boulder, Colorado, USA.

Cary, L. E. 1966. A study of forest margins. M.S. thesis, University of Wyoming, Laramie, Wyoming, USA.

Despain, D. G. 1973. Vegetation of the Big Horn Mountains, Wyoming in relation to substrate and climate. *Ecological Monographs* 43: 329–355.

Doering, W. R., and R. G. Reider. 1992. Soils of Cinnabar Park, Medicine Bow Mountains, Wyoming, USA: indicators of park origin and persistence. *Arctic and Alpine Research* 24: 27–39.

Doyle, K. M. 1997. Fire, environment and early forest succession in a heterogeneous Rocky Mountain landscape, northwestern Wyoming. Ph.D. dissertation, University of Wyoming, Laramie, Wyoming, USA.

Dunnewald, T. J. 1930. Grass and timber soils distribution in the Big Horn Mountains. *Journal of the American Society of Agronomy* 22: 577–586.

Forman, R.T.T. 1995. *Land mosaics.* Cambridge University Press, Cambridge, UK.

Franklin, J. F. 1989. Towards a new forestry. *American Forests* (November/December): 37–44.

Griggs, R. F. 1938. Timberlines in the northern Rocky Mountains. *Ecology* 19: 548–564.

Hansen, A. J., T. A. Spies, F. J. Swanson, and J. L. Ohmann. 1991. Conserving biodiversity in managed forests. *BioScience* 41: 382–392.

Harmon, M. E., J. F. Franklin, F. J. Swanson, P. Sollins, S. V. Gregory, J. D. Lattin, N. H. Anderson, S. P. Cline, N. G. Aumen, J. R. Sedel, G. W. Liendaemper, K. Cromack, Jr., and K. W. Cummins. 1986. Ecology of coarse woody debris in temperate ecosystems. *Advances in Ecological Research* 15: 133–302.

Jackson, W. N. 1957. Some soil characteristics of several grassland-timber transitions in the Big Horn Mountains and the Laramie Plains. M.S. thesis, University of Wyoming, Laramie, Wyoming, USA.

Knight, D. H. 1994. *Mountains and plains: the ecology of Wyoming landscapes.* Yale University Press, New Haven, Connecticut, USA.

Lynch, E. A. 1998. Origin of a park-forest vegetation mosaic in the Wind River Range, Wyoming. *Ecology* 79: 1320–1338.

Mears, B., Jr. 1993. Geomorphic history of Wyoming and high-level erosion surfaces. Pages 608–626 *in* A. W. Snoke, J. R. Steidtmann, and S. M. Roberts, editors, *Geology of Wyoming.* Vol. 2. Geological Survey of Wyoming. Laramie, Wyoming, USA.

MicroImages, Inc. 1996. TNTmips, version 5.3. Lincoln, Nebraska, USA.

Miles, S. R., and P. C. Singleton. 1975. Vegetational history of Cinnabar Park in Medicine Bow National Forest, Wyoming. *Soil Science Society of America Proceedings* 39: 1204–1208.

Patten, D. T. 1963. Vegetation patterns in relation to environments in the Madison Range, Montana. *Ecological Monographs* 33: 375–406.

Peet, R. K. 1988. Forests of the Rocky Mountains. Pages 63–101 *in* M. G. Barbour and W. D. Billings, editors, *North American Terrestrial Vegetation.* Cambridge University Press, New York, New York, USA.

Pickett, S.T.A., and M. L. Cadenasso. 1995. Landscape ecology: spatial heterogeneity in ecological systems. *Science* 269: 331–334.

Reed, R. A., J. Johnson-Barnard, and W. L. Baker. 1996. Fragmentation of a forested Rocky Mountain landscape, 1950–1993. *Biological Conservation* 75: 267–277.

Romme, W. H., and D. H. Knight. 1981. Fire frequency and subalpine forest succession along a topographic gradient in Wyoming. *Ecology* 62: 319–326.

Sala, O. E., W. J. Parton, L. A. Joyce, and W. K. Lauenroth. 1988. Primary production of the central grassland region of the United States. *Ecology* 69: 40–45.

Spies, T. A., J. F. Franklin, and T. B. Thomas. 1988. Coarse woody debris in Douglas fir forests of western Oregon and Washington. *Ecology* 69: 1689–1702.

Stahelin, R. 1943. Factors influencing the natural restocking of high altitude burns by coniferous trees in the central Rocky Mountains. *Ecology* 24: 19–30.

Stohlgren, T. J., and R. R. Bachand. 1997. Lodgepole pine (*Pinus contorta*) ecotones in Rocky Mountain National Park, Colorado, USA. *Ecology* 78: 632–641.

Stohlgren, T. J., R. R. Bachand, Y. Onami, and D. Binkley. 1998. Species-environment relationships and vegetation patterns: effects of spatial scale and tree life-stage. *Plant Ecology* 135: 215–228.

Tinker, D. B., C.A.C. Resor, G. P. Beauvais, K. F. Kipfmueller, C. I. Fernandes, and W. L. Baker. 1998. Watershed analysis of forest fragmentation by clear-cuts and roads in a Wyoming forest. *Landscape Ecology* 13: 149–165.

Turner, M. G., W. H. Romme, R. H. Gardner, and W. W. Hargrove. 1997. Effects of patch size and fire patterns on early post-fire succession on the Yellowstone Plateau. *Ecological Monographs* 67: 411–433.

U.S. Geological Survey. 1987. Digital elevation models. *Data Users Guide.* Department of the Interior, U.S. Geological Survey, Reston, Virginia, USA.

3

Disturbance Patterns in Southern
Rocky Mountain Forests

Thomas T. Veblen

INTRODUCTION

The pattern of landscape diversity in the Southern Rocky Mountains
has been described as resulting from "two superimposed vegetation patterns: the distribution of species along gradients of limiting factors, and
patterns of disturbance and recovery within the communities at each
point along the environmental gradients" (Romme and Knight 1982).
The previous chapter (D. H. Knight and W. A. Reiners, *this volume*)
has emphasized the first pattern whereas this chapter emphasizes the
role of natural disturbance in creating landscape patterns. Although
human impacts on fundamentally natural disturbances such as fires
and insect outbreaks are included, other chapters treat disturbances of
exclusively human origin such as logging and road construction.

A conceptual framework for analyzing the characteristics and consequences of disturbance is the concept of *disturbance regime*, or the
spatial and temporal characteristics of disturbances in a particular landscape (Paine and Levin 1981, White and Pickett 1985). The key descriptors of a disturbance regime are: (1) spatial distribution, (2) frequency, (3) size of the area disturbed, (4) mean return interval, (5)
predictability, (6) rotation period, (7) magnitude or severity, and (8)
the synergistic interactions of different kinds of disturbances. Within
an area of otherwise homogeneous habitat, variations in these parameters are major determinants of landscape heterogeneity and, consequently, must be considered in evaluating the fragmentation caused
by forest cutting and road construction. Although numerous case studies
have been done on vegetation and ecosystem response to disturbance

for the Southern Rocky Mountains, relatively little work has been done on disturbance regimes per se. To inform discussions of the relationship of landscape patchiness to natural disturbances and issues of fragmentation, this chapter will emphasize four "key" questions about disturbance regimes:

1. How do disturbance regimes vary along environmental gradients?
2. How have humans altered natural disturbance regimes?
3. How do disturbance interactions affect vegetation responses as well as the occurrence and spread of subsequent disturbances?
4. How does climatic variability affect disturbance regimes and vegetation response to disturbances?

It will quickly become evident that answers to these questions are very incomplete for the Southern Rocky Mountains. This realization is important both in guiding future research and as a caveat to incorporating the tentative knowledge of disturbance patterns into discussions of fragmentation issues. Although the geographical scope of this review is from central Wyoming to southern Colorado, studies conducted in northern Colorado will be emphasized. For this region, it will be convenient to distinguish the lower elevation montane forests of mainly ponderosa pine and Douglas fir from subalpine forests of mainly Engelmann spruce, subalpine fir, and lodgepole pine (Marr 1961).

FIRE

Historical Documentation of Fire and Its Effects

The earliest reports on the conditions of forest reserves (precursors to national forests) in the 1890s describe landscapes that had recently burned, and much of that burning was attributed to fires ignited by Native Americans mainly for the purpose of driving game (Jack 1899, Sudworth 1899). The observations of early settlers and the high fire frequencies during the prehistoric period (see following section) strongly imply that Native Americans had a quantitatively significant influence on the number of ignitions. Nevertheless, the percentages of fires ignited by humans versus lightning are unknown. During the mid-1800s period of exploration and early settlement (ca. 1850 to 1910), fires were frequently set by EuroAmericans to facilitate prospecting, to justify salvage logging, or to clear brush to find escaped cattle (Jack 1899, Sudworth 1899, Tice 1872, Fossett 1880). At least 20% of the South Platte Reserve had been burned so severely by the 1890s that regeneration had failed, apparently due to destruction of seed sources by repeated burns at the same sites in time spans of less than ten years (Jack 1899). Alternatively, regeneration may have failed due to drought that was reportedly responsible for the death of mature ponderosa pine in the same area in the 1880s (Jack 1899). In Boulder County in 1871, there were 51 indictments for illegal forest fires (Tice 1872), implying that contemporary observers perceived a trend towards an unwanted increase in fire occurrence during the latter half of the nineteenth century. Similarly, photographs taken near the turn of the century indicate that vast areas of the Southern Rocky Mountains had been recently burned (Jack 1899, Sudworth 1899, Veblen and Lorenz 1991).

Tree-Ring Based Studies of Fire History

Fire history in forested areas can be described quantitatively on the basis of two types of tree-ring evidence: dates of fire scars (the fire interval approach) or the age of stands that regenerated following stand-replacing fires (the stand origin approach). Because most fire histories of dense subalpine forests have been derived from mapping postfire stands whereas fire histories of open montane forests of ponderosa pine and Douglas fir are from fire-interval data, fire history statistics for the subalpine and montane zones usually are not directly comparable. Furthermore, the reliability of both fire history techniques is limited by numerous problems associated with the collection of the field evidence of fire as well as analytical procedures (Johnson and Gutsell 1994, Finney 1995, Kipfmueller and Baker 1998a). Quantitative comparisons of summary fire statistics for different study areas rarely are valid because of differences in the sizes of the areas sampled, sampling skill and effort, and methods of computing fire statistics. Given these caveats, the interpretation of fire history studies in this chapter will emphasize qualitative differences in fire regimes (e.g., high frequency surface fires versus low frequency crown fires), temporal trends within the same study area, and regional synchrony of fire events.

Differences in Fire Regimes by Habitat

A strong contrast exists in dominant fire type between the subalpine and montane zones (Romme and Knight 1981, Peet 1988). The continuous fuels of dense Engelmann spruce, subalpine fir, and lodgepole pine forests generally permit widespread stand-replacing or crown fires. In contrast, most fires in the open ponderosa pine woodlands of the lower montane zone are surface fires carried mainly by grass fuels. However, these two modal fire types represent opposite ends of a continuum of fire intensity that can occur in both elevational zones. For example, in ponderosa pine forests, stand-replacing fires are documented for both the fire exclusion period and the prehistoric landscape (Veblen and Lorenz 1986; Shinneman and Baker 1997).

Although statistical comparison of fire parameters from different fire history studies is not feasible, there are consistent qualitative differences in the fire regimes of the subalpine and montane zones. The average time between recurrent fires to the same stand or small area (e.g., $<1 km^2$) in subalpine forests has been roughly estimated to be 100 to 500 years versus 5 to 40 years in open woodlands in the lower montane zone (Rowdabaugh 1978, Clagg 1975, Gruell 1985, Romme 1982, Romme and Knight 1981, Peet 1988). In the subalpine zone in southern Wyoming, fire rotation (i.e., time required to burn the entire study area once) has been estimated at 182 years (for 1569–1996 A.D.) for a 3,241-ha area (Kipfmueller 1997), and in northwestern Colorado at 521 years (for 1633–1992 A.D.) for a 594-ha area of subalpine forest (Veblen et al. 1994). The longer fire rotation for the northwestern Colorado site may reflect a moister habitat or topographic restriction of fire spread into the small, high elevation valley where the study was conducted. In contrast, fire rotation in a 113-ha area of open ponderosa pine woodland in the lower montane zone of the Colorado Front Range is estimated at 29 years over the period 1679–1996 (conservatively assuming that years in which $\geq25\%$ of the trees were scarred were years in which most of the sample area burned; Veblen et al., *unpublished data*). In 73 km^2 of subalpine forest in Yellowstone National Park, evidence was found of only 15 fire years since 1600 (Romme 1982). In contrast, in only 1.13 km^2 of open ponderosa pine woodland in the Colorado Front Range evidence was found of 35 fire years since 1679 (Veblen et al. 1996). Although the subalpine zone is clearly characterized by infrequent large fires, repeated burns at short intervals (i.e., <10 years) also occasionally have occurred (Sudworth 1899).

Changes in Fire Regimes over Time

In the context of current forest fragmentation, it is important to consider how EuroAmericans have altered fire regimes over the present century, and in turn may have altered size or intensity of disturbance which affects the spatial heterogeneity of the landscape (Baker 1994). The modern "fire exclusion" period beginning in the early 1900s refers to both suppression of lightning-ignited fires and cessation of widespread, intentional burning by humans. It is widely believed that in comparison with the nineteenth century, the present century has been a period of reduced fire occurrence throughout the Southern Rocky Mountains (Peet 1988, Knight 1994). However, the validity of this generalization and its ecological consequences vary according to elevation and specific sites. Due to the long fire intervals typical of subalpine forests, the past approximately 80 years of fire suppression have not necessarily had much influence on rates of fire recurrence in some areas of subalpine forests (Romme and Despain 1989, Clagg 1975).

In the montane zone of the Southern Rocky Mountains there is a consistent pattern of reduced fire frequency during the fire exclusion period (Table 3.1). The magnitude of this decline appears small when measured as changes in mean fire return intervals because the computations for the fire exclusion period must be truncated at the date of the most recent fire which in many cases is early in the 1900s. However, simple comparison of the numbers of fire years in periods of approximately equal length before and after the initiation of fire exclusion indicates a 2- to over 14-fold decline in fire occurrence during the fire exclusion period (Table 3.1). The much greater impact of fire exclusion on fire occurrence in the montane zone, compared to the subalpine zone, reflects the inherently higher fire frequency permitted by fuel conditions at low elevation.

In the context of a book on forest fragmentation it is important to emphasize that fire suppression has promoted some forest patch *coalescence* in the montane zone during most of this century. Comparison of historical and modern landscape photographs as well as analyses of tree population age structures document the spread of ponderosa pine and Douglas fir trees into some former grasslands (Gruell 1985; Veblen and Lorenz 1991; Mast et al. 1998). This major change in the montane forests is widely attributed to elimination of the frequent surface fires that formerly prevented seedling survival at most sites. However, climatic variability and changes in herbivore populations also may have influenced the expansion of ponderosa pine woodlands. For example, in southwestern ponderosa pine forests, tree establishment at some sites corresponds with periods of increased moisture availability (Cooper 1960, White 1985), and in western Montana periodic drought is believed to limit Douglas fir expansion into grasslands (Koterba and Habeck 1971). For the Colorado Front Range, climatic influences on ponderosa pine establishment also have been hypothesized, but any association between seedling establishment and short periods (1–5 years) of climatic variation remains elusive (Mast et al. 1998). Confounding influences from livestock grazing make it difficult to detect

Table 3.1. Fire regime descriptors from fire history studies in southern Wyoming and Colorado. Time periods are: NA = the Native American period (pre-1840); ES = the EuroAmerican settlement period; and MFE = the modern fire exclusion period. Years used to define these periods in each study are given in parentheses below the respective mean fire return intervals. For computation of mean fire return intervals (MFI) only complete fire intervals (i.e., fire-scar to fire-scar) within each indicated period were used, except for the two subalpine forest sites where MFIs were computed as the period length divided by the number of intervals. "No. of intervals" is the number of fire intervals in the entire record. "No. of trees sampled" is the number of fire-scarred trees sampled. For computation of the ratios of the number of fire events, the NA period was shortened to approximate the lengths of the ES and MFE periods (i.e., 44 to 74 years).

Location (Source)	Number of trees sampled	Number of intervals	Mean fire return interval			Ratio of fire years	
			NA	ES	MFE	ES/NA	ES/MFE
Montane forests							
Wintersteen Park, northern Front Range (Laven et al. 1980)	n.d.	20	66.0 (1708–1839)	17.8 (1840–1905)	27.3 (1906–1949)	n.d.	13/4
Southern Rocky Mountain Park (Skinner and Laven 1983)	>20	15	21.5 (1703–1839)	12.8 (1840–1928)	6.5 (1929–1942)	6/3	6/3
Fourmile Canyon, northern Front Range (Goldblum and Veblen 1992)	72	14	31.8 (1721–1858)	8.1 (1859–1920)	28.0 (1921–1949)	8/3	8/2
Eldorado Springs, northern Front Range (Veblen et al. 1996)	55	32	8.2 (1703–1858)	4.4 (1859–1920)	no fires (1921–1990)	14/4	14/0
Subalpine forests							
Medicine Bow Range (Kipfmueller 1997)*	73	51	9.4 (1569–1867) 33.1	1.9 (1868–1911) 10.8	3.5 (1912–1996) 28.0	16/5 3/2	16/9 3/2
Taylor Park, Southwestern Colorado (Zimmerman and Laven 1984)	28	38	12.5 (1759–1833)	2.4 (1834–1908)	3.4 (1909–1976)	32/21	32/7

*The top line refers to all fires and the lower line refers to only stand-replacing fires.

any influences of climatic variation on seedling establishment (Mast et al. 1998). Overgrazing by livestock in the late 1800s to early 1900s also has been suggested as an explanation of ponderosa pine increases (Marr 1961). Heavy grazing can reduce competition from grasses and expose bare mineral soil for tree seedling establishment, but tree invasion of grasslands has been continuous during the recent several decades of declining livestock impact (Veblen and Lorenz 1986; Mast et al. 1998). Although the timing and rate of ponderosa pine expansion during the present century probably have been influenced by short-term climatic variation and changes in grazing pressures, without the shift from a high-frequency fire regime to nearly total fire exclusion, this tree expansion is unlikely to have taken its present course. In contrast, in the subalpine zone, conifer invasion into grasslands is linked more strongly to climatic variation or to decreased pressure from livestock (Dunwiddie 1977, Jakubos and Romme 1993). In ponderosa pine woodlands in New Mexico, a decline in fire frequency in the early nineteenth century coincides with increased grazing by sheep that would have reduced fine fuels (Savage and Swetnam 1990). Similar relationships of livestock introduction and decreased fire spread due to fuel reduction probably exist for the Colorado-Wyoming region.

Increased density of ponderosa pine stands during the period of fire exclusion has changed the susceptibility of these forests to stand-replacing fires, pathogen infestation, and perhaps insect outbreak. Qualitatively, it is obvious that very sparse ponderosa pine woodlands did not support crown fires due to lack of woody fuel continuity. Quantitatively, however, the increase in area newly capable of supporting crown fires is difficult to estimate because even prior to any significant effects of fire exclusion some stand-replacing fires occurred in ponderosa pine forests (Veblen and Lorenz 1986, Shinneman and Baker 1997). At more mesic sites, initially open stands of ponderosa pine now have understories of suppressed Douglas fir that are susceptible to insect-caused mortality that further increases the hazard of stand-replacing fires. Dwarf mistle-toe populations are well known to accumulate in both ponderosa pine and lodgepole pine stands where fires have been excluded, and the weakening effects of these hemi-parasites may increase stand-susceptibility to other pests and fire (Zimmerman and Laven 1984; Kipfmueller and Baker 1998b).

A second pattern of altered fire regimes documented for some parts of the Southern Rocky Mountains is an increase in fire frequency in the latter half of the nineteenth century due to burning by EuroAmerican settlers (Table 3.1; Rowdabaugh 1978, Laven et al.

1980, Skinner and Laven 1983, Goldblum and Veblen 1992, Kipfmueller 1997). Although this pattern is also found in additional fire history studies for the Sangre de Cristo Mountains, Colorado (Alington 1998) and the southern Front Range (Donnegan 1999), other studies in progress in Colorado do not report the same pattern (W. Romme, *personal communication*; P. Brown, *personal communication*). For the montane zone of the northern Colorado Front Range, fire dates from 526 trees from 41 sites indicate a nearly two-fold increase in the mean annual percentage of recorder trees recording fire scars for the period 1851 to 1920 in comparison with the previous 70 years (Veblen et al. 1996). Locations of fire-scarred trees in the northern Front Range indicate that there was also an increase in the frequency of large (i.e., >25 ha) burns during the late nineteenth century (Laven et al. 1980, Goldblum and Veblen 1992). Thus, the increased fire frequency associated with settlement was not exclusively an increase in small fires. The importance of large fires during the EuroAmerican settlement period is also consistent with the abundance in today's landscape of extensive, postfire stands of ponderosa pine, Douglas-fir and/or lodgepole pine that originated mostly between 1850 and 1910 (Clements 1910; Zimmerman and Laven 1984; Veblen and Lorenz 1986; Peet 1988; Hadley and Veblen 1993; Parker and Parker 1994; Kipfmueller 1997; Mast et al. 1998). As discussed below, the homogeneity of stand age and structure over such large areas may be influencing fire hazard and susceptibility to pathogen and insect attack at a landscape scale in the Southern Rocky Mountains.

INSECT OUTBREAKS

The most important insect pests of the Southern Rocky Mountains, all native species, are: mountain pine beetle, Douglas fir bark beetle, spruce beetle and western spruce budworm. All of the bark beetles tend to attack larger trees (typically >10–20 cm in diameter) and their attacks are normally lethal. They bore through the bark, create egg galleries, mate, and deposit eggs in the phloem layer. They carry with them fungi, which, in conjunction with the beetle's excavations, results in blockage of water- and nutrient-conducting tissue, killing the tree. In contrast, western spruce budworm is a defoliating moth with larvae that feed on needles and cones. Its attacks may or may not be lethal to the tree depending on numerous factors as discussed in a following section.

Mountain Pine Beetle

In the Southern Rocky Mountains the mountain pine beetle primarily attacks live ponderosa and lodgepole pines; during epidemics, nearly 100% of overstory trees can be killed over many square kilometers (Schmid and Mata 1996). In the montane zone, outbreaks may convert mixed-aged stands to young stands of ponderosa pine or accelerate succession towards Douglas fir (Amman 1977). In the subalpine zone, elimination of the overstory lodgepole pine by a beetle outbreak can accelerate succession towards the more shade-tolerant Engelmann spruce and subalpine fir.

Mountain pine beetle outbreaks may recur in the same general region within about 20 years and may recur in the same stand in about 50 to 100 years depending on how much of the original stand was killed by beetles (Schmid and Amman 1992). Durations of outbreaks are quite variable (e.g., 2 to 14 years) and may decline rapidly if weather becomes unfavorable to the beetle populations (Schmid and Mata 1996). Numerous mountain pine beetle outbreaks have occurred during the twentieth century throughout the Southern Rocky Mountains (Roe and Amman 1970). It is widely believed that increased stand densities associated with fire exclusion in this century have increased the susceptibility of stands to outbreaks of mountain pine beetle (Roe and Amman 1970, Schmid and Mata 1996). However, no long-term (e.g., based on tree-ring records) studies have been done on the frequency or duration of outbreaks to examine this hypothesis. Also this hypothesis ignores the fact that the larger trees (i.e., those most susceptible to beetle attack) were removed from stands that subsequently have experienced outbreaks. Occurrence of extensive outbreaks in the late 1800s and early 1900s (Roe and Amman 1970) indicates that not all outbreaks can be attributed to the stand structural changes resulting from modern fire exclusion. Outbreaks are believed to increase the likelihood of fire occurrence over a period of about two years while the dead leaves persist on the trees (Schmid and Amman 1992), but longer-term influences on flammability may be quite complex. The fall of the dead leaves may also temporarily decrease fuel continuity in the canopy, but subsequent ingrowth of understory trees in combination with fall of dead trees eventually may increase fire hazard (Knight 1987). Fire-injured trees are generally more susceptible to attack by mountain pine beetle (Amman and Ryan 1991).

Douglas Fir Bark Beetle

The Douglas fir bark beetle can cause widespread mortality of Douglas fir in the Southern Rocky Mountains, and its epidemics appear to have arisen during and expanded following outbreaks of western spruce budworm (Schmid and Mata 1996). Outbreaks have been observed to last from 5 to over 10 years, and intervals between outbreaks in the same areas may be on the order of 15 to 35 years (Hadley and Veblen 1993, Schmid and Mata 1996). Many of the same potential interactions with fire previously mentioned for mountain pine beetles apply to Douglas fir beetles (Cates and Alexander 1982).

Spruce Beetle

The spruce beetle in the Southern Rocky Mountains mainly infests Engelmann spruce (Alexander 1987, Schmid and Mata 1996). Endemic spruce beetle populations infest fallen trees and scattered live trees but during outbreaks can kill most canopy spruce over extensive areas. Spruce less than 10 cm in diameter usually are not attacked, nor are the subalpine fir, and their accelerated growth following the death of canopy trees can be used to date outbreaks (Veblen et al. 1991*b*). Stands containing large (i.e., >55 cm diameter) spruce and especially those in valley bottom sites are the most susceptible to outbreaks. Blowdowns or the accumulation of logging debris are usually the immediate triggers of outbreaks (Schmid and Frye 1977), which is an important distinction from outbreaks of mountain pine or Douglas fir beetle.

In 1939 a strong windstorm blew down extensive areas of subalpine forest in western Colorado, promoting the growth of endemic spruce beetle populations into the largest recorded epidemic of the twentieth century that killed 4.3 billion board feet of timber in White River, Grand Mesa, and Routt National Forests (Massey and Wygant 1954). Tree-ring methods and historical photographs document the occurrence of a spruce beetle outbreak in the mid-1800s in an area of northwestern Colorado at least as large as the 1940s outbreak (Baker and Veblen 1990; Veblen et al. 1991*b*, 1994). This widespread spruce beetle outbreak in the mid-1800s, as well as outbreaks recorded in fossil records (Feiler and Anderson 1993), occurred prior to any significant impact of EuroAmericans on the subalpine forests of northwestern Colorado in the form of either logging or fire suppression. Thus, widespread spruce beetle outbreaks are clearly a natural component of disturbance regimes in the subalpine zone.

Spruce beetle outbreaks result in a massive shift in dominance in basal area from spruce to fir due both to mortality of large spruce and the ingrowth of formerly suppressed seedlings and saplings of sub-alpine fir that are typically the most abundant tree species in the understory (Veblen et al. 1991*c*). Some new seedling establishment of spruce and fir is favored but not of the seral lodgepole pine, probably due to lack of heat for opening its serotinous cones and inhibition of seedling establishment by an already established understory. Spruce beetle outbreaks probably increase the hazard of fire ignition during a relatively short period of two to five years when fine fuels from dead needles and twigs are more abundant. The slow decay and fall rate of the dead-standing trees (Hinds et al. 1965) implies that there is an increased potential for more intense fire over many decades, but effects on stand flammability are complicated by the reduced continuity of fuels in the canopy.

The frequency of severe outbreaks in the same stand is limited by lack of trees large enough to be susceptible to beetle attack (Schmid and Frye 1977). At a stand scale, lack of large-diameter spruce for 70 to 100 years after a severe outbreak or a stand-replacing fire prevents that stand from being attacked even when surrounding older forest is attacked (Veblen et al. 1994, Schmid and Mata 1996). However, at a landscape scale, the White River area was affected by two major outbreaks in a span of only about 100 years (Veblen et al. 1991*b*). At a smaller scale in a 594-ha area of subalpine forest in northwestern Colorado, tree-ring methods documented three extensive spruce beetle outbreaks since the early 1700s (Veblen et al. 1994). Mean return interval and rotation period were 117 and 259 years, respectively, which made disturbance by spruce beetle more important, at least spatiotemporally, than disturbance by fire in this valley.

Western Spruce Budworm

The western spruce budworm primarily defoliates Douglas fir and white fir in the Southern Rocky Mountains (Schmid and Mata 1996). Extensive defoliation by budworm over several years can produce high levels of tree mortality. Suppressed trees and trees stressed because of poor site conditions suffer higher rates of mortality (Cates and Alexander 1982). Young, vigorous postfire stands may show minimal defoliation by budworm whereas multitiered stands with high stem densities and a range of tree sizes are more severely affected (Hadley and Veblen 1993). Spruce budworm outbreaks in mixed stands of Douglas fir and ponderosa pine tend to shift dominance towards pine (Hadley and Veblen 1993). During outbreaks, western spruce budworm larvae also consume cones and seeds which further impedes the ability of stands

Table 3.2. Major historic insect outbreaks in the northern Colorado Front Range. *Source:* Barrows (1936) and Schmid and Mata (1996).

Mountain pine beetle	Western spruce budworm	Douglas fir beetle
1920s	Early 1940s	Mid-1930s
1930s	Late 1950s	Early 1950s
Late 1950s	Late 1970s–1980s	Mid-1980s
Mid-1970s		

to recover from attacks (Schmid and Mata 1996). During this century, several outbreaks of western spruce budworm and Douglas fir bark beetle have greatly altered the structure and composition of the montane forests of the northern Colorado Front Range (Table 3.2; Hadley and Veblen 1993). Durations of outbreaks are highly variable but average about eleven years (Swetnam and Lynch 1993). Tree-ring studies indicate that since the early eighteenth century epidemics in the Southern Rocky Mountains have occurred at a frequency of about 20 to 33 years in the same stands (Swetnam and Lynch 1989, Shimek 1996).

Given the apparently greater susceptibility of stands with suppressed understories of Douglas fir saplings, it is likely that fire exclusion during this century is creating a more homogeneous landscape of increased susceptibility to budworm outbreaks. Studies from Montana to New Mexico suggest that since the early 1900s budworm outbreaks have become increasingly severe and synchronous over larger areas (McCune 1983, Anderson et al. 1987, Swetnam and Lynch 1989, Hadley and Veblen 1993). Increased nineteenth century burning in the upper montane zone also would have created extensive areas of postfire even-aged stands that more or less synchronously become susceptible to budworm outbreaks (Hadley and Veblen 1993). During the initial decades of stand development, these postfire stands are not highly susceptible to outbreaks, but as stands continue to age they take on a multitiered structure with subcanopy populations of suppressed Douglas fir that increase stand susceptibility to outbreaks. This hypothesis is consistent with a period of reduced budworm outbreaks in the Front Range from the 1880s through the 1920s that is followed by several widespread and severe outbreaks (Swetnam and Lynch 1989, Shimek 1996).

WIND

Exceptionally strong windstorms occasionally cause extensive blowdowns in the forests of the Southern Rocky Mountains, especially in the subalpine zone, and are important determinants of stand development patterns (Alexander 1987, Veblen et al. 1989). In the subalpine zone, frequency of high wind events may be greater; the rugged terrain creates greater turbulence, and the probability of heavy snow loads is greater (Alexander 1987). In the subalpine zone most tree species also are shallow rooted and development of dense, postfire stands increases stand susceptibility to blowdown (Alexander 1987). Single windstorms can produce enormous blowdowns. For example, in 1987, a tornado blew down 6,000 ha of forest in the Teton Wilderness (Fujita 1989, Knight 1994), and, in 1997, easterly winds of 200–250 km/hr blew down over 8,000 ha of forest on the western slope of the Park Range, Colorado, in Routt National Forest (USDA Forest Service 1998). In addition to these rare but spectacularly large blowdowns, small blowdowns of 0.2 to several hectares are common in the subalpine forests (Alexander 1964, Veblen et al. 1991*a*).

Despite the importance of small and large blowdowns to the dynamics of the subalpine forests, few studies have been done on either the frequencies or consequences of such events. Windthrow is greater where topographic or logging patterns constrict and therefore accelerate wind speed (Alexander 1964). Other features that increase the hazard of windthrow in relation to cutting operations include shallow soils, poorly drained soils, location on leeward cutting boundaries, dense stands, infestation by root and butt rots, and steeper slopes (Alexander 1964). Time elapsed since last fire, and therefore stage of seral development, is an important determinant of the successional consequences of disturbance by blowdown. For example, a 1973 blowdown of a 15-ha stand of a 350-year-old postfire forest in Rocky Mountain National Park accelerated succession from dominance by lodgepole pine towards subalpine fir and Engelmann spruce (Veblen et al. 1989). Similarly, comparison of wind disturbances in old-growth spruce-fir stands versus an adjacent approximately 250-year-old postfire stand revealed the latter to be less susceptible to small blowdowns (<0.3 ha) (Veblen et al. 1991*a*). As postfire stands dominated by lodgepole pine age, they appear to become more susceptible to moderate-sized blowdown (e.g., >10 ha), and blowdowns strongly accelerate succession towards spruce and fir (Veblen et al. 1989). This change, in turn, increases stand susceptibility to spruce beetle outbreak (Schmid and Frye 1977). Thus, where humans have altered forest structures through changes in fire regimes and logging they have also altered the potential response to natural windstorms. Although disturbance by wind should be sensitive to changes in atmospheric circulation patterns that change either the frequency of windstorms or the directions of major gusts, no long-term data evaluate whether such changes have occurred over the last several centuries in the Southern Rocky Mountains.

INFLUENCES OF CLIMATIC VARIATION ON DISTURBANCE REGIMES
Fire

Although the focus of this book is on fragmentation caused by humans, it is important to recognize that variation in regional climate is also an important influence on landscape heterogeneity through its effects on fire and insect disturbances. On an interannual scale, synchronous occurrence of fire-scar dates from areas too large for fire to have spread from a single ignition point is strong evidence that regional climate is influencing fire regimes. For example, widespread burning in 1879 and 1880 is recorded in early, albeit fragmentary, documentary sources (Sudworth 1899, Jack 1899, Plummer 1912) as well as tree-ring studies of fire history from southern Wyoming to southern Colorado (i.e., Skinner and Laven 1983, Zimmerman and Laven 1984, Goldblum and Veblen 1992, Kipfmueller 1997, Veblen et al. 1996). Other individual years that recorded fire scars at disjunct locations over this large area include 1684, 1809, 1872, and 1893 (Kipfmueller 1997) which suggests that at a regional scale climatic anomalies increase fire hazard over extensive areas.

In the montane zone of the northern Colorado Front Range, comparison of tree-ring records of fire and climatic variation from 1600 to the beginning of fire suppression in 1920 indicates that fire is strongly associated with below average spring precipitation during the fire year and with above average spring moisture availability two to three years prior to the fire year (Veblen et al., *in press*). These records also show that for the two to three years following increased spring precipitation associated with El Niño events, fire occurrence increases. ENSO (El Niño–Southern Oscillation) signals are also found in fire records from ponderosa pine woodlands in Arizona and New Mexico (Swetnam and Betancourt 1990). North of the Front Range, however, sensitivity to ENSO events weakens (Kiladis and Diaz 1989), and it is likely that mid-latitude circulation anomalies will have greater influences on fire regimes. From an understanding of the effects of interannual variation on fire regimes, it may be possible to link longer-term trends in fire occurrence to longer-lasting (i.e., multidecadal) changes in atmospheric circulation patterns such as frequencies and intensities of ENSO events. However, the challenge is to discriminate between the influences of human activities and climatic variation on fire regimes.

Despite the availability of instrumental climatic records and more complete fire records (e.g., USDA Forest Service and National Park data) for the present century, it is difficult to clearly relate long-term changes in fire regimes to climatic variation. For all the national forests of northern Colorado, there appears to be a trend towards increasing numbers for all fires, lightning-ignited fires, and forested area burned per year during the 1970s and 1980s (Fig. 3.1). Increases in areas burned during the last few decades of the twentieth century generally for the western United States (Auclair and Bedford 1994, Balling et al. 1992) have multiple and nonmutually exclusive explanations. These explanations include: (1) improved accuracy of estimates of areas burned based on the use of aerial photographs since ca. 1940; (2) fire suppression effects on fuel accumulation; (3) adoption of "let burn" policies during the 1970s and 1980s in some areas; (4) altered fuel conditions due to increased insect-caused tree mortality; and (5) for some areas, increased temperatures.

Although it has been hypothesized that a trend towards warmer temperatures over the past few decades has contributed to increased burning and insect outbreaks generally in western North America (Auclair and Bedford 1994), for the Rocky Mountain region the evidence is equivocal. Analysis of approximately 100 years of climatic trends based on 79 climatic stations from northern Montana to southern Colorado reveals substantial differences in temperature and precipitation trends according to seasonality, latitude, and elevation, rather than a regionally uniform warming trend (T. Kittel, *personal communication*). For example, in the northern Colorado Front Range for high elevations there is evidence of a post-1951 decline in mean annual temperature in contrast to warming at the same time in adjacent low elevations (Williams et al. 1996). Furthermore, widespread fire occurrence at low elevation can be favored by enhanced production of fine fuels associated with above-average moisture availability (Veblen et al. 1996), whereas widespread fires in the subalpine zone are favored mainly by drought (Clagg 1975, Romme and Despain 1989, Renkin and Despain 1992). Thus, asynchrony in climatic trends with elevation as well as differential climatic sensitivity of fire regimes at high versus low

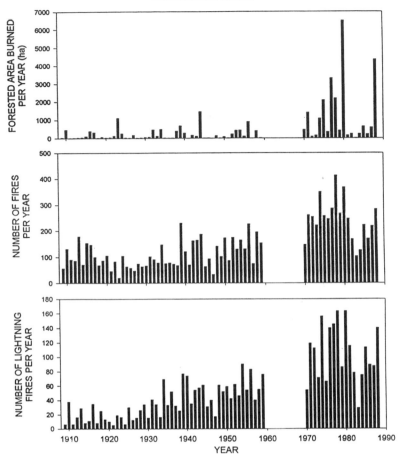

Fig. 3.1. Records of fire occurrence from five national forests in Colorado: Pike, Arapaho, Roosevelt, Routt, and White River National Forests for 1909 to 1988. No data are available for 1960–1969.

elevations greatly complicate the determination of causal influences of regional climatic variation on trends in fire regimes.

Insect Outbreaks

Weather profoundly affects the life cycles of insect pests as well as the capability of trees to respond to insect attacks, yet the effects of climatic variation on the occurrence of insect outbreaks are poorly understood (Swetnam and Lynch 1993, Logan et al. 1995). For example, mortality of mountain pine beetle is increased by cold winters, and cool temperatures are believed to be the major restriction on mountain pine beetle outbreaks at high elevations (Logan et al. 1995). Generally, warmer temperatures promote bark beetle outbreaks both through their favorable influence on the life cycle of the insect and drought-related declines in the tree's ability to withstand attack (Frye et al. 1974, Amman 1977). However, nonclimatic factors related to stand structure also play such important roles that the association of outbreaks with particular types of weather is difficult to verify quantitatively.

Although it has long been believed that drought predisposes Douglas fir stands to outbreaks of western spruce budworm (Cates and Alexander 1982), recent research from Colorado and New Mexico suggests that wet periods may favor outbreaks. For example, in northern New Mexico tree-ring records of outbreaks from 1690 to 1989 indicate a tendency for outbreaks to coincide with years of increased spring precipitation (Swetnam and Lynch 1993). These records contrast with findings for the northwestern United States and eastern Canada where shorter-term records indicate an association of budworm outbreaks with periods of moisture deficit (Kemp et al. 1985). Tree-ring records from the northern Colorado Front Range indicate an association of initiation dates of budworm outbreaks with a sequence of one year of below-average spring moisture availability followed by a couple of years of above-average moisture availability (Veblen et al., *unpublished data*). Although the mechanisms relating budworm population dynamics and tree susceptibility to attack are not clear (Swetnam and Lynch 1993), there is strong evidence that climatic variation influences the occurrence of budworm outbreaks. However, nonclimatic changes in stand structures may play an equal or greater role.

CONCLUSIONS

Returning to the four key questions about disturbance that were stated in the introduction to this chapter, it is evident that there are only preliminary and partial answers to those questions for the Southern Rocky Mountain forests. For example, in a broad sense, subalpine forests are characterized mainly by stand-replacing fires whereas lower montane forests support more surface fires, but robust quantitative analyses of fire behavior along elevational gradients are lacking. Similarly, although potential links among different disturbance types in the Southern Rocky Mountains are widely recognized and numerous examples are given in this review and elsewhere (e.g., Knight 1987), there are few studies that quantitatively document these linkages (e.g., Malanson and Butler 1984, Suffling 1993, Veblen et al. 1994). In terms of human impacts on fire regimes in the montane zone, the pattern of fire exclusion during this century is well documented for many sites throughout the Southern Rocky Mountains. The increase in burning associated with late nineteenth century EuroAmerican settlement is strong for some areas and absent for others; it may be limited to areas of more intensive land use such as the mining areas of the northern Colorado Front Range. Vegetation managers should regard both trends as common patterns that for any particular area must be corroborated by fire history studies based on adequate numbers of sample trees and sample sites. The high degree of spatial variation in fire history associated with differences in habitat and human activities implies that many more fire history studies are required in the Southern Rocky Mountains.

In contrast to the quantitatively large impact of fire exclusion on fire frequencies in the montane zone, in the subalpine zone fire exclusion over the past 70 to 90 years probably has only moderately increased mean fire return intervals from their pre-twentieth century levels. This needs to be recognized in evaluating forest health issues in the subalpine zone. For example, extensive outbreaks of spruce beetles, such as the mid-1800s and 1940s outbreaks affecting most of northwestern Colorado, cannot be attributed to fire exclusion. In contrast, for the montane zone there is strong evidence of changes in stand structures and susceptibility to insect pests during the fire exclusion period. For example, in the montane zone of the northern Colorado Front Range there is evidence of a shift during the twentieth century towards a more homogeneous landscape of stands that are increasingly susceptible to both insect outbreaks and stand-replacing fires. Even within the montane zone, however, there is substantial variation in disturbance history and patterns of vegetation change, and some of the generalizations made in this review may not be valid for a particular site. In discussion of management options, it is important to recognize the high degree of variation in disturbance histories along environmental gradients and to avoid taking generalizations out of their appropriate context.

Interannual climatic variability can create conditions favorable to exceptionally widespread burning in individual years as well illustrated by the 1988 Yellowstone fires, and multidecadal climatic variation potentially can have similarly dramatic influences on patterns of disturbance by fire and insects. In the context of forest fragmentation, it is important to consider the potentially large role of climatic variation in altering disturbance regimes and vegetation patterns. For the forests of the western United States in general, it has been suggested that recent increases in fire and insect outbreaks reflect a combination of synchronization of forest structures by nineteenth century burning, fuel accumulation under modern fire exclusion, and fire-promoting weather associated with more frequent El Niño events since the mid-1970s (Auclair and Bedford 1994). Although the Southern Rocky Mountains appear to conform to that general pattern, much more site-specific research is needed on how humans and climatic variation affect disturbance patterns and landscape structure (Baker 1994, 1995). A better understanding of landscape patterns in relation to disturbance patterns requires that researchers more fully consider the potential influences of both humans and climatic variation on disturbance regimes.

ACKNOWLEDGMENTS

This review benefited from collaborative work with many colleagues and students including: W. L. Baker, J. Donnegan, K. S. Hadley, T. Kitzberger, D. C. Lorenz, A. J. Rebertus, M. Reid, S. Shimek, T. Stohlgren, T. W. Swetnam, and R. Villalba. For comments on the manuscript I thank W. L. Baker, P. Brown, J. Donnegan, D. C. Lorenz, and W. H. Romme.

LITERATURE CITED

Alexander, R. R. 1964. Minimizing windfall around clear cuttings in spruce-fir forests. *Forest Science* 10: 130–142.

Alexander, R. R. 1987. Ecology, silviculture and management of the Engelmann spruce-subalpine fir type in the central and Southern Rocky Mountains. USDA Forest Service, Agricultural Handbook No. 659.

Alington, K. 1998. Fire history and landscape pattern in the Sangre de Cristo mountains, Colorado. Ph.D. thesis, Colorado State University, Fort Collins, Colorado, USA

Amman, G. D. 1977. The role of the mountain pine beetle in lodgepole pine ecosystems: impact on succession. Pages 3–18 *in* W. J. Mattson, editor, *Arthropods in forest ecosystems: proceedings in the life sciences.* Springer-Verlag, New York, New York, USA.

Amman, G. D., and K. C. Ryan. 1991. Insect infestation of fire-injured trees in the Greater Yellowstone Area. USDA Forest Service, Research Note INT-398, Intermountain Forest and Range Experiment Station, Ogden, Utah, USA.

Anderson, L., C. E. Carlson, and R. H. Wakimoto. 1987. Forest fire frequency and western spruce budworm in western Montana. *Forest Ecology and Management* 22: 251–260.

Auclair, A.N.D., and J. A. Bedford. 1994. Conceptual origins of catastrophic forest mortality in the western United States. *Journal of Sustainable Forestry* 2: 249–265.

Baker, W. L. 1994. Restoration of landscape structure altered by fire suppression. *Conservation Biology* 8: 763–769.

Baker, W. L. 1995. Longterm response of disturbance landscapes to human intervention and global change. *Landscape Ecology* 10: 143–159.

Baker, W. L., and T. T. Veblen. 1990. Spruce beetles and fires in the nineteenth century subalpine forests of western Colorado. *Arctic and Alpine Research* 22: 65–80.

Balling, R. C., Jr., G. A. Meyer, and S. G. Wells. 1992. Climate change in Yellowstone National Park: is the drought-related risk of wildfires increasing? *Climatic Change* 22: 35–45.

Barrows, J. S. 1936. Forest insect problems of the Rocky Mountain National Park. Unpublished report, Rocky Mountain National Park, Estes Park, Colorado, USA.

Cates, R. H., and H. Alexander. 1982. Host resistance and susceptibility. Pages 212–263 *in* J. B. Mitton and K. B. Sturgeon, editors, *Bark beetles in North American conifers*. University of Texas Press, Austin, Texas, USA.

Clagg, H. B. 1975. Fire ecology in high-elevation forests in Colorado. Master's thesis. Colorado State University, Fort Collins, Colorado, USA.

Clements, G. E. 1910. The life history of lodgepole burn forests. USDA Forest Service, Bulletin 79:7–56.

Cooper, C. F. 1960. Changes in vegetation, structure, and growth of southwestern pine forests since white settlement. *Ecological Monographs* 30: 129–164.

Donnegan, J. 1999. Climatic and human influences on fire regimes in Pike National Forest. Ph.D. thesis, University of Colorado, Boulder, Colorado, USA.

Dunwiddie, P. W. 1977. Recent tree invasion of subalpine meadows in the Wind River Mountains, Wyoming. *Arctic and Alpine Research* 9: 393–399.

Feiler, E. J., and R. S. Anderson. 1993. The paleoecology of Dome Creek Meadow, Bear River Corridor, Garfield County, Colorado. Unpublished report to the USDA Forest Service, Steamboat Springs, Colorado, USA.

Finney, M. A. 1995. The missing tail and other considerations for the use of fire history models. *International Journal of Wildland Fire* 5: 197–202.

Fossett, F. 1880. *Colorado—its gold and silver mines, farms and stock ranges, and health and pleasure resorts.* C. G. Crawford, New York, USA.

Frye, R. H., H. W. Flake, and C. J. Germain. 1974. Spruce beetle winter mortality resulting from record low temperatures in Arizona. *Environmental Entomologist* 3: 752–754.

Fujita, T. T. 1989. The Teton-Yellowstone tornado of 21 July 1987. *Monthly Weather Review* 117: 1913–1940.

Goldblum, D., and T. T. Veblen. 1992. Fire history of a ponderosa pine/Douglas fir forest in the Colorado Front Range. *Physical Geography* 13: 133–148.

Gruell, G. E. 1985. Indian fires in the interior west: a widespread influence. Pages 68–74 *in* J. E. Lotan, editor, *Proceedings: Symposium and Workshop on Wilderness Fire*. USDA Forest Service, General Technical Report INT-GTR-182.

Hadley, K. S., and T. T. Veblen. 1993. Stand response to western spruce budworm and Douglas fir bark beetle outbreaks, Colorado Front Range. *Canadian Journal of Forest Research* 23: 479–491.

Hinds, T. E., F. G. Hawksworth, and R. W. Davidson. 1965. Beetle-killed Engelmann spruce: its deterioration in Colorado. *Journal of Forestry* 63: 536–542.

Jack, J. G. 1899. Pikes Peak, Plum Creek, and South Platte Reserves. Twentieth Annual Report of the United States Geological Survey to the Secretary of the Interior, 1898–1899. United States Government Printing Office, Washington, D.C., USA.

Jakubos, B., and W. H. Romme. 1993. Invasion of subalpine meadows by lodgepole pine in Yellowstone National Park, Wyoming. *Arctic and Alpine Research* 25: 382–390.

Johnson, E. A., and S. L. Gutsell. 1994. Fire frequency models, methods and interpretations. *Advances in Ecological Research* 25: 239–287.

Kemp, W. P., D. O. Everson, and W. G. Wellington. 1985. Regional climatic patterns and western spruce budworm outbreaks. USDA Forest Service Cooperative State Research Service Technical Bulletin Number 1693.

Kiladis, G. N., and H. F. Diaz. 1989. Global climatic anomalies associated with extremes in the Southern Oscillation. *Journal of Climate* 2: 1069–1090.

Kipfmueller, K. F. 1997. A fire history of a subalpine forest in southeastern Wyoming. Master's thesis, University of Wyoming, Laramie, Wyoming, USA.

Kipfmueller, K. F., and W. L. Baker. 1998a. A comparison of three techniques to date stand-replacing fires in lodgepole pine forests. *Forest Ecology and Management* 104: 171–177.

Kipfmueller, K. F., and W. L. Baker. 1998b. Fires and dwarf mistletoe in a Rocky Mountain lodgepole pine ecosystem. *Forest Ecology and Management* 108: 77 84.

Knight, D. H. 1987. Parasites, lightning, and the vegetation mosaic in wilderness landscapes. Pages 59–83 *in* M. G. Turner, editor, *Landscape heterogeneity and disturbance.* Springer-Verlag, New York, New York, USA.

Knight, D. H. 1994. *Mountains and plains: the ecology of Wyoming landscapes.* Yale University Press, New Haven, Connecticut, USA.

Koterba, W. D., and J. R. Habeck. 1971. Grasslands of the North Fork Valley, Glacier Naional Park, Montana. *Canadian Journal of Botany* 49: 1627–1636.

Laven, R. D., P. N. Omi, J. G. Wyant, and A. S. Pinkerton. 1980. Interpretation of the fire scar data from a ponderosa pine ecosystem in the central Rocky Mountains, Colorado. USDA Forest Service, General Technical Report RM-81.

Logan, J. A., P. V. Bolstad, B. J. Bentz, and D. L. Perkins. 1995. Assessing the effects of changing climate on mountain pine beetle dynamics. Pages 92–105 *in* R. W. Tinus, editor, *Interior west global change workshop.* USDA Forest Service, General Technical Report RM-GTR-262.

Malanson, G. P., and D. R. Butler. 1984. Avalanche paths as fuel breaks: implications for fire management. *Journal of Environmental Management* 19: 229–238.

Marr, J. W. 1961. Ecosystems of the east slope of the Front Range in Colorado. *University of Colorado Studies Series in Biology* 8.

Massey, C. L., and N. D. Wygant. 1954. Biology and control of the Engelmann spruce beetle in Colorado. USDA, Circular No. 944.

Mast, J. N., T. T. Veblen, and M. E. Hodgson. 1997. Tree invasion within a pine/grassland ecotone: an approach with historic aerial photography and GIS modeling. *Forest Ecology and Management* 93: 187–194.

Mast, J. N., T. T. Veblen, and Y. B. Linhart. 1998. Disturbance and climatic influences on age structure of ponderosa pine at the pine/grassland ecotone, Colorado Front Range. *Journal of Biogeography* 25: 743–767.

McCune, B. 1983. Fire frequency reduced two orders of magnitude in the Bitteroot Canyons, Montana. *Canadian Journal of Forest Research* 13: 212–218.

Paine, R. T., and S. A. Levin. 1981. Intertidal landscapes: disturbance and the dynamics of pattern. *Ecological Monographs* 51: 145–178.

Parker, A. J., and K. C. Parker. 1994. Structural variability of mature lodgepole pine stands on gently sloping terrain in Taylor Park Basin, Colorado. *Canadian Journal of Forest Research* 24: 2020–2029.

Peet, R. K. 1988. Forests of the Rocky Mountains. Pages 63–101 *in* M.B. Barbour and W.D. Billings, editors, *North American terrestrial vegetation.* Cambridge University Press, Cambridge, UK.

Plummer, F. G. 1912. Forest fires: their causes, extent and effects, with a summary of recorded destruction and loss. USDA Forest Service Bulletin 117.

Renkin, R. A., and D. G. Despain. 1992. Fuel moisture, forest type, and lightning-caused fire in Yellowstone National Park. *Canadian Journal of Forest Research* 22: 37–45.

Roe, A. L., and G. D. Amman. 1970. The mountain pine beetle in lodgepole pine forests. USDA Forest Service Research Paper INT-71.

Romme, W. H. 1982. Fire and landscape diversity in Yellowstone National Park. *Ecological Monographs* 52: 199–221.

Romme, W. H., and D. G. Despain. 1989. Historical perspective on the Yellowstone fires of 1988. *BioScience* 39: 695–699.

Romme, W. H., and D. H. Knight. 1981. Fire frequency and subalpine forest succession along a topographic gradient in Wyoming. *Ecology* 62: 319–326.

Romme, W. H., and D. H. Knight. 1982. Landscape diversity: the concept applied to Yellowstone Park. *BioScience* 32: 664–670.

Rowdabaugh, K. M. 1978. The role of fire in the ponderosa pine-mixed conifer ecosystem. Master's thesis, Colorado State University, Fort Collins, Colorado, USA.

Savage, M., and T. W. Swetnam. 1990. Early 19th century fire decline following sheep pasturing in a Navajo ponderosa pine forest. *Ecology* 71: 2374–2378.

Schmid, J. M., and G. D. Amman. 1992. Dendroctonus beetles and old-growth forests in the Rockies. Pages 51–59 *in* M. R. Kaufmann, W. H. Moir, and R. L. Bassett, editors, *Old-growth forests in the Southwest and Rocky Mountain regions.* USDA Forest Service, General Technical Report RM-213.

Schmid, J. M., and R. H. Frye. 1977. Spruce beetle in the Rockies. USDA Forest Service, General Technical Report RM-49.

Schmid, J. M., and S.A. Mata. 1996. Natural variability of specific forest insect populations and their associated effects in Colorado. USDA Forest Service General Technical Report RM-GTR-275.

Shimek, S. W. 1996. A dendrochronological history of western spruce budworm (*Choristoneura occidentalis* Freeman) infestations and outbreaks in the northern Colorado Front Range. Master's thesis. University of Colorado, Boulder, Colorado, USA.

Shinneman, D. J., and W. L. Baker. 1997. Nonequilibrium dynamics between catastrophic disturbances and old-growth forests in ponderosa pine landscapes of
the Black Hills. *Conservation Biology* 11: 1276–1288.

Skinner, T. V., and R. D. Laven. 1983. A fire history of the Longs Peak region of
Rocky Mountain National Park. Pages 71–74 *in Proceedings of the seventh confer-
ence on fire and forest meteorology*, April 25–28, Fort Collins, CO. American
Meteorological Society, Boston, Massachusetts, USA.

Sudworth, G. B. 1899. White River Plateau Timber Land Reserve. Pages 117–179
*in Twentieth Annual Report of the United States Geological Survey, Part V. Forest
Reserves.* United States Government Printing Office, Washington, D.C., USA.

Suffling, R. 1993. Induction of vertical zones in sub-alpine valley forests by ava-
lanche-formed fuel breaks. *Landscape Ecology* 8: 127–138.

Swetnam, T. W., and J. L. Betancourt. 1990. Fire-southern oscillation relations in the
southwestern United States. *Science* 249: 1017–1020.

Swetnam, T. W., and A. M. Lynch. 1989. A tree-ring reconstruction of western
spruce budworm history in the Southern Rocky Mountains. *Forest Science* 35:
962–986.

Swetnam, T. W., and A. M. Lynch. 1993. Multi-century, regional-scale patterns of
western spruce budworm outbreaks. *Ecological Monographs* 63: 399–424.

Tice, J. H. 1872. *Over the plains and on the mountains.* Industrial Age Printing, St.
Louis, Missouri, USA.

USDA Forest Service. 1998. Preliminary assessment of blowdown on Routt
National Forest, October 1997. Rocky Mountain Research Station, unpublished report.

Veblen, T. T., K. S. Hadley, and M. S. Reid. 1991*a*. Disturbance and stand development of a Colorado subalpine forest. *Journal of Biogeography* 18: 707–716.

Veblen, T. T., K. S. Hadley, M. S. Reid, and A. J. Rebertus. 1989. Blowdown and
stand development in a Colorado subalpine forest. *Canadian Journal of Forest
Research* 19: 1218–1225.

Veblen, T. T., K. S. Hadley, M. S. Reid, and A. J. Rebertus. 1991*b*. Methods of
detecting past spruce beetle outbreaks in Rocky Mountain subalpine forest.
Canadian Journal of Forest Research 21: 242–254.

Veblen, T. T., K. S. Hadley, M. S. Reid, and A. J. Rebertus. 1991*c*. Stand response to
spruce beetle outbreak in Colorado subalpine forests. *Ecology* 72: 213–231.

Veblen, T. T., K. S. Hadley, E. M. Nel, T. Kitzberger, M. Reid, and R. Villalba. 1994.
Disturbance regime and disturbance interactions in a Rocky Mountain subalpine forest. *Journal of Ecology* 82: 125–135.

Veblen, T. T., T. Kitzberger, and J. Donnegan. 1996. Fire ecology in the wildland/
urban interface of Boulder County. Report to the City of Boulder Open Space,
Boulder, Colorado, USA.

Veblen, T. T., T. Kitzberger, and J. Donnegan. *In press*. Climatic and human influences on fire regimes in ponderosa pine forests in the Colorado Front Range.
Ecological Applications.

Veblen, T. T., and D. C. Lorenz. 1986. Anthropogenic disturbance and recovery
patterns in montane forests, Colorado Front Range. *Physical Geography* 7: 1–24.

Veblen, T. T., and D. C. Lorenz. 1991. *The Colorado Front Range: a century of ecological change.* University of Utah Press, Salt Lake City, Utah, USA.

White, A. S. 1985. Presettlement regeneration patterns in a southwestern ponderosa pine stand. *Ecology* 66: 589–594.

White, P. S., and S. T. A. Pickett. 1985. Natural disturbance and patch dynamics: an introduction. Pages 3–13 *in* S.T.A. Pickett and P. S. White, editors, *The ecology of natural disturbance and patch dynamics.* Academic Press, Inc., Orlando, Florida, USA.

Williams, M. W., M. Losleben, N. Caine, and D. Greenland. 1996. Changes in climate and hydrochemical respones in a high-elevation catchment, in the Rocky Mountains, USA. *Limnology and Oceanography* 41: 939–946.

Zimmerman, G. T., and R. D. Laven. 1984. Ecological implications of dwarf mistletoe and fire in lodgepole pine forests. Pages 123–131 *in* G. G. Hawksworth and R. F. Scharpf, editors, *Proceedings of the symposium on the biology of dwarf mistletoes.* United States Department of Agriculture Forest Service, General Technical Report RM-111.

4

Measuring and Analyzing Forest Fragmentation in the Rocky Mountains and Western United States

William L. Baker

INTRODUCTION

Direct habitat loss is globally the most significant threat to species, but habitat fragmentation is considered "the principal threat to most species in the temperate zone" (Wilcove et al. 1986). There are many effects of fragmentation, but the adverse effects of fragmentation arise in part because timber harvesting, clearing for agriculture, roads, and other land uses have ramifications well beyond the area directly affected by these activities. In the Amazon, 230,324 km^2 is deforested, but an additional 341,052 km^2 is edge habitat adjoining deforested areas; the total area affected by deforestation is more than 2.5 times the deforested area (Skole and Tucker 1993). Similarly, in the Medicine Bow National Forest, the actual area affected by timber harvesting may be 2.5–3.5 times the area of clear-cuts and roads (Reed et al. 1996a). While these ratios vary with the species or process that is considered, forest fragmentation generally has a greater effect than might be anticipated. It is insufficient, for example, to evaluate fragmentation due to timber harvesting by simply calculating the amount of harvested land area or the silvicultural rotation (Smith, *this volume*), as this ignores most of the known effects of fragmentation. The subject of this chapter is the measurement and analysis of forest fragmentation in the Rocky Mountains.

Why should we measure and analyze forest fragmentation? One answer is that simply counting up acres harvested or miles of transmission lines does not fully account for the environmental impacts of our land uses. This full accounting is required, under the National Environmental

Policy Act (NEPA), for all proposed federal actions. This requirement is also implied by the National Forest Management Act, because fragmentation may affect the viability and diversity of species (Keiter, *this volume*). Fragmentation has been shown to affect species in Western forests (Beauvais, *this volume*; Hansen and Rotella, *this volume*). Another answer is that efforts directed at sustaining individual species have been costly and in some cases ineffective (LaRoe 1993). An alternative to a "fine-filter" (species-level) approach is to use a "coarse filter" directed at managing ecosystems and landscapes, which could indirectly sustain 85–90% of the species (Hunter 1991, Kauffman et al. 1994). Fine-filter attention is still needed for the 10–15% of species that may require special management (Kauffman et al. 1994). Analyzing patterns in landscapes, such as those resulting from fragmentation of habitat by human land uses, is an essential part of the coarse-filter strategy. However, measurement and analysis of forest fragmentation are not ends in themselves; we need to know the condition of our landscapes to know how to modify management practices to minimize adverse effects.

Should we measure and analyze forest fragmentation at the project level or only when a plan for a large private or public forest is revised? An analysis of fragmentation is essential to plan revisions, completed every 10 years for national forests, but some have suggested that an analysis of each individual project's contribution to fragmentation is not needed (Estill 1996). However, individual projects often perceived to have little impact may in aggregate lead to significant cumulative effects (Preston and Bedford 1988, Council on Environmental Quality 1993). Analysis of the contributions of a proposed project to forest fragmentation can lead to a design that minimizes fragmentation and cumulative effects, a key to successful coarse-filter management.

How should we measure and analyze forest fragmentation? Several steps are involved, with decisions to be made at each step. First, we must make the necessary maps of the landscape, depicting the patchiness resulting from environmental variation and human and natural disturbances. In the process, we must define what a patch is, what an edge is, how many classes of forest patches there will be, and the depth of the edge-affected area. Second, we will need to obtain the necessary data and address basic questions about the data, such as their resolution and the minimum mapping unit to be used. Third, we will need to choose the landscape metrics or indices that we will use to quantify fragmentation, then choose appropriate computer software to complete the analyses. Next, we need to plan the analysis to address cumulative effects, consider the limitations of our approach with regard to the range of natural variability of the landscape, determine whether to use a census or sampling, and decide how to address potential sources of error and variation that may affect the results. Finally, our analysis is incomplete until we have evaluated and interpreted the results in the context of other scientific work already completed. The following sections address these steps in the fragmentation analysis.

LANDSCAPE MAPS

Forest fragmentation is most often conceptualized using a patch-corridor-matrix framework (Forman 1995). Most landscapes contain discrete patches produced by natural disturbances (Veblen, *this volume*) and underlying environmental variation (D. H. Knight, *this volume*). These landscapes can be decomposed into: (1) patches, (2) corridors, which are linear features, such as streams, transmission lines, and roads, and (3) matrix, which is the predominant, connected background in which the patches and corridors are embedded (Forman 1995). Some landscapes are all patches, while other landscapes may contain only a rather featureless matrix, but most landscapes contain a mix of patches, corridors, and matrix. Some landscapes may contain gradients in forest composition and structure that do not suggest "patchiness" (Haines-Young and Chopping 1996), where methods for continuous data may be more appropriate (Li and Reynolds 1995). A focus on patches dominates fragmentation analysis, but development of corridor- and connectivity-based analysis is needed (e.g., Schumacher 1996). In Rocky Mountain landscapes, topographic variation is sharp and disturbances are commonly severe, so that distinctly bounded patches are common. This chapter will thus focus on patch-based measurement of fragmentation. Before maps of landscape patchiness can be constructed, we must determine what is a patch, what is an edge, and how many types of patches there are, because these affect all the traditional indices of landscape structure, such as patch size and shape.

What Is a Patch?

How we measure fragmentation depends upon how we conceptualize a patch in the landscape. Patches are not arbitrarily defined, but reflect underlying processes and consequent structures in landscapes. However, while natural processes such as fires may produce real patches of successional vegetation, organisms and other processes may not always respond to this patchiness. Large predators, such as wolves, for example, may focus on prey rather than forest structure, so that a distinction between early- and late-successional vegetation patches is relatively unimportant to their habitat requirements. Fires may burn through forests differing slightly in age with little response to the age difference if fuel loads are similar. It is thus important to distinguish between processes that produce patchiness in landscapes and functional responses of organisms and other processes to patchiness in landscapes. Both are important and must be part of a general assessment of fragmentation, but they require separate considerations.

Rocky Mountain landscapes contain real patchiness from several sources (Forman 1995). First, variation in the underlying environment may lead to patchiness reflected in differences in vegetation (D. H. Knight, *this volume*). Second, natural and human disturbances create patches (Veblen, *this volume*). The third source is remnants of formerly continuous vegetation, such as woodlots in an agricultural mosaic, which are relatively uncommon in Rocky Mountain forests. A fourth type is an introduced patch, such as the buildings or tree plantations created by people. There may be some other minor patch types, but most patchiness in Rocky Mountain landscapes reflects an environmental mosaic overlain by natural and human disturbance patches, with concentrations of introduced and remnant patches where human activities are greatest.

Other species may perceive patchiness at different scales and in a different manner than the environmental, disturbance, remnant, and introduced patches that we humans may identify. A grizzly bear may select habitat at scales of kilometers (Agee et al. 1989), while a beetle may be sensitive to patchiness at the meter scale (Wiens and Milne 1989). The patches organisms perceive may reflect their individual resource needs, so coniferous forest patches that we might distinguish may be indistinguishable to a deer using them only for cover. The patchiness produced by environmental variation, disturbances, and human activities can be objectively mapped once the processes that lead to the patchiness are understood, but organism-focused patchiness can only be determined and mapped by studying each organism.

Two other ways to define patchiness are based on special values and landscape functions other than the provision of habitat for species. Humans assign special value to some patches, such as an exceptionally old bristlecone pine forest patch in a landscape of old bristlecone pine forests. The energy budget of a landscape depends in part on the albedo of the vegetation or soil surface (Ryszkowski 1992), which may vary little between age classes of coniferous forests. So, a map of energy-based patchiness would differ from a map of disturbance-based patchiness. However, the analysis of special value and function-based patchiness has not been developed.

While patches in a landscape could be mapped in different ways, depending on analysis goals, there is still a sound basis for general assessment of forest fragmentation. A general assessment would focus on the patchiness from natural and human processes (e.g., environment, disturbance, and human activities), with complementary analyses for individual species, special values, and other landscape functions, where these maps would differ.

Some ecologists might argue that there is little value in understanding how the landscape patchiness from natural and human processes has changed unless this change can be linked to an effect upon a particular species or process of interest. They also worry that landscape patchiness may simply represent human-perceived patchiness. However, there are many species (e.g., microbes) and processes (e.g., mutualism, competition) whose ecological response to changing landscape structure will never be fully understood. Moreover, the patch structure that is mapped on the landscape scale is surely influenced by human perception, but aims to reflect real processes and patterns (e.g., fire patches) that occur at this spatial scale and that are important in ecosystem functioning. Thus the basis of the coarse-filter approach to landscape management is to manage ecosystems and biodiversity by managing landscape structure itself, because this structure reflects natural processes important to ecosystems and because we will never fully understand or be able to manage all the individual linkages of this structure with other processes and species.

What Is an Edge? Another Part of Patch Definition

The extent of a patch is often ultimately defined by the location and characteristics of its edges, and environmental variation and disturbances produce edges that vary qualitatively and in their environmental effects. Just as with patch definition, edges may be defined by a physical change in microenvironment, vegetation structure, or other change produced by the natural or human process that created a patch. However, edges can also be defined functionally, by the response of organisms or other processes to the patch. In the Rocky Mountains, relatively fixed environmental features, such as large streams, wetlands, lakes, meadows, or rock outcrops and talus slopes may form comparatively high-contrast edges to forests. Some natural disturbances, such as snow avalanches, large mass movements, or exceptionally severe fires may also form high-contrast edges. Other natural disturbances, such as typical fires or insect outbreaks, are impermanent and not spatially fixed, and may leave dead trees that stay standing for decades to more than a century, so that the edge with adjoining forests is not typically sharp.

Many human-created edges are relatively permanent and spatially fixed, although land use changes can quickly alter this. Some human-created edges adjoin wide land uses (e.g., major highways, reservoirs), and there is little doubt that an edge is created, while others (e.g., small canals, trails, fences) are more subtle, and may not always form distinctive edges. Roads vary depending upon the standard to which they are constructed and their level of use. The Black Hills National Forest divided roads into primitive, secondary, and primary, and assigned different fragmentation effects to each category (USDA Forest Service 1996). The U.S. Forest Service Region 2 transportation database (R2TF) categorizes road functions as arterial, collector, and local, but has many other descriptors (USDA Forest Service 1993), so whether a road fragments could be specified using this database.

Timber harvesting produces different types and amounts of edge, depending upon the silvicultural technique, but all silvicultural techniques used in the Rocky Mountains may produce edges and distinct patches on the landscape. The main techniques used in the central and Southern Rockies include thinning, patch- and strip-clear-cutting, seed-tree cutting, simulated and two- and three-step standard shelterwood, group shelterwood, individual tree selection, and group selection (Alexander 1986 *a, b;* Sheppard and Alexander, *no date*). Diagrams of these harvest units suggest that clear-cuts, seed-tree cuts, and the seed-cut of a shelterwood all produce distinct edges with adjoining forest (Fig. 4.1). The visual distinctness of the edge on the ground or in an aerial photograph suggests that there is also a microenvironmental difference across the edge (Vaillancourt 1995). Functional responses to clear-cut edges have been reviewed in other chapters (e.g., Baker and Dillon, *this volume*). The edge produced by the seed-cut of a shelterwood persists through the overstory removal cut, and does not disappear until the regenerated trees grow to approximately the height of the adjoining uncut forest. The edge from a shelterwood harvest is not only visually apparent but also affects some species in Rocky Mountain forests (Crompton 1994). Group selection also produces a distinct edge, as groups may approach 1 ha in size, and fragmentation by group selection cuts affects some species in Rocky Mountain subalpine forests (Keller and Anderson 1992). Aerial photography of a portion of

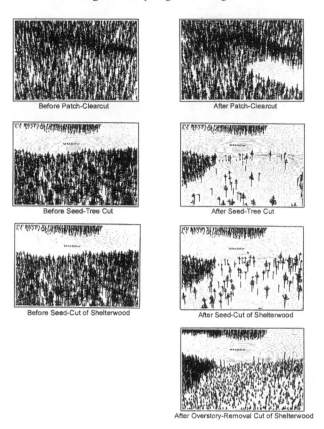

Figure 4.1. Major types of even-aged silvicultural treatments used in the Rocky Mountains and their effects on edges. Reproduced from the Black Hills National Forest, Draft Environmental Impact Statement for the Proposed Revised Land and Resource Management Plan (1994).

the Medicine Bow National Forest shows that uneven-aged silvicultural techniques, including individual tree selection and group selection also produce distinct edges that contribute to fragmentation (Fig. 4.2). Group selection may be the most fragmenting silvicultural technique, because it creates more edge per unit of harvested area than with any other technique. Thinning may also lead to a distinct edge, depending on the basal area goal.

How Many Classes of Forest Patches?

How many forest cover types, how many different age classes of a single cover type, and which types of roads or other land uses form

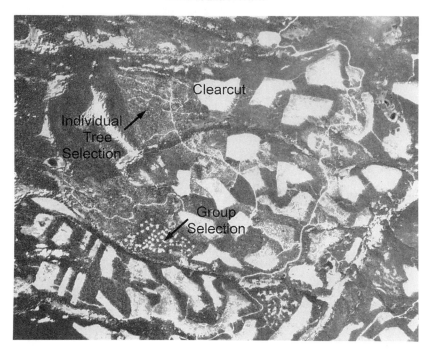

Figure 4.2. A portion of the Medicine Bow National Forest, along Sand Lake Road, illustrating major types of timber harvesting and the patchiness visible in 1:20,000 scale aerial photographs.

patch edges will all affect the outcome of a fragmentation analysis. Patch identification and mapping are limited by the precision and resolution of available data, as well as by agency data collection policies and procedures. Patches are most often determined by what is visible in remote-sensing imagery, such as aerial photographs or satellite images, used in agency forest mapping, or if patches can be located and mapped in the field. Patches are also created by human activities, such as timber harvesting, that may be mapped at the time of the activity.

As a result, there is some consistency to the classes that have been used in previous studies in the Rocky Mountains and the western United States (Table 4.1). Cover types typically represent major dominant forest types, although some studies focus on a single category of forest (e.g., old growth). Western studies have included 3 to 18 forest, shrubland, grassland, and other cover types. It may be desirable to use finer categories, such as habitat types or plant associations (e.g., Johnston

Table 4.1. Cover types and successional stages of forest used in previous studies of forest fragmentation in the western United States.

Authors	Location	Cover Types	Structural or Successional Stages or Stand-Origin Periods
Baker 1994	Medicine Bow Mts., Wyoming	9 forests, 2 shrublands, 3 grasslands/herbaceous, 1 wetland, 2 nonvegetated, 1 water	a. 4 stand-origin periods 1550–present b. 23 stand-origin periods 1550–present
Diaz et al. 1993	Western Oregon & Washington	Continuous canopy forest vs. openings	None, other than natural or created openings
Groom & Schumacher 1993	Olympic Mts., Washington	Old growth forest vs. other forest	None, other than old growth
Hann et al. 1994	Southwestern Montana	3 forests, 1 shrubland/grassland	a. 4 structural stages b. 3 stand-development stages
Harris 1984	Western Oregon	Old-growth forest vs. other forest	None, other than old growth
Lehmkuhl et al. 1994	Eastern Oregon & Washington	13 forests, 1 nonforest	5 structural stages
̄owsky and Knight, this volume	Northern Colorado	5 forests	3 structural stages
McGarigal and McComb 1995	Western Oregon	3 forests, 5 nonforests	6 structural stages, 2 canopy closure types
Miller et al. 1996	Northern Colorado	Not distinguished	3 structural stages
Morrison 1994	Olympic Mts., Washington	Old growth forest vs. other forest	None, other than old growth
O'Hara et al. 1994	Southwestern Montana	2 forests, 1 nonforest	7 structural stages
Reed et al. 1996a, b	Medicine Bow Mts., Wyoming	3 forests, 1 shrubland, 3 grasslands/herbaceous, 1 wetland, 2 nonvegetated, 1 water	7 structural stages
Ripple et al.1991a	Cascade Mts., Oregon	Managed forest vs. natural forest	None, other than "managed" forest
Shinneman 1996	Black Hills, South Dakota	6 forests, 2 shrublands, 2 grasslands/herbs	a. 9 structural stages
Shinneman & Baker, this volume		1 nonvegetated	b. 4 stand-origin periods 1650–present
Spies et al. 1994	Cascade Mts., Oregon	Closed-canopy forest vs. other forest and water	None, other than closed-canopy forest
Tinker et al. 1998	Bighorn Mts., Wyoming	8 forests, 3 shrublands, 2 grasslands/herbaceous, 2 water	Clear-cuts, blowdowns, and burns only

Table 4.2. Typical forest structural stages in use in the Rocky Mountain Region of the Forest Service. Abbreviations used include: cc = crown cover, dbh = diameter at breast height.

Stage	Meaning
1	Grass/forb, 0–10% cc
2	Shrub/seedling, < 1" dbh trees, 11–100% cc
3A	Poles/saplings, 1–9" dbh trees, 11–40% cc
3B	Poles/saplings, 1–9" dbh trees, 41–70% cc
3C	Poles/saplings, 1–9" dbh trees, 71–100% cc
4A	Mature, > 9" dbh trees, 11–40% cc
4B	Mature, > 9" dbh trees, 41–70% cc
4C	Mature, > 9" dbh trees, 71–100% cc
5	Late successional or old-growth

1987), but this has seldom occurred (see Hann et al. 1994, O'Hara et al. 1994) because most national and private forests lack the necessary maps. The temporal dimension of forest development has typically been represented by structural stages (Table 4.2), as stand-origin dates or more precise successional data are seldom available. However, structural stages are not defined based upon the formation of edges with adjoining patches, and where harvesting dates or other data are available, they may be used to better define patches (e.g., Reed et al. 1996*b*). The present common approach is thus to use a combination of forest cover types and structural stages, even though other categories may better represent the patch structure.

Research on fragmentation has focused on timber harvest units and, to a lesser extent, roads and the built environment (e.g., towns, suburbs, exurban developments) as edge-forming agents. Most studies of timber-harvesting effects (Table 4.1) do not include roads as the edge of a forest patch, although roads form distinct edges in terms of microenvironment and have effects on adjoining forests (Baker and Dillon, *this volume*). Roads also significantly decrease patch size and interior area and increase the number of patches and the amount of patch edge (Shinneman 1996; Shinneman and Baker, *this volume*; Reed et al. 1996*a*; Tinker et al. 1998). Including roads as edges is thus an important part of a general fragmentation analysis (Baker and Knight, *this volume*; Baker and Dillon, *this volume*). No studies to date in the West appear to have analyzed the effects of including trails, canals, transmission lines, fences, reservoirs, or railroads as patch edges, in part because of lack of digital data but also because they appear to be lesser sources of fragmentation in many landscapes. R. L. Knight (*this volume*) has considered the edge area created by trails, but not the dissection of patches and other fragmenting effects of trails.

In retrospective studies and in projections of the future forest, it is necessary to know when a patch edge may merge into the surrounding forest due to succession. The rate at which this occurs depends upon the environment of the patch. In my experience on the Medicine Bow National Forest in Wyoming, clear-cuts since World War II still form a distinct edge with adjoining forests 40 to 50 years after they were cut. Similar periods are likely for edges from seed-cuts (and the subsequent overstory removal) and the seed-tree cut of a shelterwood to disappear. Diaz et al. (1993) report that periods of 14 to 100 years are needed in forests of the northwestern United States, with the low end in moist, coastal forests and the high end in high elevation forests. Additional research is required to more precisely determine the time needed in our region. Edges produced by human land uses (Table 4.3) are semi-permanent and remain until intentionally changed by management.

Table 4.3. Types of potential natural- and human-created edges in Rocky Mountain landscapes.

Natural		
streams	lakes	forest age classes
meadows	game trails	rock outcrops/talus/mass movements
wetlands	snow avalanche paths	
Human		
roads	canals	fences
trails	timber harvest units	railroads
transmission lines	reservoirs	built environment

How Deep Is the Edge?

The influence of the edge environment extends some distance into the adjoining forest, creating core area and edge area zones inside a patch (Fig. 4.3), but the depth-of-edge influence (DEI) depends upon the variable analyzed (Table 4.4). The DEI also varies with the direction the edge faces, the type of forest, and other aspects of the physical setting (Chen et al. 1993, 1995; Baker and Dillon, *this volume*). For some microclimatic phenomena on certain days there is no edge effect,

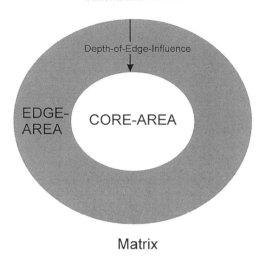

Figure 4.3. Zones created inside a patch by an edge.

but more typically maximum depths are in the 50–100 m range (Table 4.4). The maximum DEI measured in Western forests is >240 m (Chen et al. 1995). There are many studies, other than those cited in Table 4.4, in which an edge effect was identified or in which a more general effect of fragmentation was identified, but DEI was not measured (e.g., Rosenberg and Raphael 1986, Hejl 1992, Beauvais 1997).

Previous studies of fragmentation in the western United States have used DEIs of 50 m (Shinneman 1996; Reed et al. 1996*a*; Tinker et al. 1998; Lowsky and Knight, *this volume*), 100 m (Ripple et al. 1991*a*, Diaz et al. 1993, Spies et al. 1994, Shinneman 1996, Reed et al. 1996*a*), 180 m (Baker 1994), or even 399 m (Groom and Schumacher 1993). Based on available data (Table 4.4) and past studies, a series of increasing depths including perhaps 0 m, 25 m, 50 m, 100 m, and 200 m may be appropriate for general assessments of fragmentation, as these DEIs span the spectrum of potential DEIs observed in Western forests.

What Is a Corridor?

Corridors are linear connecting features, such as roads, trails, transmission lines, and streams, but can be wider features connecting patches across a landscape (Forman 1995). Connectivity is widely recognized to be important in maintaining the viability of species dependent upon dispersal and other forms of movement (Schreiber 1988, McCullough

Table 4.4. Depth-of-edge influences (DEI) measured at edges of timber harvest units (usually clear-cuts) in western U.S. forests. DEI is: (1) the point along the edge-to-interior gradient when the value reaches two-thirds of the interior value (see Chen et al. 1992), (2) subjectively estimated by examining scatterplots of variables versus distance from the forest edge (see Chen et al. 1995), or (3) the minimum distance inside the forest where typical interior-forest temperatures are reached (see Laurance and Yensen 1991).

Authors	Location	Edge Response Relative to Interior	DEI(m)
MICROCLIMATE			
Chen et al. 1995	WA	Growing season mean daily air temperature higher	180–240
Vaillancourt 1995	WY	Growing season instantaneous air temperature higher	<20
Chen et al. 1995	WA	Growing season mean daily soil temperature higher	60–120
Laurance and Yensen 1991	ID	Growing season instantaneous soil temperature higher	2 to 19
Chen et al. 1995	WA	Growing season mean daily relative humidity lower	>240
Vaillancourt 1995	WY	Growing season instantaneous relative humidity lower	50–70
Chen et al. 1995	WA	Growing season mean daily short-wave radiation higher	15–60
Vaillancourt 1995	WY	Growing season instantaneous sunlight intensity higher	30–50
Chen et al. 1995	WA	Growing season mean daily wind velocity higher	>240
Chen et al. 1995	WA	Growing season mean daily soil moisture lower or higher	0–90
VEGETATION			
Chen et al. 1992	WA	Canopy cover lower	44
Vaillancourt 1995	WY	Canopy cover lower	30–50
Frost 1992	CA	Canopy cover lower	60
Chen et al. 1992	WA	Tree density lower	43–85
Vaillancourt 1995	WY	Live tree density lower	30–50
Chen et al. 1992	WA	Relative growth rate higher	26–53
Chen et al. 1992	WA	Number of dead trees (blowdown) higher	56–125
Gratkowski 1956	OR	Number of dead trees (blowdown) higher	<60 mostly, but to 366
Vaillancourt 1995	WY	Number of dead trees (blowdown) higher	20–30
Frost 1992	CA	Number of dead trees (blowdown) higher	60
Chen et al. 1992	WA	Number of seedlings, depending on species, higher/lower	41–92
Vaillancourt 1995	WY	Number of seedlings, depending on species, higher/lower	30–50
Frost 1992	CA	Number of seedlings, depending on species, higher/lower	60
Frost 1992	CA	Understory shrub cover higher, ground cover lower	60
Frost 1992	CA	Understory species richness higher	60m
MAMMALS			
Hanley 1983	WA	Deer and elk use greater	>200
BIRDS			
Crompton 1994	SD	Bird use, depending on species, higher or lower	to 125
Ruefenacht and Knight, *this vol.*	CO	Bird use, depending on species, higher or lower	>100

1996). Patch-based indices do not directly measure connectivity and its fragmentation by land uses. Some patch-based indices do reflect dispersal-related connectivity to some extent (Schumacher 1996), but more direct measures of connectivity are available (e.g., Bridgewater 1987). However, no computer software is readily available for analyzing connectivity, and there has been no analysis of fragmentation using connectivity indices in landscapes of the western United States.

DATA ISSUES
Data Needs and Sources

For an adequate analysis of patch-based forest fragmentation, several map layers are needed (Fig. 4.4). First, the essential patchiness produced by environmental variation and natural disturbances is

Map Layers for Fragmentation Analysis

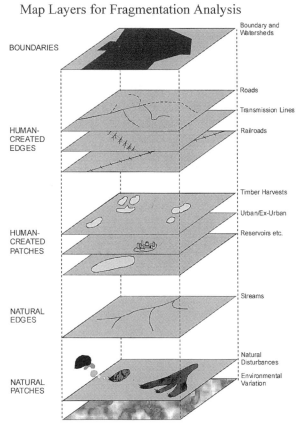

Figure 4.4. Major sets of maps needed for fragmentation analysis.

contained in a map combining cover types and structural or successional stages. These patches may be bounded by streams, particularly larger streams (Tinker et al. 1998). Second, the patches created by humans need to be in separate map layers so they can be individually overlaid on the natural patches map. In the Rocky Mountains, a map of timber-harvesting units and the built environment (e.g., buildings, parking lots, etc.), where relevant, is needed. Maps of human-created edges are essential, including roads, transmission lines, and railroads. A number of optional maps might also be used. Also necessary are maps of the forest boundary, watershed or sampling-area boundaries, and private or state land inside the analysis area.

These maps may come from a variety of sources. For cover types and structural stages, the best source is aerial photography supplemented by field inventories. This is the approach used to build the Rocky Mountain Regional Information System (RMRIS) database used in this region, Region 2, of the Forest Service (USDA Forest Service 1994). Satellite imagery can be classified to the cover-type level, although there are problems in separating some Rocky Mountain forest types, but structural stage information cannot presently be obtained with precision from satellite images. Tinker et al. (1998) used satellite imagery classified to cover type in their analysis of the Bighorn National Forest.

For linear features (edge-forming agents) the U.S. Geological Survey has digital data for hydrography and transportation. The U.S. Geological Survey's Global Land Information System web page (http://edcwww.cr.usgs.gov/webglis) can be searched for data relevant to forest fragmentation including hydrography (flowing water, standing water, and wetlands) and transportation, in three layers: (1) roads and trails, (2) railroads, and (3) pipelines, transmission lines, and miscellaneous transportation features. Data are available in 1:100,000 and 1:24,000 scales. Tinker et al. (1998) found that the 1:100,000 scale road and streams coverages contained major features, but lacked many smaller features. The U.S. Forest Service is now constructing GIS coverages in ARC/INFO (ESRI, Inc. 1994) of linear features, including most of the necessary map layers. Their roads coverages are derived from U.S. Geological Survey 1:24,000 maps, supplemented by aerial photo interpretation, field surveys, and in some cases mapping using geographical positioning systems (C. Tolbert, *personal communication*).

Each data source has limitations and advantages. Satellite imagery has the advantage that an objective classification can be completed for a large land area, and 30-m resolution Landsat imagery is widely available, with finer resolutions now becoming available. However, successional data are not readily obtained from Landsat data. Roads are not very visible in 30-m Landsat data, yet they are visible enough to require difficult removal procedures to create base maps free of human-created edges (Tinker et al. 1998). Aerial photography from national mapping efforts, such as the National Aerial Photography Program, may contain information down to 1-m resolution. Aerial photography typically requires manual interpretation and time-consuming orthorectification to make spatially precise maps. Roads, however, are very visible in typical aerial photography.

The U.S. Forest Service RMRIS database (USDA Forest Service 1994) also has advantages and limitations, in part because it was not designed for landscape-scale analyses, such as analyses of fragmentation. RMRIS was originally a tabular computer database linked to mylar overlays on U.S. Geological Survey 1:24,000-scale quadrangles, but now is being linked to GIS coverages in ARC/INFO (ESRI, Inc. 1994). The database was developed over a period of more than a decade, and it is uncertain how consistent the mapping and database development have been. The database is spatially incomplete for many regional forests, as the most detailed data are typically not collected until a timber sale is planned. Moreover, records of timber harvesting prior to World War II are scant. There are two other problems that I have identified in working with RMRIS data: (1) polygon boundaries are not always revised when a harvesting action takes place inside a polygon, and (2) structural stages are often based on the tallest overstory trees that are present, not whether the predominant vegetation creates an edge with adjoining forests. Also, harvesting may divide a polygon, but it will often still be recorded as a single polygon, significantly underestimating the fragmentation impact. In the Black Hills National Forest, the seed-cut of a shelterwood harvest is considered to result in Structural Stage 4A (USDA Forest Service 1996), which is mature forest, yet a seed-cut next to an unharvested mature forest in Stage 4A would produce a distinct edge. The structural stage or harvesting system needs revision so that harvests that produce edges result in a different structural stage.

Resolution and Minimum Mapping Unit

Several aspects of the resolution of the data may affect the outcome of fragmentation analyses. Many indices vary with the pixel resolution or level of aggregation of the data, when raster data are used (Turner et al. 1989), so it is important to report the pixel resolution used in the analysis. Pixel resolutions used in Western studies include 10 m, 25 m, 50 m, and 100 m (see citations in Table 4.1). The national forest in Region 2 with the largest north-south and east-west extent is the Pike/ San Isabel, which is approximately 295 km by 150 km. With a 50-m pixel resolution, this forest would fit in an approximately 6000 row by 3000 column raster. This raster size may be approaching the limit of present software and hardware for calculating fragmentation indices. Some fragmentation indices can be calculated on subsampled areas and then totaled across the subsamples, but others are not easily calculated unless the entire area is analyzed as a whole. While 50-m resolution is probably adequate for patches and for depth-of-edge influences (using multiples of 50 m), many linear features such as roads and streams are not usually 50-m wide. Until technology improves, analysis at the national forest scale may need to use 50-m resolution pixels, but analysis of individual watersheds can use 10-m resolution pixels (Tinker et al. 1998) more compatible with the width of linear features. The U.S. Geological Survey's "Land use and land-cover data," with a minimum mapping unit of 4 ha, are insufficient for analyzing forest fragmentation, although useful for other purposes (Hunsaker et al. 1994).

A related concern is the minimum mapping unit (MMU). Typically, the MMU is about 1 ha in the U.S. Forest Service RMRIS database. With a 10-m resolution pixel, there are 100 pixels in a 1-ha area, while with a 50-m resolution pixel there are only 4 pixels. Clearly, for analyses at the national forest level using a 50-m pixel resolution, a 1-ha MMU is near the limit of what can be mapped adequately, but for watershed-scale analyses using a 10-m pixel resolution, there is a need for a finer MMU. Rocky Mountain forests often are interrupted by small meadows and wetlands that contribute significantly to natural patchiness. In a Wisconsin study, the number of lakes identified was still increasing as the pixel resolution approached 20 m, suggesting that MMUs of 0.04 ha may not be too small (Benson and MacKenzie 1995), but additional research is needed to identify the needed MMU for Rocky Mountain forest openings.

CHOICE OF FRAGMENTATION INDICES

A wide variety of indices or metrics (all called "indices" here) that quantify fragmentation can be calculated, but which should be used? Which are the essential indices is influenced by: (1) expected changes as fragmentation occurs, (2) actual changes documented in past research, and (3) importance to particular organisms or processes. Many indices in several broad categories can be calculated by available computer programs (Table 4.5), so software is not generally limiting.

Fragmentation, by definition, involves the breakup of continuous landscapes containing large patches into smaller, often more numerous and less connected patches, with less forest cover, or, in Rocky Mountain landscapes, often less cover of old-growth forest (Buskirk et al., *this volume*). Thus, measures related to patch size, density, cover, and distance (Table 4.5) are appropriate to quantify these effects. Because the creation of edges by roads, timber harvesting, and other land uses (Table 4.3) often increases edge area, decreases core area, and increases the length of patch edge or perimeter, it is also appropriate to measure core area and edge area size, density, cover, distance, and edge/perimeter ratio (Table 4.5). Human land uses often lead to more geometric, less irregular patch boundaries (e.g., Krummel et al. 1987), so that patch shape and fractal dimension might also be appropriate measures. Fragmentation implies significant changes in the proportions of cover types in a landscape, so measures of landscape diversity and texture may be relevant (Table 4.5). Thus, all the broad categories of measures may be relevant, simply based on our understanding of fragmentation.

Past studies of fragmentation in the western United States have often used a common suite of indices that appears responsive to fragmentation (Table 4.6). Some indices that have been popular, but have not shown a meaningful response to fragmentation in the West include fractal dimension, Shannon diversity, and dominance. Other diversity and texture indices have not been consistent (Table 4.5). Fractal dimension and contagion are also poor indicators of potential dispersal success in fragmented Western landscapes (Schumacher 1996) and have a number of theoretical and practical problems that suggest they should be replaced with new indices (Frohn 1998). The common indices, that do consistently respond, measure the major components of patchiness in landscapes, including cover, size, density, shape, edge, and distance.

Species have also shown a significant response to the landscape structure measured by most of this set of common indices, where these indices have been used in the western United States (Table 4.5). Moreover, no other indices have yet been found to be consistently significant for species. However, only a few studies have empirically evaluated the relationship between indices and species presence or abundance (Table 4.7), and additional research is needed. For many other studies, a general feature such as edge, not specifically measured by a

Table 4.5. Landscape indices that can be calculated using three GIS programs. *CBC* = not directly output, but can be calculated from the program's output; for r.le "out" means that the index is obtained by specifying the out parameter. The last two columns of the table contain: (1) the number of authors of general fragmentation analyses, out of the number who used the index (the authors reviewed are in Table 4.1), whose results suggest that the index changes in a meaningful or significant way in response to fragmentation, and (2) the number of authors of studies of the relationship of species and indices, out of the number who used the index (the authors reviewed are in Table 4.7), whose results suggest that a species is sensitive to changes in the index.

Index	FRAGSTATS 2.0	r.le 2.2	Display (8/93)	No. Authors (1)	(2)
Patch, core area and edge area cover					
Cover of patches	TA	CBC	X	6/6	7/7
Cover of core areas	TCA	CBC	-	6/7	0/1
Cover of edge areas	CBC	CBC	-	3/3	—
Cover of patches by size class	—	CBC	CBC	1/1	—
Patch, core area and edge area size and ratios					
Size of each patch	AREA	out	X	—	—
Size of each patch's core area	CORE	out	—	—	—
Size of each patch's edge area	CBC	out	—	—	—
Mean patch size	MPS	s1	X	13/13	5/6
Mean core area size	MCA1, MCA2	c1, CBC	—	6/6	1/1
Mean edge area size	CBC	c3	—	1/1	—
Median patch size	—	—	CBC	1/1	—
Median core area size	—	—	—	1/1	—
St. dev. of patch size	PSSD	s2	CBC	4/5	0/1
St. dev. of core area size	CASD1, CASD2	c2, CBC	—	2/3	0/1
St. dev. of edge area size	—	c4	—	—	—
Coeff. var. patch size	PSCV	CBC	CBC	2/2	1/2
Coeff. var. core area size	CACV1, CACV2	CBC	—	2/2	1/1
Number of patches by size class	—	s5	X	8/8	—
Number of core areas by size class	—	c9	—	3/3	—
Largest patch (%)	LPI	CBC	CBC	4/4	1/1
Ratios of core area, edge area and patch-area	CAI, MCAI, TCAI	CBC	—	5/5	2/2
Patch, core area and edge area density					
Number of patches	NP	a7	X	6/7	0/1
Number of core areas	NCA	—	—	0/1	0/1
Number of core areas in each patch	NCORE	—	—	—	—
Density of patches	PD	CBC	—	7/7	3/4
Density of core areas	CAD	—	—	3/3	1/1

Continued on next page

Table 4.5—*Continued*

Index	FRAGSTATS 2.0	r.le 2.2	Display (8/93)	No. Authors (1)	(2)
Patch shape					
Shape of each patch: perim./area (P/A)	—	out	CBC	—	—
Shape of each patch: corrected perim./area (CP/A)	SHAPE	out	—	—	—
Shape of each patch: related circum. circle (RCC)	—	out	—	—	—
Mean patch shape: P/A	—	h1/m1	CBC	1/2	—
Mean patch shape: CP/A	MSI	h1/m2	—	4/8	3/4
Area-weighted mean patch shape: CP/A	AWMSI	—	—	1/2	0/1
Mean patch shape: RCC	—	h1/m3	—	—	—
St. dev. of patch shape: P/A	—	h2/m1	CBC	—	—
St. dev. of patch shape: CP/A	—	h2/m2	—	1/1	—
St. dev. of patch shape: RCC	—	h2/m3	—	—	—
No. patches by shape index class: P/A	—	h5/m1	—	—	—
No. patches by shape index class: CP/A	—	h5/m2	—	2/2	—
No. patches by shape index class: RCC	—	h5/m3	—	—	—
Fractal dimension					
Fractal dimension of each patch	FRACT	CBC	CBC	—	1/1
Perim./area fractal dimension	DLFD	f1	X	1/5	1/1
Grid fractal dimension	—	—	X	—	—
Prob. dens. funct. fractal dimension	—	—	X	—	—
Mean patch fractal dimension	MPFD	CBC	CBC	1/1	1/1
Area-weighted mean patch fractal dimension	AWMPFD	—	CBC	—	—
Patch edge/perimeter					
Perimeter length of each patch	PERIM	out	X	—	—
Edge contrast index for each patch	EDCON	—	—	—	—
Patch perimeter length	TE	e1,p1	X	4/5	2/3
Patch perimeter density	ED	CBC	CBC	6/6	3/3
Mean patch perimeter length	CBC	p2	CBC	3/3	1/1
St. dev. patch perimeter length	CBC	p3	CBC	—	—
Contrast-weighted edge density	CWED	—	—	3/3	2/2
Total edge contrast index	TECI	—	—	2/2	1/1
Mean edge contrast index	MECI	—	—	1/1	1/1
Area-weighted mean edge contrast index	AWMECI	—	—	0/1	0/1
Diversity					
Richness of patch types	PR	d1	X	1/1	—
Richness density of patch types	PRD	CBC	CBC	1/1	—
Relative richness of patch types	RPR	CBC	CBC	—	—
Shannon index of patch type diversity	SHDI	d2	X	1/6	1/2

Continued on next page

Table 4.5—*Continued*

Index	FRAGSTATS 2.0	r.le 2.2	Display (8/93)	No. Authors (1)	(2)
Diversity—contd.					
Shannon evenness index of patch type diversity	SHEI	CBC	CBC	1/1	—
Dominance index of patch type diversity	CBC	d3	X	1/5	1/2
Simpson's index of patch type diversity	SIDI	d4	CBC	1/1	2/2
Simpson's evenness index of patch type diversity	SIEI	CBC	CBC	1/1	1/1
Modified Simpson's evenness index of patch type diversity	MSIEI	CBC	CBC	1/1	1/1
Texture					
Contagion	CONTAG	t1	X	3/7	1/2
Angular second moment	—	t2	—	1/2	—
Inverse difference moment	—	t3	—	—	—
Entropy	—	t4	—	0/1	—
Contrast	—	t5	—	2/2	—
Juxtaposition					
Interspersion and juxtaposition index	IJI	—	—	—	2/2
Mean juxtaposition index	—	j1	—	—	—
St. dev. juxtaposition index	—	j2	—	—	—
Distance					
Nearest-(same type) neighbor dist. for each patch	NEAR	out	—	—	—
Nearest-(any diff. type) neighbor dist. for each patch	—	out	—	—	—
Nearest-(partic. type) neighbor dist. for each patch	—	out	—	—	—
Mean all-adjacent neighbor dist.	—	n1	—	—	—
Mean nearest-(same type) neighbor dist.	MNN	n1	—	4/4	2/2
Mean nearest-(any diff. type) neighbor dist.	—	n1	—	—	—
Mean nearest-(partic. type) neighbor dist.	—	n1	—	—	0/1
St. dev. all-adjacent neighbor dist.	—	n2	—	—	—
St. dev. nearest-(same type) neighbor dist.	NNSD	n2	—	—	—
St. dev. nearest-(any diff. type) neighbor dist.	—	n2	—	—	—
St. dev. nearest-(partic. type) neighbor dist.	—	n2	—	—	—
Coeff. var. nearest-(same type) neighbor dist.	NNCV	—	—	—	—
No. distances by distance class	—	n5	—	—	—
Proximity index	PROXIM	—	—	1/1	—
Mean proximity index	MPI	—	—	—	—
Spatial pattern					
Dispersion	CBC	CBC	CBC	0/2	—

particular landscape index, has been shown to be significant for a species (e.g., Hejl 1992, Crompton 1994). These studies do not make clear to which measure of edge (i.e., length, area) the species is responding, so particular indices cannot be recommended. The diversity and texture indices included in the common set (Table 4.6) are tenta-

Table 4.6. A common set of indices for measuring forest fragmentation in the Rocky Mountains and the West. This list was derived from Table 4.5 by including indices that have been used more than twice and, in a high percentage of uses, show meaningful or significant responses to fragmentation and/or to which a species responds significantly, based on the studies in Table 4.7.

Cover
  Percent cover of patches (by cover type/structural stage)
  Percent cover of core areas (overall and by cover type/structural stage)
  Percent cover of edge areas (overall and by cover type/structural stage)
Size
  Mean or median patch size (overall and by cover type/structural stage)
  Mean or median core area size (overall and by cover type/structural stage)
  St. dev. or coeff. of var. of patch size (overall and by cover type/structural stage)
  St. dev. or coeff. of var. of core area size (overall and by cover type/structural stage)
  Density of patches by size class
  Density of core areas by size class
  Largest patch (%) (overall and by cover type/structural stage)
  Ratio of mean/median core area size to mean/median patch size (overall and by
    cover type/structural stage)
Density
  Density of patches (overall and by cover type/structural stage)
  Density of core areas (overall and by cover type/structural stage)
Shape
  Mean/median patch shape: corrected perimeter/area (Patton) index (overall and
    by cover type/structural stage)
Edge/Perimeter
  Edge density or contrast-weighted edge density (overall and by cover type/
    structural stage)
  Mean/median patch perimeter length (overall and by cover type/structural stage)
Distance
  Mean/median nearest-neighbor (same type) distance (by cover type/structural
    stage)
Diversity
  Index needed? Possibly Simpson's index of patch type diversity
Texture
  Index needed? Possibly contrast

---

tive, as they have only been used in a few cases, and additional research is needed.

One could argue that a particular index need not be part of a general assessment unless it has been shown to be significant for a species found in the area under study. However, it is important to meet both coarse-filter and fine-filter goals. The broad overlap between indices found to record fragmentation and indices to which species respond (Table 4.5) suggests that this set of common indices is likely to prove useful in both coarse-filter and fine-filter assessments in the West. However, the present spectrum of species-oriented studies is biased toward the west coast part of the West and the spotted owl (Table 4.5). Particular landscapes and particular species may, of course, respond to only part of the set (e.g., McGarigal and McComb 1995).

Some of the common set of indices (Table 4.6) may be correlated or have narrow ranges of response, but this does not necessarily mean they are redundant and that some should be discarded. Hargis et al. (1997) evaluated the response of a set of indices to simulated landscape patterns; their graphs may be useful in interpreting index values. Although some indices may be correlated, these indices measure different quantities, and the quantities themselves are of interest, in some cases because they have known, direct effects on species (Table 4.5) or

Table 4.7. Authors reporting significant empirical relationships between individual species and fragmentation indices in western United States forests.

Author(s)	Location	Subject
Beauvais 1997	Bighorn Mountains, Wyoming	Mammals
Carey et al. 1992	Southwestern Oregon	Spotted owl
Hunter et al. 1995	Northwestern California	Spotted owls
Lehmkuhl and Raphael 1993	Olympic Peninsula, Washington	Spotted owls
Lehmkuhl et al. 1991	Southern Washington Cascades	Birds, mammals, amphibians
McGarigal and McComb 1995	Oregon Coast Range	Birds
Raphael et al. 1995	Western Washington	Marbled murrelets
Ribe et al. 1998	Western Oregon	Spotted owls
Ripple et al. 1991b	Western Oregon	Spotted owls
Ripple et al. 1997	Southwestern Oregon	Spotted owls
Rosenberg and Raphael 1986	Northwestern California	Birds, mammals, amphibians, and reptiles

because they are readily understood (e.g., patch size). Although simulations have identified indices that may be generally correlated, and thus redundant (Li and Reynolds 1994), it is not yet clear that indices correlated in one place will always be correlated, as the correlation may be in part a property of the landscape, rather than the indices. Thus it remains worthwhile to measure a suite of indices. Some value is also found in maintaining consistency in what is measured, so that comparisons can be made among forests and over time in a single forest. While the common set of indices will likely be improved by additional research, this set contains the essential indices now known to be significant indicators of fragmentation and its effects on species in the West.

COMPUTER SOFTWARE

Three specialized programs have been used in the central and Southern Rockies to calculate indices of fragmentation, but other software can be used. The major programs include FRAGSTATS (McGarigal and Marks 1995), the r.le programs (Baker and Cai 1992) and DISPLAY (Flather and MacNeal 1993). An example of the use of FRAGSTATS in the western United States is Tinker et al. (1998), while the r.le programs were used by Reed et al. (1996*a, b*) and DISPLAY was used by Lehmkuhl et al. (1994). Other software includes APACK (Mladenoff et al. 1995), PATREC (Baskent and Jordan 1995), SPAN (Turner 1990), and software by Timmins and Hunsaker (1996). Commercial GIS packages, such as ARC/INFO (ESRI Inc. 1994), can also be used to obtain some indices, such as patch size.

Computer programs, of course, have advantages and disadvantages. FRAGSTATS is a stand-alone program that can run under DOS or UNIX, and uses ASCII files, binary files, ARC/INFO files, ERDAS files, and IDRISI files, while DISPLAY can only use ASCII files. The r.le programs operate within the GRASS GIS (USA-CERL 1994) on a UNIX operating system. GRASS can read ARC/INFO, ERDAS, IDRISI, tif, gif, tga, ASCII, and other file formats. A version of GRASS for Windows, called GRASSLAND, is available (L.A.S., Inc. 1996), and there is a version of the r.le programs for GRASSLAND.

These three programs can calculate many indices, but FRAGSTATS and the r.le programs are the most complete (Table 4.5), and can calculate most of the set of common indices (Table 4.6). Both programs can output indices by class or group (e.g., lodgepole pine forest patches versus spruce/fir forest patches). The distance-measuring algorithms of FRAGSTATS appear to be slower and more limited than those of the r.le programs. FRAGSTATS has fewer texture and shape algorithms

(Table 4.5), and has more rigid output formats. However, FRAGSTATS has more extensive core area and patch adjacency measures. The r.le programs, because they are embedded within GRASS, can easily use the GIS for preprocessing and analysis, while for FRAGSTATS the user must output preprocessed files from the GIS and read them into the program. The r.le programs contain a separate program (r.le.setup) that allows the user to specify or draw regions, sampling units, or moving windows that are circular or rectangular and can be any size or number. These regions, sampling units, or moving windows can then be used as sampling areas, and indices can be calculated and output for each area separately. This method is useful when it is desirable to calculate indices for watersheds or other regions (e.g., Baker 1994), but it is also possible to do this using a GIS along with FRAGSTATS (Tinker et al. 1998). The r.le programs can also be used to create GIS maps of core areas, edge areas, or maps in which the patch attribute is the value of a particular fragmentation index.

The size of area that can be analyzed as a whole is still limited by computer capabilities, primarily memory, but areas the size of entire national forests can now be analyzed at modest resolution (e.g., 50-m pixels). In a trial I did, neither FRAGSTATS nor the r.le programs could analyze an entire Landsat TM scene containing several hundred thousand patches on a Pentium Pro machine with 128 Mb of RAM. However, I have used the r.le programs to analyze rasters with dimensions >5,000 rows by 5,000 columns containing >50,000 patches on such a machine.

The manner in which patches are "traced" controls patch definition by the software. These programs typically trace along the boundary of a patch to outline the patch extent; at each pixel the program searches neighbors for another pixel with the same attribute. If tracing is 4-neighbor, so that only pixels above and below in the same column or to the left or right in the same row are examined, then patches will not extend at a diagonal across single-pixel-wide features, such as roads and streams. If tracing is 8-neighbor, then patches may extend across single-pixel-wide features that run at a diagonal, because all eight neighbors of a pixel are searched. It is important to use only 4-neighbor tracing if patch-boundaries are determined by narrow features, such as roads or streams. Using 4-neighbor tracing will yield smaller patches and affect many other patch measures, so it is important to report which choice is used. FRAGSTATS and the r.le programs offer both 4-neighbor and 8-neighbor tracing, but DISPLAY uses only 4-neighbor tracing.

ANALYSIS FRAMEWORK
Cumulative Effects Using Spatial and Temporal Comparisons

The goal of a general assessment of forest fragmentation is often to determine the cumulative effects of land uses in present landscapes and the potential future impacts of these uses. Cumulative effects, under the U.S. National Environmental Policy Act (NEPA), occur when individual minor actions, such as a single clear-cut or transmission line, add up to significant effects when accumulated over time and/or space (Preston and Bedford 1988). In the case of forest fragmentation, these effects have accumulated due to the persistence of past timber harvest units, roads, and other patch- and edge-forming land uses (Table 4.3) on the landscape.

To determine cumulative effects of forest fragmentation on Rocky Mountain landscapes requires a comparison to a landscape without the fragmenting land use of interest. This comparison is obtained using either: (1) a spatial approach, in which the comparison is made with nearby landscapes that are comparatively free of the land use of interest (Kauffman et al. 1994), or (2) a temporal approach, in which the condition of the landscape prior to the onset of the land use of interest is reconstructed. These two approaches use the standard scientific technique of isolating the variable of interest, in this case the particular land use, in time or space so that its effect can be identified apart from competing effects of other variables.

The spatial approach uses reference areas that are comparatively free of the land use as a basis for comparison. Reference areas are wilderness areas, roadless areas, research natural areas, or other protected areas in which the primary sources of patchiness are natural environmental variation and disturbances, rather than the land uses of interest. While comparing aggregate areas of wilderness with aggregate areas outside wilderness is useful (Lowsky and Knight, *this volume*), the most meaningful spatial comparisons rely on matching a managed landscape with a similar reference area, so the only variable that differs is the land use of interest. Baker (1994) used cluster analysis of cover types to match individual watersheds to a corresponding reference area, but other multivariate techniques might be used, based on physiographic setting, geology, or other environmental variables. Once the match is made, appropriate indices can be calculated and compared (e.g, Baker 1994). Limitations of this approach are that: (1) some of the difference in index values may result from imperfections in the match, (2) there may be no corresponding reference area (Baker 1994),

(3) the data for reference areas, such as wilderness areas and roadless areas, are often lacking, and (4) even remote areas may have been affected by fire suppression, altering the patch structure.

The temporal approach relies on a variety of techniques to reconstruct the landscape prior to the land use of interest (Kauffman et al. 1994). One technique is to use historical aerial photos, satellite images, maps, and other records to reconstruct the landscape prior to the land use (Ripple et al. 1991*a*, Groom and Schumaker 1993, Hann et al. 1994, Lehmkuhl et al. 1994, Morrison 1994). A limitation of this is that aerial photography and maps are rare prior to the 1930s and 1940s. Also, an interpretation from these old sources may differ from a contemporary interpretation because recent photography is color, of higher quality, or has a different scale or resolution. Also, interpretations of historical photography cannot be field-checked, while recent agency maps have been at least partially field-checked. A second technique is to use a GIS or other means to reconstruct the original landscape by replacing present land uses with prior conditions. Clear-cuts, for example, can be restored to the mature forest condition found prior to harvesting; forests that are 120 years old in 2000 are reconstructed to have been 20-year-old forests in 1900 (e.g., Diaz et al. 1993, Reed et al. 1996*b*, Tinker et al. 1998). A limitation of this is that it is often unclear whether the area was a distinct patch or part of an adjoining patch in the original forest. After the reconstruction, the cumulative effects of fragmentation can be determined by analyzing the patchiness, using landscape indices (see following paragraph) in comparisons (e.g., 1900 vs. 2000).

The power of this temporal approach is that the effects of individual land uses and their joint contribution to fragmentation can be disentangled and quantified. To do so, indices first are calculated for the reconstructed landscape prior to the land uses. Then, the land uses are overlaid individually onto the reconstructed landscape, the patch borders are adjusted accordingly, and the indices are recalculated (e.g., Reed et al. 1996*a*, Shinneman 1996, Tinker et al. 1998). Reed et al. (1996*b*) overlaid maps of cumulative harvesting of a forest by decade to quantify the temporal development of fragmentation since World War II. Shinneman (1996) compared natural patchiness with the patchiness produced by roads using a GIS. Tinker et al. (1998): (1) reconstructed a base map of natural vegetation and disturbance patches (BASE), (2) overlaid a map of roads on BASE to quantify the separate added effect of roads, (3) overlaid a map of timber harvesting units on BASE to quantify the separate added effect of harvesting, then (4) overlaid both roads and harvest-unit maps to quantify the joint effects of these land uses. Temporal reconstruction combined with overlay analysis is the most valuable technique for analyzing the cumulative effects of individual agents and their joint contribution to fragmentation.

Snapshots and the Range of Natural Variability

Both temporal reconstructions and spatial comparisons rely upon the state of the landscape at particular instants in time, and yet landscape structure is continually changing due to natural disturbances, climatic change, and other factors. Ideally, we would like to compare the present landscape to the range of natural variability (RNV) of the landscape (Swanson et al. 1994), rather than the state of the landscape at a single instant. However, seldom is it possible to reconstruct the state of the landscape at more than one instant prior to historical land uses. An alternative would be to use valid simulation models of the processes, such as fires, that produce natural patchiness to simulate natural variation in the landscape (e.g., Boychuk and Perera 1997). However, spatial modeling of natural processes in landscapes is still in its infancy (Mladenoff and Baker 1999). Another approach is to compare among several reference areas, assuming that spatial variation in natural landscape patchiness is similar to temporal variation (Baker 1994), but this idea is untested. In general, analyses of forest fragmentation will be limited to temporal reconstructions of the landscape at a single instant in time prior to the land uses of interest.

Sampling or Census and Appropriate Scales

Fragmentation can occur at a variety of spatial scales, from the regional scale to the scale of whole forests, individual watersheds or landscapes, and even individual patches in a watershed. A general assessment of forest fragmentation may need to consider all these scales. At the regional scale, the important sources of forest fragmentation are major highways, urban and exurban developments, and concentrations of land uses, such as clear-cuts and roads. Because the central concern from fragmentation at the regional scale is potential loss of major corridors and linkages to adjoining land areas, a qualitative analysis of the effects of fragmenting agents at this scale may suffice. At the patch scale, the placement of a road, a transmission line, or a timber-harvest unit may or may not cause the patch to be broken into smaller pieces or increase the amount of edge in the patch.

Most significant is the aggregate effect of land uses on patches throughout the landscape, best analyzed by focusing on the national forest scale and smaller sampling areas within the forest. The national forest scale is a fundamental scale at which to analyze forest fragmentation. Measuring indices of forest fragmentation at the scale of a whole national forest is now feasible (Baker 1994, Tinker et al. 1998). The national forest scale alone is insufficient, however, as it is important to identify parts of the forest that are more fragmented than others.

The forest may be divided into sampling areas and a suite of indices calculated for each area (e.g., Baker 1994, Tinker et al. 1998). A logical sampling area to use is the watershed, which has functional significance, and watershed-level information is particularly useful in understanding the impacts of forest fragmentation on aquatic ecosystems and the hydrologic regime (Montgomery et al. 1995). However, watersheds can be delineated at a variety of levels (e.g., 6th level), and watersheds may vary considerably in size at the same level. Because some landscape indices are affected by the size of the sampling area, it may be necessary to avoid area-sensitive indices or merge smaller watersheds into larger units to avoid size discrepancies. An alternative to watersheds is to divide the forest into equal-area units or to use equal-area rectangular or circular units to sample the forest.

When using sampling, rather than a complete census, several concerns arise. First, to be valid, a random selection of locations to sample and an unbiased placement of sampling boundaries is preferred. The sample needs to achieve adequate spatial coverage, a sufficient number of sampling areas, and appropriate size relative to the patches. Ripple et al. (1991*a*) chose fifteen sampling areas at random, while Lehmkuhl et al. (1994) selected a spatially-stratified random sample of watersheds to ensure geographical coverage of a large area. Diaz et al. (1993), in contrast, subjectively selected the boundaries and locations of landscapes based on a priori criteria, a procedure that does not ensure that an unbiased sample is obtained. When the analysis is of an individual national forest, avoiding the problems associated with sampling and simply obtaining a complete census of the forest, using watersheds or other divisions of the land area, is clearly now possible and desirable (Baker 1994, Tinker et al. 1998).

Bracketing Potential Sources of Variation and Error

Several sources of variation, error, or uncertainty, together, may influence the outcome of the analysis of fragmentation. The depth-of-edge influence, described earlier, is imperfectly known and varies among different variables, such as microclimate and vegetation. The patches in the landscape can be defined using different criteria, or assuming that different agents form edges. Land-cover data may contain classification errors. When maps are overlaid, as when roads are overlaid on a vegetation map, there may be slivers or single-pixel patches that appear where boundaries do not match. Do these represent real patches that are small as a consequence of poor road placement or are they errors in one or both maps? Should the edge of a sampling area be included as edge when measuring the length of patch perimeter? The analyst must decide how to treat these many small uncertainties and potential errors; together these may significantly influence the results of the analysis.

Because in some cases it is impossible to determine which answer to these questions is correct, a useful approach is to bracket the range of potential choices and report the results as a range of outcomes or to complete a formal error analysis. Reed et al. (1996*b*) and Shinneman (1996) used different patch maps, representing alternative patch conceptions. Reed et al. (1996*a*) compared fragmentation with (1) no depth-of-edge influence, (2) 50-m depth-of-edge influence, and (3) 100-m depth-of-edge influence. Miller et al. (1996) compared using: (1) no roads as patch boundaries, (2) only gravel roads as patch boundaries, and (3) all roads as patch boundaries. Shinneman (1996) considered single-pixel patches resulting from overlays to be both real and to be errors. More formal procedures for analyzing errors in landscape indices that are due to land-cover misclassification can also be used (e.g., Hess and Bay 1997).

COMPARISON AND INTERPRETATION OF FINDINGS

The value of landscape indices is that they are quantitative measures of changes in the landscape useful in various comparisons, but comparisons require comparable data and analysis. The primary constraint on direct comparisons is the need for similar definitions of patches, similar edge-forming agents, the same DEI, similar data source and interpretation process, comparable pixel resolution and minimum mapping unit, and of course the same index. The development of software, such as FRAGSTATS and the r.le programs, has made possible wide use of standard indices. However, there is wide variation in the other factors when studies are compared (Table 4.1). Pixel resolution alone varies from 10 m to 100 m, some studies include roads as patch boundaries, others do not, and only a few studies include a combination of several cover types with several structural stages, while many focus on binary maps (e.g., old growth versus other forest). Comparing absolute values of indices between most studies due to these differences is not presently feasible, but comparing trends resulting from fragmentation is still possible.

The common set of indices (Table 4.6) shows a consistent trend or pattern of response that suggests a syndrome of fragmentation in the West (Table 4.8; Tinker et al. 1998). This syndrome indicates a landscape being transformed from one containing comparatively few, large, but variable-sized patches of often old forest with large core areas, into a landscape with more numerous, smaller, more uniform-sized patches with small core areas and much edge area. This set of common responses is also reflected in two principal components analyses that show that many of these variables all load highly on one or two components (Baker 1994, Tinker et al. 1998). In contrast, a principal components analysis of land use patterns throughout the United States did not identify this same suite of changes (Riitters et al. 1995). The consistency in the pattern of change across Western public forests, and divergence from patterns of general U.S. land use change, may reflect the consistency of dispersed-patch timber harvesting and road construction on Western lands. Our forests are consistently turning into "a mosaic of roads, recent cuts, and managed younger forests, as well as the edge habitat adjoining these components" (Shinneman and Baker, *this volume*). This significant Western pattern of forest fragmentation is quite different from that in agricultural landscapes, such as those of the eastern United States.

This syndrome of fragmentation is perhaps useful for evaluating results of individual future studies (Table 4.8), but other comparisons that are useful include: (1) among parts of a forest, (2) over time in a

Table 4.8. Syndrome of fragmentation in the western United States. This syndrome was compiled from the common patterns of response in the studies cited in Table 4.1.

Decline in patch size, more uniform patch sizes (decrease in st. dev.)
More small patches and fewer large patches
Decline in cover, size, and density of core areas
Increase in cover, size, and density of edge areas
Increased ratio of edge area size to patch size
Increase in the number or density of patches
More compact or uniform patch shapes
Increased total length of edge or edge density, but less edge per patch (reflecting smaller patches)
Late-successional patches smaller and initially closer together (since they are more fragmented), but later farther apart

single forest, (3) among different fragmenting agents, and (4) among alternative proposals for future land use. First, within an individual forest, there may be watersheds with little or no fragmentation and watersheds that are severely fragmented, lacking any old-growth interior forest area. This reflects in part the occurrence of protected areas (Lowsky and Knight, *this volume*), but also patterns of road development and historical management emphases (Baker 1994, Tinker et al. 1998). Second, trends over time document that fragmentation has progressed continuously since World War II, but changes in management have shifted the rate and pattern of fragmentation (Reed et al. 1996*a*). Third, comparisons among fragmenting agents indicate that roads are a more significant source of fragmentation than are timber-harvesting units (Reed et al. 1996*b*, Shinneman 1996, Tinker et al. 1998). Difficulties in projecting future landscapes have precluded widespread simulation of future fragmentation under alternative management plans, but valid simulation models of logging are now available (Tinker and Baker, *this volume*).

Together, these comparisons suggest that even though Rocky Mountain forests are naturally patchy, human land uses have significantly fragmented the forests. The pattern of fragmentation is not like that in agricultural landscapes, but it is significant nonetheless, and has been shown to affect species. The purpose of these analyses, of course, is to lead us toward redesigning our land uses so they have minimal impact (e.g., Baker and Knight, *this volume*).

Best Practices in Fragmentation Analysis

The science of fragmentation analysis is still evolving, but this review suggests there are some common threads that together represent the present state-of-the-art in methodology (Table 4.9). The essential ideas are to make maps that include all the sources of natural patchiness and human-created fragmentation, obtain a complete census of a forest and its watersheds or other sampling subdivisions, calculate the common set of indices (Table 4.6), analyze cumulative effects using temporal comparisons and overlays, bracket sources of variability and error, and compare and interpret results relative to past studies, as well as among watersheds, over time, and among proposed management alternatives, if they exist. This set of practices will lead to more complete and comparable results to encourage better land management and facilitate long-term assessments of our changing forest landscapes.

Table 4.9. Recommended best practices in fragmentation analysis, based on this review of methods applied in fragmentation analyses in the western United States.

Maps of natural patches and edges
 Use cover types and forest structural stages or more detailed data if available
 Use streams as natural edges

Maps of human-created patches and edges
 Include all the patches and edges created by timber harvesting: clear-cuts, shelterwood cuts, seed-tree cuts, group-selection cuts, and individual-tree selection
 Include all the built environment: urban, exurban, and rural developments, power stations, airports, and miscellaneous other developments
 Include roads, transmission lines, and railroads as patch edges

Scales
 Regional-scale qualitative analysis of fragmentation
 Forest-scale analyses using 50-m or better pixel resolution
 Watershed-scale analyses using 10-m or better pixel resolution

Census or sampling
 Complete census is feasible now; sampling should not be used at forest scale or watershed scale

Bracket sources of variability and error
 Bracket variability by using 0, 25, 50, 100, and 200-m DEI
 Bracket sources of potential error (e.g., overlay slivers) if they cannot be resolved

Tracing
 Use 4-neighbor tracing so that features one single-pixel-wide are treated as patch edges

Indices
 Calculate at least the common set of indices (Table 4.6) for each major cover type

Analyze cumulative effects
 Make temporal comparisons between the present landscape and the landscape prior to the land uses of interest, or between projected future landscapes and the landscape prior to the land uses of interest
 Overlay the individual agents of fragmentation and analyze the separate contribution of each agent to the total extent of fragmentation

Compare and interpret results
 Compare results to those from other studies completed in the western United States (Table 4.1) and to the syndrome (Table 4.8)
 Compare among watersheds within a forest
 Compare over time within the study area, preferably using decade-by-decade analyses
 Compare among proposed alternative land use plans

FUTURE WORK/RESEARCH NEEDS

Some areas of fragmentation analysis are in need of additional research and development. Currently, no software is available for measuring connectivity of landscapes, and there is a need to develop procedures for analyzing connectivity. Analysis of fragmentation at the regional scale is poorly developed. Additional research is needed on the sensitivity of diversity and texture indices to fragmentation, as no completely satisfactory indices have emerged. Developing new standards for minimum mapping units is important, so that small features such as meadows and other openings in the forest are mapped in the future. Present databases used by the U.S. Forest Service need to be redesigned so that polygon boundaries are redrawn following timber harvest and so that structural stages reflect edges.

There will always be a need for individually designed studies of fragmentation, but it would be beneficial to establish uniform procedures for general assessments of fragmentation, so that results can be compared among forests and regions. This chapter identifies widely used approaches that have proven successful with the idea that these may represent a common working framework.

ACKNOWLEDGMENTS

I appreciate peer reviews by William Ripple and Curtis Flather.

LITERATURE CITED

Agee, J. K., S.C.F. Stitt, M. Nyquist, and R. Root. 1989. A geographic analysis of historical grizzly bear sightings in the North Cascades. *Photogrammetric Engineering and Remote Sensing* 55: 1637–1642.

Alexander, R. R. 1986*a*. Silvicultural systems and cutting methods for old-growth spruce-fir forests in the Central and Southern Rocky Mountains. General Technical Report, U.S. Forest Service, Rocky Mountain Forest and Range Experiment Station RM-126.

Alexander, R. R. 1986*b*. Silvicultural systems and cutting methods for old-growth lodgepole pine forests in the Central Rocky Mountains. General Technical Report, U.S. Forest Service, Rocky Mountain Forest and Range Experiment Station RM-127.

Baker, W. L. 1994. Landscape structure measurements for watersheds in the Medicine Bow National Forest using GIS analysis. Final Report, Challenge Cost-Share Agreement between Department of Geography & Recreation, University of Wyoming and Routt–Medicine Bow National Forest, Laramie, Wyoming, USA.

Baker, W. L., and Y. Cai. 1992. The r.le programs for multiscale analysis of landscape structure using the GRASS geographical system. *Landscape Ecology* 7: 291–302.

Baskent, E. Z., and G. A. Jordan. 1995. Characterizing spatial structure of forest landscapes. *Canadian Journal of Forest Research* 25: 1830–1849.

Beauvais, G. P. 1997. Mammals in fragmented forests in the Rocky Mountains: community structure, habitat selection, and individual fitness. Ph.D. dissertation, Univ. of Wyoming, Laramie, Wyoming, USA.

Benson, B. J., and M. D. MacKenzie. 1995. Effects of sensor spatial resolution on landscape structure parameters. *Landscape Ecology* 10: 113–120.

Boychuk, D., and A. H. Perera. 1997. Modeling temporal variability of boreal landscape age-classes under different fire disturbance regimes and spatial scales. *Canadian Journal of Forest Research* 27: 1083–1094.

Bridgewater, P. B. 1987. Connectivity: an Australian perspective. Pages 195–200 *in* D. A. Saunders, G. W. Arnold, A. A. Burbidge and A.J.M. Hopkins, editors. *Nature conservation: the role of remnants of native vegetation.* Surrey Beatty & Sons, Chipping Norton, Australia.

Carey, A. B., S. P. Horton, and B. L. Biswell. 1992. Northern spotted owls: influence of prey base and landscape character. *Ecological Monographs* 62: 223–250.

Chen, J., J. F. Franklin, and T. A. Spies. 1992. Vegetation responses to edge environments in old-growth Douglas-fir forests. *Ecological Applications* 2: 387–396.

Chen, J., J. F. Franklin, and T. A. Spies. 1993. Contrasting microclimates among clear-cut, edge, and interior of old-growth Douglas-fir forest. *Agricultural and Forest Meteorology* 63: 219–237.

Chen, J., J. F. Franklin, and T. A. Spies. 1995. Growing-season microclimatic gradients from clear-cut edges into old-growth Douglas-fir forests. *Ecological Applications* 5: 74–86.

Council on Environmental Quality. 1993. Incorporating biodiversity considerations into environmental impact analysis under the National Environmental Policy Act. Council on Environmental Quality, Executive Office of the President, Washington, D.C., USA.

Crompton, B. J. 1994. Songbird and small mammal diversity in relation to timber management practices in the northwestern Black Hills. Master's thesis, University of Wyoming, Laramie, Wyoming, USA.

Diaz, N., J. Kertis, and D. Peter. 1993. Quantitative assessment of current and historic landscape structure. Unpublished Report, U.S. Forest Service, Regional/Subregional Ecological Assessment, Portland, Oregon, USA.

ESRI Inc. 1994. *Understanding GIS: the ARC/INFO method.* Version 7 for UNIX and Open VMS. Environmental Systems Research Institute, Inc., Redlands, California, USA.

Estill, E. 1996. NEPA streamlining. Memorandum of May 24, 1996, to Forest Supervisors, Rocky Mountain Region, U.S. Forest Service, Lakewood, Colorado, USA.

Flather, C. H., and R. MacNeal. 1993. DISPLAY spatial analysis computer program. U.S. Forest Service, Rocky Mountain Research Station, Fort Collins, Colorado, USA.

Forman, R.T.T. 1995. *Land mosaics: the ecology of landscapes and regions.* Cambridge University Press, Cambridge, UK.

Frohn, R. C. 1998. *Remote sensing for landscape ecology: new metric indicators for monitoring, modeling, and assessment of ecosystems.* Lewis Publishers, Boca Raton, Florida, USA.

Frost, E. J. 1992. The effects of forest-clear-cut edges on the structure and composition of old-growth mixed conifer stands in the western Klamath mountains. M.A. Thesis, Humboldt State Univ., Arcata, California, USA.

Gratkowski, H. J. 1956. Windthrow around staggered settings in old-growth Douglas-fir. *Forest Science* 2: 60–74.

Groom, M. J., and N. Schumacher. 1993. Evaluating landscape change: patterns of worldwide deforestation and local fragmentation. Pages 24–44 *in* P. M. Kareiva, J. G. Kingsolver, and R. B. Huey, editors. *Biotic interactions and global change.* Sinauer Associates, Inc., Sunderland, Massachusetts, USA.

Haines-Young, R., and M. Chopping. 1996. Quantifying landscape structure: a review of landscape indices and their application to forested landscapes. *Progress in Physical Geography* 20: 418–445.

Hanley, T. A. 1983. Black-tailed deer, elk, and forest edge in a western Cascades watershed. *Journal of Wildlife Management* 47: 237–242.

Hann, W., R. E. Keane, C. McNicoll, and J. Menakis. 1994. Assessment techniques for evaluating ecosystem, landscape, and community conditions. Pages 237–253, *in* M. E. Jensen and P. S. Bourgeron, editors. *Eastside forest ecosystem health assessment. Volume II: Ecosystem management: principles and applications General Technical Report.* U.S. Forest Service, Pacific Northwest Research Station PNW-GTR-318.

Hargis, C. D., J. A. Bissonette, and J. L. David. 1997. Understanding measures of landscape pattern. Pages 231–261 *in* J. A. Bissonette, editor. *Wildlife and landscape ecology: effects of pattern and scale.* Springer, New York, New York, USA.

Harris, L. D. 1984. *The fragmented forest.* University of Chicago Press, Chicago, Illinois, USA.

Hejl, S. J. 1992. The importance of landscape patterns to bird diversity: a perspective from the northern Rocky Mountains. *The Northwest Environmental Journal* 8: 119–137.

Hess, G. R., and J. M. Bay. 1997. Generating confidence intervals for composition-based landscape indices. *Landscape Ecology* 12: 309–320.

Hunsaker, C. T., R. V. O'Neill, B. L. Jackson, S. P. Timmins, D. A. Levine, and D. J. Norton. 1994. Sampling to characterize landscape pattern. *Landscape Ecology* 9: 207–226.

Hunter, J. E., R. J. Gutiérrez, and A. B. Franklin. 1995. Habitat configuration around spotted owl sites in northwestern California. *The Condor* 97: 684–693.

Hunter, M. L., Jr. 1991. Coping with ignorance: the coarse-filter strategy for maintaining biodiversity. Pages 266–281 *in* K. A. Kohm, editor. *Balancing on the brink of extinction: the Endangered Species Act and lessons for the future.* Island Press, Covelo, California, USA.

Johnston, B. C. 1987. Plant associations of Region Two. U.S. Forest Service, Rocky Mountain Region, R2-ECOL-87-2.

Kaufmann, M. R., R. T. Graham, D. A. Boyce, Jr., W. H. Moir, L. Perry, R. T. Reynolds, R. L. Bassett, P. Mehlhop, C. B. Edminster, W. M. Block, and P. S.

Corn. 1994. An ecological basis for ecosystem management. General Technical Report, U. S. Forest Service, Rocky Mountain Forest and Range Experiment Station RM-246.

Keller, M. E., and S. H. Anderson. 1992. Avian use of habitat configurations created by forest cutting in southeastern Wyoming. *The Condor* 94: 55–65.

Krummel, J. R., R. H. Gardner, G. Sugihara, R. V. O'Neill, and P. R. Coleman. 1987. Landscape patterns in a disturbed environment. *Oikos* 48: 321–324.

LaRoe, E. T. 1993. Implementation of an ecosystem approach to endangered species conservation. *Endangered Species Update* 10(3&4): 3–6.

L.A.S., Inc. 1996. *GRASSLAND user's guide for Windows 95 and Windows NT, Version 1.0.* Logiciels et Applications Scientifiques (L.A.S.), Inc., Montreal, Quebec, Canada.

Laurance, W. F., and E. Yensen. 1991. Predicting the impacts of edge effects in fragmented habitats. *Biological Conservation* 55: 77–92.

Lehmkuhl, J. F., P. F. Hessburg, R. L. Everett, M. H. Huff, and R. D. Ottmar. 1994. Historical and current forest landscapes of eastern Oregon and Washington. General Technical Report, U.S. Forest Service, Pacific Northwest Research Station PNW-GTR-328.

Lehmkuhl, J. F., and M. G. Raphael. 1993. Habitat pattern around northern spotted owl locations on the Olympic Peninsula, Washington. *Journal of Wildlife Management* 57: 302–315.

Lehmkuhl, J. F., L. F. Ruggiero, and P. A. Hall. 1991. Landscape-scale patterns of forest fragmentation and wildlife richness and abundance in the southern Washington Cascade Range. Pages 425–442, *in* L. F. Ruggiero, K. B. Aubry, A. B. Carey, and M. H. Huff, technical coordinators. *Wildlife and vegetation of unmanaged Douglas-fir forests.* U.S.D.A. Forest Service, General Technical Report PNW-GTR-285, Portland, Oregon. .

Li, H., and J. F. Reynolds. 1994. A simulation experiment to quantify spatial heterogeneity in categorical maps. *Ecology* 75: 2446–2455.

Li, H., and J. F. Reynolds. 1995. On definition and quantification of heterogeneity. *Oikos* 73: 280–284.

McCullough, D. R., editor. 1996. *Metapopulations and wildlife conservation.* Island Press, Covelo, California, USA.

McGarigal, K., and B. J. Marks. 1995. *FRAGSTATS: spatial pattern analysis program for quantifying landscape structure.* General Technical Report, U.S. Forest Service, Pacific Northwest Research Station PNW-GTR-351.

McGarigal, K., and W. C. McComb. 1995. Relationships between landscape structure and breeding birds in the Oregon Coast Range. *Ecological Monographs* 65: 235–260.

Miller, J. R., L. A. Joyce, R. L. Knight, and R. M. King. 1996. Forest roads and landscape structure in the Southern Rocky Mountains. *Landscape Ecology* 11: 115–127.

Mladenoff, D. J., and W. L. Baker, editors. 1999. *Spatial modeling of forest landscape change.* Cambridge University Press, Cambridge, UK.

Mladenoff, D. J., Y. Xin, M. A. White, and J. Boeder. 1995. *APACK 2.0 spatial analysis package.* Unpublished documentation, Department of Forest Ecology and Management, University of Wisconsin, Madison, Wisconsin, USA.

Montgomery, D. R., G. E. Grant, and K. Sullivan. 1995. Watershed analysis as a framework for implementing ecosystem management. *Water Resources Bulletin* 31: 369–386.

Morrison, P. H. 1994. GIS applications perspective: development and analysis of a chronosequence of late-successional forest ecosystem data layers. Pages 77–90 *in* V. A. Sample, editor. *Remote sensing and GIS in ecosystem management*. Island Press, Washington, D.C., USA.

O'Hara, K. L., M. E. Jensen, L. J. Olsen, and J. W. Joy. 1994. Applying landscape ecology theory to integrated resource planning: two case studies. Pages 225–236 *in* M. E. Jensen and P. S. Bourgeron, editors. *Eastside forest ecosystem health assessment, Volume II: Ecosystem management: principles and applications*. General Technical Report, U.S. Forest Service, Pacific Northwest Research Station PNW-GTR-318.

Preston, E. M., and B. L. Bedford. 1988. Evaluating cumulative effects on wetland functions: a conceptual overview and generic framework. *Environmental Management* 12: 565–583.

Raphael, M. G., J. A. Young, and B. M. Galleher. 1995. A landscape-level analysis of marbled murrelet habitat in western Washington. Pages 177–189 *in* C. J. Ralph, G. L. Hunt, Jr., M. G. Raphael, and J. F. Piatt, editors. *Ecology and conservation of the marbled murrelet*. U.S.D.A. Forest Service, General Technical Report PSW-GTR-152.

Reed, R. A., J. J. Johnson-Barnard, and W. L. Baker. 1996*a*. Contribution of roads to forest fragmentation in the Rocky Mountains. *Conservation Biology* 10: 1098–1106.

Reed, R. A., J. J. Johnson-Barnard, and W. L. Baker. 1996*b*. Fragmentation of a forested Rocky Mountain landscape, 1950–1993. *Biological Conservation* 75: 267–277.

Ribe, R., R. Morganti, D. Hulse, and R. Shull. 1998. A management driven investigation of landscape patterns of northern spotted owl nesting territories in the high Cascades of Oregon. *Landscape Ecology* 13: 1–13.

Riitters, K. H., R. V. O'Neill, C. T. Hunsaker, J. D. Wickham, D. H. Yankee, S. P. Timmins, K. B. Jones, and B. L. Jackson. 1995. A factor analysis of landscape pattern and structure metrics. *Landscape Ecology* 10: 23–39.

Ripple, W. J., G. A. Bradshaw, and T. A. Spies. 1991*a*. Measuring forest landscape patterns in the Cascade Range of Oregon, USA. *Biological Conservation* 57: 73–88.

Ripple, W. J., D. H. Johnson, K. T. Hershey, and E. C. Meslow. 1991*b*. Old-growth and mature forests near spotted owl nests in western Oregon. *Journal of Wildlife Management* 55: 316–318.

Ripple, W. J., P. D. Lattin, K. T. Hershey, F. F. Wagner, and E. C. Meslow. 1997. Landscape composition and pattern around northern spotted owl nest sites in southwest Oregon. *Journal of Wildlife Management* 61: 151–158.

Rosenberg, K. V., and M. G. Raphael. 1986. Effects of forest fragmentation in Douglas-fir forests. Pages 263–272 *in* J. Verner, M. L. Morrison, and C. J. Ralph, editors. *Wildlife 2000: modeling habitat relationships of terrestrial vertebrates*. University of Wisconsin Press, Madison, Wisconsin, USA.

Ryszkowski, L. 1992. Energy and material flows across boundaries in agricultural landscapes. Pages 270–284 *in* A. J. Hansen and F. di Castri, editors. *Landscape boundaries: consequences for biotic diversity and ecological flows.* Springer-Verlag, New York, New York, USA.

Schreiber, K.- F., editor. 1988. *Connectivity in landscape ecology.* Münster Geographische Arbeiten 29, Ferdinand Schöningh, Paderborn.

Schumacher, N. H. 1996. Using landscape indices to predict habitat connectivity. *Ecology* 77: 1210–1225.

Sheppard, W. D., and R. R. Alexander. *No date.* Overview to silvicultural systems in the Central Rocky Mountains. USDA Forest Service, Rocky Mountain Forest and Range Experiment State, Fort Collins, Colorado, USA.

Shinneman, D. J. 1996. An analysis of range of natural variability, roads, and timber harvesting in a Black Hills ponderosa pine forest landscape. M.A. thesis, University of Wyoming, Laramie, Wyoming, USA.

Skole, D., and C. Tucker. 1993. Tropical deforestation and habitat fragmentation in the Amazon: satellite data from 1978 to 1988. *Science* 260: 1905–1910.

Spies, T. A., W. J. Ripple, and G. A. Bradshaw. 1994. Dynamics and pattern of a managed coniferous forest landscape in Oregon. *Ecological Applications* 4: 555–568.

Swanson, F. J., J. A. Jones, D. O. Wallin, and J. H. Cissel. 1994. Natural variability—implications for ecosystem management. Pages 80–94 *in* M. E. Jensen and P. S. Bourgeron, editors. *Eastside forest ecosystem health assessment, Volume II: Ecosystem management: principles and applications.* General Technical Report, U.S. Forest Service, Pacific Northwest Research Station PNW-GTR-318.

Timmins, S. P., and C. T. Hunsaker. 1996. Tools for visualizing landscape pattern in large geographic areas. Pages 473–477 *in* M. F. Goodchild, L. T. Steyaert, B. O. Parks, C. Johnston, D. Maidment, M. Crane, and S. Glendinning, editors. *GIS and environmental modeling: progress and research issues.* GIS World Books, Fort Collins, Colorado, USA.

Tinker, D. B., C.A.C. Resor, G. P. Beauvais, K. F. Kipfmueller, C. I. Fernandes, and W. L. Baker. 1998. Watershed analysis of forest fragmentation by clear-cuts and roads in a Wyoming forest. *Landscape Ecology* 13: 149–165.

Turner, M. G. 1990. Spatial and temporal analysis of landscape patterns. Landscape *Ecology* 4: 21–30.

Turner, M. G., R. V. O'Neill, R. H. Gardner, and B. T. Milne. 1989. Effects of changing spatial scale on the analysis of landscape pattern. *Landscape Ecology* 3: 153–162.

USA-CERL. 1994. *GRASS user's reference manual.* U.S. Army Construction Engineering Research Laboratory, Champaign, Illinois, USA.

USDA Forest Service. 1993. *R2TF, Region 2 district production data model: transportation features, version 1.0.1.93.* U.S. Forest Service, Engelwood, Colorado, USA.

USDA Forest Service. 1994. *RMRIS, Rocky Mountain Regional Information System user's guide.* U.S. Forest Service, Engelwood, Colorado, USA.

USDA Forest Service. 1996. Black Hills National Forest, Final Environmental Impact Statement, 1996 Revised Land and Resource Management Plan, Forest Service, Custer, South Dakota, USA.

Vaillancourt, D. A. 1995. Structural and microclimatic edge effects associated with clear-cutting in a Rocky Mountain forest. Master's thesis, University of Wyoming, Laramie, Wyoming, USA.

Wiens, J. A., and B. T. Milne. 1989. Scaling of 'landscapes' in landscape ecology, or, landscape ecology from a beetle's perspective. *Landscape Ecology* 3: 87–96.

Wilcove, D. S., C. H. McLellan, and A. P. Dobson. 1986. Habitat fragmentation in the temperate zone. Pages 237–256 *in* M. E. Soulé, editor. *Conservation biology: the science of scarcity and diversity.* Sinauer Associates, Sunderland, Massachusetts, USA.

Part Two

Anthropogenic Causes of Forest Fragmentation in the Southern Rocky Mountains

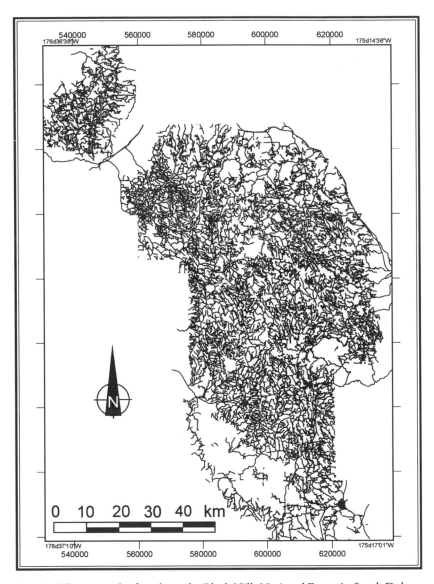

Fig. 5.1. The network of roads on the Black Hills National Forest in South Dakota and Wyoming as of 1996. Map data are from the Black Hills National Forest, Custer, South Dakota.

5

Roads and Forest Fragmentation in the Southern Rocky Mountains

William L. Baker and Richard L. Knight

INTRODUCTION

We have created an impressive network of roads over the surface of the earth in only a century of automobile use. In the U.S. National Forests alone there are over 600,000 km of roads, enough to circle the earth 15 times (Coghlan and Sowa 1998). Yet, the length of roads does not fully capture the effects of roads on landscapes and biodiversity. Often what is most remarkable is how much of the landscape is near a road (Fig. 5.1). For example, several large U.S. national parks have 30% or more of their land area within 1 km of a paved road (Schonewald-Cox and Buechner 1992), and by 1988 about 35% of the Olympic National Forest was within 114 m of a road (Morrison 1994).

Perhaps Robert Frost's well-known sentiment about "the road not taken" (Lathem 1969) underlies the desire to place roads where rapid travel has not previously been possible, covering the landscape. Yet, we do this without fully considering the effects that extend beyond the road surface itself and our brief moment of passing along the road en route to another place. Other values belie the simplicity of our road design and placement, often based only on the economic efficiency of transportation or the desire to access a certain valued product in part of the landscape (e.g., Dean 1997). Just as in other areas of natural resource management (Knight and Bates 1995), we are now reconsidering how to integrate noneconomic values with the need for economic efficiency (e.g., Evink et al. 1996, Canters et al. 1997). Fundamental to this consideration in the southern Rockies is a fuller evaluation of the potential fragmenting effects of forest roads.

Forest fragmentation is often equated with increasing isolation of small, remnant forest patches due to agricultural clearing (Curtis 1956), but roads also fragment forests even if little permanent clearing is done. Roads are an example of internal fragmentation associated in general with linear features, such as roads, power lines, and railroads (Goosem 1997). Roads, indeed, are the most significant agent of forest fragmentation in national forests of the southern Rockies (Reed et al. 1996, Tinker et al. 1998).

Roads fragment by changing landscape structure and by directly and indirectly affecting species. The primary potential effects of roads on the landscape are the dissection of vegetation patches, an increase in edge-affected area and decline in interior area, and an increasing uniformity of patch characteristics, such as shape and size (e.g., Reed et al. 1996). A focus on these landscape and community changes is a "coarse-filter" strategy for managing biodiversity, in which the assumption is that if communities and landscape patterns are well managed, then so will many species (e.g., Hunter 1991). Species may respond indirectly to these landscape changes, but also experience direct mortality on the roads and from increased human access to nearby areas, a loss or gain of habitat to the road area and its vicinity, and may find the road a barrier or conduit for movement (Schonewald-Cox and Buechner 1992, Forman and Hersperger 1996). When these effects are well known, then crafting a corresponding "fine-filter" strategy, focusing on individual species' needs, will be practical (Hunter 1991).

The road network inside national forests in the southern Rockies is sufficiently extensive to have widespread ecological effects (Table 5.1). About 45,000 km of roads in total are found. Road density varies by a factor of six from the low-density Shoshone National Forest to the high-density Black Hills National Forest (Fig. 5.1), reflecting the amount of wilderness or other roadless area and the extent of timber harvesting. The Medicine Bow National Forest also has very high density, but its value is offset by averaging with the Routt National Forest. The other six forests in Table 5.1 have a road density clustering around 0.5 km/km^2. A review suggests that "road density exhibits an apparent threshold of ca. 0.6 km/km^2, above which natural populations of certain large vertebrates decline" (Forman et al. 1997). Most forests in U.S. Forest Service Region 2 are approaching or have exceeded this value, so effects on large vertebrates might be expected. In the following sections we review current knowledge of ecological effects of roads, methods for measuring and analyzing fragmentation by roads, and emerging ideas about using landscape ecological planning to minimize the effects of roads on landscapes.

Table 5.1. Roads in forested parts of Region 2 of the U.S. Forest Service (Wyoming, South Dakota, Colorado) as of 1997. National grasslands are not included. Data are from the U.S. Forest Service R2TF database. Note that road densities are for the entire national forest, including roadless areas, and would be higher in only the roaded parts of these forests.

| | Length | | Road density | |
Forest	km	mi.	km/km^2	$mi./mi^2$
Shoshone	2,581	1,604	0.26	0.42
Pike–San Isabel	3,956	2,458	0.44	0.71
White River	3,541	2,200	0.45	0.72
Grand Mesa, Uncompahgre, Gunnison	5,607	3,484	0.47	0.75
Arapaho-Roosevelt	3,681	2,287	0.50	0.80
Rio Grande–San Juan	8,288	5,150	0.55	0.88
Bighorn	2,606	1,619	0.58	0.94
Routt–Medicine Bow	7,190	4,466	0.80	1.29
Black Hills	7,435	4,620	1.47	2.37
Total	44,885	27,888		

ECOLOGICAL EFFECTS

Because of the sheer number and distribution of roads in forests of the southern Rockies, and the accompanying use of these roads, one would be naive to think that roads did not also affect our natural heritage. Forest roads most often were constructed for timber harvesting but now also serve recreational uses. In a recent survey of the causes of decline of federally threatened and endangered species, outdoor recreation was found to be second only to water development. Motorized recreation was one of the chief contributing factors (Losos et al. 1995).

In the following sections, we summarize some studies of road-edge effects and direct effects of roads and road use on biodiversity (Table 5.2). A generalization from these studies is that roads and their adjacent environments qualify as a distinct habitat and have a number of fine-filter and coarse-filter effects (Hunter 1991). Fine-filter (species- and population-level effects) include: (1) the direct effects of roads on biodiversity, (2) the road-effect zone, and (3) the effects of roads on movement of organisms. Coarse-filter effects include losses of ecologically valuable communities and landscape changes from roads (Table 5.2).

Table 5.2. Known fragmenting effects of roads on species, communities, and landscapes, and appropriate measures of each effect.

	Buffer Analysis	Patch Analysis	Connectivity Analysis
SPECIES (FINE-FILTER)			
Direct effects			
Direct habitat loss/gain to roads and adjoining built area	Road length/area		
Direct mortality on roads	Road area		
Road-effect zone			
Habitat loss/gain due to avoidance area surrounding roads and built area	Road-effect area		
Increased access	Road-effect area		
Increased mortality from hunting			
Increased harassment of wildlife near roads			
Increased woodcutting and trampling along roads			
Increased human-set fires/other disturbances			
Potential indirect effects of landscape changes (see below)			
Increased edge species/decreased interior species		Edge area Interior area Patch size Patch type	
Perils of small populations			
Loss/gain of important natural disturbance patches			
Pollution effects	Road-effect area		

Direct Effects on Biodiversity

A direct loss of habitat is due to the road itself and the adjoining built environment (e.g., homes, businesses, buildings, parking). While forest roads may be only 3–5 m wide, the right-of-way is often 10–30 m wide, which means 1–3 ha of road area per km of road (Norse 1990). In the Black Hills National Forest, the most heavily roaded forest in the region, about 1.5–4.5% of the land area, then, is directly occupied by roads. However, the adjoining built area and the road-effect zone, discussed in the next section, add to this figure. Roads are often placed in high value habitats, such as along streams and through wetlands. This road placement was particularly important in a study of grizzly bears, as the habitats most often associated with roads were especially valuable to bears because they contained high quality foods (McLellan and Shackleton 1988).

One reason some wildlife species avoid roads is the elevated mortality from roads, both directly from humans and indirectly from collisions with vehicles. An estimated one million vertebrates a day are killed on roads in the United States (Lalo 1987). In Florida, vehicles are believed responsible for most deaths of many large, slowly reproducing animals including black bear, key deer, and the Florida panther (Harris and Gallagher 1989). A conservative estimate of the number of deer killed by automobiles during one year in the United States is 500,000 (Romin and Bissonette 1996). Forest carnivores (e.g., wolves, wolverine, bears) in the Rockies are especially vulnerable to road mortality, because they have low fecundity and large home ranges that often include road crossings (Ruediger 1996, Paquet and Callaghan 1996, Gibeau and Heuer 1996). Annual mortality on major roads and railroads in Banff National Park in Canada may be 25% of adult coyotes, 9–11% of black bears, and 3–5% of cougars (Gibeau and Heuer 1996). In a hunted population of elk in north-central Idaho, the probability of an elk being killed increased with road and hunter densities (Unsworth et al. 1993). Others have suggested that closing roads may reduce mortality rates on elk (Leptich and Zager 1991, Stalling 1994).

Other species, especially amphibians and reptiles, are vulnerable to road mortality. Large numbers of frogs and toads are killed crossing roads as they move to wetlands during the breeding season (van Gelder 1973, Gittins 1983, Cooke 1995). Snakes are attracted to roads for warmth where they are susceptible to vehicle mortality (Bernardino and Dalrymple 1992, Rosen and Lowe 1994). Small forest mammals are also killed, with greater numbers dying on wider roads (Oxley et al. 1974). Predators and scavengers are killed while feeding on road-killed wildlife, as are other species attracted to roads because of salts or vegetation, or because roads facilitate winter travel (Woods and Munro 1996, Gibeau and Heuer 1996). Collectively, the magnitude of road-killed wildlife may cause some road corridors to serve as biological sinks, areas where mortality is sufficiently high so as to offset population growth (Forman et al. 1997).

Road-Effect Zone

A zone of influence, called the "road-effect zone," parallels roads (Forman 1995). This zone is the combined result of avoidance by wildlife, a variety of effects associated with human access, indirect effects of changes in the landscape, and pollution from the road (Table 5.2). The width of the road-effect zone may vary with aspect, slope, and with the type of road and the level of persecution or protection directed to species. The Arapaho-Roosevelt National Forest, for example, used a road-effect measure that varies with terrain slope, whether the landscape is open, and forest structure (USDA Forest Service 1997). The road-effect zone may contain an altered microenvironment, relative to interior forests. For example, roads as narrow as 5 m alter the thermal environment, and 10-m wide roads may create a thermal road-effect zone more than 100 m into the adjoining forest (Saunders et al., 1998).

It is not always clear whether animals are responding to the road itself or to the altered environment of the edge habitat along the road. Surveys of songbirds in two national forests of northern Minnesota found 24 species of birds more abundant along roads than away from roads (Hanowski and Niemi 1995). Close to half these species were associated with edges, including species that use roads as corridors to locate food (e.g., American crow and blue jay). Similarly, songbirds were counted adjacent to and away from roads in coniferous forests in Montana (Hutto et al. 1995). The proportion of observations that came from on-road and off-road counts varied significantly among species. Edge-associated species (e.g., chipping sparrow, American robin) were most numerous along roads, and forest-interior species (e.g., western tanager, golden-crowned kinglets) were most numerous away from roads. These differences in bird communities were attributed to structural changes in vegetation along and away from roads.

Similar findings exist for mammals. Mule deer and elk in Colorado were more numerous 200 m or more from road edges (Rost and Bailey

1979). Based on fecal pellet counts in the winter range, deer showed a stronger avoidance of roads than did elk. Both species were less common along heavily traveled than narrow, unpaved roads. Likewise, elk on spring range in southwestern Montana avoided feeding within sight of roads (Grover and Thompson 1986). Perhaps the best study to date of how roads result in decreased use of an area by wildlife was done on elk in coniferous forests of southern Oregon (Cole et al. 1997). In this study vehicle access was experimentally limited by gating secondary and spur roads. Elk were monitored by radio transmitters both before and after the roads were closed. During road closures, elk moved less than when roads were open and also experienced greater survival. This finding corroborates a study done on elk in Montana which also reported reduced elk movements following road closures (Basile and Lonner 1979).

Whether wildlife is persecuted apparently influences distribution near roads. For example, in areas open to hunting, bears avoid roads (Reiffenberger 1974, Hamilton 1978, Brown 1980, Villarrubia 1982). In contrast, in protected areas, where hunting is prohibited and visitors seek to view wildlife, bears may be attracted to roads. However, in the Pisgah National Forest in North Carolina, black bears avoided using roads in both protected and unprotected areas (Powell et al. 1996). In Yellowstone National Park, grizzly bears were less common than expected within 0.4–2.0 km of a road (Green et al. 1997). In addition, grizzly bears substantially underused carcasses for feeding if they occurred within 400 m of roads.

In general, wildlife appear to have the ability to learn and adjust to favorable or unfavorable conditions and avoid areas where disturbance or mortality is high (Knight and Temple 1995). Elk, for example, learn to avoid areas where disturbance is excessive (Craighead et al. 1973, Geist 1978, Cole et al. 1997). Likewise, wolves may transmit avoidance behavior to subsequent generations either through direct learning or genetically based behavioral traits (Thurber et al. 1994). The upshot is that human presence, facilitated by road access, may cause otherwise suitable areas to be avoided by wildlife.

Roads are also sources of pollutants, and some, such as lead, can have significant effects on wildlife (Harrison and Dyer 1984). Lead and nitrogen from automobile exhaust may accumulate in soils up to about 200 m from a road, and the nitrogen may lead to increased plant growth followed by increased invertebrate herbivory (Angold 1997). Lichens suffer decreased growth or may be lost along roadsides, possibly due to pollution (Angold 1997). Soil pH near roads may be elevated by addition of calcareous road dust, and the altered soil may lead to vegetation changes (Auerbach et al. 1997). Vegetation changes along edges, such as road edges, are reviewed in Baker and Dillon (*this volume*).

The road-effect zone often preferentially contains ecologically valuable habitats. Late successional ponderosa pine forest patches, in a representative part of the Black Hills National Forest, are rare in the landscape, but between one-quarter and one-third of the remaining late-successional forest is within 100 m of a road (Shinneman 1996; Shinneman and Baker, *this volume*). In a representative part of the Medicine Bow National Forest, both old-growth spruce-fir and aspen forests are disproportionately located within 100 m of a road (Reed et al. 1996). Roads often follow streams or cross wetlands and other areas that play significant roles in species' life cycles or are areas of high species diversity (McLellan and Shackleton 1988, Baker 1990). In the North Fork of the Flathead River drainage in British Columbia, nearly 9% of the area was unavailable to grizzly bears because of their avoidance of roads, and this 9% was habitat with especially high quality foods (McLellan and Shackleton 1988).

Connectivity Effects

Roads can deter or prevent movement of some animals. Mountain goats experienced a variety of difficulties crossing roads in Glacier National Park including: (1) unsuccessful crossing attempts, (2) separations of nannies from kids, (3) alterations of crossing routes during successful crossings, and (4) delay of crossing to crepuscular periods (Singer 1978). Bobcats crossed paved roads in Wisconsin forests less than expected, possibly to minimize interactions with vehicles and humans (Lovallo and Anderson 1996). Black bears in North Carolina forests were most likely to cross abandoned roads and least likely to cross interstate highways (Brody and Pelton 1989). Wolves and bears in Yellowstone and Banff National parks also avoid crossing roads, especially major roads (Ruediger 1996, Paquet and Callaghan 1996).

Roads can also serve as conduits for the spread of nonnative (exotic) plants or native animals. The successful establishment of nonnative plant species can have long-term effects on the viability of native plant communities. Roads serve as important conduits for the spread of exotic species, particulary plants (Forman 1991, Panetta and Hopkins 1991). A study in Glacier National Park examined alien plant species at different distances from roads (Tyser and Worley 1992). Fifteen alien species were recorded, with the number of species declining out to the furthermost transects. These results suggest that these species were invading along the roads. Forest carnivores, in particular, appear to use roads for winter movement in deep snow, so the road system alters and enhances their movement (Paquet and Callaghan 1996). Tires may also aid in the spread of fungal spores that are important disease agents (Bennett 1991).

Landscape Changes Due to Roads

Roads have the potential to dissect patches, increase the number of patches, decrease the size of patches, make patches more compact, and increase the isolation (distance) between patches (Miller et al. 1996; Reed et al. 1996; Shinneman 1996; Shinneman and Baker, *this volume*). Associated with these changes is an increase in the proportion of the patch that is edge area and a decline in the proportion that is interior area (Reed et al. 1996; Shinneman and Baker, *this volume*), defined by the depth-of-edge influence discussed in the last section. Patches also may become more uniform in total area, edge area, and interior area, reflected in a decline in the standard deviation of these measures (Reed et al. 1996). Other measures that respond to fragmentation by roads include the fractal dimension, which is a measure of patch boundary complexity (Miller et al. 1996), contrast, which is a measure of texture (Reed et al. 1996), the number of patches by size class (Miller et al. 1996), as well as the number or percent cover of large patches (Shinneman and Baker, *this volume*).

Studies in the Black Hills National Forest (BHNF) (Shinneman 1996; Shinneman and Baker, *this volume*) and the Medicine Bow National Forest (MBNF) (Reed et al. 1996) show that roads significantly change these fragmentation measures, more so than do other sources of fragmentation (Reed et al. 1996, Tinker et al. 1998). Patch number increases as much as 4.7 times in the BHNF and 2.6 times in the MBNF when roads are overlaid on vegetation patches. Mean patch interior size declines from 19.6 ha to 4.5 ha on the BHNF and from 12.6 ha to 4.3 ha on the MBNF when roads are overlaid. Mean patch compactness, measured by the corrected perimeter per area index (Baker and Cai 1992) declines on the BHNF from 2.2 to 1.7 and on the MBNF from 2.0 to 1.8 when roads are overlaid, indicating more compact patch shapes. On the BHNF, the standard deviations of patch area and interior area are only about one-quarter of the value without roads, reflecting increasing uniformity in patch size as a result of roads. These trends mirror the syndrome of fragmentation in the western United States (Baker, *this volume*).

Roads have an added effect of leading to other human uses, such as timber harvesting and outdoor recreation, that also are fragmenting (Sader 1995; Mertens and Lambin 1997; R. L. Knight, *this volume*). In the Rocky Mountains, roads and logging are associated, as roads are most often built for this purpose (Fig. 5.2).

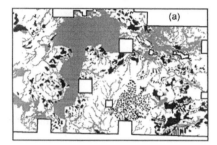 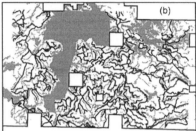

Fig. 5.2. The close association between (a) clear-cuts, shown in solid black, and (b) roads, shown as black lines, in the Tie Camp area on the Medicine Bow National Forest in southeastern Wyoming. Gray shaded area is Encampment River Wilderness and other areas considered unsuitable for timber harvesting. Square white areas are non-Federal land. [Reprinted, with permission, from Conservation Biology Vol. 10, p. 1101].

Measurement and Analysis
Mapping the Road System

Mapping a road system accurately is not a trivial task, as available data sources have limitations. Small roads may be <10 m wide, so only the largest roads can be mapped using conventional satellite images. However, new satellites with 1–5 m resolution will facilitate road mapping (Wynne and Carter 1997). Conventional aerial photographs available nationwide are adequate for mapping most roads, as are U.S. Forest Service photographs at larger scales. U.S. Geological Survey digital line graphs at 1:100,000 scale are complete, but incomplete at 1:24,000 scale. Terrain- and aircraft-induced distortions in aerial photographs (Wolf 1983) are not uniformly removed by manual procedures. Orthophotos, such as U.S. Geological Survey digital orthoquads, are corrected for distortion, but coverage is incomplete. When forest personnel have mapped roads using geographical positioning systems, locations from U.S. Geological Survey maps or digital line graphs are often found to be imprecise (J. Varner, *personal communication*), and spatial errors remain a problem.

Measuring Forest Fragmentation by Roads

A few aspects of forest fragmentation by roads can be measured using aggregate measures, such as road density and total road length, but an adequate analysis requires measuring the individual known fine-filter and coarse-filter effects (Table 5.2) using buffer analysis, patch analysis, and connectivity analysis, as explained in the following sections.

Aggregate Measures. Certain large vertebrates abandon forested areas when roads are built or road densities exceed a threshold, and road density, an aggregate index of road effects, has thus been widely used. These vertebrates include the gray wolf (Mech 1970, Jensen et al. 1986), Rocky Mountain elk (Lyon and Ward 1982, Unsworth et al. 1993), and wolverine (Hornocker and Hash 1981). Other species, including moose (Crete and Taylor 1981, Timmermann and Gallath 1982), white-tailed deer (Sage et al. 1983), and brown bear (Elgmork 1978, Knick and Kasworm 1989), may experience lower populations in heavily roaded areas. A road density of about 0.6 km/km^2 appears to be the threshold for maintaining viable populations of wolves and mountain lions (Thiel 1985, Van Dyke et al. 1986, Jensen et al. 1986, Mech et al. 1988, Mech 1989). Likewise, elk used areas in north-central Idaho with road densities <2.5 km/km^2, and 80% of observations were in areas with road densities <0.6 km/km^2 (Unsworth et al. 1993).

Aggregate measures of roads, such as road density and total length of roads, may be useful indices of road effects on these species, but are insufficient measures of fragmentation. Road density, for example, lacks correlation with the extent of deforestation or timber harvesting, or with the important landscape and community changes that accompany roads (Liu et al. 1993, Miller et al. 1996, Reed et al. 1996, Tinker et al. 1998). Aggregate measures are insensitive to spatial patterns of roads, so two landscapes with similar road density may have very different levels of fragmentation (Liu et al. 1993, Tinker et al. 1998). However, road length is a useful measure of some fine-filter effects, including direct habitat loss or gain from roads, and the length of potential barriers or deterrents to movement.

Buffer Analysis. Part of an adequate quantification of road effects is to use a geographic information system (GIS) to analyze the road area and the adjoining road-effect zone. The GIS is used to add, on both sides of the road, a buffer representing the road-effect zone discussed earlier in this chapter. Buffer analysis measures both known effects on species (fine-filter) and community and landscape changes (coarse-filter).

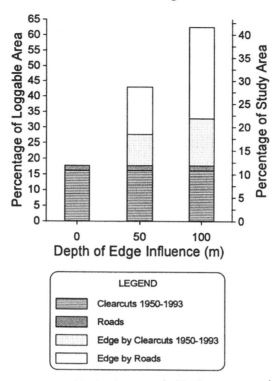

Fig. 5.3. The percentage of the landscape in the Tie Camp area on the Medicine Bow National Forest occupied by clear-cuts, roads, and edge habitat versus depth-of-edge influence. The percentage of loggable area is defined as the percentage of area suitable for logging that is occupied by clear-cuts, roads, and edge habitat. [Reprinted, with permission, from Conservation Biology Vol. 10, p. 1102]

Fine-filter effects include the immediate loss/gain of habitat from the road and associated built environment, the avoidance/attraction of the area near the road, access-related effects, and changes in edge/interior species due to the increase in edge from the road (Table 5.2). Coarse-filter measures include the area of the buffer zone, which is the area of road-induced edge habitat, and the kinds and areas of communities in the buffer zone relative to the surrounding landscape (e.g., Treweek and Veitch 1996).

Buffer analyses generally show that the actual road area is small, but the road-effect zone is large when summed across the entire length of roads. In a representative part of the Medicine Bow National Forest in southeastern Wyoming, the amount of edge along roads is about twice the amount of edge around clear-cuts (Fig. 5.3), assuming a 100-m road-effect zone and about 25% of the landscape is within 100 m of a road (Reed et al. 1996). In a representative part of the Black Hills National Forest, about 36% of the landscape is within 100 m of a road (Shinneman 1996; Shinneman and Baker, *this volume*). Of course, the area within road-effect zones is dependent upon the depth-of-edge influence, but the depth-of-edge influence in Rocky Mountain forests is often 100 m or greater (Baker, *this volume*).

Patch Analysis. Another essential measure of the effects of roads is the change in the mosaic of vegetation patches in the landscape. Changes in patch structure are coarse-filter indicators of potential fine-filter

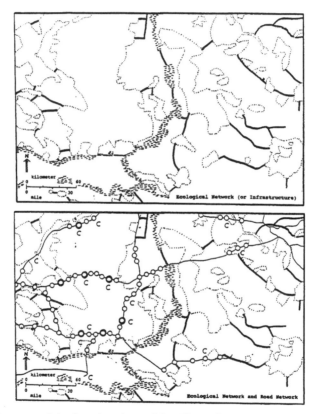

Fig. 5.4. In connectivity-based analysis of the effects of roads, a basic technique is to overlay the ecological infrastructure with the road network or human infrastructure to identify problem areas or bottlenecks needing mitigation. Dotted lines enclose patches of natural vegetation, dashed areas are water, a thick line is a major corridor for wildlife movement, a large circle is an existing or planned wildlife overpass or tunnel, a small circle is an existing or planned faunal pipe, tunnel, or culvert, and C is a bottleneck to be addressed. [Reprinted, with permission, from Trends in Addressing Transportation Related Wildlife Mortality, Florida Dept. of Transportation, p. 11].

effects (Table 5.2), such as increases in edge species and decreases in interior species, as well as a host of potential small population problems, including demographic stochasticity, genetic deterioration, and social dysfunctions that may lead to local extinctions (Wilcove 1986). The best method to analyze patch measures of fragmentation by roads is the overlay technique (Baker, *this volume*). In the overlay technique, the patch structure of a map of the landscape prior to the construction of roads is analyzed. Roads are then overlaid on this map to form new patch edges, and the patch structure is reanalyzed (e.g., Reed et al. 1996). The analyst must determine which types of roads form patch edges, which may be uncertain, but an effective approach to this problem is to complete the analysis using a variety of assumptions about which roads form edges (Miller et al. 1996; Baker, *this volume*). Past research suggests that several measures of patch structure are important (Table 5.2). A patch analysis of road effects was discussed in the section on "Landscape Changes Due to Roads."

Connectivity Analysis. Roads also affect the "ecological infrastructure" (van Selm 1988, Harms and Knaapen 1988). Individual animals require particular places and use these places dynamically, moving from one to another. The set of necessary places and movement routes is the ecological infrastructure for that species. An integration of the infrastructures for a variety of species can identify the common and essential ecological infrastructure for a region (van Selm 1988, Harms and Knaapen 1988). Human places and their movement routes (e.g., roads) constitute a corresponding human infrastructure.

In connectivity analysis, the purpose is to measure to what extent the human infrastructure interrupts the ecological infrastructure. Part of this measurement is accomplished by overlaying human places (e.g., built environment, clear-cuts) on the mosaic of natural vegetation patches, as discussed in the previous section, but that analysis does not address movement routes. The best approach again is to use the overlay technique (Baker, *this volume*) in which the ecological infrastructure is mapped and its connectivity is evaluated, after which the human infrastructure is overlaid and the connectivity of the ecological infrastructure is recalculated (e.g., Fig. 5.4). Quantitative indices of connectivity can be used (Kozova et al. 1986), but the overlay maps can also be simply used to identify locations where conflicts occur (Forman and Hersperger 1996).

Cumulative Effects. As discussed previously (Baker, *this volume*), cumulative effects occur because individually insignificant human land uses accumulate in the landscape to have a significant overall effect; this is clearly the case with roads, because roads have accumulated (Fig. 5.1). Because each individual road project is potentially an incremental addition leading to significant cumulative effects, analysis of cumulative effects is needed for each project. To determine cumulative effects, either a spatial or temporal approach can be used (Baker, *this volume*). The temporal approach, using the overlay technique, is best, as it minimizes confounding effects that may cloud spatial comparisons. The road network at the present time can be overlaid, using a GIS, on the reconstructed landscape prior to the development of the road system. By completing buffer analyses, patch analyses, and connectivity analyses in a before/after comparison, the cumulative effects of the road system can be determined (Reed et al. 1996, Tinker et al. 1998). Of course, comparing these two landscapes to the landscapes of the future is also appropriate, if additional change in the road network is projected.

LANDSCAPE ECOLOGICAL PLANNING AND MANAGEMENT OF ROADS

Separate planning approaches are needed for future roads and for roads that are already in place, but minimizing road effects may be a consistent goal. As discussed earlier, nearly all the fragmenting effects of roads are adverse for native biological diversity, so that minimizing these adverse effects may be considered a universal goal of planning (Southerland 1995). Future roads may be designed to minimize fragmentation by minimizing their length and optimizing their placement, but the only options for existing roads are to close them, move them, or mitigate their fragmenting effects.

Planning New Roads

The road network is already so extensive that the first principle of planning, if fragmentation is a concern, is to minimize construction of new roads. If new roads must be constructed, then the primary planning consideration becomes their placement, and to a lesser extent their design, considered at multiple spatial scales (Baker, *this volume*). At each scale, the goal is to minimize adverse effects on species (fine-filter) and landscape changes (coarse-filter). Interaction occurs between scales. If a route is chosen well at the regional or forest scale, then good design at the watershed or road-segment scales may be less difficult to obtain, and vice versa.

At the regional scale, the primary concern is whether roads will interrupt between-forest movement linkages, unless potential effects

Table 5.3. Some possible approaches to road placement to minimize forest fragmentation.

Buffer analysis: Place roads by analyzing contents of the road-effect zone, using the maximum expected depth-of-edge influence:

Avoid double jeopardy; place associated land uses inside the road-effect zone and as near the road as possible, so the road-effect zone is not expanded

Timber harvest units	Rest areas	Campgrounds	Powerlines
Buildings	Waysides	Oil and gas pads	

Avoid including valuable ecological elements inside the road-effect zone

Old growth forest	Riparian areas	Winter ranges	Cliffs and caves
Sensitive species' habitat	Wetlands	Interior forests	

Patch analysis: Place roads by analyzing the effects of alternative routes on patch measures

Avoid dissecting large patches containing interior forest

Avoid introducing new natural-disturbance barriers; place roads along natural fire breaks

Avoid placing roads along natural higher-value edges

Forest-riparian	Clifflines	Forest-wetland

Avoid increasing the amount of edge and decreasing the amount of interior; place roads:

Along age-class boundaries inside forests

Along natural lower-value edges

Across lower-value elements

Connectivity analysis: Place roads by analyzing the effects of alternative routes on connectivity

Avoid crossing natural linkages

Cross streams below tributaries, rather than around headwaters or above tributaries

Switchback up part of a hillside rather than gradually crossing the whole hillside

---

also exist in certain locations on ecologically significant patch structures or other valuable landscape elements. Linkages between forests may be used rarely, but rare movements can be critical to longterm viability of some species (Boone and Hunter 1996). Much literature has focused on design of regional linkage networks (e.g., Hudson 1991, Noss 1983, 1992, Meffe and Carroll 1997), and the critical concern in road placement is to avoid or minimize the interruption of linkages by roads.

The second scale is that of entire national forests, where the central issues are whether roads can be placed so they will not intersect parts of the forest containing high ecological values (e.g., clusters of wetlands, old-growth forests, elk winter range) or whether roads can be placed to have few adverse effects on connectivity, not altering movement pathways for large vertebrates or subdividing populations of sensitive species inside the forest. Road placement at the forest-wide scale also determines whether new roads add significantly to fragmentation by dissecting concentrations of large natural patches or increasing the amount of edge in a part of the forest containing a high concentration of interior forests. While initial planning at the forest-wide scale may be qualitative, it is essential to quantitatively analyze which of several alternative routes minimizes fragmentation, by using buffer analysis, patch analysis, and connectivity analysis (e.g., Treweek and Veitch 1996). These same concerns are repeated at the watershed scale and the road-segment scale.

Do general principles exist for planning road placement to minimize forest fragmentation? Forman and Hersperger (1996) suggest the main techniques include avoidance, mitigation (reducing and minimizing impacts), and compensation (providing an enhancement elsewhere, such as road closure, to compensate an unavoidable loss). Many useful suggestions have been made for road design using ecological principles (e.g., Southerland 1995, Dramstad et al. 1996, Forman and Hersperger 1996, Forman et al. 1997). Using these ideas and some ideas that follow from our measurement and analysis framework, some avoidance guidelines can be suggested (Table 5.3). These guidelines must be evaluated in individual cases, but they illustrate methods of minimizing fragmentation in road placement. Mitigative approaches are discussed below.

Minimum fragmentation road placement and design emphasize ecological values, but other values must be considered. People dependent upon commodity extraction may wish to emphasize transportation efficiency over other values, as has dominated our thinking about road locations (e.g., Dean 1997). Aesthetic values have also been important; one can drive through a large part of the Medicine Bow National Forest, a heavily fragmented forest (Reed et al. 1996), and see hardly a clear-cut and little of the road network. Indeed, this widespread use of roadside forest strips and viewshed planning to place commodity uses out of direct public view (Williamson and Calder 1973) has greatly expanded the area of the road-effect zone. Moreover, the desire to drive through or up to high-value habitats (e.g., old growth forest, wetlands, lakes) has led to fragmentation of some of our most important landscape elements. An example is the placement of roads (and trails) directly adjacent to nearly all streams and rivers, so that very little high-value riparian habitat is outside a road-effect zone. An alternative is to place roads so that road-effect zones do not intersect these elements, then include a foot trail or road access to a few examples of the element. Roads can also be designed in ways that will offset or minimize some of the adverse fine-filter effects (Table 5.2), such as direct mortality, that cannot be minimized simply by road placement (see Southerland 1995 and references therein).

Potential Restorative/Mitigative Measures

An extensive road network is in place in most forests (Table 5.1), and little, if any, of this network was designed to minimize fragmentation, so a logical question is whether road closures or other methods can mitigate or restore fragmented conditions. Temporary closures are attempted by using steel gates, earth berms, or other structures to prevent entry. The effectiveness of temporary closures in deterring vehicular entry has been questioned (Predator Project 1996), and the road may still allow foot or bicycle access by hunters and recreationists. Closed, but not obliterated roads may still elicit an avoidance response in some animals (McLellan and Shackleton 1988), and a number of other fine-filter effects (Table 5.2), particularly on plants, are not decreased by temporary closures. Moreover, temporary closures still have potentially significant community and landscape effects (Table 5.2). The advantage of temporary closures is that not all the transportation value of the road is lost.

Nonetheless, full restoration requires complete obliteration and revegetation of the road, which can lead to eventual reversal of nearly all the fine-filter and coarse-filter effects (Table 5.2). Forman and Collinge (1996) suggest identifying lowest-value landscape elements for "first-removals" and highest-value elements as "last stands" as a means to lower the adverse effects of more random land transformations. In restoration of landscapes fragmented by roads, we might similarly identify which roads are the best first-removals for obliteration. The roads that have the lowest transportation, access, or other value combined with the highest adverse fragmentation impact may be the best first-removals. Obvious candidates for first removal, then, are dead-end roads that go into the center of large, otherwise unfragmented natural patches as well as roads that are redundant, while candidates for last removal are essential arterial roads that cannot feasiblely be removed.

Mitigative measures focused on wildlife crossing roads that have met with success have been nicely reviewed and will not be repeated here (Forman and Hersperger 1996, Forman et al. 1997). These measures include amphibian tunnels, pipes, culverts, and underpasses and overpasses. In the most elaborate schemes, multimillion dollar "landscape connector" structures that are >100 m wide may allow whole faunas and even natural disturbances to cross roads (Forman and Hersperger 1996). Spatial analysis using GIS can aid in identifying areas in which mitigative structures may be most effective (e.g., Gilbert and Wooding 1996).

ACKNOWLEDGMENTS

We appreciate the assistance of Lois Bacnensky in the Region 2 office of the U.S. Forest Service, who supplied us with the road data for Table 5.1. We also appreciate the review of this chapter by Michael Soule.

LITERATURE CITED

Angold, P. G. 1997. The impact of a road upon adjacent heathland vegetation: effects on plant species composition. *Journal of Applied Ecology* 34: 409–417.

Auerbach, N. A., M. D. Walker, and D. A. Walker. 1997. Effects of roadside disturbance on substrate and vegetation properties in Arctic tundra. *Ecological Applications* 7: 218–235.

Baker, W. L. 1990. Species richness of Colorado riparian vegetation. *Journal of Vegetation Science* 1: 119–124.

Baker, W. L., and Y. Cai. 1992. The r.le programs for multiscale analysis of landscape structure using the GRASS geographical information system. *Landscape Ecology* 7: 291–302.

Basile, J. V., and T. N. Lonner. 1979. Vehicle restrictions influence elk and hunter distribution in Montana. *Journal of Forestry* 77( ): 155–159.

Bennett, A.F. 1991. Roads, roadsides and wildlife conservation: a review. Pages 99–117 *in* D. A. Saunders and R. J. Hobbs, editors. *Nature conservation 2: the role of corridors.* Surrey Beatty & Sons, Chipping Norton, Australia.

Bernardino, F. S., Jr., and G. H. Dalrymple. 1992. Seasonal activity and road mortality of the snakes of the Pa-hay-okee wetlands of Everglades National Park, USA. *Biological Conservation* 62: 71–75.

Boone, R. B., and M. L. Hunter, Jr. 1996. Using diffusion models to simulate the effects of land use on grizzly bear dispersal in the Rocky Mountains. *Landscape Ecology* 11: 51–64.

Brody, A. J., and M. R. Pelton. 1989. Effects of roads on black bear movements in western North Carolina. *Wildlife Society Bulletin* 17: 5–10.

Brown, W. S. 1980. Black bear movements and activities in Pocahontas and Randolph counties, West Virginia. M.S. thesis, West Virginia University, Morgantown.

Canters, K., A. Piepers, and D. Hendriks-Heersma, editors. 1997. Habitat fragmentation & infrastructure: proceedings of the international conference "Habitat fragmentation, infrastructure and the role of ecological engineering," 17–21 September 1995, Maastricht—The Hague, The Netherlands. Ministry of Transport, Public Works and Water Management, Directorate-General for Public Works and Water Management, Road and Hydraulic Engineering Division, Delft, The Netherlands.

Coghlan, G., and R. Sowa. 1998. National forest road system and use. USDA Forest Service, Engineering Staff, Washington, D.C.

Cole, E. K., M. D. Pope, and R. G. Anthony. 1997. Effects of road management on movement and survival of Roosevelt elk. *Journal of Wildlife Management* 61: 1115–1126.

Cooke, A. S. 1995. Road mortality of common toads (*Bufo bufo*) nearing a breeding site, 1974–1994. *Amphibia-Reptilia* 16: 87–90.

Craighead, J. J., F. C. Craighead, Jr., R. L. Ruff, and B. W. O'Gara. 1973. Home ranges and activity patterns of non-migratory elk of the Madison drainage herd as determined by biotelemetry. *Wildlife Monograph* 33.

Crete, M., and R. J. Taylor. 1981. Optimization of moose harvest in southwestern Quebec. *Journal of Wildlife Management* 45: 598–611.

Curtis, J. T. 1956. The modification of mid-latitude grasslands and forests by man. Pages 721–736 *in* W. L. Thomas, editor. *Man's role in changing the face of the earth.* University of Chicago Press, Chicago.

Dean, D. J. 1997. Finding optimal routes for networks of harvest site access roads using GIS-based techniques. *Canadian Journal of Forest Research* 27: 11–22.

Dramstad, W. E., J. D. Olson, and R.T.T. Forman. 1996. *Landscape ecology principles in landscape architecture and land-use planning.* Harvard University Graduate School of Design and Island Press, Washington, D.C., and American Society of Landscape Architects.

Elgmork, K. 1978. Human impact on a brown bear population *Ursus arctos* L. *Biological Conservation* 13: 81–103.

Evink, G. L., P. Garrett, D. Zeigler, and J. Berry, editors. 1996. *Trends in addressing transportation related wildlife mortality.* Florida Department of Transportation, Tallahassee, Florida.

Forman, R.T.T. 1991. Landscape corridors: from theoretical foundations to public policy. Pages 71–84 *in* D.A. Saunders and R.J. Hobbs, editors. *Nature conservation 2: the role of corridors.* Surrey Beatty, Chipping Norton, Australia.

Forman, R.T.T. 1995. *Land mosaics: the ecology of landscapes and regions.* Cambridge University Press, Cambridge.

Forman, R.T.T.. and S. K. Collinge. 1996. Nature conserved in changing landscapes with and without spatial planning. *Landscape and Urban Planning* 37: 129–135.

Forman, R.T.T., D. S. Friedman, D. Fitzhenry, J. D. Martin, A. S. Chen, and L. E. Alexander. 1997. Ecological effects of roads: toward three summary indices and an overview for North America. Pages 40–54 *in* K. Canters, A. Piepers, and D. Hendriks-Heersma, editors. Habitat fragmentation & infrastructure: proceedings of the international conference "Habitat fragmentation, infrastructure and the role of ecological engineering" 17–21 September 1995, Maastricht—The Hague, The Netherlands. Ministry of Transport, Public Works and Water Management, Directorate-General for Public Works and Water Management, Road and Hydraulic Engineering Division, Delft, The Netherlands.

Forman, R.T.T., and A. M. Hersperger. 1996. Road ecology and road density in different landscapes, with international planning and mitigation solutions. Pages 1–22 *in* G. L. Evink, P. Garrett, D. Zeigler, and J. Berry, editors. *Trends in addressing transportation related wildlife mortality.* Florida Department of Transportation, Tallahassee, Florida.

Geist, V. 1978. Behavior. Pages 283–296 *in* J.L. Schmidt and D.L. Gilbert, editors. *Big game of North America: ecology and management.* Stackpole Books, Harrisburg, Pennsylvania.

Gibeau, M. L., and K. Heuer. 1996. Effects of transportation corridors on large carnivores in the Bow River Valley, Alberta. Pages 1–13 *in* G.L. Evink, P. Garrett, D. Zeigler, and J. Berry, editors. *Trends in addressing transportation related wildlife mortality.* Florida Department of Transportation, Tallahassee, Florida.

Gilbert, T., and J. Wooding. 1996. An overview of black bear roadkills in Florida 1976–1995. Pages 1–15 *in* G.L. Evink, P. Garrett, D. Zeigler, and J. Berry, editors. *Trends in addressing transportation related wildlife mortality.* Florida Department of Transportation, Tallahassee, Florida.

Gittins, P. 1983. Road casualties solve toad mysteries. *New Scientist* 97: 530–531.

Goosem, M. 1997. Internal fragmentation: the effects of roads, highways, and powerline clearings on movements and mortality of rainforest vertebrates. Pages 241–255 *in* W.F. Laurance and R.O Bierregaard, Jr., editors. *Tropical forest remnants: ecology, management, and conservation of fragmented communities.* The University of Chicago Press, Chicago.

Green, G. I., D. J. Mattson, and J. M. Peek. 1997. Spring feeding on ungulate carcasses by grizzly bears in Yellowstone National Park. *Journal of Wildlife Management* 61: 1040–1055.

Grover, K. E., and M. J. Thompson. 1986. Elk in the Elkhorn Mountains, Montana. *Journal of Wildlife Management* 50: 466–470.

Hamilton, R. J. 1978. Ecology of the black bear in southeastern North Carolina. M.S. thesis, University of Georgia, Athens.

Hanowski, J. M., and G. J. Niemi. 1995. A comparison of on- and off-road bird counts: do you need to go off road to count birds accurately? *Journal of Field Ornithology* 66: 469–483.

Harms, W. B., and J. P. Knaapen. 1988. Landscape planning and ecological infrastructure: the Randstad study. Pages 163–167 *in* K.-F. Schreiber, editor. *Connectivity in landscape ecology.* Schoningh, Paderhorn.

Harris, L. D., and P. B. Gallagher. 1989. New initiatives for wildlife conservation: the need for movement corridors. Pages 11–34 *in* G. Mackintosh, editor. *Preserving communities and corridors.* Defenders of Wildlife, Washington, D.C.

Harrison, P. D., and M. I. Dyer. 1984. Lead in mule deer forage in Rocky Mountain National Park, Colorado. *Journal of Wildlife Management* 48: 510–517.

Hornocker, M. G., and H. S. Hash. 1981. Ecology of the wolverine in northwestern Montana. *Canadian Journal of Zoology* 59: 1286–1301.

Hudson, W. E., editor. 1991. *Landscape linkages and biodiversity.* Island Press, Washington, D.C.

Hunter, M. L., Jr. 1991. Coping with ignorance: the coarse-filter strategy for maintaining biodiversity. Pages 266–281 *in* K. A. Kohm, editor. *Balancing on the brink of extinction: the Endangered Species Act and lessons for the future.* Island Press, Washington, D.C.

Hutto, R. L., S. J. Hejl, J. F. Kelly, and S. M. Pletschet. 1995. A comparison of bird detection rates derived from on-road versus off-road point counts in northern Montana. Pages 103–110 *in* C.J. Ralph, J. R. Sauer, and S. Droege, editors. *Monitoring bird populations by point counts.* General Technical Report, U.S. Forest Service, Pacific Southwest Research Station PSW-GTR-149.

Jensen, W. F., T. K. Fuller, and W. L. Robinson. 1986. Wolf (*Canis lupus*) distribution on the Ontario-Michigan border near Sault Ste. Marie. *Canadian Field Naturalist* 100: 363–366.

Knick, S. T., and W. Kasworm. 1989. Shooting mortality in small populations of grizzly bears. *Wildlife Society Bulletin* 17: 11–15.

Knight, R. L., and S. F. Bates, editors. 1995. *A new century for natural resources management.* Island Press, Washington, D.C.

Knight, R. L., and S. A. Temple. 1995. Origin of wildlife responses to recreationists. Pages 81–91 *in* R.L. Knight and K.J. Gutzwiller, editors. *Wildlife and recreationists: coexistence through management and research.* Island Press, Washington, D.C.

Kozova, M., K. Smitalova, and A. Vizyova. 1986. Use of measures of network connectivity in the evaluation of ecological landscape stability. *Ekologia* (Czechoslovakia) 5: 187–202.

Lalo, J. 1987. The problem of road kill. *American Forests* September-October: 50–52, 72.

Lathem, E. C., editor. 1969. *The poetry of Robert Frost.* Holt, Rinehart and Winston, New York.

Leptich, D. J., and P. Zager. 1991. Road access management effect on elk mortality and population dynamics. Pages 128–131 in L. J. Lyon and T. N. Lonner, editors. *Elk vulnerability symposium.* Montana State University, Bozeman.

Liu, D. S., L. R. Iverson, and S. Brown. 1993. Rates and patterns of deforestation in the Philippines: application of geographic information system analysis. *Forest Ecology and Management* 57: 1–16.

Losos, E., J. Hayes, A. Phillips, D. Wilcove, and C. Alkire. 1995. Taxpayer-subsidized resource extraction harms species. *BioScience* 45: 446–455.

Lovallo, M. J., and E. M. Anderson. 1996. Bobcat movements and home ranges relative to roads in Wisconsin. *Wildlife Society Bulletin* 24: 71–76.

Lyon, L. J., and A. L. Ward. 1982. Elk and land management. Pages 443–477 *in* J.W. Thomas and D.E. Towell, editors. *Elk of North America.* Stackpole Books, Harrisburg, Pennsylvania.

McLellan, B. N., and D. M. Shackleton. 1988. Grizzly bears and resource-extraction industries: effects of roads on behaviour, habitat use and demography. *Journal of Applied Ecology* 25: 451–460.

Mech, L. D. 1970. *The wolf: ecology and behavior of an endangered species.* Doubleday, New York, New York.

Mech, L. D. 1989. Wolf population survival in an area of high road density. *American Midland Naturalist* 121: 387–389.

Mech, L. D., S. H. Fritts, G. L. Radde, and W. J. Paul. 1988. Wolf distribution and road density in Minnesota. *Wildlife Society Bulletin* 16: 85–87.

Meffe, G. K., and C. R. Carroll, and contributors. 1997. *Principles of conservation biology.* 2nd edition, Sinauer Associates, Sunderland, Massachusetts.

Mertens, B., and E. F. Lambin. 1997. Spatial modelling of deforestation in southern Cameroon: spatial disaggregation of diverse deforestation processes. *Applied Geography* 17: 143–162.

Miller, J. R., L. A. Joyce, R. L. Knight, and R. M. King. 1996. Forest roads and landscape structure in the southern Rocky Mountains. *Landscape Ecology* 11: 115–127.

Morrison, P. H. 1994. GIS applications perspective: development and analysis of a chronosequence of late-successional forest ecosystem data layers. Pages 77–90 *in* V.A. Sample, editor. *Remote sensing and GIS in ecosystem management.* Island Press, Washington, D.C.

Norse, E. A. 1990. *Ancient forests of the Pacific Northwest.* Island Press, Washington, D.C.

Noss, R. F. 1983. A regional landscape approach to maintain diversity. *BioScience* 33: 700–706.

Noss, R. F. 1992. The wildlands project: land conservation strategy. *Wild Earth* (Special Issue): 10–25.

Oxley, D. J., M. B. Fenton, and G. R. Carmody. 1974. The effects of roads on populations of small mammals. *Journal of Applied Ecology* 11: 51–59.

Panetta, F. D., and A. J. M. Hopkins. 1991. Weeds in corridors: invasion and management. Pages 341–351 *in* D. A. Saunders and R. J. Hobbs, editors. *Nature conservation 2: the role of corridors.* Surrey Beatty, Chipping Norton, Australia.

Paquet, P., and C. Callaghan. 1996. Effects of linear developments on winter movements of gray wolves in the Bow River Valley of Banff National Park, Alberta. Pages 1–21 *in* G.L. Evink, P. Garrett, D. Zeigler, and J. Berry, editors. *Trends in addressing transportation related wildlife mortality.* Florida Department of Transportation, Tallahassee, Florida.

Powell, R. A., J. W. Zimmerman, D. E. Seaman, and J. E. Gilliam. 1996. Demographic analysis of a hunted black bear population with access to a refuge. *Conservation Biology* 10: 224–234.

Predator Project. 1996. 1995 Roads Scholar project: summary of results. Unpublished report, Predator Project, Bozeman, Montana.

Reed, R. A., J. Johnson-Barnard, and W. L. Baker. 1996. Contribution of roads to forest fragmentation in the Rocky Mountains. *Conservation Biology* 10: 1098–1106.

Reiffenberger, J. C. 1974. Range and movements of West Virginia black bear during summer and autumn 1973. *Proceedings of the eastern Workshop on Black Bear Management and Research* 2: 139–142.

Romin, L. A., and J. A. Bissonette. 1996. Deer vehicle collisions: status of state monitoring activities and mitigation efforts. *Wildlife Society Bulletin* 24: 276–283.

Rosen, P. C., and C. H. Lowe. 1994. Highway mortality of snakes in the Sonoran Desert of southern Arizona. *Biological Conservation* 68: 143–148.

Rost, G. R., and J. A. Bailey. 1979. Distribution of mule deer and elk in relation to roads. *Journal of Wildlife Management* 43: 634–641.

Ruediger, B. 1996. The relationship between rare carnivores and highways. Pages 1–7 *in* G.L. Evink, P. Garrett, D. Zeigler, and J. Berry, editors. *Trends in addressing transportation related wildlife mortality*. Florida Department of Transportation, Tallahassee, Florida.

Sader, S. A. 1995. Spatial characteristics of forest clearing and vegetation regrowth as detected by Landsat Thematic Mapper imagery. *Photogrammetric Engineering and Remote Sensing* 61: 1145–1151.

Sage, R. W., W. C. Tierson, G. F. Mattfeld, and D. F. Behrend. 1983. White-tailed deer visibility and behavior along forest roads. *Journal of Wildlife Management* 47: 940–962.

Saunders, S. C., J. Chen, T. R. Crow, and K. D. Brosofske. 1998. Hierarchical relationships between landscape structure and temperature in a managed landscape. *Landscape Ecology* 13: 381–395.

Schonewald-Cox, C., and M. Buechner. 1992. Park protection and public roads. Pages 373–395 *in* P. L. Fiedler and S. K. Jain, editors. *Conservation biology: the theory and practice of nature conservation, preservation, and management*. Chapman and Hall, New York.

Shinneman, D. J. 1996. An analysis of range of natural variability, roads, and timber harvesting in a Black Hills ponderosa pine forest landscape. M.A. Thesis, University of Wyoming, Laramie, Wyoming.

Singer, F. J. 1978. Behavior of mountain goats in relation to U.S. Highway 2, Glacier National Park, Montana. *Journal of Wildlife Management* 42: 591–597.

Southerland, M. T. 1995. Conserving biodiversity in highway development projects. *The Environmental Professional* 17: 226–242.

Stalling, D. 1994. Road closed: making bulls less vulnerable. *Bugle* Fall: 107–115.

Thiel, R. P. 1985. Relationship between road densities and wolf habitat suitability in Wisconsin. *American Midland Naturalist* 113: 404–407.

Thurber, T. M., R. O. Peterson, T. D. Drummer, and S. A. Thomasma. 1994. Gray wolf response to refuge boundaries and roads in Alaska. *Wildlife Society Bulletin* 22: 61–68.

Timmerman, H. R., and R. Gollath. 1982. Age and sex structure of harvested moose related to season manipulation and access. *Alces* 18: 301–328.

Tinker, D. B., C.A.C. Resor, G. P. Beauvais, K. F. Kipfmueller, C. I. Fernandes, and W. L. Baker. 1998. Watershed analysis of forest fragmentation by clear-cuts and roads in a Wyoming forest. *Landscape Ecology* 13: 149–165.

Treweek, J., and N. Veitch. 1996. The potential application of GIS and remotely sensed data to the ecological assessment of proposed new road schemes. *Global Ecology and Biogeography Letters* 5: 249–257.

Tyser, R. W., and C. A. Worley. 1992. Alien flora in grasslands adjacent to road and trail corridors in Glacier National Park, Montana (U.S.A.). *Conservation Biology* 6: 253–262.

Unsworth, J. W., L. Kuck, M. D. Scott, and E. O. Garton. 1993. Elk mortality in the Clearwater drainage of northcentral Idaho. *Journal of Wildlife Management* 57: 495–502.

USDA Forest Service. 1997. Draft environmental impact statement. Arapaho and Roosevelt National Forests and Pawnee National Grassland, Fort Collins, Colorado.

Van Dyke, F. B., R. H. Brocke, H. G. Shaw, B. B. Aukerman, T. P. Hemker, and F. G. Lindzey. 1986. Reactions of mountain lions to logging and human activity. *Journal of Wildlife Management* 50: 95–102.

van Gelder, J. J. 1973. A quantitative approach to the mortality resulting from traffic in a population of *Bufo bufo* L. *Oecologia* 13: 93–95.

van Selm, A. J. 1988. Ecological infrastructure: a conceptual framework for designing habitat networks. Pages 63–66 *in* K.-F. Schreiber, editor. *Connectivity in landscape ecology.* Schoningh, Paderhorn.

Villarrubia, C. R. 1982. Movement ecology and habitat utilization of black bears in Cherokee National Forest, Tennessee. M.S. thesis, University of Tennessee, Knoxville.

Wilcove, D. S. 1986. From fragmentation to extinction. *Natural Areas Journal* 7: 23–29.

Williamson, D. N., and S. W. Calder. 1973. Visual resource management of Victoria's forests: a new concept for Australia. *Landscape Planning* 6: 313–341.

Wolf, P. R. 1983. *Elements of photogrammetry.* 2nd ed., McGraw-Hill, New York.

Woods, J. G., and R. H. Munro. 1996. Roads, rails and the environment: wildlife at the intersection in Canada's western mountains. Pages 1–7 *in* G.L. Evink, P. Garrett, D. Zeigler, and J. Berry, editors. *Trends in addressing transportation related wildlife mortality.* Florida Department of Transportation, Tallahassee, Florida.

Wynne, R. H., and D. B. Carter. 1997. Will remote sensing live up to its promise for forest management? *Journal of Forestry* 95(10): 23–26.

6

Forestry Practices and Forest Fragmentation in the Southern Rocky Mountains

Frederick W. Smith

INTRODUCTION

Concerns about biodiversity have led us to view forest practices in the context of how they affect landscape patterns and how these changes in landscape patterns affect habitat, often described as fragmentation. Fragmentation is variously defined but seems to be generally understood as a change in landscape character from natural to human dominated. Fragmentation in forests may best be described as a process which begins at low levels of human intervention in the landscape and ends with small remnants of natural vegetation isolated in a matrix of human-dominated vegetation structure (Hunter 1996). Fragmentation begins with human incursions into a previously natural landscape, proceeding from dissection to perforation to fragmentation as activity increases. In this process, the size of natural ecosystems is reduced and they are increasingly isolated. Fragmentation of forests is most commonly associated with changes in land use where small forest remnants become isolated in a matrix dominated by agriculture or urban land use (Hunter 1996).

Forestry in much of the Southern Rockies does not result in land use change, especially in the extensive public forests of the region. Urbanization and increased recreational use of forests may impact forest structure and biodiversity and is covered in other chapters in this volume. However, most forestry practices occur in landscapes where the forested ecosystem will remain forested. Here, forestry practices will often shift the successional or structural status of the forest, but will not lead to isolation of forest remnants in a matrix of nonforest land use. Where land use is not changed (e.g. forest remains forest, but the structure is altered) fragmentation may or may not occur. For example, a clear-cut must be extensive enough to constitute a barrier to plant or animal movement in order to cause habitat fragmentation (Spies et al. 1994). The impact of forestry practices on landscape pattern will depend on how much area is affected, the intensity of disturbance caused by a practice, and how forestry disturbances are distributed on the landscape.

WHAT IS THE CURRENT STRUCTURE OF ROCKY MOUNTAIN FORESTS?

Perhaps the most striking feature of Southern Rocky Mountain forests is their variability. For example, forests cover about 34% of Colorado, largely confined to the western half of the state. Even within areas dominated by forests, forest is interspersed with nonforest vegetation types including meadows, parks, and alpine. The heterogeneity of forest vegetation is a response to great differences in environment over small spatial scales and complex disturbances regimes. Forests of the Southern Rockies span great environmental extremes and form upper and lower treelines where elevation differences of 2,700 m can occur over distances of 40 km (Peet 1988). Precipitation and temperature vary with elevation, and therefore, the vegetation we see on a forest landscape is strongly patterned by elevation.

Natural disturbances have played a major role in shaping these heterogeneous forests. Some disturbances are spectacular in size and intensity—removing forest overstory from large areas—but occurring infrequently. Over 4,000 ha of montane forest burned in a single day on the Buffalo Creek fire of 1996 in the foothills south of Denver, Colorado, and 8,000 ha of subalpine forest was blown down in a few hours in a single wind event on the Routt National Forest on 1997. A continuous spruce beetle outbreak removed dominant Engelmann spruce trees from a substantial area (tens of thousands of hectares) of the White River Plateau between 1939 and 1953. These disturbances affect large areas but might occur on cycles operating over hundreds of years.

Other disturbances are less apparent but are equally important in shaping the forest landscape of the Southern Rockies. These chronic disturbances remove single trees or small groups and may operate at different scales in time and space. A small fire may burn a portion of a hectare, but there may be many of them in a year, and they occur year in and year out. Mountain pine beetle is endemic in pine forests, and individuals or small groups of trees may be killed in a landscape each year.

The structure of Southern Rocky Mountain forests has been heavily influenced by human activity, especially activities associated with the northern European derived settlement and immediate post settlement era between approximately 1860 and 1920. This was a period of rapid demographic change in the West and a period of extensive exploitation of mineral and natural resources. Forests were disturbed on an unprecedented scale either by tree cutting or by fires. Trees were harvested for mine timbers, ties for railroad construction and maintenance, and for building materials. Large and frequent fires associated with these activities were sometimes inadvertent—ignited from human activity such as railroading or started in fuels such as slash from timber harvest. They were sometimes intentional—set to clear land of trees to support domestic livestock grazing. The settlement era was followed by a period of fire suppression that has lasted until the present. Effective fire suppression in the Southern Rockies may well have excluded fire as a significant ecological disturbance from about the 1930s in many areas.

The activities of the settlement era have left a legacy which continues to dominate the structure of Southern Rocky Mountain forests. Over 50% of the forests on Forest Service land in Colorado have origin dates between 1867 and 1927 (USDA Forest Service 1987). Stand origin dates are based on the age of large trees in a forest stand, presumably indicating the occurrence of tree regeneration following a stand-replacing disturbance. While they do not identify particular disturbances and they reflect tree age rather than specific disturbance, they do give a general picture of forest disturbance history as well as current forest age structure. When forests are stratified by forest type, over 60% of low- and mid-elevation forests (e.g., lodgepole pine, aspen, and ponderosa pine) originated within this period, consistent in time and space where the impact that settlement era activities would be concentrated. A lesser amount of forests at high elevation originated at this time.

As a legacy of the settlement era disturbances, a majority of forests in the Southern Rockies are between 70 and 130 years old, largely even-aged, effectively mature, middle-aged forests. They regenerated following large disturbances including logging and fire in the settlement era. These forests often are extensive in size and homogeneous in structure containing high density of small- and medium-sized trees. Less than 10% of forests are under 70 years old and about 15% of forests are over 200 years old (Fig. 6.1). Disturbances that caused stand renewal were much less frequent in the years following the settlement era. During the settlement era, about 1% of the forest was disturbed and

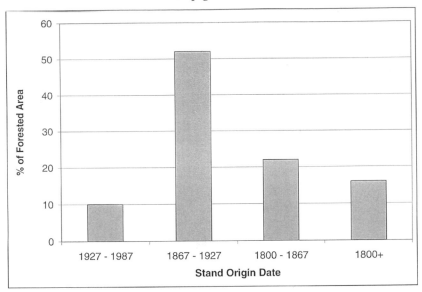

Figure 6.1. Over 50% of forests in National Forest in Colorado and Wyoming originated following disturbances in the settlement era. Only 10% of forests have originated because of disturbances in the last 60 years.

regenerated each year, but in the subsequent 60 years the rate was less than 0.2% per year. This reduction is most probably due to a reduction in the amount of logging and reduced fire amounts because of effective fire suppression.

WHAT IS THE CURRENT MAGNITUDE OF FORESTRY PRACTICES?

Forestry practices in the Southern Rockies fall into three major categories: practices that result in regeneration and forest renewal (reproduction methods), practices to alter growth by reducing tree density (thinning), and practices to reduce insect and disease incidence (forest health). Reproduction methods may be intended to produce an even-aged stand (e.g., clear-cut and shelterwood) by completely removing the forest canopy in one or more entries or may perpetuate an uneven-aged stand (e.g., selection) where the canopy is never fully removed from the area. The USDA Forest Service reports the amount of activities in annual silviculture accomplishment reports. I used these data for five recent years (1992 to 1996) to construct an overview of the level of forestry activity in the region (Table 6.1).

Table 6.1. The level of silvicultural practices in the Forest Service Rocky Mountain Region (Colorado and Wyoming) from the 1992–1996 Silviculture Activities Report. Suitable lands in the Region are 1.62 million ha and total forest lands are 5.18 million ha.

Forest Practices	Area per year (ha)	Percentage of suitable lands	Percentage of forest land
Regeneration Cut—Forest opening	1805	0.11%	0.03%
Regeneration Cut—Selection	1248	0.08%	0.02%
Thinning	471	0.03%	0.01%
Forest Health	1594	0.10%	0.03%

Forest renewal activities for the national forests in Colorado and Wyoming totaled 3,013 ha per year (about 60% even-aged methods and 40% uneven-aged methods) (USDA 1996). There are 1.6 million ha of lands suited for timber production and 5.2 million ha of forest in national forests of the Rocky Mountain Region in Colorado and Wyoming. "Lands suited for timber production" is a designation generally identifying land outside of reserves, having reasonable wood production capability and occurring on slopes which permit harvesting activity. Using these Forest Service figures as an indicator of harvesting activity in the region, 0.2% of lands suited for timber production and 0.06% of all forested lands are subject to reproduction cuttings in a year. Partial cuttings for purposes other than regeneration (e.g., thinning and forest health) impact another 2066 ha per year, 0.13% of lands suited for timber production and 0.04% of all forested lands. At this level of activity, 20% of lands suited for timber production and 6% of all forested lands would be subject to regeneration treatments over a century.

The disturbance regime on a forest is a combination of silviculture and natural disturbances. The disturbance regime is characterized by the size and timing of disturbances and determines the rate of turnover of forest stands and the age and size class structure of a forest. Fire occurrence data for the past 25 years coupled with current forest renewal silviculture activities can provide a sense of the disturbance regime and its implications on the future structure of a forest. Data for the Arapaho-Roosevelt National Forest in northeast Colorado are used to illustrate these trends (Table 6.2). Silvicultural activities account for about 155 ha regenerated forest in a year while fires disturb an average of 232 ha on a forest of ~405,000 forested ha. The silvicultural rotation

Table 6.2. The current disturbance regime on the Arapaho-Roosevelt National Forest in Colorado. Cutting is taken from the 1992–1996 Silviculture Activities Report. Annual area burned is the average of the period from 1972–1997 from the forest fire records. The disturbance rotation is the time required to disturb the total area of forest lands at the current cutting and fire disturbance rate.

Disturbance	Area ($ha\ yr^{-1}$)	Percentage of Forest Land	Disturbance Rotation
Regeneration cutting	157	0.04%	2500
Fire	232	0.06%	1667
Total	389	0.10%	1000

for the forest is over 2,500 years at this rate of disturbance, and when coupled with recent fires, the disturbance rotation is still about 1,000 years. These figures paint a picture of a relatively low level of silvicultural impact on the landscape. These disturbance intervals are longer and well outside the range expected for montane and even high-elevation subalpine forest types in the region. This level of disturbance may not be sustainable and fire and insect disturbances may well increase in the future. In the interim, the forest landscape will become older and more homogeneous. The average age of forest stands will increase, they will be more dense, and multiple story canopies will develop in places.

WHAT IS THE IMPACT OF FOREST PRACTICES ON LANDSCAPE PATTERNS?

Forestry activities such as harvesting and road building perforate landscapes to some degree and, in extreme cases, cause fragmentation. The way that these activities are implemented can have a major influence on the amount of impact they have on landscape character, and ultimately, habitat and biodiversity. Forest cutting followed by conversion to other land uses has the most significant effects for forest fragmentation. Clearing of forest land for agricultural use is rare in the Southern Rockies, but there is increasing perforation and perhaps fragmentation of habitat as more houses and housing subdivisions are built in forests.

Silvicultural activities perforate a landscape for a time between the creation of an opening and revegetation and growth of forest cover. Revegetation of Southern Rocky Mountain forests occurs over moderate time scales, with considerable variability among forest types. Lodge-pole pine forests tend to regenerate rapidly and recover to ceiling leaf area and high net primary production in about 50 years (Long and Smith 1992). Engelmann spruce forests may have a stand initiation period lasting several years and development of multiple age classes make take 250 years (Aplet et al. 1988). Associated road access may impact landscape structure and habitat more severely than forest open-ings made through cutting. Forest openings that are scaled to natural disturbance patterns may do the least harm in terms of disruption of habitat. For a given volume or area harvested, cutting in many small units creates large amounts of edge habitat and most reduces interior habitat. Cutting a given area in few, large units would create less edge and would have the potential to leave more interior habitat intact, causing less perforation of the forest.

Forest cutting and harvest in the Southern Rockies from the 1970s through the 1990s has often occurred as small units widely dispersed on the landscape. This cutting pattern emerged for several reasons, some forestry related, some wildlife related, and some socially related. There is an impression that small openings have less visual impact in a landscape than large openings, and therefore small harvest units will be more acceptable to the general public. This is coupled with a per-ception on the part of the public (and perhaps biologists and forest managers) that small openings have less environmental impact than do large openings.

There are silvicultural considerations that have led to the common use of small openings to secure regeneration. Growing timber can be a marginal economic activity in the Southern Rockies because of moder-ate growth rates, long rotations, and market conditions. Under these circumstances, natural regeneration rather than plantation forestry is the most common regeneration technique. Where natural regenera-tion is used, seed to establish the next generation must come from within or adjacent to the area being regenerated. Conifer species in the Southern Rockies (e.g., ponderosa pine, non-serotinous lodgepole pine, Engelmann spruce) produce wind-disseminated seed. In openings, areas to be regenerated must be small or narrow enough so that sufficient seed can be blown in from adjacent standing trees to regenerate the area. This consideration limits the size of openings to the effective seed dissemination distance.

Management for goals other than timber has also led to the silvi-cultural prescription of small regeneration openings. Water yield is an important use of Southern Rockies forests and is a historically important management goal on national forest lands. Water yield from subalpine forests can be increased by ~30% by cutting strips or small openings of about 5 tree heights in diameter in a continuous mature forest canopy where about 50% of the landscape is in openings (Troendle and King 1985, 1987). Group shelterwood openings and small clearcuts of 1 to 3 ha have been used to create these water yield enhancement treatments (Alexander 1987). The small openings are cut into a large designated area such as a whole or partial watershed, opening 30–50% of the area.

Management of forest for elk and deer habitat is one of the major reasons for the use of small unit sizes for forest renewal cutting in the Southern Rockies. Managing for high elk and deer populations is an important goal of state wildlife agencies and the land management agencies. Guidelines for managing forest habitat for elk call for maintaining 60% of an area in forage, 20–30% in security cover and 10–20% in thermal cover (Thomas et al. 1979). High quantities of high quality forage are produced in forest openings and the guidelines call for small openings (~10 ha) of restricted width (<183 m) to ensure complete use of openings because elk and deer limit their use of openings to small distances from escape cover. These guidelines have had a substantial impact on the design of silvicultural practices. The guidelines are used to design silvicultural treatments involving forest harvest and they are implemented explicitly for habitat improvement projects to maintain or increase elk and deer populations.

ARE THERE WAYS TO APPLY FORESTRY PRACTICES TO REDUCE FRAGMENTATION TYPE EFFECTS?

The amount of perforation and habitat fragmentation caused by a given level of forestry activities can be managed. The design of cutting patterns has a profound effect on landscape structure in the short term, and cutting patterns establish a legacy that impacts future management options (Franklin and Forman 1987). For example, patterns created by strip clear-cutting of 40 to 50 years ago in lodgepole pine forests dominate landscape structure in parts of the Medicine Bow National Forest. These long, narrow areas are well regenerated, but still contrast with adjacent forest. Current management is difficult where there is a desire to break up these geometric patterns, reduce edge, and restore patch dimensions to the historic fire-dominated landscape.

A starting point to consider for designing patches created from forestry activity is the structure of natural disturbances. For example,

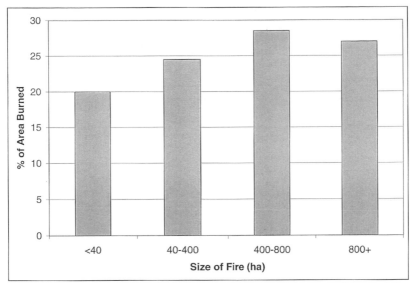

Figure 6.2. The proportion of the forested area burned in fires of different sizes is similar for small (<40 ha) to very large fires (>800 ha) on the Arapaho-Roosevelt National Forest for the period 1972–1997.

while there are many small fires in a year on the Arapaho-Roosevelt National Forest, much of the area burned occurs in fires of large size (Fig. 6.2). While 20% of the total area burned is by fires <40 ha, ~60% of the area burned is in fires of 400 ha and larger. Openings created by forestry activities could be scaled with these natural disturbance sizes in mind to build a landscape more comparable to the historic landscape. Also, the proportion of a landscape in patches of different sizes should be examined with respect to the natural disturbance regime. Indeed, the interiors of openings created by fire, insects, or wind are not homogeneous and this should also be considered when attempting to modify harvesting to more closely approximate natural disturbance. A mix of opening sizes in a landscape over time and space would produce a heterogeneous landscape with a variety of patch sizes, stand structures, and forest successional stages. Current management tends to produce small, regular, and internally homogeneous openings and patches.

Placing larger openings and patches in a landscape by cutting would reduce perforation and habitat fragmentation for a given harvest level (Li et al. 1993). However, this may prove difficult to implement.

Attempts to practice forestry at larger disturbance scales will need to find acceptance with stakeholders. Large openings may be socially unpopular, may impact visual quality, and may not provide as effective elk and deer habitat as do small forest openings.

Openings created by timber harvest are not identical to openings created by disturbances such as fire, insects, or wind. Stands which develop under management will differ from stands that develop without management. However, managed and unmanaged forest stands do share some common characteristics while there are some important differences. Again, a starting point to consider for reducing the habitat fragmentation caused by silvicultural operations is the benchmark of historic forest conditions. For example, conditions in openings should be compared to conditions following disturbance from fire, insects, or wind. The structure of established stands should be compared to the structure of stands that would have occurred without management in the historic landscape.

Harvesting removes a significant amount of tree bole biomass from a stand while most natural disturbances leave tree boles largely intact on site either as dead snags or as downed coarse woody debris. Site preparation can remove significant amounts of coarse woody debris and forest floor organic matter. Silvicultural management in developing stands tends to simplify stand structure by creating regular spacing of trees, by leaving trees of uniform size, and by removing trees of unwanted species.

Stand-level changes can occur as part of silvicultural activities which can alter the forest landscape and habitat whether the area is clearfelled or partially cut. While not as dramatic as the forest opening/mature forest contrasts in a landscape, they are important to landscape structure and silviculture. The structure of mature forests and openings created by fire are characterized by the presence of snags and coarse woody debris. Snags are often removed as part of a harvesting activity for safety reasons. Snags may be removed along road systems in harvest areas by fuelwood cutters. Coarse woody debris is usually added to the system by the felling of cull logs, but might be removed in the site preparation operation by burning or mechanical treatment to facilitate regeneration. Thinnings may simplify forest structure by reducing species diversity of trees in a stand, by reducing size diversity, and by creating a regular spacing pattern.

Management can be adjusted to reduce some of the differences between managed and unmanaged stands. Existing snags and trees to provide replacement snags can be left in harvesting operations. Site preparation activities can be evaluated and applied as a minimal approach to accomplish stand regeneration goals. Site disturbance, removal of down coarse woody debris, and forest floor disturbance could be reduced to only what is required to secure adequate regeneration. This approach would increase the amount of biological legacies from the previous forest to the next generation, but may create risks of fire and/or insect outbreaks. Intermediate treatments in stands can be modified to allow more irregularity in the post-treatment stand including variation in spacing, tree size, and species composition. Also there are choices of silvicultural systems that can ameliorate the effects of harvesting. Uneven-aged management and multi-aged stand structures (e.g., reserve tree silviculture systems) can be used to approximate natural forest structures and to maintain a large tree canopy strata on a forest site.

Conclusions

1. A significant portion of forest stands and forest landscapes in the Southern Rockies are human created and are a legacy of the extensive disturbances associated with the settlement era.

2. Significant areas of Southern Rocky Mountain forests are dominated by dense, even-aged stands of ~90–140 years in age after a century of recovery where there has been a low level of timber harvest and an active program of fire suppression. The landscape this creates is probably less diverse than in the past.

3. We can expect disturbances such as fire, insects, and disease to increase in these dense, even-aged forests.

4. Our current level of silviculture activities is low. We impact a small portion of the landscape by direct silvicultural activity and reduce the occurrence of natural disturbances by active fire suppression.

5. The way that silvicultural practices have been applied in small, dispersed cutting units has caused disproportionately large perforation and fragmentation type effects when compared to the small amount of the acres harvested. This cutting pattern occurred in order to reduce perceived ecological impact, to minimize visual impact, to improve wildlife habitat for edge-preferring species (especially elk), and to increase water yield.

6. Silvicultural activities should be scaled to the size characteristic of natural disturbances to perpetuate the landscape structures that reduce disruptions in habitat.

7. Silvicultural practices that seek to maintain late-seral structural attributes in managed stands—such as maintaining and creating snags, coarse woody debris, and spatial heterogeneity—can be used

to restore historic stand structures and to reduce the impacts of forestry activities on habitat disruption.

Literature Cited

Alexander, R. R. 1987. Ecology, silviculture, and management of the Engelmann spruce-subalpine fir type in the central and Southern Rocky Mountains. USDA Forest Service Handbook No. 659.

Aplet, G., R. Laven, and F. W. Smith. 1988. Patterns of community development in Colorado Engelmann spruce-subalpine fir forests. Ecology 69:312–319.

Hunter, M. L. 1996. Fundamentals of conservation biology. Blackwell Science, Cambridge.

Li, H., J. F. Franklin, F. J. Swanson, and T. A. Spies. 1993. Developing alternative forest cutting patterns: a simulation approach. Landscape Ecology. 8:63–75.

Franklin, J. F. and R. T. T. Forman. 1987. Creating landscape patterns by forest cutting. Landscape Ecology 1:5–18.

Long, J. N., and F. W. Smith. 1992. Volume increment in *Pinus contorta* var. *latifolia*: the influence of stand development and crown dynamics. Forest Ecology and Management 53:53–64.

Peet, R. K. 1988. Forests of the Rocky Mountains, pp165–208. *in* (Barbour, M. G. and Billngs, W. D., eds.) North American Terrestrial Vegetation.

Spies, T. A., W. J. Ripple, and G. A. Bradshaw.1994. Dynamics and pattern of a managed coniferous forest landscape in Oregon. Ecological Applications 4:555–568.

Thomas, J. W., H. Black, Jr., R. J. Scherzinger and R. J. Pedersen. 1979. Deer and elk pp. 104–127. *in* (J. W. Thomas, ed) Managing wildlife habitats in managed forests: the Blue Mountains of Oregon and Washington. USDA Forest Service Agriculture Handbook No. 553.

Troendel, C. A., and R. M King. 1985. The effect of timber harvest on the Fool Creek watershed, 30 years later. Water Resources Bulletin 21:1915–1922

Troendel, C. A., and R. M King. 1987. The effect of partial and clear-cutting on streamflow at Deadhorse Creek, Colorado. Journal of Hydrology 90:145–157.

USDA Forest Service. 1987. Inventory of national forest system lands administered by Region 2. USDA Rocky Mountain Region,

USDA Forest Service. 1997. Silvicultural Activity Report. USDA Rocky Mountain Region, Denver, CO.

7

Forest Fragmentation and Outdoor Recreation in the Southern Rocky Mountains

Richard L. Knight

INTRODUCTION

Although we are willing to concede that anything humans do to excess can have harmful effects on biological diversity, outdoor recreation has traditionally been spared much of this recrimination. Whereas individuals may blame logging, livestock grazing, water development, and mining as the major causes of endangerment of species, we are reluctant to believe that outdoor recreation—our principle use of public lands—has much impact. The facts show otherwise. In a recent survey of the major causes of endangerment of federally listed species on public lands in the United States, outdoor recreation was found to be second only to water-development projects as the principle cause of species declines (Fig. 7.1; Losos et al. 1995). Other summaries support the contention that outdoor recreation is not benign (Ream 1980, Boyle and Samson 1985, Hammitt and Cole 1987, Knight and Gutzwiller 1995). On public wildland areas, outdoor recreation may be the chief threat to native biodiversity. Outdoor recreation of wilderness areas has increased about ten-fold in the past 40 years (Cole and Landres 1996). Cole and Landres estimated that by 1992, total wilderness recreation use probably exceeded eighteen million visitor-days. They further documented that visitation had increased greatly in Alaska and in desert regions of the American West and was occurring more frequently during nontraditional use seasons, particularly during winter.

The principal ways that recreation activities result in altered species populations include harvest, disturbance, habitat modification,

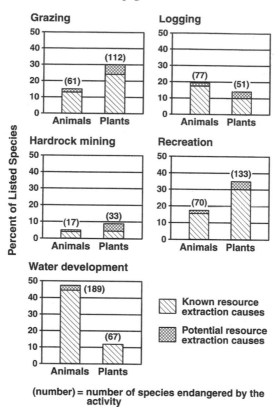

Fig. 7.1. Percentage of federally listed U.S. plants and animals affected by resource extraction uses on public lands. Numbers in parentheses are number of species (Losos et al. 1995).

and pollution (Fig. 7.2; Knight and Cole 1995*a*). Harvest involves immediate death from hunting, fishing, trapping, or collecting. Disturbance, intentional or otherwise, occurs when species are agitated by recreationists. Recreationists can also modify vegetation, soil, water, and even microclimates. Finally, species are affected when their habitats are contaminated with discarded human food or foreign objects, such as tangled fishing line or engine oil.

Collectively, these categories of impacts can affect individuals, populations, and communities (Fig. 7.2; Gutzwiller 1995, Knight and Cole 1995*a*). Some of these effects are often of short duration, for example, an elevated heart rate or alteration of behavior. Other impacts may result in altered distribution and numbers of a popu-

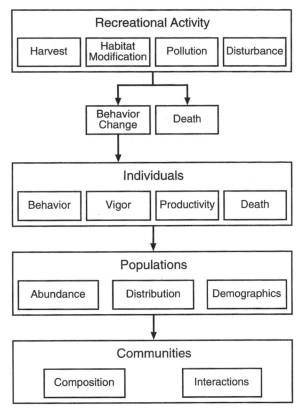

Fig. 7.2. A conceptual model of wildlife responses to recreationists (Knight and Cole 1995*a*).

lation or even different composition of plant and animal communities (Skagen et al. 1991, Wood 1993).

Given that outdoor recreation may affect biodiversity, the question of whether outdoor recreation fragments forests in general, and in the Southern Rocky Mountains in particular, is important. Although outdoor recreation is a single term, it embodies an enormous variety of different uses of wildlands that vary at spatial and temporal scales as well as in numbers (Pomerantz et al. 1988). For example, snowmobile activity can be spatially and temporally concentrated and at times, such as weekends and holidays, can be enormously popular. Similarly, rock climbers do not climb on all cliffs throughout the year. They are concentrated temporally (weekends versus weekdays, warm seasons versus cold seasons), and spatially (tall cliffs that are vertical or overhanging).

Also, the numbers of climbers is influenced by proximity to roads, urban areas, public versus private lands, and other factors.

Of these diverse types of outdoor recreation, which ones might have the ability to fragment forests? Certainly motorized recreation and the use of roads has this ability (see Baker and Knight, *this volume*). Likewise, use of trails and specific locations where recreationists gather, such as campsites, picnic sites, rest areas, and viewing sites, all have the ability to either internally fragment forests or perforate them (Fig. 7.3; Forman 1995). For the 258 federally threatened and endangered species within the United States whose decline on public lands was primarily attributed to outdoor recreation (Losos et al. 1995), hiking was second only to off-highway vehicle use as a cause for species declines (Fig. 7.4). This chapter summarizes what is known regarding recreational trails and site-specific locations such as campsites and presents information regarding the number of trails that occur on public land forests in the southern Rockies. It concludes with management recommendations and research needs.

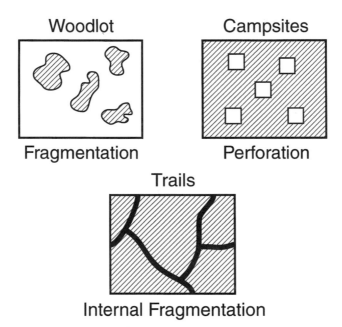

Fig. 7.3. Illustration of fragmentation and perforation. Trails internally fragment landscapes; fixed-site recreational facilities (campgrounds, picnic areas, overlooks) perforate areas.

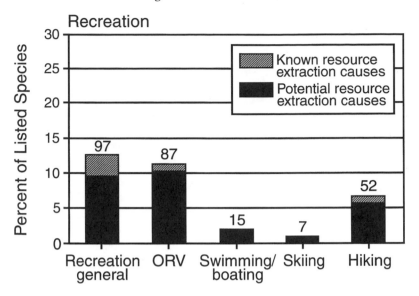

Fig. 7.4. Specific outdoor recreation activities that contribute to the endangerment of federally listed U.S. species on public lands. Numbers on columns are number of species (Losos et al. 1995).

RECREATIONAL TRAILS

Trails are used by a variety of recreationists, including hikers, equestrians, mountain bikers, and off-highway motorists. During winter months trails are often used by skiers or snowmobilers. Whereas trails are defined by a central strip of repeated disturbance and have distinctive margins affected by travel and maintenance, they are normally more curvilinear, quieter, less polluted and more likely to change location than roads (Forman 1995). Trails fragment landscapes by dissection, that is they subdivide an area using equal-width lines (Forman 1995). Fragmentation is defined as the breaking up of a habitat or land type into smaller parcels (Buskirk et al., *this volume*). In this sense, trails internally fragment a landscape.

The critical question regarding the magnitude of effects trails have in fragmenting forest landscapes concerns the "trail distance effect," that is, the width of effects that radiate outward from trails. In addition, trails may contribute to forest fragmentation if they inhibit wildlife movement across trails or if they serve as conduits for invasive plants and animals.

Two studies have addressed trail distance effects on wildlife in forests of the Southern Rocky Mountains. Miller et al. (1998) found that songbird populations were reduced in the vicinity of trails in ponderosa pine forests along the Colorado Front Range (Fig. 7.5). For certain bird species populations did not return to control levels until more than 300 m outward from the trails (at control sites). In addition, Miller et al. (1998) found that songbirds experienced increased nest failure close to trails (Fig. 7.6). Nest success continued to increase for more than 200 m from trails suggesting that the trail distance effect for nest predation is considerable.

The second study that examined wildlife responses to recreational trails in forests of the Southern Rocky Mountains was also conducted

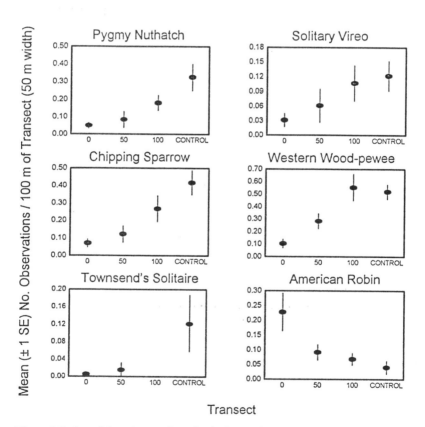

Fig. 7.5. Index of abundance of songbirds detected along transects 0, 50, and 100 m away from trails, and control transects in ponderosa pine forests, City of Boulder Open Space and Mountain Parks, Boulder, Colorado. Vertical lines denote one standard error (Miller et al. 1998).

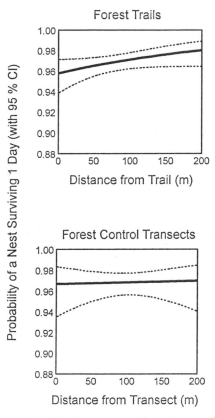

Fig. 7.6. Predicted probability that a nest will survive one day at a given distance from trails and control transects within ponderosa pine forests, City of Boulder Open Space and Mountain Parks, Boulder, Colorado. Calculated from 162 nests. Dotted lines denote 95% confidence interval (CI) (Miller et al. 1998).

on open space in Boulder, Colorado (Miller et al., *unpublished data*). In this study both American robins and mule deer showed heightened responses to people along trails. For example, the probability that a robin 10 m from a trail would flush by a pedestrian was 80% (Fig. 7.7). If a mule deer was 80 m from a trail, there was a 40% probability it would become alert to a pedestrian on the trail and a 10% chance it would flush (Fig. 7.8). No differences were found in responses by robins if the pedestrian was alone or with a dog on leash. The presence of a dog with a pedestrian, however, resulted in a much greater response by mule deer. For example, if a pedestrian was alone and a mule deer was 40 m from a trail, there was less than a 10% chance that

American Robin

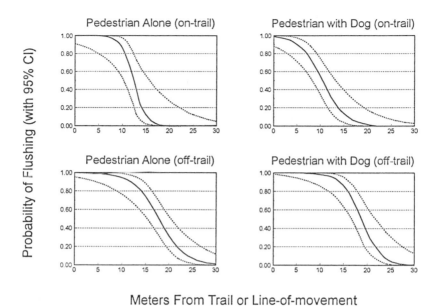

Fig. 7.7. The probability that an American robin will flush at a given distance from pedestrians and dogs, both on and off trails, City of Boulder Open Space and Mountain Parks, Boulder, Colorado. Dotted lines denote 95% confidence interval (CI) (Miller et al., *unpublished data*).

the mule deer would be flushed. If the pedestrian had a dog on leash the probability of the deer being flushed increased to almost 80% (Fig. 7.8).

Other species show aversion to recreational trails. In a study of grizzly bears in the Jewel Basin Hiking Area in the Northern Rocky Mountains of Montana, Mace and Waller (1996) found that bears avoided trails during summer and autumn. In addition, the probability of grizzly bear use increased as the distance to trails increased. Indeed, bears selected areas at considerable distances from trails (greater than 2,130 m).

Recreational trails during winter months are often used by snowshoers and cross-country skiers. In a study of elk responses to skiers in Yellowstone National Park, the authors found that the median distance at which elk started to move when approached was 400 m (Cassirer et al. 1992). This was in an area where elk were not ha-

Mule Deer

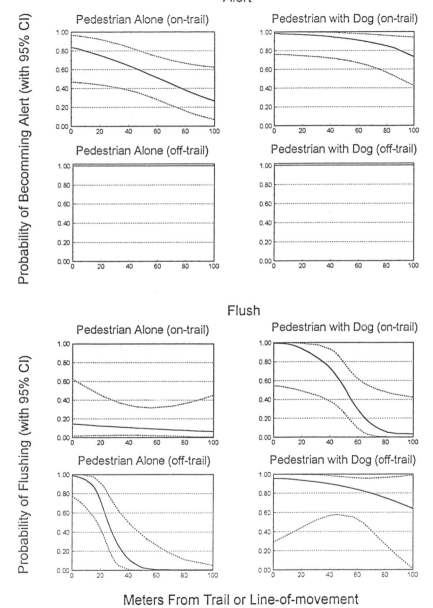

Fig. 7.8. Probability that a mule deer will become alert or flush at a given distance from pedestrians and dogs, both on and off trails, City of Boulder Open Space and Mountain Parks, Boulder, Colorado. Dotted lines denote 95% confidence intervals (CI) (Miller et al., *unpublished data*).

bituated to people. Following disturbance in this area, 78% of the elk left the drainage and returned, on average, within 2 days in the absence of other activity. In some instances the elk did not return to the drainage. The authors concluded that cross-country skiers would have to be kept more than 650 m from elk wintering areas and that skiers would have to remain at distances greater than 1,700 m to avoid disturbing elk.

These studies suggest that wildlife respond to humans associated with recreational trails. Wildlife also show alterations in their behavior to humans in areas without trails. A series of detailed experiments conducted in subalpine forests of southeastern Wyoming showed that human visitation in forests without trails altered bird behavior and displaced birds (Gutzwiller et al. 1994, Riffell et al. 1996, Gutzwiller et al. 1997). These studies were significant because they demonstrated that recreational activities away from trails were displacing birds from habitat that was otherwise suitable. In effect, such displacement generated gaps in resources for birds because, although the resources were still present, species that were sensitive to human intrusion would not be able to utilize them.

Other studies support these findings. In a study of pedestrians with and without dogs, both on and off of trails, in coniferous forests near Boulder, Colorado, Miller et al. (*unpublished data*) found that both birds and mammals became alert and flushed at greater distances from people and dogs when they were off trails (Figs. 7.7 and 7.8). Likewise, in a study of marmot responses to hikers on and off trails in Switzerland, the strongest response by marmots was shown to hikers when they strayed away from trails (Mainini et al. 1993). Recreationists off trails constitute a form of disturbance that is unpredictable whereas recreationists on trails may be perceived by wildlife as predictable. The study near Boulder, Colorado found that both birds and deer showed a reduced response to people and dogs when they were on trails than when away from trails (Figs. 7.7 and 7.8).

Recreational trails also affect native plant communities. Researchers in the Rocky Mountains have documented how trails allow exotic plant species to invade natural areas and have substantiated that the trail distance effect applies to plant as well as wildlife communities. In montane forests of Rocky Mountain National Park, Colorado, Benninger-Truax et al. (1992) found that plant species composition was altered by proximity to trails and by the level of trail use. Because they found that exotic species occurred along trails they concluded that recreation trails serve as conduits for movements of these species into natural areas. In addition, their findings demonstrated that trail corridors in Rocky Mountain National Park provide habitat for vegetation different from that of the forest interior.

In Glacier National Park, Montana, Tyser and Worley (1992) determined that back-country trails served as conduits for the invasion of exotic species. In addition, they found that exotic species extended out beyond 100 m from trails, the limits of their transects. Because they did not detect a decline in these species at 100 m they surmised that the trail distance effect was even greater than what they had measured.

SITE-SPECIFIC RECREATION AREAS

Site-specific recreational areas, such as campgrounds, picnic areas, and wildlife viewing areas, have the potential to perforate forests if they exhibit a disturbance-distance effect outward from the edges (Fig. 7.3). Studies suggest that these areas do alter the wildlife and plant communities within their perimeters (Frissell and Duncan 1965, Hooper et al. 1973, Cole 1981, Kuss and Graefe 1985), however, whether they exhibit an edge distance effect is unknown.

TRAILS AND SITE-SPECIFIC AREAS IN THE SOUTHERN ROCKY MOUNTAINS

Researchers who have examined whether a trail distance effect exists for plant and wildlife communities have all documented effects. Although the depth of this distance effect is dependent upon a variety of factors (e.g., species, season, time, weather, topography, and vegetation [Knight and Cole 1995*b*]), it is believed to be at least 100 m. Accordingly, to estimate how much of the forests of the Southern Rocky Mountains is affected by trails, I have calculated the area within 100 m on either side of recreation trails on U.S. Forest Service lands in Wyoming and Colorado (Table 7.1). Of the 56,034 km^2 of forest lands that are managed by the U.S. Forest Service in Colorado, 3,255 km^2 are affected (6%). Of the 19,480 km^2 of forest land administered by the Forest Service in Wyoming, 1,006 km^2 (5%) are affected.

Road density is a critical statistic explaining the presence or absence of certain wildlife species in wildlands (Baker and Knight, *this volume*). Although trail density has not been examined to see whether similar effects occur, it is reasonable to suppose that similar consequences might occur (e.g., Mace and Waller 1996). Accordingly, I also present trail densities for the forest lands administered by the U.S. Forest Service in Wyoming and Colorado (Table 7.1). The densities range from 0.13 to 0.47 km/km^2 in Wyoming forest lands to 0.26 to 0.54 km/km^2 in Colorado. Further studies are necessary before managers will know whether these numbers are useful in explaining presence/absence and persistence of sensitive species.

The number of campgrounds, picnic areas, and overlooks also varies considerably within the national forests of the Southern Rockies (Table 7.1). These numbers are presented only as a basis for some future comparison after biologists have examined whether a distance effect is associated with fixed-site recreational areas. Once that distance effect is known, coupled with the perimeter of these areas, one could calculate the total area affected.

Table 7.1. Total length of trails (km), trail density (km/km^2) and campgrounds, picnic areas, and overlooks in forested parts of U.S. Forest Service (Wyoming, Colorado) as of 1997. National Grasslands are not included. Data are from USDA Forest Service regional files.

Forest Name	Trail Length	Trail Density	Number of Trails	Campgrounds, Picnic Areas, Overlooks
Colorado				
Pike–San Isabel	2,438	0.54	102	17
White River	2,359	0.30	64	Unknown
Grand Mesa, Uncompaghre, Gunnison	3,432	0.29	51	38
Arapaho-Roosevelt	2,655	0.36	51	22
Rio Grande–San Juan	3,923	0.26	74	15
Routt	1,467		27	7
Wyoming				
Bighorn	2,114	0.47	36	Unknown
Medicine Bow	571	0.13	33	Unknown
Shoshone	2,346	0.24	32	Unknown

MANAGEMENT RECOMMENDATIONS

Ecological traps are landscape components where generalist species, such as predators, competitors, and parasites, are attracted to habitat edges (e.g., Temple and Carey 1988). This, in turn, results in reduced populations of specialist species, often those species of conservation concern. Because trails may result in increased populations of generalist species that increase predation, nest parasitism by brownheaded cowbirds, and competition with specialist species, trails meet the criteria of ecological traps. The net result of increased numbers of generalist species is a decline in species sensitive to humans and those that have specialized ecological niches. The collective result is that trails may result in altered species composition of wildlife and plant communities, with more generalist and fewer specialist species.

This observation and the observed trail distance effect discussed earlier suggest that the density and distribution of trails has the potential to alter biological diversity within an area. Because trails show the characteristics of ecological edges, where they are placed might be of considerable ecological importance (Knight and Temple 1995, Larson 1995). For example, it would be strategic before building any new trails, or when considering rerouting trails, to place trails so they parallel existing human-created edges or rights-of-way, rather than bisect contiguous, undisturbed areas.

Historically, trails have been placed along riparian areas, often in immediate proximity to streams and rivers and along lake shores. Although humans are strongly attracted to waterways, trails need not always be placed next to them. This is particularly relevant because riparian corridors play a disproportionate role in maintaining regional biodiversity (Naiman et al. 1993). Trail placement that alternates next to and away from waterways would create areas adjacent to water free of human disturbance (Fig. 7.9). This recommendation regarding trail placement should also hold for other unique or sensitive landscape features, such as cliffs. Cliffs support elevated biodiversity, often including species found no where else (Camp and Knight 1997). Placing trails adjacent to cliffs, either at the base or along the top, may displace a variety of species (Knight and Cole 1995*b*, Parikesit et al. 1995).

Trails also occur through or adjacent to other sensitive areas. For example, trails that bisect critical wildlife habitat or sensitive plant communities could be designed or rerouted to minimize disturbing these species. In some cases, this may involve determining the landscape that is actually viewed by wildlife from a sensitive location such as a nest or feeding site (viewshed; Camp et al. 1997). Locating trails and site-specific recreation areas in sites with abundant topographic relief and providing security areas in drainages adjacent to those where recreation occurs might also minimize disturbance and energy costs (Stalmaster 1980, Cassirer et al. 1992, Larson 1995).

Managers can think strategically about rerouting or closing trails. By reducing trail densities adjacent to wilderness areas, de facto wildlands on multiple-use areas are created. When trails are being designed or rerouted, a biological assessment should be included. Even today when trails are designed, little or no consideration is given to biological

Fig. 7.9. Possible locations of trails and waterways. The upper figure shows the traditional approach, where the trail parallels the water. The middle and lower figures show alternative placements of trails to minimize negative ecological effects.

concerns. Following their construction, monitoring of trails is essential. By measuring biological effects associated with trails before and following their completion, managers have the opportunity to learn whether harmful trail effects are occurring. This approach will also allow managers to contribute to our understanding of trail effects (Gutzwiller 1993).

Because trails serve as conduits for exotic species, weed-management programs should be established to control invasive species. These programs could monitor the status of established exotic species and the arrival of new species (Tyser and Worley 1992). In addition, trailsides could be rehabilitated using native seed mixes. Because hay and manure of pack stock may contain seeds of exotic species, people using pack stock could be required to use weed-free feed.

The predictability of human activity appears to have a clear effect on wildlife with individuals showing elevated responses to unpredictable activities. Accordingly, activities on trails, where wildlife may have grown accustomed to seeing people, elicits reduced responses from wildlife compared to activities away from trails (Cassirer et al. 1992; Mainini et al. 1993; Knight and Cole 1995b; Miller et al., *unpublished data*). Managers of natural areas should encourage recreationists to stay on-trail. Compliance with this type of recommendation will be enhanced if managers explain how visitors' behavior can harm wildlife and that visitors can minimize their impacts by staying on-trail (Klein 1993).

Four categories of restrictions exist that may facilitate the coexistence of trail-based recreationists and wildlife: spatial, temporal, behavioral, and visual (Knight and Temple 1995). Spatial restrictions are often used to separate recreationists from wildlife. Flushing response and flight distance between people and wildlife are often used to determine these spatial requirements (Knight and Temple 1995, Richardson and Miller 1997). Temporal restrictions are a management option for periods (e.g., daily, seasonal) when wildlife use critical resources, such as wintering, feeding, breeding, or roosting areas. Although spatial and temporal restrictions on human activities associated with trails are often used in concert, alteration of human behavior is also possible. Because such things as noise, speed, and type of recreational activity elicit different responses from wildlife, aspects of these categories could be modified to minimize the impacts of recreationists (Klein 1993). Researchers have noted that wildlife are often less affected when visually shielded from human activities. Components of visual screening that can reduce wildlife response to disturbance along trails include the position of the animal near the trail in relation to the location of the vegetation or topographic features (e.g., cliff, slope)(Larson 1995). For example, when screening vegetation is near the source of disturbance (trail), as opposed to near the animals, it may allow animals to use areas closer than usual to the trail.

Finally, when public lands cannot be stewarded by natural resource managers, land managers should consider closing areas. Traditionally, other uses of public lands have incorporated closures and rest. For example, livestock grazing is allowed during only a portion of the year and forests are reseeded and allowed to grow back after logging. If land management agencies continue to see their operating budgets reduced and have inadequate personnel to ensure stewardship, closures should be considered. To do otherwise and see areas degraded from overuse would be irresponsible.

Evidence is encouraging that many recreationists will be amenable to these suggestions. A recent survey of birdwatchers found that their primary motivation was to contribute to wildlife conservation (McFarlane 1994). This study highlighted two important points. First, people care about wildlife; indeed, it may often be the primary motivation for going outdoors. Second, people's goals can change over time as they gain greater insights and appreciation for nature. When people understand that outdoor recreation, unmanaged, can alter plant and animal communities, natural resource managers will experience greater compliance in building a level of coexistence between recreationists and biodiversity.

Research Needs

Little research exists that documents the effects of recreational trails and fixed-site recreational areas on biological diversity in the Southern Rocky Mountains. For example, of the two studies that have examined bird responses to trails (Miller et al. 1998, Miller et al., *unpublished data*), each was done in urban matrices. Although this is not the case for studies of plant communities associated with trails (e.g., Benninger-Truax et al. 1992, Tyser and Worley 1992), additional studies are needed to confirm the emerging generalization that trails alter the natural communities through which they pass. For example, would a study of trail effects on wildlife communities show a different response in a wildland rather than urban matrix?

Likewise, we do not know the effects of different trail densities (km trail/km^2) on wildlife species. This phenomenon has been demonstrated for a variety of wildlife species in relation to road densities (Baker and Knight *this volume*), which suggests a similar pattern might exist for different densities of trails.

In addition to generalized studies of trails and recreation, little is known about how different types of recreational activities affect wildlife and plant communities. Klein (1993) detected that wildlife responses varied sharply with type of recreationist (e.g., joggers, birdwatchers, photographers). This observation begs the question whether the principal users of recreational trails (pedestrians, mountain bikers, equestrians, cross-country skiers) affect wildlife differently. This concern is particularly relevant because many land management agencies restrict one or more of these activities on trails, often giving the reason that they are concerned with the effects of types of recreational activities on wildlife and plant communities.

Although we know that fixed-site recreational areas alter the plant and wildlife communities within their boundaries, we do not know whether they have an influence beyond their perimeters. Because these areas differ widely in size as well as use, studies which examine how these variables shape plant and wildlife responses would be useful.

Finally, research needs to examine how the placement and design of recreational trails and facilities affect biological diversity (Knight and Temple 1995, Larson 1995). Although some biologists suggest that trails should not be placed in sensitive areas (e.g., riparian and cliff sites), no one has yet examined how altering trail placement affects wildlife and plant species. Campsites could be designed or placed to ensure adequate spatial and visual restrictions that would allow sensitive wildlife to exist nearby. Such sites could be situated so patches or strips of vegetation lie between them and necessary wildlife habitat. Existing understory vegetation could be maintained, and both horizontal and vertical heterogeneity of vegetation could be increased, allowing for greater species diversity as well as minimizing overt effects of disturbance. Considering the number of fixed-site facilities constructed every year on public lands, the opportunity to design research projects that look at different facility designs should be apparent.

ACKNOWLEDGMENTS

I owe a special debt to my graduate students who have helped me in so many ways. In particular, the research of R. Camp, S. Miller, and C. Miller proved instrumental to my thinking on how outdoor recreation alters native biological diversity. In addition, the insights and contributions of D. Cole, K. Gutzwiller, G. Orians, and S. Skagen have been invaluable. Kevin Gutzwiller and Bill Romme kindly reviewed a draft of this mansucript.

LITERATURE CITED

Benninger-Truax, M., J. L. Vankat, and R. L. Schaefer. 1992. Trail corridors as habitat and conduits for movement of plant species in Rocky Mountain National Park, Colorado, USA. *Landscape Ecology* 6: 269–278.

Boyle, S. A., and F. B. Samson. 1985. Effects of nonconsumptive recreation on wildlife: a review. *Wildlife Society Bulletin* 13: 110–116.

Camp, R. J., and R. L. Knight. 1997. Cliff bird and plant communities in Joshua Tree National Park, California, USA. *Natural Areas Journal* 17: 110–117.

Camp, R. J., D. T. Stinton, and R. L. Knight. 1997. Viewsheds: a complementary management approach to buffer zones. *Wildlife Society Bulletin* 25: 612–615.

Cassirer, E. F., D. J. Freddy, and E. D. Ables. 1992. Elk responses to disturbance by cross-country skiers in Yellowstone National Park. *Wildlife Society Bulletin* 20: 375–381.

Cole, D. N. 1981. Vegetational changes associated with recreational use and fire suppression in the Eagle Cap Wilderness, Oregon: some management implications. *Biological Conservation* 20: 247–270.

Cole, D. N., and P. B. Landres. 1996. Threats to wilderness ecosystems: impacts and research needs. *Ecological Applications* 6: 168–184.

Forman, R.T.T. 1995. *Land mosaics.* Cambridge University Press, Cambridge, England.

Frissell, S. S., Jr., and D. P. Duncan. 1965. Campsite preferences and deterioration in the Quetico-Superior Canoe country. *Journal of Forestry* 63: 256–260.

Gutzwiller, K. J. 1993. Serial management experiments: an adaptive approach to reduce recreational impacts on wildlife. *Transactions of the North American Wildlife and Natural Resources Conference* 58: 528–536.

Gutzwiller, K. J. 1995. Recreational disturbance and wildlife communities. Pages 169–181 *in* R. L. Knight and K. J. Gutzwiller, editors. *Wildlife and recreationists: coexistence through management and research.* Island Press, Washington, D.C., USA.

Gutzwiller, K. J., E. A. Kroese, S. H. Anderson, and C.A. Wilkins. 1997. Does human intrusion alter the seasonal timing of avian song during breeding periods? *Auk* 114: 55–65.

Gutzwiller, K. J., R. T. Wiedenmann, K. L. Clements, and S. H. Anderson. 1994. Effects of human intrusions on song occurrence and singing consistency in subalpine birds. *Auk* 111: 28–37.

Hammitt, W. E., and D. N. Cole. 1987. *Wildland recreation ecology and management.* John Wiley & Sons, New York, New York, USA.

Hooper, R. G., H. S. Crawford, and R. F. Harlow. 1973. Bird density and diversity as related to vegetation in forest recreational areas. *Journal of Forestry* 71: 766–769.

Klein, M. L. 1993. Waterbird behavioral responses to human disturbances. *Wildlife Society Bulletin* 21: 31–39.

Knight, R. L., and D. N. Cole. 1995*a*. Wildlife responses to recreationists. Pages 51–69 *in* R. L. Knight and K. J. Gutzwiller, editors. *Wildlife and recreationists: coexistence through management and research.* Island Press, Washington, D.C., USA.

Knight, R. L., and D. N. Cole. 1995*b*. Factors that influence wildlife responses to recreationists. Pages 71–79 *in* R. L. Knight and K. J. Gutzwiller, editors. *Wildlife and recreationists: coexistence through management and research.* Island Press, Washington, D.C., USA.

Knight, R. L., and K. J. Gutzwiller, editors. 1995. *Wildlife and recreationists: coexistence through management and research.* Island Press, Washington, D.C., USA.

Knight, R. L., and S. A. Temple. 1995. Wildlife and recreationists: coexistence through management. Pages 327–333 *in* R. L. Knight and K. J. Gutzwiller, editors. *Wildlife and recreationists: coexistence through management and research.* Island Press, Washington, D.C., USA.

Kuss, F. R., and A. R. Graefe. 1985. Effects of recreational trampling on natural area vegetation. *Journal of Leisure Research* 17: 165–183.

Larson, R. A. 1995. Balancing wildlife viewing with wildlife impacts: a case study. Pages 257–270 *in* R. L. Knight and K. J. Gutzwiller, editors. *Wildlife and recreationists: coexistence through management and research.* Island Press, Washington, D.C., USA.

Losos, E., J. Hayes, A. Phillips, D. Wilcove, and C. Alkire. 1995. Taxpayer-subsidized resource extraction harms species. *BioScience* 45: 446–455.

Mace, R. D., and J. S. Waller. 1996. Grizzly bear distribution and human conflicts in Jewel Basin Hiking Area, Swan Mountains, Montana. *Wildlife Society Bulletin* 24: 461–467.

Mainini, B., P. Neuhaus, and P. Ingold. 1993. Behavior of marmots *Marmota marmota* under the influence of different hiking activities. *Biological Conservation* 64: 161–164.

McFarlane, B. L. 1994. Specialization and motivations of birdwatchers. *Wildlife Society Bulletin* 22: 361–370.

Miller, S. G., R. L. Knight, and C. K. Miller. 1998. Influence of recreational trails on breeding bird communities. *Ecological Applications* 8: 162–169.

Naiman, R. J., H. Decamps, and M. Pollock. 1993. The role of riparian corridors in maintaining regional biodiversity. *Ecology* 31: 209–212.

Parikesit, P., D. W. Larson, and U. Matthes-Sears. 1995. Impacts of trails on cliff-edge forest structure. *Canadian Journal of Botany* 73:943–953.

Pomerantz, G.A., D.J. Decker, G.R. Goff, and K.G. Purdy. 1988. Assessing impact of recreation on wildlife: a classification scheme. *Wildlife Society Bulletin* 16:58–62.

Ream, C. H. 1980. Impacts of backcountry recreationists on wildlife: an annotated bibliography. USDA Forest Service General Technical Report INT-81.

Richardson, C. T., and C. K. Miller. 1997. Recommendations for protecting raptors from human disturbance: a review. *Wildlife Society Bulletin* 25: 634–638.

Riffell, S. K., K. J. Gutzwiller, and S. H. Anderson. 1996. Does repeated human intrusion cause cumulative declines in avian richness and abundance? *Ecological Applications* 6: 492–505.

Skagen, S. K., R. L. Knight, and G. H. Orians. 1991. Human disturbance of an avian scavenging guild. *Ecological Applications* 1: 215–225.

Stalmaster, M. V. 1980. Management strategies for wintering bald eagles in the Pacific Northwest. Pages 49–67 *in* R. L. Knight, G. T. Allen, M. V. Stalmaster, and C. W. Servheen, editors. *Proceedings of the Washington bald eagle symposium.* The Nature Conservancy, Seattle, Washington, USA.

Temple, S. A., and J. R. Carey. 1988. Modeling dynamics of habitat-interior bird populations in fragmented landscapes. *Conservation Biology* 2: 340–347.

Tyser, R. W., and C. A. Worley. 1992. Alien flora in grasslands adjacent to road and trail corridors in Glacier National Park, Montana (U.S.A.). *Conservation Biology* 6: 253–262.

Wood, A. K. 1993. Parallels between old-growth forest and wildlife population management. *Wildlife Society Bulletin* 21: 91–95.

8

Fragmentation by Inholdings and Exurban Development

David M. Theobald

INTRODUCTION

Rapid population growth throughout the Rocky Mountain West is causing another wave of extensive and long-lasting landscape transformation. The land use change that has generated the greatest concern recently is conversion of agricultural and forested land into low-density residential development, commonly referred to as exurban and ranchette. This type of conversion is especially prevalent along the Front Range and in the high mountain valleys of the Southern Rocky Mountains.

While roughly three-quarters of the forests in Colorado occur on public land (mostly federal), exurban development of private lands is an important component of forest fragmentation. Private land dissects the public land ownership pattern, follows the dendritic valley and stream-bottom patterns, and extends upslope to the forest fringe. Not only is 80% of forested land within 3 km of private land areas (including inholdings), private land is found at key locations, such as winter ranges and migration corridors, throughout the Southern Rocky Mountains. Changes in the use of private land adjacent to forested areas influence the ecological functioning and impact the management of ecological processes (such as forest fire suppression).

My objectives here are to describe the extent, rates, and patterns of private land development, focusing on inholdings and exurban development, and to examine the potential effects on habitat loss and fragmentation of the Southern Rocky Mountain landscape. A brief overview of the land use change driving this transformation is provided, followed by an analysis of the extent and trajectories of land use changes. Historical, current, and future development patterns, both at regional and landscape scales, are described and potential landscape fragmentation effects are examined. Finally, a few considerations are offered for refining the way in which landscape fragmentation is typically approached, to more adequately reflect both the natural variation found and the type of development occurring in the Southern Rocky Mountain landscape. Most of the analyses are based on data from Colorado, because the majority of the Southern Rockies are located in central Colorado, and because land use trends in Colorado are a bellwether for the Rocky Mountain region in general (Riebsame et al. 1996).

Land Use Change in the Rocky Mountain West

The Rocky Mountain states (Arizona, Colorado, Idaho, Montana, Nevada, New Mexico, Utah, and Wyoming) are experiencing dramatic landscape transformation, principally in the form of conversion of agricultural land to residential land use. This widespread land use change is fueled by rapid population growth rates two to three times the rest of the United States from 1990 to 1996. Population growth in the Rocky Mountains averaged 2.1% growth annually, compared to 0.9% for the remainder of the United States (U.S. Census Bureau 1997). Nineteen of the 281 Rocky Mountain counties exceeded 6% annual growth. Population growth was even more rapid in the Southern Rocky Mountains—the western and Front Range counties in Colorado—and averaged 3.1%. Ten of the 58 Southern Rocky Mountain counties exceeded 6% annual growth. The Rocky Mountain states are projected to grow by nearly 6.5 million additional people by the year 2025 (U.S. Census Bureau 1998), so that in the span of one generation, this region faces the addition of the combined 1996 populations of Colorado, Montana, and New Mexico. Though periods within the past 150 years have had equal or greater rates of growth, the magnitude and extent of the landscape change caused by this population growth are unprecedented. One clear indication of this is urban sprawl, where the density of a city decreases while the overall population increases (Diamond and Noonan 1996).

Though much of the recent growth is focused on large urban areas, rural areas have also exhibited remarkable growth. Nationwide, rural populations began growing at a faster rate than urban areas due to urban emigration in the 1970s; a brief migratory "turn-around" back to cities occurred in the 1980s (Fuguitt and Beale 1996), but the Rocky Mountain region did not experience this (Cromartie 1994).

Today, the large federal lands remain an important factor attracting immigrants to the Rocky Mountain region (Rudzitis and Streatfield 1992). Nearly 7% of all Rocky Mountain residents have immigrated since 1990.

Unlike previous booms in the Rocky Mountain west, current changes are driven by growth of the secondary and tertiary economy—services, recreation, and information businesses (Cromartie 1994, Power 1996, Beyers 1996), a new appreciation for the quality-of-life of small towns and rural areas (Nelson 1992), and amenity migration, in which people choose residential location based more on recreational and aesthetic qualities rather than job location (Ulman 1954, Jobes 1993, Nelson 1997). However, a clear analysis of the transition from extractive to service-based economies is complicated by standard federal data collection efforts, particularly the categories used in the U.S. Department of Commerce's Regional Economic Information System. Their classification schemes do not resolve some of the nuances important to tracking the New West economy (Wirth Forum 1998). For example, one of the most common misconceptions about the service economy is that they only provide low-paying "burger-flipper" jobs. However, hospital workers such as doctors, nurses, and technicians are included in the service category of federal economic statistics (Wirth Forum 1998).

Resource-based economies, such as agriculture and forestry, and wide open spaces have been and continue to be defining characteristics of this region (Riebsame et al. 1997). The amount of land in agricultural use has increased steadily since the late 1800s, reaching an apex in the 1960s. However, since 1978, the Rocky Mountain states have lost over 3,400 km² of agricultural land annually (U.S. Census of Agriculture 1993).

Defining a Development Gradient

One of the major challenges to understanding the potential ecological effects of land use change is to make socio-economic and ecological data commensurable. A number of conceptual gradients depicting human-dominated landscapes have been formulated, including the Beale code (Butler and Beale 1993) and the "modification gradient," which distinguishes urban, suburban, cultivated, managed, and natural landscapes (Forman and Godron 1986). However, the urban-rural gradient suggested by McDonnell and Pickett (1990) offers the benefit of defining an urban-rural gradient in terms of measurable factors, such as population density. This approach provides a way to link ecological processes to measures of human disturbance in human-dominated ecosystems (McDonnell and Pickett 1990, Medley et al. 1995).

Common land use databases, such as USGS LU/LC (Anderson et al. 1976) and Census Bureau, make a simple distinction between urban and non-urban. These data are useful for broad-scale, general analyses, but are limited by not identifying areas that are being encroached by low-density development. The Natural Resource Inventory (NRI) database distinguishes between high- and low-density development but is limited to broad-scale analysis because of the coarseness of the analytical unit (roughly county-level) (NRCS 1995). Finer-scale data that distinguish development densities are needed to understand the spatial pattern of land use change and to assess the ecological and social implications of these changes (Theobald et al. 1996, Theobald and Hobbs 1998, Wirth Forum 1998). Effects of ecological disturbance are known to result from houses in rural areas with housing densities far below the typical definition of "urban" (Theobald et al. 1997). For example, gray fox avoid using habitat in areas with housing densities as low as 1 unit per 13 ha (Harrison 1997).

Here I quantify the development gradient concept using housing density rather than population density because housing density is strongly related to changes on the landscape and can be measured at a fine scale. Population density is frequently used as a gradient, but population-based statistics belie the magnitude of landscape change. Population data underestimate the magnitude of human influence on the local landscape because they are tied to the place of primary residence. Recognizing the distinction between population and housing density data is especially important in the Rocky Mountains, which has a high proportion of vacation and second houses—the vacancy rate in 1990 averaged 29% (compared to 14% for the rest of the U.S.) and can be as high as 83%.

Housing density is measured on a continuous scale, but, for convenience, five levels of development density—urban, suburban, exurban, ranchette, and rural are distinguished. Urban areas are defined as having greater than 123.5 units per km^2, assuming 2.2 people per house, which is substantially lower than the Census Bureau's definition of urban based on 1,605 people or 281.5 houses per km^2 (McDonnell et al. 1997). The relatively low thresholds are used to differentiate better patterns of low-density development. Exurban areas are low-density areas with between 6.2 and 24.7 units per km^2. Ranchette areas have between 3.1 and 6.2 units per km^2, while rural areas have less than 3.1 units per km^2.

Inholdings, rather than fitting within this gradient concept, are isolated, small-acreage (<1 km^2) remnant private land holdings created by mining claims, townsites, or homesteads that perforate public land ownership. The total area of inholdings in the western states is estimated to be less than 40,500 ha (Pearson 1993), but, because the inholdings are scattered across the landscape, they pose difficulties for land management and potentially fragment habitat. These inholdings are generally more difficult to develop, though there have been a few highly visible cases of "threatened" development (Pearson 1993, Hearn 1998). Developed inholdings are generally used for summertime cabins (e.g., in the old Marble, Colorado, townsite) or for year-round residents as a result of intense housing pressure and lack of affordable housing in nearby exurban lands (e.g., Lake Irwin near Crested Butte) (Olgeirson 1994, Anderson 1995). Roads, driveways, outbuildings, and associated infrastructure, in addition to houses, can result in direct habitat loss and cause potential fragmentation.

METHODS

I estimated the amount and type of land cover that occurs on and near the different housing densities to determine the extent and trend of potential fragmentation by exurban development in the Southern Rocky Mountains. A number of landscape indices were calculated for both the whole state of Colorado and for a smaller study site in the Blue River Valley in Summit County. Computing these indices at two scales provides a broad perspective for a large region, complemented with a detailed analysis using finer-scale vegetation and development data.

Land Use/Cover

A useful source of land use/cover data is the Natural Resource Inventory (NRI) (NRCS 1995). Rather than being a census of agricultural land, the NRI provides detailed sampling of land use for 1982, 1987, and 1992. This database was developed using a systematic, stratified-random sampling of aerial photo-interpreted points (NRCS 1997) and distinguishes not only agricultural from forested land use, but from urban areas as well (Table 8.1). Information on urban land use is absent in the Census of Agriculture data.

Data on land use change are generally reported as summary statistics that are averaged across a broad region. This averaging hides spatial patterns of land use change and dynamics of important land use conversions. For example, most observers of western land use change have assumed that the major contributor to loss of agricultural land is

Table 8.1. Land use and cover categories derived from the NRI database (NRCS 1995).

Category	Description
Agriculture	Includes standard classes such as cropland, pastureland, and rangeland. Also includes Conservation Reserve Program lands, which are typically in the Miscellaneous category.
Federal	Lands identified in public ownership.
Forest	Forested lands, and includes some grazed forested lands.
Miscellaneous	Includes farmsteads and special agroforestry uses such as Christmas tree farms and greenhouses.
Rural Transportation	Includes highways, paved, gravel, and dirt roads.
Urban (high density)	Includes urban and built-up areas, in densities with greater than 1 unit per 10 acres.
Urban (low density)	Includes smaller built-up areas, in densities with less than 1 unit per 10 acres.
Water	Permanent open water bodies.

conversion to residential land use. This assumption is based largely on the relationship between places of population growth and agricultural loss (e.g., Knight 1994, Theobald et al. 1996, Frank 1997). To test this assumption and to understand the components of land use change, I calculated the trajectories of land use from 1982 to 1992 using the NRI database.

An inadequacy of both the Census of Agriculture and NRI data is that they are limited when examining spatially-explicit, landscape-level land use change because their smallest unit of analysis is at the county level (roughly). To examine development trends that occur directly on different vegetation types and estimate the extent of potential vegetation fragmentation and loss by development, I used the USGS Land Use/Land Cover 1:250,000 series to map broad vegetation cover types, such as forested, agricultural, rangeland, and wetlands.

Housing Density

For detailed housing density patterns, I developed maps of private land development densities based on 1990 U.S. Census Bureau block-group level data. A block-group is a subdivision of a census tract and contains between 250 and 550 housing units. Housing density was calculated by dividing the number of housing units by the area of a block-group. I removed public lands and areas greater than 3,280 m in elevation and greater than 20% slope because large-scale development in these areas is difficult. Because block-group size varies in response to development density, suburban and urban areas are fairly well mapped, with polygons as small as a couple of hectares. Areas with low housing density are mapped at a coarser resolution, using fairly large polygons (some approaching one thousand hectares), which leads to large areas being mapped at the same density. A finer resolution of housing density is available in the block-level data even in low-density areas in the central mountains of Colorado. However, historical comparisons (and future projections) are difficult to make because of the data collection methodologies changed slightly from the 1980 to 1990 censuses.

For the landscape-scale analysis, I used maps of housing density at a quarter-section (65 ha) resolution, based on county tax assessor data for 1960, 1990, and projected to 2020 (Theobald and Hobbs 1998), which provided finer-resolution housing density with better detail in rural areas. The fine-scale housing density data are complemented with fine-scale vegetation data from a classified Landsat TM image (30 m pixel).

RESULTS

Colorado lost over 360 km² of agricultural land annually (U.S. Census of Agriculture 1993). One-third of agricultural land in Colorado is cropland, and the remainder is pasture/rangeland. This distinction is important because conversion to cropland resulted in major changes in native vegetation and ecosystems, but conversion to pasture/rangeland use caused some change to the native vegetation and habitat, while still providing significant wildlife habitat. The NRI data suggest that overall conversion of agricultural land occurred at a slower pace in Colorado, at a rate of 146 km² annually (Table 8.2).

Forested land was also lost, but at a slower rate of 105 km² annually. High-density urban land use increased by 60 km² annually (a rate of 3.8%), and low-density urban land use increased by 16 km² annually (a rate of 3.9%). For the Western Slope and Front Range counties of Colorado, agricultural acreage gained 8 km² annually. Forested land use lost 101 km², and high-density urban gained 6 km² annually (a rate of 3.8%), but low-density urban gained 12 km² (a rate of 13.2%).

While the net loss of agricultural land use in Colorado from 1982 to 1992 was 1,460 km², over 3,210 km² were converted from agricultural land use, while 1,750 km² were converted to agricultural land use (Table 8.3). Over 890 km² of agricultural land (61%) were converted

Table 8.2. Land use and cover change in Colorado and the Southern Rocky Mountain portion of Colorado for 1982, 1987, and 1992. These data are from the NRI database (NRCS 1995). The agricultural category included CRP lands.

Land Use Category	Area in Colorado (km²)			Annual growth rate (%) 1982–92	Area (km²) gained 1982–92	Area in western and Front Range of CO (km²)			Annual growth rate (%) 1982–92	Area (km²) gained 1982–92
	1982	1987	1992			1982	1987	1992		
Agriculture	145724	144466	144257	-0.1	-147	47079	47186	47181	0.0	10
Federal	95970	96625	96815	0.1	85	91497	91101	91295	0.0	-20
Forest	16261	16042	15197	-0.6	-106	13622	13402	12601	-0.8	-102
Miscellaneous	4260	4427	4638	0.9	38	3088	3232	3356	0.9	27
Rural Transportation	2478	2498	2534	0.2	6	889	910	934	0.5	4
Urban (high density)	2741	3292	3786	3.8	105	1565	1820	2161	3.8	60
Urban (low density)	383	431	533	3.9	15	104	157	242	13.2	14
Water	1785	1819	1841	0.3	6	1091	1126	1165	0.7	7

Table 8.3. Transition matrix of land use trajectories for Colorado from 1982 (rows) and 1992 (columns). Data from NRI database (NRCS 1995).

Land Use in 1982	Agriculture	Federal	Forest	Misc.	Rural Trans.	Urban (high)	Urban (low)	Water	TOTAL 1982
Agriculture	142421	1508	183	455	93	760	138	78	145636
Federal	691	95037	127	57	0	0	0	0	95911
Forest	850	161	14869	80	4	217	56	13	16251
Misc.	129	51	2	4042	3	23	0	6	4258
Rural Transportation	32	0	6	0	2432	0	0	6	2476
Urban (high)	0	0	0	0	0	2739	0	0	2739
Urban (low)	0	0	0	0	0	44	339	0	383
Water	47	0	0	0	0	0	0	1736	1784
Total 1992	144169	96756	15188	4635	2532	3784	533	1840	269438

from agricultural to urban land use, but no areas of urban land use were converted back out of urban. Over 180 km^2 of agricultural land were converted to forest, while over 850 km^2 of forest were converted to agriculture.

For the Western Slope and Front Range counties of Colorado, the net gain of agricultural land use was 100 km^2. However, over 510 km^2 of agricultural land were converted to urban uses, and over 230 km^2 were converted to urban from forested land use. Clearly, while the net amount of agricultural land converted is a striking figure, averaging across a broad geographic region hides the fact that over twice the net amount was actually converted. Some areas of agricultural land use, most likely near fast-growing urban areas, were lost, while other areas, such as rural counties in northwestern Colorado, gained agricultural lands from conversion from forest land (e.g., over 680 km^2 from 1982 to 1992) (Fig. 8.1).

Conversion of Agricultural to Urban Land Use

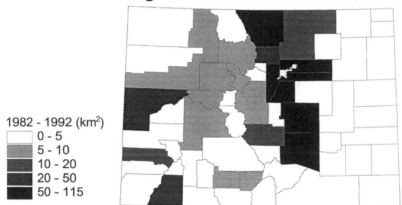

Fig. 8.1. County-level agricultural to urban conversion from 1982 to 1992. Data are from the NRI database (NRCS 1995).

Regional Scale

Because densities can be differentiated, maps of housing density at the regional scale offer a means to refine our understanding of rates of development (Figs. 8.2, 8.3, and 8.4). They detail not only the development of the Front Range, but also the growth of some small mountain towns, such as Breckenridge and Aspen. Historical, current, and projected (1960, 1990, and 2020) housing development patterns

Housing Density in 1960

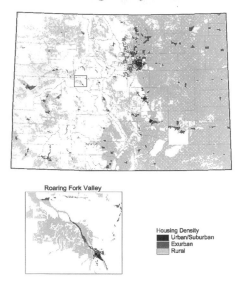

Fig. 8.2. Housing density in Colorado for 1960. Data are from Census Bureau block-group level. *Urban* is defined as >123.5 units/km², *suburban* as <123.5 units/ km², *exurban* as <24.7 units/km², *ranchette* as <6.2 units/km², and *rural* as <3.1 units/km².

Housing Density in 1990

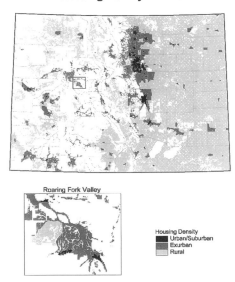

Fig. 8.3. Housing density in Colorado for 1990. Data are from Census Bureau block-group level. See Fig. 8.2 for density definitions.

Housing Density in 2020

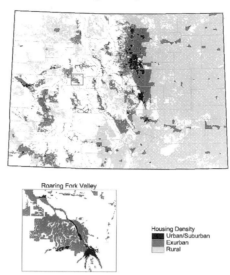

Fig. 8.4. Housing density in Colorado for 2020. Data are projected by using county-level population projections from the Colorado State demographer's office and forcing the new population into the block groups in the same proportion as was found in 1990. Population is converted to housing density by assuming the same ratio of people to houses (by block-group). This model likely overestimates the housing densities in urban and suburban areas, and underestimates the housing density in lower-density areas. See Fig. 8.2 for density definitions.

provide data not only on the spatial expanse of development, but also on the rates of development (Table 8.4).

The fastest growing category of development was exurban, which grew nearly 240 km² annually from 1960 to 1990. The area covered in suburban and higher densities in 1990 was 91% of the area estimated to be in urban land use in the NRI data set. This statistic supports the earlier assertion that development occurring at densities at or less than exurban are not resolved well in the NRI data base.

The amount of each land use/cover class was calculated for different development densities (Table 8.5). Roughly 21% of the forest land cover in Colorado was developed, and this increased slightly. From 1960 to 1990, an additional 205 km² of forest cover were developed. Perhaps more important, development intruded into forest cover, especially in the form of exurban development, which constituted only 2% of all developed areas of forest cover in 1960, but increased to 13% in 1990 and is projected to be 23% in 2020. In contrast, roughly

Table 8.4. Total area and trends of development by category in Colorado using Census block-group data.

Development	Area (km²)			Annual Growth (%)
Category	1960	1990	2020	1960–1990
Urban	429	1343	1764	7.1
Suburban	425	1250	1817	6.4
Exurban	2796	10192	16812	8.8
Ranch	2808	7518	10022	5.5
Rural	139162	128331	119227	–0.2
Vacant	4556	1546	542	–2.2

96% of the agricultural land cover and 61% of range land cover had some level of development. Exurban development constituted only 2% in 1960, 7% in 1990, and a projection of 10% in 2020 of agricultural land, and 1%, 4%, and 8% in the rangeland cover category and 8%, 16%, and 20% in wetland land cover, respectively. Housing density on nonforested lands within 3.2 km of the forest fringe has quadrupled from 1960 to 1990, and is projected to double from 1990 to 2020. These data also show a slight trend of housing density increasing faster in areas closer to the forest fringe (within 0.4 km) as compared to areas further away (within 3.2 km of the edge).

Landscape Scale

The broad regional-scale land use trends described above are supported by results from landscape-scale studies. In the East River Valley in Gunnison County, the amount of agricultural land that has been converted to residential has doubled every decade since 1960 (Theobald et al. 1996). Similar rates of changes and patterns occurred in the Blue River Valley in Summit County (Fig. 8.5).

Fragmentation of vegetation by development was measured by calculating the distance from every quarter-section in the county to the nearest development type (Fig. 8.6). The degree of fragmentation in Summit County varies considerably depending upon the housing density assumed to represent development. Fragmentation has been fairly dramatic since 1960, especially since the emergence of a few micro-urban areas (e.g., Silverthorne and Dillon). The degree of fragmentation levels off between 1980 and 1990 but will likely increase based on projected land use patterns. Using rural densities, the average distance in the county to developed areas ranges from 2 to 4 km.

Table 8.5. Cross-tabulated area (km²) of development density by land use/cover classes.

Development Density	Agriculture			Forest			Range			Wetlands		
	1960	1990	2020	1960	1990	2020	1960	1990	2020	1960	1990	2020
Urban	4	191	314	1	13	43	4	106	188	0	2	4
Suburban	53	416	631	16	88	199	28	276	471	2	9	18
Exurban	1167	3803	5650	357	2412	4243	495	2880	5808	45	93	113
Ranch	1324	2646	3350	698	1885	2397	512	2727	4029	40	49	70
Rural	52024	47841	44966	17035	13914	11526	68369	65503	61886	488	42	378

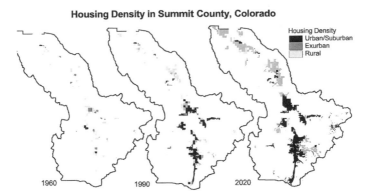

Fig. 8.5. Housing density in Summit County 1960, 1990, and 2020. Housing density data were calculated by aggregating parcel-level information from the county tax assessor's office by quarter-sections (65 ha). The future housing scenario assumes "business-as-usual," that is, it reflects the current zoning in place and the population projections from the Colorado State Demographer's Office. See Theobald and Hobbs (1998) for more details on the forecast model.

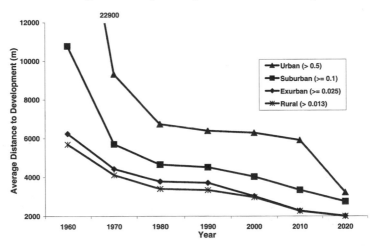

Fig. 8.6. Fragmentation of development in Summit County, as measured by the average distance to development (m). Note that the average distance ranges considerably depending upon the density threshold that is assumed to cause fragmentation and that the average distance to urban in 1960 is 22,900 m (off the scale). Fragmentation has been fairly dramatic since 1960, especially considering the rise of a few micro-urban areas (Silverthorne and Dillon). The pattern steadies between 1980 and 1990, but considerable fragmentation is likely based on the projected land use patterns. In general, concentrated development around micro-urban areas will reduce fragmentation, while dispersed development will increase fragmentation.

Certain vegetation types are more likely to be affected by the potential fragmentation of development. For instance, aspen is generally closer to exurban development than conifer, but aspen is generally further from suburban development than conifer. This trend shows that lower density exurban development is occurring in areas that contain higher proportions of aspen vegetation in the Blue River Valley.

DISCUSSION

Data from regional- and landscape-scale studies support the conclusion that there is substantial and expanding impact on natural vegetation by development in Colorado. However, quantifying the extent of habitat fragmentation caused by development and measuring long-term species population trends are more difficult. Two major impediments exist. First, while some empirical research shows that development disturbs habitat (e.g., Vogel 1989, Harrison 1997), little work has established long-term effects on population viability and for broad assemblages of species. Development impacts habitat principally in two ways: by removing or altering native vegetation and through increased human and human-related activity (Knight and Mitchell 1997, Theobald et al. 1997). For example, the diversity of native bird species is largely dependent on the amount of native vegetation present (e.g., Mills et al. 1989) and distances at which wildlife "flush" from human presence (Rodgers and Smith 1995).

These impacts affect wildlife in a number of different ways, for example, decreasing the size of critical winter ranges, blocking wildlife movement corridors, and spreading exotic plants. Furthermore, efforts to quantify disturbance effects of development are complicated because development does not affect all species equally (Theobald et al. 1997, White et al. 1997). A considerable time lag often occurs in the response of local populations of wildlife to disturbance (Soule 1991), and much of our understanding of habitat fragmentation comes from research done outside the Rocky Mountain West (Romme 1997; Buskirk et al., *this volume*).

A second impediment to measuring potential landscape fragmentation by development is that the current conception of habitat fragmentation, from the fields of landscape ecology and conservation biology, does not adequately incorporate the heterogeneity of habitat found in this region, nor the varying degree of impacts of development. Typically, three aspects of a landscape—patch, edge, and matrix—provide the basis for calculating landscape fragmentation (Forman and Godron 1986; Baker, *this volume*). Landscape fragmentation is characterized as a break-up of a continuous landscape containing large habitat patches into smaller, usually more numerous and less-connected patches (Noss et al. 1997). This conception of fragmentation, rooted in island biogeography theory (MacArthur and Wilson 1967), has framed some useful thinking about landscape structure, for example, in distinguishing between habitat patches and the surrounding "inhabitable" matrix. However, this approach needs to be refined to reflect a functional perspective and incorporate gradients in habitat and matrix quality, in development density and pattern, and in the degree of impact on habitat by development.

Five factors need to be addressed as a first step towards refining a methodology to calculate fragmentation caused by development. The area of degraded or 'lost' habitat due to development is not simply the intersection of the habitat and development areas. Rather, the amount of loss or degree of impact depends both on the density and type of development, and the sensitivity of species and ecosystems to development. Potential fragmentation by development also depends on the distance from development at which species are disturbed. Evidence exists showing that 100 to 500 m disturbance distance is a reasonable estimate (Theobald et al. 1997), though this distance is species specific. Because the density of development varies across space and some species show a nonlinear response to housing density (Miller et al. 1997), it follows that the gradient of development should be considered. Whether a patch is isolated due to fragmentation by development depends largely on the short-term movement and long-term dispersal abilities of a species and the configuration of habitat patches. Species may be able to span two patches if they are reachable via "stepping stone" patches. Finally, if development reduces the net area of habitat, such that it no longer provides ample habitat for area-sensitive species, then fragmentation has occurred. Understanding habitat fragmentation requires resolving a number of functional responses—responses that are likely to be species specific—and that methods to calculate fragmentation must improve to more adequately address these responses and the gradients found in natural and human systems.

CONCLUSION

Data from both regional and landscape scales showed a marked transformation of land use throughout Colorado. The net loss of agricultural lands is occurring rapidly, at a rate between 145 km^2 to 364 km^2 per year. The analysis of land use trajectories, however, showed that land use change dynamics in this region are more complex than a simple summary statistic. In fact, loss of agricultural land has occurred at over twice the rate suggested by the net statistics. About 28% of the loss of agricultural land and 17% of the loss of forested land can be attributed directly to conversion to urban use. The detailed housing density data showed a rapid intrusion of exurban development into agricultural and, especially, forested land.

The current extent and continued pace of development clearly warrant concern for habitat loss and fragmentation. Housing density data and the development gradient approach offer useful ways to link socio-economic patterns to ecological responses that will improve our ability to understand the potential consequences of development. However, a fundamental challenge for scientists, land managers, and planners is to design new patterns of development that minimize impacts on natural processes and landscape patterns (Romme 1997). Clustering development in a limited portion of a parcel, in place of typical dispersed "ranchette" development, can substantially reduce the amount of habitat loss and fragmentation at the scale of an individual subdivision (Theobald et al. 1997), but the potential impacts of numerous clustered developments dispersed throughout a valley need to be considered from a broader scale.

ACKNOWLEDGMENTS

I wish to thank the reviewers of an earlier draft for their useful comments. This research was supported by the Great Outdoors Colorado Trust Fund and the Colorado Division of Wildlife.

LITERATURE CITED

Anderson, J. R., E. E. Hardy, J. T. Roach, and W. E. Witmer. 1976. A land use and land cover classification system for use with remote sensor data. USGS Professional Paper 964, 1976. USGS, Reston, Virginia, USA.

Anderson, L. 1995. Developer proposes 41 new homesites at Irwin. *Chronicle & Pilot.* Crested Butte, Colorado. April 28.

Beyers, W. B. 1996. Explaining the new service economies of the rural west. Pacific Northwest Regional Economics Conference, Portland, Oregon, USA.

Butler, M. A., and C. L., Beale. 1993. Rural-urban continuum codes for metro and nonmetro counties. Agriculture and Rural Economy Division, Economic Research Service, U.S. Department of Agriculture. Staff Report No. 9425.

Cromartie, J. 1994. Recent demographic and economic changes in the West. Statement before the House Committee on Natural Resources Hearing on "The Changing Needs of the West." April 7, 1994. Economic Research Service, U.S. Department of Agriculture.

Diamond, H. L., and P. F. Noonan. 1996. *Land use in America.* Island Press, Washington, D.C., USA.

Forman, R.T.T., and M. Godron. 1986. *Landscape Ecology.* John Wiley & Sons, New York, New York, USA.

Frank, A. P. 1997. Measuring farmland conversion: a proposal for an agricultural lands conversion pressure index and a commitment to agriculture index. Colorado Department of Agriculture. Denver, Colorado, USA.

Fuguitt, G. V., and C. L. Beale. 1996. Recent trends in nonmetropolitan migration: toward a new turnaround. *Growth and Change* (Spring): 156–174.

Harrison, R. L. 1997. A comparison of gray fox ecology between residential and undeveloped rural landscapes. *Journal of Wildlife Management* 61: 112–122.

Hearn, K. 1998. On the offensive: developer Tom Chapman. *High Country News* 30(3): 10. Paonia, Colorado, USA.

Jobes, P. C. 1993. Population and social characteristics in the Greater Yellowstone Ecosystem. *Society and Natural Resources* 6: 149–163.

Knight, R. L. 1994. What happens when ranches die? *Colorado Rancher & Farmer*, October: 8–10.

Knight, R. L., and J. Mitchell. 1997. Subdividing the West. Pages 272–274 *in* G.K. Meffe and C.R. Carroll, editors. *Principles of Conservation Biology*. Sinauer Associates, Sunderland, Massachusetts, USA.

MacArthur, R. H., and E. O. Wilson. 1967. *The theory of island biogeography*. Princeton University Press, Princeton, Massachusetts, USA.

McDonnell, M. J., and S.T A. Pickett. 1990. Ecosystem structure and function along urban-rural gradients: An unexploited opportunity for ecology. *Ecology* 71: 1232–1237.

McDonnell, M. J., S.T.A. Pickett, P. Groffman, P. Bohlen, R. V. Pouyat, W. C. Zipperer, R. W. Parmelee, M. M. Carreiro, and K. Medley. 1997. Ecosystem processes along an urban-to-rural gradient. *Urban Ecosystems* 1: 21–36.

Medley, K. E., M. J. McDonnell, and S.T.A. Pickett. 1995. Forest-landscape structure along an urban-to-rural gradient. *The Professional Geographer* 47: 159–168.

Miller, J. R., D. M. Theobald, and N. T. Hobbs. 1997. Characterization of urban-rural gradients and effects on avian assemblages. *12ᵗʰ Annual Symposium of the U.S.-International Association for Landscape Ecology*. Durham, North Carolina, USA.

Mills, G. S., J. B. Dunning, J. B., Jr., and J. M. Bates. 1989. Effects of urbanization of breeding bird community structure in southwestern desert habitats. *Condor* 91: 416–428.

NRCS 1995. 1992 National Resources Inventory, Natural Resources Conservation Service, CD-ROM #1, West Region.

NRCS 1997. Instructions for collecting 1997 National Resources Inventory Data, Natural Resources Conservation Service, Resources Inventory and Geographic Information Systems Division. http://www.ncg.nrcs.usda.gov/nri/inst_toc.html.

Nelson, A. C. 1992. Characterizing exurbia. *Journal of Planning Literature* 6: 350–368.

Nelson, P. B. 1997. Migration, sources of income, and community change in the nonmetropolitan Northwest. *The Professional Geographer* 49: 418–430.

Noss, R. F., M. A. O'Connell, and D. D. Murphy. 1997. *The science of conservation planning: habitat conservation under the Endangered Species Act.* Island Press, New York, New York, USA.

Olgeirson, I. 1994. Ghost Towns' revival haunting. *The Denver Post.* (May 30). Page: B1. Denver, Colorado, USA.

Pearson, M. 1993. The private parts of paradise. *Wilderness* (Spring): 20–27.

Power, T. M. 1996. *Lost landscapes and failed economies: the search for a value of place.* Island Press, Washington, D.C., USA.

Riebsame, W. E., H. Gosnell, and D. M. Theobald. 1996. Land use and landscape change in the Colorado mountains I: theory, scale, and pattern. *Mountain Research and Development* 16: 395–405.

Riebsame, W. E., H. Gosnell, and D. M. Theobald. 1997. *Atlas of the new West: portrait of a changing region.* Norton Press, New York, New York, USA.

Rodgers, J. A., Jr., and H. T. Smith. 1995. Set-back distances to protect nesting bird colonies from human disturbance in Florida. *Conservation Biology* 9: 89–99.

Romme, W. H. 1997. Creating pseudo-rural landscapes in the Mountain West. Pages 139–161 *in* J. I. Nassauer, editor. *Placing nature: culture and landscape ecology.* Island Press, New York, New York, USA.

Rudzitis, G., and R. A. Streatfield. 1992. The importance of amenities and attitudes: a Washington example. *Journal of Environmental Systems* 22: 269.

Soule, M. E. 1991. Land use planning and wildlife maintenance: guidelines for conserving wildlife in an urban landscape. *Journal of the American Planning Association* 57: 313–323.

Theobald, D. M., H. Gosnell, and W. E. Riebsame. 1996. Land use and landscape change in the Colorado mountains II: a case study of the East River Valley, Colorado. *Mountain Research and Development* 16: 407–418.

Theobald, D. M., J. M. Miller, and N. T. Hobbs. 1997. Estimating the cumulative effects of development on wildlife habitat. *Landscape and Urban Planning* 39: 25–36.

Theobald, D. M. and N. T. Hobbs. 1998. Forecasting rural land use change: a comparison of regression- and spatial transition-based models. *Geographical & Environmental Modelling* 2: 57–74.

Ullman, E. 1954. Amenities as a factor in regional growth. *Geographic Review* 44: 119–132.

U.S. Census Bureau. 1997. County population estimates.

U.S. Census Bureau. 1998. Projections of the Total Population of States. Population Paper Listing #47, Population Projections for States, by Age, Sex, Race, and Hispanic Origin: 1995 to 2025.

U.S. Census of Agriculture. 1993. Final County File. Washington, D.C. The Bureau of Census.

Vogel, W. O. 1989. Response of deer to density and distribution of housing in Montana. *Wildlife Society Bulletin* 17: 406–413.

White, D., P. G. Minotti, E. M. Preston. 1997. Assessing risks to biodiversity from future landscape change. *Conservation Biology* 11: 349–360.

Wirth Forum 1998. *The Wirth Forum on Growth, Sustainability, and the Future of the West.* University of Colorado, Boulder, USA.

Part Three

Biodiversity Responses to Forest Fragmentation in the Southern Rocky Mountains

9

Mammalian Responses to Forest Fragmentation in the Central and Southern Rocky Mountains

Gary P. Beauvais

INTRODUCTION

The responses of mammals to human-caused fragmentation of forests in the Central and Southern Rocky Mountains are poorly understood. Studies of habitat use by mammals in managed forests of the region are taxonomically biased towards ungulates and small rodents; habitat relationships of forest carnivores and bats are very poorly known. Likewise, few studies have investigated habitat use at the landscape scale; instead they have considered stands or patches as units of analysis. The inherent landscape quality of forest fragmentation means that small-scale analyses are of limited use. By contrast, in the Pacific Northwest the longer debate over wildlife and forestry has led to more research at broader spatial scales (e.g., Rosenberg and Raphael 1986, Lehmkuhl et al. 1991).

Increasing awareness of human impacts on Rocky Mountain forests (Reed et al. 1996, Tinker et al. 1998) likely will generate more studies of habitat use, but such studies necessarily are constrained temporally and spatially. Although they may clarify current and local relationships, they tend to ignore historical and regional processes. Modern faunas are determined primarily by these larger-scale processes, and only secondarily by intra-community dynamics (Ricklefs 1987). Accordingly, the distribution of mammals in the Rocky Mountains is a legacy of regional forest fragmentation that occurred 10,000 years ago. The management implications of current patterns of habitat use will be apparent only when interpreted in this broader context.

THE REGION

My area of analysis extends from the southern limit of the Sangre de Cristo Mountains to the northern Pryor Range, and from the Wasatch Mountains in the west to the Black Hills and Front Range in the east (Fig. 9.1). Although this includes some areas (e.g., Wyoming

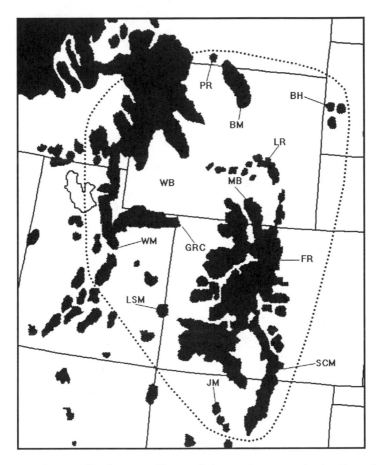

Fig. 9.1. Current distribution of boreo-alpine environments in the Central and Southern Rocky Mountain region. Dotted line encloses the area discussed in text. Dark areas are the combined ranges of alpine tundra, lodgepole pine, sub-alpine fir, and Engelmann spruce (modified from Little 1971). Letters refer to place names mentioned in text: BH = Black Hills, BM = Big Horn Mountains, FR = Front Range, GRC = Green River Canyon, JM = Jemez Mountains, LR = Laramie Range, LSM = La Sal Mountains, MB = Medicine Bow Mountains, PR = Pryor Range, SCM = Sangre de Cristo Mountains, WB = Wyoming Basin, WM = Wasatch Mountains.

Basin, northern Colorado Plateau) that are technically outside of the Central and Southern Rocky Mountain provinces, forests in these areas are similar ecologically to those on the main chain of the Rockies. Data for some species from the Central and Southern Rocky Mountains are so few that information from these nearby regions is valuable in describing patterns of habitat use.

Plant communities in this region vary strongly with elevation, grading from grassland and shrub-steppe at low elevations to conifer forest at intermediate and tundra at the highest elevations. Distributions of some mammals closely track these broad-scale vegetational patterns (Fitzgerald et al. 1994, Merrill et al. 1996), allowing the identification of three basic groups of mammals in the region (see Table 9.1):

1. Forest-adapted mammals (e.g., southern red-backed vole, snowshoe hare, American marten). Many species in this group reach the southern limits of their ranges in the Central and Southern Rocky Mountains and are much more widespread to the north (Armstrong 1977, Kirkland 1981). Because of strong affinities to coniferous forest, species in this group are most influenced by forest management.

Table 9.1. Species mentioned in text. Species are grouped according to affinities to conifer forest (forest-adapted mammals), open vegetation (open-country mammals), or several vegetation types (generalist mammals).

Forest-adapted mammals	Generalist mammals	Open-country mammals
Masked shrew	Deer mouse	American pika
Dusky shrew	Montane vole	Lemming
Common water shrew	Least chipmunk	Black-tailed prairie-dog
Silver-haired bat	Western jumping mouse	Yellow-bellied marmot
Southern red-backed vole	Weasel	American badger
Western heather vole	Red fox	Pronghorn
Water vole	Bobcat	Bighorn sheep
Northern flying squirrel	Coyote	Mountain goat
Red squirrel	Gray wolf	American bison
Abert's squirrel	Mountain lion	Muskox
American marten	Black bear	
Fisher	Grizzly bear	
Snowshoe hare	Mule deer	
Canada lynx	Elk	
Wolverine		
Moose		

2. Generalist mammals (e.g., deer mouse, mule deer, coyote). Most members are widespread throughout the region (Armstrong 1977, Kirkland 1981) and occur in a variety of vegetation types and elevational zones. Forest management activities can influence distributions locally, but broad environmental tolerances produce relatively contiguous populations regionally.

3. Open-country mammals (e.g., black-tailed prairie-dog, American badger, pronghorn). Because species in this group prefer open vegetation like grassland and shrub-steppe, forest management has minimal impacts on their distributions. Important exceptions (e.g., bighorn sheep, American pika) are adapted to alpine tundra or other open environments surrounded by coniferous forest.

HISTORICAL BIOGEOGRAPHY OF THE REGION

The glacial-interglacial cycles of the Pleistocene Epoch (2.0–0.01 million years ago) repeatedly altered the distributions of plant and animal communities. Cold climates and glaciers forced biota to lower elevations and latitudes. During the last glacial maximum, about 18,000 years ago, life zones in the Rocky Mountains were at least 600–800 m lower in elevation than today (Wells 1966, Whitlock 1993). Much of the Yellowstone Plateau and central Colorado were covered by alpine glaciers, and unglaciated mountains supported tundra and tundra-steppe (Whitlock 1993). The mammalian fauna at high elevations was correspondingly more arctic in character: muskox (Walker 1982) and lemmings (Martin et al. 1979) were common in such sites, and the alpine-adapted American pika, currently fragmented in distribution, existed in widespread, contiguous populations (Hafner and Sullivan 1995).

Valley bottoms and plains currently in grasslands and xeric-adapted shrubs were dominated by subalpine forests in the late Pleistocene. Most of the modern Great Plains (Axelrod 1985), Great Basin (Wells 1983), and desert southwest (Lomolino et al. 1989) supported contiguous forests of spruce and pine. The flora and fauna of these late-Pleistocene forests differed somewhat from those of modern forests. Besides including now extinct taxa (e.g., mammoth, saber-toothed cat; Anderson 1984), the communities of these forests exhibited greater local coexistence of species now restricted to different life zones (Guthrie 1984, Patterson 1984).

Still, the wider distribution of coniferous forest resulted in wider distributions of extant forest-adapted mammals (Walker 1987). The late-Pleistocene ranges of western heather voles and American martens extended well into the central Great Basin, and other boreo-alpine species (e.g., American pika, yellow-bellied marmot) occurred throughout the now-arid lowlands of the region (Grayson 1987). Similarly, late-Pleistocene remains of American martens and wolverines are known from central Nebraska and eastern Colorado (Graham and Graham 1994), and those of dusky shrews, yellow-bellied marmots, and other boreo-alpine taxa have been found as far south as the Mexican border (Patterson 1984).

Rapid climatic warming at the Pleistocene-Holocene transition (12,000–10,000 years ago) caused an upward and northward contraction of coniferous forest, which fragmented populations of forest-adapted mammals. Forest-dwelling species were eliminated first from lowlands converting to open vegetation, then from patches of forest isolated on small mountain ranges like the La Sal and Jemez mountains (Brown 1971, Patterson 1984). The ranges of open-country mammals were correspondingly increased. Interestingly, xeric-adapted ponderosa pine probably expanded northward into the region in response to Holocene warming, allowing expansion of the range of Abert's squirrels, which associate closely with ponderosa pine. However, even ponderosa pine was restricted to lower mountain slopes, and populations of Abert's squirrels still are fragmented at a regional scale (Davis and Brown 1989, Lamb et al. 1997).

CURRENT MAMMALIAN DISTRIBUTIONS

At a regional scale, forest-adapted mammals are the most spatially restricted group of mammals in the Central and Southern Rocky Mountains. Whereas most open-country and generalist mammals form relatively contiguous populations, forest-adapted mammals occur in metapopulations (especially of the mainland-island type; Hanski and Simberloff 1997) and in some truly isolated populations. A few mammals strongly associated with coniferous forest can disperse across large expanses of nonforest vegetation; for example, Abert's squirrels have apparently crossed up to 57 km of grassland and open woodland in Arizona (Davis and Brown 1989). Also, forest-dwelling bats have obvious dispersal advantages over nonvolant mammals. However, most forest-adapted mammals do not disperse below the elevation limit of conifers, and lowland occurrences of even the widest-ranging species (e.g., Canada lynx, wolverine) are rare (Maj and Garton 1994) and usually involve dispersing subadults whose fitness likely is low (Banci 1994, Koehler and Aubry 1994).

Where isolated, forest-adapted mammals occur in smaller populations than farther north and thus likely are subject to a suite of factors that increase their risk of local extinction. These risks include a loss of genetic variability through inbreeding and genetic drift, two of the main factors in the so-called extinction vortex (Gilpin and Soule 1986, Caughley and Gunn 1996). Low genetic variability has been documented in isolated populations of montane chipmunks (Dobson et al. 1987, Sullivan 1996) and American pikas (Hafner and Sullivan 1995) in the region, and likely occurs in populations of other forest- and alpine-adapted species.

Although immigrants can alleviate genetic and demographic problems (Mills and Allendorf 1996), forest-adapted mammals (excluding bats) rarely disperse between isolated mountain ranges. Forest-adapted mammals have failed to recolonize insular ranges in the Great Basin (Brown 1971, Grayson 1987) and the Southwest (Patterson 1984). Western heather voles have not colonized the Big Horn Mountains (Merrill et al. 1996), and water voles, northern flying squirrels, and fishers apparently have failed to reach the Southern Rockies (Hall 1981, Fitzgerald et al. 1994). This lack of recolonization suggests that populations of some forest-adapted mammals in Colorado are true Pleistocene relicts with no genetic connection to northern populations. Populations on peninsular forests like those in the Medicine Bow and Sangre de Cristo mountains likely exchange few individuals with neighboring populations, and are at risk of future isolation by disturbances to connecting corridors of forest.

This spatial isolation has allowed forest-adapted mammals in the region to diverge from more northern populations, as indicated by patterns of subspeciation. The Wyoming Basin and Green River Canyon form the range boundaries of many forest-dwelling subspecies; the conversion of this area from forest to shrub-steppe eliminated the last connection between conifer forests of Colorado and those to the west and north (Findley and Anderson 1956, Kirkland 1981). Other subspecies are restricted to only a few mountain ranges in the region, and truly insular ranges support several endemic subspecies. These include snowshoe hare, pika, and least chipmunk in the Big Horn Mountains (Hall 1981). Morphological, behavioral, and genetic analyses confirm the divergence among mountain ranges of populations of red squirrels (Lindsay 1987), Abert's squirrels (Lamb et al. 1997), American pikas (Hafner and Sullivan 1995), and least chipmunks (Sullivan 1985), and suggest that more subspecific designations may be warranted.

Although some of this genetic differentiation likely is due to founder effects (few individuals in an initial population) and subsequent genetic drift (Hartl 1988, Caughley and Gunn 1996), some may be functional. Ten thousand years of relative isolation on the edge of a species' geographic range likely is long enough for populations to accumulate adaptive changes; for example, the robust skull morphology of red squirrels in the Black Hills may be an adaptation for feeding on ponderosa pine cones (Lindsay 1987), and is presumably under strong genetic control. Locally-adapted populations are irreplaceable evolutionary units with substantial conservation value, and as such are of significant management concern. Indeed, the U.S. Endangered Species Act grants special protection to threatened populations with unique genetic or morphological characters (Pennock and Dimmick 1997), raising the possibility that some small populations of forest-adapted mammals in the region could qualify for statutory protection.

HABITAT ASSOCIATIONS

Euro-Americans obviously have affected mammals in the Rocky Mountains via deliberate eradications (e.g., grizzly bear, American bison), restorations (e.g., elk, gray wolf), and translocations to new, extralimital sites (e.g., mountain goat, moose). The effects of more indirect actions, like timber harvest and road building, are less apparent. Some evidence suggests that such actions have contributed to local extinctions. American martens were eliminated from the Black Hills and apparently the Laramie Range as forestry activities increased, and major reductions in Canada lynx and wolverine populations in Colorado were similarly timed. Throughout North America, large mammals commonly disappear from forests surrounded by land converted to other uses, including mountain ranges surrounded by agricultural land (Picton 1979) and national parks surrounded by multiple-use forest (Glenn and Nudds 1989, Newmark 1995).

Of more use to managers are studies that directly relate forestry practices to habitat quality for individual species in the region, but such studies are rare. Further, habitat quality is ultimately a function of reproductive fitness (Fretwell 1972), which is difficult to measure in free-ranging populations and thus rarely investigated in the field. Abundance or intensity of use (habitat selection) are typically used to indicate habitat quality, even though these can be decoupled from fitness (Van Horne 1983). However, following Ruggiero et al. (1988), I consider patterns of abundance and intensity of use as reliable information about the environments needed for population persistence, and I have summarized these patterns for mammals in the region in Tables 9.2–9.4.

Forest-Adapted Mammals

Species in this group strongly prefer undisturbed forest. Several species (e.g., southern red-backed vole, American marten) prefer forest and avoid dry and open patches, including clear-cuts, at both the stand (Table 9.2) and landscape (Table 9.4) scales. Some of the same species are most abundant in late-seral stands with large trees and large and abundant coarse woody debris (Table 9.3). This association with later seral stages also is indicated by a preference for spruce-fir stands (Table 9.2) and landscapes dominated by spruce-fir (Table 9.4), because spruce-fir generally reaches a climax condition following pine on mesic sites in the region (Buttrey and Gillam 1984, Johnson and Fryer 1989).

Most forest-adapted mammals use habitat similarly in Rocky Mountain forests and in more northern forests (e.g., Pierce and Peek 1984, Millar et al. 1985, Buskirk and Ruggiero 1994), but some regional differences are important. In particular, habitat use by snowshoe hares may differ strongly between the two regions. In contrast to their association with spruce and fir in southern forests (Tables 9.2–9.4), snowshoe hares (and Canada lynx) preferred 20-yr old stands of lodgepole pine in northwestern Montana (Koehler et al. 1979) and Washington (Koehler 1990). This preference may be due to more mesic conditions in northern forests, which could increase the habitat effectiveness of early-seral stands by increasing densities of saplings and mid-story shrubs. However, the paucity of information on snowshoe hare habitat use makes interregional comparisons difficult.

Habitat preferences of most forest-dwelling bats in the region are essentially unknown. The single study (Mattson et al. 1996) performed in this region documents a clear preference for late-seral ponderosa pine by roosting silver-haired bats in the Black Hills. Studies from Canada (Barclay et al. 1988, Vonhof 1996) and the Pacific Northwest (Perkins and Cross 1988, Thomas 1988) indicate that mature stands are preferred roosting sites for various bats in various forest types. Some of the same species preferentially forage in clear-cuts (Erickson and West 1996), suggesting that a mosaic of openings and mature stands is optimal habitat. However, ecological differences may preclude the direct application of these results to more southern and interior Western forests.

The effects of roads on forest-adapted mammals in this region also are largely unstudied. Although high road densities may increase trapping mortality of forest furbearers in northern areas, trapping pressure is relatively low in southern forests. Road surfaces and right-of-ways are poor habitat for red-backed voles in forests of Canada (Douglass

Table 9.2. Use of stand- and patch-types by some mammals commonly occurring in forests of the Central or Southern Rocky Mountains. Table includes only statistically significant (*P*<0.10) patterns of habitat use from studies performed in the Central or Southern Rocky Mountain region. Multivariate analyses of habitat use are not included. + = preference for that environment; – = avoidance of that environment. + or – after a letter indicates significantly higher or lower values of the attribute signified by that letter in that environment. A = abundance; F = foraging; R = resting; U = general use.

Species	CONIFER FOREST	PONDEROSA PINE	LODGEPOLE PINE	SPRUCE-FIR	MIXED CONIFER	ASPEN	WILLOW	WET MEADOW	DRY MEADOW	SHRUB	CLEAR CUT (ASPEN)	CLEAR CUT (CONIFER)	BURN	TALUS	MESIC SOIL	XERIC SOIL	REFERENCES
FOREST-ADAPTED MAMMALS																	
Dusky shrew				A+													Raphael 1988
Masked shrew				A+													Raphael 1988
Common water shrew			-		-												Jenniges 1991
S. red-backed vole			+	A+	+										A+		Raphael 1988; Nordyke and Buskirk 1991; Campbell and Clark 1980; Jenniges 1991
Snowshoe hare				U+								U-					Wolfe et al. 1982; Crouch 1985
Abert's squirrel		F+ A+										U- F-					Pedersen et al. 1987
American marten				R+													Buskirk et al. 1989; Wilbert 1992
Moose			-			+ U+ -	+ U+			U+							Oedekoven and Lindzey 1987; Nowlin 1985; Van Dyke et al. 1995
GENERALIST MAMMALS																	
Deer mouse			-	-					+	-						A+	Campbell and Clark 1980; Jenniges 1991
Least chipmunk			-	-		-			+	-							Jenniges 1991
Montane vole			-	A+	-	+		+	-								Raphael 1988; Jenniges 1991
W. jumping mouse			+	-	-	+		+		+							Raphael 1988; Jenniges 1991
Black bear					U+					-							Grogan 1997
Mountain lion									U-	U+		U-					Van Dyke et al. 1986; Logan and Irwin 1985
Elk	F- R-		-	+		F- R-	-	F+ R+	+ R+ F+	- F- U+ R-	R-	U+ R- F+	U+ E+				Crouch 1985; Davis 1977; Oedekoven and Lindzey 1987; Sawyer 1997; Lonner 1975; Canon et al. 1987; Collins and Urness 1983
Mule deer		F- R-				F- R-		F+ R-	F- R- R+	U+ R- F+ R-	F- R-	F+	U+	F- R-			Kufeld et al. 1988; Davis 1977; Oedekoven and Lindzey 1987; Thomas and Irby 1990; Collins and Urness 1983
OPEN-COUNTRY MAMMALS																	
Mountain goat	U-									U-				U+			Haynes 1994

Table 9.3. Relationships between microhabitat (within-stand) structures and some mammals commonly occurring in forests of the Central or Southern Rocky Mountains. Table includes information only from studies performed in the Central or Southern Rocky Mountain region. Multivariate patterns of habitat use are not included. + or – after a letter indicates a positive or negative relationship, respectively, between the habitat attribute and the mammal attribute signified by that letter. A = abundance; F = foraging; R = resting; U = general use; X = probability of occurrence.

	GROUND COVER	MIDSTORY COVER	CANOPY COVER	% SPRUCE AND FIR IN CANOPY	TREE DENSITY	SERAL STAGE	LOG COVER	LOG SIZE	DISTANCE TO LOG	LOG DECAY CLASS	SNAG BASAL AREA	TREE BASAL AREA	SNAG ABUNDANCE	SNAG SIZE	TREE SIZE	HORIZONTAL VISIBILITY	REFERENCES
FOREST-ADAPTED MAMMALS																	
Silver-haired bat	X+ A+										U+	U+		U+	U+	U+	Mattson et al. 1996
S. red-backed vole					X-	A+			X+	X- A+							Nordyke and Buskirk 1991; Raphael 1988; Wywialowski and Smith 1988
Red squirrel					A+										A+		Beauvais and Buskirk *unpub. manuscript*
Snowshoe hare		U+			A+		U+ R+	R+							A+		Wolfe et al. 1982; Beauvais and Buskirk *unpub manuscript*
American marten			U- R+	U+	R-					R-			U+ A- R+	R+			Corn and Raphael 1992; Hargis and Bissonette 1997; Wilbert 1992
Moose		U+			U+						U+	U+			U+		Van Dyke 1995
GENERALIST MAMMALS																	
Least chipmunk	X+				A-	A-											Nordyke and Buskirk 1988; Crompton 1994
Deer mouse		X+				A-											Nordyke and Buskirk 1988; Crompton 1994
W. jumping mouse						A+											Raphael 1988
Elk						U+											Lonner 1975
OPEN-COUNTRY MAMMALS																	
Bighorn sheep																U+	Risenhoover and Bailey 1980

Table 9.4. Relationships between macrohabitat (landscape) patterns and some mammals commonly occurring in forests of the Central or Southern Rocky Mountains. Table includes information only from studies performed in the Central or Southern Rocky Mountains. Multivariate patterns of habitat use are not included. + or – after a letter indicates a positive or negative relationship, respectively, between the habitat attribute and the mammal attribute signified by that letter. A = abundance; F = foraging; R = resting; U = general use; X = probability of occurrence.

	FOREST-ADAPTED MAMMALS							GENERALIST MAMMALS						OPEN-COUNTRY MAMMALS		
REFERENCES	Mattson et al. 1996	Beauvais and Buskirk unpub manuscript	Wywialowski and Smith 1988; Beauvais and Buskirk unpub. manuscript	Beauvais and Buskirk unpub. manuscript	Beauvais and Buskirk unpub. manuscript	Hargis and Bissonette 1997	Beauvais and Buskirk unpub. manuscript	Beauvais and Buskirk unpub. manuscript	Beauvais and Buskirk unpub. manuscript	Logan and Irwin 1985	Rost and Bailey 1979; Sawyer 1997; Beauvais and Buskirk unpub. manuscript	Rost and Bailey 1979; Kufeld et al. 1988	Mattson 1997	Haynes 1994	Wakelyn 1987	Svendsen 1974
FOREST COVERAGE				A+	A+	A+		A-	A-							A-
SPRUCE-FIR COVERAGE		A+	A+		A+		A+			A-						
CLEARCUT EDGE DENSITY						A-		A+			A+					
DISTANCE TO FOREST													F-			
DISTANCE TO WATER	U+		X-													
DISTANCE TO FOREST EDGE										U-						
DISTANCE TO PATCH EDGE												U-				
DISTANCE TO ROAD											U+	U+				
ROAD DENSITY											U-					
SLOPE										U+	U-				A+	
TOPOGRAPHIC RELIEF														U+	A+	
	Silver-haired bat	Dusky shrew	S. red-backed vole	Red squirrel	Snowshoe hare	American marten	Moose	Least chipmunk	Weasel	Mountain lion	Elk	Mule deer	Grizzly bear	Mountain goat	Bighorn sheep	Yellow-bellied marmot

1977) and the Pacific Northwest (Adams and Geis 1983). Also, moose may experience some of the negative effects that roads confer on generalist ungulates like elk and mule deer; for example, motorized recreation can alter moose behavior in the winter (Colescott 1996).

Generalist Mammals

Disturbance of mature forest improves habitat quality for many generalist mammals. Although they occur in a wide variety of vegetation types and elevational zones, deer mice and least chipmunks prefer dry and open types in this (Table 9.2) and more northern (e.g., Millar et al. 1985, Kirkland 1990) regions. When these species occur in forests, abundances decrease with increasing seral stage (Table 9.3). Mule deer and elk preferentially forage in open patches, including clear-cuts (Table 9.2), and concentrate activities near the edges between forest and open vegetation (Table 9.4; Irwin and Peek 1983). Clear-cutting (Wallmo et al. 1972, Regelin et al. 1974) and burning (Hobbs and Spowart 1984, Canon et al. 1987) can increase forage for ungulates, and clear-cuts on mesic sites can improve forage for black bears (Irwin and Hammond 1985). Mule deer and elk may prefer recent burns over clear-cuts for foraging, presumably because of the cover provided by standing dead trees (Davis 1977).

By contrast, high road densities reduce, in some cases sharply, habitat quality for some generalist mammals and can even negate the positive effects of forage production for ungulates (Lyon and Jensen 1980). Mule deer and elk avoid roads by several hundred meters (Table 9.4; Lyon 1983, Witmer and deCalesta 1985). Likewise, legal hunting mortality on game species is positively correlated with road density (Unsworth et al. 1993), suggesting that illegal harvest varies similarly. Motorized and nonmotorized recreation disturb wintering elk (Cassirer et al. 1992) and mule deer (Freddy et al. 1986), and residential development within forests reduces security habitat (Huber 1992; Theobald, *this volume*).

To the extent that roads increase human-caused mortality, large carnivores likely experience the most negative effects of high road densities. The combination of legal and illegal hunting is the most limiting factor on the growth of populations of mountain lions (Anderson et al. 1992) and black bears (Beck 1991) in the region, and grizzly bears in Montana and southern Canada (Wieglus et al. 1994, Mace et al. 1996). Mountains lions (Van Dyke et al. 1986), grizzly bears (McClellan and Shackleton 1988), black bears (McCutchen 1990), and gray wolves (Mech et al. 1988) avoid roads and highly-roaded areas in many North American forests. Large roadless areas with minimal human presence are probably the most critical habitat elements for large carnivores (Noss et al. 1996), including even the more forest-adapted wolverine (Banci 1994).

Roads may allow other generalist mammals to expand their ranges locally, but almost no research has examined this question in this region. In Canada (Douglass 1977) and the Pacific Northwest (Adams and Geis 1983), generalist rodents reach relatively high densities on forest roads. Packed snow-machine trails may allow coyotes, red foxes, and bobcats to expand their winter ranges into high-elevation forests (G. P. Beauvais, *personal observations*), which could be detrimental to forest-adapted species like American marten and Canada lynx. Coyotes, especially, are suspected of being important predators of and competitors with species adapted to the deep snow of western forests.

Open-Country mammals

Bighorn sheep populations in the Rocky Mountains have been significantly fragmented over the last 150 years, and are subject to many of the small-population processes that challenge forest-adapted mammals (Smith et al. 1991, FitzSimmons et al. 1995). Although disease is a primary management concern, reforestation of migration corridors has substantially reduced habitat quality (Wakelyn 1987, Risenhoover et al. 1988). Clear-cutting or burning of traditional migration routes can reverse these effects and improve forage (Hobbs and Spowart 1984). These actions may also benefit the small, introduced populations of mountain goats in the region, but Haynes (1994) cautions against increased human activities of any kind near mountain goats. The negative effects that roads and human presence have on generalist ungulates probably also apply to bighorn sheep and mountain goats (MacArthur et al. 1979, MacArthur et al. 1982). Also, if removal of forest and increased road densities result in more livestock use, disease transmission from livestock to bighorn sheep may cancel any positive forage effects (Smith et al. 1991).

We clearly need more research on mammal distributions in the region, including descriptions of the basic habitat preferences of many taxa. Some rather common species (e.g., yellow-bellied marmots, western heather voles) appear infrequently or not at all in Tables 9.1–9.4 because of the lack of rigorously collected and analyzed data on habitat use in managed forests. Studies that relate landscape-scale patterns of vegetation and roads to population viability are most lacking. There may be a threshold in the amount of forest or spruce-fir forest below which some forest-adapted mammals cannot persist. A similar threshold may exist for the effect of road densities on large carnivores. Studies of animal movements in patchy forests may reveal patch types, sizes, or juxtapositions that facilitate dispersal and population connectivity. At a regional scale, comparisons of the genetic composition of populations of forest-adapted mammals, especially those on insular and peninsular ranges, is needed to identify populations with unique conservation value.

CONCLUSIONS

We know that distributions of forest-adapted mammals are already fragmented on a regional scale, and persistent clear-cutting, and possibly road building, threaten to fragment them at finer scales. In contrast, most open-country and generalist mammals form larger and more contiguous populations, and respond positively to the vegetation changes that accompany clear-cutting. At a local scale, replacement of forest-adapted mammals by habitat generalists may not change species richness or diversity, but at a regional scale such replacement essentially makes rare species even rarer and common species more common (Beauvais 1997). Additionally, it may reduce or even eliminate genetically unique populations of forest-adapted mammals. Therefore, the most prudent conservation strategy is to bias management in favor of forest-adapted species.

Given the goal of protecting this group, one approach would be to reduce clear-cutting and rely more on harvest techniques with less impact on stand and landscape structure. The specific responses of forest-adapted mammals in the Rocky Mountains to alternative harvest techniques are poorly known, but most species prefer stands with at least some tree cover to clear-cuts. Retaining downed logs and snags in harvested stands may be as important as retaining live trees; logs and snags are critical to species like American marten (Buskirk and Ruggiero 1994), Canada lynx (Koehler and Aubry 1994), and several bats (Rabe et al. 1998), and are recruited very slowly in Rocky Mountain forests. From the perspective of forest-adapted mammals, the most critical difference between stands regenerating after natural disturbances (e.g., fires, blowdowns) and stands regenerating after clear-cutting may be the abundance of coarse woody debris in the former, and the lack of it in the latter.

Because many forest-adapted mammals have strong associations with spruce-fir forest, managers should especially protect and enhance coverage of this forest type. Spruce-fir, currently, is rarely clear-cut in the region. However, clear-cutting stands of late-seral lodgepole pine with the potential to convert to spruce-fir obviously reduces future spruce-fir coverage. Again, partial harvesting techniques may allow timber extraction from late-seral stands without reducing the viability of emerging spruce and fir trees, and thus may maintain habitat quality for forest-adapted species.

Partial harvesting techniques, however, are not appropriate in every situation or on a widespread basis. In some scenarios clear-cutting is preferable for conserving mammals, such as for facilitating seasonal movements for isolated populations of bighorn sheep. More generally, partial harvesting requires more roads to extract an equivalent amount of timber as from clear-cutting, and increased road densities clearly reduce habitat quality for ungulates and especially large carnivores. Thus, to maintain viable populations of all native mammals, forest managers face the difficult task of simultaneously reducing clear-cutting and road densities, while still extracting timber.

Ultimately, the most effective way to integrate timber production and mammal conservation may be to mimic natural disturbance patterns by clustering clear-cuts together (Romme et al., *this volume*). Done properly, such a strategy could minimize losses of habitat quality for forest-adapted mammals, large carnivores, and ungulates by maintaining large, interconnected blocks of mature and roadless forest. However, on forests with already high densities of clear-cuts and roads, maintaining current habitat conditions may not ensure the long-term persistence of some of these species. In such situations, road closures and reduced timber harvest may be unavoidable.

Our limited knowledge of habitat use by mammals in Rocky Mountain forests suggests that human actions, especially clear-cutting and road building, are shifting mammalian communities toward more generalist and human-tolerant species at the expense of forest- and wilderness-adapted species. More intensive research on distributions and responses to human actions is needed to fully understand this effect. However, until such information is available, management activities should favor forest-adapted and road-sensitive species. The rate of forest succession in the Rocky Mountains is so slow that management actions taken today will determine forest structure, and thus habitat quality for native mammals, for decades.

Literature Cited

Adams, L. W., and A. D. Geis. 1983. Effects of roads on small mammals. *Journal of Applied Ecology* 20: 403–415.

Anderson, A. E., D. C. Bowden, and D. M. Kattner. 1992. The puma on the Uncompahgre Plateau, Colorado. Technical Publication No. 40. Colorado Division of Wildlife, Denver, Colorado, USA.

Anderson, E. 1984. Who's who in the Pleistocene: a mammalian bestiary. Pages 40–89 *in* P. S. Martin and R. G. Klein, editors. *Quaternary extinctions: a prehistoric revolution.* University of Arizona Press, Tucson, Arizona, USA.

Armstrong, D. M. 1977. Distributional patterns of mammals in Utah. *Great Basin Naturalist* 37: 457–474.

Axelrod, D. I. 1985. Rise of the grassland biome, central North America. *Botanical Review* 51: 163–201.

Banci, V. 1994. Wolverine. Pages 99–127 *in* L. F. Ruggiero, K. B. Aubry, S. W. Buskirk, L. J. Lyon, and W. J. Zielinski, technical editors. *The scientific basis for conserving forest carnivores: American marten, fisher, lynx, and wolverine in the western United States.* USDA Forest Service General Technical Report RM–254.

Barclay, R.M.R., P. A. Faure, and D. R. Farr. 1988. Roosting behavior and roost selection by migrating silver-haired bats (*Lasionycteris noctivagans*). *Journal of Mammalogy* 69: 821–825.

Beauvais, G. P. 1997. Mammals in fragmented forests in the Rocky Mountains: community structure, habitat selection, and individual fitness. Ph.D. Dissertation. University of Wyoming, Laramie, Wyoming, USA.

Beck, T.D.I. 1991. Black bears of west-central Colorado. Technical Publication No. 39. Colorado Division of Wildlife, Denver, Colorado, USA.

Brown, J. H. 1971. Mammals on mountaintops: nonequilibrium insular biogeography. *American Naturalist* 105: 467–478.

Buskirk, S. W., S. C. Forrest, M. G. Raphael, and H. J. Harlow. 1989. Winter resting site ecology of marten in the central Rocky Mountains. *Journal of Wildlife Management* 53: 191–196.

Buskirk, S. W., and L. F. Ruggiero. 1994. American marten. Pages 7–37 *in* L. F. Ruggiero, K. B. Aubry, S. W. Buskirk, L. J. Lyon, and W. J. Zielinski, technical editors. *The scientific basis for conserving forest carnivores: American marten, fisher, lynx, and wolverine in the western United States.* USDA Forest Service General Technical Report RM–254.

Buttrey, R. F., and B. C. Gillam. 1984. Ecosystem descriptions. Pages 43–71 *in* R. L. Hoover and D. L. Wills, editors. *Managing forested lands for wildlife.* Colorado Division of Wildlife, Denver, Colorado, USA.

Campbell, T. M., and T. W. Clark. 1980. Short-term effects of logging on red-backed voles and deer mice. *Great Basin Naturalist* 40: 183–189.

Canon, S. K., P. J. Urness, and N. V. DeByle. 1987. Habitat selection, foraging behavior, and dietary nutrition of elk in burned aspen forest. *Journal of Range Management* 40: 433–438.

Cassirer, E. F., D. J. Freddy, and E. D. Ables. 1992. Elk responses to disturbance by cross country skiers in Yellowstone National Park. *Wildlife Society Bulletin* 20: 375–381.

Caughley, G., and A. Gunn. 1996. *Conservation biology in theory and practice.* Blackwell Science, Inc., Cambridge, Massachusetts, USA.

Colescott, J. H. 1996. Moose-willow interactions in riparian communities. Master's thesis. University of Wyoming, Laramie, Wyoming, USA.

Collins, W. B., and P. J. Urness. 1983. Feeding behavior and habitat selection of mule deer and elk on northern Utah summer range. *Journal of Wildlife Management* 47: 646–663.

Corn, J. G., and M. G. Raphael. 1992. Habitat characteristics at marten subnivean access sites. *Journal of Wildlife Management* 56: 442–448.

Crompton, B. J. 1994. Songbird and small mammal diversity in relation to timber management practices in the northwestern Black Hills. Master's thesis. University of Wyoming, Laramie, Wyoming, USA.

Crouch, G. L. 1985. Effects of clear-cutting a subalpine forest in central Colorado on wildlife habitat. USDA Forest Service Research Paper RM–258.

Davis, P. R. 1977. Cervid responses to forest fire and clear-cutting in southeastern Wyoming. *Journal of Wildlife Management* 41: 785–788.

Davis, R., and D. E. Brown. 1989. Role of post-Pleistocene dispersal in determining the modern distribution of Abert's squirrel. *Great Basin Naturalist* 49: 425–434.

Dobson, M. L., C. L. Pritchett, and J. W. Sites, Jr. 1987. Genetic variation and population structure in the cliff chipmunk, *Eutamias dorsalis*, in the Great Basin of western Utah. *Great Basin Naturalist* 47: 551–561.

Douglass, R. J. 1977. Effects of a winter road on small mammals. *Journal of Applied Ecology* 14: 827–834.

Erickson, J. L., and S. D. West. 1996. Managed forests in the western Cascades: the effects of seral stage on bat habitat use patterns. Pages 215–227 *in Bats and Forests Symposium*: October 19–21, 1995, Victoria, British Columbia, Canada. British Columbia Ministry of Forests Research Program.

Findley, J. S., and S. Anderson. 1956. Zoogeography of the montane mammals of Colorado. *Journal of Mammalogy* 37: 575–577.

Fitzgerald, J. P., C. A. Meaney, and D. M. Armstrong. 1994. *Mammals of Colorado*. University Press of Colorado, Boulder, Colorado, USA.

Fitzsimmons, N. N., S. W. Buskirk, and M. H. Smith. 1995. Population history, genetic variability, and horn growth in bighorn sheep. *Conservation Biology* 9: 314–323.

Freddy, D. J., W. M. Bronaugh, and M. C. Fowler. 1986. Responses of mule deer to disturbance by persons afoot and snowmobiles. *Wildlife Society Bulletin* 14: 63–68.

Fretwell, S. D. 1972. *Populations in a seasonal environment*. Princeton University Press, Princeton, New Jersey, USA.

Gilpin, M. E., and M. E. Soule. 1986. Minimum viable populations: processes of species extinction. Pages 19–34 *in* M. E. Soule, editor. *Conservation biology: the science of scarcity and diversity*. Sinauer Associates, Inc., Sunderland, Massachusetts, USA.

Glenn, S. M., and T. D. Nudds. 1989. Insular biogeography of mammals in Canadian parks. *Journal of Biogeography* 16: 261–268.

Graham, R. W., and M. A. Graham. 1994. Late Quaternary distribution of *Martes* in North America. Pages 26–58 *in* S. B. Buskirk, A. S. Harestad, M. G. Raphael, and R. A. Powell, editors. *Martens, sables, and fishers: biology and conservation*. Cornell University Press, Ithaca, New York, USA.

Grayson, D. K. 1987. The biogeographic history of small mammals in the Great Basin: observations on the last 20,000 years. *Journal of Mammalogy* 68: 359–375.

Grogan, R. G. 1997. Black bear ecology in southeast Wyoming. Master's thesis. University of Wyoming, Laramie, Wyoming, USA.

Guthrie, R. D. 1984. Mosaics, allelochemics, and nutrients: an ecological theory of late-Pleistocene megafaunal extinctions. Pages 259–298 *in* P. S. Martin and R. G. Klein, editors. *Quaternary extinctions: a prehistoric revolution*. University of Arizona Press, Tucson, Arizona, USA.

Hafner, D. J., and R. M. Sullivan. 1995. Historical and ecological biogeography of Nearctic pikas (Lagomorpha: Ochotonidae). *Journal of Mammalogy* 76: 302–321.

Hall, E. R. 1981. *The mammals of North America.* Volume 1. Second Edition. John Wiley and Sons, New York, New York, USA.

Hanski, I., and D. Simberloff. 1997. The metapopulation approach, its history, conceptual domain, and application to conservation. Pages 5–26 *in* I. A. Hanski and M. E. Gilpin, editors. *Metapopulation biology: ecology, genetics, and evolution.* Academic Press, San Diego, California, USA.

Hargis, C. D., and J. A. Bissonette. 1997. Effects of forest fragmentation on populations of American marten in the intermountain west. Pages 437–451 *in* G. Proulx, H. N. Bryant, and P. M. Woodard, editors. *Martes: taxonomy, ecology, techniques, and management.* Provincial Museum of Alberta, Edmonton, Alberta, Canada.

Hartl, D. L. 1988. *A primer of populations genetics.* Second edition. Sinauer Associates, Inc., Sunderland, Massachusetts, USA.

Haynes, L. A. 1994. Mountain goat habitat of Wyoming's Beartooth Range: implications for management. *Biennial Symposium of the Northern Wild Sheep and Goat Council* 8: 325–339.

Hobbs, N. T., and R. A. Spowart. 1984. Effects of prescribed fire on nutrition of mountain sheep and mule deer during winter and spring. *Journal of Wildlife Management* 48: 551–560.

Huber, T. P. 1992. Integrated remote sensing and GIS techniques for elk habitat management. *Journal of Environmental Systems* 22: 325–339.

Irwin, L. L., and F. M Hammond. 1985. Managing black bear habitats for food items in Wyoming. *Wildlife Society Bulletin* 13: 477–483.

Irwin, L. L., and J. M. Peek. 1983. Elk, *Cervus elaphus,* foraging related to forest management and succession in Idaho. *Canadian Field-Naturalist* 97: 443–447.

Jenniges, J. J. 1991. Habitat utilization of birds and small mammals in the north fork of the Little Snake River. Master's thesis. University of Wyoming, Laramie, Wyoming, USA.

Johnson, E. A., and G. I. Fryer. 1989. Population dynamics in lodgepole pine-Engelmann spruce forests. *Ecology* 70: 1335–1345.

Kirkland, G. L., Jr. 1981. The zoogeography of the mammals of the Uinta Mountains region. *Southwestern Naturalist* 26: 325–339.

Kirkland, G. L., Jr. 1990. Patterns of initial small mammal community change after clear-cutting of temperate North American forests. *Oikos* 59: 313–320.

Koehler, G. M. 1990. Population and habitat characteristics of lynx and snowshoe hares in north central Washington. *Canadian Journal of Zoology* 68: 845–851.

Koehler, G. M., and K. B. Aubry. 1994. Lynx. Pages 74–98 *in* L. F. Ruggiero, K. B. Aubry, S. W. Buskirk, L. J. Lyon, and W. J. Zielinski, technical editors. *The scientific basis for conserving forest carnivores: American marten, fisher, lynx, and wolverine in the western United States.* USDA Forest Service General Technical Report RM–254.

Koehler, G. M., M. G. Hornocker, and H. S. Nash. 1979. Lynx movements and habitat use in Montana. *Canadian Field Naturalist* 93: 441–442.

Kufeld, R. C., D. C. Bowden, and D. L. Schrupp. 1988. Habitat selection and activity patterns of female mule deer in the Front Range, Colorado. *Journal of Range Management* 41: 515–522.

Lamb, T., T. R. Jones, and P. J. Wettstein. 1997. Evolutionary genetics and phylogeography of tassel-eared squirrels (*Sciurus aberti*). *Journal of Mammalogy* 78: 117–133.

Lehmkuhl, J. F., L. F. Ruggiero, and P. A. Hall. 1991. Landscape-scale patterns of forest fragmentation and wildlife richness and abundance in the southern Washington Cascade range. Pages 425–442 *in* L. F. Ruggiero, K. B. Aubry, A. B. Carey, and M. H. Huff, technical coordinators. *Wildlife and vegetation of unmanaged Douglas-fir forests.* USDA Forest Service General Technical Report PNW–285.

Lindsay, S. L. 1987. Geographic size and non-size variation in Rocky Mountain *Tamiasciurus hudsonicus*: significance in relation to Allen's rule and vicariant biogeography. *Journal of Mammalogy* 68: 39–48.

Little, E. L., Jr. 1971. *Atlas of United States trees.* Volume 1. USDA Forest Service Miscellaneous Publication 1146.

Logan, K. A., and L. L. Irwin. 1985. Mountain lion habitats in the Big Horn Mountains, Wyoming. *Wildlife Society Bulletin* 13: 257–262.

Lomolino, M. V., J. H. Brown, and R. Davis. 1989. Island biogeography of montane forest mammals in the American Southwest. *Ecology* 70: 180–194.

Lonner, T. N. 1975. Elk use-habitat type relationships on summer and fall range in Long Tom Creek, southwestern Montana. Pages 101–109 *in* S. R. Hieb, editor. *Proceedings of the Elk-Logging Roads Symposium.* University of Idaho, Moscow, Idaho, USA.

Lyon, L. J. 1983. Road density models describing habitat effectiveness for elk. *Journal of Forestry* 81: 592–595.

Lyon, L. J., and C. E. Jensen. 1980. Management implications of elk and deer use of clear-cuts in Montana. *Journal of Wildlife Management* 44: 352–362.

MacArthur, R. A., V. Geist, and R. H. Johnston. 1982. Cardiac and behavioral responses of mountain sheep to human disturbance. *Journal of Wildlife Management* 46: 351–358.

MacArthur, R. A., R. H. Johnston, and V. Geist. 1979. Factors influencing heart rate in free-ranging bighorn sheep: a physiological approach to the study of wildlife harassment. *Canadian Journal of Zoology* 57: 2010–2021.

Mace, R. D., J. S. Waller, T. L. Manley, L. J. Lyon, and H. Zuuring. 1996. Relationships among grizzly bears, roads, and habitat in the Swan Mountains, Montana. *Journal of Applied Ecology* 33: 1395–1404.

Maj, M. and E. O. Garton. 1994. Appendix B: fisher, lynx, wolverine summary of distribution information. Pages 169–175 *in* L. F. Ruggiero, K. B. Aubry, S. W. Buskirk, L. J. Lyon, and W. J. Zielinski, technical editors. *The scientific basis for conserving forest carnivores: American marten, fisher, lynx, and wolverine in the western United States.* USDA Forest Service General Technical Report RM–254.

Martin, L. D., B. M. Gilbert, and S. A. Chomko. 1979. *Dicrostonyx* (Rodentia) from the late Pleistocene of northern Wyoming. *Journal of Mammalogy* 60: 193–195.

Mattson, D. J. 1997. Selection of microsites by grizzly bears to excavate biscuitroot. *Journal of Mammalogy* 78: 228–238.

Mattson, T. A., S. W. Buskirk, and N. L. Stanton. 1996. Roost sites of the silver-haired bat (*Lasionycteris noctivagans*) in the Black Hills, South Dakota. *Great Basin Naturalist* 56: 247–253.

McClellan, B. N., and D. M. Shackleton. 1988. Grizzly bears and resource-extraction industries: effects of roads on behaviour, habitat use and demography. *Journal of Applied Ecology* 25: 451–460.

McCutchen, H. E. 1990. Cryptic behavior of black bears (*Ursus americanus*) in Rocky Mountain National Park, Colorado. *International Conference of Bear Research and Management* 8: 65–72.

Mech, L. D., S. H. Fritts, G. L. Radde, and W. J. Paul. 1988. Wolf distribution and road density in Minnesota. *Wildlife Society Bulletin* 16: 85–87.

Merrill, E. H., T. W. Kohley, and M. E. Herdendorf. 1996. *Wyoming terrestrial vertebrate species atlas.* Wyoming Cooperative Fish and Wildlife Research Unit. University of Wyoming, Laramie, Wyoming, USA.

Millar, J. S., D.G.L. Innes, V. A. Loewen. 1985. Habitat use by non-hibernating small mammals of the Kananaskis Valley, Alberta. *Canadian Field-Naturalist* 99: 196–204.

Mills, L. S., and F. W. Allendorf. 1996. The one-migrant-per-generation rule in conservation and management. *Conservation Biology* 10: 1509–1518.

Newmark, W. D. 1995. Extinctions of mammal populations in western North American parks. *Conservation Biology* 9: 512–526.

Nordyke, K. A., and S. W. Buskirk. 1988. Evaluation of small mammals as ecological indicators of old-growth conditions. Pages 353–358 *in* R. C. Szaro, K. E. Severson, and D. R. Patton, technical editors. *Management of amphibians, reptiles, and small mammals in North America.* USDA Forest Service General Technical Report RM–166.

Nordyke, K. A., and S. W. Buskirk. 1991. Southern red-backed vole, *Clethrionomys gapperi*, populations in relation to stand succession and old-growth character in the central Rocky Mountains. *Canadian Field-Naturalist* 105: 330–334.

Noss, R. F., H. B. Quigley, M. G. Hornocker, T. Merrill, and P. C. Paquet. 1996. Conservation biology and carnivore conservation in the Rocky Mountains. *Conservation Biology* 10: 949–963.

Nowlin, R. A. 1985. Distribution of moose during occupation of vacant habitat in northcentral Colorado. Ph.D. dissertation. Colorado State University, Fort Collins, Colorado, USA.

Oedekoven, O. O., and F. G. Lindzey. 1987. Winter habitat-use patterns of elk, mule deer, and moose in southwestern Wyoming. *Great Basin Naturalist* 47: 638–643.

Patterson, B. D. 1984. Mammalian extinction and biogeography in the Southern Rocky Mountains. Pages 247–293 *in* M. H. Nitecki, editor. *Extinctions.* University of Chicago Press, Chicago, Illinois, USA.

Pedersen, J. C., R. C. Farentinos, and V. M. Littlefield. 1987. Effects of logging on habitat quality and feeding patterns of Abert squirrels. *Great Basin Naturalist* 47: 252–258.

Pennock, D. S., and W. W. Dimmick. 1997. Critique of the evolutionarily significant unit for "distinct population segment" under the U.S. Endangered Species Act. *Conservation Biology* 11: 611–619.

Perkins, J. M., and S. P. Cross. 1988. Differential use of some coniferous forest habitats by hoary and silver-haired bats in Oregon. *Murrelet* 69: 21–24.

Picton, H. D. 1979. The application of insular biogeographic theory to the conservation of large mammals in the northern Rocky Mountains. *Biological Conservation* 15: 73–79.

Pierce, D. J., and J. M. Peek. 1984. Moose habitat use and selection patterns in north-central Idaho. *Journal of Wildlife Management* 48: 1335–1343.

Rabe, M. J., T. E. Morrell, H. Green, J. C. DeVos, Jr., and C. R. Miller. 1998. Characteristics of ponderosa pine snag roosts used by reproductive bats in northern Arizona. *Journal of Wildlife Management* 62: 612–621.

Raphael, M. G. 1988. Habitat associations of small mammals in a subalpine forest, southeastern Wyoming. Pages 359–367 *in* R. C. Szaro, K. E. Severson, and D. R. Patton, technical editors. *Management of amphibians, reptiles, and small mammals in North America.* USDA Forest Service General Technical Report RM–166.

Reed, R. A., J. Johnson-Barnard, and W. L. Baker. 1996. Fragmentation of a forested Rocky Mountain landscape, 1950–1993. *Biological Conservation* 75: 267–277.

Regelin, W. L., O. C. Wallmo, J. Nagy, and D. R. Dietz. 1974. Effect of logging on forage values for deer in Colorado. *Journal of Forestry* 72: 282–285.

Ricklefs, R. E. 1987. Community diversity: relative roles of local and regional processes. *Science* 235: 167–171.

Risenhoover, K. L., and J. A. Bailey. 1980. Visibility: an important habitat factor for an indigenous, low-elevation bighorn herd in Colorado. *Proceedings of the Biennial Symposium of the Northern Wild Sheep and Goat Council* 2: 18–27.

Risenhoover, K. L., J. A. Bailey, and L. A. Wakelyn. 1988. Assessing the Rocky Mountain bighorn sheep management problem. *Wildlife Society Bulletin* 16: 346–352.

Rosenberg, K. V., and M. G. Raphael. 1986. Effects of forest fragmentation on vertebrates in Douglas-fir forests. Pages 263–272 *in* J. Verner, M. L. Morrison, and C. J. Ralph, editors. *Wildlife 2000: modeling habitat relationships of terrestrial vertebrates.* University of Wisconsin Press, Madison, Wisconsin, USA.

Rost, G. R., and J. A. Bailey. 1979. Distribution of mule deer and elk in relation to roads. *Journal of Wildlife Management* 43: 634–641.

Ruggiero, L. F., R. S. Holthausen, B. G. Marcot, K. B. Aubry, J. W. Thomas, and E. C. Meslow. 1988. Ecological dependency: the concept and its implications for research and management. *Transactions of the North American Wildlife and Natural Resources Conference* 53: 115–126.

Sawyer, H. H. 1997. Evaluation of a summer elk model and sexual segregation of elk in the Big Horn Mountains, Wyoming. Master's thesis. University of Wyoming, Laramie, Wyoming, USA.

Smith, T. S., J. T. Flinders, and D. S. Winn. 1991. A habitat evaluation procedure for Rocky Mountain bighorn sheep in the intermountain west. *Great Basin Naturalist* 51: 205–225.

Sullivan, R. M. 1985. Phyletic, biogeographic, and ecologic relationships among montane populations of least chipmunks (*Eutamias minimus*) in the southwest. *Systematic Zoology* 34: 419–448.

Sullivan, R. M. 1996. Genetics, ecology, and conservation of montane populations of Colorado chipmunks (*Tamias quadrivittatus*). *Journal of Mammalogy* 77: 951–975.

Svendsen, G. E. 1974. Behavioral and environmental factors in the spatial distribution and population dynamics of a yellow-bellied marmot population. *Ecology* 55: 760–771.

Thomas, D. W. 1988. The distribution of bats in different ages of Douglas-fir forests. *Journal of Wildlife Management* 52: 619–626.

Thomas, T. R., and L. R. Irby. 1990. Habitat use and movement patterns by migrating mule deer in southeastern Idaho. *Northwest Science* 64: 19–27.

Tinker, D. B., C. A. Resor, G. P. Beauvais, K. F. Kipfmueller, C. I. Fernandes, and W. L. Baker. 1998. Watershed analysis of forest fragmentation by clear-cuts and roads in a Wyoming forest. *Landscape Ecology* 13: 149–165.

Unsworth, J. W., L. Kuck, M. D. Scott, and E. O. Garton. 1993. Elk mortality in the Clearwater drainage of northcentral Idaho. *Journal of Wildlife Management* 57: 495–502.

Van Dyke, F. 1995. Microhabitat characteristics of moose winter activity sites in south-central Montana. *Alces* 31: 27–33.

Van Dyke, F. G., R. H. Brocke, H. G. Shaw, B. B. Ackerman, T. P. Hemker, and F. G. Lindzey. 1986. Reactions of mountain lions to logging and human activity. *Journal of Wildlife Management* 50: 95–102.

Van Dyke, F., B. L. Probert, and G. M. Van Beek. 1995. Seasonal habitat use characteristics of moose in south-central Montana. *Alces* 31: 15–26.

Van Horne, B. 1983. Density as a misleading indicator of habitat quality. *Journal of Wildlife Management* 47: 893–901.

Vonhof, M. J. 1996. Roost-site preferences of big brown bats (*Eptesicus fuscus*) and silver-haired bats (*Lasionycteris noctivagans*) in the Pend d'Oreille valley in southern British Columbia. Pages 62–80 *in Bats and Forests Symposium*: October 19–21, 1995, Victoria, British Columbia, Canada. British Columbia Ministry of Forests Research Program.

Wakelyn, L. A. 1987. Changing habitat conditions on bighorn sheep ranges in Colorado. *Journal of Wildlife Management* 51: 904–912.

Walker, D. N. 1982. A late Pleistocene *Ovibos* from southeastern Wyoming. *Journal of Paleontology* 56: 486–491.

Walker, D. N. 1987. Late Pleistocene/ Holocene environmental changes in Wyoming: the mammalian record. Pages 334–392 *in* R. W. Graham, H. A. Semken, Jr., and M. A. Graham, editors. *Late Quaternary mammalian biogeography and environments of the Great Plains.* Illinois State Museum Scientific Papers, Volume 22.

Wallmo, O. C., W. L. Regelin, and D. W. Reichert. 1972. Forage use by mule deer relative to logging in Colorado. *Journal of Wildlife Management* 36: 1025–1033.

Wells, P. V. 1966. Late Pleistocene vegetation and degree of pluvial climatic change in the Chihuahuan desert. *Science* 153: 971–975.

Wells, P. V. 1983. Paleobiogeography of montane islands in the Great Basin since the last glaciopluvial. *Ecological Monographs* 53: 341–382.

Whitlock, C. 1993. Postglacial vegetation and climate of Grand Teton and southern Yellowstone National Parks. *Ecological Monographs* 63: 173–198.

Wieglus, R. B., F. L. Bunnell, W. L. Wakkinen, and P. E. Zager. 1994. Population dynamics of Selkirk Mountain grizzly bears. *Journal of Wildlife Management* 58: 266–272.

Wilbert, C. J. 1992. Spatial scale and seasonality of habitat selection by martens in southeastern Wyoming. Master's thesis. University of Wyoming, Laramie, Wyoming, USA.

Witmer, G. W., and D. S. deCalesta. 1985. Effect of forest roads on habitat use by Roosevelt elk. *Northwest Science* 59: 122–125.

Wolfe, M. L., N. V. Debyle, C. S. Winchell, and T. R. McCabe. 1982. Snowshoe hare cover relationships in northern Utah. *Journal of Wildlife Management* 46: 662–670.

Wywialowski, A. P., and G. W. Smith. 1988. Selection of microhabitat by the red-backed vole, *Clethrionomys gapperi*. *Great Basin Naturalist* 48: 216–223.

10

Bird Responses to Forest Fragmentation

Andrew J. Hansen and Jay J. Rotella

INTRODUCTION

In the 1970s, studies in the agriculturally-dominated landscapes of the eastern United States documented a suprising trend. Seemingly suitable forest stands that were small in area were devoid of several species of birds that typically occur in such habitats (Lynch and Whitcomb 1978, Whitcomb et al. 1981). Similar trends were soon discovered in Europe, Australia, and elsewhere (Terborgh 1989, Saunders et al. 1991). The ecological changes associated with habitat fragmentation are now well known and many conservation plans are designed to minimize fragmentation (Thomas et al. 1990, Suring et al. 1993). However, it is important to ask how well the lessons learned about forest fragmentation in heavily forested biomes apply to the Rocky Mountains, where relatively open forests are naturally interspersed with grasslands and shrublands. We address this question for birds in the Southern Rocky Mountains.

In contrast to the Eastern Deciduous Forest, habitats of the Rockies have been patchy and variable throughout pre-European settlement times due to interactions of abiotic gradients and disturbance (D. H. Knight, *this volume;* Veblen, *this volume*). Interactions among climate, soils, topography, and disturbance cause grasslands, coniferous forests, and deciduous forests to interdigitate to extents that vary dramatically with local topographic setting and disturbance history. This "natural fragmentation" may have selected for species that are relatively tolerant to the patch sizes, edge types, and isolation effects that have resulted in species extinctions in other ecosystems (Buskirk et al., *this volume*).

We are no longer in pre-European settlement times, however. Modern human land use has dramatically altered vegetation patterns across much of the Rockies. While logging has further fragmented habitats in some locations, livestock grazing and fire exclusion have resulted in a pronounced expansion of closed-canopy coniferous forest elsewhere (Arno 1980, Gruell et al. 1982). In more productive valley bottoms, agriculture and rural residential development have altered habitats, landscape connectivity, and biotic processes like predation (Theobald, *this volume*; Hansen and Rotella, 1999).

The relative effects of these different human-driven trajectories of landscape change on native species are poorly understood in the Southern Rocky Mountains. Certainly, understanding will not be gained by only considering a simple story of the forest being fragmented and replaced by expanding agriculture. Rather, in the Rockies we should examine interactions among species life histories, abiotic factors, natural disturbance, and human land use.

We explore the influence of these changes in landscape patterns on Southern Rocky Mountains birds in the context of two hypotheses. Hansen and Urban (1992) and Hansen et al. (1992) suggested that the effects of habitat fragmentation on biodiversity reflect: (1) the life history attributes of the species in the community, and (2) the specific trajectory of landscape change. In this chapter, we first compare the life history attributes of birds in the Southern Rocky Mountains to those in other biomes to evaluate their likely sensitivities to landscape change. We then describe three common trajectories of landscape change in the Southern Rockies and review current knowledge of bird responses to these landscape trajectories. Finally, we draw conclusions for management and future research. As we shall see, forest fragmentation by logging is only one of the challenges that landscape managers will face in the Southern Rocky Mountains.

LIFE HISTORY ATTRIBUTES

Life history attributes (LHA) such as migratory strategy, reproductive potential, and home range size set constraints on the types and spatial and temporal scales of resources that organisms can exploit. Examples of bird species that are sensitive to forest fragmentation in eastern forests include neotropical migrants with low reproductive potential that have nest types that are vulnerable to nest predators and brood parasites (Whitcomb et al. 1981). Hansen and Urban (1992) hypothesized that communities from different geographical locations have different suites of LHA and that these differences will cause communities to respond differently to landscape change. In comparing the LHA of birds in the Pacific Northwest (PNW) to those in the EDF, Hansen and Urban found that no species in the Pacific Northwest had the set of traits that characterized the group of birds most sensitive to forest fragmentation in the Eastern deciduous forest. They concluded the Pacific Northwest bird community was likely to be less sensitive to forest fragmentation than the Eastern deciduous forest community.

What LHAs characterize birds in the Southern Rockies? Based on pre-European settlement landscape dynamics in the Rockies, we predict that Southern Rocky Mountains bird communities have the following traits (presented relative to traits of Eastern deciduous forest birds):

1. Relatively more species dependent upon structurally complex, open-canopy habitats because of the high disturbance frequency here.
2. Relatively fewer closed-canopy forest associates because of abundance of nonforest and open forest habitats.
3. Relatively fewer conifer edge or interior specialists because the gradient from early-seral to late-seral habitats is less extreme here.

The rationale for the first two predictions is that many species in a community are adapted to the most common habitat types. Disturbances such as wildfire and abiotic constraints resulted in structurally complex, open-canopy habitats being common across the Rockies in pre-European settlement times, while closed canopy conifer forests were likely less common (Veblen, *this volume*).

The logic behind the third prediction is based on what we term the Biomass Accumulation Hypothesis (Fig. 10.1). According to this hypothesis, species will more finely partition resources from forest edge to forest interior when there is high contrast in biomass accumulation along the gradient. In the Pacific Northwest, for example, the equitable environment allows mature and old-growth forests to have relatively high net primary productivity and accumulate very high levels of vegetative biomass relative to early successional forests. Vegetation abundance strongly influences microclimate, ecological processes, and distribution of organisms (e.g., Franklin and Forman 1987). Further, while moving between early-successional and mid-to-late successional patches, wind speed and light levels are reduced while soil moisture increases (Chen et al. 1995). These changes in microclimate influence decomposition rates (Klein 1989) and the structure and composition of understory vegetation (Ranney et al. 1981). Even biotic interactions like predation vary with vegetation structure (Martin 1993). The result is a steep gradient in resources and conditions from forest edge to forest interior. This steep gradient should allow for resource specialization and niche partitioning, such that some species specialize on either edge or interior habitats. In the Southern Rocky Mountains, in contrast, abiotic factors constrain net primary productivity and biomass accumulation to lower levels and mid-to-late seral forests often have relatively open canopies. Consequently, we expect less of a difference in vegetation structure, microclimate, and ecological processes between forest edge and interior. Hence, we predict that fewer species in the Southern Rocky Mountains will specialize on either forest edges or interiors. As forest fragmentation benefits edge specialists and hinders

BIOMASS ACCUMULATION HYPOTHESIS

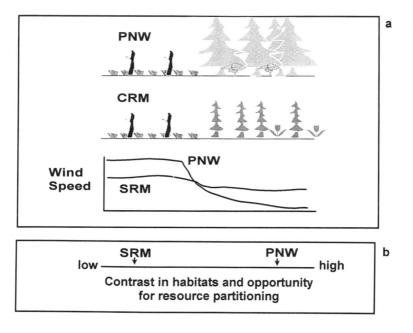

Fig. 10.1. The Biomass Accumulation Hypothesis predicts that differing biomass accumulation influences relative differences in forest edge and interior habitats and the number of species that specialize on edge or interior habitats. (a) Biomass accumulation is greater in late-seral forests compared to early seral habitats in the PNW than in the SRM. Consequently, microclimate and ecological processes differ more along the gradient from edge to interior in the PNW than SRM. Consequently (b), more species are likely to specialize on either edge or interior habitats in the PNW and other ecosystems with high biomass accumulation.

interior specialists, we expect fewer species to respond to fragmentation in the Southern Rocky Mountains compared to the PNW and other ecosystems with high biomass accumulation.

We examined these predictions by drawing on five studies that rated the LHA of birds in different locations. Hansen and Urban (1992) compared the LHA of an Eastern deciduous forest bird community from southern Maryland (Whitcomb et al. 1981) with a Pacific Northwest bird community from western Oregon. Miller and Knight (1995) did a similar analysis of LHA of birds in the Colorado Rocky Mountains. These studies were used to estimate the number of bird species from each of these three communities in each of three life history guilds: structurally complex open-canopy specialists, closed-canopy specialists, and fragmentation-sensitive species as defined by Whitcomb et al. (1981). To assign species to a fourth guild (closed-canopy interior specialists) we drew on Hansen et al. (1994), who quantified bird abundances along transects from clear-cuts to mature and old-growth forest interiors in western Oregon, and on Ruefenacht (1997), who did a similar study in conifer forests of the Colorado Rockies. As each of these previous works are case studies with no estimates of variance, it was not possible to assess the statistical significance of differences in species distributions among guilds.

The results indicated that a substantially larger percentage of the species from the Southern Rocky Mountains were associated with open-canopy forests that contained large trees or snags than was the case for the Eastern deciduous forest or Pacific Northwest communities (Table 10.1). Also as predicted, relatively fewer species were associated with

Table 10.1. Representation of species in life history guilds in three forest biomes: the Southern Rocky Mountains (SRM), the Eastern Dedicuous Forest (EDF) and the Pacific Northwest (PNW). Data for the first three guilds come from Hansen and Urban (1992a) and Miller and Knight (1995). Data for the last guild are from Whitcomb et al. (1981), Hansen et al. (1994), and Ruefenacht (1997).

Guild	SRM (98 Species)	EDF (74 Species)	PNW (75 Species)
Structurally complex	4 (14%)	6 (8%)	6 (8%)
Open-canopy	19 (19%)	22 (30%)	25 (33%)
Closed-canopy			
Fragmentation sensitive	1 (1%)	8 (11%)	0 (0%)
Closed-canopy interior	2 of 30	15of 62	2 of 20
	species studied (6%)	species studied (24%)	species studied (10%)

closed-canopy forests in the Southern Rocky Mountains than in the Pacific Northwest or Eastern deciduous forest. Moreover, only one Southern Rocky Mountains species (the veery) had the suite of LHA that Whitcomb et al. (1981) found characterized the eight Eastern deciduous forest species that were most sensitive to forest fragmentation. Finally, a lower percentage of species in the Southern Rocky Mountains were significantly more abundant in forest interiors than near forest edges created by clear-cuts (6%, brown creeper and red-breasted nuthatch) than was the case in the Pacific Northwest (10%, Swainson's thrush and Stellar's jay) or the Eastern deciduous forest (24%).

Forests in the Eastern deciduous forest study area were fragmented by agriculture and residential development, rather than by clear-cuts, as was the case in the other two biomes. As discussed later in this paper, we would expect stronger negative edge effects in human-dominated landscapes such as those found in the Eastern deciduous forest. Our analysis suggests that the bird community in the Southern Rocky Mountains is characterized by LHA that may cause the community to be less sensitive to forest fragmentation and more sensitive to lack of natural disturbance (such as wildfire) than the communities in the Eastern deciduous forest or Pacific Northwest. The LHA of the Southern Rocky Mountains community may reflect both the prevalence of forest/grassland ecotones in pre-European settlement times and the relatively small difference in biomass accumulation between early- and late-seral forest patches in the Southern Rocky Mountains. Because relatively few studies of these topics have been done in the Pacific Northwest and Southern Rocky Mountains, these conclusions should be seen as preliminary.

Trajectory of Landscape Change

Hansen et al. (1992) suggested that forest fragmentation by agricultural land uses is only one of several trajectories of landscape change occurring around the world. They additionally modeled bird response to forest fragmentation by forest plantations and afforestation following abandonment of agriculture. They found that the bird community responded very differently to each of these landscape trajectories. Hence, knowledge of the nature of landscape change is critical to understanding long-term biodiversity trends. What are the typical trajectories of landscape change in the Southern Rocky Mountains today? Below we describe three trajectories: (1) expansion of conifer forests resulting from fire exclusion, (2) forest fragmentation due to logging, and (3) habitat conversion and alteration from rural residential development. Fire, as a natural agent of forest fragmentation, is the oldest type of landscape trajectory; logging has been the most prevalent type in recent history and has been the most studied form of landscape change; and residential development is the most recent. We summarize the changes in landscape pattern associated with each trajectory and predict the response of the Southern Rocky Mountains bird community. We then review relevant studies on actual bird responses to these changes.

Fire Exclusion

Studies of fire scars on trees have revealed that the fire frequency has shifted from relatively high to very low throughout the Rockies, especially at low to mid elevations (Arno et al. 1997, Swetnam and Baisam 1996). This dramatic reduction is thought to be the product of both fuel reduction from livestock grazing and human fire suppression. Vegetation has responded dramatically to this change in fire regime. Photo comparisons have revealed substantial encroachment of grasslands by forests and an increase in tree density and canopy cover in conifer stands in southwest Montana (Gruell 1983). Simultaneously, deciduous forest types have declined in abundance in many areas. For example, Gallant et al. (1998) reconstructed vegetation composition and structure in a watershed in the Centennial Mountains, Idaho, from 1850 to present. They found that aspen cover was reduced by about 80% over this time period, while mature conifer forest increased in area, patch size, and connectivity. Moreover, this response of vegetation to fire exclusion appears to be ongoing. Simulation studies in Zion National Park, Utah, suggest that conifer forest expansion may continue for another 100 years under the current fire regime (D. Roberts, *personal communication*). This increase in forest area and fuel loads is likely to eventually lead to an increase in large, severe fires (Veblen, *this volume*).

Hence, the likely landscape change under this trajectory is an increase in the area, patch size, connectivity, and density of mature conifer forest and a concomitant fragmentation of grasslands and deciduous forest types (Table 10.2). Severe fires would reverse this trend and lead to an overall increase in the grain size of the landscape (Veblen, *this volume*). Therefore, we predict an increase in the abundance of species associated with dense conifer forests and large forest patches and a reduction in species specializing on early seral conifer forests, grasslands, and deciduous stands. Habitats for this latter group of species would increase following the infrequent severe fires. However, these early successional habitats may be too isolated in space and time to support viable populations of these species.

Existing studies suggest that this landscape change will strongly influence the bird community. Deciduous habitats including aspen, cottonwood, and willow stands were found to support substantially higher species richness than any other cover type in a study area in the Greater Yellowstone Ecosystem (Hansen et al., 1999). Several bird species specialized on these habitat types and were not present in other habitats. Similarly, several grassland specialists are found in the Rockies, and many of these species exhibited substantial population reductions in recent decades (Dobkin 1992). As deciduous and grassland habitats are reduced, several bird species are likely to suffer increasing rates of local extinction.

Table 10.2. Predicted changes in landscape pattern and bird responses under three landscape trajectories in the Southern Rocky Mountains.

Trajectory	Landscape Pattern	Bird Reponse
Fire Suppression	Non-Fire Periods: Increase in mature conifer area, patch size, connectivity, stand density; decrease in grassland and deciduous area, patch size, connectivity. Severe Fire Periods: expansion of grasslands and deciduous; contraction of coniferous forest.	Non-Fire Periods: Increase in species associated with conifer habitats and large conifer patches; decrease in early seral conifer, grassland, deciduous species. Severe Fire Periods: Increase in early seral conifer, grassland, deciduous species. Long term:Reduction in species richness due to spatial/temporal isolation of habits.
Logging	Decrease in mature conifer area, core area, patch size/shape variation, connectivity, stand structural complexity; decrease in disturbance patch structural complexity, variation in patch size/shape.	Loss of closed-canopy species, forest-interior species, structural-complexity associated species; expansion of early-seral, structurally-simple associated species.
Rural Residential Development	Habitat conversion, reduced patch size, simpler patch shape, reduced connectivity for native species, increased connectivity for invasive species, more abrupt ecotones, altered biotic interactions.	Increase in some nest predators/brood parasites; lowered reproductive success in deciduous-associated species; loss of deciduous-associated species.

Another consequence of fire exclusion is a reduction in stand-replacement fires and early-successional forest habitats. Hutto (1995) studied birds in several recent burns in Montana and Idaho. Of 87 species detected in these burns, 15 species were strongly associated with them, being found more frequently in recent burns than other cover types. Some of these species, such as the black-backed woodpecker, were virtually restricted to recently burned sites. Habitat area, patch size, and connectivity is likely greatly reduced for these species in post-settlement times. Even if fire exclusion leads to major fires over the next 50 years, it is not clear if local populations can persist during the long intervals between fires.

Another possible consequence of fire exclusion is loss of species associated with open-canopy mature conifer forests such as ponderosa pine forests. These forests were maintained by frequent ground fires and are now undergoing invasion by Douglas fir and true fir and dramatic increases in stand density. Unfortunately, we are not aware of any studies of bird response to increases in stand density in ponderosa pine forests. We also predict that closed-canopy forest species will expand under fire exclusion. However, key studies have yet to be done.

In summary, conifer expansion under fire exclusion is a very prevalent trajectory of landscape change throughout the Rocky Mountains. Conservationists and landscape managers have only recently begun to acknowledge the substantial changes in vegetation associated with this trajectory and research on ecological consequences remains underdeveloped. Initial studies suggest substantial impacts on bird species abundances.

Logging

A second common trajectory of landscape change in the Rockies is driven by clear-cut logging. Staggered-setting clear-cut logging has been widely employed on some of the national forests in the region. Its effects on landscape patterns have been similar to those documented in other regions in fragmenting conifer forests and reducing within-stand structural complexity (e.g., Hansen et al. 1991, Ripple et al. 1991, Mladenoff et al. 1993). For example, Reed et al. (1996) quantified landscape change under logging during 1950–1993 in the Medicine Bow National Forest in southeast Wyoming. They found a decrease in forest mean patch size and mean patch shape and an increase in total edge.

How might landscape patterns under logging compare with those of pre-European settlement times? A. J. Hansen and R. Patten (*unpub-*

lished data) compared spatial patterns created by clear-cut logging in Targhee National Forest, Idaho, during 1950–1990 with those created by wildfire in the adjacent Yellowstone National Park. Approximately 50% of each landscape remained in closed-canopy forest. Because wildfire burned in large linear strips as driven by wind, the forest remaining in the burned landscape was much less fragmented than that in the logged landscape. Mean core area (area >100 m from an edge) was about five times greater in the burned landscape. Disturbance patches also differed between the two landscapes. Patches created by fire were larger, more variable in size, more complex in shape, and better connected than those created by logging units. They also had much higher levels of within-stand heterogeneity for variables such as live trees, snags, and fallen trees.

Selective timber harvest is also common in the Rockies. However, we are not aware of studies quantifying the effects of this type of logging on landscape patterns. We predict that staggered-setting clear-cut logging would lead to a loss of species associated with within-stand structural complexity and interiors of closed-canopy forests (Table 10.2).

In our evaluation of current knowledge of bird response to fragmentation due to logging, we recognize three components of landscape change associated with fragmentation: loss of total area of the habitat, decrease in patch size and associated increase in edge, and increasing patch isolation. Each of these components of fragmentation due to logging may elicit unique responses from species and communities. Because relatively few studies of bird response to fragmentation have been completed in the Southern Rocky Mountains, we reviewed studies of logging effects in conifer forests from throughout western North America.

Area of Habitat. Most ecologists assume that the average abundance of a species in a landscape is related to the area of suitable habitat across the landscape. Thus, as the area of a habitat is reduced through fragmentation, we expect that species abundances will drop and some species will suffer local extinction. The best test of these ideas in western coniferous forests was by McGarigal and McComb (1995) working in coastal Oregon (Table 10.3). They found that the abundance of 10 of 15 late-seral associated bird species was significantly ($p < 0.10$) related to area of late-seral forest. Hence, in western forests, as elsewhere, we can expect species to be reduced in abundance if the area of their habitats is reduced through habitat fragmentation.

Patch Size and Edge. As stated earlier, several species of birds have been found to be rare or missing from small forest patches in the Eastern deciduous forest (Terborgh 1989). This loss of species could result from altered microclimate, nutrient cycling, vegetation structure, and/ or predation rates due to loss of interior habitat with decreasing patch size (Ranney et al. 1981, Robinson and Wilcove 1994). However, such strong effects of decreased patch size have generally not been found in coniferous forests in western North America (Table 10.3). In each of four studies we reviewed, only a small percentage (7–20%) of species exhibited significantly lower abundance in small patches or near forest edges. No species showed a significant response to patch size or edge across all of the studies, and no species were absent from small patches. Similarly, species richness was not found to be significantly related to patch size or distance from edge. The two studies that examined predation on artificial nests found that rates did not differ from forest edge to interior, quite in contrast to similar studies in the Eastern deciduous forest (e.g., Wilcove 1985, Small and Hunter 1988).

Patch Isolation. The third component of fragmentation, patch isolation, sometimes reduces species abundances and richness due to reduced immigration. However, the two studies on isolation in western coniferous forests found little or no effect on species abundances or diversity (Table 10.3).

In total, studies on patch size, edge, and patch isolation suggest that the spatial configuration of habitat (controlling for area) does not influence birds in western coniferous forests as much as in some other biomes. This result may be at least partially explained by the nature of land use in the expanding matrix (Schmiegelow et al. 1997). The agricultural and rural residential development that fragments the Eastern deciduous forest favors nest predators and brood parasites (brown-headed cowbirds) that strongly influence birds in forest fragments (Terborgh 1989). In all the studies we reviewed from western coniferous forests, natural factors or logging were the agents of fragmentation. Nest predators and cowbirds were not found to be more abundant in more fragmented landscapes in these studies. These results suggest that research in the West should focus on potential differences in the effects of fragmentation between landscapes driven by logging and those driven by agriculture and rural residential development.

Landscape Setting. An often overlooked aspect of landscape pattern that is relevant to the impacts of fragmentation is the location of habitats relative to biophysical gradients (Hansen and Rotella, 1999). The Rocky Mountains are characterized by strong gradients in topography, climate, and soils. Ecological processes like primary productivity vary across these abiotic gradients. Both abiotic patterns and the

Table 10.3. Summary of studies of bird response to forest fragmentation in coniferous forests of western North America.

Study	Design	Species Responses	Community Responses
Habitat area			
McGarigal and McComb 1995, (Oregon Coast Range)	30 subbasins stratified by area and spatial configuration of late-seral forest.	Abundance of 10 of 15 late-seral associates related to habitat area.	Not studied.
Patch Size and Edge			
Keller and Anderson 1992, (southeastern Wyoming)	Compared natural true fir stands with those fragmented by logging.	Abundance of 2 of 15 species showed significant negative relationship with fragmentation.	Not studied.
Schmiegelow et al. 1997, (north central Alberta)	Compared isolated fragments of 4 sizes, connected fragments, and controls.	Abundance of 6 of 30 species was lower in connected fragments than controls; abundance of 7 of 37 species was lower in isolated fragments than controls.	Species richness did not dif among three treatments.
Ruefenacht 1997, lorado Rockies)	Compared edge and interior habitats for meadow/forest and clear-cut/forest edges.	Abundance of 5 of 39 species was higher in forest interior than on meadow/forest edge; abundance of 2 of 30 species was higher in forest interior than on clear-cut/forest edge.	Predation on artificial nests not differ between edge a interior.
Vega 1993, (Oregon Cascades)	Examined artificial nest predation from clear-cut/forest edge to forest interior.	Not studied.	Predation did not differ betv edge and interior.
Schieck et al. 1995, (Vancouver Is., British Columbia)	Compared old-growth forest tracts of different size.	The abundance of 1–3 (depending on statistical test) species of late-seral associates was related to patch size.	Richness of late-seral associ was not related to patch siz
Patch Isolation			
McGarigal and McComb 1995, (Oregon Coast Range)	30 subbasins stratified by area and spatial configuration of late-seral forest.	Abundance of 1 of 15 late-seral associates was higher in less fragmented subbasins.	Not studied.
Schmiegelow et al. 1997, (north central Alberta)	Compared isolated fragments of 4 sizes, connected fragments, and controls.	Percent of species with lower abundance in fragments and controls did not differ between isolated and connected fragments.	Slightly less species turnove connected than isolated fragments.
Truchi et al. 1995, (Colorado Rockies)	Compared aspen patches differing in isolation.	Not studied.	Species richness was not related to patch isolation.

related ecological processes can strongly influence the distribution and abundance of vertebrates. For example, in mature lodgepole pine forests in the Greater Yellowstone Ecosystem, we found that the abundances of several species and species richness significantly related to elevation, snowmelt date, and normalized difference vegetation index, a measure of vegetation productivity (Hansen et al., *in review*). Moreover, initial demographic studies suggest that some low-elevation forests serve as population source habitats for some bird species (Hansen et al., *in review*). These results suggest that low-elevation conifer forests may merit special consideration in managing biodiversity. Logging has often been centered on more productive, low-elevation forests, presumably with negative effects on some forest birds. The challenge is to tailor timber harvest to biophysical gradients to better optimize biodiversity and wood-production objectives.

RURAL RESIDENTIAL DEVELOPMENT

The most rapidly expanding land use in many locations in the Rockies is rural residential development. Population growth in the Rockies is among the fastest in the United States (Riebsame et al. 1997), and many of the immigrants are choosing to live in rural locations (Theobald, *this volume*). Initial studies suggest that rural residential development results in conversion of natural habitats; reduced patch size, shape complexity and connectivity of native habitats, and increased connectivity for invasive species (Theobald et al. 1996).

Perhaps as important as what landscape changes result from this development is where in the landscape these changes are occurring. We have hypothesized that people in the northern Rockies have disproportionately settled in those places in the landscape that are most important for native species (Hansen and Rotella, 1999). These places tend to be the productive valley bottoms that are well watered and support deciduous forests or productive conifer forests.

Consequently, we predict that rural residential development will result in reduced habitat area for bird species, especially those specializing on deciduous forests and low-elevation conifer forests. Many of these species may also suffer local extinction due to increased nest predation and brood parasitism.

Relatively few studies have quantified the effects of rural residential development on birds in the Rockies. The few that have show striking results. V. Saab (1999) examined bird communities in cottonwood forests of different sizes along the South Fork of Snake River in southeast Idaho. The 57 patches were stratified by the surrounding landscape matrix: either seminatural habitats or agriculture and rural residential development. Saab found that 71% of the variation in bird species richness was explained by landscape matrix, patch size, patch proximity, and patch vegetation structure. Large, well-connected patches in a seminatural matrix were highest in species richness. The abundances of many individual bird species showed similar trends. Saab also found that nest predators and brood parasites were most abundant in cottonwood patches in the agricultural and rural residential matrix.

In the Greater Yellowstone Ecosystem, we found (Hansen et al., 1999) that bird abundance and richness were significantly higher in deciduous forests (cottonwood, aspen, willow) than in other cover types. We speculated that these "hot spot" habitats act as population source areas for some species due to the high vegetation structure and productivity in these habitats. Preliminary field studies of nest success and population modeling revealed that this was the case for aspen habitats. However, cottonwood stands appeared to be population sinks. In this study area, aspen occurs in a seminatural matrix while cottonwood is surrounded by agriculture and rural residential development. These intense land uses favor nest predators and brood parasites and have likely caused these cottonwood stands to change from a population source habitat for some native birds to a population sink.

As rural residential development expands in the Rockies, we can expect local extinctions of bird species as population source habitats are increasingly converted to sink habitats. To the extent that rural residential development is disproportionately focused on deciduous habitats and low-elevation coniferous forests, we may find that local extinctions occur even in landscapes where average human density is relatively low.

Interactions among Landscape Drivers

While many landscapes in the Southern Rocky Mountains may be experiencing only one of these trajectories of change, some places are likely subjected to two or even three trajectory types. Interactions among these trajectories may lead to complex relationships. For example, logging near rural residential development will possibly have a larger effect than logging in seminatural forests because the predators and parasites favored by this development will be able to penetrate logged forest. Also, fire exclusion may be more vigorous near residences, hastening the loss of deciduous, grassland, and shrubland habitats. Understanding these interactions among landscape drivers will be a challenge.

CONCLUSIONS

How do birds respond to forest fragmentation in the Southern Rocky Mountains? Perhaps this question is a subset of those we should ask to better understand the influence of human activities on Rocky Mountain ecosystems. The more general questions are what are the major factors that affect landscape change in this region, what are the resulting trajectories of landscape change, and how are ecological processes and native species responding to this change?

Forest fragmentation by logging is the trajectory of change best studied in the Southern Rocky Mountains. There is good reason to expect that reductions in the area of forest habitats resulting from logging will lead to reductions in some species abundances and ultimately to local extinctions. However, the influence of forest spatial configuration on native birds here appears to be rather weak, based on current studies. These studies have not yet identified any particular species that are obviously sensitive to forest spatial configuration. Bird community-scale responses have also been weak in these studies. These results may be due to the fact that species in the region have developed life history attributes that are well adapted to the natural fragmentation that was typical over much of the Southern Rocky Mountains in pre-European settlement times and to the lower biomass accumulation in this region. However, the results could also be due to too few studies being completed to date or to the possibility that landscapes studied have not yet undergone sufficient fragmentation to cause strong responses by native species. How extensive is forest fragmentation by logging in Southern Rocky Mountains? Key studies on this topic are yet to be done. Substantial fragmentation has been documented on particular national forests such as the Medicine Bow in Wyoming (Reed et al. 1996) and the Targhee National Forest in Idaho. In some other national forests, however, timber harvest has been minimal, or partial logging has been used instead of clear-cutting.

We speculate that much more land area in Southern Rocky Mountains is likely undergoing forest expansion under fire exclusion than is being influenced by logging. Again, key data on forest expansion are not available. Because the expansion has been occurring over decades and is slow relative to our individual observation times, we often do not perceive the radical change in forest area, forest density, and loss of grasslands and deciduous forests. This trajectory is likely having a large impact on native species. Even with logging as mentioned above, net habitat area for closed-canopy conifer associates has likely experienced a substantial net increase across the region. At the same time, species requiring structurally complex early successional conifer forest habitats, grasslands, shrublands, and deciduous forests have likely declined dramatically. Over the longer term, this trajectory is likely to lead to major changes in the grain size of the landscape (Veblen, *this volume*). The less frequent fires of the future are likely to be much larger in size and more severe. Hence, the landscape dynamic is changing from frequent, small, lower severity fires in pre-European settlement times to infrequent, large, high severity fires in future times. The consequences of this change for ecological processes and native species are not well known.

Rural residential development likely covers less area than either logging or forest expansion across the region. However, such development may be having a larger effect than its area would suggest because it may be concentrated on the places in the landscape that are hot spots for native species abundance and richness, and function as population source areas (Hansen and Rotella, 1999). Through habitat conversion and alteration of biotic interactions (e.g., predation) within remaining hot spot habitats, the value of these habitats for maintaining viable populations of native species may be substantially reduced.

How can we better understand and manage these changes? This book is evidence that we need to expand our research paradigm to better understand the drivers, types, and rates of change in landscape patterns, and consequences for species and processes. The simple model of forest fragmentation derived from the EDF is insufficient here in the Southern Rocky Mountains, and research needs to be better tailored to the regional situation. We would also benefit from better understanding the influence of abiotic factors on ecological processes, biodiversity, and human settlement in the region. To the extent that strong gradients in topography, climate, and soils strongly influence ecological and socioeconomic patterns in the region, management plans should consider these gradients. Hansen and Rotella (1999) offer several guidelines for land use allocation and silviculture in landscapes with strong abiotic controls. (An example of landscape-scale management is offered in Romme et al., *this volume*). Similarly, Hansen et al. (1999) offer an approach for managing biodiversity at local to regional scales that focuses increasing research and management on the species and places in a planning area that are most at risk.

Beyond attempting to maintain key habitats, future management will likely be increasingly focused on restoration of degraded habitats. Excellent opportunities exist to use prescribed fire and ecological forestry to expand the area of aspen groves, grasslands, and early successional, structurally complex seral stages (e.g., Aplet, *this volume*).

Managing the rate and consequences of rural residential development offers a special challenge because development occurs mostly on private lands. Increasingly, scientists and public land managers need to work with local government officials to develop knowledge, data, and management alternatives that include suites of incentives and regulations to meet biodiversity, socioeconomic, and other objectives.

Fortunately, viable populations of native species still remain in many Rocky Mountain landscapes, and we have time to engage in this new era of cooperative research and management.

Literature Cited

Arno, S. F. 1980. Forest fire history in the Northern Rockies. *Journal of Forestry* 78(8): 460–465.

Arno, S. F., H. Y. Smith, and M. A. Krebs. 1997. Old growth ponderosa pine and western larch stand structures: influences of pre-1900 fires and fire exclusion. USDA Forest Service Intermountain Research Station INT-RP-495.

Chen, J., J. F. Franklin, and T. A. Spies. 1995. Growing-season microclimatic gradients extending into old-growth Douglas-fir forests from clear-cut edges. *Ecological Applications* 5: 74–86.

Dobkin, D. S. 1992. Neotropical migrant landbirds in the Northern Rockies and Great Plains. USDA Forest Service Northern Region. Publication No. R1-93-34. Missoula, Montana, USA.

Franklin, J., and R. Forman. 1987. Creating landscape patterns by forest cutting: ecological consequences and principles. *Landscape Ecology* 1: 5–18.

Gallant, A., A. J. Hansen, J. Councilman, D. Monte, and D. Betz. 1998. *Vegetation dynamics under natural and human drivers during 1856–1996 in the East Beaver Creek Watershed, Centennial Mountains, Idaho.* Montana State University, Bozeman, Montana, USA.

Gruell, G. E. 1983. Fire and vegetative trends in the Northern Rockies: interpretations from 1871–1982. General Technical Report INT-158. USDA Forest Service Intermountain Forest and Range Experimental Station.

Gruell, G. E., W. C. Schmidt, S. F. Arno, and W. J. Reich. 1982. Seventy years of vegetative change in a managed ponderosa pine forest in western Montana — implications for resource management. General Technical Report INT-130. USDA Forest Service Intermountain Forest and Range Experimental Station.

Hansen, A. J., J. A. Peterson, E. G. Horvath, P. Lee, and K. R. Purcell. 1994. Which vertebrates respond to forest edges in the Pacific Northwest? Unpublished report. Forest Science Department, Oregon State University, Corvallis, Oregon, USA.

Hansen, A. J., and J. R. Rotella. 1999. Abiotic factors. *In* M. Hunter, editor. *Maintaining Biodiversity in Forest Ecosystems.* Cambridge University Press, Cambridge, UK.

Hansen, A. J., J. R. Rotella, and M. L. Kraska. 1999. Dynamic habitat and population analysis: a filtering approach to resolve the biodiversity manager's dilemma. *Ecological Applications* 9(4): 1459–1476.

Hansen, A. J., T. Spies, F. Swanson, and J. Ohmann. 1991. Lessons from natural forests: implications for conserving biodiversity in managed forests. *BioScience* 41: 382–392.

Hansen, A. J., and D. L. Urban. 1992. Avian response to landscape pattern: the role of species life histories. *Landscape Ecology* 7: 163–180.

Hansen, A. J., D. Urban, and B. Marks. 1992. Avian community dynamics: the interplay of landscape trajectories and species life histories. Pages 170–195 *in* A. J. Hansen and F. di Castri, editors. *Landscape boundaries: consequences for biotic diversity and ecological flows.* Springer-Verlag Ecological Studies Series, New York, New York, USA.

Hutto, R. L. 1995. Composition of bird communities following stand-replacement fires in Northern Rocky Mountain (USA) conifer forests. *Conservation Biology* 9: 1041–1058.

Keller, M. E., and S. H. Anderson. 1992. Avian use of habitat configurations created by forest cutting in southeastern Wyoming. *The Condor* 94: 55–65.

Klein, B. C. 1989. Effects of forest fragmentation on dun and carrion beetle communities in Southern Amazonia Brazil. *Ecology* 70: 1715–1725.

Lynch, J. F., and R. F. Whitcomb. 1978. Effects of the insularization of the eastern deciduous forest on avifaunal diveriisty and turnover. Pages 461–489 *in* A. Marmelstein, editor. *Classification, inventory, and analysis of fish and wildlife habitat.* USDI Fish and Wildlife Service, Washington, D.C., USA.

Martin, T. E. 1993. Nest predation and nest sites: new perspectives on old patterns. *BioScience* 43: 523–532.

McGarigal, K., and W. C. McComb. 1995. Relationships between landscape structure and breeding birds in the Oregon Coast Range. *Ecological Monographs* 65: 235–260.

Miller, J. R., and R. L. Knight. 1995. Life-history traits of the Southern Rocky Mountain avifauna. Unpublished report. Department of Biology, Colorado State University, Fort Collins, Colorado, USA.

Mladenoff, D. J., M. A. White, J. Pastor, T. R. Crow. 1993. Comparing spatial pattern in unaltered old-growth and disturbed forest landscapes. *Ecological Application* 3: 294–306.

Ranney, J. W., M. C. Bruner, and J. B. Levenson. 1981. The importance of edge in the structure and dynamics of forest islands. Pages 67–96 *in* R. L. Burgess and D. M. Sharpe, editors. *Forest island dynamics in man-dominated landscapes.* Springer-Verlag, New York, New York, USA.

Reed, R., J. Johnson-Barnard, and W. L. Baker. 1996. Fragmentation of a forested Rocky Mountain landscape, 1950–1993. *Biological Conservation* 75: 267–277.

Riebsame, W. E., H. Gosnell, and D. Theobald. 1997. *Atlas of the new West: portrait of a changing region.* W. W. Norton & Co., New York, New York, USA.

Ripple, W. J., G. A. Bradshaw, and T. A. Spies. 1991. Measuring forest landscape patterns in the Cascade Range of Oregon, USA. *Biological Conservation* 57: 73–88.

Robinson, S. K., and D. S. Wilcove. 1994. Forest fragmentation in the temperate zone and its effects on migratory songbirds. *Bird Conservation International* 4: 233–241.

Ruefenacht, B. 1997. Songbird communities along natural and clear-cut forest edges. Ph.D. dissertation. Department of Fisheries and Wildlife, Colorado State University, Fort Collins, Colorado, USA.

Saab, V. 1999. Importance of spatial scale to habitat use by breeding birds in riparian forests: a hierarchical analysis. *Ecological Applications* 9: 135–151.

Saunders,, D. A., R. J. Hobbs, and C. R. Margules. 1991. Biological consequences of ecosystem fragmentation: a review. *Conservation Biology* 5: 18–32.

Schieck, J., K. Lertzman, B. Nyberg, and R. Page. 1995. Effects of patch size on birds in old-growth montane forests. *Conservation Biology* 9: 1072–1084.

Schmiegelow, F.K.A., C. S. Machtans, and S. J. Hannon. 1997. Are boreal birds resilient to forest fragmentation? An experimental study of short-term community responses. *Ecology* 78: 1914–1932.

Small, M. F., and M. L. Hunter. 1988. Forest fragmentation and avian nest predation in forested landscapes. *Oecologia* 76: 62–64.

Suring, L., D. Crocker-Bedford, R. Flynn, C. Hale, G. Iverson, M. Kirchhoff, T. Schenck, L. Shea, and K. Titus. 1993. A proposed strategy for maintaining well-distributed, viable populations of wildlife associated with old-growth forests in southeast Alaska. Interagency Committee, USDA Forest Service, Juneau, Alaska, USA.

Swetnam, T. W., and C. H. Baisan. 1996. Historical fire regime patterns in the southwestern United States since AD 1700. Pages 11–32 *in* C. D. Allen, technical editor. *Fire effects in southwestern forests, proceedings of the second La Mesa Fire Symposium*, March 29–31, 1994, Los Alamos, New Mexico. USDA Forest Service General Technical Report RM-GTR-286.

Terborgh, J. 1989. *Where have all the birds gone?* Princeton University Press, Princeton, New Jersey, USA.

Theobald, D. M., H. Hosnell, and W. E. Riebsame. 1996. Land use and landscape change in the Colorado Mountains II: a case study of the East River Valley. *Mountain Research and Development.* 16: 407–418.

Thomas, J. W., E. D. Forsman, J. B. Lint, C. Meslow, B. Noon, and J. Vernen. 1990. A conservation strategy for the northern spotted owl: a report of the interagency scientific committee to address the conservation of the northern spotted owl. USDA Forest Service, Portland, Oregon, USA.

Turchi, G. M., P. L. Kennedy, D. L. Urban, and D. Hein. 1995. Bird species richness in relation to isolation of aspen habitats. *Wilson Bulletin* 107: 463–474.

Vega, R. 1993. Bird communities in managed conifer stands in the Oregon Cascades: habitat associations and nest predation. Master's thesis. Oregon State University, Corvallis, Oregon, USA.

Whitcomb, R. F., C. S. Robbins, J. F. Lynch, B. L. Whitcomb, K. Klimkiewicz, and D. Bystrak. 1981. Effects of forest fragmentation on avifauna of the eastern deciduous forest. Pages 125–205 *in* R. L. Burgess and D. M. Sharpe, editors. *Forest island dynamics in man-dominated landscapes.* Springer-Verlag, New York, New York, USA.

Wilcove, D. S. 1985. Nest predation in forest tracts and the decline of migratory songbirds. *Ecology* 66: 1211–1214.

11

Plant and Vegetation Responses to Edges in the Southern Rocky Mountains

William L. Baker and Gregory K. Dillon

Introduction

Forest fragmentation is a global issue concerning biological diversity. In the Rocky Mountains and western United States, the pattern of fragmentation differs from the agricultural-clearing sequence that is the common image. Instead, the syndrome of fragmentation in the western United States is to transform a landscape containing large patches, varying in size, but with substantial interior area, into a landscape with comparatively small, uniform-sized patches with small interior and much edge area, in which "edge effects" are apparent (Baker, *this volume*). Edge effects are the suite of differences in microenvironment and biota across edges between forest and nonforest or early successional vegetation (Opdam et al. 1993, Murcia 1995). Edge effects were long considered beneficial to wildlife, but now are increasingly recognized as more complex, and often detrimental to biological diversity (Yahner 1988, Murcia 1995).

Edge effects are modified by other potential effects (Fig. 11.1). Disturbance effects occur because the edge environment may favor or discourage certain kinds of disturbance (e.g., Laurance 1997). Matrix effects occur because the composition and management of the adjoining opening affect the propagule rain and disturbances reaching into the forest edge (Janzen 1983). Higher-order effects occur when the direct response of one organism leads to a subsequent response in a different organism, possibly affecting still others (Terborgh 1992). An example is a decline in a pollinator that subsequently affects the survival of a plant. Lags may occur in the appearance of edge effects because

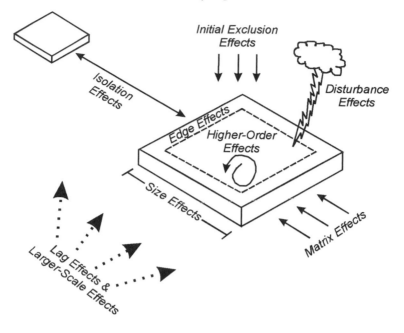

Fig. 11.1. Edge effects and major modifying effects that alter the response of plants to the edge.

of higher-order effects and because organisms, such as long-lived trees, may simply respond slowly (Opdam et al. 1993).

In the following sections we review these effects in more detail, and attempt to identify known and potential patterns of response of Rocky Mountain plants to edges. First we review the potential ecological effects of edges on plants, based on the global literature. Then, we examine the extent of known effects in the Rocky Mountains. Finally, we present initial results of a study of the effects of road edges on plants.

POTENTIAL ECOLOGICAL EFFECTS OF EDGES ON PLANTS
Differentiation of Edge and Interior Forest

The forest edge microenvironment becomes distinct from the interior at edge creation. Relative to interiors, edges most often have higher mean light levels, air and soil temperature, vapor pressure deficit, and wind speed, and lower relative humidity and soil moisture (Table 11.1), but the edge environment may also be more variable than the interior (Chen et al. 1993). The edge environment is generally brighter, hotter, and drier than the interior, and species most often appear to be responding to gradients in light, temperature, and moisture. Soil conditions (especially pH, moisture, and nutrients) may also differ from those in the interior (Matlack 1994, Jose et al. 1996).

Differences in edge and interior vegetation arise from demographic responses to the edge microenvironment (Table 11.2). Natality rates, growth rates, and mortality rates may all be affected. Recruitment often increases overall, increasing understory tree density in edges (Table 11.2). Overall growth rates appear to increase in edges relative to interiors, leading to increases in tree basal area (Table 11.2). Canopy tree mortality from both stress and blowdown is consistently elevated in edges, leading to lowered canopy cover and foliage thickness (Table 11.2).

Initially, forest edges adjoining openings reflect the original interior forest, but a sequence of microenvironmental and vegetational responses typically follows edge creation. An initial increase in stem density may occur within 1–2 years of edge creation, but may reach a peak, effectively sealing the edge, within 10–30 years in temperate-zone deciduous forests (Ranney et al. 1981, Brothers and Spingarn 1992, Matlack 1994), or perhaps 5 years in tropical forests (Williams-Linera 1990*a*). Edge-interior differences may persist for 50 or more years after the edge seals (Matlack 1994, Kupfer 1996) and may be permanent (Ranney et al. 1981). Edges about 270 years old in New Jersey oak-hickory forests retain vegetation differences between edge and interior (Wales 1972). However, the microenvironmental differences between edge and interior typically decline as the edge seals (Matlack 1994).

Geographic variation in the relative importance of and rates of natality, growth, and mortality processes leads to differences in how the edge vegetation develops. In tropical and warm temperate settings, closure of the edge by accelerated growth of understory trees and rapid regeneration leads to high tree density and basal area in the edge relative to the interior (e.g., Williams-Linera 1990*a* and Table 11.2). In contrast, in cool temperate settings, where accelerated growth and regeneration are slower to seal the edge, mortality and disturbance processes may dominate for decades, leading to lower tree density and basal area in edges relative to interiors (e.g., Chen et al. 1992 and Table 11.2).

Response of Plants to the Edge

Plants can be classified as edge-restricted, edge-oriented, interior-restricted, interior-oriented, and ubiquitous (Ranney et al. 1981, Frost

Table 11.1. Microenvironmental trends from forest edges into forest interiors, the reported trend, the type of edge, and the depth-of-edge influence (DEI), where measured. A dash indicates that a transect was not used, but comparisons between edge and interior were done.

Trend	Location and edge vegetation	DEI
Light intensity (usually PAR) high in edges relative to interiors		
Chen et al. 1993	Washington conifer forests/clear-cuts	—
Luken and Goessling 1995	Kentucky mixed hardword/cropland	5 m
Burke and Nol 1998	Ontario deciduous forests/abandoned fields	5 m
Cadenasso et al. 1997	New York deciduous forests/abandoned fields	1–7 m
Young and Mitchell 1994	New Zealand podocarp-broadleaf forest/pasture	10 m
MacDougall and Kellman 1992	Belize riparian forests/savanna	10 m
Jose et al. 1996	Indian montane tropical forests/natural grasslands	15 m
Kapos 1989	Amazon rainforests/pastures	40 m
Matlack 1993*a*	Pennsylvania/Delaware old forests/cropland	0–44 m
Brothers and Spingarn 1992	Indiana old-growth forests/cropland	20–50 m
Vaillancourt 1995	Wyoming subalpine forests/clear-cuts	30–50 m
Chen et al. 1995	Oregon & Washington conifer forests/clear-cuts	15–60 m
Air temperature high in edges relative to interiors		
Chen et al. 1993	Washington conifer forests/clear-cuts	—
Brothers and Spingarn 1992	Indiana old-growth forests/cropland	<8 m
Cadenasso et al. 1997	New York deciduous forests/abandoned fields	1–10 m
Turton and Freiberger 1997	Australian tropical rainforests/pastures	10 m
Williams-Linera 1990*a*	Panama tropical rainforests/shifting cultivation	15 m
Vaillancourt 1995	Wyoming subalpine forests/clear-cuts	<20 m
Matlack 1993*a*	Pennsylvania/Delaware old forests/cropland	0–24 m
Jose et al. 1996	Indian montane tropical forests/natural grasslands	>30 m
Young and Mitchell 1994	New Zealand podocarp-broadleaf forest/pasture	30–50 m
Chen et al. 1995	Oregon & Washington conifer forests/clear-cuts	180–240 m
Air temperature no different in edges and interiors		
Burke and Nol 1998	Ontario deciduous forests/abandoned fields	5 m
Relative humidity low in edges relative to interiors		
Chen et al. 1993	Washington conifer forests/clear-cuts	—
Brothers and Spingarn 1992	Indiana old-growth forests/cropland	<8 m
Cadenasso et al. 1997	New York deciduous forests/abandoned fields	5–14 m
Williams-Linera 1990*a*	Panama tropical rainforests/shifting cultivation	15 m
Jose et al. 1996	Indian montane tropical forests/natural grasslands	>30 m
Matlack 1993*a*	Pennsylvania/Delaware old forests/cropland	0–50 m
Vaillancourt 1995	Wyoming subalpine forests/clear-cuts	50–70 m
Chen et al. 1995	Oregon & Washington conifer forests/clear-cuts	>240 m
Relative humidity no different in edges and interiors		
Burke and Nol 1998	Ontario deciduous forests/abandoned fields	5 m
Vapor pressure deficit high in edges relative to interiors		
Chen et al. 1993	Washington conifer forests/clear-cuts	—
Kapos et al. 1997	Amazon rainforests/pastures	10 m

Continued on next page

Table 11.1—*Continued*

Trend	Location and edge vegetation	DEI
Vapor pressure deficit high in edges relative to interiors (contd.)		
Turton and Freiberger 1997	Australian tropical rainforests/pastures	10 m
Matlack 1993*a*	Pennsylvania/Delaware old forests/cropland	0–50 m
Young and Mitchell 1994	New Zealand podocarp-broadleaf forest/pasture	30–50 m
Kapos 1989	Amazon rainforests/pastures	60 m
Vapor pressure deficit no different in edges and interiors		
Camargo and Kapos 1995	Amazon rainforests/pastures	—
Wind speed high in edges relative to interiors		
Chen et al. 1993	Washington conifer forests/clear-cuts	—
Raynor 1971	New York pine plantation/abandoned field	60 m
Chen et al. 1995	Oregon & Washington conifer forests/clear-cuts	>240 m
Soil temperature high in edges relative to interiors		
Chen et al. 1993	Washington conifer forests/clear-cuts	—
Burke and Nol 1998	Ontario deciduous forests/abandoned fields	5 m
Brothers and Spingarn 1992	Indiana old-growth forests/cropland	<8 m
Cadenasso et al. 1997	New York deciduous forests/abandoned fields	3–21 m
Jose et al. 1996	Indian montane tropical forests/natural grasslands	30 m
Turton and Freiberger 1997	Australian tropical rainforests/pastures	30 m
Chen et al. 1995	Oregon & Washington conifer forests/clear-cuts	60–120 m
Soil moisture low in edges relative to interiors		
Burke and Nol 1998	Ontario deciduous forests/abandoned fields	5 m
Kapos 1989	Amazon rainforests/pastures	20 m
Jose et al. 1996	Indian montane tropical forests/natural grasslands	30 m
Kapos et al. 1997	Amazon rainforests/pastures	80 m
Chen et al. 1995	Oregon & Washington conifer forests/clear-cuts	0–90 m
Litter moisture low in edges relative to interiors		
Matlack 1993*a*	Pennsylvania/Delaware old forests/cropland	0–50 m
Soil moisture no different in edges and interiors		
Cadenasso et al. 1997	New York deciduous forests/abandoned fields	—
Soil moisture high in edges relative to interiors		
Chen et al. 1993	Washington conifer forests/clear-cuts	—
Soil moisture trend complex from edges to interiors		
Camargo and Kapos 1995	Amazon rainforests/pastures	—
Soil pH low in edges relative to interiors		
Jose et al. 1996	Indian montane tropical forests/natural grasslands	30 m
Soil organic carbon low in edges relative to interiors		
Jose et al. 1996	Indian montane tropical forests/natural grasslands	30 m
Soil nitrogen low in edges relative to interiors		
Jose et al. 1996	Indian montane tropical forests/natural grasslands	30 m
Soil phosphorus low in edges relative to interiors		
Jose et al. 1996	Indian montane tropical forests/natural grasslands	30 m

1992, Kupfer and Malanson 1993). Species representing these groups occur in both eastern deciduous forests and western conifer forests in the United States (Ranney et al. 1981, Frost 1992, Matlack 1994) and in Indian montane tropical forests (Jose et al. 1996), suggesting that edge-interior differences are often sufficient to support different floras. However, in some cases, only a small amount of, or no interior-restricted flora occurs (Gysel 1951, Ranney et al. 1981, Williams-Linera 1990*b*, Palik and Murphy 1990, Fraver 1994). Edge-restricted or edge-oriented species are often shade-intolerant, while interior-restricted or interior-oriented species are shade tolerant (Table 11.2). Disturbance-adapted species and nonnative or exotic species also appear to favor edges (Table 11.2). In western conifer forests, the interior-oriented species may be the largest group and include obligately mycorrhizal members of the *Ericaceae* and *Orchidaceae,* species dependent on cool, moist environments, and species dependent on old-growth forest conditions (Frost 1992). Plants most vulnerable to edge effects may include these interior-oriented species, species with low growth or reproductive potential, species lacking tolerance to disturbance, and species with poor competitive ability or poor dispersal ability (Frost 1992).

Plant dispersal may be affected by edges. Plants in the edge environment are disproportionately exposed to seed dispersal vectors, such as wind and animals, and thus may dominate the regional seed rain (Ranney et al. 1981). Fleshy fruits along forest edges, relative to interiors, may have a greater probability of dispersal by birds (Thompson and Willson 1978). The presence of edge species means that natural openings in patch interiors may become dominated by vagile edge species, when in large areas of interior forest a different set of species would dominate in natural openings (Ranney et al. 1981; Laurance 1991, 1997; Kupfer et al. 1997).

Depth-of-Edge Influence

The depth-of-edge influence (DEI) is the distance, from the edge of the opening into the forest, over which the edge differs from the forest interior. DEI is typically measured along a transect, but transects have sometimes been too short to reach the true interior, and interiors may not be free of confounding disturbances (Murcia 1995). While DEI has traditionally been measured as a perpendicular response to a linear edge, in reality edge effects extend in from all directions and the DEI is consequently deeper in corners (Malcolm 1994).

Vegetational DEI's generally have been estimated to be 60 m or less for most variables, regardless of location, but geographic variation

Table 11.2. Vegetation trends from forest edges into forest interiors, the reported trend, the type of edge, and the depth-of-edge influence (DEI), where measured. A dash indicates that a transect was not used, so DEI is not available, but comparisons between edge and interior were done.

Trend	Location and edge vegetation	DEI
GROWTH RATE		
Growth rate high in edges relative to interiors		
Young and Mitchell 1994	New Zealand podocarp-broadleaf forests/pasture	—
Williams-Linera 1990*b*	Panama tropical rainforests/shifting cultivation	—
Bierregaard et al. 1992	Amazon tropical rainforests/pastures	25 m
Chen et al. 1992	Oregon & Washington conifer forests/clear-cuts	26–53 m
UNDERSTORY DENSITY (RECRUITMENT)		
Understory tree (saplings, seedlings) density or basal area high in edges relative to interiors		
Brothers 1993	Indiana old-growth forests/cropland	—
Hadley and Savage 1996	Oregon noble fir forests/natural grassland	—
Kupfer and Malanson 1993	Iowa riparian forests/river cutbank	—
Luken et al. 1991	Kentucky deciduous forests/powerline corridor	—
de Casenave et al. 1995	Argentina semi-arid forests/natural grassland	—
Fraver 1994	North Carolina mixed hardwood forests/cropland	10 m
Wales 1972	New Jersey oak-hickory forests/cropland	10–20 m
Ranney et al. 1981	Wisconsin deciduous forests/cropland	10–30 m
Williams-Linera 1990*a*	Panama tropical rainforests/shifting cultivation	20 m
Bierregaard et al. 1992	Amazon tropical rainforests/pastures	25 m
Vaillancourt 1995	Wyoming subalpine forests/clear-cuts	30–50 m
Frost 1992	California old-growth conifer forests/clear-cuts	60 m
Chen et al. 1992	Oregon & Washington conifer forests/clear-cuts	16–137 m
Understory tree (saplings, seedlings) density or basal area low in edges relative to interiors		
Young and Mitchell 1994	New Zealand podocarp-broadleaf forests/pasture	—
Turton and Freiberger 1997	Australian tropical rainforests/pastures	30 m
Chen et al. 1992	Oregon & Washington conifer forests/clear-cuts	62–81 m
Understory tree (saplings, seedlings) density no different in edges and interiors		
Palik and Murphy 1990	Michigan deciduous forests/cropland	5–45 m
UNDERSTORY COVER		
Understory foliage thickness or leaf area high in edges relative to interiors		
de Casenave et al. 1995	Argentina semi-arid forest/natural grassland	—
Camargo and Kapos 1995	Amazon rainforests/pastures	—
Miller and Lin 1985	Connecticut red maple forests/cropland	15 m
Malcolm 1994	Amazon rainforests/pastures	35 m
Understory shrub cover high in edges relative to interiors		
de Casenave et al. 1995	Argentina semi-arid forests/natural grassland	—
Matlack 1993*a*	Pennsylvania/Delaware old forests/cropland	0–40 m
Frost 1992	California old-growth conifer forests/clear-cuts	60 m
Understory ground cover low in edges relative to interiors		
Frost 1992	California old-growth conifer forests/clear-cuts	60 m

Continued on next page

Table 11.2—*Continued*

Trend	Location and edge vegetation	DEI
DENSITY OR BASAL AREA OF CANOPY TREES		
Canopy tree density or basal area high in edges relative to interiors		
Kupfer and Malanson 1993	Iowa riparian forests/river cutbank	—
Luken et al. 1991	Kentucky deciduous forests/powerline corridor	—
Young and Mitchell 1994	New Zealand podocarp-broadleaf forests/pasture	—
Ranney et al. 1981	Wisconsin deciduous forests/cropland	15 m
Palik and Murphy 1990	Michigan deciduous forests/cropland	5–20 m
Wales 1972	New Jersey oak-hickory forests/cropland	10–20 m
Burke and Nol 1998	Ontario deciduous forests/abandoned fields	20 m
Canopy tree density or basal area low in edges relative to interiors		
de Casenave et al. 1995	Argentina semi-arid forests/natural grassland	—
Viana et al. 1997	Brazil Atlantic tropical forests/cropland	—
Burke and Nol 1998	Ontario deciduous forests/abandoned fields	10 m
Vaillancourt 1995	Wyoming subalpine forests/clear-cuts	30–50 m
Chen et al. 1992	Oregon & Washington conifer forests/clear-cuts	43–85 m
COVER OF CANOPY TREES		
Canopy tree cover low in edges relative to interiors		
Laurance 1991, 1997	Australian tropical rainforests/pastures	—
Williams-Linera 1990*a,b*	Panama tropical rainforests/shifting cultivation	—
Camargo and Kapos 1995	Amazon rainforests/pastures	—
Chen et al. 1992	Oregon & Washington conifer forests/clear-cuts	44 m
Vaillancourt 1995	Wyoming subalpine forests/clear-cuts	30–50 m
Frost 1992	California old-growth conifer forests/clear-cuts	60 m
Canopy tree cover high in edges relative to interiors		
Turton and Freiberger 1997	Australian tropical rainforests/pastures	—
Overstory foliage thickness low in edges relative to interiors		
Malcolm 1994	Amazon rainforests/pastures	60 m
MORTALITY		
Tree mortality (blowdown and other causes) high in edges relative to interiors		
Lovejoy et al. 1986	Amazon tropical rainforests/pastures	—
Williams-Linera 1990*a*	Panama tropical rainforests/shifting cultivation	—
Viana et al. 1997	Brazil Atlantic tropical forests/cropland	—
Hadley and Savage 1996	Oregon noble fir forests/natural grassland	—
Vaillancourt 1995	Wyoming subalpine forests/clear-cuts	20–30 m
Young and Mitchell 1994	New Zealand podocarp-broadleaf forests/pasture	30–50 m
Esseen 1994	Swedish boreal forests/clear-cuts	>56 m
Gratkowski 1956	Oregon conifer forests/clear-cuts	<60 m
Frost 1992	California old-growth conifer forests/clear-cuts	60 m
Bierregaard et al. 1992	Amazon tropical rainforests/pastures	60 m
Ferreira and Laurance 1997	Amazon rainforests/pastures	100 m
Laurance et al. 1997	Amazon rainforests/pastures	100 m
Chen et al. 1992	Oregon & Washington conifer forests/clear-cuts	56–125 m
Kapos et al. 1997	Amazon tropical rainforests/pastures	200 m
Laurance 1991	Australian tropical rainforests/pastures	200–500 m

Continued on next page

Table 11.2—*Continued*

Trend	Location and edge vegetation	DEI
SPECIES FAVORED BY EDGES OR INTERIORS		
Forest edge tree species (often shade-intolerant species) high in edges relative to interiors		
Whitney and Runkle 1981	Ohio old-growth forests/cropland	—
Kupfer and Malanson 1993	Iowa riparian forests/river cutbank	—
Luken et al. 1991	Kentucky deciduous forests/powerline corridor	—
Young and Mitchell 1994	New Zealand podocarp-broadleaf forests/pasture	—
Kupfer 1996	Ohio old-growth forests/roads	—
Chen et al. 1992	Oregon & Washington conifer forests/clear-cuts	—
MacDougall and Kellman 1992	Belize riparian forests/savanna	10 m
Palik and Murphy 1990	Michigan deciduous forests/cropland	5–20 m
Wales 1972	New Jersey oak-hickory forests/cropland	10–20 m
Ranney et al. 1981	Wisconsin deciduous forests/cropland	10–30 m
Frost 1992	California old-growth conifer forests/clear-cuts	60 m
Forest interior tree species (often shade-tolerant species) low in edges relative to interiors		
Whitney and Runkle 1981	Ohio old-growth forests/cropland	—
Young and Mitchell 1994	New Zealand podocarp-broadleaf forests/pasture	—
Kupfer 1996	Ohio old-growth forests/roads	—
Chen et al. 1992	Oregon & Washington conifer forests/clear-cuts	—
Fox et al. 1997	Australian temperate rainforests/pasture	5 m
Palik and Murphy 1990	Michigan deciduous forests/cropland	5–20 m
MacDougall and Kellman 1992	Belize riparian forests/savanna	10 m
Ranney et al. 1981	Wisconsin deciduous forests/cropland	10–30 m
Frost 1992	California old-growth conifer forests/clear-cuts	60 m
Species composition (not just trees) or life forms change from edge to interior		
Kupfer 1996	Ohio old-growth forests/roads	—
Kupfer and Malanson 1993	Iowa riparian forests/river cutbank	—
de Casenave et al. 1995	Argentina semi-arid forests/natural grassland	—
Palik and Murphy 1990	Michigan deciduous forests/cropland	5–20 m
Wales 1972	New Jersey oak-hickory forests/cropland	10–20 m
Ranney et al. 1981	Wisconsin deciduous forests/cropland	10–30 m
Burke and Nol 1998	Ontario deciduous forests/abandoned fields	25–35 m
Jose et al. 1996	Indian montane tropical forests/natural grasslands	30 m
Matlack 1994	Pennsylvania/Delaware old forests/cropland	<40 m
Frost 1992	California old-growth conifer forests/clear-cuts	60 m
Fraver 1994	North Carolina mixed hardwood forests/cropland	60 m
Disturbance-adapted tree species high in edges relative to interiors		
de Casenave et al. 1995	Argentina semi-arid forest/natural grassland	—
Williams-Linera 1990*a*	Panama tropical rainforests/shifting cultivation	20 m
Laurance 1991, 1997	Australian tropical rainforests/pastures	200 m
Mycorrhizal-dependent species low in edges relative to interiors		
Frost 1992	California old-growth conifer forests/clear-cuts	60 m
Exotic species high in edges relative to interiors		
Fox et al. 1997	Australian temperate rainforests/pasture	5 m
Luken and Goessling 1995	Kentucky mixed hardword forests/cropland	6 m
Burke and Nol 1998	Ontario deciduous forests/abandoned fields	10 m
Brothers and Spingarn 1992	Indiana old-growth forests/cropland	20–50 m
Fraver 1994	North Carolina mixed hardwood forests/cropland	10–60 m

Continued on next page

Table 11.2—*Continued*

Trend	Location and edge vegetation	DEI
DIVERSITY		
Total species richness high in edges relative to interiors		
de Casenave et al. 1995	Argentina semi-arid forests/natural grassland	—
Frost 1992	California old-growth conifer forests/clear-cuts	30 m
Fraver 1994	North Carolina mixed hardwood forests/cropland	20–40 m
Total species richness low in edges relative to interiors		
Fox et al. 1997	Australian temperate rainforests/pasture	—
Total species richness no different in edges and interiors		
Matlack 1994	Pennsylvania/Delaware old forests/cropland	<40 m
Tree species richness high in edges relative to interiors		
Brothers 1993	Indiana old-growth forests/cropland	—
Ranney et al. 1981	Wisconsin deciduous forests/cropland	10–30 m
Understory species richness low in edges relative to interiors		
Frost 1992	California old-growth conifer forests/clear-cuts	60 m
Understory species richness high in edges relative to interiors		
Kupfer and Malanson 1993	Iowa riparian forests/river cutbank	—
Ranney et al. 1981	Wisconsin deciduous forests/cropland	10–30 m

in demographic responses leads to variation in DEIs (Table 11.2). DEIs tend to be lowest in eastern U.S. forests, intermediate in tropical forests, and greatest in the mountainous western United States, when data are available for a particular variable at all three places (e.g., understory tree density; Table 11.2). The deepest DEIs for increased understory density, lowered canopy tree cover, increased mortality, and species favored by edges or interiors are predominantly in the mountainous western United States (Chen et al. 1992, Frost 1992, Vaillancourt 1995). An exception to this trend is the deep DEI for elevated tree mortality in tropical rainforests, which may extend to 200 m or more, in part because of damage from tropical cyclones (Laurance 1991, Kapos et al. 1997).

Microenvironmental DEIs generally are also 60 m or less, but often are shorter than vegetational DEIs and can be much longer (Table 11.1). Several variables extend as far as 240 m in temperate forests of the U.S. Pacific Northwest (Chen et al. 1995). Many microenvironmental DEIs have large ranges, as they vary between aspects, time of day, season, and age of the edge. The trend along the gradient from edge to interior is often unimodal, gradually increasing or decreasing with distance. However, the trend may also be bimodal or have other forms, because vegetational responses in the immediate edge area may produce microenvironmental shadows and other complex effects

(Murcia 1995, Camargo and Kapos 1995). Geographical trends in microenvironmental DEI may be similar to vegetational trends, but are less consistent (Table 11.1).

Sun-facing edges often, but not always (Brothers and Spingarn 1992, Kupfer 1996), have the deepest DEI (Wales 1972; Ranney et al. 1981; Palik and Murphy 1990; Brothers and Spingarn 1992; Matlack 1993*a*, 1994; Fraver 1994; Young and Mitchell 1994; Chen et al. 1995). Microclimate effects may be greatest on southwest-facing edges and least at northeast-facing edges in the north temperate zone (Chen et al. 1995). Aspect effects on edges from microclimate are slight in the tropics (Ferreira and Laurance 1997), except some distance from the equator, where east- and west-facing edges, penetrated more deeply by low sun angles, may have higher seedling or tree densities (Turton and Freiburger 1997, Viana et al. 1997).

Modifying Effects: Disturbance, Matrix, Higher-Order Interactions, and Lags

Natural disturbances may be increased or altered in edge environments relative to interiors, and may significantly affect the DEI. Edges may have elevated rates of treefall gap formation (Bierregaard et al. 1992, Hadley and Savage 1996, Camargo and Kapos 1995, Kapos et al. 1997). Edges that face the wind typically have higher blowdown rates (Esseen 1994, Vaillancourt 1995, Laurance 1991, 1997). Elevated treefalls and blowdown may extend as far as 500 m into tropical rainforests prone to cyclones (Laurance 1991), with the most striking increase in elevated gap areas extending 200 m into rainforests in Australia and Brazil (Laurance 1991, Kapos et al. 1997). Blowdown can extend to over 350 m from an edge in temperate forests subject to strong cyclones (Gratkowski 1956). Edges may promote increased defoliation during insect outbreaks (Kouki et al. 1997).

Disturbance by human activities (e.g., trampling, grazing, woodcutting) in the edge zone may affect the edge vegetation. Cattle grazing rainforest edges from adjoining pastures may open the canopy, lower species richness, and lead to increased weedy and early successional species, effectively increasing the DEI (Williams-Linera 1990*a*, Fox et al. 1997). Cattle grazing may also delay the development of edge-interior differentiation during succession of young stands (Palik and Murphy 1990). In deciduous forest patches in a suburban setting in Delaware, 14 major categories of human disturbances (e.g., dumps, campsites, building rubble) were found, and 95% of disturbances occurred within 82 m of the forest edge (Matlack 1993*b*). Proximity of a road increased this distance (Matlack 1993*b*). Human impacts in these suburban forest edges have more significant effects than does the altered microclimate of the edge (Matlack 1993*b*). Human disturbances may increase local diversity in fragments, but, by increasing the DEI, regional diversity may decline as interior-forest species have difficulty regenerating (Levenson 1981, Hoehne 1981).

The composition of the adjacent opening and natural disturbances occurring in it may also affect the edge environment. In a floodplain opening abutting a forest, diversity may be high because of the many microenvironments produced by disturbance, and disturbances may prevent the forest edge from increasing in basal area as typically occurs adjoining more stable openings (Kupfer and Malanson 1993). Fires burning into tropical gallery forests from adjoining savannas may benefit some trees by providing unique microsites for regeneration, but these fires do not appear likely to eliminate other trees (Kellman et al. 1996).

The size of the opening and human activities occurring in it may affect the edge environment as well. Road edges, for example, may be very different from clear-cut or field edges. Because roads are maintained openings susceptible to constant external influence (e.g., automobile traffic), they may experience higher levels of human disturbances. Also, the width of a road may affect the composition of edge vegetation (Kupfer 1996). The opening can be a source of propagules, and the management of the opening determines the potential propagule pool (Janzen 1983). When the forest edge adjoins a road, the potential propagule pool, often containing exotics, may be transported along the length of the edge by automobiles (Schmidt 1989). Both road and trail corridors in the Rocky Mountains have been shown to have increased abundance of exotic plant species (Benninger-Traux et al. 1992, Tyser and Worley 1992). However, exotic species are not correlated with trails and natural disturbances (e.g., tree falls) in Indiana old-growth forests, in part because these disturbances do not increase light levels appreciably (Brothers and Spingarn 1992). When fire is used to clear an opening in the tropics, its intensity affects the subsequent diversity of butterflies in fragments (Bierregaard et al. 1992) and is likely to also affect the subsequent pool of plant propagules that may invade the fragment. Disturbances (e.g., wind) from the opening may increase canopy gap density, and propagules from the opening may be able to dominate in these gaps, eventually transforming the canopy in some settings (Janzen 1983). Fragments also experience an altered natural disturbance regime because disturbances that originated outside the area of the fragment when it was part of continuous forest no longer spread into the fragment area (Baker 1989).

Secondary interactions or "ripple effects" can have significant long-term effects that may not appear as rapidly as direct demographic effects, such as enhanced tree mortality, due to altered microclimatic changes. Secondary interactions include direct effects on herbivores, predators, pollinators, or other animals that then secondarily affect plants (e.g., Aizen and Feinsinger 1994). However, third or higher-order effects may occur as a rippling sequence (Janzen 1983). For example, herbivores, such as deer, that are attracted to edges of openings, may significantly alter the survival of seedlings of canopy trees, eventually affecting the composition of the forest as far as 8 km into the forest (Alverson et al. 1988). If fragmentation favors seed predators, such as woodland mice, over seed dispersers, such as birds, then bird-dispersed plants may suffer reduced dispersal and ultimately decline (Santos and Telleria 1994). In contrast, small woodlots in Wisconsin have experienced a decline in wind-dispersed plants, and are now dominated by bird-dispersed species and species depending on vegetative reproduction (Hoehne 1981). In other cases, edges may also favor some seed dispersers, such as squirrels, who may increase the natality of certain trees in edges (Sork 1983). Competitive interactions may intensify in small fragments, leading to different outcomes than in continuous forest interiors (Laurance 1997). Positive feedbacks may also occur: proliferation of light-loving lianas near tropical forest edges may increase susceptibility to wind damage, further opening the canopy, favoring more lianas (Laurance 1991).

These higher-order effects may require decades or centuries to play out fully. Many plants differ from animals in that they may live for decades or hundreds of years and can persist vegetatively for long periods (Kellman et al. 1996). As a consequence, demographic adjustments to edge creation may be very slow, and may require the passage of several generations of long-lived trees, which could take centuries (Kellman et al. 1996). Moreover, some indirect responses or ripple effects may not follow until after these initial direct responses of dominant trees, prolonging the time required for adjustment.

EFFECTS OF EDGES ON ROCKY MOUNTAIN VEGETATION

Only a few studies have been done on the effects of edges on vegetation in mountainous forests of the western United States, and, while these studies hint at common processes and responses, much remains unstudied. The DEI for many vegetational and microenvironmental variables is greater in these forests than in most other forests studied to date throughout the world (Tables 11.1 and 11.2). This large DEI could arise because the edges studied in western forests by Chen et al. (1992), Frost (1992), and Vaillancourt (1995) were only 10–26 years old, younger than many edges studied in other forests. DEI has been shown to diminish with age at a single site in forests of the eastern United States (Ranney et al. 1981, Matlack 1994), with edge closure estimated to occur between 10 and 30 years. However, edges of this age do appear to have a smaller DEI in eastern forests (e.g., Matlack 1994) than western edges of similar age. Another possible explanation for the large DEI in western forests is that the trees are taller, allowing the altered microenvironment to penetrate deeper (J. Chen, *personal communication*). However, montane forests in the Rocky Mountains with comparatively large DEI are not exceptionally tall.

The comparatively large DEI in western forests may also reflect the rates of recruitment, growth, and mortality in response to edge creation, combined with the characteristics of the flora. The dominance of tree mortality over growth and recruitment is reflected in the lack of closure of western forest edges after 10–15 years (Chen et al. 1992). In both eastern U.S. and tropical forests, a tree and shrub flora occurs that rapidly responds to treefall gaps and also does well in edge environments (Wales 1972, Janzen 1983, Matlack 1994). While treefalls occur in western forests, no such distinct flora occurs with high dispersal capability and rapid growth (Veblen 1986, Spies et al. 1990). Instead, trees responding positively to edges represent comparatively slow-growing, shade-intolerant conifers or deciduous trees capable of vegetative sprouting (Frost 1992, Vaillancourt 1995). The absence of a pre-adapted flora to rapidly close the edge may reflect the long-standing dominance of large natural disturbances, as opposed to treefall gaps, in western forests, and the tendency for disturbances to be revegetated from surviving above-ground or under-ground vegetative structures (Doyle et al., 1998). A significant response to initial opening of the edge is a flush of understory shrub growth and accelerated growth of established understory trees (Frost 1992, Chen et al. 1992). The large DEI in Western forests may also, in part, be due to ongoing disturbance in the edge environment by management activities, which slows down the vegetation recovery process (J. Chen, *personal communication*).

Only a few modifying effects on Rocky Mountain forest edges are known, largely because of insufficient research. Increased blowdown rates extend 20–30 m into subalpine forests adjacent to clear-cuts, particularly on edges facing prevailing winds (Vaillancourt 1995). Blowdown is greater on moderate to steep slopes, on topographic saddles, and where winds are accelerated by gaps or narrow valleys upwind (Alexander 1964). Almost nothing is known about whether edges experience increased human disturbances or exotic species invasion (but see following section). While it is logical to expect that characteristics of the opening (e.g., road versus clear-cut) will affect the response of plants to the edge, almost nothing is known about this in the West (but also see the following section). Finally, no studies have been done on potential higher-order effects and time lags.

EFFECTS OF ROAD EDGES ON ROCKY MOUNTAIN VEGETATION

Roads are the most significant contributors to the present fragmentation syndrome in Rocky Mountain forests (Reed et al. 1996; Baker and Knight, *this volume*), yet road edges in the Rocky Mountains and elsewhere remain largely unstudied. Consequently, no estimates have been made of DEI for road edges in the Rocky Mountains. While such data do exist for clear-cut edges (Vaillancourt 1995), processes leading to edge effects along roads may differ. We are studying the effects of road edges on vegetation in Rocky Mountain coniferous forests, and we present initial results here.

The primary objective of the study is to estimate mean DEI for vegetation in road edges in subalpine forests dominated by lodgepole pine, subalpine fir, and Engelmann spruce. We hypothesized that the abundance of exotic species, and their invasion into adjacent forests, may be higher at road edges because of the potential for seed dispersal along roads. Also, because roads are narrow, linear openings, we hypothesized that the DEI would be shorter and less pronounced than in clear-cut edges.

During July and August of 1997, 11 sites adjacent to forest roads on the Medicine Bow–Routt National Forest of southeastern Wyoming and the Arapaho-Roosevelt National Forest in northern Colorado were sampled. Sites were restricted to where a road was constructed through mature forest (i.e., forests never subjected to timber harvest or other management activities). Also, each site had to meet certain criteria (e.g., be more than 100 m from clear-cuts, other roads and riparian areas, and have a slope <20 degrees) to minimize confounding variables. At each site, trees (>5 cm dbh) were counted, by species and 5-cm dbh size-class, in 5 m x 100 m belt transects parallel to the road and located at the forest edge and 10, 20, 30, 40, 60, 80, 100, and 120 m in from the forest edge. Percent cover of all understory trees (<5 cm dbh) and other species of vascular plants were also estimated in twenty-five 1 m x 2 m quadrats nested inside each of the belt transects, as well as at the edge of the road surface (the road ditch). This sampling design was intended to characterize the growth and abundance of canopy trees, seedlings and saplings, and individual understory species along the edge-to-interior gradient. The design also allowed for the identification of changes in overall species composition and presence of exotic species with distance from the edge.

Initial results suggest that vegetation does respond differently to road edges than to clear-cut edges in the same area. Canopy trees, for example, appear to have very little consistent response to road edges. Regardless of species, stem density, basal area, and mean dbh do not consistently increase or decrease along the edge-to-interior gradient. Several possible reasons for this are hypothesized. First, the road edges sampled appear to be lacking the trend found by Vaillancourt (1995) of increased mortality close to the edge. Because roads are narrow, linear openings (mean opening width = 13.5 m; n = 11), as opposed to wider clear-cut openings, wind may lack the fetch necessary to cause blowdown mortality. Second, the persistence of frequent disturbances such as roadside harvesting may prevent the establishment of consistent edge-to-interior trends. Lastly, the relatively slow-growing canopy dominants may simply require one or more generations to respond to edge creation. Supporting this, the only two sites that have edges greater than 50 years old are also the only sites at which any edge-to-interior trends are apparent. These responses remain unclear, however, as the trends at these two sites are exactly opposite.

If canopy trees are simply slow to respond, one might expect to see earlier responses in the recruitment of seedlings and saplings in the understory. Lodgepole pine recruitment exhibited the clearest trends. Seedlings and saplings appear to have their highest frequencies at the road ditch and forest edge when lodgepole pine is the dominant canopy or understory tree (Fig. 11.2a). In addition, at sites where subalpine fir is the dominant tree species, recruitment of lodgepole pine has a distinct peak at the forest edge (Fig. 11.2b). Both patterns are consistent with the concept that lodgepole pine is generally shade-intolerant and would thrive in areas of increased sunlight. Subalpine fir also shows a consistent pattern at sites where it is the dominant understory tree, despite the composition of the canopy. In these cases, subalpine fir frequencies are at their lowest at the ditch, peak at approximately 10 m from the edge and fluctuate around a mean value past 20 m (Fig. 11.2c). This pattern suggests that at sites where subalpine fir is al-

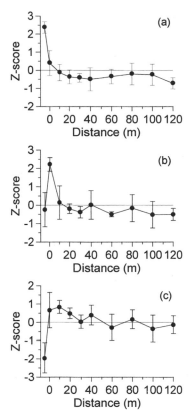

Fig. 11.2. Standardized score (z-score), from the mean understory frequency at each site averaged between sites, versus distance from the forest edge for: (a) lodgepole pine where it is the dominant species (n = 5), (b) lodgepole pine where subalpine fir is dominant (n = 4), and (c) subalpine fir where it is the understory dominant (n = 6). Error bars represent +/− 1 standard deviation from the between-site mean.

ready successful in the understory because of its shade-tolerance, it is able to take advantage of increased resources (i.e., sunlight) near the edge, but cannot thrive at the road surface because the sunlight is too intense. Frequent disturbances may further inhibit the establishment of subalpine fir seedlings at the ditch. Engelmann spruce, although commonly present in the understory, has no consistent patterns along the gradient. Overall, the pattern of increased recruitment near the edge is consistent with that found by Vaillancourt (1995) at clear-cut edges (Table 11.2), indicating that both clear-cut and road edges in Rocky Mountain forests could possibly seal, given enough time (i.e., at least one full generation).

Table 11.3. Abbreviated list of edge-restricted plant species. Species listed were found only in quadrats at the road ditch and forest edge. The total number of sites sampled was 11.

Species	# Sites	Native	Seeded
Rough bentgrass	8	Yes	No
Western pearlyeverlasting	2	Yes	No
Drummond's rockcress	5	Yes	No
Smooth brome	3	No	No
Thistle	2	No	No
Orchardgrass	3	No	Yes
Blue wildrye	2	Yes	Yes
Spreading groundsmoke	3	Yes	No
Drummond's rush	2	Yes	No
Alpine timothy	5	Yes	No
Timothy	6	No	Yes
Annual bluegrass	3	Yes	No
Canada bluegrass	3	No	No
Kentucky bluegrass	4	No	No
Red sandspurry	10	No	No
Alsike clover	2	No	Yes
White clover	3	No	No

Patterns of understory species composition are not fully analyzed. Many sites are strongly dominated by grouse whortleberry throughout the gradient, with many other species occurring sporadically and in much lower abundance. Therefore, if responses to the road edge are present, they may be difficult to detect in most species. One pronounced response, however, found at almost all sites is the differentiation of the flora at the road ditch and forest edge from that of the forest understory. As expected, many species, including exotics, that are not typical of the forest understory have established at the road ditch and forest edge (Table 11.3). Some of these have been seeded for erosion control, while others are disturbance-adapted species that were either present in the regional seed bank or introduced after road construction (Table 11.3). These species could be referred to as edge-restricted, as they were not found at any locations deeper than the forest edge.

Contrary to our hypothesis, no widespread invasion of exotics occurred from roads into the forest understory. While one exotic (common dandelion) was occasionally present, but not abundant, toward the interior, most were consistently edge-restricted. Most likely, the failure of these species to invade the forest understory is due to the relatively undisturbed soil and dominance of grouse whortleberry past the edge. However, because exotic species are common near the edge, any disturbance to the canopy, groundcover, or soil that would create conditions like those at the edge could increase their abundance.

Overall, initial analyses suggest that the DEI of road edges is smaller than that at clear-cut edges. Vaillancourt (1995) found increased understory tree density and decreased canopy tree density up to 30–50 m from clear-cut edges (Table 11.2). In contrast, increased recruitment of understory trees appears restricted to <20 m from a road edge, with no apparent trends in canopy density. Also, exotic species invasion, a potentially detrimental effect of road edges, appears to be primarily limited to the road ditch and forest edge. However, these data indicate only vegetation trends in response to road edges. Data on microenvironmental trends (e.g., Saunders et al., 1998), as well as pollution effects (e.g., Angold 1997) and human disturbances (e.g., Matlack 1993*b*) may be necessary to more accurately estimate the extent of the road edge environment.

MANAGEMENT AND CONSERVATION

The presence of an edge zone in fragments means that fragments below some minimum size are essentially entirely edge, lacking interior. This minimum size appears in some cases to be 2–4 ha, based on species concerns (Levenson 1981, Ranney et al. 1981, Matlack 1994), but perhaps 5–10 ha or more in cool- or cold-temperate settings, based on disturbances and measured DEIs (Chen et al. 1992, Esseen 1994). However, for certain important microenvironmental parameters, such as wind speed, fragments less than 64 ha in area are effectively all edge (Chen et al. 1995). Even large patches have significant edge area. Patches of 1,000 ha would have 22–42% of their total area influenced by edge effects, depending on patch shape, while patches of 500 ha would have 30–58% of their area affected by edge, assuming a 100-m DEI (Ferreira and Laurance 1997). In Australian tropical forests, isolated reserves less than 350–650 ha in area are likely to lose interior-forest species because of a disturbance-induced DEI of 200 m (Laurance 1991). In two central Rocky Mountain forests, roads alone have reduced mean patch sizes to 4.3–4.5 ha (Baker and Knight, *this volume*), sizes that are, on average, 100% edge for a DEI of 120 m, 75% edge for a DEI of 60 m, and 30% edge for a DEI of 20 m.

What are the best land uses adjacent to a fragment if the goal is to minimize edge effects? Placing tree plantations next to harvested forest edges may decrease the microenvironmental edge effect (Bierregaard et al. 1992). In the tropics, seeds are predominantly animal-dispersed, and edge effects include elevated treefall gaps that can be invaded by seeds from the adjoining openings (Janzen 1983). Fragment edges may seal within a few years, diminishing the DEI (Williams-Linera 1990*a*). In this case, the best adjoining use may be cropland, since the propagule pool will be diminished (Janzen 1983). In temperate forests, the edge may take decades to seal and a greater abundance of wind-dispersed seeds diminishes the spread, relative to animal-dispersed seeds, of species from openings. In this case, perhaps sealing the edge is more important than worrying about the propagule pool, so the best adjacent use may be secondary succession or a tree plantation, rather than low cropland. Roads may be best placed inside the successional area or a tree plantation and away from the forest edge, so that their propagule pool is transported into successional vegetation, rather than into old forest.

Several aspects of timber harvest and road design may be used to minimize the edge effect. First, concentrating harvest areas, rather than dispersing them, would decrease the amount of edge created. Disturbance effects could be minimized by not placing clear-cuts, or other harvest units that produce high-contrast edge, in areas at high risk for blowdown (Alexander 1964). When feasible, native trees could also be planted near edges to accelerate sealing of the edge. Use of harvest methods that do not create high-contrast edges may also minimize microclimate effects. To decrease the effects of roads on adjoining forest, roads should be made as narrow as possible and avoid going through patches of old forest. In addition, seed mixes used in the ditch and bank areas should include only native species, and human-caused disturbances (livestock grazing, motorized vehicle use, wood-cutting) should be kept to a minimum along roads. Whenever possible, roads should be obliterated once their purpose is fulfilled, and the regeneration of native understory species in the former road encouraged.

Research Needs

Many basic questions about Rocky Mountain forest edges remain unanswered. How rapidly do edges seal, and does this vary with the type of opening (e.g., road, clear-cut)? How does variation in natality, growth, and mortality with environment (e.g., slope, aspect) affect the pattern of response of edge vegetation? Are secondary processes, such as competition and succession, modified in the edge? How important are higher-order effects? How do natural edges differ from those created by human activities? We are turning much of our forest into edge before we have the answers to these questions.

ACKNOWLEDGMENTS

We appreciate peer reviews by John Kupfer and Jiquan Chen.

LITERATURE CITED

Aizen, M. A., and P. Feinsinger. 1994. Forest fragmentation, pollination, and plant reproduction in a Chaco dry forest, Argentina. *Ecology* 75: 330–351.

Alexander, R. R. 1964. Minimizing windfall around clear cuttings in spruce-fir forests. *Forest Science* 10: 131–142.

Alverson, W. S., D. M. Waller, and S. L. Solheim. 1988. Forests too deer: edge effects in northern Wisconsin. *Conservation Biology* 2: 348–358.

Angold, P. G. 1997. The impact of a road upon adjacent heathland vegetation: effects on plant species composition. *Journal of Applied Ecology* 34: 409–417.

Baker, W. L. 1989. Landscape ecology and nature reserve design in the Boundary Waters Canoe Area, Minnesota. *Ecology* 70: 23–35.

Benninger-Traux, M., J. L. Vankat, and R. L. Schaefer. 1992. Trail corridors as habitat and conduits for movement of plant species in Rocky Mountain National Park, Colorado, USA. *Landscape Ecology* 6: 269–278.

Bierregaard, R. O., Jr., T. E. Lovejoy, V. Kapos, A. Augusto dos Santos, and R. W. Hutchings. 1992. The biological dynamics of tropical rainforest fragments: a prospective comparison of fragments and continuous forest. *BioScience* 42: 859–866.

Brothers, T. S. 1993. Fragmentation and edge effects in central Indiana old-growth forests. *Natural Areas Journal* 13: 268–275.

Brothers, T. S., and A. Spingarn. 1992. Forest fragmentation and alien plant invasion of central Indiana old-growth forests. *Conservation Biology* 6: 91–100.

Burke, D. M., and E. Nol. 1998. Edge and fragment size effects on the vegetation of deciduous forests in Ontario, Canada. *Natural Areas Journal* 18: 45–53.

Cadenasso, M. L., M. M. Traynor, and S.T.A. Pickett. 1997. Functional location of forest edges: gradients of multiple physical factors. *Canadian Journal of Forest Research* 27: 774–782.

Camargo, J.L.C., and V. Kapos. 1995. Complex edge effects on soil moisture and microclimate in central Amazonian forest. *Journal of Tropical Ecology* 11: 205–221.

Chen, J., J. F. Franklin, and T. A. Spies. 1992. Vegetation responses to edge environments in old-growth Douglas-fir forests. *Ecological Applications* 2: 387–396.

Chen, J., J. F. Franklin, and T. A. Spies. 1993. Contrasting microclimates among clear-cut, edge, and interior of old-growth Douglas-fir forest. *Agricultural and Forest Meteorology* 63: 219–237.

Chen, J., J. F. Franklin, and T. A. Spies. 1995. Growing-season microclimatic gradients from clear-cut edges into old-growth Douglas-fir forests. *Ecological Applications* 5: 74–86.

de Casenave, J. L., J. P. Pelotto, and J. Protomastro. 1995. Edge-interior differences in vegetation structure and composition in a Chaco semi-arid forest, Argentina. *Forest Ecology and Management* 72: 61–69.

Doyle, K. M., D. H. Knight, D. L. Taylor, W.J. Barmore, and J. M. Benedict.1998. Seventeen years of forest succession following the Waterfalls Canyon Fire in Grand Teton National Park, Wyoming. *International Journal of Wildland Fire* 8: 45–55.

Esseen, P.-A. 1994. Tree mortality patterns after experimental fragmentation of an old-growth conifer forest. *Biological Conservation* 68: 19–28.

Ferreira, L. V., and W. F. Laurance. 1997. Effects of forest fragmentation on mortality and damage of selected trees in central Amazonia. *Conservation Biology* 11: 797–801.

Fox, B.J., J.E. Taylor, M.D. Fox, and C. Williams. 1997. Vegetation changes across edges of rainforest remnants. *Biological Conservation* 82: 1–13.

Fraver, S. 1994. Vegetation responses along edge-to-interior gradients in the mixed hardwood forests of the Roanoke River Basin, North Carolina. *Conservation Biology* 8: 822–832.

Frost, E. J. 1992. The effects of forest-clear-cut edges on the structure and composition of old-growth mixed conifer stands in the western Klamath mountains. Master's thesis. Humboldt State University, Arcata, California, USA.

Gratkowski, H. J. 1956. Windthrow around staggered settings in old-growth Douglas-fir. *Forest Science* 2: 60–74.

Gysel, L. W. 1951. Borders and openings of beech-maple woodlands in southern Michigan. *Journal of Forestry* 49: 13–19.

Hadley, K. S., and M. Savage. 1996. Wind disturbance and development of a near-edge forest interior, Mary's Peak, Oregon Coast Range. *Physical Geography* 17: 47–61.

Hoehne, L. M. 1981. The groundlayer vegetation of forest islands in an urban-suburban matrix. Pages 41–54 *in* R. L. Burgess and D. M. Sharpe, editors. *Ecological studies, Vol. 41: Forest island dynamics in man-dominated landscapes.* Springer-Verlag, New York, New York, USA.

Janzen, D. H. 1983. No park is an island: increase in interference from outside as park size decreases. *Oikos* 41: 402–410.

Jose, S., A. R. Gillespie, S. J. George, and B. M. Kumar. 1996. Vegetation responses along edge-to-interior gradients in a high altitude tropical forest in peninsular India. *Forest Ecology and Management* 87: 51–62.

Kapos, V. 1989. Effects of isolation on the water status of forest patches in the Brazilian Amazon. *Journal of Tropical Ecology* 5: 173–185.

Kapos, V., E. Wandelli, J. L. Camargo, and G. Ganade. 1997. Edge-related changes in environment and plant responses due to forest fragmentation in central Amazonia. Pages 33–44 *in* W. F. Laurance and R. O. Bierregaard, Jr., editors. *Tropical forest remnants: ecology, management, and conservation of fragmented communities.* The University of Chicago Press, Chicago, Illinois, USA.

Kellman, M., R. Tackaberry, and J. Meave. 1996. The consequences of prolonged fragmentation: lessons from tropical gallery forests. Pages 37–58 *in* J. Schelhas and R. Greenberg, editors. *Forest patches in tropical landscapes.* Island Press, Washington, D.C., USA.

Kouki, J., D. G. McCullough, and L. D. Marshall. 1997. Effect of forest stand and edge characteristics on the vulnerability of jack pine stands to jack pine budworm (*Choristoneura pinus pinus*) damage. *Canadian Journal of Forest Research* 27: 1765–1772.

Kupfer, J. 1996. Patterns and determinants of edge vegetation of a midwestern forest preserve. *Physical Geography* 17: 62–76.

Kupfer, J. A., and G. P. Malanson. 1993. Structure and composition of a riparian forest edge. *Physical Geography* 14: 154–170.

Kupfer, J. A., G. P. Malanson, and J. R. Runkle. 1997. Factors influencing species composition in canopy gaps: the importance of edge proximity in Hueston Woods, Ohio. *The Professional Geographer* 49: 165–178.

Laurance, W. F. 1991. Edge effects in tropical forest fragments: application of a model for the design of nature reserves. *Biological Conservation* 57: 205–219.

Laurance, W. F. 1997. Hyper-disturbed parks: edge effects and the ecology of isolated rainforest reserves in tropical Australia. Pages 71–83 *in* W. F. Laurance and R. O. Bierregaard, Jr., editors. *Tropical forest remnants: ecology, management, and conservation of fragmented communities*. The University of Chicago Press, Chicago, Illinois, USA.

Laurance, W. F., S. G. Laurance, L. V. Ferreira, J. M. Rankin-de Merona, C. Gascon, and T. E. Lovejoy. 1997. Biomass collapse in Amazonian forest fragments. *Science* 278: 1117–1118.

Levenson, J. B. 1981. Woodlots as biogeographic islands in southeastern Wisconsin. Pages 13–39 *in* R. L. Burgess and D. M. Sharpe, editors. *Ecological studies, Vol. 41: Forest island dynamics in man-dominated landscapes*. Springer-Verlag, New York, New York, USA.

Lovejoy, T. E., R. O. Bierregaard, Jr., A. B. Rylands, J. R. Malcolm, C. E. Quintela, L. H. Harper, K. S. Brown, Jr., A. H. Powell, G.V.N. Powell, H.O.R. Schubart, and M. B. Hays. 1986. Edge and other effects of isolation on Amazon forest fragments. Pages 257–285 *in* M. E. Soulé, editor. *Conservation Biology*. Sinauer Associates, Sunderland, Massachusetts, USA.

Luken, J. O., and N. Goessling. 1995. Seedling distribution and potential persistence of the exotic shrub *Lonicera maackii* in fragmented forests. *American Midland Naturalist* 133: 124–130.

Luken, J. O., A. C. Hinton, and D. G. Baker. 1991. Forest edges associated with power-line corridors and implications for corridor siting. *Landscape and Urban Planning* 20: 315–324.

MacDougall, A., and M. Kellman. 1992. The understory light regime and patterns of seedlings in tropical riparian forest patches. *Journal of Biogeography* 19: 667–675.

Malcolm, J. R. 1994. Edge effects in central Amazonian forest fragments. *Ecology* 75: 2438–2445.

Matlack, G. R. 1993*a*. Microenvironment variation within and among forest edge sites in the eastern United States. *Biological Conservation* 66: 185–194.

Matlack, G. R. 1993*b*. Sociological edge effects: spatial distribution of human impact in suburban forest fragments. *Environmental Management* 17: 829–835.

Matlack, G. R. 1994. Vegetation dynamics of the forest edge-trends in space and successional time. *Journal of Ecology* 82: 113–123.

Miller, D. R., and J. D. Lin. 1985. Canopy architecture of a red maple edge stand measured by a point drop method. Pages 59–70 *in* B. A. Hutchison and B. B. Hicks, editors. *The forest-atmosphere interaction.* D. Reidel, Dordrecht, The Netherlands.

Murcia, C. 1995. Edge effects in fragmented forests: implications for conservation. *Trends in Ecology and Evolution* 10: 58–62.

Opdam, P., R. van Apeldoorn, A. Schotman, and J. Kalkhoven. 1993. Population responses to landscape fragmentation. Pages 147–171 *in* C. C. Vos and P. Opdam, editors. *Landscape ecology of a stressed environment.* Chapman & Hall, New York, New York, USA.

Palik, B. J., and P. G. Murphy. 1990. Disturbance versus edge effects in sugar-maple/beech forest fragments. *Forest Ecology and Management* 32: 187–202.

Ranney, J. W., M. C. Bruner, and J. B. Levenson. 1981. The importance of edge in the structure and dynamics of forest islands. Pages 67–95 *in* R. L. Burgess and D. M. Sharpe, editors. *Ecological studies, Vol. 41: Forest island dynamics in man-dominated landscapes.* Springer-Verlag, New York, New York, USA.

Raynor, G. S. 1971. Wind and temperature structure in a coniferous forest and a contiguous field. *Forest Science* 17: 351–363.

Reed, R. A., J. J. Johnson-Barnard, and W. L. Baker. 1996. Contribution of roads to forest fragmentation in the Rocky Mountains. *Conservation Biology* 10: 1098–1106.

Santos, T., and J. L. Telleria. 1994. Influence of forest fragmentation on seed consumption and dispersal of Spanish juniper, *Juniperus thurifera. Biological Conservation* 70: 129–134.

Saunders, S. C., J. Chen, T. R. Crow, and K. D. Brosofske. 1998. Hierarchical relationships between landscape structure and temperature in a managed forest landscape. *Landscape Ecology* 13: 381–395.

Schmidt, W. 1989. Plant dispersal by motor cars. *Vegetatio* 80: 147–152.

Sork, V. L. 1983. Distribution of pignut hickory (*Carya glabra*) along a forest to edge transect, and factors affecting seedling recruitment. *Bulletin of the Torrey Botanical Club* 110: 494–506.

Spies, T. A., J. F. Franklin, and M. Klopsch. 1990. Canopy gaps in Douglas-fir forests of the Cascade mountains. *Canadian Journal of Forest Research* 20: 649–658.

Terborgh, J. 1992. Maintenance of diversity in tropical forests. *Biotropica* 24: 283–292.

Thompson, J. N., and M. F. Willson. 1978. Disturbance and the dispersal of fleshy fruits. *Science* 200: 1161–1163.

Turton, S. M., and H. J. Freiburger. 1997. Edge and aspect effects on the microclimate of a small tropical forest remnant on the Atherton Tableland, Northeastern Australia. Pages 45–54 *in* W. F. Laurance and R. O. Bierregaard, Jr., editors. *Tropical forest remnants: ecology, management, and conservation of fragmented communities.* The University of Chicago Press, Chicago, Illinois, USA.

Tyser, R. W., and C. A. Worley. 1992. Alien flora in grasslands adjacent to road and trail corridors in Glacier National Park, Montana (U.S.A.). *Conservation Biology* 6: 253–262.

Vaillancourt, D. A. 1995. Structural and microclimatic edge effects associated with clear-cutting in a Rocky Mountain forest. Master's thesis. University of Wyoming, Laramie, Wyoming, USA.

Veblen, T. T. 1986. Treefalls and the coexistence of conifers in subalpine forests of the central Rockies. *Ecology* 67: 644–649.

Viana, V. M., A.A.J. Tabanez, and J.L.F. Batista. 1997. Dynamics and restoration of forest fragments in the Brazilian Atlantic moist forest. Pages 351–365 *in* W. F. Laurance and R. O. Bierregaard, Jr., editors. *Tropical forest remnants: ecology, management, and conservation of fragmented communities.* The University of Chicago Press, Chicago, Illinois, USA.

Wales, B. A. 1972. Vegetation analysis of northern and southern edges in a mature oak-hickory forest. *Ecological Monographs* 42: 451–471.

Whitney, G. G., and J. R. Runkle. 1981. Edge versus age effects in the development of a beech-maple forest. *Oikos* 37: 377–381.

Williams-Linera, G. 1990 a. Vegetation structure and environmental conditions of forest edges in Panama. *Journal of Ecology* 78: 356–373.

Williams-Linera, G. 1990 b. Origin and early development of forest edge vegetation in Panama. *Biotropica* 22: 235–241.

Yahner, R. H. 1988. Changes in wildlife communities near edges. *Conservation Biology* 2: 333–339.

Young, A., and N. Mitchell. 1994. Microclimate and vegetation edge effects in a fragmented podocarp-broadleaf forest in New Zealand. *Biological Conservation* 67: 63–72.

Part Four

Case Studies of Forest Fragmentation in the Southern Rocky Mountains

12

Songbird Communities along Natural Forest Edges and Forest Clear-cut Edges

Bonnie Ruefenacht and Richard L. Knight

INTRODUCTION

The connection between the decline of neotropical migratory song-birds and forest fragmentation has gained increasing prominence in recent years (Martin and Finch 1995, Robinson et al. 1995*a*). This decline is attributed to an increase in forest edge and decrease of forest tract size. Increased levels of forest edge are believed to result in elevated levels of nest predation and brown-headed cowbird nest parasitism, as well as reduced populations of forest-interior songbirds due to reduction of habitat and competition from edge-generalist species (Sherry and Holmes 1995).

Studies of bird populations and forest edges have primarily been carried out in agricultural and suburban landscape matrices where fragmentation was due to agriculture and human settlement. These results may not be applicable to forest-dominated landscapes (Rudnicky and Hunter 1993, Yahner 1996). Few studies have been conducted in coniferous forest-dominated landscapes, and no studies compare bird communities along edges of natural openings and edges of forest clear-cuts.

Coniferous forests in the Southern Rocky Mountains are characterized by a high degree of habitat heterogeneity due to a variety of natural ecological processes such as fire, wind, insects, avalanches, and landslides (Peet 1988). Bird populations in the Southern Rocky Mountains may be less affected by anthropocentric fragmentation by virtue of their longer association with naturally fragmented landscapes (Norment 1991, Dobkin 1994). Few studies have addressed forest edge effects on bird populations in the Southern Rocky Mountain region (Keller and Anderson 1992) and fewer still have examined the dynamics of nest parasitism by cowbirds and nest predation. Because sustaining biological diversity within a region requires knowledge of regional communities and the processes that affect those communities (Finch and Ruggiero 1993), studies evaluating population status and trends of birds in western North America are critically needed (Finch 1991). Before implementing management schemes based on ideas from other bioregions (e.g., eastern deciduous forest), we would be prudent to examine whether these ideas are applicable to the Southern Rocky Mountain region (Hansen and Urban 1992).

In this study we compared bird species relative abundance, composition, nest predation, and cowbird nest parasitism between (1) edges of natural forest openings and edges of forest clear-cuts, (2) forest interiors adjacent to natural openings and forest interiors adjacent to clear-cuts, (3) edges of natural forest openings and adjacent forest interiors, and (4) between forest clear-cut edges and adjacent forest interiors.

Study Area and Methods

Our study was conducted in the Red Feather Lake District of the Roosevelt National Forest, Larimer County, Colorado (41°N 106°15'W—40°30'N 105°W). We examined lodgepole pine forests because forest clear-cutting in this region is mainly in this forest type. Undergrowth vegetation of these forest stands was dominated by common juniper, kinnikinnik, Oregon grape, and Wood's rose. Herbaceous vegetation was scarce with heartleaf arnica, beardtongue, bigflower cinquefoil, and stonecrop being the most common species (Hess and Alexander 1986).

We chose 15 clear-cut openings and 15 natural openings at random by marking all possible natural and clear-cut openings within the Red Feather Lakes District on aerial photographs, numbering them, and then selecting sites using a random numbers table. Elevation of the natural and clear-cut openings ranged from 2,500 m to 3,100 m. Natural openings were dominated by cristata, ryegrass, trisetum, and poa grass species. Dominant forbs were golden banner, groundsels, thistle, kinnikinnik, pussytoes, penstemon, and geranium. Dominant shrubs were juniper, serviceberry, Oregon grape, currant, sagebrush, shrubby cinquefoil, and buffaloberry species. Size of natural openings ranged from 0.3–62.0 ha ($\bar{X}$ = 7.0 ha, SE = 16 ha). We did not have information on age of the natural openings. Clear-cuts were ≤10 years old and were dominated by young lodgepole trees and logging debris. Size of clear-cuts ranged from 0.1–46.0 ha ($\bar{X}$ = 9.0, SE = 12 ha). Forest

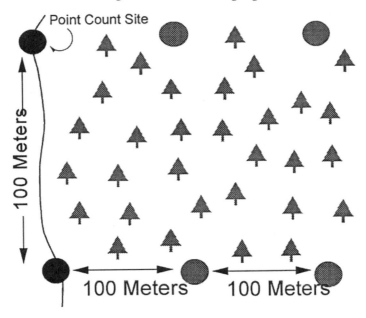

Fig. 12.1. Layout of transects for birds surveys. Birds were surveyed using 50 m radius point counts placed along edges of natural openings and clear-cuts, at 100 m into forests from natural openings and clear-cuts, and at 200 m into forests from natural openings and clear-cuts.

interiors adjacent to natural openings and clear-cuts were surrounded by lodgepole forests or forests consisting of Engelmann spruce or ponderosa pine. Field work was conducted during June–July of 1994 and 1995. The same study sites were used for both years.

Birds were surveyed using 50 m fixed radius point counts (Ralph et al. 1995). Two point count sites, 100 m apart, were arbitrarily located along the edges of natural openings and clear-cut edges (Fig. 12.1). Two point count sites were then located 100 m into forests from the two point count sites along the edges of natural openings and clear-cuts. Two additional point count sites were located 200 m into forests from the two point count sites on the edges of natural openings and clear-cuts. Thus, six survey points were established for each of the 30 sites (n = 180 survey points). Surveys were conducted from 0600 to 1000 hours and were not done during inclement weather. Study sites were surveyed once in June and again in July.

Two observers were used to survey birds for the duration of the study. Observers would occasionally survey study sites together to ensure there were no discrepancies in species identification and distance estimation. Two study sites were surveyed each day when weather conditions were ideal (i.e., minimal wind and clear skies). One observer would survey one study site while the other observer surveyed another study site. The observer waited for 5 minutes after arriving at point count sites before counting birds. All birds seen or heard during a 10 minute interval were recorded and their distances to the observer were estimated.

We placed 18 artificial nests each year at each of 11 natural sites and 11 clear-cut sites. Four of the sites used in 1995 were not used in 1994, otherwise, the same sites were used for both years of the study. In 1994, artificial nest trials of seven days in length were conducted at five natural sites and five clear-cut sites during the first week in June and at six natural sites and six clear-cut sites during the first week in July. Artificial nests were made of chicken wire ($\bar{x}$ diameter = 22 cm, SE = 7 cm; $\bar{x}$ depth = 10, SE = 4 cm) painted brown and entwined with vegetation found in the area. Two mottled Japanese quail eggs were placed in each nest. During the first trial, six nests were placed along edges, six nests were placed 50 m into forests, and six nests were placed 100 m into forests. For the second nest trial, we increased distances into forests to increase the treatment effect; six nests were placed along edges, six nests were placed 100 m into forests, and six nests were placed 200 m into forests. Each nest was placed by walking a random distance determined *a priori* (0–100 m) along the transect. Next, a random bearing determined *a priori* (0–360°) was chosen. Then we walked a random distance determined *a priori* between 0–10 m, which was used for the first nest trial, or between 0–50 m, which was used for the second nest trial and the 1995 nest trial, along the chosen bearing. Nests were either placed on the ground or in a tree ($\bar{x}$ height of nests = 1.4 m, SE = 0.4 m). Artificial nests were placed in a similar manner in 1995, but only one nest trial was conducted in mid July. All predation events were noted.

Searches for natural nests were conducted daily throughout the field season (Martin and Geupel 1993). Once a nest was found, it was checked every third day. A 6.1 m pole with a mirror attached was used to monitor high nests. For each nest, height above ground and distance to forest edge were measured and predation or parasitism events were recorded.

Data Analyses

Bird species observed at the two point counts conducted at the same distance category (i.e., edge, 100 m, and 200 m) at the same site were averaged together; we used this average to indicate relative abundance in our analyses. We did not estimate bird species densities because of low abundances for individual bird species (Buckland et al. 1993). When choosing study sites, we picked similar habitats so that any detectability biases that occurred would be the same from point count to point count. We arbitrarily determined that a species should have at least ten detections per distance category to be included in our analyses.

All of the following statistical tests were conducted at the α = 0.05 significance level. Because bird surveys were conducted for two years and each site was surveyed twice per year, we used repeated measures analysis in PROC GLM (SAS 1996) to test for differences in bird species relative abundance between seasons (June and July) and between years (1994 and 1995). If a species showed a year or season effect, the species was analyzed within year or season. Bird species relative abundances not showing any season or year effect were combined across years and seasons.

We used analysis of variance in PROC GLM (SAS 1996) to test for differences in bird species relative abundance between edges of natural opening and forest clear-cuts, 100 m into forests from natural openings and 100 m into forests from clear-cuts, and 200 m into forests from natural openings and 200 m into forests from clear-cuts. We used analysis of variance in PROC GLM (SAS 1996) to test for differences in bird species relative abundances between edges of natural openings, 100 m into forests from natural openings, and 200 m into forests from natural openings. Analysis of variance in PROC GLM (SAS 1996) was used to test for differences in bird species relative abundance between clear-cut edges, 100 m into forests from clear-cuts, and 200 m into forests from clear-cuts. Percent species similarities (Bray and Curtis 1957) for bird communities were calculated between clear-cut edges and adjacent forest interiors, between edges of natural openings and adjacent forest interiors, between edges of natural openings and clear-cut edges, and between forest interiors adjacent to natural openings and forest interiors adjacent to clear-cuts.

Birds were separated into life history categories *a priori* regarding migratory strategy, diet, nesting strategy, and seral stage association based on Ehrlich et al. (1988). Migratory strategy categories were: (a) long distance migrants that migrated to South America, (b) short distance migrants that migrated to Mexico or Central America and (c) residents that did not migrate. Birds were categorized into herbivore, omnivore, and insectivore diet categories based upon their primary diet during the breeding season. Nesting strategy categories were hole excavator, hole non-excavator, or cup nesters. Seral stage association categories were closed canopy, open canopy, or generalist. Closed canopy bird species were primarily found in coniferous forest habitat. Open canopy species were found in open habitats or along edges. Generalist birds were those that did not show a specific habitat usage. Bird species falling into these categories were combined and averaged across the 15 natural opening study sites and the 15 clear-cut study sites. Analysis of variance in PROC GLM (SAS 1996) was used to test for differences in relative abundance for these life history categories between edges of natural openings and forest clear-cut edges, between forest interiors adjacent to natural openings and forest interiors adjacent to clear-cuts, between edges of natural openings and adjacent forest interiors, and between clear-cut edges and adjacent forest interiors.

Yahner and Cypher (1987) found that artificial nests placed higher than 1.5 m above ground were disturbed more than those placed 0.5 m above ground. We used G-tests of independence with Yates' correction for continuity to determine if artificial nest predation was independent of nest height (Sokal and Rohlf 1981). For artificial nests, t-tests (PROC TTEST, SAS 1996) were used to test for predation differences between trials and years. PROC LOGISTIC (SAS 1996) was used to determine if the number of artificial nests predated differed between edges of natural openings and clear-cut edges, between forest interiors adjacent to natural openings and forest interiors adjacent to clear-cuts, between edges of natural openings and adjacent forest interiors, and between clear-cut edges and adjacent forest interiors.

For natural nests, the Mayfield procedure (Mayfield 1975, Johnson 1979) was used to calculate nest success for each natural nest. PROC REG (SAS 1996) was used to examine the relationship between nest success and distance of nests from edges, either clear-cut or natural. Because only two natural nests were parasitized, these data were not analyzed. PROC REG (SAS 1996) was used to determine if number of young fledged was influenced by distance of nests to edges or by the type of edge (natural or clear-cut) closest to nests.

Results
Bird Species Composition

We made 2,098 audible and visual observations of 40 species at both natural and clear-cut sites. The percent species similarity between edges of natural openings and adjacent forest interiors was 55%. Natural opening study sites contained ten edge species, three forest interior species, and 27 species occurred at both edges and forest interiors (Table 12.1). The percent species similarity between clear-cut edges and adjacent forest interiors was 70%. Clear-cut sites contained five edge species, two forest interior species, and 21 species occurred at both edges and forest interiors (Table 12.1). The percent species similarity between edges of natural openings and clear-cut edges was 61%.

Nine species were detected only along edges of natural openings. Warbling vireos were detected only at forest interiors adjacent to natural openings. Cordilleran flycatchers, mourning doves, olive-sided flycatchers, and white-crowned sparrows were detected at edges of natural openings and adjacent forest interiors, but were not detected at clear-cut edges or adjacent forest interiors. Red-breasted nuthatches were detected only at forest interiors, regardless of edge type. Clark's nutcrackers were detected only at clear-cut edges and adjacent forest interiors.

Bird Species Relative Abundances

Ruby-crowned kinglets differed in relative abundances during June and July for 1994 and 1995 ($F = 6.97$; $df = 12, 336$; $P < 0.001$). Thus, the relative abundances of ruby-crowned kinglets were analyzed within seasons and within years, but all other species were pooled across seasons and years. For June 1994, ruby-crowned kinglets were more abundant at forest interiors (for both 100 m and 200 m distances into forests from edges) adjacent to clear-cuts than at clear-cut edges ($F = 3.45$; $df = 2, 42$; $P = 0.0409$; Table 12.2). No other species relative abundances were different between clear-cut edges and adjacent forest interiors.

American robins were more abundant along edges of natural openings than in adjacent forest interiors (both 100-m and 200-m distances into forests from edges; $F = 3.51$; $df = 2, 42$; $P = 0.039$; Table 12.2). American robins ($F = 5.20$; $df = 1, 28$; $P = 0.0304$) and broad-tailed hummingbirds ($F = 5.80$; $df = 1, 28$; $P = 0.0229$) were more abundant along edges of natural openings than along clear-cut edges. Relative abundances of both species were not different between 100 m and 200 m distances into forests from natural openings and between 100 m and 200 m distances into forests from clear-cuts (Table 12.3).

Table 12.1. Bird species composition at edges and forest interiors of natural openings (NAT) and forest clear-cuts (CC), Roosevelt National Forest, Colorado. Field work was conducted in June–July of 1994 and 1995.

Species	Edge[1]		Forest Interior[2]		Common[3]	
	NAT	CC	NAT	CC	NAT	CC
Mourning Dove					X	
Common Nighthawk	X					
Broad-tailed Hummingbird					X	X
Northern Flicker					X	X
Williamson's Sapsucker					X	X
Hairy Woodpecker					X	X
Olive-sided Flycatcher					X	
Hammond's Flycatcher					X	X
Cordilleran Flycatcher					X	
Tree Swallow	X	X				
Steller's Jay					X	X
Gray Jay					X	X
Clark's Nutcracker						X
American Crow	X					
Common Raven	X					
Mountain Chickadee					X	X
Brown Creeper					X	X
White-breasted Nuthatch					X	X
Red-breasted Nuthatch			X	X		
House Wren	X		X			
Ruby-crowned Kinglet					X	X
Mountain Bluebird		X			X	
Townsend's Solitaire					X	X
Hermit Thrush					X	X
American Robin					X	X
Warbling Vireo			X			
Yellow-rumped Warbler					X	X
Wilson's Warbler	X					
Green-tailed Towhee	X					
Vesper Sparrow	X					
Chipping Sparrow					X	X
Dark-eyed Junco					X	X
White-crowned Sparrow					X	
Brewer's Blackbird	X					
Brown-headed Cowbird		X			X	
Western Tanager		X			X	
Pine Siskin					X	X
Pine Grosbeak	X					X
Red Crossbill					X	X
Cassin's Finch		X			X	

1. Edge species includes those found at edges or at edge and 100 m into forests from edges.
2. Forest interior species were those found at 100 m or 200 m into forests from edges or at both 100 m and 200 m into forests from edges.
3. Common species were found at both edges and forest interiors.

Table 12.2. Comparison of bird species relative abundances between edges at natural openings and adjacent forest interiors, and between clear-cut edges and adjacent forest interiors, Roosevelt National Forest, Colorado. Field work was done in June–July of 1994 and 1995. Analysis of variance in PROC GLM was used to determine significance levels.

| | Edge | | 100 m into Forests | | 200 m into Forests | | |
	$\bar{x}$	SE	$\bar{x}$	SE	$\bar{x}$	SE	P
Natural Opening							
Broad-tailed Hummingbird	1.80	0.12	1.40	0.06	1.13	0.10	0.4899
Mountain Chickadee	2.80	0.13	3.80	0.20	3.73	0.24	0.5808
Ruby-crowned Kinglet	1.60	0.20	2.67	0.16	2.53	0.18	0.5096
American Robin	2.20	0.18	0.73	0.06	0.67	0.08	0.0388
Yellow-rumped Warbler	2.53	0.12	4.20	0.16	4.40	0.18	0.0643
Dark-eyed Junco	3.87	0.17	3.07	0.22	2.33	0.22	0.4093
Clear-cut							
Mountain Chickadee	3.67	0.20	3.80	0.16	3.27	0.11	0.8154
Ruby-crowned Kinglet	0.53	0.10	2.33	0.13	2.67	0.11	0.0409*
Yellow-rumped Warbler	3.40	0.19	4.53	0.18	2.23	0.25	0.4738
Dark-eyed Junco	4.67	0.22	2.00	0.16	2.20	0.16	0.0865

* Ruby-crowned kinglets showed a significant difference between season (June and July) and between years (1994 and 1995). Significance level reported here is for Season 1, 1994.

Table 12.3. Comparison of bird species relative abundances obtained from point counts conducted at edges and forest interiors at natural openings and forest clear-cuts, Roosevelt National Forest, Colorado. Field work was done in June–July of 1994 and 1995. Analysis of variance in PROC GLM was used to determine significance levels.

| | Natural Opening | | Clear-cut | | |
	$\bar{x}$	SE	$\bar{x}$	SE	P
Edges					
Broad-tailed Hummingbird	1.80	0.12	0.53	0.07	0.0229
Mountain Chickadee	2.80	0.13	3.67	0.20	0.3488
American Robin	2.20	0.18	0.53	0.06	0.0304
Yellow-rumped Warbler	2.53	0.12	3.40	0.19	0.3253
Dark-eyed Junco	3.87	0.17	4.67	0.22	0.8566
100 m into Forests					
Gray Jay	0.87	0.06	1.13	0.07	0.4502
Mountain Chickadee	3.80	0.20	3.80	0.16	1.0000
Ruby-crowned Kinglet	2.67	0.16	2.33	0.13	0.6758
Yellow-rumped Warbler	4.20	0.16	4.53	0.18	0.7245
Dark-eyed Junco	3.07	0.22	2.00	0.16	0.3178
200 m into Forests					
Mountain Chickadee	3.73	0.24	3.27	0.11	0.6548
Ruby-crowned Kinglet	2.53	0.18	2.67	0.11	0.8701
Yellow-rumped Warbler	4.40	0.18	4.47	0.19	0.9485

Bird Life History Categories

Short distance migrants (F = 6.34; df = 1, 28; P = 0.0178) and habitat generalists (F = 7.11; df = 1, 28; P = 0.0126) were more abundant along edges of natural openings than along clear-cut edges (Table 12.4). Short distance migrants (F = 6.82; df = 1, 28; P = 0.014) and open canopy species (F = 5.37; df = 1, 28; P = 0.028) were more abundant at 100 m into forests from natural openings than at 100 m into forests from clear-cuts (Table 12.4). No life history category differed in relative abundance between 200 m distances into forests from natural openings and 200 m distances into forests from clear-cuts (Table 12.4).

Short distance migrants (F = 3.84, df = 2, 42; P = 0.029), open canopy species (F = 5.47; df = 2, 42; P = 0.008), and habitat generalists (F = 4.53; df = 2, 42; P = 0.017) were more abundant along edges of natural openings than in adjacent forest interiors (for both 100 m and 200 m distances into forests from edges; Table 12.5). Herbivores (F = 5.68; df = 2, 42; P = 0.007) and open canopy species (F = 4.64; df = 2, 42; P = 0.015) were more abundant along clear-cut edges than in adjacent forest interiors (for both 100 m and 200 m distances into forests from edges; Table 12.5). Relative abundances of residents, insectivores, omnivores, cup nesters, hole excavators, hole non-excavators, and closed canopy species were not different between edges of natural openings and clear-cut edges, between forest interiors adjacent to natural openings and forest interiors adjacent to clear-cuts, between edges of natural openings and forest interiors adjacent to natural openings, or between clear-cut edges and forest interiors adjacent to clear-cuts. We did not have enough observations to analyze long-distance migrants.

Artificial Nests

Nest predation was independent of nest height; thus, nest height was ignored in our analyses. Predation rates of artificial nests differed between years for nests placed along clear-cut edges (T = −2.55, df = 19, P = 0.0197) and nests placed at 100 m into forests from natural openings (T = −2.81, df = 20, P = 0.0109); thus, data between years were not pooled. No differences were found between the two nest trials for 1994 (T < 1.2096, df = 9, P > 0.05), so these data were combined.

In 1994 we did not detect any differences in the number of artificial nests predated between edges of natural openings and clear-cut

Table 12.4. Comparison of bird species relative abundance based on life-history categories between edges and forest interiors at natural openings and forest clear-cuts. Bird surveys were conducted using point counts during June–July of 1994 and 1995 in Roosevelt National Forest, Colorado. Analysis of variance in PROC GLM was used to determine significance levels. The comparisons in this table are between natural and clear-cut sites, at the level of edge, 100 m into the forest, and 200 m into the forest.

| | Edge | | | | | 100 m into Forests | | | | | 200 m into Forests | | | | |
| | Natural | | Clear-cut | | | Natural | | Clear-cut | | | Natural | | Clear-cut | | |
	$\bar{x}$	SE	$\bar{x}$	SE	P	$\bar{x}$	SE	$\bar{x}$	SE	P	$\bar{x}$	SE	$\bar{x}$	SE	P
Migrants															
Long Distance	0.02	0.13	0.00	0.00	NA	0.02	0.13	0.00	0.00	NA	0.00	0.00	0.02	0.13	NA
Short Distance	6.03	4.35	3.95	3.36	0.0178	4.62	2.74	3.37	2.22	0.0143	4.02	2.90	3.65	2.50	0.5636
Resident	0.08	0.33	0.22	0.56	0.1324	0.20	0.48	0.18	0.50	0.7844	0.07	0.25	0.07	0.25	0.9082
Feeders															
Herbivore	1.68	2.48	1.77	2.32	0.8700	1.10	1.24	0.70	0.87	0.1813	1.02	1.49	0.75	1.41	0.4326
Omnivore	0.15	0.40	0.33	0.73	0.1700	0.28	0.49	0.38	0.69	0.3973	0.17	0.42	0.28	0.67	0.3224
Insectivore	4.70	3.70	3.18	2.83	0.0641	4.38	2.65	3.82	2.53	0.2913	3.82	3.08	3.77	2.29	0.9355
Nesters															
Cup	4.15	3.65	2.67	2.93	0.0547	3.07	2.25	2.38	1.83	0.0816	2.80	2.38	2.47	1.85	0.4964
Hole Excavator	0.13	0.39	0.10	0.30	0.6462	0.12	0.32	0.18	0.54	0.3787	0.18	0.54	0.27	0.58	0.4267
Hole Non-excavator	1.17	1.55	1.17	1.51	1.0000	1.33	1.32	1.33	1.61	1.0000	1.05	1.40	1.00	1.03	0.8609
Seral Stage															
Open Canopy	3.15	2.94	2.30	1.83	0.1836	2.20	1.68	1.48	1.32	0.0280	1.42	1.44	1.30	1.45	0.7318
Closed Canopy	2.57	2.29	2.75	2.94	0.7340	3.38	2.14	3.12	2.20	0.5641	3.42	2.90	3.15	2.11	0.6437
Generalist	1.27	2.28	0.37	0.74	0.0126	0.53	0.83	0.38	0.72	0.3550	0.45	0.93	0.50	1.03	0.7919

Table 12.5. Comparison of bird species relative abundance based on life history categories between edges and forest interiors at natural openings and forest clear-cuts. Bird surveys were conducted using point counts during June–July of 1994 and 1995 in Roosevelt National Forest, Colorado. Analysis of variance in PROC GLM was used to determine significance levels. The comparisons in this table are between edges and forest interiors, for natural sites and for clear-cut sites.

| | Natural Opening | | | | | | | Clear-cut | | | | | | |
| | Edge | | 100 m | | 200 m | | | Edge | | 100 m | | 200 m | | |
	x̄	SE	x̄	SE	x̄	SE	P	x̄	SE	x̄	SE	x̄	SE	P
Migrants														
Long Distance	0.02	0.13	0.02	0.13	0.00	0.00	NA	0.00	0.00	0.00	0.00	0.02	0.13	NA
Short Distance	6.03	4.35	4.62	2.74	4.02	2.90	0.0293	3.95	3.36	3.37	2.22	3.65	2.50	0.5850
Resident	0.08	0.33	0.20	0.48	0.07	0.25	0.1550	0.22	0.56	0.18	0.50	0.07	0.25	0.6003
Feeders														
Herbivore	1.68	2.48	1.10	1.24	1.02	1.49	0.2307	1.77	2.32	0.70	0.87	0.75	1.41	0.0066
Omnivore	0.15	0.40	0.28	0.49	0.17	0.42	0.2084	0.33	0.73	0.38	0.69	0.28	0.67	0.8038
Insectivore	4.70	3.70	4.38	2.65	3.82	3.08	0.5208	3.18	2.83	3.82	2.53	3.77	2.29	0.3686
Nesters														
Cup	4.15	3.65	3.07	2.25	2.80	2.38	0.0950	2.67	2.93	2.38	1.83	2.47	1.85	0.8145
Hole Excavator	0.13	0.39	0.12	0.32	0.18	0.54	0.7308	0.10	0.30	0.18	0.54	0.27	0.58	0.1362
Hole Non-excavator	1.17	1.55	1.33	1.32	1.05	1.40	0.6718	1.17	1.51	1.33	1.61	1.00	1.03	0.4907
Seral Stage														
Open Canopy	3.15	2.94	2.20	1.68	1.42	1.44	0.0078	2.30	1.83	1.48	1.32	1.30	1.45	0.0151
Closed Canopy	2.57	2.29	3.38	2.14	3.42	2.90	0.2362	2.75	2.94	3.12	2.20	3.15	2.11	0.6614
Generalist	1.27	2.28	0.53	0.83	0.45	0.93	0.0165	0.37	0.74	0.38	0.72	0.50	1.03	0.6815

Table 12.6. Number of artificial nests predated for 1994 and 1995. Artificial nests were randomly placed along edges of clear-cuts and natural openings, at 50 m, 100 m, and 200 m distances into forests from edges of clear-cuts and natural openings. Six artificial nests were placed at each distance category. Artificial nests were picked up and data recorded after a 7-day interval.

1994 SEASON 1[1]

	Natural Opening				Clear-cut		
Site[2]	Edge	50 m[3]	100 m	Site	Edge	50 m	100 m
1	0	1	0	1	2	1	2
2	3	3	2	2	0	1	0
3	3	0	1	3	0	1	1
4	1	2	1	4	2	1	0
5	0	0	0	5	1	0	3

1994 SEASON 2

	Natural Opening				Clear-cut		
Site	Edge	100 m	200 m	Site	Edge	100 m	200 m
6	1	0	0	6	1	0	0
7	0	1	2	7	1	2	0
8	0	0	1	8	3	2	1
9	1	3	0	9	0	1	1
10	0	1	1	10	0	2	2
11	1	1	2				

1995

	Natural Opening				Clear-cut		
Site	Edge	100 m	200 m	Site	Edge	100 m	200 m
1	1	1	1	1	3	3	1
2	1	3	3	2	1	3	2
3	0	1	1	3	2	2	0
4	0	2	2	4	1	1	1
5	1	2	0	5	3	5	5
6	0	1	1	6	2	1	1
7	1	0	0	7	2	5	3
8	1	2	0	8	2	2	2
9	0	0	0	9	0	0	2
10	1	1	0	10	0	4	4
11	2	3	1	11	3	1	1

1. In 1994, artificial nests were placed during the first week in June (season 1) and the first week in July (season 2).

2. Site numbers are only for this table. Only four of the sites used in 1994 were used again in 1995.

3. In 1994 during the June artificial nest trials, artificial nests were placed along edges, at 50 m distances into forests from edges, and at 100 m distances into forests from edges. To increase the treatment effect, we did not place artificial nests at 50 m distances into forests from edges for all other artificial nest trials, but instead placed nests at 200 m distances into forests from edges.

edges (Wald's χ^2 = 0.0506, df = 1, P = 0.8220) or between forest interiors adjacent to natural openings and forest interiors adjacent to clear-cuts (Wald's χ^2 = 1.9005, df = 1, P = 0.1680, see Table 12.6). We found no differences in the number of artificial nests predated between edges of natural openings and adjacent forest interiors (Wald's χ^2 = 0.0105, df = 1, P = 0.7459), or between clear-cut edges and adjacent forest interiors (Wald's χ^2 = 0.0054, df = 1, P = 0.9416). In 1995 we found no differences in the number of artificial nests predated between edges of natural openings and adjacent forest interiors (Wald's χ^2 = 0.9895, df = 1, P = 0.3199) or between clear-cut edges and adjacent forest interiors (Wald's χ^2 = 0.1353, df = 1, P = 0.7130). More artificial nests, however, were predated along clear-cut edges (30% predated) and adjacent forest interiors (36% predated) than along edges of natural openings (12% predated) and adjacent forest interiors (23% predated) (Wald's χ^2 = 10.85, df = 1, P = 0.001).

Natural Nests

We found 31 bird nests of nine species (see Table 12.7). Only two nests were parasitized by cowbirds and they were both abandoned before eggs hatched. Fifteen nests were successful (i.e., fledged at least one young) and 16 nests were unsuccessful. No correlation was found between the Mayfield survival estimates and distance of nests to edges (P = 0.8384). Nests located nearest to clear-cut edges fledged more young ($\bar{x}$= 2.44, SE = 2.01 birds fledged) than nests located nearest to edges of natural openings ($\bar{x}$ = 1.09, SE = 1.50 birds fledged) (P = 0.037).

DISCUSSION

In the eastern United States declines of songbirds due to nest predation, nest parasitism, and edge effects have been noticed. We also found nest predation, nest parasitism, and edge effects in songbird communities in the Southern Rocky Mountains. An aspect of our study that has not previously been investigated was examining songbird communities along natural and human-created edges. The edges of natural openings served as a control against which bird communities of human-created edges could be compared. Edges of natural openings and adjacent forest interiors tended to have greater species richness and a different species composition than clear-cut edges and adjacent forest interiors. Several species, including American crows, common ravens, Wilson's warblers, green-tailed towhees, vesper sparrows, and Brewer's blackbirds were only observed along edges of natural openings. The Clark's nutcracker was the only species observed along clear-cut edges but

Table 12.7. Natural nest data. Searches for natural nests at clear-cut and natural opening sites were made between June and July of 1994 and 1995 in the Red Feather Lakes District of the Roosevelt National Forest, Colorado. Each nest was checked every third day and any parasitism or predation event was recorded.

No.	Species	Site	Distance	No. Young Fledged
Natural Nests for 1994				
1	Yellow-rumped Warbler	Clear-cut	200 m	2
2	Yellow-rumped Warbler	Clear-cut	100 m	Unsuccessful
3	Hermit Thrush	Clear-cut	Edge	4
4	Green-tailed Towhee	Natural	Opening	3
5	Dark-eyed Junco	Natural	Edge	Unsuccessful
Natural Nests for 1995				
1	American Robin	Natural	Edge	Unsuccessful
2	American Robin	Natural	Edge	Unsuccessful
3	American Robin	Natural	Opening	Unsuccessful
4	American Robin	Natural	Edge	Unsuccessful
5	American Robin	Natural	Edge	Unsuccessful
6	Common Snipe	Natural	Edge	Unsuccessful
7	Yellow-rumped Warbler	Natural	50 m	Unsuccessful; Parasitized
8	Hammond's Flycatcher	Clear-cut	75 m	Unsuccessful
9	Hermit Thrush	Natural	100 m	Unsuccessful
10	American Robin	Natural	Edge	3
11	American Robin	Natural	Edge	1
12	Hermit Thrush	Clear-cut	200 m	Unsuccessful
13	Hermit Thrush	Clear-cut	150 m	3
14	Hammond's Flycatcher	Natural	10 m	4
15	Dark-eyed Junco	Clear-cut	Opening	4
16	American Robin	Natural	Opening	4
17	Hammond's Flycatcher	Natural	Edge	Unsuccessful
18	Common Nighthawk	Natural	230 m	Unsuccessful
19	Vesper Sparrow	Natural	Opening	2
20	Hammond's Flycatcher	Clear-cut	50 m	4
21	Hammond's Flycatcher	Natural	15 m	Unsuccessful; Parasitized
22	Hammond's Flycatcher	Natural	50 m	2
23	White-crowned Sparrow	Natural	Edge	4
24	White-crowned Sparrow	Natural	Opening	Unsuccessful
25	Dark-eyed Junco	Natural	200 m	2
26	White-crowned Sparrow	Natural	Opening	4

was not observed along edges of natural openings. Clark's nutcracker was also observed in forest interiors adjacent to clear-cuts but was not observed in forest interiors adjacent to natural openings. Warbling vireos were only seen at forest interiors adjacent to natural openings while no species was seen only at forest interiors adjacent to clear-cuts.

Bird species were more abundant along edges of natural openings than along clear-cut edges, but bird species abundances were not different between forest interiors adjacent to natural openings and forest interiors adjacent to clear-cuts. Our findings differed from those of Keller and Anderson (1992) who studied the effects of forest fragmentation on birds in the Medicine Bow National Forest, Wyoming. They found little evidence that any species either used or avoided edges between forests and forest clear-cuts. Because we examined bird communities at both edges of natural openings and forest clear-cuts, we were able to discern differences among these two types of forest edges.

A possible explanation for why bird species relative abundance and composition differed between edges and adjacent forest interiors of natural openings and clear-cuts is differences in vegetation characteristics. Typically, the border between clear-cut openings and forests have high contrast, straight boundaries, and hard edges, which are formed when essentially closed canopy forests are opened by a forest clear-cut (Forman 1995). Edges between natural openings and forests often have low contrast, curvilinear boundaries, and soft edges, which are formed when forests and natural openings gradually coalesce forming less discernible boundaries between forests and openings. Because of the physical characteristics of hard edges and soft edges, they experience different microclimate conditions and ecological processes, which produce various edge effects (Forman and Moore 1992, Kupfer 1995, Murcia 1995).

Forest clear-cuts used in our study were littered with logs, branches, and debris left over from cutting. The high density of logs at clear-cuts prevented grasses and forbs from growing, but seeds from the pine cones did allow for regrowth of lodgepole. Natural openings had few fallen logs, substantially more ground cover, and fewer trees than clear-cut openings. The few trees that did occur in natural openings were larger and thicker than trees found in clear-cuts. Trees surrounding clear-cuts were taller, larger, and had higher crown heights than trees surrounding natural openings. Also, higher tree mortality occurred along clear-cut edges than along edges of natural openings (Ruefenacht 1998).

Forest interiors adjacent to clear-cuts had a more closed canopy, and trees were in higher densities, taller, and had higher crown heights compared to trees at forest interiors adjacent to natural openings (Ruefenacht 1998). The reason for these differences in vegetation between natural openings and clear-cuts is the result of foresters logging areas with specific tree requirements. The differences in bird species relative abundance and composition between edges of natural openings, clear-cut edges, and their adjacent forest interiors might be caused by these vegetation differences.

Within the southern Rocky Mountain region, no species of songbird has yet been designated forest interior, area-sensitive, or edge-sensitive. We found that red-breasted nuthatches were only observed in forest interiors adjacent to natural openings and clear-cuts; warbling vireos were only observed in forest interiors adjacent to natural openings. Whether these two species are indeed forest-interior specialists will require further study (Villard 1998).

Artificial and Natural Nests

Researchers have documented a trend of higher predation on artificial nests close to habitat edges as compared to forest interiors (Gates and Gysel 1978, Chasko and Gates 1982, Andrén and Angelstam 1988, Møller 1989, Santos and Telleria 1992, Burkey 1993, Nour et al. 1993, Fenske-Crawford and Niemi 1997). Our results, however, concur with those of Yahner and Wright (1985) and Ratti and Reese (1988), who found predation rates on artificial nests were independent of distance from edges.

Studies using artificial nests have shown that landscapes with higher human presence experience higher predation rates (Andrén et al. 1985, Wilcove 1985, Angelstam 1986, Andrén 1992) generally because of high relative abundances of corvid species. Our clear-cut sites were situated in a forest dominated matrix with low relative abundances of corvids rather than an agricultural dominated matrix where corvids appear to be more abundant (Miller and Knight 1993). Ratti and Reese (1988) found higher predation rates for abrupt edges than for gradual edges in Idaho. They suggested that abrupt edges might serve as travel corridors for generalist predators, an idea that agrees with our findings. In 1995 predation was lower for artificial nests located at edges of natural openings and adjacent forest interiors than nests located at clear-cut edges and adjacent forest interiors. In 1994 we found no differences in nest predation between edges of natural openings and clear-cut edges or between forest interiors adjacent to natural openings and forest interiors adjacent to clear-cuts.

For natural nests, we found that predation rates and number of birds fledged was also independent of distance of nests to edges. Again, there is contradictory evidence regarding this pattern (Paton 1994, Robinson et al. 1995*a*). Both Gates and Gysel (1978) and Chasko and Gates (1982) found higher predation rates on natural nests close to edges compared to further from edges. However, our findings agree with Yahner (1991) and Hanski et al. (1996), who found predation rates were independent of distance of natural nests to edges. We found no differences in success rates of natural nests at natural opening and clear-cut sites. Number of birds fledged, however, was higher for natural nests close to clear-cut openings than for natural nests close to natural openings.

Gates and Gysel (1978), Brittingham and Temple (1983), and Paton (1994) have shown that cowbird parasitism is elevated along edges, whereas Hahn and Hatfield (1995) found cowbird parasitism was independent of distance of nests from edges. Because of the few nests (n = 2) parasitized and the low number (n = 24) of cowbird observations, we are unable to draw any conclusions. Hejl et al. (1995) reported cowbirds were rare in lodgepole habitat and Robinson et al. (1995*b*) observed that cowbirds were uncommon in forested landscapes and in the Rocky Mountain region. Cup-nesting species were more abundant along edges of natural openings than along clear-cut edges.

Fragmenting forests by clear-cutting timber stands has been alleged by some to mimic fire (but see Hansen et al. 1991, Hejl et al. 1995). If this is the case, then bird communities associated with edges of natural openings may resemble bird communities associated with edges created by forest clear-cutting. Our findings suggest there are differences in abundance, composition, and nest predation between these different edge types. Further studies would be useful to see whether our findings have general applicability and in understanding the root causes for these differences.

Acknowledgments

We thank Larry Mullin and Dennis Lowry from the U.S. Forest Service for providing funding and other resources, and William F. Andelt, Carl E. Bock, Mike Carter, Denis J. Dean, Richard D. Laven, and Kenneth R. Wilson for their intellectual energies and editorial comments. Steve Johnson and John Bustos provided assistance with Forest Service facilities and location of sites. Jeffrey Kearns assisted during both field seasons. Funding was provided by the Rocky Mountain

Region Experimental Station of the U.S. Forest Service, Utah State University Quinney Foundation, and Colorado State University.

LITERATURE CITED

Andrén, H. 1992. Corvid density and nest predation in relation to forest fragmentation: a landscape perspective. *Ecology* 73: 794–804.

Andrén, H., and P. Angelstam. 1988. Elevated predation rates as an edge effect in habitat islands: experimental evidence. *Ecology* 69: 544–547.

Andrén, H., P. Angelstam, E. Linström, and P. Widén. 1985. Differences in predation pressure in relation to habitat fragmentation: an experiment. *Oikos* 45: 273–277.

Angelstam, P. 1986. Predation on ground-nesting birds' nests in relation to predator densities and habitat edge. *Oikos* 47: 365–373.

Bray, J. R., and J. T. Curtis. 1957. An ordination of the upland forest communities in southern Wisconsin. *Ecological Monographs* 27: 325–349.

Brittingham, M. C., and S. A. Temple. 1983. Have cowbirds caused forest songbirds to decline? *BioScience* 33: 31–35.

Buckland, S. T., D. R. Anderson, K. P. Burnham, and J. L. Laake. 1993. *Distance sampling: estimating abundance of biological populations.* Chapman and Hall, New York, New York, USA.

Burkey, T. V. 1993. Edge effects in seed and egg predation at two neotropical rainforest sites. *Biological Conservation* 66: 129–143.

Chasko, G. G., and J. E. Gates. 1982. Avian habitat suitability along a transmission-line corridor in an oak-hickory forest region. *Wildlife Monographs* 82: 1–41.

Dobkin, D. S. 1994. *Conservation and management of neotropical migrant landbirds in the northern rockies and great plains.* University of Idaho, Moscow, Idaho.

Ehrlich, P. R., D. S. Dobkin, and D. Wheye. 1988. *The birder's handbook: a field guide to the natural history of North American birds.* Simon and Schuster Inc., New York, New York, USA.

Fenske-Crawford, T. J., and G. J. Niemi. 1997. Predation of artificial ground nests at two types of edges in a forest-dominated landscape. *Condor* 99: 14–24.

Finch, D. M. 1991. Population ecology, habitat requirements, and conservation of neotropical migratory birds. USDA Forest Service, General Technical Report RM-205, Fort Collins, Colorado, USA.

Finch, D. M., and L. F. Ruggiero. 1993. Wildlife habitats and biological diversity in the rocky mountains and northern Great Plains. *Natural Areas Journal* 13: 191–203.

Forman, R.T.T. 1995. *Land mosaics: the ecology of landscapes and regions.* University Press, Cambridge, England.

Forman, R.T.T., and P. N. Moore. 1992. Theoretical foundations for understanding boundaries in landscape mosaics. Pages 236–258 *in* A. J. Hansen and F. di Castri, editors. *Landscape boundaries: consequences for biotic diversity and ecological flows.* Springer-Verlag, New York, New York, USA.

Gates, J. E., and N. R. Givven. 1991. Neotropical migrant birds and edge effects at a forest-stream ecotone. *Wilson Bulletin* 103: 204–217.

Gates, J. E., and L. W. Gysel. 1978. Avian nest dispersion and fledgling success in field-forest ecotones. *Ecology* 59: 871–883.

Hahn, D. C., and J. S. Hatfield. 1995. Parasitism at the landscape scale: cowbirds prefer forests. *Conservation Biology* 9: 1415–1424.

Hansen, A. J., T. A. Spies, F. J. Swanson, and J. L. Ohmann. 1991. Conserving biodiversity in managed forests. *BioScience* 41: 382–392.

Hansen, A. J., and D. L. Urban. 1992. Avian response to landscape pattern: the role of species' life histories. *Landscape Ecology* 7: 163–180.

Hanski, I. K., T. J. Fenske, and G. J. Niemi. 1996. Lack of edge effect in nesting success of breeding birds in managed forest landscapes. *Auk* 113: 578–585.

Hejl, S. J., R. L. Hutto, C. R. Preston, and D. M. Finch. 1995. Effects of silvicultural treatments in the Rocky Mountains. Pages 220–244 in T. E. Martin and D. M. Finch, editors. *Ecology and management of neotropical birds: a synthesis and review of critical issues.* Oxford University Press, New York, New York, USA.

Hess, K., and R. R. Alexander. 1986. Forest vegetation of the Arapaho and Roosevelt National Forests in central Colorado: a habitat type classification. Research Paper RM-266. USDA Forest Service, Rocky Mountain Forest and Range Experiment Station, Fort Collins, Colorado, USA.

Johnson, D. H. 1979. Estimating nest success: The Mayfield method and an alternative. *Auk* 96: 651–661.

Keller, M. E., and S. H. Anderson. 1992. Avian use of habitat configurations created by forest cutting in southeastern Wyoming. *Condor* 94: 55–65.

Kupfer, J. A. 1995. Landscape ecology and biogeography. *Progress in Physical Geography* 19: 18–34.

Martin, T. E., and D. M. Finch, editors. 1995. *Ecology and management of neotropical migratory birds: a synthesis and review of critical issues.* Oxford University Press, New York, New York, USA.

Martin, T. E., and G. R. Geupel. 1993. Nest-monitoring plots: methods for locating nests and monitoring success. *Journal of Field Ornithology* 64: 507–519.

Mayfield, H. F. 1975. Suggestions for calculating nest success. *Wilson Bulletin* 87: 456–466.

Miller, C. K., and R. L. Knight. 1993. Does predator assemblage affect reproductive success in songbirds? *Condor* 95: 712–715.

Møller, A. P. 1989. Nest site selection across field-woodland ecotones: the effect of nest predation. *Oikos* 56: 240–246.

Murcia, C. 1995. Edge effects in fragmented forests: implications for conservation. *Trends in Ecology and Evolution* 10: 58–62.

Norment, C. J. 1991. Bird use of forest patches in the subalpine forest-alpine tundra ecotone of the Beartooth Mountains, Wyoming. *Northwest Science* 65: 1–9.

Nour, N., E. Matthysen, and A. A. Dhondt. 1993. Artificial nest predation and habitat fragmentation: different trends in bird and mammal predators. *Ecography* 16: 111–116.

Paton, P.W.C. 1994. The effect of edge on avian nest success: how strong is the evidence? *Conservation Biology* 8: 17–26.

Peet, R. K. 1988. Forests of the Rocky Mountains. Pages 63–101 *in* M. G. Barbour and W. D. Billings, editors. *North American terrestrial vegetation*. Cambridge University Press, Cambridge, England.

Ralph, C. J., J. R. Sauer, and S. Droege. 1995. Monitoring bird populations by point counts. General Technical Report PSW-GTR-149. Pacific Southwest Research Station, Forest Service, U.S. Department of Agriculture.

Ratti, J. T., and K. P. Reese. 1988. Preliminary test of the ecological trap hypothesis. *Journal of Wildlife Management* 52: 484–491.

Robinson, S. K., F. R. Thompson, III, T. M. Donovan, D. R. Whitehead, and J. Faaborg. 1995 *a*. Regional forest fragmentation and the nesting success of migratory birds. *Science* 267: 1987–1990.

Robinson, S. K., S. I. Rothstein, M. C. Brittingham, L. J. Petit, and J. A. Grzybowski. 1995 *b*. Ecology and behavior of cowbirds and their impact on host populations. Pages 428–460 *in* T. E. Martin and D. M. Finch, editors. *Ecology and management of neotropical migratory birds: a synthesis and review of critical issues*. Oxford University Press, New York, New York, USA.

Rudnicky, T. C., and M. L. Hunter. 1993. Reversing the fragmentation perspective: effects of clear-cut size on bird species richness in Maine. *Ecological Applications* 3: 357–366.

Ruefenacht, B. 1998. Songbird communities associated with forest clear-cut edges and edges of natural openings. Ph.D. dissertation, Colorado State University, Fort Collins, Colorado, USA.

Santos, T., and J. L. Telleria. 1992. Edge effects on nest predation in Mediterranean fragmented forests. *Biological Conservation* 60: 1–5.

SAS Institute. 1996. *SAS/STAT user's guide*. Version 6.11. SAS Institute, Cary, North Carolina, USA.

Sherry, T. W., and R. T. Holmes. 1995. Summer versus winter limitation of populations: what are the issues and what is the evidence? Pages 85–120 *in* T. E. Martin and D. M. Finch, editors. *Ecology and management of neotropical migratory birds: a synthesis and review of critical issues*. Oxford University Press, New York, New York, USA.

Sokal, R. R., and F. J. Rohlf. 1981. *Biometry*. 2nd edition. W. H. Freeman and Company, New York, New York, USA.

Villard, M.A. 1998. On forest-interior species, edge avoidance, area sensitivity, and dogmas in avian conservation. *Auk* 115:801–805

Wilcove, D. S. 1985. Nest predation in forest tracts and the decline of migratory songbirds. *Ecology* 66: 1211–1214.

Yahner, R. H. 1991. Avian nesting ecology in small even-aged stands. *Journal of Wildlife Management* 55: 155–159.

Yahner, R. H. 1996. Forest fragmentation, artificial nest studies, and predator abundance. *Conservation Biology* 10: 672–673.

Yahner, R. H., and B. L. Cypher. 1987. Effects of nest location on depredation of artificial arboreal nests. *Journal of Wildlife Management* 51: 178–181.

Yahner, R. H., and A. L. Wright. 1985. Depredation on artificial ground nests: effects of age and plot age. *Journal of Wildlife Management* 49: 508–513.

13

Influence of Stand Shape, Size, and Structural Stage on Forest Bird Communities in Colorado

Michael F. Carter and Scott W. Gillihan

INTRODUCTION

Much of the research on responses by forest bird populations to habitat alteration at the landscape and stand levels has been conducted in the eastern deciduous forest (see Faaborg et al. 1995 for a review). Many of those studies were conducted on forest patches isolated by urbanization or agriculture. Forested ecosystems in the Southern Rocky Mountains are fundamentally different in structure, function, and type of anthropogenic disturbance, at landscape and stand levels, and have avian communities that reflect the specific conditions of the Rockies. Extrapolating from other geographic regions or forest types containing other avian communities may be misleading (Hansen and Urban 1992). While eastern forests are replaced or fragmented by agriculture or development, the primary agent of anthropogenic disturbance in Southern Rocky Mountain forests has been timber harvesting (Hejl 1994). The result is a local, temporary setback to an earlier seral stage, or modification of the stand structure, rather than long-term or permanent conversion to a nonforested cover type. Eastern deciduous forests were historically more homogeneous and contiguous than Southern Rocky Mountain forests. The landscape pattern in Southern Rocky Mountains is a natural mosaic of forest stands (or patches) of varying size, shape, age, and species composition. This mosaic is maintained through the effects of natural conditions and processes such as topographic diversity (Miller et al. 1996), snow avalanches (Veblen et al. 1994), snow accumulation (Billings 1969), and fire, insects, and disease (Knight 1987). However, little information is available on relationships between birds and patterns in the landscape mosaic of the Southern Rocky Mountains. An integral component of the landscape-level response of birds is their relationship with characteristics of the elements that comprise the mosaic. The purpose of this study was to examine that relationship, to determine patterns of avian distributions in spruce-fir and mixed-conifer forests in relation to patch size, shape, and structural stage.

STUDY AREA AND METHODS

This study was conducted in spruce-fir and mixed-conifer forests in the Rio Grande National Forest of southern Colorado. The spruce-fir community was dominated by Engelmann spruce and subalpine fir. Dominant tree species in the mixed-conifer (in descending order of occurrence) included Douglas fir, ponderosa pine, limber pine, quaking aspen, and white fir, with scattered Engelmann spruce, subalpine fir, piñon pine, Rocky Mountain juniper, bristlecone pine, and blue spruce. Understory vegetation in mixed-conifer was dominated by buffaloberry and common juniper.

To initially locate patches with varying characteristics, we used the U.S. Forest Service Resource Information System (RIS) database. This database contains information from aerial photography, with forest patches classified into five commonly used structural stages (R. Metzger, *personal communication*) (Table 13.1). Using these maps, we allocated point-count transects among structural stages in a stratified fashion. These transects were then placed on aerial photos for field use in conducting the counts. Because management maps were coarse-grained and structural stages at census points were often different than on

Table 13.1. Structural stage definitions.

Type	Canopy cover	dbh* of overstory trees
1	—	<12.5 cm
2	<40%	12.5–23 cm
3	>40%	12.5–23 cm
4	<40%	>23 cm
5	>40%	>23 cm

* Diameter at breast height

management maps, it was necessary to redetermine structural stage in the field. Structural stage was based on total canopy cover (as measured with a concave spherical densitometer) and an estimate of diameter at breast height of canopy trees (Table 13.1). Patch shape and size were determined for each census point on photos after the point counts were conducted. The size of the forest patch in which the census point was located was determined from aerial photographs; patch sizes in the spruce-fir part of the study were categorized as <2 ha, 4–22 ha, and >22 ha. Patch sizes in mixed-conifer were <2 ha, 2–4 ha, 4–20 ha, and >20 ha. The different categories and sizes were a function of RIS data (i.e., we collected field data to match the scale of data collected in the RIS data set). Patch shape in both forest communities was categorized from aerial photos as round, double (twice as long as wide), and triple (three times as long as wide).

The avian community was censused with a modified fixed-radius point count method (Hutto et al. 1986). Point counts (15–24) were paced 200 m apart along the transect. At each point, an observer counted all birds seen or heard during a 5-minute period, estimating the distance to birds that were within 50 m. Birds detected beyond 50 m were grouped into an unlimited distance category. Birds flying over or through the forest patch in the vicinity of the census point were noted but were excluded from data analysis. Observers started at their first census points within 0.5 hr of sunrise and conducted point counts until 1030 hours, with the goal of completing at least 20 points. Observers were trained in estimating distances, pacing, and bird identification for four days prior to beginning field work. Training consisted of simultaneous point counts where observers independently conducted a count at the same time and place and then compared what was seen and heard. We conducted simultaneous counts until we felt all observers were acting as a unit.

Analyses were conducted using only the detections within 50 m of the census point. This range severely reduced sample size, but we felt it was warranted because it helped limit detections to the stands that were being censused. Because detections were low (especially in the spruce-fir community) and did not meet assumptions for parametric statistics, bird census results were converted to presence/absence data for each species at each point. Presence was tested for a response among patch characteristics (shape, size, structural stage) using hierarchical log-linear analysis (Fienberg 1970, Hutto et al. 1986, Wilkinson et al. 1996). For each species, we constructed models that tested for interaction between presence and levels of structural stage, patch shape, and patch size either as main terms or as interactions. A model containing all third-order interactions was first tested, then interactions not contributing to the overall model fit were dropped or added in a stepwise fashion until the most parsimonious model was found that was not statistically different (p <0.05) from the fully saturated model (Wilkinson et al. 1996). Species with fewer than 24 detections were not tested because data became too sparse. For a few species where sample size was low but where high detection rates in a cell were noted, we report the proportion of detections in the cell without a significance test. For levels of significant terms, standardized parameter estimates are presented. Values greater than >2.0 are considered indicative of significant responses (negative or positive according to sign) to the respective level of a patch characteristic (Wilkinson et al. 1996). Statistical analyses were conducted with program SYSTAT (SPSS 1996).

RESULTS

In the spruce-fir forest, five observers conducted 1,089 point counts during June 9–25, 1994. Points were dropped from the analysis that occurred in forest communities other than spruce-fir (n = 6), in logged spruce-fir (n = 157), or points with no bird detections (n = 128) leaving a total of 798 point counts for analysis. A total of 46 species was detected, of which we classified 22 as being spruce-fir-associated species using Andrews and Righter (1992) and personal experience. The other 24 species, although often found in or near spruce-fir forests, were considered to be associated primarily with other habitats (e.g., meadows and willow riparian) or forest types (e.g., aspen and ponderosa pine). A statistically significant response to at least one patch characteristic was found for eight spruce-fir species. Two species (brown creeper and golden-crowned kinglet) had sample sizes less than 24 but with obvious loadings in a cell, and we report the percent of detections in the cell without a significance test (Table 13.2). Twelve species that we classified *a priori* as spruce-fir community members had insufficient sample sizes with which to conduct statistical tests (Table 13.2).

In the mixed-conifer forest, five observers conducted 1,098 point counts during June 7–22, 1995. The type of forest patch at 83 points was classified as a community other than mixed-conifer, therefore those points were dropped from the analysis. In most cases the dropped points were in pure aspen stands, which contained an avian community very different from the mixed-conifer community as a whole. However, scattered aspen trees and small aspen stands (less than ~0.5 ha) were so pervasive that we considered them an integral part of the mixed-conifer community and retained any points that included them. An additional 13 points were dropped because bird censuses were conducted after 1100 hours, when bird activity was too low to yield a representative sample of the avian community. At the remaining 1,002 points, 70 species were detected within the 50 m radius. Loglinear analysis revealed a statistically significant response to at least one patch characteristic for 21 of the 25 species judged to be mixed-conifer community members (Andrews and Righter 1992) (Table 13.2).

Discussion
Species Responding to Patch Shape

The three patch shapes differ in relative amount of edge (triple has more edge than double, which has more edge than round), and species responding to patch shape could be responding to edge. Western tanager, in mixed-conifer, was the only species that responded to shape by seeming to respond negatively to the amount of edge (Table 13.2). However, rather than a response to edges, the response of tanagers to shape is instead likely related to differences in habitat. We found that total canopy cover, overstory, and tree height increased as the amount of edge increased relative to patch shape (Gillihan, *unpublished data*). These changes indicate closure of the forest canopy, which would be unfavorable to tanagers and may explain the relationship we found. This species prefers forested areas with either natural (Johnsgard 1986) or human-made (Franzreb and Ohmart 1978) openings. The source of these habitat differences is unclear, except that "triple"-shaped patches are possibly associated with riparian areas that produce larger trees and forests with closed canopies. Regarding edges, many of the edges in our study were simple boundaries between different structural stages or forest communities rather than hard edges between open and forested areas; this was especially true for the mixed-conifer forest. It is notable that only one species showed a response to patch shape, and the response was probably an artifact.

Species Responding to Patch Size

Patch size affects both the relative amount of edge habitat (i.e., smaller patches have relatively more edge) and the degree of insularity, a function of the amount of unbroken forest surrounding the census point. Two species that prefer the smaller size classes (Table 13.2) are generally categorized as species of open forest or forest edges: American robin (Keller and Anderson 1992) and dark-eyed junco (Johnsgard 1986). Their apparent preference for small patches may be related to

Table 13.2. Influence of patch variables on presence of bird species in spruce-fir and mixed-conifer forests of the Rio Grande National Forest, Colorado, as determined by log-linear analysis. Species are listed in taxonomic order. The number of point counts and proportion of total points at which a species was detected is listed. Significant terms can be either stage, shape, or size, or interactions. "l.s." means low sample size and that the species was not tested. In the Lambda/SE of Lambda column, for significant terms, results presented are levels of patch shape (ordered as Round, Double, and Triple), patch size (ordered from smallest class to largest), and structural stage (ordered by number: Types 1, 2, 3, 4, 5). Values greater than 2 indicate cells contributing significantly to the overall log-linear model. The sign indicates positive or negative association of the cell for the patch characteristic. Description is our interpretation of the log-linear results.

Species	Forest type	n (prop.)	Sign. term(s)	x^2 to remove from model (P)	Lambda/SE of Lambda	Description
Broad-tailed hummingbird	m-c	8 (0.008)	stage	32.24 (<0.0001)	5.1, 1.5, −1.3, 0.6, −2.6	avoids Type 5, prefers Type 1
Hairy woodpecker	s-f	3 (0.003)	l.s.			
Three-toed woodpecker	s-f	3 (0.003)	l.s.			
Northern flicker	s-f	5 (0.005)	l.s.			
Williamson's sapsucker	m-c	60 (0.060)	stage	20.25 (0.0004)	−0.8, 1.6, −0.9, 4.1, −1.7	prefers Type 4
Western wood-pewee	m-c	182 (0.182)	none			
Olive-sided flycatcher	s-f	6 (0.006)	l.s.			
Hammond's flycatcher	s-f	20 (0.022)	none			
Cordilleran flycatcher	m-c	57 (0.057)	stage	17.63 (0.0015)	−2.6, 1.1, 1.6, 1.7, 2.3	avoids Type 1, prefers Type 5
	m-c	45 (0.045)	stage	19.47 (0.0006)	−1.3, −1.3, −0.9, 1.6, 4.1	prefers Type 5
Violet-green swallow	m-c	53 (0.053)	stage	10.21 (0.0370)	0.5, 2.0, −1.5, 2.0, −1.4	prefers Types 2, 4
Steller's jay	m-c	175 (0.175)	none			
Clark's nutcracker	s-f	13 (0.014)	l.s.			
	m-c	143 (0.143)	none			
Gray jay	s-f	23 (0.025)	none			
Mountain chickadee	s-f	217 (0.235)	stage	39.18 (<0.0001)	−2.3, −3.2, −1.6, 4.8, 2.9	avoids Types 1, 2, prefers Types 4, 5
	m-c	248 (0.248)	stage	28.02 (<0.0001)	−4.0, 1.6, 3.4, −0.7, 2.0	avoids Type 1, prefers Types 3, 5
Red-breasted nuthatch	s-f	9 (0.010)	l.s.			
	m-c	77 (0.077)	stage	14.17 (0.0068)	−1.7, 1.2, −0.04, −1.2, 3.3	prefers Type 5
			size	12.06 (0.0072)	0.8, 2.7, 0.4, −2.6	avoids largest size class

Species		N (proportion)	Variable	χ² (P)	Standardized residuals	Interpretation
Brown creeper	s-f	18 (0.019)	l.s.			66.7% of detections in Type 5
	m-c	29 (0.029)	stage	14.59 (0.0056)	−0.8, −0.9, 0.2, −0.9, 3.9	prefers Type 5
House wren	m-c	117 (0.117)	stage	16.52 (0.0024)	0.1, −1.3, −2.0, 3.5, 1.4	avoids Type 3, prefers Type 4
Ruby-crowned kinglet	s-f	395 (0.427)	stage	40.64 (<0.0001)	−4.6, −2.1, 2.6, 1.9, 3.5	avoids Types 1,2, prefers Types 3, 5
	m-c	317 (0.316)	stage	62.00 (<0.0001)	−3.7, −2.2, 3.8, 1.3, 6.0	avoids Types 1, 2 prefers Types 3, 5
Golden-crowned kinglet	s-f	10 (0.011)	l.s.			70% of detections in Type 5
American robin	s-f	53 (0.057)	stage	31.85 (<0.0001)	4.9, 2.0, −0.9, −1.0, −2.6	avoids Type 5, prefers Types 1,2
	m-c	311 (0.310)	stage	25.34 (<0.0001)	4.3, −1.9, −2.1, 1.9, −1.2	avoids Type 3, prefers Type 1
			size	9.45 (0.0239)	1.7, 1.8, −1.7, −1.9	avoids largest size class
Townsend's solitaire	s-f	15 (0.016)	l.s.	24.98 (0.0001)	−1.8, 4.4, −0.3, 2.2, −1.8	prefers Types 2, 4
	m-c	98 (0.098)	stage			
Hermit thrush	s-f	111 (0.120)	stage	14.22 (<0.0066)	−2.5, −0.8, 1.1, 0.6, 2.9	avoids Type 1, prefers Type 5
	m-c	178 (0.178)	stage	13.25 (0.0101)	−2.2, −0.4, 1.4, 0.5, 2.9	avoids Type 1, prefers Type 5
Warbling vireo	m-c	379 (0.379)	size	16.01 (0.0011)	2.7, 0.3, 0.6, −3.6	avoids largest size, prefers smallest
Yellow-rumped warbler	s-f	328 (0.355)	stage	15.32 (0.0041)	−3.5, 2.0, 1.4, 0.8, −0.4	avoids Type 1
	m-c	422 (0.421)	stage	55.96 (<0.0001)	−5.7, 0.3, 5.2, −1.0, 2.7	avoids Type 1, prefers Types 3, 5
Brown-headed cowbird	m-c	45 (0.045)	none			
Western tanager	m-c	241 (0.241)	stage	34.56 (<0.0001)	−3.2, 3.1, 0.6, 4.1, −2.3	avoids Types 1, 5, prefers Types 2, 4
			shape	20.98 (<0.0001)	4.4, −0.7, −3.5	avoids triple, prefers round
White-crowned sparrow	s-f	51 (0.055)	stage	30.82 (<0.0001)	3.7, 3.6, −1.9, −0.1, −2.5	avoids Type 5, prefers Types 1,2
Chipping sparrow	m-c	129 (0.129)	stage	24.78 (0.0001)	3.2, −1.2, −2.9, 3.1, 0.5	avoids Type 3, prefers Types 1, 4
Green-tailed towhee	m-c	157 (0.157)	stage	93.55 (<0.0001)	7.3, 2.2, −2.9, 1.5, −1.6	avoids Type 3, prefers Types 1, 2
Dark-eyed junco	s-f	127 (0.137)	size	8.82 (0.0121)	2.7, −0.4, −2.4	avoids largest size, prefers smallest
	m-c	181 (0.181)	stage	18.34 (0.0011)	−2.0, 1.1, 2.6, 2.4, −2.3	avoids Types 1, 5, prefers Types 3, 4
Red crossbill	s-f	7 (0.008)	l.s.			
Cassin's finch	s-f	17 (0.018)	l.s.			
Pine grosbeak	s-f	7 (0.008)	l.s.			
Evening grosbeak	m-c	274 (0.274)	stage	26.74 (<0.0001)	−2.5, −1.1, −0.4, 4.9, 0.7	avoids Type 1, prefers Type 4
Pine siskin	s-f	81 (0.088)	stage	10.39 (0.0344)	1.1, −2.1, 0.7, −0.8, 2.5	avoids Type 2, prefers Type 5
	m-c	251 (0.250)	stage	43.13 (<0.0001)	−4.3, −1.7, 4.2, 1.4, 3.4	avoids Type 1, prefers Types 3, 5

the amount of edge habitat or the proximity of other patches, including open areas. Red-breasted nuthatch, a third species showing a patch size response, apparently prefers the second smallest patches and avoids the largest patch size. Possibly, this preferred patch size is associated with cavity-nesting sites.

Warbling vireos are typically found in aspen patches (Dobkin 1994), which were common in the mixed-conifer study area. This species' apparent preference for the smallest patches and avoidance of the largest (Table 13.2) is probably a function of our analysis, in which we dropped all census points that fell within large aspen patches.

Species Responding to Structural Stage

Structural stage is defined by total canopy cover and size of overstory trees (Table 13.1), and is related to stand age. Stand age is commonly used as the habitat variable in species/habitat association studies. Several species showed a preference for the most open/youngest patches, Types 1 and 2, in one or both forest communities (Table 13.2): broad-tailed hummingbird, American robin, green-tailed towhee, and white-crowned sparrow. These species favor open forest or forest openings for foraging and/or nesting (Johnsgard 1986; Andrews and Righter 1992). A number of mixed-conifer bird species preferred the more open forest, Types 2 and 4 (Table 13.2): Williamson's sapsucker, violet-green swallow, Townsend's solitaire, and western tanager. Chipping sparrow falls in an intermediate position between these two groups, using Type 1 and Type 4 forests more frequently, reflecting the forest margin habitat they use for nesting (Johnsgard 1986). House wrens are typically associated with open and riparian forests, especially where snags or dead limbs are available for nesting cavities (Johnsgard 1986). Their avoidance of dense Type 3 and preference for the relatively more open Type 4 may be related to differences in within-patch habitat features. Other species showed a preference for the older, more closed forest stages, Types 3, 4, and 5, in one or both forest communities (Table 13.2): Hammond's flycatcher, Cordilleran flycatcher, mountain chickadee, red-breasted nuthatch, brown creeper, ruby-crowned kinglet, golden-crowned kinglet, hermit thrush, pine siskin, and evening grosbeak. All of these species have been found to be associated with older or denser forests in other studies (Farr 1993, McGarigal and McComb 1995).

The responses of two species were paradoxical. Yellow-rumped warblers strongly avoided Type 1 patches in both forest communities, and showed a preference for the denser Types 3 and 5 in mixed-conifer. However, this species has shown a negative response to patch age in other studies (Farr 1993, Manuwal and Huff 1987), suggesting a preference for less dense, more open forest. This bird was the most common species encountered in the mixed-conifer forest, and the second-most common in spruce-fir. This warbler's pervasiveness in all structural classes, save Type 1, may indicate a generalist which is accepting of most forest and structural types other than Type 1. Dark-eyed juncos demonstrated contradictory results between the two forest communities. Whether this contradiction reflects a real difference in response to forest type is unknown. Dark-eyed juncos may be responding to inherent differences between spruce-fir and mixed-conifer forests that we did not measure. Pine siskins exhibited a positive response to openings created by patch cuts and strip cuts (Keller and Anderson 1992) but a negative response to selection cuts (Franzreb and Ohmart 1978). Pine siskins were most common in Type 5 in both forest types but avoided Type 2 in spruce-fir, and preferred Type 3 and avoided Type 1 in mixed-conifer. This lack of an obvious pattern, other than preference for Type 5, could be due to the species' nonterritorial, nomadic flocking behavior as groups seek out suitable cone crops (Erskine 1977) or perhaps in response to foraging opportunities for seeds and insects on the ground (Bent 1968).

Species with No Response

Most species that did not demonstrate a response to patch characteristics (Table 13.2) are wide-ranging habitat generalists (brown-headed cowbird), hold large territories (Steller's jay, Clark's nutcracker, and gray jay), or are nomadic (red crossbill, Cassin's finch, and pine grosbeak) (Andrews and Righter 1992, Johnsgard 1986). Thus, they could be expected to occur in a variety of habitats, rather than showing an affinity for a single habitat. Also, some of these species (the corvids) breed early in the spring season and were probably no longer on territories when we conducted our censuses. Finally, some of these species (hairy woodpecker, three-toed woodpecker, northern flicker, and olive-sided flycatcher) are closely tied to within-patch features, such as snags, and thus should be expected to occur in any patch that contains such features, independent of other patch characteristics.

Study Limitations

Because an observer on the ground cannot easily determine the extent of a particular patch, confirming that a detected bird is actually in the patch being censused is not always possible. This is especially problematic in small patches, where an observer might detect birds in that patch as well as in adjacent patches, while an observer in a large patch might detect only birds within the large patch. We attempted to mitigate this effect by analyzing only the 50 m radius subset of our data—a 50 m radius yields a circle of 0.8 ha, smaller than the 2 ha maximum of the smallest patch size category. However, some census points were near patch boundaries, and some individual birds may have been recorded from adjacent patches. Because adjacent patches could have different characteristics, this factor may have masked some habitat preferences in our study.

This study relied only on the presence of a bird in a particular patch to indicate suitability of that patch. However, a species' presence is only one measure of the suitability of a particular patch; some measure of breeding success should be included as well, as the local population could be supported by immigration from other, more suitable, patches (Van Horne 1983).

Management Implications

Our results, in two forest communities, indicate that structural stage influences more Southern Rocky Mountain bird species than does patch size or shape; this may be a widespread trend in western forests. Much of the structural influence was forest-community dependent, but a strong trend is evident among the two forest communities of species using Type 5 (Table 13.3). Rosenberg and Raphael (1986) found few correlations between patch size and populations of Douglas fir species. Patch shape, especially when expressed as amount of edge, seems to be of slightly more importance. Rosenberg and Raphael (1986) identified a small number of forest-interior and area-sensitive species, and a somewhat larger number of species that appeared to avoid the "hard" edges marking the boundary of forested and clear-cut areas. The apparent limited influence of patch size and shape is probably related to the natural mosaic of Rocky Mountain forests. Rocky Mountain birds have evolved in a landscape mosaic containing a diversity of forest patch shapes, sizes, and structural stages maintained by natural disturbance events. Their evolutionary history has contributed to a need for contact with a variety of forest patches of varying shape, size, structural stage, and (for mixed-conifer) species composition. An effective management strategy for maintaining spruce-fir and mixed-conifer bird populations would be to maintain a landscape mosaic of habitat patches of varying species composition and a full complement of structural classes, especially Type 5. Ideally, management activities would yield a numerical and spatial distribution of patch shapes, sizes, and structural stages that would parallel the numerical and spatial distribution found in unmanaged forests.

Some species that responded to structural stage exhibited two basic patterns: either a continuous response or a categorical response. Hermit thrush in the spruce-fir forest provide an example of a species exhibiting a continuous response as it showed a gradual increase in abundance with increasing structural stage. An example of a species

Table 13.3. Summary of distribution of species among forest types and structural stages (see Table 13.2) for assignments of species to forest communities. Figure omits species responding to patch size (n = 4) and patch shape (n = 1).

	SPECIES COMMON TO			
	Mixed-conifer only	**Mixed-conifer**	**Spruce-fir**	**Spruce-fir only**
TYPE 1	Broad-tailed Hummingbird Chipping sparrow Green-tailed Towhee	American Robin ————————————	———— American Robin	White-crowned Sparrow
TYPE 2	Violet-green Swallow Western Tanager Green-tailed Towhee	Townsend's Solitaire	American Robin Yellow-rumped Warbler	White-crowned Sparrow
TYPE 3		Mountain Chickadee Yellow-rumped Warbler Dark-eyed Junco Pine Siskin	Ruby-crowned Kinglet	
TYPE 4	Williamson's Sapsucker Violet-green Swallow Western Tanager Chipping Sparrow Evening Grosbeak	House Wren Townsend's Solitaire Dark-eyed Junco	Mountain Chickadee	
TYPE 5	Cordilleran Flycatcher	Hammond's Flycatcher Mountain Chickadee ———— Red-breasted Nuthatch Brown Creeper —————— Ruby-crowned Kinglet ——— Hermit Thrush —————— Yellow-rumped Warbler Pine Siskin ———————	———— Mountain Chickadee ———— Brown Creeper ——— Ruby-crowned Kinglet ——— Hermit Thrush ——— Pine siskin	Golden-crowned Kinglet

with a categorical response would be the brown creeper. Creepers were relatively uncommon in all but the oldest structural class. Managers should be aware of the differing impacts of forest alteration on species that demonstrate a continuous versus a categorical response to forest structure. The abundance of those species with continuous responses would gradually change with alterations of forest from one structural class to another. These species would still be present, but at a slightly different abundance. However, species with a categorical response apparently have a threshold of tolerance for habitat change. Above that threshold, where their habitat needs are met, they are relatively common; below that threshold they are markedly less common. Brown creeper populations would decline significantly if a Type 5 forest patch was logged and set back to an earlier class. Obviously some key components of the habitat are lost when going from Type 5 to any of the lower classes. To preserve biodiversity in managed forests, managers should retain natural processes such as fire (Hutto et al. 1993) that produce habitats for woodpeckers and flycatchers (e.g., olive-sided), and human alterations such as logging should be carried out so as to mimic the timing and pattern of natural processes (Hutto et al. 1993, Hejl et al. 1995) with a clear regard for maintaining older seral stages.

The issue of juxtaposition, or the positional relationship of patches within the forest mosaic, may be more important than other landscape traits (Keller and Anderson 1992). A species might prefer a particular forest type only when it is adjacent to another type. American robins, for example, nest in seedling-sapling stages but forage in forest openings. Suitable habitat for this species includes an appropriate mix and spatial arrangement of both forest types. Given the highly heterogeneous nature of the forest in which Southern Rocky Mountain species have evolved, other species probably have similar requirements of habitat adjacency. Before a truly effective management strategy can be formulated, the interplay of species' habitat needs and forest patch juxtaposition needs to be articulated. This would require examining bird demographics in relation to the forest mosaic. Such an investigation would include bird census data, breeding data, and forest patch data analyzed with the tools of landscape ecology.

ACKNOWLEDGMENTS

We thank the members of the field crews: Chuck Aid, John Bishop, Susan Bonfield, Jim Bradley, Rich Levad, and David Pavlacky. We thank Rick Metzger, Kirk Navo, and Richard Roth for providing management perspectives in the design of this project. Funding was provided by the Rocky Mountain Region of the U.S. Forest Service and Great Outdoors Colorado Trust Fund through the Colorado Division of Wildlife. Carl Bock, David Fleck, Sallie Hejl, Richard Hutto, Richard Knight, Tony Leukering, and Chuck Preston provided helpful reviews of earlier versions of this manuscript.

Literature Cited

Andrews, R., and R. Righter. 1992. *Colorado birds*. Denver Museum of Natural History, Denver, Colorado, USA.

Bent, A. C. 1968. *Life histories of North American cardinals, grosbeaks, buntings, towhees, finches, sparrows, and allies*. Part 1. Dover Publications, Inc., New York, New York, USA.

Billings, W. D. 1969. Vegetational pattern near alpine timberline as affected by fire-snowdrift interaction. *Vegetatio* 19: 192–207.

Dobkin, D. S. 1994. *Conservation and management of neotropical migrant landbirds in the Northern Rockies and Great Plains*. University of Idaho Press, Moscow, Idaho, USA.

Erskine, A. J. 1977. Birds in boreal Canada. Canadian Wildlife Service. Report Series No. 41.

Faaborg, J., M. Brittingham, T. Donovan, and J. Blake. 1995. Neotropical migrant responses to habitat fragmentation in the temperate zone. Pages 357–380 *in* D. M. Finch and T. E. Martin, editors. *Ecology and management of migratory birds*. Oxford University Press, Oxford, UK.

Farr, D. 1993. Bird abundance in spruce forests of west central Alberta: the role of stand age. Pages 55–62 *in* D. H. Kuhnke, editor. *Birds in the boreal forest*. Proceedings of a workshop. Forestry Canada, Northwest Region, Northern Forestry Centre, Edmonton, Alberta, Canada.

Fienberg, S. E. 1970. The analysis of multidimensional contingency tables. *Ecology* 51: 419–433.

Franzreb, K. E., and R. D. Ohmart. 1978. The effects of timber harvesting on breeding birds in a mixed-conifer forest. *Condor* 80: 431–441.

Hansen, A. J., and D. L. Urban. 1992. Avian response to landscape pattern: the role of species' life histories. *Landscape Ecology* 7: 163–180.

Hejl, S. J. 1994. Human-induced changes in bird populations in coniferous forests in western North America during the past 100 years. *Studies in Avian Biology* 15: 232–246.

Hejl, S. J., R. L. Hutto, C. R. Preston, and D. M. Finch. 1995. The effects of silvicultural treatments on forest birds in the Rocky Mountains. Pages 220–244 *in* T. Martin and D. M. Finch, editors. *Population ecology and conservation of neotropical migratory birds*. Oxford University Press, New York, New York, USA.

Hutto, R. L., S. J. Hejl, C. R. Preston, and D. M. Finch. 1993. Effects of silvicultural treatments on forest birds in the Rocky Mountains: implications and management recommendations. Pages 386–391 *in* D. M. Finch and P. W. Stangel, editors. *Status and management of neotropical migratory birds.* General Technical Forest Service, U.S. Department of Agriculture.

Hutto, R. L., S. M. Pleschet, and P. Hendricks. 1986. A fixed-radius point count method for nonbreeding and breeding season use. *Auk* 103: 593–602.

Johnsgard, P. A. 1986. *Birds of the Rocky Mountains.* University of Nebraska Press, Lincoln, Nebraska, USA.

Keller, M. E., and S. H. Anderson. 1992. Avian use of habitat configurations created by forest cutting in southeastern Wyoming. *Condor* 94: 55–65.

Knight, D. H. 1987. Parasites, lightning, and the vegetation mosaic in wilderness landscapes. Pages 59–83 *in* M. G. Turner, editor. *Landscape heterogeneity and disturbance.* Springer-Verlag, New York, New York, USA.

Manuwal, D. A., and M. H. Huff. 1987. Spring and winter bird populations in a Douglas-fir forest sere. *Journal of Wildlife Management* 51: 586–595.

McGarigal, K., and W. C. McComb. 1995. Relationships between landscape structure and breeding birds in the Oregon Coast Range. *Ecological Monographs* 65: 235–260.

Miller, J. R., L. A. Joyce, R. L. Knight, and R. M. King. 1996. Forest roads and landscape structure in the Southern Rocky Mountains. *Landscape Ecology* 11: 115–127.

Rosenberg, K. V., and M. G. Raphael. 1986. Effects of forest fragmentation on vertebrates in Douglas-fir forests. Pages 263–272 *in* J. Verner, M. L.Morrison, and C. J. Ralph, editors. *Wildlife 2000: modeling habitat relationships of terrestrial vertebrates.* University of Wisconsin Press, Madison, Wisconsin, USA.

SPSS. 1996. *SYSTAT 6.0 for Windows®* SPSS, Inc., Chicago, Illinois, USA.

Van Horne, B. 1983. Density as a misleading indicator of habitat quality. *Journal of Wildlife Management* 47: 893–901.

Veblen, T. T., K. S. Hadley, E. M. Nel, T. Kitzberger, M. Reid, and R. Villalba. 1994. Disturbance regime and disturbance interactions in a Rocky Mountain subalpine forest. *Journal of Ecology* 82: 125–135.

Wilkinson, L, G. Blank, and C. Gruber. 1996. *Desktop analysis with SYSTAT.* Prentice Hall, Upper Saddle River, New Jersey, USA.

14

Effects of Wilderness Designation on the Landscape Structure of a National Forest

Jonathan F. Lowsky and Richard L. Knight

INTRODUCTION

The greatest threat to the long-term maintenance of global biological diversity is direct anthropogenic habitat alteration (Burgess and Sharpe 1981, Noss 1983, Harris 1984, Wilcox and Murphy 1985). The value of wilderness areas that are intended to sustain negligible human alteration, then, is in their ability to maintain the ecological integrity of the systems they are meant to protect. Unfortunately, even rather large reserves tend to be but remnants of greater, more contiguous systems that are strongly influenced by exogenous human-mediated processes (Schonewald-Cox 1983, Janzen 1983, 1986, Newmark 1985, Schonewald-Cox and Bayless 1986). Naturally occurring fragmentation is a process that, by definition, is essential to the maintenance of many ecosystems and contributes to ecological heterogeneity (Baker 1994, Romme 1982, Turner 1989). However, when fragmentation is the result of human activities, its effects can be devastating, critically affecting the spatial (e.g., the virtual elimination of old growth eastern deciduous forest) and temporal (e.g., roads are forever) dynamics of a system. Thus, considering protected areas within a landscape context has become increasingly important (Noss 1983, 1991, Schonewald-Cox 1983, Janzen 1986, Schonewald-Cox and Bayless 1986, Franklin 1993, Lamberson et al. 1992).

Current conservation literature focuses on the importance of wilderness, yet little attention has focused on the explicit quantification of this importance (Diamond 1975, Noss 1983, Soule and Simberloff 1986, Pickett et al. 1992). Other studies (e.g., Franklin & Forman

1987, Krummel et al. 1987, Spies et al. 1994, Wallin et al. 1994, Mladenoff et al. 1993, Turner et al. 1996) have described the landscape pattern differences and fragmentation effects resulting from the effects of forestry practices or human alteration of disturbance regimes; however, none have focused explicitly on wilderness. If wilderness areas are to be functionally significant within a greater landscape, securing the integrity of the natural landscape structure and improving upon the landscape structure of the unprotected matrix in which they are embedded is imperative. Landscape ecology involves the study of landscape patterns, the interactions among patches within a landscape mosaic, and how these patterns and interactions change over time; as such it is an approach that may be used as a valuable tool for the assessment of existing protected areas. The purpose of this study was to provide a concrete quantification of the effect that land use designation has on landscape structure.

The composition and configuration of landscape elements can affect the ecological processes of a protected area (Franklin and Forman 1987, Krummel et al. 1987, Spies et al. 1994, Wallin et al. 1994, McGarigal and Marks 1994, Mladenoff et al. 1993, Turner et al. 1996, Turner 1989). Because these attributes of a landscape can be measured, described, and quantified, they can provide insights into the degree of fragmentation that has occurred. Here, we use landscape metrics to determine whether the composition and configuration of major forest types within a wilderness system differ from the non-wilderness national forest lands surrounding it. As the first step in this process, we conducted a quantitative landscape analysis of the spatial pattern of the designated wilderness areas of the U.S. Forest Service (USFS) Arapaho-Roosevelt National Forest (ARNF) in north-central Colorado, and compared this landscape to the nonwilderness multiple-use lands of the ARNF. This analysis was conducted to determine if any discernible differences existed in landscape pattern and structure between a protected landscape and the multiple-use national forest lands in which it is embedded. If such differences can be consistently described, information useful for evaluating the ecological integrity of nature reserve systems versus the unprotected lands surrounding them can be derived, aiding in the long-term management of these areas.

The second step of our analysis was to test a series of predictions regarding the effects of land protection on landscape structure. These predictions are founded largely on the notion that once an area is protected from extractive resource use (e.g., timber harvest, mining) and anthropogenic fragmentation agents (e.g., roads, development) the overall composition and configuration of vegetation will be more suitable for the persistence of those species most sensitive to habitat alteration (e.g., area-sensitive, edge-sensitive, and isolation-sensitive [Temple 1991]) (Burke and Nol 1998, Fahrig 1998, Gaines et al. 1998, Peacock and Smith 1997, Wolff et al. 1997, MacNally and Bennett 1997, McGarigal and McComb 1995). If these predictions are indeed true, then protected areas of public lands might be disproportionately more important to the persistence of vertebrate biological diversity than the surrounding matrix and could provide a model for modification of landscape structure in human-dominated landscapes.

METHODS
Study Area

The study area was the ARNF, and only national forest lands were considered in this analysis. Although the ARNF is actually two separate national forests, they are administered and managed jointly. These forests extend southward from the Wyoming border along the backbone of the Front Range of the northern Colorado Rocky Mountains to Mount Evans, the Continental Divide and Hoosier Pass, and westward from the foothills of the Front Range to the Medicine Bow Range to the north and the Gore Range to the south. Elevation within the study area ranges from 1,752 m in the eastern foothills to 4,346 m at the highest point, Mount Evans. Forest vegetation in the ARNF ranges from xerophytic Rocky Mountain juniper dominated vegetation at the warmer, drier low elevations to mesophytic Engelmann spruce-subalpine fir dominated vegetation at the cooler, moister high elevations. The dominant forest types (comprising 99% of forest cover) are aspen, Engelmann spruce-subalpine fir, lodgepole pine, and ponderosa pine (Table 14.1).

Eight wilderness areas exist within the ARNF: Cache La Poudre, Comanche Peaks, Indian Peaks, Mount Evans, Neota, Never Summer, Rawah, and Vasquez . They vary in size from 29,634 ha (Comanche Peaks) to 3,818 ha (Cache La Poudre). Total area of the ARNF wilderness system is 119,498 ha as compared to 402,022 ha of nonwilderness area. These wilderness areas were designated between 1978 and 1980.

Cover Type Classification and Map Creation

Forest cover types were identified based on the dominant plant species that was currently (not potentially) dominant, using canopy

Table 14.1. Patch type metrics of the major forest types of the Arapaho-Roosevelt National Forest by seral stage and land use designation with totals where applicable.

Metric	Forest Type	Land Use	Seral Stage			
			Early	Mid	Late	Total
Area (ha)	Aspen	Wilderness	0.00	880.00	199.75	1079.75
		Matrix	424.00	14646.00	1526.50	16596.50
	Douglas Fir	Wilderness	14.50	544.20	1008.00	1566.70
		Matrix	174.50	10176.25	12819.75	23170.50
	Lodgepole Pine	Wilderness	241.00	18789.75	18376.50	37407.25
		Matrix	4846.00	102287.70	55372.75	162506.50
	Ponderosa Pine	Wilderness	11.00	1553.00	1681.00	3245.00
		Matrix	668.75	35719.75	16430.50	52819.00
	Spruce-Fir	Wilderness	236.50	11235.25	23099.50	34571.25
		Matrix	1467.25	22615.00	42458.00	66540.25
Mean Core Area (ha)	Aspen	Wilderness	—	5.58	12.19	17.77
		Matrix	1.79	2.61	2.40	6.80
	Douglas Fir	Wilderness	6.25	26.30	19.36	51.91
		Matrix	3.26	4.71	5.34	13.31
	Lodgepole Pine	Wilderness	36.30	72.71	80.10	189.11
		Matrix	3.07	31.34	18.21	52.62
	Ponderosa Pine	Wilderness	5.25	21.04	40.53	66.82
		Matrix	4.83	12.65	8.53	26.01
	Spruce-Fir	Wilderness	27.38	36.99	100.87	165.24
		Matrix	5.22	11.39	28.56	45.17

Mean Area Per Disjunct Core (ha)					
Aspen	Wilderness	—	5.58	7.84	13.42
	Matrix	3.81	4.04	2.40	6.44
Douglas Fir	Wilderness	6.25	24.55	23.67	48.22
	Matrix	4.41	5.44	5.82	11.26
Lodgepole Pine	Wilderness	45.38	43.14	51.47	94.61
	Matrix	4.63	19.58	13.61	33.19
Ponderosa Pine	Wilderness	5.25	17.66	39.23	56.89
	Matrix	6.11	10.20	8.26	18.46
Spruce-Fir	Wilderness	27.38	27.84	55.48	83.32
	Matrix	6.57	10.62	20.57	31.19
Patch Density (#/ha)					
Aspen	Wilderness	—	0.06	0.01	
	Matrix	0.02	0.57	0.06	
Douglas Fir	Wilderness	0.00	0.01	0.03	
	Matrix	0.01	0.28	0.32	
Lodgepole Pine	Wilderness	0.00	0.16	0.15	
	Matrix	0.20	0.61	0.53	
Ponderosa Pine	Wilderness	0.00	0.04	0.03	
	Matrix	0.02	0.46	0.30	
Spruce-Fir	Wilderness	0.01	0.18	0.15	
	Matrix	0.04	0.33	0.29	
Total Core Area Index (%)					
Aspen	Wilderness	—	44.40	54.94	
	Matrix	35.02	35.34	34.52	
Douglas Fir	Wilderness	43.10	67.66	63.39	
	Matrix	42.98	45.45	46.54	
Lodgepole Pine	Wilderness	75.31	75.07	77.58	
	Matrix	43.52	64.25	60.35	

Continued on next page

Table 14.1—*continued*

Metric	Forest Type	Land Use	Seral Stage			
			Early	Mid	Late	Total
Total Core Area Index (%) (contd.)	Ponderosa Pine	Wilderness	47.73	63.68	72.34	
		Matrix	48.41	55.88	53.50	
	Spruce-Fir	Wilderness	69.45	69.14	76.85	
		Matrix	48.34	56.85	66.87	
Edge Density (m/ha)	Aspen	Wilderness	—	1.33	0.23	
		Matrix	0.29	9.96	1.03	
	Douglas Fir	Wilderness	0.02	0.47	0.98	
		Matrix	0.09	5.26	6.52	
	Lodgepole Pine	Wilderness	0.15	11.50	10.15	
		Matrix	2.71	31.69	19.52	
	Ponderosa Pine	Wilderness	0.01	1.41	1.17	
		Matrix	0.32	13.93	6.86	
	Spruce-Fir	Wilderness	0.18	8.96	13.12	
		Matrix	0.72	8.98	12.62	
Contrast-weighted Edge Density (m/ha)	Aspen	Wilderness	—	0.48	0.08	
		Matrix	0.14	4.34	0.46	
	Douglas Fir	Wilderness	0.02	0.18	0.48	
		Matrix	0.063	2.44	3.58	
	Lodgepole Pine	Wilderness	0.09	5.02	4.76	
		Matrix	1.33	14.63	9.52	
	Ponderosa Pine	Wilderness	0.01	0.62	0.64	
		Matrix	0.16	7.47	3.76	

Spruce-Fir	Wilderness	0.08	4.84	7.49
	Matrix	0.38	4.22	6.76
Mean Nearest Neighbor (m)				
Aspen	Wilderness	—	574.88	3542.51
	Matrix	1720.53	249.99	1311.14
Douglas Fir	Wilderness	—	530.11	140.35
	Matrix	2634.93	327.20	294.94
Lodgepole Pine	Wilderness	11366.89	477.76	384.24
	Matrix	303.42	157.22	225.56
Ponderosa Pine	Wilderness	—	359.57	565.23
	Matrix	1166.39	181.98	297.79
Spruce-Fir	Wilderness	18645.64	415.71	356.22
	Matrix	851.86	271.22	247.97
Mean Proximity Index				
Aspen	Wilderness	—	23.51	4.27
	Matrix	2.46	28.20	9.27
Douglas Fir	Wilderness	0.00	12.20	10.32
	Matrix	4.41	26.58	37.45
Lodgepole Pine	Wilderness	0.01	664.96	229.54
	Matrix	18.40	1434.877	261.64
Ponderosa Pine	Wilderness	0.00	94.04	330.73
	Matrix	19.05	185.42	52.55
Spruce-Fir	Wilderness	0.00	89.07	454.89
	Matrix	14.15	80.62	415.60

cover as the measure of dominance. Nonforested patches were those never dominated or incapable of being dominated by forest trees, or lands previously having such cover and currently maintained in nonforest cover by forest management. Seral stages are developmental stages of forest stands described in terms of average age and canopy closure (Buttery and Gillam 1987). Structural stage was classified as early-, mid-, or late-seral following the work of Williams and Marcot (1991). We created a map of the ARNF rasterized (25-m cell size) from vector attribute and coverage data from the USFS Region 2 Resource Information System (RIS) using workstation ARC/INFO 6.1 geographic information system (GIS) (ESRI, Inc. 1992) consisting of the wilderness areas and the non-protected matrix of the ARNF. Each wilderness area was considered an independent element of the nature reserve system.

Analysis and Predictions

ARC/INFO 6.1 and FRAGSTATS 2.0 (raster version) software (McGarigal and Marks 1994) were used for the analysis of the structure of the landscapes in question. Throughout this paper, the term "matrix" refers to the nonwilderness national forest lands surrounding the wilderness areas of the ARNF. The predictions below were tested as null hypotheses using a suite of metrics that were chosen *a priori*. We compared the results from the wilderness areas to the matrix.

Although some landscape metrics are unitless and can, therefore, be misleading and uninformative when used as descriptors of a condition or state for a single unit or landscape, they have been used effectively when making comparisons of different landscapes of the same scale (e.g., Mladenoff et al. 1993) or the same landscape at different points in time (e.g., Ripple et al. 1991). Inferential statistics were not used in this analysis because all patches in the landscape were included in the calculations.

Composition. Prediction 1: A greater proportion of each major forest type exists in late-seral stages within wilderness areas than within the non-protected matrix .

Prediction 2: Wilderness areas should be dominated by late-seral stages whereas the matrix should be dominated by early-seral stages.

Two indices were used to characterize landscape composition: percent landscape occupied by each patch type and landscape dominance. Patch type was characterized by the species and seral stage of the dominant tree species in a patch. Landscape dominance was used to determine the extent to which a particular landscape was dominated by either a few patch types covering a large area, or by an even distribution of patch types (Turner 1989).

Configuration. Landscape configuration was characterized by four groups of metrics: (1) patch size, (2) patch shape and core area, (3) patch edge, and (4) spatial distribution of patches.

Patch Size. Prediction 3: Patch size of a given forest type should be greater in the wilderness areas than in the matrix.

Analysis and results focus on the median rather than the mean of most of the configuration metrics at the patch and class levels because it is a better measure of central tendency of a highly skewed distribution than the mean (Ott 1993). Patch area is an important indicator of habitat fragmentation. For example, bird species richness and utilization by some species are strongly correlated with patch size (e.g. Robbins et al. 1989). The total and relative area of each patch type is also important. For example, a landscape with a smaller median patch size for a given type than another landscape might be considered more fragmented.

Patch Shape. Prediction 4: Patches of a given forest type should be less euclidean within the wilderness areas than in the matrix.

Patch shape is important in determining the amount of patch edge (see Core Area). We measured patch shape using a shape index (SI) based on the McGarigal and Marks (1994) modification of Patton's formula (1975) for use in raster applications. SI measures the complexity of patch shape compared to a standard shape. It is important to note that perimeter length is biased upward in raster images because of the stair-stepping pattern of line segments, and the magnitude of this bias varies in relation to the grain or resolution of the image (McGarigal and Marks 1994). Also, because patches that have identical areas and perimeters may have different shapes, shape indexes must be considered along with core area metrics that reveal such differences.

Core Area. Prediction 5: The ratio of core area to total area should be greater in the wilderness areas than in the matrix.

Prediction 6: Forested patches within the wilderness system should have greater core area than those in the matrix.

Core area is the area within a patch beyond some specified edge distance or buffer width (Temple 1986) and is a function of patch size, patch shape, and the depth-of-edge effects. A 50 m edge distance was used in this analysis based on the review by Paton (1994). Core area was determined by eliminating edge area defined by a 50 m buffer within each patch. Two core area metrics were used in this analysis: total core area index (TCAI) and mean area per disjunct core (MCA).

TCAI quantifies the percentage of the total area comprising each patch type occupied by interior or core area. We defined mean core area as the mean area per disjunct core (McGarigal and Marks 1994). The result of this definition is that even when a patch contains two or more core areas each is considered as a separate entity, thus, the mean has greater ecological credence.

Patch Edge. Prediction 7: The ratio of edge length to total area is greater in the matrix than in the wilderness areas.

Prediction 8: The edge contrast of a given forest type is greater in the matrix than in the wilderness areas.

Edge density (ED) standardizes edge to a per-unit-area basis that permits patch type comparisons among landscapes of varying size (McGarigal and Marks 1994). ED equals zero when the entire landscape consists of a given patch type. In addition, contrast-weighted edge density (CWED) was used to evaluate edge characteristics (McGarigal and Marks 1994). Comparing edge density among landscapes may be misleading because edge types function differently. For example, the edge between a patch comprising late-seral Engelmann spruce-subalpine fir and a mid-seral patch of the same type is functionally quite different from the edge between late-seral Engelmann spruce-subalpine fir and an early-seral aspen patch. Because CWED reduces the length of each edge segment proportionate to the degree of contrast between adjoining patch types, landscapes with the same CWED are presumed to have the same amount of total edge effect from a functional perspective (McGarigal and Marks 1994).

Spatial Distribution of Patches. Prediction 9: Patches of a given forest type are more densely distributed in the matrix than in the wilderness areas.

Prediction 10: A given forest type will be distributed in larger, more evenly dispersed patches within the wilderness areas than within the matrix.

Spatial distribution was characterized by measures of patch density and Gustafson and Parker's (1994) proximity index. Patch density, like edge density, describes the number of patches on a per-area basis that permits comparisons of landscapes of varying size. A landscape with a greater density of patches of a specific patch type would be considered more fragmented than a landscape with a lower density of patches of that type (McGarigal and Marks 1994).

The proximity index considers the size and proximity of all patches with edges that are within a specified search radius of the focal patch.

The search radius used in this analysis was the greatest distance between any patches in the given landscape, thus encompassing all patches on the landscape. A patch located in a neighborhood in which the corresponding patch type is distributed in larger, more contiguous, and/or closer patches than another patch will have a larger index value (McGarigal and Marks 1994).

RESULTS

Composition

Forest cover types comprised a smaller percentage of total land area in the wilderness areas (65%) than in its matrix (94%) largely due to the extensive areas above treeline within the wilderness system. Lodgepole pine and Engelmann spruce-subalpine fir occupied more than half (60%) of the total area of the ARNF, 92% of the total forested area of the wilderness areas, and 67% of the total forested area of the matrix. Of the major forest types (those occupying greater than 5% of the forested landscape) occurring in the ARNF, only Engelmann spruce-subalpine fir occupied a greater proportion (33% more) of the wilderness areas than the matrix. Late-seral stages dominated the forested patches of the wilderness system (58%) whereas mid-seral stages dominated the matrix (58%) (see Figure 14.2).

Configuration

Patch Size. Forest patches within the wilderness system were larger than in the multiple-use matrix (see Figure 14.3). Median patch size of forested land within the wilderness areas (14.5 ha, range 0.25–2,842.25 ha) was 64% greater than in the matrix (5.25 ha, range 0.25–8,357.25 ha) (Fig. 14.2). Of the major forest types in the ARNF, only Douglas fir had a smaller median patch size in the wilderness system than in the matrix.

Whereas less than 4% of the forested patches in the matrix were larger than 100 ha, more than 13% of the wilderness patches were larger than 100 ha. The majority of forest patches within the wilderness system were greater than 10 ha (59%) but were less than 10 ha in the matrix (66%) (Fig. 14.2). A greater proportion (66%) of late-seral patches within the wilderness system were greater than 10 ha than in the matrix (27%). In addition, more than twice the proportion of late-seral patches within the wilderness system (19%) were greater than 100 ha than in the matrix (9%). The forested patches in the wilderness system had less variability in patch sizes relative to its mean (coefficient of variation [CV] = 284.18) than the matrix (CV = 585.88).

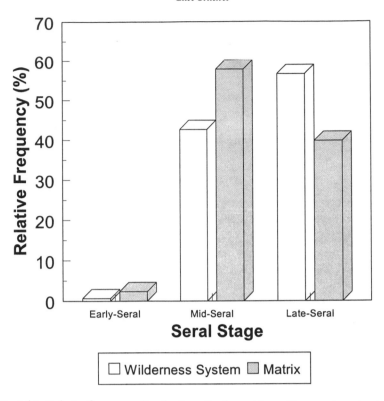

Fig. 14.1. Relative frequency distribution of early-, mid-, and late-seral patches in the wilderness areas and the matrix.

Core Area and Patch Shape. Protected forest patches had greater amounts of core area per patch, greater area per disjunct core, a greater ratio of core area to total area, and more complex shapes than matrix patches (Table 14.2). Core habitat represented a greater proportion of the total area of each major forest type in the wilderness system (Table 14.1) and all mid- and late-seral major forest types had more interior area per patch and more area per core in the wilderness system than the matrix (Table 14.1). Although the distribution of core area for both the wilderness system and the matrix was heavily skewed right, only 2% of the matrix patches had more than 100 ha of interior habitat and 52% had less than 1 ha of interior. However, 11% of wilderness areas patches had more than 100 ha of interior and only 29% had less than 1 ha of interior (Fig. 14.3).

Mean patch shape complexity was greater for all major forest types in the wilderness areas than in the matrix except early-seral ponderosa

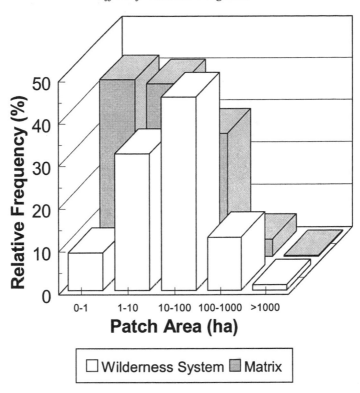

Fig. 14.2. Relative frequency distributions of patch area in the wilderness areas and the matrix.

pine. Shape complexity calculated for the wilderness areas varied from 1.00 to 17.21 and from 1.00 to 16.15 in the matrix. Although the distribution of patch shape was similar for the wilderness areas and the matrix, mean and median values were greater in the wilderness areas (Table 14.2) and the proportion of patches with shape values under 1.25 was greater in the matrix (47.12%) than in the wilderness (36.48%). The mode shape complexity value for all landscapes was 1.0 and is an artifact of the rasterization of the patch polygons. Small patches were simplified due to the 50 m^2 cell size used in the rasterization process. No patch that was greater than 1.0 ha had a shape complexity value of 1.0. The wilderness areas had greater variability in patch shape relative to its respective mean (CV = 46.78) than the matrix (CV = 42.29).

Patch Edge. Edge densities confirmed the greater level of fragmentation in the matrix. On the landscape level, the matrix contains more

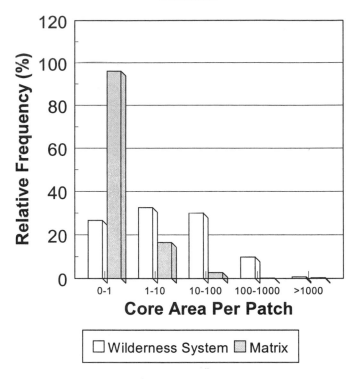

Fig. 14.3. Relative frequency distributions of core area per patch in the wilderness areas and the matrix.

than twice as much edge per hectare (78.56 m/ha) than the wilderness areas (36.12 m/ha). The density of edge decreased on both landscapes when weighted for edge contrast, yet the relative amounts of edge remained similar (i.e., more than twice the amount of contrast-weighted edge per hectare in the matrix than in the wilderness areas). All of the major forest types had a substantially greater edge density and/or contrast-weighted edge density in the matrix than in the wilderness areas except late-seral Engelmann spruce-subalpine fir (Table 14.1).

Spatial Distribution of Patches. Generally, the major forest types within the wilderness areas were more evenly distributed than in the matrix. Patch density, nearest neighbor, and contagion results all suggest that forested patches in the matrix were more clumped than in the wilderness areas. Median patch densities were more than three times greater within the matrix (mean = 0.25 ± 0.22, median = 0.28) than within each of the wilderness areas (mean = 0.16 ± 0.29, median = 0.08) (Table 14.1).

All forest types that occurred in both landscapes were more evenly distributed in the wilderness areas than in the matrix. Although the median proximity index suggests that patches of the major forest types within the wilderness areas were less isolated than in the matrix, the proximity values for each patch type were mixed (Table 14.2). Three of the five late-seral stages of the major forest types did, however, have greater proximity values in the wilderness than in the matrix while the reverse was true for the mid-seral stages (Table 14.1).

Table 14.2. Descriptive statistics of patch level metrics for the wilderness areas and multiple-use forest matrix.

| | | Landscape | |
Metric	Statistic	Wilderness Areas	Matrix
N		1080	14220
Patch Area (ha)	Mean	72.66	22.82
	SD	206.49	133.70
	Median	14.50	5.25
	Mode	0.25	0.25
	CV	284.18	585.88
	Max	2842.25	8357.25
	Min	0.25	0.25
Edge Contrast	Mean	45.04	50.69
	SD	16.85	21.96
	Median	40.00	44.74
	Mode	40.00	100.00
	CV	37.41	43.33
	Max	100.00	100.00
	Min	20.00	20.00
Shape	Mean	1.86	1.69
	SD	0.87	0.71
	Median	1.66	1.50
	Mode	1.00	1.00
	CV	46.78	42.29
	Max	17.21	16.15
	Min	1.00	1.00

Continued on next page

Table 14.2—*continued*

| Metric | Statistic | Landscape | |
		Wilderness Areas	Matrix
Disjunct Core Area (ha)	Mean	53.94	13.38
	SD	174.25	101.30
	Median	6.00	1.00
	Mode	0.00	0.00
	CV	323.06	757.18
	Max	261675.00	6300.00
	Min	0.00	0.00
Core Area Index (%)	Mean	37.63	23.63
	SD	27.27	23.12
	Median	43.62	19.05
	Mode	0.00	0.00
	CV	68.81	97.88
	Max	92.07	88.24
	Min	0.00	19.05
Near (m)	Mean	566.90	315.59
	SD	2156.00	1103.05
	Median	141.42	100.00
	Mode	50.00	50.00
	CV	380.46	349.53
	Max	41179.64	45751.53
	Min	50.00	50.00
Proximity Index	Mean	268.75	315.50
	SD	941.11	1988.87
	Median	16.63	14.79
	Mode	0.00	0.01
	CV	350.18	630.39
	Max	12119.27	41803.16
	Min	0.00	0.00

DISCUSSION

Our analysis has described the composition and configuration of the major forest types in a national forest wilderness system and compared it to its multiple-use matrix. The results of this analysis demonstrate that the protected status of the wilderness areas of the Arapaho-Roosevelt National Forest has resulted in a landscape structure that is less fragmented and contains a greater proportion of mature and old-growth forest than its surrounding matrix. These differences are largely due to the absence of anthropogenic fragmentation agents such as timber extraction, road construction, and other types of development within the wilderness areas. Although natural disturbances such as fire contribute to this structure, we suggest that because most fires on the ARNF are human-caused (USFS, *personal communication*), fire disturbance can be described as a human-caused disturbance as well. The addition of human disturbance to the multiple-use ARNF has produced a forest mosaic dominated by early- and mid-seral stages. In addition, anthropogenic disturbance in the matrix has altered the size, shape, and spatial relationship of forest patches. The result is the disruption of ecosystem processes and a landscape structure that is less conducive to the long term persistence of vertebrate species sensitive to habitat fragmentation.

Composition

Differences in vegetational composition often create distinct boundaries for many species, trophic levels, and taxonomic groups (Wiens 1989, Hansen and Urban 1992, Rusek 1992). When combined with structural contrasts, these effects are amplified (e.g., late-seral Engelmann spruce-subalpine fir/late-seral lodgepole pine versus late-seral Engelmann spruce-subalpine fir/early-seral lodgepole pine). Differences in cover type composition between the wilderness areas and the matrix can largely be attributed to elevational differences (see Buttery and Gillam 1987). However, differences in seral stage composition were due to land use designation (i.e., wilderness versus nonwilderness). The prevention of natural fragmentation processes (e.g., fire suppression) and the exclusion of anthropogenic fragmentation agents in the wilderness areas resulted in a forest mosaic dominated by late-seral stages (dominance = 0.17). The most glaring difference was the absence of early-seral aspen and ponderosa pine communities, and the near absence of early-seral patches of Douglas fir (i.e., a single patch), Engelmann spruce-subalpine fir (six patches), and lodgepole pine (five patches) in the wilderness areas. Although the ARNF wilderness areas are important for protecting a greater amount of ecologically important mature and old growth forests (Finch and Ruggiero 1993) than the surrounding matrix, the absence of early-seral forests suggests that important ecosystem processes may not be occurring that maintain the shifting steady-state mosaic that preserves landscape heterogeneity (Pickett and White 1985, Baker 1989). Shugart and West (1981) have suggested that a protected area should be at least 50 times median patch size. If this is the case, then the wilderness areas in this system all could, in the long term and without human interference (i.e., fire suppression), support a stable mosaic.

Configuration

The results of our analysis suggest that the land use designation of the wilderness areas has considerably affected the configuration of the forest communities. Most of the *a priori* predictions of the effect of protection on landscape configuration were confirmed. Patches were in fact larger with more core area and less edge in the wilderness than in the matrix and were dispersed more evenly in larger, more contiguous patches across the landscape.

Patch Area, Core Area, and Shape. Edge-sensitive species occur only in the interior of their preferred habitat and will be absent from small habitat patches with little or no true interior habitat (Temple 1986). This aspect of configuration alone demonstrates the benefit of wilderness forest patches as habitat particularly in light of the widespread decline of neotropical songbird populations (Rappole and McDonald 1994). The greater degree of patch shape complexity in the wilderness areas is offset by the greater patch size. Shape complexity becomes increasingly important as patch size decreases, maximizing edge and decreasing core area (Temple 1986). Interestingly, although core area is considered a function of area and shape, the core area and shape metrics were not correlated. Instead, core area was a direct function of patch size; the difference in patch area alone was so great that it may have dominated shape effects. Another possibility is that the lower limit of patch size was constrained by the 50 m² resolution of the rasterized data. As patch size decreased, shape became increasingly square and patches or core areas of 50 m² or less were ultimately square. Unfortunately, because shape and edge effects are greatest in small patches, the resolution chosen for this study may have reduced the accuracy of related metrics. Accordingly, we should note that this analysis was conducted under the assumption that the comparisons were assumed to be relevant because the resolution was the same for all landscapes.

Some researchers have suggested that human-influenced landscapes exhibit simpler patterns than natural landscapes (Krummel et al. 1987, O'Neill et al. 1988, Turner et al. 1989). Landscapes influenced by natural rather than anthropogenic disturbances may respond differently, with natural disturbances increasing landscape complexity.

Patch Edge. Edge effects act both independently and cumulatively to determine relative connectedness and degrees of habitat isolation (Kareiva 1990, Wiens 1990, Hansson 1990, Noss 1991). We have long recognized that altering patch boundaries by accelerated processes to abrupt edges can change both plant and animal species composition and abundances at individual microsites (Leopold 1933) and habitat heterogeneity in the landscape (Morrison et al. 1992). Formerly considered to be a desirable goal in wildlife management theory and practice (Leopold 1933), the "edge effect" is now understood to have some deleterious impacts on biological communities. This effect is particularly true when the edge in question is induced rather than the result of natural processes (Gates and Geysel 1978, Temple and Cary 1988, Klein 1989, Chen et al. 1992). Not only did the wilderness areas have less edge per hectare than the matrix, but the contrast of that edge was also lower for all major forest types. Edge contrast reflects the magnitude of difference between patches with respect to one or more ecological attributes at a given scale. In effect, as edge contrast increases, the magnitude of edge effect also increases.

Spatial Distribution of Patches. The spatial configuration of landscape elements can be crucial to the persistence of many organisms. Temple (1986) identified three categories of birds that are particularly sensitive to landscape fragmentation: area-sensitive, edge-sensitive, and isolation-sensitive. These categories can be applied to vertebrate classes and many invertebrates as well. As patch fragments become increasingly smaller and more isolated, species inhabiting these patches become susceptible to extirpation as a result of environmental, demographic, and genetic stochasticity. Several authors have claimed that patch isolation explains why fragmented habitats often contain fewer bird species than contiguous habitats (Whitcomb et al. 1981, Hayden et al. 1985, Dickman 1987). The distribution of patches across a landscape may be of particular importance for species that require habitat patches of a minimum size or specific arrangement (e.g., the northern spotted owl in the Pacific northwest [Gutierrez et al. 1985]).

The proximity index measures the arrangement and adjacency of patches in relation to each other. When examining the spatial configuration of patches of naturally fragmented forest types such as those that occur in the ARNF, the results can be unclear. Although the nearest neighbor analysis suggests lower connectivity of like patches within the wilderness areas, it also indicates a greater degree of fragmentation when considered with the patch density values. The overall picture, when considering all three metrics, is that the wilderness patches had a lesser degree of adjacency but tended to be larger and more contiguous with other forest patches than in the matrix. This result coincides with the area and density metrics if one considers that when a large patch of a given type is divided into smaller fragments overall adjacency of that type will increase whereas median patch area and the level of adjacency for that type will decrease.

Caveats and Limitations

This analysis was conducted at a very coarse grain. It was not meant to provide a panacea for all issues of conservation at the landscape level nor does it evaluate the condition of the landscape for all species at all scales. Rather, this analysis is a first step in an effort to evaluate the potential of lands that are used for a variety of purposes to support native biological diversity. In addition, ecological applications of geographic information systems are inherently prone to a wide array of error, from the original data collection and digitizing to the simplification of complex ecological patterns. Differences detected in landscape structure were limited by the resolution in the digital landscapes. Furthermore, the RIS data used for this analysis was often a mean over an entire patch. Thus, a certain degree of error is inherent in attempts to delineate ecological boundaries and assumptions must be made regarding fine grain patterns that are overshadowed. In addition, the forest types evaluated in this study were often assigned to an entire patch with no consideration of understory vegetation. Also, elevation was not considered in this study and could be a confounding factor particularly in compositional differences.

McGarigal and McComb (1995) point out that the hypothesis that wildlife populations are regulated by landscape structure is based largely on theoretical rather than empirical work. Another limitation of this type of analysis is that index and ratio estimators may have limitations, including relative inaccuracies compared to direct measurement, lack of normal distribution, and lack of information about the form of the relationship between the variables being compared (Sokal and Rohlf 1981). Indeed, because of the many ways in which composition and configuration can be measured, there are literally hundreds of possible ways to quantify landscape structure. The investigator, therefore, needs to select the metrics and scale appropriate to the question at hand. In addition, one should remember that the wilderness boundaries are artificial and some differences in the results could be an artifact of the imposition of these boundaries.

Current research suggests that different landscape metrics may reflect processes operating at different scales. The relationships between metrics, processes, and scale needs more study to understand (1) the factors that create pattern and (2) the ecological effects of changing patterns on processes. The broad scale metrics of landscape structure may provide an appropriate metric for monitoring regional ecological changes. Such an application is of particular importance because changes in broad-scale patterns (e.g., global change) can be measured with remote sensing technology, and an understanding of the pattern-process relationship will allow functional changes to be inferred.

CONCLUSIONS

As the principles of landscape ecology gain the attention of the ecological community, our inability to adequately protect biological diversity with a species-by-species approach becomes increasingly obvious (Franklin 1993). Instead, the land itself needs protection, and time is of the essence. Often, dwelling on the theory and design of hypothetical and future nature reserves is impractical. Rather, land managers and policy makers must be convinced that public lands must be managed in an ecologically sound manner while ensuring that a broad range of interests are appeased.

Many land management activities involve decisions that alter landscape patterns. Ecologists, land managers, and planners have traditionally ignored interactions between different elements in a landscape—the elements are usually treated as different systems. Results from landscape ecological studies suggest that a broadscale perspective incorporating spatial relationships is a necessary part of land use planning, for example, in decisions about the management and protection of existing protected areas.

The long-term maintenance of biological diversity may require a management strategy that places regional biogeography and landscape patterns above local concerns (Noss 1983). This study suggests that the landscape structure of lands such as USFS wilderness areas may enhance sensitive biological diversity. Protection of biological diversity, however, cannot depend upon protected areas alone, but must consider all lands that have not been fully converted (Noss 1991). The multiple-use matrix plays at least three critical roles in the conservation of biological diversity: (1) providing habitat at smaller spatial scales, (2) increasing the effectiveness of protected areas, and (3) controlling connectivity in the landscape (Franklin 1993). The future lies in the management of these lands. Hopefully, the rise of landscape ecology has altered the way scientists, policy makers, and, to a lesser extent, the public perceive conservation issues, and strides will be taken toward incorporating a landscape perspective into policies and guidelines for the management of public lands.

ACKNOWLEDGMENTS

We would like to thank K. Wilson and D. Dean for invaluable discussion, review, and advice. Judy Terrel provided indispensable help in manuscript preparation.

LITERATURE CITED

Baker, W.L. 1989. Landscape ecology and nature reserve design in the boundary waters canoe area, Minnesota. *Ecology* 70:23–35.

Burgess, R.L., and D.M. Sharpe, editors. 1981. Forest island dynamics in man-dominated landscapes. Springer-Verlag, New York, USA.

Buttery, R. F. and B. C. Gillam. 1987. Forested ecosystems. Pages 43–72 *in* R. L. Hoover and D. L. Wills editors. *Managing forested lands for wildlife*. Colorado Division of Wildlife in cooperation with USDA Forest Service, Rocky Mountain Region, Denver, CO, USA.

Chen, J., J. F. Franklin, and T. A. Spies. 1992. Vegetation responses to edge environments in old-growth Douglas fir stands. *Ecological Applications* 2:387–396.

Diamond, J. M. 1975. The island dilemma: lessons of modern biogeographic studies for the design of natural preserves. *Biological Conservation* 7:129–146.

Dickman, C. R. 1987. Habitat fragmentation and vertebrate species richness in an urban environment. *Journal of Applied Ecology* 24:337–351.

ESRI, Inc. 1992. ARC/INFO 6.1. Redlands, CA.

Finch, D., and L. F. Ruggierro. 1993. Wildlife habitats and biological diversity in the Rocky Mountains and northern Great Plains. *Natural Areas Journal* 13:191–203.

Forman, R.T.T, and M. Godron. 1986. *Landscape Ecology*. John Wiley & Sons, New York.

Franklin, J. F. 1993. Preserving biodiversity: species, ecosystems, or landscapes? *Ecological Applications* 3:202–205.

Gates, J. E., and L. W. Geysel. 1978. Avian nest dispersion and fledgling success in field-forest ecotones. *Ecology* 59:871–883.

Gustafson, E. J., and G. R. Parker. 1994. Using an index of habitat patch proximity for landscape design. *Landscape and Urban Planning* 29:117–120.

Hansen, A. J., and D. L. Urban. 1992. Avian response to landscape pattern: The role of species' life histories. *Landscape Ecology* 7:163–180.

Hansson, L. 1990. Spatial dynamics in fluctuating vole populations. Oecologia 85:213–217.

Hardt, R. A., and R. T. T. Forman. 1989. Boundary form effects on woody colonization of reclaimed surface mines. *Ecology* 70:1252–1260.

Harris, L. D. 1984. *The fragmented forest: island biogeography theory and the preservation of biotic diversity*. University of Chicago Press, Chicago, Illinois, USA.

Hayden, I. J., J. Faaborg, and R. L. Clawson. 1985. Estimates of minimum area requirements for Missouri forest birds. *Missouri Academy of Science* 19:11–22.

Janzen D. 1983. No park is an island: increase in interference from outside as park size decreases. *Oikos* 41:402–410.

Janzen D. 1986. The eternal external threat. Pages 286–303 *in* M. E. Soule, editor. *Conservation Biology: The science of scarcity and diversity.* Sinauer Associates, Sunderland, Massachusetts, USA.

Kareiva, P. 1990. Population dynamics in spatially complex environments: theory and data. *Philosophical Transactions of the Royal Society*, London, Great Britain 330:175–181.

Klein, B. C. 1989. Effects of forest fragmentation on dung and carrion beetle communities in central Amazonia. *Ecology* 70:1715–1725.

Krummel, J. R., R. H. Gardener, G. Sugihara, R. V. O'Neill, and P. R. Coleman. 1987. Landscape patterns in a disturbed environment. *Oikos* 48:321–324.

Lamberson, R. H., R. McKelvey, B. R. Noon, and C. Voss. 1992. A dynamic analysis of northern spotted owl viability in a fragmented forest landscape. *Conservation Biology* 6:505–512.

Leopold, A. 1933. *Game management.* Scribner, New York, USA.

McGarigal, K., and B.J. Marks. 1994. *FRAGSTATS: spatial pattern analysis program for quantifying landscape structure Ver. 2.0.* U.S. Forest Service General Technical Report PNW 351.

McGarigal, K., and W. C. McComb. 1995. Relationships between landscape structure and breeding birds in the Oregon Coast range. *Ecological Monographs* 65:235–260.

Mladenoff, D. J., M. A. White, J. Pastor, and T. R. Crow. 1993. Comparing spatial pattern in unaltered old-growth and disturbed forest landscapes. *Ecological Applications* 3:294–306.

Morrison, M. L., B. G. Marcot, and R. W. Mannan, editors. 1992. Wildlife-habitat relationships: concepts and applications. The University of Wisconsin Press, Madison, WI.

Newmark, W. D. 1985. Legal and biotic boundaries of western North American national parks: A problem of congruence. *Biological Conservation* 33:197–208.

Noss, R. F. 1983. A regional landscape approach to maintain diversity. *BioScience* 33:700–706.

Noss, R. F. 1991. *Protecting habitats and biological diversity. part i: guidelines for regional reserve systems.* National Audubon Society, New York, USA.

O'Neill, R. V., J. R. Krummel, R. H. Gardener, G. Sugihara, B. Jackson, D. L. DeAngelis, B. T. Milne, M. G. Turner, B. Zygmunt, S. W. Christensen, V. H. Dale, and R. L. Graham. 1988. Indices of landscape pattern. *Landscape Ecology* 1:153–162.

Ott, R.L. 1993. *An introduction to statistical methods and data analysis.* Duxbury Press, Belmont, California, USA.

Paton, P. W. 1994. The effect of edge on avian nest success: How strong is the evidence? *Conservation Biology* 8:17–26.

Patton, D. R. 1975. A diversity index for quantifying habitat "edge". *Wildlife Society Bulletin* 3:171–173.

Pickett, S. T. A., V. T. Parker, and P. L. Fielder. 1992. The new paradigm in ecology: implications for conservation biology above the species level. Pages 65–88 *in* P. L. Fielder and S. K. Jain, editors. *Conservation biology: the theory and practice of nature conservation preservation and management.* Chapman and Hall, New York, USA.

Pickett, S. T. A., and P. S. White, editors. 1985. *The ecology of natural disturbances and patch dynamics.* Academic Press, Orlando, Florida, USA.

Rappole, J. H., and M. V. McDonald. 1994. Cause and effect in population declines of migratory birds. *Auk* 111:652–660.

Ripple, W. J., G. A. Bradshaw, and T. A. Spies. 1991. Measuring forest landscape patterns in the Cascade Range of Oregon, USA. *Biological Conservation* 57:73–88.

Robbins, C. S., D. K. Dawson, and B. A. Dowell. 1989. Habitat area requirements of breeding forest birds of the middle Atlantic states. *Wildlife Monographs* 103.

Romme, W. H. 1982. Fire and landscape diversity in subalpine forests of Yellowstone National Park. *Ecological Monographs* 52:199–221.

Rusek, J. 1992. Distribution and dynamics of soil organisms across ecotones. Pages 196–216 *in* A. J. Hansen and F. di Castri editors. *Landscape boundaries, consequences for biotic diversity and ecological flows.* Springer-Verlag, New York, USA.

Schonewald-Cox, C. M. 1983. Guidelines to management: a beginning attempt. Pages 414–445 *in* C. M. Schonewald-Cox, S. M. Chambers, B. Mac Bryde and L. Thomas editors. *Genetics and conservation.* Benjamin Cummings, Menlo Park, California, USA.

Schonewald-Cox, C. M. and J. W. Bayless. 1986. The boundary model: a geographical analysis of design and conservation of nature reserves. *Biological Conservation* 38:305–322.

Shugart, H. H. and D. C. West. 1981. Long-term dynamics of forest ecosystems. *American Scientist* 69:647–652.

Sokal, R. R., and F. J. Rohlf. 1981. *Biometry.* Freeman Press, San Francisco, USA.

Soule, M. E. and D. Simberloff. 1986. What do genetics and ecology tell us about the design of nature reserves? *Biological Conservation* 35:19–40.

Spies, T. A., W. J. Ripple, and G. A. Bradshaw. 1994. Dynamics of a managed coniferous forest landscape in Oregon. *Ecological Applications* 4:555–568

Temple, S. A. 1986. Predicting impacts of habitat fragmentation on forest birds: a comparison of two models. Pages 301–304 *in* J. Verner, M.L. Morrison, and C.J. Ralph, editors. *Wildlife 2000: Modeling Habitat Relationships of Terrestrial Vertebrates.* University of Wisconsin Press, Madison, Wisconsin, USA.

Temple, S. A. 1991. The role of dispersal in the maintenance of bird populations in a fragmented landscape. *Acta Congressus Internationalis* 20:2298–2305.

Temple, S. A. and J. R. Cary. 1988. Modeling dynamics of habitat-interior bird populations in fragmented landscapes. *Conservation Biology* 2:340–347.

Turner, M. G. 1989. Landscape ecology: The effect of pattern on process. *Annual Review of Ecological Systems* 20:171–197.

Turner, M. G., R. H. Gardener, V. H. Dale, and R. V. O'Neill. 1989. Predicting the spread of disturbance in heterogeneous landscapes. *Oikos* 55:121–127.

Wiens, J. A. 1989. *The ecology of bird communities, Volume 2.* Cambridge University Press, Cambridge, Great Britain.

Wiens, J. A. 1990. Habitat fragmentation and wildlife populations: The importance of autecology, time, and landscape structure. *Transactions 19th IUJB Congress*, Trondheim 1989.

Wilcox, B. A. and D. D. Murphy. 1985. Conservation strategy: the effects of fragmentation on extinction. *American Naturalist* 125:879–887.

Williams, B., and B. Marcot. 1991. Use of biodiversity indicators for analyzing and managing forest landscapes. *Transactions of the North American Wildlife and Natural Resources Conference* 56:613–627.

15

Impact of Logging and Roads on a Black Hills Ponderosa Pine Forest Landscape

Douglas J. Shinneman and William L. Baker

INTRODUCTION

Landscape level analysis is widely acknowledged as an important component of ecosystem and biodiversity management (Forman and Godron 1986, Grumbine 1990, Turner et al. 1995). Furthermore, pre-EuroAmerican landscape characteristics are increasingly advocated as valuable references for determining the range of natural variability of ecosystems (Kaufmann et al. 1994, Lehmkuhl et al. 1994). Range of natural variability refers to ranges in the composition, structure, and dynamics of ecosystems before EuroAmerican influence. Ecosystems outside their range of natural variability may not sustain native species, especially species that depend specifically on diminished pre-EuroAmerican components and processes (Swanson et al. 1994). Thus, to perpetuate native species diversity, restoration of range of natural variability conditions may be required. This type of coarse-filter approach to maintaining native biodiversity may be more effective than single-species conservation efforts (Hunter et al. 1988).

Departure from the range of natural variability on U.S. national forests is often the result of management activities, especially road construction and timber harvesting, that have fragmented forest ecosystems. Fragmentation is the decrease in patch size, decline in interior habitat, increase in edge habitat, and increase in distance between patches accompanying the breakup of continuous habitats by human activities (Noss and Csuti 1994). Fragmentation is not restricted to landscapes impacted by agricultural clearing (e.g., Fahrig and Merriam 1985), as the large forest patches that are a component of the range of natural variability for many national forests are now often diminished in extent and connectivity (Harris 1984, Hunter 1990, Baker 1994, Morrison 1994) and much interior habitat has been replaced by edge habitat. Edge effects are reviewed in other chapters (Baker and Dillon, *this volume*; Baker, *this volume*; R. L. Knight, *this volume*). Roads can also contribute to edge and edge effect by subdividing otherwise continuous interior forest areas (Schonewald-Cox and Buechner 1992, Reed et al. 1996*a*). Roads and road edge habitat can have many deleterious ecological impacts (Baker and Knight, *this volume*).

A landscape-level, geographic information system (GIS) analysis of the effects of logging and road construction can assist in determining the degree of fragmentation of the pre-EuroAmerican landscape (Baker 1994; Morrison 1994; Baker, *this volume*). Yet most previous studies of fragmentation using GIS (Ripple et al. 1991, Mladenoff et al. 1993, Reed et al. 1996*b*) have not considered the contribution of roads. However, timber harvesting and roads may affect 2.5 to 3.5 times the area of land actually harvested (Reed et al. 1996*a*). Thus, such an analysis could benefit the U.S. Forest Service, which has advocated managing national forests within their range of natural variability (Kaufmann et al. 1994, Swanson et al. 1994).

An interesting application of the range of natural variability concept to landscapes is in the Black Hills of South Dakota and Wyoming, where the U.S. Forest Service has recently presented its Black Hills National Forest Revised Land and Resource Management Plan (USDA Forest Service 1996*a*). Our range of natural variability assessment of the Black Hills National Forest suggests that large patches of dense, old forest were a component of the pre-EuroAmerican landscape (Shinneman and Baker 1997). The U.S. Forest Service, in contrast, originally interpreted the Black Hills forest range of natural variability as "naturally fragmented" with widespread "open forest conditions" and advocated extensive logging to return to this structure (USDA Forest Service 1994*a*). Although the U.S. Forest Service has since reexamined this pre-EuroAmerican landscape analysis (USDA Forest Service 1996*b*) and has accepted some alternative assessments (e.g., Shinneman 1996, Parrish et al. 1996), it has still recommended increasing road construction and maintaining past levels of logging to thin and break up dense forests, which are largely attributed to fire suppression (USDA Forest Service 1996*a, b*). However, a significant limitation of the U.S. Forest Service plan, in addition to problems with the original range of natural variability assessment

(Shinneman and Baker 1997), is that the impact of logging and road construction on the contemporary landscape structure has not been adequately quantified. This lack of quantification, we believe, is a general limitation of many national forest planning analyses.

We hypothesized that the Black Hills National Forest had been substantially fragmented by timber harvesting and roads. To examine this hypothesis we: (1) quantified contemporary Black Hills forest landscape structure and the contribution of roads and timber harvesting to this structure, and (2) determined the status of the remaining large, dense, late-successional forest (LSF) patches, that have been especially targeted for timber harvest.

STUDY AREA

The Black Hills are an island mountain range completely surrounded by prairies, located in western South Dakota and northeastern Wyoming (Fig. 15.1). Topography generally consists of rounded to rugged hills in the central region, surrounded by a fairly level plateau dissected by steep, narrow valleys (Alexander 1987). Elevations range from about 1,070 m to 2,200 m. Elevational vegetation zones are inconspicuous, with only slight climatic differences between low and high elevations (Hoffman and Alexander 1987).

Although the Black Hills contain a diverse assemblage of species that are also found in the Rocky Mountains, boreal forests, Great Plains, and eastern deciduous forests (Stephens 1973), the forests are dominated by expansive stands of ponderosa pine. Dispersed within these pine forests are patches of white spruce, quaking aspen, bur oak, paper birch, other hardwood species, and grassy mountain "parks" (Hoffman and Alexander 1987). The pine forests have been intensively managed for more than a century, with practically all areas having been harvested or thinned at least twice (Alexander 1987), and currently 70% of the 503,299 ha Black Hills National Forest is available for timber production, primarily through shelterwood logging techniques (USDA Forest Service 1996*b*). As a result, the ponderosa pine forests consist of two-storied managed stands, even-aged managed stands, and unmanaged younger stands, while old-growth forest is sparse and mostly dispersed in small remnant patches (Alexander 1987). Moreover, few remaining areas are roadless, none larger than 7,300 ha (USDA Forest Service 1994*a*).

Our study area (Fig. 15.1) straddles the Wyoming/South Dakota border and includes 37,233 ha of the Black Hills National Forest (including 5,101 ha of private inholdings). Elevations range from

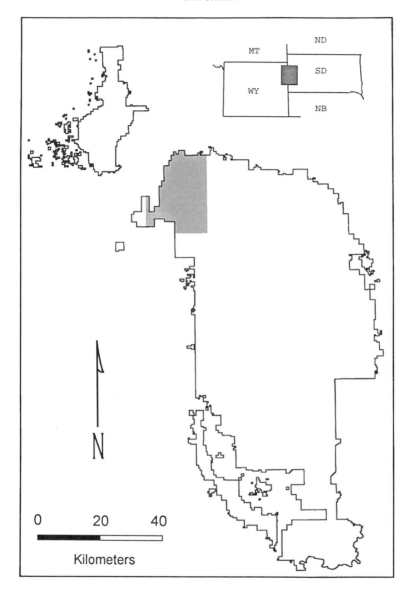

Fig. 15.1. The study area location (shaded) in the Black Hills National Forest (outlined) of South Dakota and Wyoming.

1,129 m to 2,044 m. This area was chosen because it has a representative mix of Black Hills National Forest conditions, including a dominant cover of 50–135 year old ponderosa pine forests, typical timber harvest activities, an identified roadless area, and average road density levels. A quantitative comparison (Shinneman 1996) documents that the vegetation in the study area is representative of the whole Black Hills National Forest in terms of percent cover of the vegetation attributes.

METHODS
Data Sources and GIS Procedures

Data sources included the Rocky Mountain Resource Information Systems (RMRIS) database updated through 1995 (USDA Forest Service 1994*b*), digitized 1993 USFS road data, and USFS-identified old-growth polygon data. The RMRIS database contains information (e.g., cover type) for polygons primarily derived from USFS aerial photo interpretation with some ground-truthing. We used a few of the original RMRIS category values and reclassed others into more useful subdivisions (Table 15.1).

These data were loaded into an ARC/INFO GIS vector-based coverage (ESRI, Inc. 1995) provided by the U.S. Forest Service and then converted into vector- and raster-based maps in the GRASS GIS (USA-CERL 1994). Several GRASS programs were used to analyze these data. The r.le programs (Baker and Cai 1992) were used to calculate indices of landscape structure for the study area. The study area required a 28.46 km x 19.74 km rectangular coverage, and a 10 m pixel resolution (2,846 rows by 1,974 columns) was selected. Thus, road width was also set at 10 m.

The USFS RMRIS and road data have two pertinent limitations. First, recent timber harvest activities could not be analyzed directly, as actual harvest boundaries are not always recorded in the RMRIS database. Instead, harvest types and sizes are sometimes merely recorded as occurring within already existing polygons mapped prior to the recent harvesting, even though these individual harvests often alter polygon shape and area. Moreover, during database updates, changes resulting from harvest activities are not necessarily recorded. Thus, patches created by recent logging are imperfectly reflected in the Black Hills National Forest polygon maps and RMRIS database. The second limitation is that the Black Hills National Forest road data have not been field-checked with a global positioning system (GPS), which would identify the many temporary logging roads that are not otherwise mapped but often receive persistent use (e.g., illegal 4x4 trails). Thus, the 1993 road data may significantly underestimate the current road network on the Black Hills National Forest, as was found on another forest (Reed et al. 1996*a*).

Table 15.1. The original RMRIS categories, the GRASS GIS reclassed categories, and the associated polygon/patch attributes for each, which were used to produce the vegetation patch and late successional forest (LSF) maps. Abbreviations (e.g., TAA, 3c) are those used in RMRIS.

Category	*Polygon/Patch Attribute*	
Cover Type	GRA = Grasslands	TPP = Ponderosa Pine
(Original RMRIS category)	GFE = Fescues	TWS = White Spruce
Dominant vegetative or non-vegetative	TAA = Aspen	SHR = Shrublands
land cover	TBO = Bur Oak	SMS = Mountain Mahogany
	TPB = Paper Birch	NFL = Nonvegetated Site
		TOH = Other Hardwoods
Habitat Structural Stage	1 = Grass-Forb, <10% CC	
(Original RMRIS category)	2 = Shrub-Seedling, <1" DBH, 11–100% CC	
Code describing the current	3a = Sapling-Pole, 1–9" DBH, 11–40% CC	
structural stage, canopy cover (CC),	3b = Sapling-Pole, 1–9" DBH, 41–70% CC	
diameterat breast height (DBH)	3c = Sapling-Pole, 1–9" DBH, 71–100% CC	
	4a = Mature, >9" DBH, 11–40% CC	
	4b = Mature, >9" DBH, 41–70% CC	
	4c = Mature, >9" DBH, 71–100% CC	
	5 = Old-growth	
Tree Size	N = Nonstocked	
(Original RMRIS category)	E = Established seedlings (<1" DBH)	
Classification of the site based on	S = Small/Sapling: (1.0–4.9" DBH)	
the stocking and size of live trees	M = Medium: (5.0–8.9" DBH)	
	L = Large: (9.0–15.9" DBH)	
	V = Very large: (>16.0" DBH)	
Crown Cover Percent Class	1–9%	25–49%
(RMRIS category reclassed in GRASS)	10–24%	50–74%
Vegetation crown cover percent ranges		75–100%
Year Historical Class	Pre-EuroAmerican: 1650–1859	
(RMRIS category reclassed in GRASS)	Early settlement: 1860–1897	
Vegetation year of origin values	Early national forest years: 1898–1945	
reclassed into historical time periods	Modern national forest years: 1946–1995	

Landscape Structure Analysis

Landscape structure is defined by the attributes of different patches in the landscape, such as size, shape, diversity, and spatial arrangement. Patch edge, edge effect, and patch interior (i.e., the portion of the patch not influenced by the edge effect) also define landscape structure (Thomas et al. 1979, Forman and Godron 1986). This landscape mosaic of patch attributes can influence species distributions and ecosystem functions (Pickett 1994). Thus, we selected a set of indices to measure these attributes in the contemporary Black Hills forest landscape (Table 15.2).

The Black Hills National Forest landscape has a vegetation patch mosaic that reflects the spatial influences of natural disturbance, environmental gradients, and extensive forest harvesting that has varied from earlier intensive clearing to contemporary partial cutting. Thus, patch types are primarily distinguished by variation in forest cover types, age or structural stages, and tree densities (Alexander 1987), in contrast to more readily identifiable clearcut patches (e.g., Reed et al. 1996*b*). For this study, we combined attributes to produce two maps: a cover type/habitat structural stage (cov/hab) map and a cover type/year history class (cov/year) map. For example, in the cov/hab map a patch might consist of ponderosa pine in the 3B structural stage (see Table 15.1). These related patch maps have different landscape structures, emphasizing slightly different aspects of the vegetation patchiness produced by disturbance.

The impact of past harvest activities and roads on the landscape structure was determined by comparing landscape structure analyses for two additional contrasting patch conceptions (Fig. 15.2). In addition to the vegetation-defined patches described above (Fig. 15.2a), patches were also considered to be simply the land area between the

Table 15.2. Landscape structure indices calculated. (Indices explained in detail in Baker and Cai 1992.)

Total number of patches	Total edge area (ha)
Percent of landscape covered by a patch type	Total length of all patch perimeters
Density of patches (no./ha)	Frequency distribution of patches by size class
Mean patch size (ha)	Frequency distribution of patch interiors by size class
Median patch size (ha)	Mean shape (corrected perimeter/area: $(0.282 \times \text{perim.})/(\text{area})^{1/2}$
Standard deviation of patch size	Standard deviation of patch shape
Mean interior size (ha)	Contagion
Median interior size (ha)	Dominance
Standard deviation of patch interior size	Entropy
Total interior area (ha)	Shannon diversity

roads, ignoring vegetation attributes, to indicate the patchiness that roads alone create on the landscape (Fig. 15.2b). Also, because roads create abrupt edges that separate otherwise equivalent patches (Schonewald-Cox and Buechner 1992), the road-defined and vegetation-defined patch structures were combined, creating vegetation

(a)   **(b)**   **(c)**

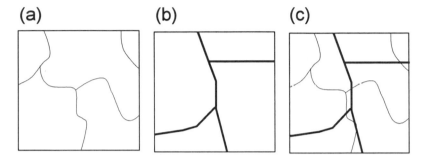

Fig. 15.2. The three patch conceptions, with (a) vegetation-defined patches only, (b) road-defined patches only, and (c) the vegetation patches further delineated by road edges.

patches further delineated by roads (Fig. 15.2c).

Identification and Analysis of Late-Successional Forest Patches

Black Hills old-growth ponderosa pine consists of both an open-canopy and a dense multistory form (Mehl 1992). To focus on the spatial attributes of contemporary dense LSF patches in the Black Hills landscape, we first needed to identify these areas. However, except for the RMRIS category "old growth score," which is very incomplete for the Black Hills National Forest, no single category consistently identifies a range of valuable LSF characteristics. Moreover, after reviewing the USFS-identified old-growth forest polygon data for RMRIS category value content (for the entire Black Hills National Forest) in the GRASS GIS, we found these polygon data inadequate for identifying old-growth forest patches (see Fig. 15.3). For example, 26.6% of the land area of these patches with available year-origin data contains forests less than 98 years old and 74.7% is less than 135 years old (Fig. 15.3b). Thus, the USFS-identified old-growth patches contain too much young forest to be considered old-growth (Mehl 1992), and were not analyzed in further detail.

Because old-growth forest is rare on the Black Hills (Alexander

1987) and not adequately identified, we combined several relevant RMRIS categories to identify patches representing a range of LSF characteristics. The specific LSF criteria employed in this analysis were based upon contemporary (Mehl 1992) as well as historical (Graves 1899) descriptions of dense, old-growth, Black Hills ponderosa pine. The attribute data were obtained from the year historical class, habitat structural stage, canopy cover class, and tree size category GRASS maps (Table 15.1), and patches containing these attributes were overlaid in GIS to find all areas meeting combinations of these LSF criteria. However, almost no patches were identified that met Mehl's (1992) old-growth standard, requiring >160-year-old stands. Therefore, we used less stringent criteria and created two different LSF maps. LSF map 1

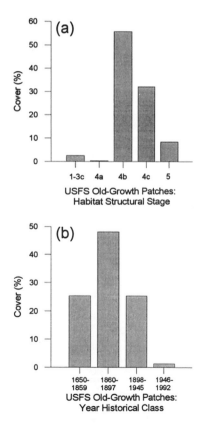

Fig 15.3. The percent land area in (a) the habitat structural stages and (b) the year historical classes for the USFS-identified old-growth patches. Values were calculated for the entire Black Hills National Forest.

required stands with structural stages 4c and 5, trees older than 135 years, large to very large trees, and 50% or greater crown cover. LSF map 2 was identical to map 1 except we included stands as young as 98 years and added structural stage 4b. LSF map 1 covered 0.97% (310.86 ha) of the study area and LSF map 2 covered 20.53% (6,597.14 ha). We then examined the landscape structure and spatial context of the LSF patches using the first 14 indices in Table 15.2, with and without the effects of roads. We also determined the mean and standard deviation of distance between these patches.

RESULTS

Landscape Structure Measures

We found 1,331.2 km of mapped roads on the study area, with an average road density of 3.6 km/km^2. The study area landscape (including private land) as defined by only roads consists of patches with a mean size of 139.0 ha (Table 15.3). Patch size frequency is not evenly distributed around the mean, as 67.3% of the road-defined patches are under 100 ha. Yet only 10.8% of the study area landscape is covered by patches under 100 ha (Table 15.3). Two fairly large patches were defined by roads, at 3,809.7 ha and 3,690.5 ha. However, the

Table 15.3. Landscape structure statistics for road-defined patch map. Patches were delineated by road edges; patch interiors by depth of edge influences. Road-defined patch map total area = 37,233.28 ha.

Index	Value
No. of patches	263
Patch density (no./km^2)	0.71
Mean patch size (ha)	138.98
SD patch size (ha)	375.37
Median patch size (ha)	34.49
Percent area in patches <100 ha	10.81
Mean interior size (ha) with 50 m edge effect	113.06
SD interior size (ha) with 50 m edge effect	325.98
Median interior size (ha) with 50 m edge effect	21.57
Mean interior size (ha) with 100 m edge effect	90.26
SD interior size (ha) with 100 m edge effect	281.00
Median interior size (ha) with 100 m edge effect	12.50
Total length of roads (km)	1331.15
Road density (km/km^2)	3.58

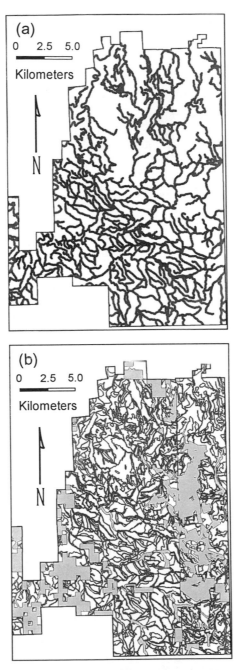

Fig. 15.4. The edge habitat (in black) on the study area with (a) 100 m depth-of-edge influence from roads only and (b) 50 m depth-of-edge influence from both roads and vegetation patches for the cov/hab vegetation patch map. Light gray shading on the cov/hab map represents private land or areas without data.

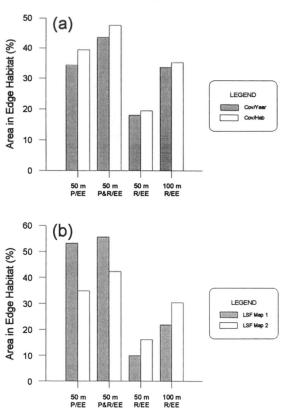

Fig. 15.5. The percent land area in edge habitat with various depth-of-edge influences from roads and adjacent patches for (a) the vegetation patch maps and (b) the LSF maps. P/EE = patch edge effect only, P&R/EE = patch and road edge effect, and R/EE = road edge effect only.

true size of these large patches may be considerably smaller, as not all roads have been mapped and considerable recent logging activity has occurred in one of these large patches (see Methods section). Road edge habitat constitutes a large portion of the study area (Figs. 15.4, 15.5a). Roads alone occupy 1.8% of the landscape. With a 50 m depth-of-edge influence, roads and road edge habitat encompass 20.2% of the study area and, with a 100 m depth-of-edge influence, 36.3% of the study area is road/road edge habitat. Road edge habitat has also resulted in mostly small- to moderate-sized patch interiors (Table 15.3).

Patch sizes in the original cov/hab and cov/year patch maps, where the effects of roads are excluded, are generally small. In both maps the mean patch sizes are under 50 ha (Table 15.4), and most patches are under 25 ha. A few patches of 500–2,000 ha were also found within

Table 15.4. Landscape structure statistics for the vegetation patch maps with and without road edges. The cov/hab map has a total area of 30,687.50 ha and the cov/year map has a total of 25,588.24 ha, based on pixels with available data for the RMRIS categories used in each map.

Index	Cov/hab map		Cov/year map	
	Without Roads	*With Roads*	*Without Roads*	*With Roads*
No. of patches	948	4425	577	2773
Patch density (no./ha)	0.03	0.14	0.02	0.11
Mean patch size (ha)	32.37	6.81	44.35	9.08
SD patch size (ha)	79.40	22.09	123.52	27.83
Median patch size (ha)	11.20	0.11	13.72	0.10
Percent area in patches <100 ha	49.86	75.22	39.19	68.35
Total patch perimeter (km)	3745.01	5012.56	2657.46	3647.86
Patch perimeter density (m/ha)	122.03	163.34	103.85	142.56
Mean shape	2.16	1.67	2.12	1.65
SD shape	0.80	0.64	0.76	0.62
Contagion	4.77	4.73	4.20	4.16
Dominance	1.51	1.51	1.42	1.42
Entropy	2.22	2.26	1.58	1.62
Shannon	1.96	1.96	1.42	1.42

each of these maps.

Division of these generally small vegetation-defined patches by roads reduces average patch size by nearly 80% in both maps (Table 15.4). This reduction is partly the result of thin strips of some patches being "sliced" off by roads, creating many small patch fragments, and possibly skewing the mean. However, even if these small slivered patch fragments are removed from consideration (all 1 pixel patches), roads still reduce average patch sizes by nearly 70% for both maps (to 10.1 ha and 13.5 ha). Roads also significantly increase the total land area covered by small patches in the study area (Table 15.4). For instance, the total area in the cov/hab map covered by patches under 100 ha increases from 49.9% to 75.2% after patch division by roads. Other effects of roads include a five-fold increase in patch density, an increased compactness of patch shapes, and a decline in variation in patch size and shape (Table 15.4).

Roads also increase the total amount of edge and edge habitat on the vegetation patch landscapes. The total patch perimeter (a relative measure of edge) and density of patch perimeter on both maps

Table 15.5. Interior patch size statistics for the vegetation-defined patch maps. Interiors were measured after assuming patch edge effects (P/EE) only (i.e., with no roads on the landscape), patch and road edge effects, and road edge effects (R/EE) only.

Index	No Roads & 50 m P/EE	50 m R/EE & 50 m P/EE	50 m R/EE only	100 m R/EE only
Cov/hab map				
Mean interior size (ha)	19.60	3.62	5.59	4.49
SD interior size (ha)	59.18	15.16	18.87	16.06
Median interior size (ha)	3.59	0.00	0.01	0.00
Cov/year map				
Mean interior size (ha)	29.07	5.19	7.57	6.12
SD interior size (ha)	96.37	19.38	24.23	20.73
Median interior size (ha)	5.16	0.00	0.01	0.01

increase by about one-third when the road edges are added to vegetation patch edges (Table 15.4). The cov/hab map has 39.5% of the study area within edge habitat, assuming a 50 m depth-of-edge influence from patches only, 19.4% assuming a 50 m depth-of-edge influence from roads only, and increases to 47.6% when a 50 m depth-of-edge influence from patches and roads is combined (Fig. 15.5a).

However, this large amount of edge habitat produces a complex pattern on the study area landscape (Figs. 15.5a and 15.5b) and, thus, is an important structural component. This pattern of edge habitat has a significant influence on already small mean patch interior sizes (Table 15.5). With a 50 m depth-of-edge influence from adjacent patches and roads, mean interior sizes are 3.6 ha for the cov/hab map and 5.2 ha for the cov/year map. Even assuming no edge habitat exists between adjoining vegetation patches on the entire landscape (e.g., as might be the case between ponderosa pine patches in structural stages 4b and 4c), the average interior is still small (<8.0 ha) for both maps, because road edge effect is so significant (Table 15.5).

The landscape diversity measures (Table 15.4) are less informative. The cov/hab map reveals a somewhat more diverse landscape (higher Shannon diversity value) and greater dispersion of equivalent patch types (higher entropy value) than the cov/year map, likely a result of the greater number of patch types identified in the cov/hab map. The contagion value calculated for both maps demonstrates a fairly high degree of clumping of relatively few patch types, while the dominance results indicate that these same patch types cover much of the landscape. These measures reflect the relatively few ponderosa pine patch types that constitute the greater portion of each map's landscape. When road edges are considered, these texture and diversity measures were

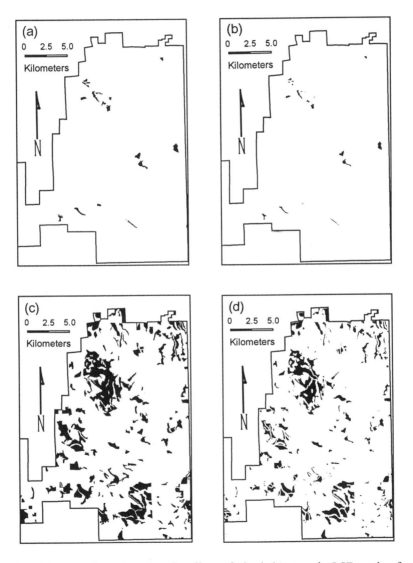

Fig. 15.6. Maps demonstrating the effects of edge habitat on the LSF patches for: (a) map 1 and (c) map 2 without edge habitat; and (b) map 1 and (d) map 2 with a 50 m depth-of-edge influence from roads and adjacent patches.

not noticeably influenced.

Late-Successional Forest (LSF) Analysis

We found little LSF in the study area. Only 0.76% of the study area contains forests in habitat structural stage 5, which is often equated with old-growth forest, and only 0.97% of the study area meets the criteria we used in generating LSF map 1 (Fig. 15.6). Patch sizes in both LSF maps are generally very small and are substantially reduced after division from road edges (Table 15.6). Even without considering roads, no patches larger than 50 ha were found in LSF map 1, and only three patches are larger than 250 ha in LSF map 2 (including a large 1,402.4 ha patch in the Sand Creek Roadless Area). Mean patch sizes without roads are 14.1 ha and 42.0 ha for LSF maps 1 and 2, respectively, and 4.4 ha and 8.9 ha, respectively, with roads. These small mean patch sizes with roads are due in part to the small 1-pixel patches created, which, if removed from consideration, would result in mean patch sizes of 7.2 ha and 13.6 ha for LSF maps 1 and 2, respectively. Thus, roads reduce LSF patch sizes by 49–79%.

Edge habitat is a significant component of LSF patch structure (Fig. 15.6), producing a very small mean LSF patch interior area (Table 15.7) and comprising a large percentage of the LSF patch area (Fig. 15.5b). For instance, a 50 m depth-of-edge influence around all roads

Table 15.6. Landscape index measures for the LSF patch maps with and without road edges.

Index	LSF map 1 Without Roads	LSF map 1 With Roads	LSF map 2 Without Roads	LSF map 2 With Roads
No. of patches	22	70	157	728
Mean patch size (ha)	14.13	4.40	42.03	8.94
SD patch size (ha)	11.53	8.97	119.29	46.35
Median patch size (ha)	10.46	0.04	14.11	0.08
% LSF area in patches <100	100.00	100.00	47.74	66.28
Total length of edge (km)	53.72	59.74	688.76	905.66
Edge density (m/LSF ha)	172.88	192.36	104.40	137.28
Mean shape	1.94	1.51	2.02	1.63
SD shape	0.50	0.49	0.75	0.62
Mean distance (m)	801.30		268.00	
SD distance (m)	1,050.30		455.00	

Table 15.7. Interior patch area size statistics for LSF patches. Interiors were measured after assuming patch edge effects (P/EE) only (i.e., with no roads on the landscape), patch and road edge effects, and road edge effects (R/EE) only.

Index	No Roads & 50 m P/EE	50 m R/EE & 50 m P/EE	50 m R/EE only	100 m R/EE only
LSF map 1				
Mean interior size (ha)	6.62	1.98	4.00	3.47
SD interior size (ha)	7.47	5.10	8.55	7.79
Median interior size (ha)	3.84	0.00	0.00	0.00
LSF map 2				
Mean interior size (ha)	27.37	5.23	7.60	6.30
SD interior size (ha)	92.34	34.62	43.60	28.34
Median interior size (ha)	6.28	0.00	0.01	0.00

and adjacent non-LSF patches results in a 2.0 ha and 5.2 ha mean LSF patch interior for LSF maps 1 and 2, respectively (Table 15.7), and 55.5% and 42.3% of the LSF patch area is in edge habitat for LSF maps 1 and 2, respectively (Fig. 15.5b). Assuming no edge habitat exists between LSF and non-LSF patch types, road-edge influence still results in small mean LSF interior sizes (Table 15.7), and the proportion of total LSF patch area in edge habitat is still fairly large. For instance, 30.5% of LSF area in map 2 is within edge habitat with a 100 m depth-of-edge influence from roads only (Fig. 15.5b). Also, the median patch in both maps has virtually no interior area, assuming only a 50 m road-edge effect (Table 15.7).

Mean distances between the LSF patches in both maps and variation around the mean indicate that the patches are fairly evenly dispersed (Table 15.6, Fig. 15.6). Thus, LSF habitat is typically distant from similar habitat on the study area landscape. Mean distance from the edge of each LSF patch to the edge of the nearest LSF patch is 801.3 m for LSF map 1 and 268.0 m for LSF map 2. However, there are areas where several LSF patches are clustered (Fig. 15.6).

DISCUSSION
Forest Fragmentation

Previous research on forest fragmentation has often relied on comparing structural indices between managed forest landscapes and similar but less-altered landscapes to determine if changes in certain indices indicate forest fragmentation has occurred (e.g., Lehmkuhl et al.

1994, Spies et al. 1994). However, no large unaltered landscapes remain on the Black Hills National Forest with which to compare our results, as even the remaining roadless areas have been subjected to some past harvest activities (USDA Forest Service 1994*a*). Moreover, extensive past timber harvest and widely used partial cutting procedures make historical aerial photo interpretation of past Black Hills forest landscapes difficult and inconclusive. Thus, these two conventional methods were not available for this study. However, two factors indicate that the study area's pre-EuroAmerican forest has been fragmented by timber harvesting and roads.

First, a recent natural variability assessment (Shinneman and Baker 1997) provides strong evidence that much of the pre-EuroAmerican Black Hills forest landscape generally contained large patches, including substantial areas of dense, old forest. In our study area alone, there was evidence of patches of dense, old-growth forest larger than 6,000 ha in the pre-EuroAmerican forest. Even without considering roads, most of the contemporary landscape consists of a mosaic of small- to moderate-sized patches, small interiors, and a considerable amount of edge length as a result of timber harvesting (Tables 15.4 and 15.5). Furthermore, large patches of dense, old-growth forest, using a modest definition (Mehl 1992), are now absent from the study area. The most stringent set of old-growth criteria used in this research (LSF map 1), which did not represent dense old-growth forest by Mehl's (1992) standards, identified small, isolated patches that covered only 1.0% of the study area landscape (Table 15.6, Figs. 15.6a and 15.6b).

The second factor that indicates the pre-EuroAmerican forest structure has been fragmented is that the current network of roads did not exist in the pre-EuroAmerican Black Hills landscape. Roads on our study area reduced mean patch sizes and patch interior sizes by at least 70%, increased the coverage of small patches on the landscape by 40–50%, increased the total patch perimeter by more than a third, and created much more compact patch shapes, with reduced variation in size and shape, in both vegetation maps (Tables 15.4 and 15.5). Roads and road edge habitat alone may cover more than one third of the study area (Fig. 15.5a), assuming a 100-m depth-of-edge influence. This estimate is a much greater percentage of the landscape affected by roads than the approximately 22% of the landscape reported on the Medicine Bow National Forest in southeastern Wyoming (Reed et al. 1996*a*). Roads and road edge habitat also further divide the already small and dispersed LSF patches and create extremely small LSF patch interiors (Tables 15.6 and 15.7). Indeed, the median LSF patch lacks any interior habitat.

Although these changes in the pre-EuroAmerican Black Hills landscape structure may not now represent the extreme fragmentation created by more disruptive agricultural clearing or clearcut logging, the pattern of structural change is similar. Smaller patch sizes, increased edge and edge habitat, decreased interior habitat, loss of old-growth forest, and general habitat isolation have been found to be key indicators of forest fragmentation in clearcut forest landscapes (e.g., Ripple et al. 1991, Lehmkuhl et al. 1994, Reed et al. 1996*a*). Although fewer studies have been conducted for managed second-growth forests without clear-cutting as the dominant harvest method (such as in the Black Hills), similar changes in landscape structure have also been documented in these types of forests. For instance, Mladenoff et al. (1993) compared a managed, second-growth forest landscape to a nearby wilderness and determined that patches in the second growth forest were generally smaller, had less complex shapes, were more isolated from similar habitat, and contained less old-growth than in the wilderness forest landscape. The Black Hills landscape, like many public forest landscapes subjected to timber harvesting, may retain forest cover and appear to be highly connected, but the old-growth component of the landscape is isolated in a sea of younger-aged forests consisting primarily of edge habitat produced by harvesting and roads.

The contribution of roads to fragmentation has not been widely assessed, with only a few studies specifically considering their impact on landscape structure (e.g., Reed et al. 1996*a*, Tinker et al. 1998). For example, Morrison (1994) demonstrated that logging significantly reduced the size and total area of old-growth patches on the Olympic Peninsula and that roads contributed to the amount of edge effect on these remaining old-growth patches. Allen (1994) used a GIS to demonstrate that road density in managed ponderosa pine/mixed conifer forests can be extremely high but did not specifically assess structural effects. While our study demonstrates similar results, it also shows that roads impact several indices of landscape structure by altering individual patch characteristics such as size, shape, and interior area (Tables 15.4–15.7) and greatly increasing edge and edge habitat (Table 15.4, Figs. 15.3 and 15.4). These same general trends, but to a lesser extent, have been reported for the Medicine Bow National Forest (Reed et al. 1996*a*) and Bighorn National Forest (Tinker et al. 1998).

While these results suggest the Black Hills landscape is heavily fragmented, this research probably greatly underestimates the true level of fragmentation of pre-EuroAmerican forest conditions. Recent harvest activity is not always accurately reflected in the RMRIS database, and roads are likely more extensive than has been mapped. These findings should also be generally applicable to the entire Black Hills National Forest, because the RMRIS category values, road densities, and logging histories are similar for the study area and the Black Hills National Forest as a whole.

Implications for Native Species Diversity

These fragmented conditions can lead to habitat isolation for some species, insufficient habitat for old-growth-dependent species, and increased habitat for edge-related species. Edge effects may even exist between patches of the same forest type with different ages or structural stages (Harris 1984, Hunter 1990, Bradshaw 1992). Also, different forest structural stages created by past clear-cut or partial harvest techniques can affect species diversity between treated and untreated stands (Harris 1984, Hansen et al. 1995), and the landscape configuration and proportional area of these patches may affect species abundance across broader scales (McGarigal and McComb 1995). On the Black Hills National Forest, Crompton (1994) demonstrated that shelterwood harvest activities affect songbird species diversity, as species composition differed between interior untreated forest, interior treated forests (thinned by shelter-wood harvests), and edge habitat (which he measured into both the adjacent treated and untreated patches). For instance, he found that: (1) total numbers of timber-gleaning insectivore species and certain interior-associated species were generally lower in recently harvested stands compared to unharvested stands, (2) only the largest untreated old-forest patches (>1,000 ha) contained the full suite of forest interior-associated birds known to the Black Hills, (3) certain species demonstrated an aversion for the edge habitat occurring between cut and uncut patches, and (4) some species were only found in certain patch types, such as the ovenbird which was found only in the interiors of untreated, dense, mixed conifer-deciduous forest patches on the Black Hills National Forest. Similarly, Dykstra (1996) demonstrated that Black Hills bird species composition differed even between moderately dense (41–70% canopy cover [CC]) sapling or pole sized stand of trees and very dense (>70% CC) mature or old-growth forest, as a result of the structural differences between these patch types (e.g., large vs. small trees, presence vs. absence of standing snags and downed old trees, different understory components). For example, Dykstra found that accipiters such as the northern goshawk were absent from the younger, modestly dense (41–70% CC) treated stands on his study area while present in the older, denser (>71% CC) untreated stands. Other research has indicated that the northern goshawk may be dependent upon large patches of dense, old-growth ponderosa pine (e.g., Crocker-Bedford 1990), and this species is not faring well in the Black Hills (USDA Forest Service 1996*b*).

However, although the current Black Hills forest mosaic does affect birds, the effects on other species require further study. In particular, species dependent on interior, wilderness, and old-growth habitats may be negatively affected, as these conditions are now rare on the study area and the Black Hills as a whole. Several species have been documented as rare or sensitive on the Black Hills, and they may be particularly vulnerable to the scarcity of these habitat types (USDA Forest Service 1996*b*). For instance, the mountain lion may be sensitive to areas with high road densities (Van Dyke et al. 1986), and this species also has a tenuous hold in the Black Hills (Turner 1974, USDA Forest Service 1996*b*).

Implications for Management and Range of Natural Variability Restoration

Initial USFS recommendations to maintain current levels of logging and increase road construction to restore the forest to within its range of natural variability (USDA Forest Service 1994*a*) were flawed. Initial USFS assessment methods primarily relied upon summarizing RMRIS data (USDA Forest Service 1994*a*). Although the U.S. Forest Service made an effort to duplicate our landscape structure analysis methods in the Black Hills National Forest Final Environmental Impact Statement (Price, *unpublished manuscript;* USDA Forest Service 1996*b*), this "revised" version of our research failed to adequately identify important patch characteristics, incorrectly measured landscape structure, did not compare the current managed landscape structure to pre-EuroAmerican landscapes, and ignored the spatial status of old-growth forests altogether (D. J. Shinneman, *unpublished manuscript*). These inadequate analyses, combined with a lack of comprehensive digitized spatial data for forest harvest activities, initial over-estimations of old-growth, and under-estimations of the spatial extent of road impacts, have probably led to the misinterpretations of the current forest structural conditions on the Black Hills.

Our study demonstrates that the Black Hills National Forest is presently a highly fragmented landscape, with high road density, patchy forest conditions, much edge and little interior habitat, few large interior areas, and very little dense old-growth forest (Tables 15.3–15.7). Moreover, these conditions represent a significant deviation from the large patches and dense old forests, which are a component of the Black Hills range of natural variability (Shinneman and Baker 1997). Thus, widespread application of a proposed thinning and fragmenting management strategy will move the forest farther from its range of natural variability by decreasing patch size and increasing patch edge in an already severely fragmented landscape.

In contrast to USFS recommendations, our analysis suggests that restoration of the Black Hills National Forest landscape to its range of natural variability will require: (1) restoration and maintenance of some large patches in order to regain large interior areas, (2) restoration of large areas of dense old-growth forest in order to increase rare interior old-growth habitat, (3) a strategy for road closures, as well as careful site selection for new roads, to reduce road edge habitat on the landscape, and (4) a management plan that maintains or restores connectivity between large core areas with similar habitat, in order to reduce the degree of habitat isolation for species dependent on habitats such as old-growth forest (e.g., Noss and Harris 1986). For example, the largest dense LSF patch on our study area (see Fig. 15.6c) exists in the Sand Creek watershed (the only USFS-identified roadless area on the study area) and could serve as a core LSF habitat area.

Our study demonstrates that significant forest fragmentation can occur in landscapes other than agricultural or clearcut areas, as evidenced by the changes in landscape structure indices in this managed, but non-clearcut forest. Roads add to fragmentation by dividing otherwise continuous patches, adding edge habitat, and decreasing interior area. Timber harvesting and roads in western coniferous forest landscapes produce a pattern of fragmentation different from that in cleared landscapes with isolated woodlots. Public forest landscapes may never be completely cleared. However, these forests may be transformed into a mosaic of roads, recent cuts, and managed younger forests, as well as the edge habitat adjoining these components, as is now the pattern in the Black Hills.

Acknowledgments

We appreciate the assistance of everyone at the Bearlodge and Spearfish Ranger Districts of the Black Hills National Forest who helped us obtain information and assisted us in many ways. We especially appreciate the help of Pam Johnson and Elizabeth Stiller. We also thank

Richard Knight for his peer review of this chapter.

LITERATURE CITED

Alexander, R. R. 1987. Silviculture systems, cutting methods, and cultural practices for Black Hills ponderosa pine. USDA Forest Service General Technical Report, RM-139, Fort Collins, Colorado, USA.

Allen, C. D. 1994. Ecological perspective: linking ecology, GIS, and remote sensing to ecosystem management. Pages 111–139 *in* V. A. Sample, editor. *Remote sensing and GIS in ecosystem management.* Island Press, Washington, D.C., USA.

Baker, W. L. 1994. Final report: landscape structure measurements for watersheds in the Medicine Bow National Forest using GIS analysis. Department of Geography and Recreation, University of Wyoming, Laramie, Wyoming, USA.

Baker, W. L., and Y. Cai. 1992. The r.le programs for multiscale analysis of landscape structure using the GRASS geographical information system. *Landscape Ecology* 7: 291–302.

Bradshaw, F. J. 1992. Quantifying edge effect and patch size for multiple-use silviculture: a discussion paper. *Forest Ecology and Management* 48: 249–264.

Crocker-Bedford, D. C. 1990. Goshawk reproduction and forest management. *Wildlife Society Bulletin* 18: 262–269.

Crompton, B. J. 1994. Songbird and small mammal diversity in relation to timber management practices in the northwestern Black Hills. Master's thesis, University of Wyoming, Laramie, Wyoming, USA.

Dykstra, B. L. 1996. Effects of harvesting ponderosa pine on birds in the Black Hills of South Dakota and Wyoming. Master's thesis, South Dakota State University, Brookings, South Dakota, USA.

ESRI, Inc. 1995. *Understanding GIS: the ARC/INFO method.* Environmental Systems Research Institute, Inc., Redlands, California, USA.

Fahrig, L., and G. Merriam. 1985. Habitat patch connectivity and population survival. *Ecology* 66: 1762–1768.

Forman, R.T.T., and M. Godron. 1986. *Landscape ecology.* John Wiley and Sons, New York, New York, USA.

Graves, H. S. 1899. The Black Hills Forest Reserve. Pages 67–164 *in The nineteenth annual report of the survey, 1897–1898, Part V, Forest Reserves.* Department of the Interior, U.S. Geological Survey, Washington, D.C., USA.

Grumbine, R. E. 1990. Protecting biological diversity through the greater ecosystem concept. *Natural Areas Journal* 10: 114–120.

Hansen, A. J., W. C. McComb, R. Vega, M. G. Raphael, and M. Hunter. 1995. Bird habitat relationships in natural and managed forests in the west Cascades of Oregon. *Ecological Applications* 5: 555–569.

Harris, L. D. 1984. *The fragmented forest.* University of Chicago Press, Chicago, Illinois, USA.

Hoffman, G. R., and R. R. Alexander. 1987. Forest vegetation of the Black Hills National Forest of South Dakota and Wyoming: a habitat type classification. USDA Forest Service, Rocky Mountain Forest and Range Experiment Station, Research Paper RM-276.

Hunter, M. L. 1990. *Wildlife, forests, and forestry: principles of managing forests for biodiversity.* Prentice Hall, Englewood Cliffs, New Jersey, USA.

Hunter, M. L., G. L. Jacobson, Jr., and T. Webb III. 1988. Paleoecology and the coarse-filter approach to maintaining biological diversity. *Conservation Biology* 2: 375–385.

Kaufmann, M. R., R. T. Graham, D. A. Boyce, Jr., W. H. Moir, L. Perry, R. T. Reynolds, R. L. Basset, P. Mehlop, C. B. Edminster, W. M. Block, and P. S. Corn. 1994. An ecological basis for ecosystem management. USDA Forest Service, Rocky Mountain Forest and Range Experiment Station, Technical Report RM-246.

Lehmkuhl, J. F., P. F. Hessburg, R. L. Everett, M. H. Huff, and R. D. Ottmar. 1994. Historical and current forest landscapes of eastern Oregon and Washington. USDA Forest Service General Technical Report PNW-GTR-328.

McGarigal, K., and W. C. McComb. 1995. Relationships between landscape structure and breeding birds in the Oregon Coast Range. *Ecological Monographs* 65: 235–260.

Mehl, M. S. 1992. Old-growth descriptions for the major forest cover types in the Rocky Mountain region. Pages 106–120 *in* M. R. Kaufmann, W. H. Moir, and R. L. Bassett, technical coordinators. *Old-growth forests in the Southwest and Rocky Mountain regions.* USDA Forest Service, Rocky Mountain Forest and Range Experiment Station, General Technical Report RM-213.

Mladenoff, D. J., M. A. White, J. Pastor, and T. R. Crow. 1993. Comparing spatial pattern in unaltered old-growth and disturbed forest landscapes. *Ecological Applications* 3: 294–306.

Morrison, P. H. 1994. GIS application perspective: development and analysis of a chronosequence of late-successional forest ecosystem data layers. Pages 77–90 *in* V. A. Sample., editor. *Remote sensing and GIS in ecosystem management.* Island Press, Washington, D.C., USA.

Noss, R. F., and B. Csuti. 1994. Habitat fragmentation. Pages 237–264 *in* G. K. Meffe and C. R. Carroll, editors. *Principles of conservation biology.* Sinauer Associates, Sunderland, Massachusetts, USA.

Noss, R. F., and L. D. Harris. 1986. Nodes, networks and MUM's: preserving diversity at all scales. *Environmental Management* 10: 299–309.

Parrish, J. B., D. J. Herman, and D. J. Reyher. 1996. A century of change in Black Hills forest and riparian ecosystems. USDA Forest Service Agricultural Experiment Station Publication, B 722.

Pickett, S.T.A. 1994. Essay 9a: mosaics and patch dynamics. Pages 242–243 *in* G. K. Meffe and C. R. Carrol, editors. *Principles of conservation biology.* Sinauer Associates, Sunderland, Massachusetts, USA.

Reed, R. A., J. Johnson-Barnard, and W. L. Baker. 1996*a*. Contribution of roads to forest fragmentation in the Rocky Mountains. *Conservation Biology* 10: 1098–1106.

Reed, R. A., J. Johnson-Barnard, and W. L. Baker. 1996*b*. Fragmentation of a forested Rocky Mountain landscape, 1950–1993. *Biological Conservation* 75: 267–277.

Ripple, W. J., C. A. Bradshaw, and T. A. Spies. 1991. Measuring forest landscape patterns in the Cascade Range of Oregon, USA. *Biological Conservation* 57: 73–88.

Schonewald-Cox, C., and M. Buechner. 1992. Park protection and public roads. Pages 373–395 *in* P. L. Fiedler and S. K. Jain, editors. *Conservation biology: the theory and practice of nature conservation, preservation and management.* Chapman and Hall, New York, New York, USA.

Shinneman, D. J. 1996. An analysis of range of natural variability, roads, and timber harvesting in a Black Hills ponderosa pine forest landscape. Master's thesis, University of Wyoming, Laramie, Wyoming, USA.

Shinneman, D.J., and W.L. Baker. 1997. Nonequilibrium dynamics between catastrophic disturbances and old-growth ponderosa pine landscapes of the Black Hills. *Conservation Biology* 11: 1276–1288.

Spies, T. A., W. J. Ripple, and G. A. Bradshaw. 1994. Dynamics and pattern of a managed coniferous forest landscape in Oregon. *Ecological Applications* 4: 555–568.

Stephens, H. A. 1973. *Woody plants of the North Central Plains.* University of Kansas Press, Lawrence, Kansas, USA.

Swanson, F. J., J. A. Jones, D. O. Wallin, and J. H. Cissel. 1994. Natural variability: implications for ecosystem management. Pages 80–94 *in* M. E. Jensen and P. S. Bourgeron, editors. *Volume II. Ecosystem management: principles and applications.* USDA Forest Service General Technical Report PNW-GTR-318.

Thomas, J. W., C. Maser, and J. E. Rodiek. 1979. Edges. Pages 48–59 *in* J.W. Thomas, editor. *Wildlife habitats in managed forest: the Blue Mountains of Oregon and Washington.* USDA Forest Service Agriculture Handbook. No. 553.

Tinker, D. B., C.A.C. Resor, G. P. Beauvais, K. F. Kipfmueller, C. I. Fernandes, and W. L. Baker. 1998. Watershed analysis of forest fragmentation by clearcuts and roads in a Wyoming forest. *Landscape Ecology* 13: 149–165.

Turner, R. W. 1974. *Mammals of the Black Hills of South Dakota and Wyoming.* University of Kansas, Lawrence, Kansas, USA.

Turner, M. G., R. H. Gardner, and R. V. O'Neill. 1995. Ecological dynamics at broad scales. *BioScience Supplement: Science and Biodiversity Policy.* 29–35.

USA-CERL. 1994. *Grass 4.1 user's reference manual.* U.S. Army Construction Engineering Research Laboratory, Champaign, Illinois, USA.

USDA Forest Service. 1994a. Draft environmental impact statement for the Black Hills National Forest revised land and resource management plan. USDA Forest Service, Custer, South Dakota, USA.

USDA Forest Service. 1994b. Rocky Mountain resource information system user's guide. Rocky Mountain Region, Denver, Colorado, USA.

USDA Forest Service. 1996a. 1996 Revision: land and resource management plan for the Black Hills National Forest. USDA Forest Service, Custer, South Dakota, USA.

USDA Forest Service. 1996b. Final environmental impact statement for the Black Hills National Forest revised land and resource management plan. USDA Forest Service, Custer, South Dakota, USA.

Van Dyke, F. G., R. H. Brocke, and H. G. Shaw. 1986. Use of road track counts as indices of mountain lion presence. *Journal of Wildlife Management* 50: 102–109.

16

Using the LANDLOG Model to Analyze the Fragmentation of a Wyoming Forest by a Century of Clear-cutting

Daniel B. Tinker and William L. Baker

INTRODUCTION

The fragmentation of forest landscapes by commercial timber harvesting has become an important source of land management debate over the last few years. The identification of fragmentation as a significant issue facing foresters is complicated by the inability of managers and researchers to agree as to exactly what constitutes fragmentation. While natural processes such as fire, avalanches, and blowdowns often produce altered forest patterns, these mosaics typically exhibit different structural characteristics than those produced by timber harvest (Mladenoff et al. 1993). Reed et al. (1996a) defined fragmentation as "a change in landscape structure that typically, but not universally, includes smaller patch sizes, smaller patch perimeter lengths, greater distances between patches, more edge habitat, and less interior habitat (habitat not affected by human-created boundaries)." As timber harvesting in Rocky Mountain coniferous forests continues, fragmentation of contiguous stands of previously unharvested forest results in small, isolated remnants of old-growth forest in a matrix of younger, regenerating stands.

Recent studies have identified fragmentation resulting from human alterations of forest landscapes (Mladenoff et al. 1993; Miller et al. 1996; Reed et al. 1996a, 1996b; Tinker et al. 1998). In addition, several studies have begun to address specific questions regarding the effects of the spatial patterning of timber harvest on wildlife habitat (Bettinger et al. 1997; Beauvais, *this volume*) and bird nesting success (Robinson et al. 1995). Other research has focused on simulating the effects of various timber harvesting regimes on landscape structure (Franklin and Forman 1987, Li et al. 1993, Wallin et al. 1994, Gustafson 1996, Gustafson and Crow 1996). However, these studies were not quantitatively predictive, and did not attempt to estimate the long-term, cumulative effects of present patterns of human alteration of forest landscapes.

Our approach differs from previous studies in that we used existing timber harvest guidelines and practices to simulate clear-cutting in the Medicine Bow National Forest in southeastern Wyoming in order to quantify and compare changes in landscape structure over a 100-year period. Previous studies of the present landscape of the Medicine Bow National Forest have shown it to be significantly fragmented by timber harvesting and roads compared to the period prior to the onset of widespread clear-cutting in the 1950s (Baker 1994; Reed et al. 1996*a, b*).

For this study, we used LANDLOG, a spatially-explicit, dynamic simulation model modified from an existing disturbance simulation model (DISPATCH; Baker et al. 1991), in concert with the landscape structure analysis program r.le (Baker and Cai 1992) to simulate timber harvest in the Medicine Bow National Forest according to its current guidelines (USDA Forest Service 1985). The simulations were performed within the GRASS 4.1 GIS (USA-CERL 1994) to analyze the long-term effects of clear-cutting on landscape structure, as well as to evaluate the sustainability of harvesting timber as it is currently practiced. We hypothesized that harvestable stands of lodgepole pine would be depleted during the 100-year simulation, and we expected specific changes in landscape structure, such as an increase in the number of patches, a decrease in the amount of core, or interior, area of the patches, and an increase in the amount of patch edge. Besides the actual simulation and quantification of the periodic and cumulative changes in forest structure, our objectives included an evaluation of the LANDLOG model, which shows promise as a planning tool for forest managers and silviculturists.

STUDY AREA

The Medicine Bow National Forest in southeastern Wyoming includes a portion of the Medicine Bow Mountains. Our study area, located about 75 km west of Laramie, includes the majority of the Laramie District of the Medicine Bow National Forest (Fig. 16.1). The climate in the Medicine Bow Mountains is characterized by long, cold winters and short, cool summers, with most of the precipitation

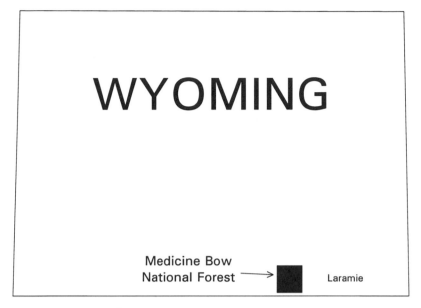

Fig. 16.1. Location of the Medicine Bow National Forest, southeastern Wyoming.

occurring during the winter as snow. The forest vegetation is dominated by lodgepole pine, Engelmann spruce, and subalpine fir, with scattered smaller patches of aspen, Douglas fir, limber pine, and ponderosa pine (Alexander et al. 1986). Understory vegetation is often dominated by dwarf huckleberry and buffaloberry. Our study area is approximately 45 km east-west and 60 km north-south, and is represented in the computer by a raster of 894 columns by 1,209 rows with a pixel-resolution of 50 m.

METHODS

Map Preparation

Digital vector maps representing vegetative cover type, clear-cuts, forest stand age, forest boundary, and riparian areas were obtained from the Medicine Bow National Forest. In addition, a vector map was obtained that contained all of the areas in the Laramie District of the Medicine Bow National Forest that have been classified as suitable for timber extraction. This map was based on harvest suitability requirements of the area, which included criteria such as soil type and stability, elevation, vegetation type, and slope and aspect (C. Tolbert, *personal communication*). The Sheep Mountain Wildlife Refuge, located

339

on the eastern edge of the Laramie District, along with all roadless areas and alpine regions of the Snowy Range, were excluded from the study based on designation by the Medicine Bow National Forest as unsuitable for present or future timber harvest. All vector coverages were converted to raster format at 10 m resolution using the GRASS 4.1 GIS, and were then resampled to 50 m resolution for subsequent map preparation and use during the simulation. Using the "r.mapcalc" command in GRASS 4.1, all riparian areas were removed from the initial SUITABLE map, creating a new map we called SUITNEW, as riparian areas are also considered unsuitable for harvesting.

Based on an initial analysis of clear-cut placement in the Medicine Bow National Forest between 1985 and 1993, over 95% of the scheduled clear-cuts designated under the 1984 Medicine Bow National Forest Plan were located in lodgepole pine stands. We therefore remade the vegetation cover map using "r.mapcalc" to create a coverage containing only lodgepole pine stands. This lodgepole pine coverage was then combined with the map of suitable areas to create a map of suitable lodgepole pine forests (SUITLP). Finally, the SUITLP map was combined with a map of ages of lodgepole pine stands within the study area to produce the base map used for the simulation (SUITAGELP). No current digital coverages of roads exist for the Medicine Bow National Forest, therefore the effects of roads as agents of fragmentation were not measured in this study.

Model Simulation

The LANDLOG model was used to simulate timber harvesting in the Medicine Bow National Forest over a period of 100 years. Harvest guidelines in the Medicine Bow National Forest Forest Plan (USDA Forest Service 1985) were followed as closely as possible in order to simulate clear-cutting as it has been practiced since 1985. According to the 1984 Forest Plan for the Medicine Bow National Forest, the minimum age at which a suitable stand of lodgepole pine could be cut is 90 years.

We analyzed the actual timber harvesting since 1984 to obtain the parameter values needed to run the model. The common pattern of commercial timber harvesting in the Medicine Bow National Forest since 1985 has been the timber-sale approach. Under this plan, large areas of the forest are designated as timber sale areas, within which multiple clear-cuts are placed. We estimated the average size of timber sale areas to be approximately 550 ha. Based on an analysis of the digital map of 1985–1994 clear-cuts, using the r.le program (Baker and Cai 1992), the average number of clear-cuts per year was 87.4 (s.d. = 44.3) and the average size clear-cut was 6.23 ha (s.d. = 6.31). The sizes of clear-cuts were tallied in 25 size-classes from 1–>24 ha. This empirical distribution was randomly sampled by the model, so that the actual variation in clear-cut size was represented in the simulations. Additionally, the average distance between clear-cuts made between 1985–1994 was calculated and used to position simulated clear-cuts. Following traditional management practice, new clear-cuts were not placed adjacent to existing cuts or regenerating stands of lodgepole pine less than 21 years of age (D. Carr, *personal communication*). Therefore, at each yearly time-step, 50 m buffers were placed around all patches under 21 years of age, including recent clear-cuts. Once a patch reached 21 years of age, the buffer was removed and new cuts could then be placed adjacent to these former openings. All pixels within the study area were increased in age by one year through an annual update subroutine; in this way, the model was both spatially and temporally dynamic, and cuts of a young age at the beginning of the simulation became available for re-harvest at some time during the 100-year simulation.

At each yearly time-step, new timber-sale areas and clear-cuts within each timber-sale area were randomly located within the study area using a random number generator, and the size of each cut was randomly selected from the size distribution described above. Each clear-cut was then spread using an algorithm designed to create patches shaped like actual clear-cuts. If the model was unable to spread a clear-cut because the initial point was located in a patch which was smaller than the selected cut size, the location subroutine would relocate the clear-cut to another harvestable patch. If, after 100 such attempts, the model was still unable to locate and spread a clear-cut, the model would stop under the assumption that harvestable forest has been depleted. Ten replications of the 100-year simulation were performed, and results from the landscape structure analyses of all ten replicates were averaged.

Model Validation

The LANDLOG model was validated by comparing actual changes in landscape structure from 1985–1993 with simulated changes for the same period. To accomplish this, we first recreated the 1985 landscape by replacing all clear-cuts made from 1985–1993 back into the vegetation cover maps, and then ran the model for a 9-year period. Ten replications were performed to assess the accuracy and precision of the model's predictive capability relative to the actual 1993 map. Over 80% of the 25 indices measured by the r.le landscape structure analysis program (described in a following section) were validated for use in the simulations. A complete description of the validation procedure for the LANDLOG model is presented elsewhere (Baker 1999).

Landscape Structure Analysis

Following each 10-year period of simulation, raster maps of the forest were saved for analysis of landscape structure by the r.le programs (Baker and Cai 1992). The amount of harvestable area, defined as all suitable lodgepole pine patches >90 years old, was calculated at the initiation of the simulation and at 10-year intervals for a period of 100 years of simulated harvest. A variety of other landscape indices, known to measure forest fragmentation in the Rocky Mountains (Baker, *this volume*), were calculated (Table 16.1). An explanation of each index is in Baker and Cai (1992). Changes in these indices were also calculated at 10-year intervals, and compared over the entire 100-year simulation period to identify both periodic and cumulative changes to landscape structure.

Before the analyses were done, patches were reclassified into 12 age classes (Table 16.1). This reclassification was done to eliminate unrealistic edges such as would occur when two adjacent patches differed in age by only a few years. The structure of the age classification was based on the following assumptions: 1) during the first 100 years of stand development, edges of stands which differ by 20 years of age are discernable both from ground observations and aerial photographs; 2) between 100 and 400 years of age, changes in canopy structure, and therefore edge characteristics, seem to be identifiable when stands differ by approximately 50 years; and 3) once a stand reaches 400 years of age, the ragged canopies associated with climax stands of lodgepole pine change very little until altered by some disturbance event.

All edge-related analyses were based on a 50 m depth-of-edge influence. This estimate may be considered conservative, because other studies have suggested that edge effects may be detected at greater distances than 50 m from the edge of a patch (Chen et al. 1992; Vaillancourt 1995).

RESULTS

Because our age-class divisions imposed upon the data prior to the landscape structure analysis created an age class of 80–100 years old, the amount of harvestable timber must be estimated by lodgepole

Table 16.1. Landscape indices used to analyze structural changes in lodgepole pine forests as a result of the simulated clear-cutting. See Baker and Cai (1992) for an explanation of each index.

___

Age
   Mean patch age
   Standard deviation of patch age
   Mean pixel age
   Standard deviation of pixel age

Cover
   Percent cover of lodgepole pine forest by age-class (yrs): 1–20, 21–40, 41–60, 61–80, 81–100, 101–150, 151–200, 201–250, 251–300, 301–350, 351–400,   400+

Size
   Mean core area (ha), assuming a depth-of-edge influence of 50 meters
   Standard deviation of core area
   Mean core area by age-class (ha): 1–20, 21–40, 41–60, 61–80, 81–100, 101–150, 151–200, 201–250,251–300, 301–350, 351–400, 400+, assuming a depth-of-edge influence of 50 meters
   Mean patch size (ha)
   Standard deviation of patch size

Density
   Total number of patches
   Number of patches by age-class (yrs): 1–20, 21–40, 41–60, 61–80, 81–100, 101–150, 151–200, 201–250,251–300, 301–350, 351–400, 400+
   Number of patches by size-class (ha): 0.25–2.49, 2.50–4.99, 5.00–7.49, 7.50–9.99, 10.00–12.49, 12.50–24.99, 25.00–49.99, 50.00–124.99, 125.00+

Edge/perimeter
   Mean edge area (ha), assuming a depth-of-edge influence of 50 meters
   Standard deviation of edge area
   Total edge length (ha)

Diversity
   Patch richness
   Shannon diversity
   Dominance
   Inverse Simpson's

Distance
   Mean distance between forest patches >200 years old
   Standard deviation of distance between forest patches >200 years old

___

pine stands within the areas of suitable harvest that are older than 80, rather than 90, years of age. Therefore, these estimates of the absolute amount of harvestable timber may be slightly overestimated, but the relative changes that occurred during the simulation period are nevertheless revealing. Using this age classification, cover of harvestable lodgepole pine decreased by approximately one-third, from 63% of the suitable area in 1997 to 41% in 2097, following 100 years of simulated harvesting (Fig. 16.2). However, if the percentage of the landscape covered by the 80–100 year age class is assumed to be divided equally between the 80–90 and 90–100 year age classes, and using 90 years of age as the minimum harvestable age of lodgepole pine, the estimates of harvestable timber in 1997 and 2097 would be 54.5% and 34.5%, respectively. The magnitude of decrease is very similar to that calculated when a minimum age of 80 years is used. The percentage of the study area covered by younger stands was affected much differently than harvestable-aged stands. The percentage of the landscape covered by stands from 41–60 years of age increased more than seven-fold from 2% to 15%, while stands that were 61–80 years of age increased in percent cover of the landscape from 6% to 15% (Fig. 16.2). There was very little change in percent cover of the two youngest age classes (Fig. 16.2).

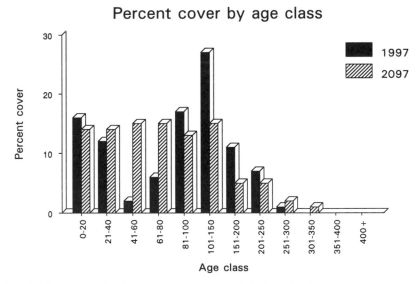

Fig. 16.2. Changes in the percentage of suitable lodgepole pine forest area by age class over a 100-year simulation of timber harvesting.

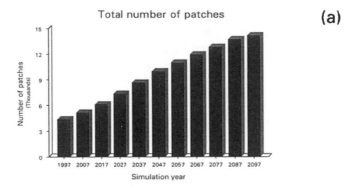

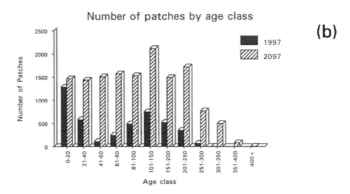

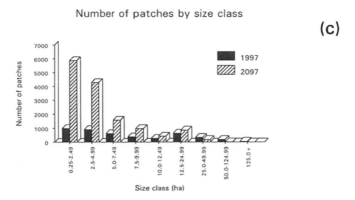

Fig. 16.3. Three indices regarding number of patches: (a) changes in the total number of patches within the study area over a 100-year simulation period; (b) number of patches in each of twelve age classes in 1997 (solid bars) and 2097 (hatched bars); (c) number of patches in each of nine size classes in 1997 (solid bars) and 2097 (hatched bars).

The total number of patches in the study area increased over three-fold in a nearly linear fashion, from 4,410 patches when the simulation began (1997) to 14,181 patches after 100 years (2097) (Fig. 16.3a). The distribution of this increase across the twelve age classes was quite variable; however, the number of patches increased in all classes (Fig. 16.3b). The 21–40, 61–80, 81–100, 101–150, and 201–250 age classes showed three-to six-fold increases in the number of patches, while the 41–60 year age class exhibited a thirteen-fold increase (Fig. 16.3b). The four oldest age classes experienced the largest proportional changes (10- to 50-fold increases), but these classes contained fewer patches when the simulation began, so the absolute increases in the number of patches were less than in the younger age classes. The 0–20 year age class increased only slightly in the number of patches (Fig. 16.3b).

The largest increases in the number of patches occurred within the smallest size classes. Patches 0.25–2.49 ha in size increased six-fold following 100 years of timber harvest, while patches from 2.5–9.99 ha increased from 2.5 to 4.5 times their original numbers (Fig. 16.3c). The intermediate size classes (10–24.99 ha) increased in the number of patches only by approximately 1.5 times. Notably, the three largest size classes all showed large decreases in the number of patches. The number of patches that were 25–49.99 ha in size decreased by almost half, while patches in the largest two size classes (50–125+ ha) were almost completely eliminated (Fig. 16.3c).

Mean core area for all patches at the initiation of the simulation was 7.0 ha (Fig. 16.4a). This value decreased nearly linearly through the first 50 years of the simulation to 2.04 ha. A much lower rate of change was observed during the final 50 years, resulting in a final mean core area of only 1.1 ha (Fig. 16.4a). The standard deviation of the mean core area also decreased in a relatively linear fashion during the first half of the simulations, from an initial value of 21.4, then decreased asymptotically to a final value of 2.6 (Fig. 16.4a). With regard to changes in core area within the twelve age classes, the five youngest age classes from 0–100 years old experienced decreases in core area of 49%–86%, while the five age classes from 100–350 years of age all experienced decreases greater than 90% (Fig. 16.4b). The two oldest age classes actually increased in core area due to the fact that there were no patches within these two classes when the simulation began; therefore, the core area was zero at that time.

The mean patch size for all stands of lodgepole pine was reduced by almost 50% during the first 40 years of the simulation, from 14.78

ha at year 0 to 7.50 ha at year 40 (Fig. 16.5a). The rate of decrease in patch size leveled off following year 50 and the mean patch size at year 100 was 4.55, a total decrease from year 0 of almost 70% (Fig. 16.5a). Standard deviation of the mean patch size was reduced by over 83% during the 100 years of simulated clear-cutting (Fig. 16.5a).

The mean age of lodgepole pine stands across the entire study area was reduced from 98.2 years in 1997 to 85.4 years in 2097 (Fig. 16.5b). This decrease was nearly linear during the first 70 years of the

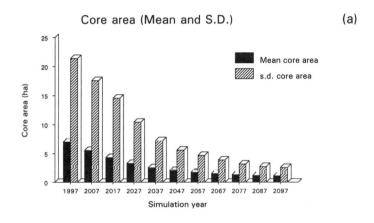

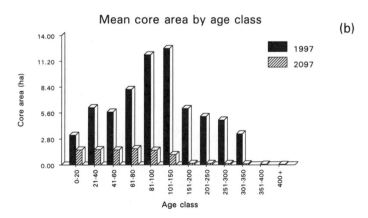

Fig. 16.4. Core area measures: (a) Changes in mean and standard deviation of core area (ha) for the study area at 10-year intervals from 1997–2097; (b) Changes in mean core area for each of twelve age classes.

simulation, after which the rate of decrease leveled off and seemed to reach some minimum threshold. Patch age standard deviation was relatively unchanged throughout the 100 year simulation (Fig. 16.5b).

Mean patch edge area averaged across all stands of lodgepole pine in the study area decreased by 55%, from 7.8 ha in 1997 to 3.5 ha in 2097 (Fig. 16.6a). However, the total amount of edge across the landscape more than doubled, from 12,399 ha in 1997 to 28,734 ha in 2097 (Fig. 16.6b). In addition, the patch edge-to-core area ratio almost tripled, from 1.10 to 3.13 during the 100-year simulation (Fig. 16.7). The standard deviation of mean edge size was reduced from 13.33 ha in 1997 to 3.51 ha in 2097, a reduction of 74% (Fig. 16.6a).

The diversity indices changed relatively little during the simulations (Table 16.2). For example, the richness index increased from 9 to 11 during the simulation as a result of the appearance of stands within the oldest age classes which were not present at all when the simula-

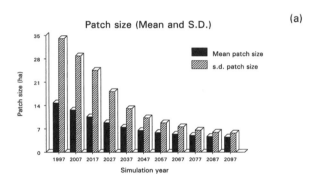

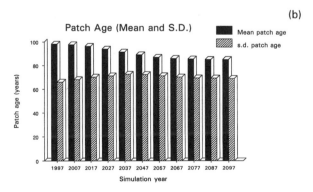

Fig. 16.5. Changes in mean (solid bars) and standard deviation (hatched bars) of (a) patch size and (b) patch age over the 100-year simulation at 10-year intervals.

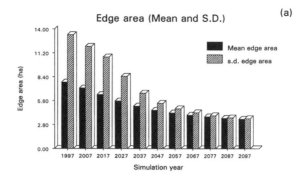

(a)

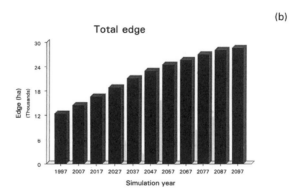

(b)

Fig. 16.6. Changes in (a) mean (solid bars) and standard deviation (hatched bars) of mean patch edge area and (b) total patch edge area over the 100-year simulation at 10-year intervals.

tions began. Shannon diversity increased slightly from 1.8 to 2.0. The Inverse Simpson average also showed a minimal increase from a value of 5.07 in 1997 to 6.66 in 2097. Dominance was unchanged after the 100 years of simulated clear-cutting from an initial value of 0.40, although this measure did fluctuate slightly during the simulation.

The mean distance between lodgepole pine stands >200 years of age decreased rapidly during the first 50 years of the simulations, followed by a period of considerably smaller decreases (Fig. 16.8). The average distance between these older stands was 473 m in 1997 and decreased to 161 m in 2097. The standard deviation of this distance measure also decreased, but to a much larger extent. In 1997 the standard deviation was 1,341 m and in 2097 this value was 249 m. Much of this decrease (>80%) also occurred during the first 50 years of the simulation (Fig. 16.8).

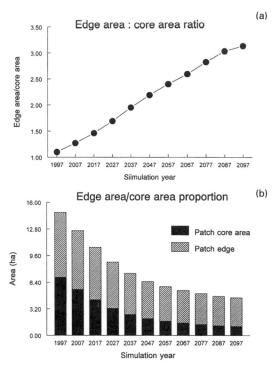

Fig. 16.7. Changes in (a) the edge area/core area ratios; and (b) the proportion of patch area composed of core area (solid bars) and edge area (hatched bars) over the 100-year simulation at 10-year intervals.

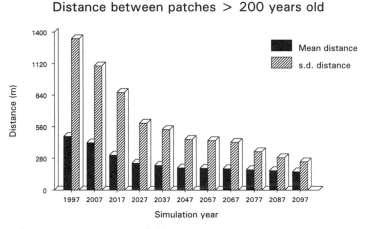

Fig. 16.8. Changes in mean (solid bars) and standard deviation (hatched bars) of mean distance between patches >200 years of age over the 100-year simulation at 10-year intervals.

DISCUSSION

Changes in Landscape Structure

Landscape structure changes predicted by the LANDLOG model seem to represent what has been identified as a "fragmentation syndrome" (Tinker et al. 1998; Baker, *this volume*). This syndrome is characterized by a suite of changes that are highly correlated, and include an increase in the number of patches, a reduction in core area, and an increase in the amount of edge across the landscape.

The 41% of harvestable timber that remained following 100 years of simulated clear-cutting (using a minimum harvestable age of 80 years for analysis purposes) suggests that current timber removal practices may be sustainable at the century scale, yet produce a landscape that is highly fragmented. (Notably, when the minimum harvestable age is assumed to be 90 years, available harvestable timber is reduced further to 34.5%.) Also, the classification of stands which regenerated from previous clear-cuts as harvestable assumes that they have reached not only the minimum age, but the minimum size requirements for harvest, and that the culmination of mean annual increment has occurred. Although much work has been done on the natural history and silvicultural characteristics of lodgepole pine, given that this is the first harvest rotation in much of the Rocky Mountain coniferous forests, these assumptions may prove to be invalid. Additionally, many other site characteristics such as elevation, slope, aspect, and nutrient and moisture availability can greatly affect the development of regenerating stands of lodgepole pine. For example, stands of lodgepole pine in the Bighorn National Forest in north-central Wyoming that were clear-cut in the 1950s have changed relatively little since harvested (G. Beauvais, *personal communication*). In this study, the largest increases in percent cover of the landscape were observed in the youngest age classes (Fig. 16.2), and the resulting forests were dominated by a matrix of young stands, rather than a matrix of older stands of lodgepole pine.

The relatively small decrease in mean patch age from 98 years of age to 85 years of age over the 100 year simulation was surprising, yet the results have important management implications. Following the simulations, the average age of the forest was reduced below the minimum harvestable age of 90 years (Fig. 16.5b). With the removal and conversion of many of the older stands to young, regenerating clearcuts, we expected that the mean patch age would shift to a much younger average age within the study area. The relative stability in age

351

structure may be due to the dynamic nature of the model, and of the forest itself, whereby older stands that are removed are continually replaced by aging younger stands. Standard deviation of the mean patch age was also stable during the simulation (Fig 16.5b), largely because the range of patch ages was maintained throughout the 100 years of simulation, even though the ages were redistributed across the range.

The three-fold increase in total number of patches and the bias of the increase towards younger stands demonstrates the tendency of clear-cut timber harvesting to fragment more mature forest (Figs. 16.3a and 16.3b). Clear-cutting appears to create more numerous older stands as well (Fig. 16.3b), but this probably reflects the perforation of large, intact, old stands by clear-cuts, leading to fewer large stands (Fig. 16.3c). In fact, all of the increase in the number of patches across the landscape occurred within the smaller size classes (0.25–24.99 ha), with clear-cutting resulting in the near elimination of large stands >50 ha (Fig. 16.3c).

An increase in the number of patches corresponds with a decline in patch core area. As the number of patches increased, core area decreased, which could cause a reduction in suitable habitat for many interior, forest-dwelling animals (Ruggiero et al. 1994), and a shift in species composition of some communities of neotropical migrant birds (Dobkin 1994). The overall large decrease in core area from this simulation (Fig. 16.4a) suggests that these effects on interior habitat and species composition may be quite severe, especially given that the greatest decreases in core area occurred in the oldest patches (Fig. 16.4b). The decrease in core area corresponds highly with decreases in mean patch size across the landscape. Intuitively, as patch size decreases, so must the amount of interior habitat. Our simulations produced an average patch size of only 4.5 ha after 100 years of simulation (Fig. 16.5a), a value smaller than the amount of core area that existed before the simulation began (7.0 ha; Fig. 16.4a). Ripple et al. (1991) also found that clear-cut harvesting was associated with, among other things, a decrease in patch size.

At the start of the simulation, the standard deviations of both mean core area and patch size were quite large (Fig. 16.4a), suggesting a heterogeneous landscape containing a broad range of patch and core area sizes. The marked decrease in the standard deviation of mean core area and patch size indicates a trend towards the production of a forest which contains patches that are smaller and more similar in size than in the landscape prior to harvesting. Other studies have documented decreased complexity of forest patch structure as a result of clear-cuts and roads in Colorado, Wyoming, and South Dakota (Miller et al. 1996; Reed et al. 1996*a*, *b*; Shinneman 1996; Tinker et al. 1998).

Mean edge length for individual patches decreased (Fig. 16.6a); this might suggest that the adverse effects of patch edges (Chen et al. 1992, Vaillancourt 1995) are not evident in these forests following simulated clear-cutting. However, the decrease in mean edge length produced by our simulations is directly related to mean patch size (i.e., as mean patch size decreases, so does mean edge length). A better measurement of depth-of-edge effects may be the ratio of edge area per patch to core area per patch. Our results show that the edge area/core area ratio increased by a factor of three, indicating that while core area decreased during the 100-year simulation, the amount of edge per unit of core area increased (Fig. 16.7).

In this study, total edge increased by 130% (Fig. 16.6b). Murcia (1995) suggested that edges created by young secondary growth surrounding older matrix forest highlight differences in structural complexity and biomass, and very different microclimates may co-exist on either side of the created edge. The 74% reduction in the standard deviation of mean edge size is similar to that observed in other patch indices from this study, and also suggests the production of a landscape which is becoming more similar in structure (Fig. 16.6a).

Diversity indices were relatively unchanged during the entire simulation (Table 16.2). Many measures of diversity are associated with major land-use changes such as the conversion of natural areas to agriculture or exurban communities (Mladenoff et al. 1993). Our

Table 16.2. Diversity indices measured using r.le.

Simulation Year	Richness	Shannon diversity	Dominance	Inverse Simpson's
1997	9	1.80	0.40	5.07
2007	9	1.81	0.39	4.96
2017	9	1.80	0.40	4.90
2027	9	1.87	0.33	5.45
2037	10	1.93	0.37	6.20
2047	10	2.00	0.31	6.74
2057	10	2.00	0.30	6.76
2067	10	1.99	0.31	6.68
2077	10	2.01	0.29	6.81
2087	11	2.02	0.38	6.85
2097	11	2.00	0.40	6.66

simulations, however, were not associated with strict land use changes, but rather identified conversions of the age structure of lodgepole pine stands. We would therefore not expect large changes in the diversity indices. However, repeated harvesting of lodgepole pine stands may result in a decrease in landscape diversity over longer periods of time. For example, many lodgepole pine stands develop into spruce-fir climax stands through natural secondary succession. These old-growth stands may become rare as the landscape is converted into a more homogeneous matrix of young lodgepole pine forests.

The decrease in the average distance between stands >200 years old (Fig. 16.8) seems counterintuitive at first, because forest fragmentation is often associated with the isolation of old-growth forest patches (Murcia 1995, Franklin and Forman 1987, Noss and Csuti 1994). However, the stronger force that is driving the spatial and structural changes to older forest patches following this simulation may be fragmentation (Buskirk et al., *this volume*), rather than isolation. For example, the average distance between existing large, intact older patches at the beginning of the simulation (473 m) was longer than that following 100 years of clear-cutting (161 m) because small clear-cuts fragment these large, old patches into numerous, smaller patches that contribute many short distances to the calculation of mean distance. Standard deviation of distance decreased as did other standard deviation measures, suggesting that distances between older patches are becoming more similar, as is the landscape as a whole. While we did not measure it directly, it is undoubtedly the large, old-forest patches that are becoming isolated by fragmentation into numerous, small old-forest patches.

Temporal Landscape Change Thresholds

Many of the changes imposed upon the landscape structure by clear-cutting occurred during the first 40–50 years of the simulation (Figs. 16.4a, 16.5a, 16.5b, 16.6a, 16.6b, 16.8). This period of marked directional transformation was followed, in most cases, by a leveling-off period, as if some threshold had been reached. Because of the 100-year duration of this simulation, we cannot possibly predict if this trend would continue, or if forest structure would once again begin to change. We suggest that indices such as mean patch size, mean core area, and mean edge area are constrained from any further reductions in size by the inability of the model to place subsequent clear-cuts within many of the patches until they have reached the minimum harvestable age and were surrounded by harvestable lodgepole pine.

However, the rate of increase in the total number of patches (Fig. 16.3a) seems to be just beginning to decline, suggesting that the maximum threshold for this landscape metric has not been reached.

Usefulness of the LANDLOG Model

As is the case with many ecological models, LANDLOG has limitations: most spatial models are only as good as the maps from which they run. In addition, many important ecosystem variables are inevitably excluded from the models due to the inability of most computer systems to operate such a complex simulation. However, our model does provide good baseline information from which other studies can be built, and it may help in identifying related ecological trends that are important areas of future research. Simulation models such as LANDLOG are extremely useful to begin to understand the long-term consequences of current management policies. Alternative approaches derived from present USDA Forest Service planning software such as FORPLAN, or that use other spatial optimization algorithms (e.g., Bettinger et al. 1997) do not provide valid spatial representations of the landscape pattern resulting from timber harvesting. Clearly, a wait-and-see approach may not provide adequate information in a timely enough manner to prevent irreparable damage to our forest landscapes. Because restoration of fragmented landscapes requires decades (Baker 1995), a change in landscape management is needed now if the goal is to minimize fragmentation.

CONCLUSIONS

Our model predicts that the present timber harvest regime as set out by the 1984 Forest Plan in the Medicine Bow National Forest will result in continued and significant forest fragmentation as a result of clear-cutting. The expected degree of fragmentation is actually much higher because the spatial arrangement and density of roads could not be considered (Reed et al. 1996a; Tinker et al. 1998). The results from this study and others (Reed et al. 1996a, b; Miller et al. 1996; Tinker et al., 1998) suggest that, if present trends continue, forest fragmentation will result in a landscape structure which little resembles pre-EuroAmerican landscapes. The ecosystem consequences of such structural changes are discussed elsewhere in this volume (Beauvais, *this volume*). Because of socio-economic considerations, many forest managers are reluctant to consider alternative harvest regimes and are, in fact, reticent to expend any resources on measuring and monitoring the state of the landscape with respect to fragmentation (USDA Forest

Service, 1996) until specific effects of these structural alterations have been identified. This reluctance is unfortunate, as research continues to suggest that fragmentation of national forests as a result of timber harvest and roadbuilding is occurring at an alarming rate (Reed et al. 1996*a*, *b*; Tinker et al. 1998).

As commercial timber harvesting in the Rocky Mountains enters its second half-century, managers and researchers have the responsibility to try to ensure that the decisions regarding future harvesting regimes are made responsibly and are based on the best information available. Results from this study indicate that clear-cutting, as it is presently practiced in the Medicine Bow National Forest, produces highly fragmented forests and landscapes. Perhaps more importantly, our results suggest the use of models such as LANDLOG may assist managers in developing harvesting policies that are both productive and sustainable, yet do not negatively impact biotic diversity and landscape structure as do present practices.

ACKNOWLEDGMENTS

We thank Carol Tolbert and Dave Carr of the Laramie District of the Medicine Bow National Forest Supervisors Office in Laramie, Wyoming for their help with map preparation and information regarding current timber harvest policy. We also wish to thank Gary Beauvais for a thoughtful and careful review of an earlier draft of the chapter.

LITERATURE CITED

Alexander, R. R., G. R. Hoffman, and J. M. Wirsing. 1986. Forest vegetation of the Medicine Bow National Forest in Southeastern Wyoming: a habitat type classification. USDA Forest Service Research Paper INT–271.

Baker, W. L. 1995. Longterm response of disturbance landscapes to human intervention and global change. *Landscape Ecology* 10: 143–159.

Baker, W. L. 1994. Landscape structure measurements for watersheds in the Medicine Bow National Forest using GIS analysis. Report by Dept. of Geography & Recreation, University of Wyoming to the Routt–Medicine Bow National Forest, Laramie, Wyoming, USA.

Baker, W. L. 1999. Spatial simulation of the effects of human and natural disturbance regimes on landscape structure. *In* D. J. Mladenoff and W. L. Baker, editors. *Spatial modeling of forest landscapes*. Cambridge University Press, Cambridge, UK.

Baker, W. L., and Y. Cai. 1992. The r.le. programs for multiscale analysis of landscape structure using the GRASS geographical information system. *Landscape Ecology* 7: 291–302.

Baker, W. L., S. S. Egbert, and F. F. Frazier. 1991. A spatial model for studying the

effects of climatic change on the structure of landscapes subject to large disturbances. *Ecological Modelling* 56: 109–125.

Bettinger, P., J. Sessions, and K. Boston. 1997. Using Tabu search to schedule timber
harvests subject to spatial wildlife goals for big game. *Ecological Modeling* 94:
111–123.

Chen, J., J. F. Franklin, and T. A. Spies. 1992. Vegetation responses to edge environments in old-growth Douglas-fir forests. *Ecological Applications* 2: 387–396.

Dobkin, D. S. 1994. Conservation and management of neotropical migrant landbirds
in the Northern Rockies and Great Plains. University of Idaho Press. Moscow,
Idaho, USA.

Franklin, J. F., and R.T.T. Forman. 1987. Creating landscape patterns by forest
cutting: ecological consequences and principles. *Landscape Ecology* 1: 5–18.

Gustafson, E. J. 1996. Expanding the scale of forest management: allocating timber
harvests in time and space. *Forest Ecology and Management* 87: 27–39.

Gustafson, E. J., and T. R. Crow. 1996. Simulating the effects of alternative forest
management strategies on landscape structure. *Journal of Environmental Management* 46: 77–94.

Li, H., J. F. Franklin, F. J. Swanson, and T. A. Spies. 1993. Developing alternative
forest cutting patterns: a simulation approach. *Landscape Ecology* 8: 63–75.

Miller, J. R., L. A. Joyce, R. L. Knight, and R. M. King. 1996. Forest roads and
landscape structure in the Southern Rocky Mountains. *Landscape Ecology* 11:
115–127.

Mladenoff, D. J., M. A. White, J. Pastor, and T. R. Crow. 1993. Comparing spatial
pattern in unaltered old-growth and disturbed forest landscapes. *Ecological Applications* 3: 294–306.

Murcia, C. 1995. Edge effects in fragmented forests: implications for conservation.
Trends in Ecology and Evolution 10: 58–62.

Noss, R. F., and B. Csuti. 1994. Habitat fragmentation. Pages 237–264 *in* G. K.
Meffe and C. R. Carroll editors. *Principles of conservation biology.* Sinauer Associates, Inc., Sunderland, Massachusetts, USA.

Reed, R. A., J. Johnson-Barnard, and W. L. Baker. 1996a. The contribution of roads
to forest fragmentation in the Rocky Mountains. *Conservation Biology* 10: 1098–
1106.

Reed, R. A., J. Johnson-Barnard, and W. L. Baker. 1996b. Fragmentation of a forested Rocky Mountain landscape, 1950–1993. *Biological Conservation* 75: 267–
277.

Ripple, W. J., G. A. Bradshaw, and T. A. Spies. 1991. Measuring forest landscape
patterns in the Cascade Range of Oregon, USA. Biological Conservation 57:
73–88.

Robinson, S. K., F. R. Thompson, III, T. M. Donovan, D. R. Whitehead, and J.
Faaborg. 1995. Regional forest fragmentation and the nesting success of migratory birds. *Science* 267: 1987–1990.

Ruggiero, L. F., K. B. Aubry, S. W. Buskirk, L. J. Lyon, and W. J. Zielinski. 1994. The
scientific basis for conserving forest carnivores: American marten, fisher, lynx,
and wolverine in the western United States. USDA Forest Service General

Technical Report RM–254, Rocky Mountain Forest and Range Experiment Station, Ft. Collins, Colorado, USA.

Shinneman, D. J. 1996. An analysis of range of natural variability, roads, and timber harvesting in a Black Hills ponderosa pine forest landscape. Master's Thesis, University of Wyoming, Laramie, Wyoming, USA.

Tinker, D. B., C.A.C. Resor, G. P. Beauvais, K. F. Kipfmueller, C. I. Fernandes, and W. L. Baker. 1998. Watershed analysis of forest fragmentation by clear-cuts and roads in a Wyoming forest. *Landscape Ecology* 13: 149–165.

USA-CERL. 1994. *GRASS 4.1 User's Manual.* United States Army Corps of Engineers Construction Engineering Research Laboratory, Champaign, Illinois, USA.

USDA Forest Service. 1985. Medicine Bow National Forest and Thunder Basin National Grassland Land and Resource management plan. Rocky Mountain Region, USA.

USDA Forest Service. 1996. NEPA Streamlining report to District Forest Supervisors from Elizabeth Estill, Regional Forest Supervisor.

Vaillancourt, D. A. 1995. Structural and microclimatic edge effects associated with clear-cutting in a Rocky Mountain forest. Master's thesis, University of Wyoming, Laramie, Wyoming, USA.

Wallin, D. O., F. J. Swanson, and B. Marks. 1994. Landscape pattern response to changes in pattern generation rules: land-use legacies in forestry. *Ecological Applications* 4: 569–580.

Part Five

Management Implications of Forest Fragmentation in the Southern Rocky Mountains

17

A Landscape Approach to Managing Southern Rocky Mountain Forests

Gregory H. Aplet

INTRODUCTION

Forest fragmentation resulting from road construction, timber management, recreation, and other factors has become a topic of increasing importance to wildland managers. Known to have effects on wildlife through influences on predator and parasite densities, habitat patch size, and barriers to migration, fragmentation also has visual impacts, changes the character of the vegetation mosaic, and facilitates the movement of exotic species. Forest management, through its influence on vegetation and land use, can directly affect the rate and direction of fragmentation on managed lands. The purpose of this paper is to briefly review the effects of fragmentation on the naturalness of wildland ecosystems, to consider the role of forest management in restoring and maintaining naturalness, and to propose an approach to management that will lead to the restoration and maintenance of natural structure and reduce fragmentation in Rocky Mountain forests.

EFFECTS OF TRADITIONAL FOREST MANAGEMENT

The basic qualities of any ecosystem can be described in terms of composition, structure, and function, where composition describes the abundance of ecosystem components, such as plant and animal communities, water, and nutrients; structure describes their physical distribution in space; and function describes the processes through which composition and structure interact, including predation, decomposition, and disturbances such as windstorms and floods (Landres et al. 1998). A further refinement of this notion is offered by Jenny (1941,

1980), who suggests that the state of an ecosystem (i.e., its composition and structure) is a function of a relatively small set of factors, including climate, topographic relief, soil parent material, the pool of available organisms, and disturbance. Jenny considers only the time since the last major disturbance, but disturbance ecologists now recognize the importance of other aspects of disturbance (White and Pickett 1985); hence, Jenny's disturbance factor should probably be considered as a multifactor "disturbance regime." It is through the interactions of these "state factors" that ecosystem composition and structure are determined.

This simple model can be applied to the analysis of human impacts on ecosystems through timber management. While the relationship between deforestation and climate has been debated for generations, it does not appear that traditional timber management has had a large effect on regional climate. Timber management does not usually dramatically alter topography, except where road construction on slopes changes hydrology and causes landslides. Soil parent material is likewise unaffected by timber management. Alternatively, timber management can have dramatic effects on ecosystems where it alters the organism state factor. Though the practice is not common in the western United States, timber management often employs fast growing species planted outside of their native range. The introduction of new species and the eradication of undesirable ones represent a direct alteration of ecosystem composition and structure by altering the organism state factor.

By far, though, the most pervasive impact of timber management on ecosystems has been the alteration of disturbance regimes. The ecological effect of forest management has been to alter the pattern, intensity, and frequency of disturbance to create a forest of desired composition, structure, and function. Traditionally, the objective of forest management has been timber production, and silviculture has employed either even- or uneven-aged management to achieve that objective. Under even-aged management, (e.g., clear-cutting, seed tree, shelterwood, coppice), the objective is to establish a single cohort of trees on a site where the canopy trees have been removed, grow trees until stand-level productivity drops to an unacceptable level, and again regenerate the site. Under uneven-aged management (e.g., single tree or group selection), the objective is to maintain an optimum level of "growing stock" in a stand that will yield harvests of consistent volume and composition over time without removing the canopy.

These systems can effectively produce timber, but their widespread use can alter ecosystem composition, structure, and function. Even-aged management maintains the forest in structurally simple, young stands with patch sizes and orientations determined as much by operating constraints as by ecological factors. Uneven-aged management maintains the forest landscape in a structurally uniform, all-aged condition, without the patch structure of natural forests (Aplet 1994, O'Hara 1998). These differences are maintained through the active imposition of a disturbance regime suited not to the maintenance of ecosystem diversity but to the production of timber volume. According to Noss (1993), timber management results in the following seven effects: younger forests, simplified stands, smaller patches, isolated patches, fewer fires, more roads, and more endangered species. With the exception of the direct alteration of the fire regime and more endangered species (which may be more the ultimate result of the others), all of these effects may be described as fragmentation, defined here as the alteration of the spatial arrangement of components of the forest ecosystem.

Thus, fragmentation has significant effects on ecosystems by altering the fundamental aspect of structure. This can feed back to ecosystem composition, such as the bird community, and functions, such as migration and predation, and is of great concern to wildland managers. But perhaps the reason fragmentation has become such a hot issue among those concerned about the future of wildland ecosystems is not because of its secondary effects, but because it is so obvious at the human scale. Roadcuts, clear-cuts, and powerline corridors are easily seen and offend many people's sense of what a forest should look like. Fragmentation changes the appearance of the forest from something natural to something artificial.

FORESTRY AND NATURALNESS

To many, the quality of naturalness is inherent in the definition of forest. In its 1990 report, the National Research Council Committee on Forestry Research described the similarities and differences between agriculture and forestry: "The most important similarities between forestry and agriculture are in our shared scientific roots. . . . Silviculture is the scientific counterpart of horticulture or agronomy. . . . But critical differences exist between forestry and agriculture. Whereas agricultural fields are of human creation, most forests are essentially developed by natural systems" (NRC 1990).

The NRC's description of the essential difference between forests and agricultural fields mirrors the observations of Aldo Leopold almost fifty years ago in the section of The Land Ethic entitled "Land health and the A-B cleavage": "In my own field, forestry, group A is quite content to grow trees like cabbages, with cellulose as the basic forest commodity. . . . Group B, on the other hand, sees forestry as fundamentally different from agronomy because it employs natural species, and manages a natural environment rather than creating an artificial one" (Leopold 1949).

Thus, the quality of naturalness distinguishes a forest from an agricultural field, vineyard, or orchard. At a 1992 conference entitled *Defining Sustainable Forestry*, participants described the essence of sustainable forestry from a diversity of perspectives. Following the meeting, the conference organizers summarized the results as follows: "To an increasing number of people, a forest that is not 'natural' is not sustainable. . . . Naturalness is a desired condition, not simply because of its aesthetic appeal, which should not be trivialized, but because it represents the highest likelihood of achieving Leopold's most famous objective: 'to keep every cog and wheel' " (Aplet et al. 1993). To a large extent, it is fragmentation through timber management and road construction that is perceived to be responsible for the loss of naturalness in managed forests. Restoration of natural pattern represents an important step toward achievement of sustainable forestry.

DEFINING NATURALNESS

Defining sustainability as the maintenance of naturalness is an important first step, but it raises as many questions as it answers. Definitions of naturalness have proven elusive due to concerns about the role of humans in ecosystems, the dynamic nature of ecosystems, and the imprecision attending definitions of ecosystems and communities (Shrader-Frechette and McCoy 1995, Hunter 1996), but recent attempts have coalesced around the notion of wholeness. The most natural ecosystems are the most whole; they possess all of the components of the ecosystems that historically dominated the land (Landres et al. 1998). In North America, these are the ecosystems that existed for the several centuries prior to European colonization. The Australian Heritage Commission (1995) defines natural cover as "an area of land or water which essentially retains its pre-European cover." Elsewhere in the world, natural ecosystems may reflect the historical influence of indigenous cultures.

Recently, the equation of naturalness, or natural conditions, with historical conditions has been expressed through the use of such terms as natural variability (Swanson et al. 1994), range of natural variability (Caraher et al. 1992, Landres et al. 1998), reference variability (Manley et al. 1995), and historical range of variability (Morgan et al. 1994). In each of these descriptions, it is understood that ecosystem behavior is dynamic but constrained though time by bounded fluctuations in the factors affecting ecosystem condition, especially climate and disturbance (Aplet and Keeton 1999). Natural ecosystems are those with the composition, structure, and function typical of the period prior to the massive disruptions of disturbance regimes and species composition that accompanied European colonization of North America (Aplet and Keeton 1999). In North America, this period consists of most of the last two thousand years. Elsewhere in the world, where indigenous cultures maintain the land uses and technologies of the last several centuries, "natural" conditions may be maintained even where human use and occupancy are high.

The equation of naturalness with historical ecosystem conditions does not reflect an arbitrary preference for the past. Instead, it recognizes that the conditions that sustained species and other ecosystem components in the past are the conditions most likely to sustain those same components into the future. Recent innovative approaches to management by the U.S. Forest Service reflect this philosophy. According to Manley et al. (1995), "[R]estoring and maintaining landscape conditions within distributions that organisms have adapted to over evolutionary time is the management approach most likely to produce sustainable ecosystems." Likewise, the recently completed Landscape Assessment of the Interior Columbia Basin Ecosystem Management Project (Quigley and Arbelbide 1997) concluded, "[T]he endemic biota of the Basin will have the fewest risks to population persistence if regional and landscape vegetation patterns approximate those in which the biota have adapted over the last two millennia."

PATTERN VERSUS PROCESS

Thus, naturalness and the historical range of variability of ecosystems are tightly linked. But what is it about those ecosystems that determines naturalness? Ecosystems can be described in terms of composition, structure, and function. In other words, pattern and process, where pattern (i.e., composition and structure) describes ecosystem components and their arrangement (i.e., how it looks), and process (i.e., function) describes interactions (i.e., how it works). Landres et al. (1998) maintain that naturalness includes both pattern and process. That is, an ecosystem is natural if it maintains characteristic composition and structure *and* continues to function according to historical processes.

An alternative way to regard naturalness is to think of it as encompassing only pattern. That is, an ecosystem is natural if it maintains characteristic composition and structure, regardless of how it came to possess those qualities. The advantage of separating pattern from process in the discussion of naturalness is that it opens up a role for management in the restoration of natural conditions. This relationship can be conceived as a two-dimensional graph with axes of pattern and process (Fig. 17.1). Pattern ranges from artificial (or novel) to natural (or typical of historical conditions), and process ranges from controlled (tightly managed) to free (or "self-willed" as Thoreau referred to wilderness [Turner 1996]). Under this construction, presettlement aboriginal influences are included among natural processes and reflect the "will of the land." Ecosystems that are most natural and free are the most wild, but managed land can be natural as well. The process of bringing land under tighter control in order to increase naturalness is called restoration (Fig. 17.2).

Classes of Ecosystems

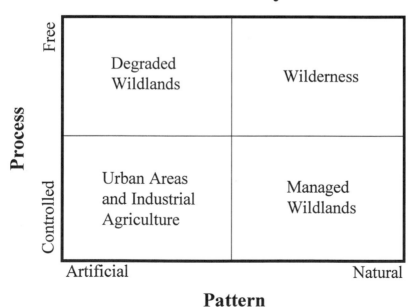

Fig. 17.1. Ecosystems can be described in terms of pattern and process, where pattern ranges from artificial to natural and process ranges from controlled to free.

Effects of Management

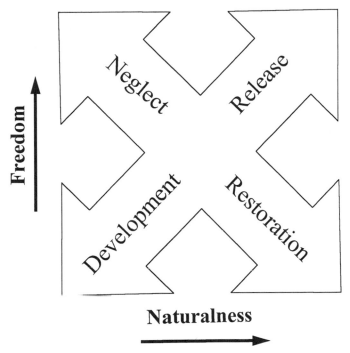

Fig. 17.2. Management decisions may move an ecosystem in a number of directions with respect to pattern and process. Restoration brings the system under control in order to increase naturalness. By minimizing human impacts, wilderness managers seek to keep lands free without degrading naturalness, a process described here as release. Naturalness can also be reduced—intentionally through the process of development or unintentionally through neglect.

MANAGING FOR NATURALNESS

The argument thus far has been that sustainable forestry requires the restoration and maintenance of a quality known as naturalness, and that naturalness equates to the pattern (composition and structure) of historical ecosystems. To the extent that traditional forestry's main effect on ecosystems has been fragmentation, sustainable forestry consists of the reversal of fragmentation to restore natural vegetation structure to the landscape. But how? Designing forest management treatments to restore natural structure requires that we first be able to describe natural structure and then turn those *de*scriptions into *pre*-scriptions for management.

Not long ago, simply describing the nature of the landscape mosaic was enormously difficult. The science of landscape ecology, which focuses on describing and understanding the dynamics of landscape pattern, is only a few years old. Fortunately, recent advances in computerized geographic information systems and spatial statistics now allow complex landscape mosaics to be described using a variety of measurements. Collectively, these descriptions allow landscape structure to be objectively characterized. For example, Ripple et al. (1991) showed how several landscape variables changed over time following clear-cut logging in the Pacific Northwest (Fig. 17.3). The same kinds of variables can be developed to describe the structure of natural forests as well.

Just as ecosystem characteristics fluctuate over time and space, measures of landscape structure are not static. They, too, fluctuate within a historical range of variability. Applying this concept at the scale of the forest stand, Lundquist and Ward (1995) described a range of desired conditions for a number of spatial variables within a forest stand in New Mexico (Table 1 in Lundquist and Ward 1995). Baker (1992) described variability in attributes of the landscape mosaic, including characteristic distributions of patch size and fire frequency and intensity (Fig. 17.4). If distributions typical of natural forest landscapes can be developed, those distributions can be used to develop prescriptions for a forest management regime that will restore or maintain natural structure and, hence, minimize fragmentation.

STANDS AND LANDSCAPES

Traditionally, forest management has been focused at the scale of the forest stand. Forests are divided into convenient homogeneous units and regenerated through the process of timber harvest. Landscape considerations have been, first, the maintenance of a steady flow of timber from a "regulated" forest and, second, the heeding of constraints on cutting unit dispersion and water quality. Generally, little attention has been paid at the stand or landscape scales to maintaining forest structure.

Managing to restore natural structure will require new attention at both the stand and landscape scales. Natural disturbances function differently across forest types, and maintaining these variations will require understanding the effects of natural disturbance. For example, in the Colorado Rockies, forests occupy essentially three elevation bands: ponderosa pine at the lowest elevations, Engelmann spruce-

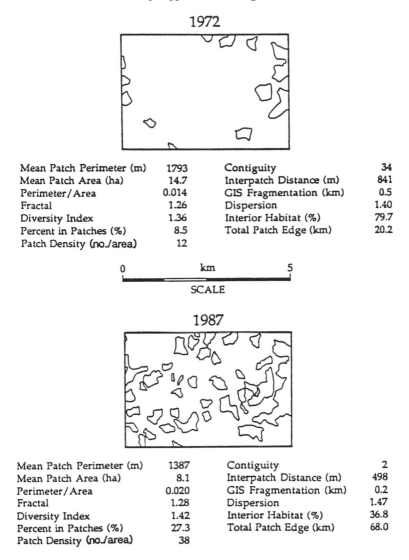

1972

Mean Patch Perimeter (m)	1793	Contiguity	34
Mean Patch Area (ha)	14.7	Interpatch Distance (m)	841
Perimeter/Area	0.014	GIS Fragmentation (km)	0.5
Fractal	1.26	Dispersion	1.40
Diversity Index	1.36	Interior Habitat (%)	79.7
Percent in Patches (%)	8.5	Total Patch Edge (km)	20.2
Patch Density (no./area)	12		

0   km   5

SCALE

1987

Mean Patch Perimeter (m)	1387	Contiguity	2
Mean Patch Area (ha)	8.1	Interpatch Distance (m)	498
Perimeter/Area	0.020	GIS Fragmentation (km)	0.2
Fractal	1.28	Dispersion	1.47
Diversity Index	1.42	Interior Habitat (%)	36.8
Percent in Patches (%)	27.3	Total Patch Edge (km)	68.0
Patch Density (no./area)	38		

Fig. 17.3. Ripple et al. (1991) used a number of statistics to measure changes in landscape structure following clear-cut logging in the Pacific Northwest (from Ripple et al. 1991).

subalpine fir at the highest elevations, and lodgepole pine in between. Frequent, low-intensity fire dominates the disturbance regime in ponderosa pine, a forest type in which uneven-aged management has been suggested as consistent with natural processes (O'Hara 1998). Lodgepole pine stands at low elevations tend to burn catastrophically at 50–150-year intervals (Peet 1988) and thus may be managed using

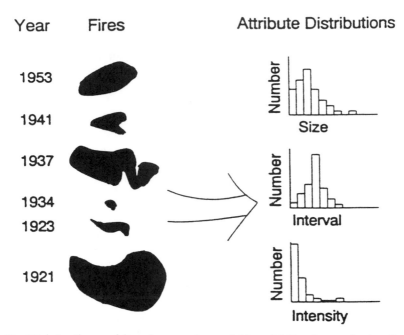

Fig. 17.4. Attributes of disturbance regimes exhibit variability that can be described as characteristic distributions (from Baker 1992).

even-aged methods (Aplet 1994). In the spruce-fir zone, dynamics are more complex, reflecting a transition from even-aged to uneven-aged structure over time (Aplet et al. 1988). These stands may present opportunities for more complex, synthetic approaches to timber management (Aplet 1994, O'Hara et al. 1994).

Managing to maintain natural structure at the landscape scale requires descriptions of landscape dynamics that are far better than our current understanding allows. Highly dissected landscapes and strong environmental gradients assure that patch dynamics in the Southern Rockies are complex. To restore and maintain natural landscape structure, stand-level treatments must be conducted in ways that sustain pattern over larger areas. This represents terra incognita for foresters, and the development of these treatments must be approached cautiously. Attention must be given to research and experimentation in a framework of adaptive management to assure that, in the words of the great silviculturist Thornton Munger, "untested innovations will not get ahead and get off the trail of nature's silvical laws" (as quoted in Curtis 1998).

CHALLENGES

A forest management system patterned after natural disturbance is appealing, if it results in a more natural pattern and a reduction in both biological and visual impacts on the forest ecosystem. Unfortunately, application of such a system presents a number of formidable challenges.

First, basing timber management on patterns of natural disturbance does not address the problem of roads. Roads are now recognized as one of the most difficult challenges of wildland managers (Noss and Cooperrider 1994). Roads not only fragment the forest by creating edge habitat and permanently bare soil, but they also cause disruptions to hydrology, contribute sediment to streams, aid in the dispersal of exotic species, and facilitate long-term changes in land use (V. Dale, *personal communication*). While there are ways of engineering roads to reduce these impacts, timber management, even if it is based on natural patterns, will continue to require roads. Except where operations can be conducted without roads (e.g., helicopter logging), roads and their fragmenting effects will continue to challenge wildland managers.

Second, anthropogenic disturbance is additive, not substituted. Natural disturbances will continue to shape the forest, whether managers impose disturbance on the system or not. Thus, management cannot simply mimic natural disturbance. Nevertheless, managers can work with natural disturbance regimes to tailor disturbances that are more like natural disturbances than they have been in the past. This may increase the frequency of disturbance but not radically alter the overall regime. In some cases, such as where fire has been, and will continue to be, suppressed, management-induced disturbance can be substituted for natural (or historically anthropogenic) fire without changing the disturbance frequency.

Third, the kind of disturbance introduced by timber management is novel. Very few natural disturbances remove trees from the forest. Even the most severe forest fires generally do not consume live trees, and even if they do, the post disturbance environment of an intense fire is very different from that left by a logging operation. Fires kill understory vegetation, consume duff, and leave a mineral soil without the physical soil disturbance produced by logging. Other disturbances, such as windstorms, insect outbreaks, disease epidemics, and avalanches, each leave their own characteristic mark on the forest that is different from logging. Forest management based on the replication of natural disturbance must be attentive to these differences.

Fourth, disturbance regimes are enormously complex. Just as disturbances differ in type, they vary in size, shape, intensity, timing, location, orientation, and other factors (White and Pickett 1985, Baker 1992). Just knowing which factors to include in a prescription is not simple. Designing a system that not only captures this variability, but does it in the right proportions, will be extremely difficult—but it is important. As ecologist Norm Christensen (1988) has observed: "In many ecosystems, one of the most important consequences of fire (or natural disturbance in general) is to maintain landscape heterogeneity. The simulation and maintenance of that heterogeneity is one of the most significant challenges to natural landscape managers."

Even where the disturbance regime seems fairly straightforward, such as in a crown-fire ecosystem like lodgepole pine, simply describing the historical disturbance regime can be extremely time-consuming and costly. In a detailed study of fire history in Douglas-fir forests in Oregon, Morrison and Swanson (1990) determined the outlines and historical intensities of all fires on two 1,940 ha plots for the past several centuries. The differences between the sites suggest that fire histories differ significantly across the landscape. Understanding these differences will be important to the development of prescriptions based on natural disturbance but will require a tremendous amount of future research.

Another factor complicating the application of natural disturbance to forest management is scale. Many natural disturbances, especially in the Southern Rockies, occur at scales well beyond those of traditional management. As the Yellowstone fires of 1988 showed, fire in lodgepole pine can occur as events of hundreds of thousands of hectares in a single year. The spruce beetle outbreak on the White River National Forest in the 1940s killed spruce over hundreds of thousands of hectares (Veblen et al. 1991). The 1997 blowdown of over 8,000 ha of Engelmann spruce-subalpine fir forest on the Routt National Forest in Colorado showed that even windstorms can occur at scales that do not fit neatly into traditional management regimes.

In general, management should not seek to replicate the most extreme events, as these are likely rare and additive to a management regime (Manley et al. 1995). However, the proper scale of management-induced disturbance should be informed by the scale of natural disturbance, and this may often be significantly larger than current limits in place on the national forests (Aplet 1994). In these cases, it may be appropriate to concentrate cutting units in one place to create one large disturbance, rather than dispersing that same area across the landscape in 16.2 ha blocks (Franklin and Formann 1987). In other cases, it may be appropriate to let nature do the disturbing, and, if timber is to be removed, salvage some of the dead trees. In any case, determining the proper scale for management intervention remains a challenge.

Finally, the greatest challenge to the use of natural pattern as a guide to management may be the condition of the land itself. In some cases, conditions are now so unlike historical ecosystems that they lack precedent. In ponderosa pine forests of Colorado's Front Range, as throughout the West, fire suppression has promoted the growth of unprecedented densities of understory saplings that now carry fire into the canopy. Reintroducing fire must be done with great care and will often require thinning and other treatments beforehand. Where exotic species have invaded or native seed sources have been depleted, historical disturbances may produce very unexpected results. As the Landscape Assessment of the Interior Columbia Basin Ecosystem Management Project (Quigley and Arbelbide 1997, p. 908) concluded:

> If native landscape patterns were more common, a change toward [properly functioning landscape systems] could be achieved simply by conserving the systems through mimicking disturbances with human production activities and reaping the benefits of both commodities and amenities.
>
> However, since most landscapes (subbasins) are currently far from functioning properly, a substantial change in trend may not be possible for a long time. This is particularly true with traditional commodity landscape patterns, where slow growing elements, such as large old trees or bunchgrasses, have been "lost."

Frissell and Bayles (1996) put it more succinctly: "If there ever was a free lunch, we already ate it."

CONCLUSIONS

While fraught with challenges, the patterning of management-induced disturbances after natural disturbances represents an opportunity to reduce forest fragmentation through the restoration of natural pattern to forest ecosystems. This process should be approached cautiously, focusing on those parts of the landscape that have been most altered through anthropogenic disturbance in the past and avoiding areas of high ecological integrity, such as roadless areas (Quigley and Arbelbide 1997). The following steps should be followed in any attempt to restore naturalness to managed landscapes:

1. Determine historical composition, structure, and function,
2. Assess current conditions,

3. Identify those places on the landscape that have departed the least from historical conditions and those elements of the ecosystem that are rare or threatened,
4. Protect those places from further degradation,
5. Develop methods for moving altered landscapes toward natural conditions,
6. Test methods on a portion of the landscape,
7. Implement restoration on the degraded landscape in an adaptive management framework.

Finally, all of the preceding must be tempered with a healthy dose of reality. The aforementioned challenges are formidable. Roads, natural disturbance, complexity, ignorance, and the condition of the land all frustrate the restoration of natural pattern through management. Additionally, economic barriers are enormous. The research, application development, methods, and monitoring necessary to apply these concepts will be costly. New markets will need to be developed in some places, and new administrative tools and processes will also be needed. Nevertheless, despite these challenges and frustrations, the tailoring of management actions to emulate the patterns of natural ecosystems holds considerable promise to mitigate some of the fragmenting effects of forest management in the Southern Rockies.

LITERATURE CITED

Aplet, G. H. 1994. Beyond even- vs. uneven-aged management: toward a cohort-based silviculture. *Journal of Sustainable Forestry* 2: 423–433.

Aplet, G. H., R. D. Laven, and F. W. Smith. 1988. Patterns of community dynamics in Colorado Engelmann spruce-subalpine fir forests. *Ecology* 69: 312–319.

Aplet, G. H., N. Johnson, J. T. Olson, and V. A. Sample. 1993. Conclusion: prospects for a sustainable future. Pages 309–314 *in* G. H. Aplet, N. Johnson, J. T. Olson, and V.A. Sample, editors. *Defining sustainable forestry.* Island Press, Covelo, California, USA.

Aplet, G. H., and W. S. Keeton. 1999. Application of historical range of variability concepts to the conservation of biodiversity. Pages 71–86 *in* R. K. Baydack, H. Campa III, and J. B. Haufler, editors. *Practical approaches to the conservation of biological diversity.* Island Press, Covelo, California, USA.

Australian Heritage Commission. 1995. *National wilderness inventory handbook.* Second edition. R. Lesslie and M. Maslen, preparers. A. J. Law, Commonwealth Government Printer, Canberra, Australia.

Baker, W. L. 1992. The landscape ecology of large disturbances in the design and management of nature reserves. *Landscape Ecology* 7: 181–194.

Caraher, D. L., J. Henshaw, F. Hall, W. H. Knapp, B. P. McCammon, J. Nesbitt, R. J. Pedersen, I. Regenovitch, and C. Tietz. 1992. Restoring ecosystems in the

Blue Mountains: a report to the regional forester and the forest supervisors of the Blue Mountain forests. USDA Forest Service Pacific Northwest Region, Portland, Oregon, USA.

Christensen, N. L. 1988. Succession and natural disturbance: paradigms, problems, and preservation of natural ecosystems. Pages 62–86 *in* J. K. Agee and D. R. Johnson, editors. *Ecosystem management for parks and wilderness.* University of Washington Press, Seattle, Washington, USA.

Curtis, R. O. 1998. "Selective Cutting" in Douglas-fir: history revisited. *Journal of Forestry* 96(7): 40–46.

Franklin, J. F., and R.T.T. Formann. 1987. Creating landscape patterns by forest cutting: ecological consequences and principles. *Landscape Ecology* 1: 5–18.

Frissell, C. A., and D. Bayles. 1996. Ecosystem management and the conservation of aquatic biodiversity and ecological integrity. *Water Resources Bulletin* 32: 229–240.

Hunter, M. L. 1996. Benchmarks for managing ecosystems: are human activities natural? *Conservation Biology* 10: 695–697.

Jenny, H. 1941. *Factors of soil formation.* McGraw-Hill, New York, New York, USA.

Jenny, H. 1980. *Soil genesis with ecological perspectives.* Springer-Verlag, New York, New York, USA.

Landres, P. B., P. S. White, G. Aplet, and A. Zimmerman. 1998. Naturalness and natural variability: definitions, concepts, and strategies for wilderness management. Pages 41–50 *in* David L. Kulhavy and Michael H. Legg, editors. *Wilderness & natural areas in eastern North America: research, management and planning.* Nacogdoches, Texas: Stephen F. Austin University, Arthur Temple College of Forestry, Center for Applied Studies.

Leopold, A. 1949. *A Sand County almanac.* Oxford University Press, New York, New York, USA.

Lundquist, J. E., and J. P. Ward, Jr. 1995. Describing the conditions of forest ecosystems using disturbance profiles. Pages 128–134 *in* L. G. Eskew, compiler. *Forest health through silviculture.* Proceedings of the 1995 National Silviculture Workshop; May 8–11, 1995. Mescalero, New Mexico. USDA Forest Service General Technical Report RM-GTR-267. Fort Collins, Colorado, USA.

Manley, P., G. E. Brogan, C. Cook, M. E. Flores, D. G. Fullmer, S. Husari, T. M. Jimerson, L. M. Lux, M. E. McCain, J. A. Rose, G. Schmitt, J. C. Schuyler, and M. J. Skinner. 1995. Sustaining ecosystems: a conceptual framework. USDA Forest Service Pacific Southwest Region R5-EM-TP-001. San Francisco, California, USA.

Morgan, P., G. H. Aplet, J. B. Haufler, H. C. Humphries, M. M. Moore, and W. D. Wilson. 1994. Historical range of variability: a useful tool for evaluating ecosystem change. *Journal of Sustainable Forestry* 2: 87–111.

Morrison, P. H., and F. J. Swanson. 1990. Fire history and pattern in a Cascade Range landscape. USDA Forest Service General Technical Report PNW-GTR-254.

Noss, R.F. 1993. Sustainable forestry or sustainable forests? Pages 17–43 *in* G. H. Aplet, N. Johnson, J. T. Olson, and V.A. Sample, editors. *Defining sustainable forestry.* Island Press, Covelo, California, USA.

Noss, R. F., and A. Y. Cooperrider. 1994. *Saving nature's legacy: protecting and restoring biodiversity.* Island Press, Covela, California, USA.

National Research Council (NRC). 1990. *Forestry research: a mandate for change.* Committee on Forestry Research, National Research Council. National Academy Press, Washington, D.C., USA.

O'Hara, K. L. 1998. Silviculture for structural diversity: a new look at multiaged systems. *Journal of Forestry* 96(7): 4–10.

O'Hara, K. L., R. S. Seymour, S. D. Tesch, and J. M. Guldin. 1994. Silviculture and our changing profession: leadership for shifting paradigms. *Journal of Forestry* 92(1): 8–13.

Peet, R. K. 1988. Forests of the Rocky Mountains. Pages 63–102 *in* M. G. Barbour, and W. D. Billings, editors. *North American terrestrial vegetation.* Cambridge University Press, Cambridge, UK.

Quigley, T. M., and S. J. Arbelbide, technical editors. 1997. An assessment of ecosystem components in the interior Columbia Basin and portions of the Klamath and Great Basins. Volume 2. *In* T. M. Quigley, technical editor. *The Interior Columbia Basin Ecosystem Management Project: Scientific Assessment.* USDA Forest Service, Pacific Northwest Station. General Technical Report PNW-GTR-405. Portland, Oregon, USA.

Ripple, W. J., G. A. Bradshaw, and T. A. Spies. 1991. Measuring forest landscape patterns in the Cascade Range of Oregon, USA. *Biological Conservation* 57: 73–88.

Schrader-Frechette, K. S., and E. D. McCoy. 1995. Natural landscapes, natural communities, and natural ecosystems. *Forest and Conservation History* 39: 138–142.

Swanson, F. J., J. A. Jones, D. O. Wallin, and J. H. Cissel. 1994. Natural variability—implications for ecosystem management. Pages 80–94 *in* R. L. Everett, team leader. *Ecosystem management: principles and applications. Volume II of the Eastside Forest Ecosystem Health Assessment.* USDA Forest Service General Technical Report PNW-GTR-318.

Turner, J. 1996. *The abstract wild.* University of Arizona Press, Tucson, Arizona, USA.

Veblen, T. T., K. S. Hadley, M. S. Reid, and A. J. Rebertus. 1991. The response of subalpine forests to spruce beetle outbreak in Colorado. *Ecology* 72: 213–231.

White, P. S., and S.T.A. Pickett. 1985. Natural disturbance and patch dynamics: an introduction. Pages 3–13 *in* S.T.A. Pickett and P.S. White, editors. *The ecology of natural disturbance and patch dynamics.* Academic Press, Orlando, Florida, USA.

18

Using Natural Disturbance Regimes as a Basis for Mitigating Impacts of Anthropogenic Fragmentation

William H. Romme, M. Lisa Floyd, David Hanna,
and Jeffery S. Redders

Introduction

Profound changes are taking place in the public's attitudes towards wildland ecosystems and their management in the Southern Rocky Mountains. From a previous emphasis on producing commodities and maintaining a few select species, a shift has been made towards sustaining entire ecosystems, including the biodiversity, ecological processes, and evolutionary legacies that make up these systems (Kaufmann et al. 1994, Christensen et al. 1996, Vogt 1997), as well as a renewed emphasis on outdoor recreation (R. L. Knight, *this volume*). Sustaining entire ecosystems—while still producing necessary goods and services for the human component of those ecosystems—requires fundamentally different kinds of management strategies than were employed in the past. Path breaking development of just such a "new forestry" has begun in several areas, notably the Pacific Northwest and southwestern United States (e.g., Hansen et al. 1991, Swanson and Franklin 1992, Covington and Moore 1994, Kohm and Franklin 1997). In this chapter, we lay some groundwork for new management strategies in Southern Rocky Mountain landscapes by synthesizing what is known about the "natural" disturbance regimes of forest ecosystems in our region—the kinds, frequencies, intensities, and extents of disturbances that partially shaped the biota of this region over thousands of years—and suggesting ways in which management-related disturbances can be designed to mimic the natural disturbances to which these systems are adapted.

Four general ideas underlie all of what follows. First, forest ecosystems in the Southern Rocky Mountains have a long history of disturbance by fire, wind, insects, and other agents, and the native biota have a fascinating variety of adaptations that allow them to endure or even thrive in the presence of such disturbances (Reice 1994). However, during the last century we have subjected forest ecosystems to intensities and kinds of disturbances that lie outside the range of disturbances to which these systems are adapted. The result has been degradation or loss of key ecological components and processes (Hobbs and Huenneke 1992, Quigley et al. 1996, Swanson et al. 1997). In this chapter we develop a coarse-filter approach to ecosystem management based on the premise that we can minimize losses of biodiversity and ecological function by making our human-imposed disturbance regimes resemble as closely as possible the natural disturbance regimes under which the biota evolved.

The second general idea of this chapter is that the pronounced elevational and topographic variability of the Southern Rocky Mountain region has produced a great variety of vegetation types, each with its own distinctive landscape structure and disturbance regime. Therefore, issues related to natural ecological patterns and processes, disturbance regimes, and the magnitude of human-induced changes need to be evaluated individually for each vegetation type. Considerable risk exists in extrapolating from one vegetation type to another because of some profound differences in ecology and history.

A third general idea is that we are not starting with a "blank slate" in terms of choices and options in management, but that we have several important legacies of past human use and management that must be dealt with in developing future management strategies. This sense of a "cultural landscape" has been well developed in some other regions, (e.g., New England; Foster 1993), but it is not fully appreciated in the Mountain West (Dahms and Geils 1997). Some of the historical legacies in our region, such as fire exclusion and over-cutting of mature ponderosa pine trees during the early 1900s, reduce our management options today. In this chapter we identify some of these legacies, and suggest ways to compensate for what society may now regard as poor choices in the past.

The fourth general idea underlying this analysis is that our understanding of the ecology of forest systems in the Southern Rocky Mountains is still inadequate to permit complete confidence in our management decisions today. We must acknowledge that we are going to make some mistakes. However, the seriousness of these mistakes can be reduced by placing forest management into a consciously experimental framework and by carefully observing the system's response to our well intentioned efforts (e.g., testing explicit ecological hypotheses with each timber sale, prescribed burn, or road closure) and modifying our actions appropriately as we learn more about the system. In other words, we need to practice adaptive management (Christensen et al. 1996).

This chapter is structured around these four major ideas. First, we describe and justify a concept of reference conditions against which we will compare current ecological conditions and disturbance regimes. We then evaluate lower-elevation and higher-elevation landscapes, which represent two ends of the spectrum of variability among forest types in the Southern Rockies. We consider the disturbance regimes that prevailed during the reference period, the major legacies of the last century of land use and management, and potential opportunities and challenges for modifying our present management approaches to make our disturbances more closely resemble the natural disturbance regimes.

THE CONCEPT OF REFERENCE CONDITIONS

To evaluate current ecological conditions, we need a benchmark or reference period of ecological integrity to compare with the present (Leopold 1966). The several hundred years just prior to the arrival of European settlers in the nineteenth century provides such a benchmark. We refer to this period from about 1500 to about 1860 as the *period of indigenous settlement*, to distinguish it from the period of EuroAmerican settlement that began in the mid to late 1800s.

We emphasize that the period of indigenous settlement was *not* a time of stasis—climatically, ecologically, or culturally (Whitney 1994). Nevertheless, compared with the most recent 130 years, the period from about 1500–1860 was a time of relatively consistent environmental and cultural conditions in this region. We also point out that our goal today should not be to recreate all of the ecological conditions of the 1500s through 1800s. Achievement of such a goal would be impossible, given the climatic, cultural, and ecological changes that have occurred in the last century; it also would be unacceptable socially, economically, and politically. We agree with Dahms and Geils (1997) that the reference period was not completely "natural" or preferable in all ways to today's landscape. However, the period of indigenous settlement does appear to have been a time when the ecosystems of the Southern Rocky Mountain region were intact and functioning well. These ecosystems supported rich biodiversity, conserved soils and nutrients, and ran on solar energy (Kaufmann et al. 1994).

The magnitude and extent of indigenous people's influences on ecosystems of the Southern Rocky Mountains is one of the big questions in our region. Whitney (1994) evaluated the effects of indigenous people in northeastern North America prior to European settlement. He concluded that people significantly altered ecosystems in coastal regions, major river valleys, and around the Great Lakes, but that human impacts were minimal in much of northern New England and the Allegheny Plateau. We expect that the situation was similar in the Southern Rocky Mountains—local sites of intense human effects but extensive areas with little human influence—but we emphasize that more research is needed on this important question.

LOW-ELEVATION LANDSCAPES
Disturbance Regimes of the Reference Period

One of the most extensive forest types at lower elevations in the Southern Rocky Mountains is ponderosa pine forest, growing in pure stands or mixed with Douglas fir and/or white fir (Peet 1988, Knight 1994). A characteristic fire regime of frequent, nonlethal fires, with roughly 5–20 year intervals between successive fires at any given point in the landscape, has been documented for ponderosa pine forests throughout the American West (e.g., Swetnam and Baisan 1996; Agee 1997; Veblen, *this volume*). These low-intensity fires consumed litter and killed small trees and above-ground portions of shrubs and herbs but generally did not kill large trees or below-ground perennating organs of shrubs and herbs. This fire regime maintained a fine-grained mosaic of structural types, including clumps of mature pines interspersed with clumps of younger pine or all-aged mixtures and openings dominated by shrubs or herbs. Empirical reconstructions of stand structure during the period of indigenous settlement, and contemporary written accounts, indicate that many stands were very open, almost like savannas, with <100 canopy trees/ha (e.g., Swetnam and Baisan 1996, Fule et al. 1997). Other kinds of disturbances also occurred—insects, windthrow, and dwarf mistletoe (Schmid and Mata 1996; Veblen, *this volume*)—but these other disturbances probably were of secondary importance compared with the powerful influence of fire.

We must emphasize, however, that not every ponderosa pine forest had the characteristic structure and fire regime described above. Early writings also describe dense ponderosa pine forests (Shinneman and Baker 1997, Dahms and Geils 1997), and recent work in a ponderosa pine forest in the Colorado Front Range documented far longer fire intervals during the eighteenth and nineteenth centuries than have usually been reported for this forest type (M. R. Kaufmann, *personal communication*). Shinneman and Baker (1997) argue that the "typical" low-density forest structure was maintained by frequent fires in more xeric portions of the landscape, whereas ponderosa pine forests on more mesic sites had denser canopies and longer-interval fire regimes—similar to higher-elevation forest types. Unfortunately, we have no quantitative estimates of the relative proportions of the landscape characterized by these contrasting structures and disturbance regimes within ponderosa pine and warm, dry mixed conifer forest types during the period of indigenous settlement. Obtaining such information should be a high research priority.

Legacies of Past Land Use and Management in Low-Elevation Landscapes

The arrival of European miners and settlers in the late 1800s was accompanied by a brief increase in fire frequency in at least some areas (e.g., the Colorado Front Range; Veblen and Lorenz 1991). However, one of the most ubiquitous and lasting effects of European settlers was elimination of the frequent fires that formerly maintained the distinctive open structure of many ponderosa pine forests (Table 18.1). This abrupt alteration of fire regimes occurred in most of the American West around 1880, though there were exceptions (Swetnam and Baisan 1996). A principal mechanism for the change in fire regime was the introduction of large herds of livestock, with the consequent removal of the fine herbaceous fuels that formerly carried low-intensity fires through the forests. Grazing was regulated on public lands after 1934, but by this time the Forest Service was developing an effective fire control program. The result of early grazing and fire suppression has been fire intervals during the twentieth century that far exceed the intervals of previous centuries in ponderosa pine forests throughout most of the Southern Rocky Mountain region (Swetnam and Baisan 1996; Veblen, *this volume*).

A second legacy of excessive grazing in the late 1800s and early 1900s was dramatic alteration of herbaceous plant communities (Fleischner 1994). Reviewing the proposed San Juan Forest Reserve in southwestern Colorado in 1903, for example, DuBois (1903) wrote: "In low gulches and flats where large herds of cattle have been ranged year after year, the bunch grass is pulled up by the roots and gradually dies out. On overstocked cow ranges the white roots of bunchgrass can be seen all over the ground." Because almost no place escaped grazing

Table 18.1. Major legacies of past forest use and management in low-elevation forested landscapes of the Southern Rocky Mountains.

Human Activity	Direct Effects	Indirect Effects
Excessive livestock grazing in late 1800s and early 1900s	—Reduction and local extirpation of grazing—sensitive herbaceous species, e.g., native bunchgrasses	—Elimination of continuous herbaceous fuels and cessation of frequent extensive fires —Altered herbaceous composition even under more moderate grazing today
Fire exclusion since late 1800s, via livestock grazing and direct fire control	—Fire intervals of unprecedented length —Deep litter and duff layers —Dense stands of shrubs and small trees	—Risk of uncontrollable, high-intensity wildfire —Depauperate herb communities (lacking species intolerant of shade and grazing)
"High-grade" logging of large old trees in late 1800s and early 1900s	—Elimination of large trees and snags over extensive areas	—Depauperate animal communities (lacking cavity nesters) —Reduced pine seed production
Selective logging of saw timber trees in middle and late 1900s	—Development of dense stands of small trees with homogenous forest structure over extensive areas —Frequent re-entry and soil effects (e.g., compaction)	—Depauperate animal communities (lacking species of open stands and large trees) —Risk of destructive insect outbreak
Extensive road building for logging, grazing management, fire control, and outdoor recreation	—Fragmentation of the forest landscape —Easy human access in most areas —Erosion and sedimentation	—Spread of alien weeds —Human disturbance of wildlife —Easy accessibility for fire suppression or prescribed fire
Increasing human population growth and outdoor recreation	—Expanding systems of roads and trails	—Human disturbance of wildlife —Impacts associated with roads

during this time, we lack good reference areas in which to determine the pregrazing composition and structure of herbaceous communities. Nevertheless, we can make some reasonable inferences on how at least some herbaceous communities were altered. Comparisons of grazed versus ungrazed mesa tops, plus early observations of livestock behavior, indicate that several native species of bunchgrass greatly declined in abundance, and some were locally extirpated (e.g., DuBois 1903,

Arnold 1950, Rummell 1951, Johnson 1956, Madany and West 1983). Other species, including grazing-resistant natives and some introduced species, increased in abundance. Although we lack many details, it seems likely that many ponderosa pine forest understories today bear scant resemblance to their pre-1860 composition and structure, especially in areas like the Western Slope of the Rockies where native grazers such as bison were uncommon during the reference period.

Logging activities in the late 1800s and early 1900s also created a legacy of dramatically altered forest structure in ponderosa pine forests. The scale and impact of logging increased dramatically in the 1890s with the advent of railroad logging and large-scale commercial logging ventures. To be commercially feasible, a railroad logging operation had to take out nearly every merchantable tree within reach of the tracks (Whitney 1994). By the middle of the twentieth century, nearly every accessible ponderosa pine forest in the Southern Rocky Mountain region had been subjected to "high-grade" logging (i.e., removal of all or most of the large, old, yellow-bark ponderosa pine trees). Throughout the ponderosa pine zone today, except for a few impenetrable canyons and administratively protected areas, large, old ponderosa pine trees are scarce or absent.

But human-caused changes were not the only regional-scale processes occurring during the last century. A historically unique combination of events—elimination of formerly extensive fires, removal of herbaceous plants by livestock and of old trees by loggers, plus periods of unusually wet weather accompanied by large pine seed crops—all came together to produce an abundant cohort of ponderosa pine seedlings in the early twentieth century (Covington and Moore 1994). This pine cohort dominates many ponderosa pine forests throughout the Southwest today, and is conspicuous even in the rare stands that have escaped logging. Silviculture during the second half of the twentieth century has tended to selectively remove individuals of this cohort as they reach sawtimber size (20 cm diameter), thus maintaining high densities of relatively small trees. The result has not been forest fragmentation, but coalescence and homogenization of stand structure in ponderosa pine forest landscapes throughout much of the Southern Rocky Mountains.

In the lower-elevation forest landscapes that now cover much of our region, there are potential risks to long-term maintenance of biodiversity, ecosystem function, and production of commodities and amenities. Some species thrive in dense stands of ponderosa pine, but others require more open habitats such as the little glades that formerly existed between clumps of large trees. Even the species that prefer dense stands may lack sufficient numbers of large, old trees in most ponderosa pine forests today. Associated with the scarcity of large, old trees is a lack of snags, which provide nesting and perching habitat for numerous birds and mammals. Balda (1975) estimates that one third of breeding bird species in southwestern ponderosa pine forests, and 40–55% of breeding pairs, are secondary cavity nesters. Notably, snag densities are far below minimum recommended levels in many ponderosa pine forests today (Cunningham et al. 1980). Herbaceous plant species, reduced or locally extirpated by early grazing, may be unable to reestablish their former presence, even when grazing is well-regulated or eliminated, because of intense competition from woody plants and deep organic litter on the forest floor. Even ponderosa pine itself is unable to become reestablished after logging in many stands, apparently because of unsuitable seed bed conditions and competition from sprouting shrubs (Harrington 1985, 1987).

Dense ponderosa pine forests are susceptible to mountain pine beetle outbreaks (Schmid and Mata 1996). Many of the obligate, snag-nesting birds of ponderosa pine forests are insectivorous; hence the reduced density of insect predators in many stands due to lack of snags, coupled with the high density and stressed condition of the trees, creates conditions that may foster development of insect population explosions (Balda 1975).

Dense ponderosa pine forests also are at risk of uncontrollable, destructive wildfires. Current fuel conditions—litter, duff, and branchwood on the forest floor, and closely spaced tree crowns—probably are more conducive to high-intensity crown fires over extensive areas than was usually the case during the reference period (Covington and Moore 1994). The area burned by wildfires has increased sharply in the last two decades, despite ongoing fire control efforts, and recent fires in ponderosa pine forests have often been destructive crown fires rather than the surface fires that once shaped these ecosystems (Covington and Moore 1994, Agee 1997, Moir et al. 1997).

We must stress that the undesirable changes and risks described above for today's ponderosa pine forests apply at a landscape scale rather than at the scale of individual stands. Dense stands of small trees are not "bad" in and of themselves. In fact, they provide good habitat for some species, and they grow wood fiber, accumulate nutrients, and stabilize soils very effectively. Similar stands, unburned for many decades, also existed in the pre-1860 landscape. However, such stands formerly were interspersed with more open stands that had burned recently. What is unprecedented today is that a single kind of stand structure dominates the low elevation forests of the Southern Rocky Mountain region. Hence, efforts to correct some of the current problems in ponderosa pine forests must be undertaken from a landscape perspective.

Opportunities and Challenges in Low-Elevation Landscapes

Innovative approaches now are being developed to restore key ecosystem components and processes that have been lost in ponderosa pine forests as a result of a century of fire exclusion, grazing, logging, and climatic variability (Covington and Moore 1994; D. Lynch and W. H. Romme, *unpublished manuscript*). These approaches are based on re-designing our modern human disturbance regimes to mimic those of the reference period (Table 18.2).

Where the objective is to re-create more open pine stands, selective logging can be used to thin overly dense pine canopies. However, rather than cutting the larger trees, the emphasis should be on removing the smaller trees that have developed in the wake of fire exclusion and grazing. Periodic, low-intensity fires during the reference period killed small trees but left the large ones intact, and modern logging can be designed to have a similar effect. Small trees should not be harvested uniformly, but should be removed in patches, to re-create the small forest openings (scale of 0.01–0.1 ha) that formerly characterized ponderosa pine forests. Similarly, clusters of trees should be left to re-create clumps of mature pines (D. Lynch and W. H. Romme, *unpublished manuscript*).

Selective logging should be followed (or preceded) by prescribed fire to reduce slash and litter, kill above-ground portions of resprouting shrubs, and stimulate sprouting and growth of suppressed herbaceous plants (Harrington 1981). In many stands, a single prescribed fire will not be sufficient to reduce excessive litter accumulation and reinvigorate a long-suppressed herbaceous stratum (Abrahamson and Abrahamson 1996). Where Gambel oak is abundant, a single fire may actually increase the cover of this vigorously resprouting shrub, so a second or even third prescribed fire may be needed at short intervals (2–5 years) to temporarily reduce the oak's competitiveness and provide an opportunity for pine seedlings and herbs to become established (Harrington 1985, 1987). Following initial treatment, a program of periodic prescribed burning should be implemented, mimicking the variability in fire intervals and seasons of burning that characterized the reference period. Initially, all fires may need to be manager-ignited

Table 18.2. Major opportunities and challenges for mitigating adverse effects of past and present human activity in low-elevation forested landscapes of the Southern Rocky Mountains.

Objective	Possible Mitigating Action(s)	Ecological Rationale
Restore large trees; reduce density of small trees and saplings in some stands	Log selectively to remove predominantly small and intermediate size classes; retain remaining large trees	Some stands in reference period were low-density (<100 stems/ha) and contained trees of all sizes
Restore large snags and fallen logs	Restore large tree component (source of future snags and logs); close some roads to reduce losses to firewood gatherers	Large snags and fallen logs were key structural and functional components of reference period forests
Reduce depth and mass of duff and litter on forest floor	Initiate and maintain prescribed fire programs	Frequent, low-intensity fires regularly reduced litter and duff layers during reference period
Reduce risk of uncontrollable wildfire and insect outbreak	Utilize prescribed fire; also thin some stands mechanically to reduce tree density	Fire was a keystone process in pre-1860 forests that maintained open stand structure with reduced risk of high-intensity fire and insect outbreak
Restore plant species intolerant of shade and livestock grazing, and animal species intolerant of dense stands of small trees	Thin stands, introduce prescribed fire, regulate livestock grazing; active reintroduction of native species may be needed in some places	Reference period fire regime and absence of livestock grazing maintained suitable habitat for many specialized plant and animal species
Reduce spread and local expansion of competitive, alien weeds	Control local weed populations before logging or prescribed burning to prevent rapid increase and spread	Certain alien species have unprecedented competitive effects on native biota; may threaten integrity of native flora and ecological function of forests

during spring and fall, but once fuel loads and canopy structures have been restored to something more like their reference condition, lightning ignitions may be allowed to burn in midsummer as well as fall and spring.

Grazing must be regulated, either by fencing or temporarily closing livestock allotments, because both native and domestic ungulates will be attracted by the increased quantity and quality of forage in the burned stands. Excessive grazing may wipe out the gains in herbaceous vegetation that have been obtained through treatment by prescribed fire and logging (Johnson 1956). Finally, given that we have much experience in degrading ecosystems, but little in restoring them, we must clearly acknowledge and capitalize upon the experimental nature of this approach. A research component should be built into the restoration program, with clearly formulated ecological questions and hypotheses to be rigorously tested by the treatment. Adequate funding for the research must be assured from the outset.

Several challenging issues must be addressed in restoration projects of this kind. First, the logging may be uneconomic because of lack of markets for small-diameter material (D. Lynch and W. H. Romme, *unpublished manuscript*). Development of new markets and technologies utilizing small-diameter pine should be a priority if this kind of restoration is to be applied at a broad scale. Thinning and prescribed fire may accelerate the invasion or local expansion of alien weeds if preventive measures are not implemented (Hobbs and Huenneke 1992). These activities also can facilitate the spread of dwarf mistletoe (Hawksworth and Wiens 1995)—a problem for timber production, but actually a potential benefit from a wildlife habitat standpoint (Bennetts et al. 1996). If thinning and burning are followed by dry summers and poor seed crops, the treatment may lead simply to increased cover of Gambel oak rather than establishment of new herbaceous plants and pine seedlings. Fire may kill disproportionate numbers of older trees, the very individuals that need to be maintained, because of heavy fuel loads around their bases. Hand removal of litter and conducting initial burns in the fall are methods that may be used to reduce fire-caused mortality of large, old trees (Swezy and Agee 1991, Covington and Moore 1994). One of the most difficult issues facing prescribed fire programs in many parts of the Rockies is the growing risk of property loss and liability associated with expensive homes now being built in long-unburned ponderosa pine forests adjacent to public lands or on private inholdings (Theobald, *this volume*).

Despite these potential difficulties, the combined program of selective logging, prescribed fire, grazing management, and research is necessary to effectively restore the structural elements and ecological processes that have been lost in some ponderosa pine forests. Logging alone will not reduce surface fuel loads or stimulate the growth of long-suppressed herbaceous plants. Nor will prescribed fire by itself thin the canopy adequately, because most of the trees in many stands are not small enough to be killed by a low-intensity surface fire.

High-Elevation Landscapes
Disturbance Regimes of the Reference Period

Major forest types at higher elevations in the Southern Rocky Mountains include spruce-fir, lodgepole pine, aspen, and cool wet mixed conifer forests (Peet 1988, Knight 1994). The two most important and ubiquitous kinds of disturbance during the period of indigenous settlement were stand-destroying fire and bark beetle outbreaks (Baker and Veblen 1990; Veblen et al. 1994; Veblen, *this volume*). Rare but extensive lethal fires left a lasting imprint on the landscape in the form of patches of forest undergoing succession more or less synchronously. Return intervals of major, stand-destroying fires varied with elevation, topography, and geographic area, but generally were in the hundreds of years (Veblen, *this volume*). Mountain pine beetle and spruce beetle populations periodically erupted into major outbreaks that killed large-diameter lodgepole pine or Engelmann spruce trees, respectively, over extensive areas (Schmid and Mata 1996). Return intervals of extensive mountain pine beetle and spruce beetle outbreaks were shorter than the intervals between successive, stand-destroying fires, but still were in the range of decades to centuries (Veblen et al. 1994; Veblen, *this volume*). In addition, some disturbances were caused by snow avalanches, extensive windthrow, and other insects and fungi (Schmidt and Mata 1996; Veblen, *this volume*), but their effects generally were more localized or less intense than the effects of fire and bark beetles.

Legacies of Past Land Use and Management in High-Elevation Landscapes

Effects of twentieth-century fire suppression are not as clear in high-elevation landscapes as in low-elevation landscapes of the Southern Rocky Mountains. Few large fires occurred during the twentieth century, but given the long fire-return intervals that naturally characterize these systems, the current fire-free intervals may not be far outside the range of variability in fire intervals that characterized the period of indigenous settlement. Certainly the time that has elapsed since the last fire in any individual stand is not unprecedented, but larger landscape units (e.g., watersheds) may have gone for longer than usual without a large fire. Fire frequency increased briefly during the late nineteenth century period of European settlement in at least some parts of the Southern Rocky Mountains (e.g., the Front Range; Veblen and Lorenz 1991). Although fire suppression has been the general policy throughout most of the twentieth century, our experience with the 1988 Yellowstone fires and with recent fires in the Canadian Rockies (Romme and Despain 1989, Bessie and Johnson 1995, Weir et al. 1995) suggests that even modern fire control techniques may be ineffective in high-elevation forests burning under severe fire weather conditions. Thus, the principal reasons for the paucity of extensive high-elevation fires during this century may be related more to lack of ignitions or wet weather conditions than to human fire suppression. The possibility also exists that large, Yellowstone-like fires will occur in high-elevation forests of the Southern Rocky Mountains within the next few decades, regardless of fire-control efforts (Agee 1997). The behavior and ecological effects of the few high-elevation fires that have occurred during this century, though stand-destroying, do not appear much different from those of fires during the period of indigenous settlement (Romme and Despain 1989, Turner et al. 1997).

Other human activities since the late 1800s have produced important changes in disturbance regimes and vegetation structure of high-elevation landscapes (Table 18.3). These impacts are related mainly to timber cutting and to the extensive network of roads that has been constructed to support logging, fire control, and recreation (Baker and Knight, *this volume*). In some ways, these kinds of disturbance are novel—unprecedented in the history of the landscape—and as such they may potentially cause more serious changes in these ecological systems than the fires, insect outbreaks, and other disturbances that the biota have experienced throughout their evolutionary history. In portions of the Southern Rocky Mountains, these activities did not occur extensively until after World War II.

The most conspicuous anthropogenic disturbance in high-elevation forests of the late twentieth century is clearcut logging (Table 18.3). This method was used in most forest types during the 1950s–1970s but is now less frequent in spruce-fir because of problems in stand regeneration. Although a relatively small proportion of the total land area was affected by clearcutting without adequate reforestation, the legacies of this activity will last for many decades or centuries. Direct effects include a reduction in total forest area and fragmentation of interior forest (i.e., mature forest that is not close to a forest edge). Indirect effects include a reduction in the future timber base, as well as reduced habitat quality for some old-growth forest species that are sensitive to habitat alteration. The legacy of clearcuts without reforestation is not altogether "bad," as most of these areas appear to have adequate plant cover (mostly herbs rather than trees), and the

Table 18.3. Major legacies of past forest use and management in high-elevation forested landscapes of the Southern Rocky Mountains.

Human Activity	Direct Effects	Indirect Effects
Clearcut logging, without adequate tree regeneration	—Reduction in total forest area —Fragmentation of interior forest	—Reduction in future timber base —Reduced habitat quality for plant and animal species of interior forests —Improved habitat for nonforest and edge species
Clearcut logging, with adequate tree regeneration	—Fragmentation of interior forest —Development of successional stands that lack snags and large coarse woody debris —Homogeneous disturbance intensity throughout logging units —Shift to younger stand age classes, especially on productive portions of landscape	—Reduced habitat quality for old-growth plant and animal species —Inadequate habitat for some early successional species (cavity nesters and perching birds) —Risk of long-term reduction of soil organic matter and soil microbial activity —Reduced landscape heterogeneity and sharper stand boundaries, compared to former fire-created patterns —Restriction of old-growth forests to less productive sites
Partial timber cuts	—Reduced structural contrast between logged and unlogged areas —Accumulation of small coarse woody debris (slash) on forest floor	—Eventual loss of large trees, snags, and large coarse woody debris, with associated effects on soil structure and biota —Eventual reduction in habitat quality for old-growth plant and animal species —Extensive road system and frequent entry required
Extensive road building for logging, grazing management, recreation, and fire control	—Fragmentation of the forest landscape —Easy human access in most areas —Erosion	—Spread of alien weeds —Human disturbance of wildlife —Easy accessibility for fire suppression or prescribed fire
Fire suppression	—Some reduction in total area burned, compared to previous century (maybe less than is often thought)	—Loss of habitat for early postfire successional species —False sense of security with regard to future uncontrollable fires
Increasing human population growth and outdoor recreation	—Expanding systems of roads and trails	—Human disturbance of wildlife —Impacts associated with roads

removal of the forest probably increased stream flow and improved habitat for nonforest species.

Regeneration of forest cover after clearcutting is usually assured in some areas, especially aspen forests. Effects of clearcutting in these areas are more subtle than in clearcuts lacking regeneration—but are still potentially significant (Table 18.3). Clearcutting, even when followed by regeneration, results in fragmentation of interior forests and a shift in the forest patch mosaic to younger age classes (e.g., Tinker et al. 1998). Moreover, the intensity of organic matter removal in clearcutting is unprecedented in the evolutionary history of these forests, because fires, windstorms, and insect outbreaks all leave most of the large woody material in place (Spies 1997, Wei et al. 1997). Indeed, young stands developing after clearcutting are structurally very different from young stands developing after stand-destroying fire (Hutto 1995). In particular, regenerating clearcuts lack large dead trees, both standing and fallen. Clearcuts also lack the blackened soil, the temporary reduction in herbaceous plant cover, and brief nutrient pulse associated with fire. The intensity of disturbance tends to be more spatially homogeneous in logged areas than in naturally disturbed areas, and edges between disturbed and undisturbed patches are sharper (Hansen et al. 1991).

Since the 1970s, silvicultural methods have emphasized partial cutting techniques rather than clearcutting in some spruce-fir forests. Although partial cutting has less immediate impact than clearcutting, its long-term legacies may be just as significant, particularly if the partial cutting is simply the first entry in a long-term even-aged management strategy (Table 18.3). If partial cutting emphasizes removal of large trees, a gradual shift to smaller size classes occurs. Large snags and fallen logs, key structural elements for many wildlife species and soil processes, gradually disappear.

Of all the novel kinds of disturbances that humans have brought to forests of the Southern Rocky Mountains during the last century, roads may be the most ubiquitous and significant long-term legacy of our activities (Baker and Knight, *this volume*). Roads affect both lower-elevation and higher-elevation landscapes. They are unprecedented features in the ecological history of the region (Forman 1995) and can cause greater fragmentation of mature forests than clearcutting (Tinker et al. 1998). Roads and trails may be conduits for the spread of alien weeds and barriers to the movement of some sensitive native species (Forman 1995; Baker and Dillon, *this volume*). Roads also allow easy entry for humans and facilitate human disturbance of wildlife.

Opportunities and Challenges in High-Elevation Landscapes

Since the 1970s, planners generally have emphasized small logging units widely dispersed across the landscape. The rationale has been to reduce visual impacts of clearcuts, enhance tree regeneration, and buffer soil erosion. However, recent empirical and theoretical studies have demonstrated that this strategy maximizes fragmentation of interior and old-growth forest (Forman 1995, Franklin et al. 1997). Moreover, the natural disturbance regime generally produced few large disturbance patches rather than many small patches, and the native biota appear well adapted to large as well as small disturbance patches (Turner et al. 1997). Many of the problems of erosion and poor regeneration in large clearcuts actually result from roads and the lack of remnant snags and coarse woody debris, rather than clearcut size per se. Therefore, ecologists are now urging consideration of logging units that are relatively large and aggregated, with patch sizes and shapes that resemble fire-created patches (Crow and Gustafson 1997, Franklin et al. 1997). This design can reduce fragmentation of mature forest and assure at least some large patches of interior forest, and it mimics the natural disturbance regime with respect to spatial patterns of disturbance. We must emphasize, however, that the reasoning just presented deals only with the optimal spatial patterning of cutting units given some reasonable target for total timber production—it does not imply that a greater total area should be logged. On the contrary, many would argue that wood production targets in the Southern Rocky Mountains, which have decreased in many areas during the last decade, should remain low or even be reduced further because of this region's low capacity for timber growth compared with other regions, as well as the potential ecological and aesthetic effects of timber production.

Regardless of size or shape, recently logged areas in subalpine forests of the Southern Rocky Mountains usually bear little resemblance to areas of natural disturbance by fire, insects, or wind. Most conspicuous is the paucity of large standing and fallen dead trees in logged areas (Spies 1997, Hutto 1995, Wei et al. 1997). These and other "biological legacies" of the previous stand are critical structural elements for numerous species and ecological processes involved in recovery from the disturbance (Perry and Amaranthus 1997, Franklin et al. 1997, Kaila et al. 1997, Spies 1997). Therefore, Franklin et al. (1997) and others are now suggesting variable retention harvest systems, which are based on retaining some structural elements of the stand that was logged (e.g., large trees and snags) for at least the next rotation, to

Table 18.4. Major opportunities and challenges for mitigating adverse effects of past and present human activity in high-elevation forested landscapes of the Southern Rocky Mountains.

Objective	*Possible Mitigating Action(s)*	*Ecological Rationale*
Minimize fragmentation of interior forest by timber cutting operations	Cut timber in few large patches rather than in many small patches, without increasing total logged area	Most of the area disturbed by fire in pre-1860 period was burned in a few large fires rather than many small fires
Minimize fragmentation of mature forest by roads	Minimize new road building; close existing roads wherever possible; implement logging techniques that do not require roads if possible	Roads are anthropogenic landscape features that have no ecological precedence, but have negative effects on native biota
Create heterogeneous stand structure within logged areas; create softer boundaries between cutting units and uncut forest	Design logging units for less uniform cutting intensity, (e.g., mix partial cuts & clearcuts, leave patches of uncut or partially cut forest within & along edges of clearcuts)	Fire severity in large fires tends to be patchy; creates a heterogeneous post-fire environment
Provide large snags, coarse woody debris, and other biological legacies of the previous stand in logged areas	Leave most large snags & fallen logs within logged areas, as well as some large & small canopy trees that will eventually become snags & fallen logs	Fires leave great quantities of snags & coarse woody debris in all size classes; this material is important in postfire succession, wildlife habitat, & long-term soil development
Prevent the spread of alien plant species along roads and in logged areas	Plant native species in abandoned roads & logged areas, or avoid planting altogether if risk of erosion is low; minimize road building	Native plant species are capable of rapidly revegetating bare soil areas created by fire, but the natives may be less competitive than the alien species in roads and logged areas
Restore early successional communities lacking due to fire suppression	Introduce prescribed fire on a landscape scale	Young stands produced by traditional logging practices lack key structural components of recently burned habitats, so are not adequate replacement
Provide old-growth forest stands on productive sites as well as less productive sites	Retain existing old-growth stands; attempt to restore missing structural elements (e.g., snags) in previously cut stands, especially those on productive sites	Pre-1860 landscape mosaic contained some old-growth on all kinds of sites, not just unproductive

achieve three objectives: (1) "lifeboating" species and processes immediately after logging, (2) "enriching" the new forest stand with structures that otherwise would be lacking, and (3) "enhancing connectivity" between patches of unlogged forest habitat (Franklin et al. 1997). We further suggest that variable retention harvests be followed by extensive prescribed fire (not just burning of piles of slash) to rapidly decompose some of the smaller-sized organic matter, create blackened or mineral soil surfaces, and temporarily reduce herbaceous cover. These additional fire effects may be as important in natural forest recovery processes as maintaining biological legacies, though research is needed.

Managers can look for ways to minimize the extent and impact of roads, and thereby reduce the effects of these novel structures on fragmentation of interior forest habitats, dispersal of alien species, and human-caused disturbance of wildlife. A group of large, aggregated patches of timber-cutting activity may require fewer access roads than a comparable area in small dispersed patches. Necessary roads can be placed in areas that minimize their fragmenting effects (e.g., running around a large patch of mature forest rather than bisecting it) and unnecessary roads can be permanently closed (Baker and Knight, *this volume*). In some places, loggers may be able to reduce the impact of roads and skid trails by using large-wheeled tree harvesting machines or by horse-logging in winter (Table 18.4).

Finally, managers should continue efforts to restore fire as a natural process in high-elevation forests. Some of the ecological effects of fire can never be entirely simulated by logging, even with variable retention techniques, and some native species like the black-backed woodpecker are almost completely dependent upon recently burned forests (Hutto 1995). Prescribed fire in high-elevation forests, whether lightning or manager-ignited, is a challenging undertaking because of the potential for uncontrollable, high-intensity fires. However, prescribed burns may be feasible in some places, especially in relatively large wildland areas with little human development.

SUMMARY AND RECOMMENDATIONS

There are important differences in the natural disturbance regimes and in the legacies of a century of EuroAmerican activity in lower-elevation versus higher-elevation ecosystems of the Southern Rocky Mountains. In lower-elevation landscapes, fire—a keystone ecological process during the period of indigenous settlement—has been essentially removed, at least temporarily, and early grazing and logging have further altered the structure, composition, and function of ponderosa pine forests. The result has been homogenization of forest structure and loss of formerly open, savanna-like stands. As a consequence of these changes, portions of the low-elevation landscape may now be at risk of destructive wildfire, insect outbreaks, and loss of biodiversity. Relatively intensive restoration efforts, involving prescribed fire, mechanical thinning, and grazing regulation, now are needed in some places to compensate for these undesirable legacies of past human use. We face major challenges in implementing restoration of ponderosa pine forest ecosystems, including safety and liability risks of allowing fires to burn near the urban-wildland interface, the risk of increasing the spread of invasive alien weeds, and the need for long-term control of grazing and recreation activities within treated areas.

In contrast, high-elevation landscapes of the Southern Rocky Mountains probably have been altered much less by a century of fire suppression. Given naturally long intervals between large fires, the low fire frequency and consequent increase in extent and connectedness of spruce-fir forests in roadless areas during the twentieth century may not be far outside the historic range of variability. The only "restoration" now needed in many of these areas is some form of prescribed natural fire. However, road-building and logging, especially during the last half-century, have dramatically altered high-elevation landscape structure in other parts of the region. Some of the impacts of these anthropogenic disturbances are unprecedented in the evolutionary history of the biota, especially with respect to fragmentation of interior forests and the lack of large snags and fallen logs in post-disturbance environments. Changes in logging techniques, such as variable retention harvest strategies, aggregated cutting patterns, and minimized road systems, may ameliorate some of these negative effects of timber production. Major challenges involved in ecosystem management of high-elevation landscapes include economic costs and potential hazards for loggers and recreationists related to leaving large trees and snags within logged areas, as well as risks of prescribed fire in the typically heavy fuels of subalpine forests.

In this chapter, we have presented several specific recommendations for revising timber harvest methods and for active restoration of degraded structural elements and processes. We emphasize that these recommendations are intended for lands being managed primarily for commodity production. Some of the strategies may someday be appropriate in wilderness areas also, but all of the methods are experimental and the potential adverse effects are not yet fully explored. Therefore, they first should be tested in areas that already have been subjected to intensive human alterations during the last century. Wilderness and roadless areas, though not "pristine," nevertheless provide some of the best reference areas available for measuring the effects of human activities on the land, and their value for this function will only increase with time.

Research Needs: We suggest two major areas in which research is urgently needed to support the implementation of the management strategies suggested in this chapter.

(1) *Quantitative descriptions of reference ecological conditions*—In lower-elevation forest landscapes, we do not know the relative proportions during the reference period of open, savanna-like ponderosa pine forests where low-intensity fires were frequent, versus dense stands where fire was less frequent. In higher-elevation landscapes, we do not know the relative proportions of early, middle, and late successional spruce-fir forests during the reference period. Nor do we know how either of these proportions varied over time. This information is central to the concept of a historic range of variation and is needed to provide an objective basis for setting management and restoration targets at landscape scales.

(2) *Ecological effects of "new forestry" approaches in the Southern Rocky Mountains*—Research programs are under way in other regions (e.g., the Southwest and the Pacific Northwest) to evaluate the efficacy of some of the new management strategies described in this chapter. However, we must recognize that all such efforts—including prescribed burning, mechanical thinning, aggregated cutting units, and variable retention harvests—are still experimental, and may yet reveal unanticipated negative effects on biodiversity and ecosystem function. As these new techniques are used in the Southern Rocky Mountains, they should be explicitly designed and evaluated as scientific experiments. We have much to learn about potentially sustainable commodity production and basic ecosystem function from well-conceived pilot projects that apply and assess new silvicultural approaches, and ongoing evaluation is a part of adaptive management.

ACKNOWLEDGMENTS

The San Juan National Forest provided financial and logistic support for empirical studies and conceptual development of many of the ideas in this chapter. Fort Lewis College and Harvard University provided W. H. Romme with time for thinking and writing, through a sabbatical leave and a Bullard Fellowship at Harvard Forest in 1997–1998. We thank William L. Baker, Steven W. Buskirk, Dennis H. Knight, and Richard L. Knight for critical reviews of an early draft.

LITERATURE CITED

Abrahamson, W. G., and C. R. Abrahamson. 1996. Effects of fire on long-unburned Florida uplands. *Journal of Vegetation Science* 7: 565–574.

Agee, J. K. 1997. Fire management for the 21st century. Pages 191–201 *in* K. A. Kohm and J. F. Franklin, editors. *Creating a forestry for the 21ˢᵗ century: the science of ecosystem management.* Island Press, Washington, D.C., USA.

Arnold, J. F. 1950. Changes in ponderosa pine bunchgrass ranges in northern Arizona resulting from pine regeneration and grazing. *Journal of Forestry* 48: 118–126.

Baker, W. L., and T. T. Veblen. 1990. Spruce beetles and fires in the nineteenth-century subalpine forests of western Colorado, USA. *Arctic and Alpine Research* 22: 65–80.

Balda, R. P. 1975. The relationship of secondary cavity nesters to snag densities in western coniferous forests. Southwest Wildlife Habitat Technical Bulletin No. 1, USDA Forest Service, Albuquerque, New Mexico, USA.

Bennetts, R. E., G. C. White, F. G. Hawksworth, and S. E. Severs. 1996. The influence of dwarf mistletoe on bird communities in Colorado ponderosa pine forests. *Ecological Applications* 6: 899–909.

Bessie, W. C., and E. A. Johnson. 1995. The relative importance of fuels and weather on fire behavior in subalpine forests. *Ecology* 76: 747–762.

Christensen, N. L., A. M. Bartuska, J. H. Brown, S. Carpenter, C. D'Antonio, R. Francis, J. F. Franklin, J. A. MacMahon, R. F. Noss, D. J. Parsons, C. H. Peterson, M. G. Turner, and R. G. Woodmansee. 1996. The report of the Ecological Society of America committee on the scientific basis for ecosystem management. *Ecological Applications* 6: 665–691.

Covington, W. W., and M. M. Moore. 1994. Southwestern ponderosa forest structure: changes since Euro-American settlement. *Journal of Forestry* 92: 39–47.

Crow, T. R., and E. J. Gustafson. 1997. Ecosystem management: managing natural resources in time and space. Pages 215–228 *in* K. A. Kohm and J. F. Franklin, editors. *Creating a forestry for the 21ˢᵗ century: the science of ecosystem management.* Island Press, Washington, D.C., USA.

Cunningham, J. B., R. P. Balda, and W. S. Gaud. 1980. Selection and use of snags by secondary cavity-nesting birds of the ponderosa pine forest. USDA Forest Service Research Paper RM-222.

Dahms, C. W., and B. W. Geils, technical editors. 1997. An assessment of forest ecosystem health in the Southwest. USDA Forest Service General Technical Report RM-GTR-295.

DuBois, C. 1903. Report on the proposed San Juan Forest Reserve, Colorado. Unpublished report, on file at the supervisor's office, San Juan National Forest, Durango, Colorado, USA.

Fleischner, T. L. 1994. Ecological costs of livestock grazing in western North America. *Conservation Biology* 8: 629–644.

Forman, R.T.T. 1995. *Land mosaics: the ecology of landscapes and regions.* Cambridge University Press, Cambridge, UK.

Foster, D. R., 1993. Land-use history and forest transformations in central New England. Pages 91–110 *in* M. J. McDonnell and S.T.A. Pickett, editors. *Hu-*

mans as components of ecosystems. Springer-Verlag, New York, New York, USA.

Franklin, J. F., D. R. Berg, D. A. Thornburgh, and J. C. Tappeiner. 1997. Alternative silvicultural approaches to timber harvesting: variable retention harvest systems. Pages 111–139 *in* K. A. Kohm and J. F. Franklin, editors. *Creating a forestry for the 21ˢᵗ century: the science of ecosystem management.* Island Press, Washington, D.C., USA.

Fule, P. Z., W. W. Covington, and M. M. Moore. 1997. Determining reference conditions for ecosystem management of southwestern ponderosa pine forests. *Ecological Applications* 7: 895–908.

Hansen, A. J., T. A. Spies, F. J. Swanson, and J. L. Ohmann. 1991. Conserving biodiversity in managed forests. *BioScience* 41: 382–392.

Harrington, M. G. 1981. Preliminary burning prescriptions for ponderosa pine fuel reductions in southeastern Arizona. USDA Forest Service Research Note RM-402.

Harrington, M. G. 1985. The effects of spring, summer, and fall burning on Gambel oak in a southwestern ponderosa pine stand. *Forest Science* 31: 156–163.

Harrington, M. G. 1987. Phytotoxic potential of Gambel oak on ponderosa pine seed germination and initial growth. USDA Forest Service Research Paper RM-277.

Hawksworth, F. G., and D. Wiens. 1995. Dwarf mistletoes: biology, pathology, and systematics. Agriculture Handbook 709. USDA Forest Service, Washington, D.C., USA.

Hobbs, R. J., and L. F. Huenneke. 1992. Disturbance, diversity, and invasion: implications for conservation. *Conservation Biology* 6: 324–337.

Hutto, R. L. 1995. Composition of bird communities following stand-replacement fires in Northern Rocky Mountain (USA) conifer forests. *Conservation Biology* 9: 1041–1058.

Johnson, W. M. 1956. The effect of grazing intensity on plant composition, vigor, and growth of pine-bunchgrass ranges in central Colorado. *Ecology* 37: 790–798.

Kaila, L., P. Martikainen, and P. Punttila. 1997. Dead trees left in clear-cuts benefit saproxylic Coleoptera adapted to natural disturbances in boreal forest. *Biodiversity and Conservation* 6: 1–18.

Kaufmann, M. R., R. T. Graham, D. A. Boyce, Jr., W. H. Moir, L. Perry, R. T. Reynolds, R. L. Bassett, P. Mehlhop, C. B. Edminster, W. M. Block, and P. S. Corn. 1994. An ecological basis for ecosystem management. USDA Forest Service General Technical Report RM-246.

Knight, D. H. 1994. *Mountains and plains: the ecology of Wyoming landscapes.* Yale University Press, New Haven, Connecticut, USA.

Kohm, K. A., and J. F. Franklin, editors. 1997. *Creating a forestry for the 21st century: the science of ecosystem management.* Island Press, Washington, D.C., USA.

Leopold, A. 1966. *A Sand County almanac, with essays on conservation from Round River.* Ballantine Books, New York, New York, USA.

Madany, M. H., and N. E. West. 1983. Livestock grazing-fire regime interactions within montane forests of Zion National Park, Utah. *Ecology* 64: 661–667.

Moir, W. H., B. Geils, M. A. Benoit, and D. Scurlock. 1997. Ecology of southwestern ponderosa pine forests. Pages 3–27 *in* W. M. Block and D. M. Finch, technical editors. *Songbird ecology in southwestern ponderosa pine forests: a literature review.* USDA Forest Service General Technical Report RM-GTR-292.

Peet, R. K. 1988. Forests of the Rocky Mountains. Pages 46–101 *in* M. G. Barbour and W. D. Billings, editors. *North American terrestrial vegetation.* Cambridge University Press, New York, New York, USA.

Perry, D. A., and M. P. Amaranthus. 1997. Disturbance, recovery, and stability. Pages 31–56 *in* K. A. Kohm and J. F. Franklin, editors. *Creating a forestry for the 21ˢᵗ century: the science of ecosystem management.* Island Press, Washington, D.C., USA.

Quigley, T. M., R. W. Haynes, and R. T. Graham, technical editors. 1996. Integrated scientific assessment for ecosystem management in the Interior Columbia Basin. USDA Forest Service General Technical Report PNW-GTR-382.

Reice, S. 1994. Nonequilibrium determinants of biological community structure. *American Scientist* 82: 424–435.

Romme, W. H., and D. G. Despain. 1989. Historical perspective on the Yellowstone fires of 1988. *BioScience* 39: 695–699.

Rummell, R. S. 1951. Some effects of livestock grazing on ponderosa pine forest and range in central Washington. *Ecology* 32: 594–607.

Schmid, J. M., and S. A. Mata. 1996. Natural variability of specific forest insect populations and their associated effects in Colorado. USDA Forest Service General Technical Report RM-GTR-275.

Shinneman, D. J., and W. L. Baker. 1997. Nonequilibrium dynamics between catastrophic disturbances and old-growth forests in ponderosa pine landscapes of the Black Hills. *Conservation Biology* 11: 1–13

Spies, T. 1997. Forest stand structure, composition, and function. Pages 11–30 *in* K. A. Kohm and J. F. Franklin, editors. *Creating a forestry for the 21ˢᵗ century: the science of ecosystem management.* Island Press, Washington, D.C., USA.

Swanson, F. J., and J. F. Franklin. 1992. New forestry principles from ecosystem analysis of Pacific Northwest forests. *Ecological Applications* 2: 262–274.

Swanson, F. J., J. A. Jones, and G. E. Grant. 1997. The physical environment as a basis for managing ecosystems. Pages 229–238 *in* K. A. Kohm and J. F. Franklin, editors. *Creating a forestry for the 21ˢᵗ century: the science of ecosystem management.* Island Press, Washington, D.C., USA.

Swetnam, T. W., and C. H. Baisan. 1996. Historical fire regime patterns in the southwestern United States since AD 1700. Pages 11–32 *in* C. D. Allen, technical editor. *Fire effects in southwestern forests: proceedings of the second La Mesa fire symposium, Los Alamos, 1994.* USDA Forest Service General Technical Report RM-GTR-286.

Swezy, D. M., and J. K. Agee. 1991. Prescribed fire effects on fine-root and tree mortality in old-growth ponderosa pine. *Canadian Journal of Forest Research* 21: 626–634.

Tinker, D. B., C. A. C. Resor, G. P. Beauvais, K. F. Kipfmueller, C. I. Fernandes, and W. L. Baker. 1998. Watershed analysis of forest fragmentation by clearcuts and roads in a Wyoming forest. *Landscape Ecology* 13: 149–165.

Turner, M. G., W. H. Romme, R. H. Gardner, and W. W. Hargrove. 1997. Effects of fire size and pattern on early succession in Yellowstone National Park. *Ecological Monographs* 67: 411–433.

Veblen, T. T., and D. C. Lorenz. 1991. *The Colorado Front Range: a century of ecological change.* University of Utah Press. Salt Lake City, Utah, USA.

Veblen. T. T., K. S. Hadley, E. M. Nel, T. Kitzberger, M. Reid, and R. Villalba. 1994. Disturbance regime and disturbance interactions in a Rocky Mountain subalpine forest. *Journal of Ecology* 82: 125–135.

Vogt, K. A. 1997. *Ecosystems: balancing science with management.* Springer-Verlag, New York, New York, USA.

Wei, X., J. P. Kimmins, K. Peel, and O. Steen. 1997. Mass and nutrients in woody debris in harvested and wildfire-killed lodgepole pine forests in the central interior of British Columbia. *Canadian Journal of Forest Research* 27: 148–155.

Weir, J. M. H., K. J. Chapman, and E. A. Johnson. 1995. Wildland fire management and the fire regime in the southern Canadian Rockies. Pages 275–280 *in* J. K. Brown, R. W. Mutch, C. W. Spoon, and R. H. Wakimoto, technical coordinators. *Proceedings: symposium on fire in wilderness and park management.* USDA Forest Service General Technical Report INT-GTR-320.

Whitney, G. G. 1994. *From coastal wilderness to fruited plain: a history of environmental change in temperate North America from 1500 to the present.* Cambridge University Press, Cambridge, UK.

19

Law, Policy, and Forest Fragmentation in the Southern Rocky Mountains

Robert B. Keiter

Introduction

In the Southern Rockies region, forest fragmentation and related biodiversity concerns raise complex legal and policy issues. In fact, concern over the impact of timber harvesting, roading, and other human intrusions on national forest ecosystems has triggered judicial intervention into forest management practices across the public domain. In the Pacific Northwest, forest fragmentation was at the heart of the decade-long spotted owl–timber harvesting controversy, prompting a federal injunction prohibiting all logging on the west-side national forests, an unprecedented presidential summit, and a major federal interagency ecosystem management initiative. In the Southwest, a federal court has enjoined logging on the region's national forests to protect Mexican spotted owl habitat from fragmentation. In the Midwest, another federal court has invalidated portions of the Shawnee National Forest plan for failure to analyze the cumulative environmental impacts associated with timber harvesting, oil and gas leasing, and motorized recreational activities. Although the courts have not uniformly sustained environmental challenges to forest management decisions, the successful rulings nonetheless suggest that the law can be employed to address ecological fragmentation problems. For the Southern Rockies region, not surprisingly, the legal issues underlying forest fragmentation are largely the same as those involved in these other cases.

This chapter will examine how the law addresses forest fragmentation and related policy considerations. The chapter begins by outlining the principal laws governing forest management and related fragmentation concerns, namely the National Forest Management Act (NFMA), National Environmental Policy Act (NEPA), and Endangered Species Act (ESA). Next, the chapter identifies emerging ecosystem management concepts designed to address fragmentation and biodiversity concerns, and then examines the difficult legal issues that can arise under an ecosystem management approach. This examination focuses on legal compliance obligations, including the timing of judicial review, scale considerations, and adaptive management strategies. The chapter concludes with general policy observations on an ecosystem management approach to the southern Rockies fragmentation problem.

THE LAW AND FOREST FRAGMENTATION

The laws governing forest fragmentation are generally the same as those addressing ecological integrity in the national forests. In both instances, the primary laws are the National Forest Management Act (16 U.S.C. §§ 1600–1614), National Environmental Policy Act (42 U.S.C. §§ 4321–4361), and Endangered Species Act (16 U.S.C. §§ 1531–1543), though other statutes also may apply. Although these laws do not expressly address ecological fragmentation, they do govern specific human activities that promote fragmentation, such as timber harvesting, roading, recreation, inholdings, and exurban development. They also address natural phenomena that can cause fragmentation, such as wildfire, disease, insects, and windthrow. When construing and applying these laws, the courts have given considerable deference to agency legal interpretations so long as the interpretation is consistent with statutory language and congressional intent (*Chevron, USA, Inc. v. Natural Resources Defense Council,* 467 U.S. 837 (1984)). The courts, given the scientific and technical considerations involved in many resource decisions, have also tended to defer to agency expertise when reviewing management decisions, so long as the decision is based on defensible scientific information and the agency has responded to contrary scientific opinions (e.g., *Sierra Club v. Marita,* 46 F.3d 606 (7th Cir. 1995)). Nonetheless, these laws establish clearly enforceable legal standards and procedures that have been employed by the courts to overturn forest management decisions that ignore important ecological and biodiversity concerns.

National Forest Management Act

The National Forest Management Act of 1976 (NFMA) amended the Multiple Use–Sustained Yield Act of 1960 (16 U.S.C. §§ 528-531) that governs management of the national forests. The NFMA, while reaffirming the multiple-use management principle, establishes a comprehensive, forest-based, interdisciplinary land and resource planning process with a ten- to fifteen-year revision cycle (16 U.S.C. § 1604). The NFMA's legislative history indicates that it was designed to elevate non-timber resources to a coequal status with timber on the national forests and to impose limitations on clear-cut harvesting techniques (Wilkinson and Anderson 1985). The NFMA provisions have been implemented through detailed regulations originally drafted by a Committee of Scientists (16 U.S.C. § 1604(h)); the regulations contain specific resource management standards and planning requirements (36 C.F.R. Part 219). The NFMA planning process requires compliance with NEPA disclosure and public involvement procedures (16 U.S.C. §§ 1604(d), (g)(1)), and it provides for interjurisdictional coordination (16 U.S.C. § 1604(a)). Although most forest plan decisions are not subject to immediate judicial review (*Ohio Forestry Association, Inc. v. Sierra Club*, 118 S.Ct. 1665 (1998)), NFMA provisions can be judicially enforced through project decision appeals.

Because forest fragmentation can significantly reduce available habitat for forest-dwelling species, the NFMA biodiversity provision imposes ecologically important management requirements. Under this provision, a key goal of forest planning is to "provide for diversity of plant and animal communities based on the suitability and capability of the specific land area in order to meet overall multiple-use objectives, and within the multiple-use objectives of a land management plan adopted pursuant to this section, provide, where appropriate, to the degree practicable, for steps to be taken to preserve the diversity of tree species similar to that existing in the region controlled by the plan." (16 U.S.C. § 1604(g)(3)(B)). But several diversity-related regulations notwithstanding (36 C.F.R. §§ 219.26, 219.27(g)), the courts have generally given the Forest Service broad discretion in meeting its biodiversity obligations, primarily on the theory that the agency—not the courts—possesses the requisite technical expertise to make these scientific judgments. The Seventh Circuit Court of Appeals, for example, rejected the argument that the Forest Service was required to incorporate conservation biology principles into its biodiversity analysis for forest planning purposes (*Sierra Club v. Marita*, 46 F.3d 606 (7th Cir. 1995)). Other courts have reached similar results (*Colorado Environmental Coalition v. Dombeck*, 185 F.3d 1162 (10th Cir. 1999); *Sierra Club v. Espy*, 38 F.3d 792 (5th Cir. 1994); *Sierra Club v. Robertson*, 28 F.3d 753 (8th Cir. 1994), *affirming*, 810 F.Supp. 1021 (W.D. Ark. 1992)).

The courts have, however, interpreted the Forest Service's minimum viable population regulation to impose meaningful constraints on forest management decisions. Under this regulation, the Forest Service is obligated to ensure habitat "to maintain viable populations of native and desired non-native vertebrate species," which includes maintaining well distributed population segments and habitat to facilitate interaction among these segments (36 C.F.R. § 219.19). As the spotted owl litigation demonstrated, the regulation's population distribution and habitat protection requirements are designed to prohibit fragmentation that threatens the viability of forest-dwelling species. The Ninth Circuit Court of Appeals has ruled that the regulation applies to both planning and project decisions (*Inland Empire Public Lands Council v. U.S. Forest Service*, 88 F.3d 754 (9th Cir. 1996)), and that the Forest Service must ensure well-distributed, viable populations in its planning processes even after a species is listed under the Endangered Species Act (*Seattle Audubon Society v. Evans*, 952 F.2d 297 (9th Cir. 1991)). The Ninth Circuit, however, has also ruled that the minimum viable population regulation does not require the Forest Service to select the management alternative that provides the highest likelihood of species survival (*Seattle Audubon Society v. Lyons*, 80 F.3d 1401 (9th Cir. 1996)). And in *Inland Empire*, the court deferred to the Forest Service's population viability analyses, relying upon the agency's scientific expertise (*Inland Empire Public Lands Council v. U.S. Forest Service*, 88 F.3d 754 (9th Cir. 1996)). Moreover, despite a strong dissent asserting that "it is important to consider the size, configuration, and connectivity of old growth in the forest planning process," the court refused to interpret the minimum viable population regulation's habitat maintenance requirement as an absolute prohibition on forest fragmentation (*Oregon Natural Resources Council v. Lowe*, 109 F.3d 521 (9th Cir. 1997)).

The NFMA also contains specific timber harvesting requirements that can be interpreted to minimize fragmentation. These requirements include: (1) soil, slope, and watershed protections; (2) a five-year restocking requirement; and (3) limitations on clear-cutting and other harvesting methods (16 U.S.C. §§ 1604(g)(3)(E), (F)). The courts have generally enforced the five-year restocking requirement (*Sierra Club v. Cargill*, 732 F.Supp. 1095 (D. Colo. 1990); *Ayers v. Espy*, 873 F.Supp. 455 (D. Colo. 1994)), and they have been receptive to claims alleging potential soil, slope, and watershed damage (*Citizens for Environmental Quality v. United States*, 731 F.Supp. 970 (D. Colo. 1989); *Sierra Club v. Glickman*, 974 F.Supp. 905 (E.D. Tex. 1997)). But the courts have generally deferred to the Forest Service's choice of harvesting methods and rejected efforts to limit clear-cutting (e.g., *Sierra Club v. Espy,* 38 F.3d 792 (5th Cir. 1994); *Sierra Club v. Robertson,* 810 F.Supp. 1021 (W.D. Ark. 1992); Cheever 1998). In addition, the NFMA exempts salvage timber sales involving trees that have been damaged by fire, insects, disease, or windstorms from these harvesting limitations (16 U.S.C. § 1604(g)(3)(F)(iv)). And the NFMA excludes salvage sales from its harvesting size requirements (16 U.S.C. § 1604(m)).

The NFMA does not expressly address road construction in the national forests, even though roads can have severe fragmentation impacts and are costly to construct and maintain. The NFMA and the amended Resources Planning Act of 1974 (16 U.S.C. §§ 1601–1614) contain economic feasibility language (16 U.S.C. §§ 1604(g)(3)(F)(ii), 1608), but the courts have ruled that these provis ions do not require an economic feasibility analysis for individual timber sales (*Citizens for Environmental Quality v. United States,* 731 F.Supp. 970 (D. Colo. 1989)) and do not prohibit "below cost" timber sales that include road construction costs (*Thomas v. Peterson,* 753 F.2d 754 (9th Cir. 1985); *Big Hole Ranchers Ass'n, Inc. v. U.S. Forest Service,* 686 F.Supp. 256 (D.Mont. 1988)). The courts also have been reluctant to review regional road construction funding policies, even those that give priority to construction in roadless areas (*National Wildlife Federation v. Coston,* 773 F.2d 1513 (9th Cir. 1985)). But if forest planners select a management alternative with a comparatively low present net value, the NFMA requires them to explain why that alternative was selected over one with a higher present net value (*Citizens for Environmental Quality v. United States,* 731 F.Supp. 970 (D. Colo. 1989)). And the courts have sustained the Forest Service's power to close roads or trails to off-road vehicle use to minimize recreational conflicts (*Northwest Motorcycle Ass'n v. U.S. Dept. of Agriculture,* 18 F.3d 1468 (9th Cir. 1994)), which suggests similar authority might be invoked to address fragmentation concerns related to road use. Moreover, the Forest Service has announced a moratorium on new road construction into roadless areas while the agency reformulates its roading policies to address environmental, safety, and fragmentation concerns (Fed. Register, January 28, 1998, pp. 4350–4354).

National Environmental Policy Act

The National Environmental Policy Act of 1969 establishes explicit procedural requirements governing all federal agencies to ensure environmentally informed decisions and public disclosure. Under NEPA, federal agencies are required to prepare an Environmental Impact Statement (EIS) before taking any major action that significantly affects the human environment (42 U.S.C. § 4332(2)(C)). The Council on Environmental Quality has promulgated detailed regulations implementing NEPA obligations, which are designed to promote comprehensive environmental analysis of proposed federal actions (40 C.F.R. § 1500 et seq.). These NEPA procedural obligations have been subject to rigorous judicial enforcement, making NEPA the principal vehicle that courts have used to review both planning and project-level forest management decisions. However, the courts have clearly ruled that NEPA is primarily a procedural statute; it does not impose substantive limitations on forest management decisions (*Robertson v. Methow Valley Citizens Council*, 490 U.S. 332 (1989)).

The courts have used NEPA to address both forest fragmentation and cumulative impact issues. The Ninth Circuit Court of Appeals has ruled that the Forest Service must analyze the impact of proposed timber sales on wildlife corridors connecting the sale areas, a decision that should ensure fragmentation concerns are identified and addressed in the environmental analysis process (*Marble Mountain Audubon Society v. Rice*, 914 F.2d 179 (9th Cir. 1990)). The same court, however, has also ruled that the NFMA does not require the Forest Service to ensure connectivity in its forest plans; rather, the agency can address connectivity concerns in its project-level decisions under the minimum viable population regulation (*Oregon Natural Resources Council v. Lowe*, 109 F.3d 521 (9th Cir. 1997)). Regarding cumulative impacts, several courts have construed NEPA to require analysis of both the spatial and temporal environmental impacts of proposed federal actions (Keiter 1990). The Forest Service, for example, is required to consider and analyze the aggregate impacts of linked or concurrent projects, such as timber harvesting and road construction, in a single EIS and not to segment its analysis of the environmental impacts (e.g., *Thomas v. Peterson*, 753 F.2d 754 (9th Cir. 1985); *Neighbors of Cuddy Mountain v. U.S. Forest Service*, 137 F.3d 1372 (9th Cir. 1998)). The Forest Service also must disclose and consider the cumulative environmental impacts of activities occurring on adjacent lands when assessing related timbering, roading, and other projects, but not necessarily at the forest planning stage (*Resources Limited, Inc. v. Robertson*, 8 F.3d 1394 (9th Cir. 1993)). However, the courts have not required the Forest Service to extend its NFMA-based minimum viable population analysis to adjacent, nonfederal lands (*Inland Empire Public Lands Council v. U.S. Forest Service*, 88 F.3d 754 (9th Cir. 1996)).

Endangered Species Act

The Endangered Species Act establishes a clear national priority to protect species against extinction (*Tennessee Valley Authority v. Hill*, 437 U.S. 153 (1978)). Administered by the U.S. Fish and Wildlife Service (FWS) in the interior West, the ESA imposes a broad conservation obligation on all federal agencies (16 U.S.C. § 1536(a); France and Tuholske 1986). Key to application of the ESA is the initial listing decision: utilizing the best available scientific information, the FWS is obligated to determine whether a species is either endangered or threatened "throughout all or a significant portion of its range" due to destruction of its habitat, commercial exploitation, or related reasons (16 U.S.C. § 1533(a); *Northern Spotted Owl v. Hodel*, 716 F.Supp. 479 (W.D. Wash. 1988); Doremus 1997). Once a listing decision is made, the Secretary of the Interior must also designate critical habitat (*Northern Spotted Owl v. Lujan*, 758 F.Supp. 621 (W.D. Wash. 1991); Yagerman 1990). And once a species is listed, federal land management agencies must consult with the FWS to determine if proposed agency actions, such as timber sales or road construction projects, might jeopardize that species' continued existence or adversely modify its critical habitat (16 U.S.C. § 1536(b); *Thomas v. Peterson*, 753 F.2d 754 (9th Cir. 1985)). Moreover, the ESA prohibits anyone, whether on public or private land, from "taking" an endangered species by any means, which includes habitat modification that results in direct injury to species members by altering essential breeding, feeding, or sheltering behavior (16 U.S.C. § 1538(a)(1); 50 C.F.R. § 17.3; *Babbitt v. Sweet Home Chapter of Communities*, 515 U.S. 687 (1995); Cheever 1991). Thus, the presence of a wide-ranging listed species with diverse habitat needs can limit development activities presenting fragmentation risks, as has occurred with the Northern Spotted Owl, marbled murrelett, and various salmon runs in the Pacific Northwest (Flournoy 1993; Sher 1993; Weaver 1997).

In addressing forest fragmentation concerns in the southern Rockies, however, the ESA has limited application. Unlike the Pacific Northwest, where several wide-ranging, forest-dwelling species have been listed under the ESA, only a few such southern Rockies species are listed as endangered or threatened. The principal listed forest-dwelling species with habitat that extends into the southern Rockies is the Mexican Spotted Owl; other forest-dwelling species found in the Southern Rockies that are being considered for listing include the Canadian lynx and northern goshawk (*Defenders of Wildlife v. Babbitt*, 958 F.Supp.

670 (D.D.C. 1997); *Southwest Center for Biological Diversity v. Babbitt,* 926 F.Supp. 920 (D. Ariz. 1996)). Other than the Mexican Spotted Owl, none of these species has yet had a noticeable impact on logging, roading, or similar fragmentation activities in the southern Rockies (*Colorado Environmental Coalition v. Dombeck,* 185 F.3d 1162 (10th Cir. 1999); *Silver v. Babbitt,* 924 F. Supp. 976 (D. Ariz. 1995)). In Montana, however, the courts have sustained an ESA takings claim against the Forest Service for excessive road density in grizzly bear habitat (*Swan View Coalition, Inc. v. Turner,* 824 F.Supp. 923 (D. Mont. 1992)). Whether recent listing proposals for the Canadian lynx and northern goshawk or whether reintroduction proposals involving the grizzly bear or wolf might impact regional forest management decisions remains to be seen. In the absence of a listed species, of course, the ESA does not apply to forest management decisions, which would then only be required to meet the NFMA's diversity requirements.

Preservation Laws

National parks and other preserved areas, when strategically located, can ameliorate forest fragmentation concerns. For the most part, national parks, wilderness areas, wildlife refuges, and wild and scenic rivers are not subject to intensive development activities; rather, these areas are managed to preserve their natural qualities with minimal human intervention. Under the National Parks Organic Act of 1916 (16 U.S.C. §§ 1–18), the Wilderness Act of 1964 (16 U.S.C. §§ 1331–1340), the National Wild and Scenic Rivers Act of 1968 (16 U.S.C. §§ 1271–1287), and the National Wildlife Refuge System Improvement Act of 1997 (Public Law 105–57), resource managers enjoy broad authority to protect the landscape and to regulate most activities that contribute to fragmentation concerns. The courts have held, for example, that the Park Service may regulate or even prohibit recreational activities that pose a threat to park resources (e.g., *Bicycle Trails Council v. Babbitt,* 82 F.3d 1445 (9th Cir. 1996); *Conservation Law Foundation v. Hodel,* 864 F.2d 954 (1st Cir. 1989)). But these laws do not prohibit every activity that might fragment the landscape. The National Parks Organic Act allows roads and visitor facilities to be constructed within national parks, and the National Wildlife Refuge System Improvement Act only disallows incompatible activities (16 U.S.C. §§ 668dd(a)(3), (d)(3)). Moreover, the Wilderness Act contains grandfather provisions permitting some mining operations and motorized uses to continue within designated wilderness areas (16 U.S.C. §§ 1133(d)(1), (3)), and it authorizes timber harvesting within wilderness boundaries to control insects, fire, and disease (16 U.S.C. § 1133(d)(1); *Sierra Club v. Lyng,* 663 F.Supp. 556 (D.D.C. 1987)).

Nonetheless, the presence of preserved lands can help protect the ecological integrity of large landscapes. Under the NFMA, the ten- to fifteen-year forest planning cycle provides forest managers with an opportunity to reevaluate roadless areas for potential inclusion in the wilderness system and to reconsider undeveloped river corridors for inclusion in the wild and scenic rivers system (36 U.S.C. § 219.17). These recommendations should be viewed as an important tool that can be used to address fragmentation problems. In addition, the NFMA contains interjurisdictional coordination provisions that obligate forest planners to work with nearby national park and wildlife refuge managers to address shared ecological concerns (16 U.S.C. § 1604(a); Keiter 1994). Coordinated planning can—and should—be employed as a means to promote ecological integrity and to minimize fragmentation on the public domain.

Provisos

These laws may be more important collectively than any single law in promoting ecologically sound planning and management to address forest fragmentation concerns. In fact, one court has expressly noted that the aggregate impact of these laws is to sanction ecosystem management on the national forests (*Seattle Audubon Society v. Lyons,* 871 F.Supp. 1291 (W.D. Wash. 1994), *affirmed sub nom., Seattle Audubon Society v. Moseley,* 80 F.3d 1401 (9th Cir. 1996)). However, other laws governing mining, grazing, and related development activities—often dubbed "the lords of yesterday"—can undermine ecological management efforts by granting important private access rights to public resources without regard for the environmental consequences (Wilkinson 1992). Moreover, Congress has the authority to alter environmental laws, which it has done on several occasions through the appropriations process. During the height of the spotted owl controversy, Congress adopted an appropriations rider that effectively prohibited judicial enforcement of the environmental laws governing timber harvesting in the Pacific Northwest (*Robertson v. Seattle Audubon Society,* 503 U.S. 429 (1992)). More recently, Congress added a salvage timber rider to the Rescissions Act of 1995 (16 U.S.C. § 1611 note) that likewise prohibited judicial review under the environmental laws of both salvage sales and green timber sales on the national forests (*Idaho Sporting Congress, Inc. v. U.S. Forest Service,* 92 F.3d 922 (9th Cir. 1996); *Oregon Natural Resources Council v. Thomas,* 92 F.3d 792

(9th Cir. 1996)). Thus, although the existing law contains several interrelated and judicially enforceable provisions that address forest fragmentation problems, Congress has the power to alter these laws through amendments or appropriations riders to override ecological concerns.

Ecosystem Management, Fragmentation, and the Law

For forest management purposes, ecological considerations—including fragmentation and biodiversity concerns—must be addressed at appropriate spatial and temporal scales, which often extend beyond established legal boundaries and conventional, short-term planning cycles. Currently, the concept of ecosystem management is being employed to address these concerns. Although the law does not expressly mandate ecosystem management on the national forests, it can be interpreted to support ecosystem management policy initiatives (Keiter 1994, Interagency Ecosystem Management Task Force 1995*b*). Indeed, while upholding the President's Forest Plan to resolve the bitter Pacific Northwest timber controversy, the federal district court observed that "given the current condition of the forests, there is no way the agencies could comply with the environmental laws without planning on an ecosystem basis" (*Seattle Audubon Society v. Lyons,* 871 F.Supp. 1291, 1311 (W.D. Wash. 1994), *affirmed sub nom., Seattle Audubon Society v. Moseley,* 80 F.3d 1401 (9th Cir. 1996)). This section will define ecosystem management and examine the critical legal issues that it presents as a policy for addressing forest fragmentation concerns.

Ecosystem Management

The Forest Service, along with the other principal federal land management agencies, has adopted ecosystem management as a governing policy. Several different ecosystem management definitions have been advanced, though none has yet been written into law (e.g., Lackey 1998; Christensen et al. 1996; Grumbine 1994; Society of American Foresters 1993). For federal purposes, an interagency task force has defined ecosystem management in the following terms: "a method for sustaining or restoring natural systems and their functions and values. It is goal driven, and it is based on a collaboratively developed vision of desired future conditions that integrates ecological, economic and social factors. It is applied within a geographic framework defined primarily by ecological boundaries." (Interagency Ecosystem Management Task Force 1995*a*). In proposed revisions to its NFMA regulations (which have since been withdrawn), the Forest Service offered its own definition of ecosystem management, tempered by its statutory multiple-use mandate: "a concept of natural resources management wherein National Forest activities are considered within the context of economic, ecological, and social interactions within a defined area over both short- and long-terms" (Fed. Register, April 13, 1995, p. 18920; Thomas and Huke 1996). In short, the ecosystem management concept seeks to better integrate ecological and social considerations in forest management decisions and to expand the spatial and temporal scale at which these decisions are directed.

The concept of ecosystem management has also been refined and clarified through a series of related principles. Notwithstanding disagreements on some points, most observers agree on the basic content of the principles governing ecosystem management (e.g., Interagency Ecosystem Management Task Force 1995*a*; Moote et al. 1994; Grumbine 1994). First, ecosystem management goals must be socially defined through a shared vision process that incorporates ecological, economic, and social considerations (Moote et al. 1994; Cortner et al. 1994). Second, given that most ecosystems transcend conventional boundaries, ecosystem management requires coordination among federal, state, tribal, and local entities as well as collaboration with other interested parties, including private property owners (Shannon 1993; U.S. GAO 1994). Third, ecosystem management is based upon integrated and comprehensive scientific information that addresses multiple rather than single resources (Moote et al. 1994; Grumbine 1994). Fourth, ecosystem management seeks to maintain and restore biodiversity and sustainable ecosystems (Christensen et al. 1996; Grumbine 1994; Keiter 1994). Fifth, ecosystem management involves management at large spatial and temporal scales to accommodate the dynamic and sometimes unpredictable nature of natural processes (Keiter 1994; Cortner 1994). Sixth, because of its experimental nature, ecosystem management requires an adaptive management approach, which includes establishing baseline conditions, monitoring, reevaluation, and adjustment (Interagency Ecosystem Management Task Force 1995*a*; Lee 1993).

The Forest Service, applying these principles, has developed a tiered decision process for implementing ecosystem management on the national forests. Under this system, forest planning takes place at three different scales: the regional, watershed (or forest), and project (or stand) levels. At the regional level, the Forest Service is experimenting with regional assessments that are designed to identify and examine forest resources at an expansive ecological scale, as well as related social and economic trends. In several instances, these regional assessments are being done in conjunction with other federal land management agencies, with participation from state and local governments as well as other interested parties. The goal is to use the assessment data to revise forest management plans. The Interior Columbia Basin Ecosystem Management Project, which has involved both the Forest Service and Bureau of Land Management, is perhaps the best known and most advanced of these regional initiatives (e.g., USDA Forest Service and USDI BLM 1997). At the forest level, the Forest Service is obligated under the NFMA to develop and revise forest management plans, which have been used to zone national forests according to resource uses and to establish management priorities over a ten- to fifteen-year planning cycle. At the project level, the Forest Service then implements its forest plans through such site-specific decisions as individual timber sales, road construction contracts, and other management decisions. This expanded three-stage decision process is designed to enable forest managers to address fragmentation and related concerns at an appropriate ecological scale and to devise effective management strategies to maintain or restore ecosystem integrity.

The Emerging Law of Ecosystem Management

This three-stage approach to forest management, however, raises myriad legal issues that are just being addressed by the agencies and the courts. A threshold issue, with this extended planning and implementation process, is to determine when judicial review is appropriate. A second important issue, given the greatly expanded scale of planning, involves how to integrate the principal laws governing forest management—namely NFMA, NEPA, and ESA—into this spatially and temporally extended decision process. A third and related issue is how to integrate these same laws into an adaptive management process, which presupposes that management decisions are contingent, and thus subject to revision to accommodate new information. Although some answers are emerging from the courts, others can only be inferred from the laws and related judicial decisions.

Regarding the timing of judicial review, the Supreme Court has recently ruled that forest planning decisions involving alleged timber management NFMA violations generally are not ripe for judicial review until specific project decisions have been made (*Ohio Forestry Association, Inc. v. Sierra Club*, 118 S.Ct. 1665 (1998)). The decision resolves a split among the federal circuits: several courts had held that forest plans may be immediately reviewed because they make initial resource allocation decisions (e.g., *Idaho Conservation League v. Mumma*, 956 F.2d 1508 (9th Cir. 1992); *Sierra Club v. Marita*, 46 F.3d 606 (7th Cir. 1995); *Sierra Club v. Thomas*, 105 F.3d 248 (6th Cir. 1997)), while other courts had held that review was premature at the plan stage because on-the-ground changes only occurred after project-level decisions were made (e.g., *Sierra Club v. Robertson*, 28 F.3d 753 (8th Cir. 1994); *Wilderness Society v. Alcock*, 867 F.Supp. 1026 (N.D. Ga. 1994), *affirmed*, 83 F.3d 386 (11th Cir. 1996)). The Supreme Court, observing that forest plans are elaborate technical documents covering diverse lands and that forest plans may be amended or changed over time, concluded that courts should wait until individual timber sale decisions are made and specific environmental impacts can be assessed before reviewing NFMA claims. Significantly, the Court indicated that NEPA-based challenges to forest plans are ripe for immediate judicial review when plans are completed. In addition, the Court suggested that planning decisions with obvious environmental consequences, such as road construction or road opening decisions, may also be ripe for prompt judicial review. Further litigation in the lower courts will be necessary to clarify the full implications of the *Ohio Forestry Association* ruling. Yet because the ruling indicates that most timber-related forest planning decisions are not subject to immediate judicial review, forest managers may not be fully accountable in a judicial forum for the ecological ramifications of their decisions as the courts have been reluctant to require broad-scale ecological analysis of project-level decisions.

To address forest fragmentation through an ecosystem management approach, temporal and spatial scale considerations must be reconciled with the Forest Service's NFMA, NEPA, and ESA legal obligations. The primary question is what legal obligations attach at each of the three decision levels in this expanded forest planning process. Under the NFMA, forest managers are obligated to ensure consistency between the original forest plan and project-level decisions; both planning and project decisions also must comply with substantive NFMA requirements (*Inland Empire Public Lands Council v. U.S. Forest Service*, 88 F.3d 754, 757 (9th Cir. 1996); *Sierra Club v. Espy*, 38 F.3d 792, 795 (5th Cir. 1994)). To meet these consistency and compliance requirements, forest fragmentation and similar large-scale ecological concerns should be addressed initially at the forest planning stage and then reassessed at the project-level decision stage when individual timber sale, road design, and similar decisions are made. In addition, the NFMA provides that whenever a forest plan is changed to address unanticipated ecological or other concerns, the plan must be formally amended and subsequent—but not ongoing—project-level decisions must then conform with the amended plan (16 U.S.C. § 1604(f)(4); *Forest Guardians v. Dombeck,* 131 F.3d 1309 (9th Cir. 1997)). Forest planners, therefore, should consider tiering their NFMA obligations by addressing fragmentation at both the regional- and forest-level planning stages before binding resource allocation decisions are made.

At the same time, related NEPA and ESA requirements should be met throughout this three-stage decision process. As in the case of forest planning, managers should consider tiering NEPA analyses and ESA consultation obligations. NEPA analyses can be tiered by utilizing EISs, Environmental Assessments, and supplemental EISs to ensure full analysis of the ecological ramifications associated with resource decisions that present potential fragmentation concerns. Under NEPA, forest managers must consider and evaluate the cumulative environmental impacts associated with logging and other activities occurring on adjacent lands, even those that are in private ownership, though managers have discretion to do this analysis either at the programmatic or project level (*Northcoast Environmental Center v. Glickman,* 136 F.3d 660 (9th Cir. 1998); *Resources Ltd., Inc. v. Robertson,* 8 F.3d 1394, 1400–01 (9th Cir. 1994)). Under the Endangered Species Act, forest managers may be required to consult and even reconsult with the FWS at any stage in the decision process, depending upon listing decisions and the biological impacts related to fragmentation. Because the ESA requires forest managers to consult with the FWS whenever listed species might be present, the courts have ruled that new ESA listings require reconsultation on existing forest plans, because these plans constitute ongoing agency actions (*Pacific Rivers Council v. Thomas,* 30 F.3d 1050 (9th Cir. 1994); *Silver v. Babbitt,* 924 F.Supp. 976 (D. Ariz. 1995)). In short, when utilizing ecosystem management as a means to address fragmentation concerns, the Forest Service should be prepared to integrate its NFMA, NEPA, and ESA legal obligations through a complex tiering process to ensure it has fully considered the ecological impacts of its planning and project decisions.

Adaptive management, a critical dimension of ecosystem management, imposes additional legal obligations on land managers responsible for addressing fragmentation concerns. Adaptive management acknowledges that scientific knowledge is often incomplete and uncertain, which means management decisions are often contingent and should be revised as new information is acquired. According to the courts and governing regulations, the Forest Service and other federal land management agencies are required to utilize high quality scientific information to satisfy NEPA and related obligations when making management decisions (40 C.F.R. § 1500.1(b) (1997); *Sierra Club v. U.S. Dep't of Agriculture*, 116 F.3d 1482, 1997 WL 295308, **13 (7th Cir. 1997)). NEPA may not, however, require agencies to engage in an ongoing analysis of environmental consequences once a decision is made. Nevertheless, when new information about the effects of forest fragmentation or other ecological impacts becomes available, managers adhering to adaptive management principles should be prepared to amend existing forest plans, to supplement EIS analyses, and to reconsult with the FWS in order to anticipate and meet NFMA, NEPA, and ESA legal obligations.

The principal tools for implementing adaptive management obligations are inventory and monitoring. Under the NFMA, inventory and monitoring are obligatory (16 U.S.C. § 1604(g)(3)(C); 40 C.F.R. §§ 1505.3); under NEPA, agencies are only obligated to gather information when feasible (40 C.F.R. § 1502.22) and monitoring is only required when necessary to mitigate environmental consequences (40 C.F.R. §§ 1502.2, 1502.3). According to the courts, the NFMA inventory and monitoring obligations attach only when technically and financially feasible (*Inland Empire Public Lands Council v. U.S. Forest Service*, 88 F.3d 754, 762 n.12 (9th Cir. 1996)). However, when confronted with alleged NFMA minimum viable population violations based on excessive logging, the courts have enforced the Forest Service's monitoring obligations. In *Sierra Club v. Glickman* (974 F.Supp. 905 (E.D. Tex. 1997)), the district court concluded that the Forest Service violated its NFMA diversity obligations by relying upon habitat models rather than inventorying and monitoring actual population numbers to ensure minimum viable populations of neotropical songbirds. In *Sierra Club v. U.S. Dep't of Agriculture* (116 F.3d 1482, 1997 WL 295308 (7th Cir. (Ill.))), the court ruled that the Forest Service was required to gather up-to-date population data as part of its monitoring obligations rather than rely upon ten-year-old data to assess the forest plan's impacts on species populations. In sum, the courts view the NFMA and its implementing regulations as imposing affirmative monitoring obligations on forest managers to assess the impacts that logging and other potentially fragmenting activities can have on forest-dwelling species.

Framing Fragmentation Policy

Although the existing law establishes important standards and procedures that can be used to address forest fragmentation concerns, the law does not focus expressly on fragmentation as a central element in forest management policy. For the most part, fragmentation policy is being developed and defined administratively through ecosystem management and related initiatives. As a policy matter, important fragmentation issues are: the role of regional assessments in ecosystem management; the relationship between ecosystem management and consensus-based partnerships; the role of management in maintaining or mimicking natural ecological processes; and the relationship between public and private lands in addressing fragmentation concerns. Although the Forest Service and other federal land management agencies are addressing each of these concerns, Congress has also taken an active interest in them and will undoubtedly influence the policy debate. How these difficult issues are resolved will plainly influence southern Rockies forest fragmentation policy.

Under prevailing ecosystem management policies, regional assessments are becoming a central device for ensuring that the full ecological ramifications (including fragmentation impacts) of past and contemplated management decisions are understood and addressed in the planning process. The Forest Service has undertaken large-scale ecological assessments in the Interior Columbia Basin, High Sierras, and Southern Appalachians, seeking a better understanding of the impacts of past timber harvesting and related resource management policies. Similar large-scale assessments have also been employed elsewhere, including the Greater Yellowstone Ecosystem, northern forests, Great Lakes, and Chesapeake Bay regions. Congress has funded these initiatives, despite reservations over the cost and potential management implications associated with this additional layer of planning. And the Forest Service, in proposed revisions to its NFMA regulations, provided for expanded ecosystem analysis as part of the forest planning process, though these proposed changes have now been withdrawn. Moreover, Congress is considering comprehensive amendments to the NFMA that would acknowledge a role for ecosystem management (S. 1253), but the Forest Service has resisted congressional efforts to revise the existing forest planning system in favor of administrative modifications. Despite the fluidity of this situation, most observers generally agree that ecosystem-based analysis can improve forest planning and decisions. Thus, forest managers concerned about fragmentation in the Southern Rockies might consider initiating a regional assessment to identify fragmentation problems and to begin devising ecologically sound solutions.

As part of ecosystem management policy, the Forest Service and other public land management agencies have promoted the concept of cooperative stewardship, which entails using consensus-based processes to resolve difficult resource management issues. Examples of recent consensus processes include the Quincy Library Group in the central Sierra Nevada region, the Applegate Partnership in southwestern Oregon, and the Malpais Borderlands Group in southern Arizona and New Mexico (Keystone Center 1996; Yaffee et al. 1996). Although still quite controversial (Coggins 1998; Duane 1997), consensus-based partnerships acknowledge that human values play a major role in formulating natural resource policy and that local consensus on management priorities can produce more durable solutions and avoid the costs associated with administrative appeals or litigation (Keystone Center 1996; Brick 1998). Consensus-based processes also can bring private landowners into ecosystem-oriented discussions, thus creating an opportunity to integrate public and private lands for management purposes. Congress has put a partial stamp of approval on this dimension of ecosystem management by amending the Federal Advisory Committee Act (5 U.S.C. Appendix 2) to exempt state and local governments from the statute's rigorous procedural requirements (2 U.S.C. § 1534; McHarg 1995; Lynch 1996). In addition, Congress has passed legislation legitimizing the Quincy Library Group's forest management proposal for three central Sierra Nevada national forests; it addresses regional forest health problems through revised timber harvesting policies and the use of fuel breaks and prescribed fire (Fed. Register, Dec. 21, 1998, p. 70383; Marston 1997; Duane 1997). A similar consensus-based partnership initiative might be used to address southern Rockies forest fragmentation concerns, so long as the group's mission is clearly defined as reducing fragmentation to enhance ecological objectives.

In the southern Rockies, most forest fragmentation problems can be traced to human-caused disturbances, such as excessive logging, roading, and exurban development. Without such disturbances, most scientists believe that naturally evolving ecological processes would not have created such serious fragmentation problems. For forest managers, therefore, a key question is whether to rely primarily upon natural processes to solve fragmentation problems or whether to engage in intensive management to reduce fragmentation. A vital underlying concern, of course, is the appropriate human role in nature: biocentrists argue that human intervention cannot improve on natural processes, while anthropocentrists believe science can—and must—be employed to manage nature's unpredictable processes and to address negative human legacies such as excessive logging and roading. Several recent forest management proposals, including the Quincy Library Group legislation and the Interior Columbia Basin Draft EIS's preferred alternative, provide for more intensive management, including increased timber harvesting and prescribed fire, to improve forest health. Congress, however, recently defeated a proposed forest health bill that provided for accelerated salvage logging to reduce fire danger and insect damage in the western forests (H.R. 2515). If the goal is to reduce forest fragmentation, managers should not assume that intensive timber management is necessary, though active restoration efforts may be required to eliminate roads and other development scars that exacerbate fragmentation problems.

A comprehensive approach to the southern Rockies forest fragmentation problems must address management on both public and private lands. But federal natural resources law, except for the ESA's taking provision (16 U.S.C. §1538(a)), generally does not apply to private lands. Instead, state and local zoning and planning laws define ownership rights and govern development options on private lands (Keiter 1998), and the southern Rockies states have notoriously resisted strong zoning or planning requirements. These states also have not adopted strong forest practices legislation to regulate private timber lands and harvesting techniques (e.g., Endter-Wada and Dennis-Perez 1997). Moreover, with the U.S. Supreme Court's revitalization of Fifth Amendment takings doctrine (e.g., *South Carolina Coastal Council v. Lucas,* 505 U.S. 1003 (1992)) and Congress's continued interest in federal takings legislation to enhance private property rights protections (S. 781, H.R. 1534), government officials at all levels—federal, state, and local—have been increasingly reluctant to promote ecologically-based regulatory measures to address fragmentation or related concerns on private lands. Nonetheless, the FWS has employed the ESA's habitat conservation planning provisions to develop regional, cooperative solutions to endangered species problems with private landowners (16 U.S.C. § 1539(a); Ebbins 1997; Kostyack 1997). Congress may enshrine a modified version of this process into law through proposed ESA amendments (S. 1180; H.R. 2351; Ruhl 1998). Even without the compulsion of the ESA, similar cooperative approaches involving federal and state forest managers as well as private landowners may provide an effective technique for integrating private lands into a regional Southern Rockies forest fragmentation policy.

Clearly, framing an effective forest fragmentation policy for the Southern Rocky Mountains will raise difficult legal issues and pose tough policy choices. Nevertheless, the law provides some guidance in addressing fragmentation concerns. The law can be employed to promote ecosystem management in the southern Rockies national forests, which can—and should perhaps—include preparation of a regional fragmentation assessment. The law also can be used to encourage and facilitate potentially affected parties to participate in cooperative processes for formulating a regional fragmentation policy. Other related national policies, including the Forest Service's recent moratorium on new road construction, provide an opportunity to reassess regional roading policies with a view toward reducing fragmentation. Any regional forest fragmentation policy, however, must be consistent with existing law and cannot ignore that Congress has oversight responsibilities for public lands policy. But within this framework, there is substantial opportunity under the prevailing law to elevate fragmentation on the southern Rocky Mountain forest management agenda and to devise effective policies promoting ecological integrity.

LITERATURE CITED

Brick, P. 1998. Of imposters, optimists, and kings. *Chronicle of Community* 2(2): 34–38.

Cheever, F. 1991. An introduction to the prohibition against takings in section 9 of the Endangered Species Act: learning to live with a powerful species preservation law. *University of Colorado Law Review* 62: 109–199.

Cheever, F. 1998. Four failed forest standards: what we can learn from the history of the National Forest Management Act's substantive timber management provisions *Oregon Law Review* 77: 601–705.

Christensen, N., A. Bartuska, J. Brown, S. Carpenter, C. D'Antonio, R. Francis, J. Franklin, J. MacMahon, R. Noss, D. Parsons, C. Peterson, M. Turner, and R. Woodmansee. 1996. The report of the Ecological Society of America committee on the scientific basis for ecosystem management. *Ecological Applications* 6: 665–691.

Coggins, G. 1998. Of Californicators, quislings and crazies. *Chronicle of Community* 2(2): 27–34.

Cortner, H.J. 1994. Intergovernmental coordination in ecosystem management. Pages 229–242 *in* U.S. Senate, Committee on Environment and Public Works. *Ecosystem management: status and potential.* Senate Print 103–98. Congressional Research Service. U.S. Government Printing Office, Washington, D.C., USA.

Cortner, H. J., M. A. Shannon, M. G. Wallace, S. Burke, and M. Moote. 1994. *Institutional barriers and incentives for ecosystem management: a problem analysis.* Water Resources Center, University of Arizona, Tucson, Arizona, USA.

Doremus, H. 1997. Listing decisions under the Endangered Species Act: why better science isn't always better policy. *Washington University Law Quarterly* 75: 1029–1153.

Duane, T. 1997. Community participation in ecosystem management. *Ecology Law Quarterly* 24: 771–797.

Ebbins, M. 1997. Is the southern California approach to conservation succeeding? *Ecology Law Quarterly* 24: 695–706.

Endter-Wada, J., and L. Dennis-Perez. 1997. Protection or infringement of property rights? addressing concerns regarding nonfederal forest lands in Utah. *Journal of Land, Resources and Environmental Law* 17: 11–44.

Flournory, A. 1993. Beyond the "Spotted Owl problem": learning from the old-growth controversy. *Harvard Environmental Law Review* 17: 261–332.

France, T., and J. Tuholske. 1986. Stay the hand: new directions for the Endangered Species Act. *Public Land Law Review* 7: 1–19.

Grumbine, R.E. 1994. What is ecosystem management? *Conservation Biology* 8: 27–38.

Interagency Ecosystem Management Task Force. 1995 a. *The ecosystem approach: healthy ecosystems and sustainable economies. Volume I. Overview.* National Technical Information Service, Springfield, Virginia, USA.

Interagency Ecosystem Management Task Force. 1995 b. *The ecosystem approach: healthy ecosystems and sustainable economies. Volume II. Implementation issues.* National Technical Information Service, Springfield, Virginia, USA.

Keiter, R. 1990. NEPA and the emerging concept of ecosystem management on the public lands. *Land and Water Law Review* 25: 43–60.

Keiter, R. 1994. Beyond the boundary line: constructing a law of ecosystem management. *University of Colorado Law Review* 65: 293–333.

Keiter, R. 1998. Ecosystems and the law: toward an integrated approach. *Ecological Applications* 8: 332–341.

Keystone Center. 1996. *Keystone national policy dialogue on ecosystem management: implementing community-based approaches.* Keystone Center, Keystone, Colorado, USA.

Kostyack, J. 1997. Reshaping habitat conservation plans for species recovery: an introduction to a series of articles on habitat conservation plans. *Environmental Law* 27: 755–765.

Lackey, R. 1998. Seven pillars of ecosystem management. *Landscape and Urban Planning* 40: 21–30.

Lee, K. N. 1993. *Compass and gyroscope: integrating science and politics for the environment.* Island Press, Covelo, CA and Washington, D.C., USA.

Lynch, S. 1996. The Federal Advisory Committee Act: an obstacle to ecosystem management by federal agencies. *Washington Law Review* 71: 431–459.

Marston, E. 1997. The timber wars evolve into a divisive attempt at peace. *High Country News.* Sep. 17: 1. Paonia, Colorado, USA.

McHarg, H. 1995. The Federal Advisory Committee Act: keeping interjurisdictional ecosystem management groups open and legal. *Journal of Energy, Natural Resources, and Environmental Law* 15: 437–472.

Moote, M. A., S. Burke, H. J. Cortner, and M. G. Wallace. 1994. *Principles of ecosystem management.* Water Resources Research Center, University of Arizona, Tucson, Arizona, USA.

Ruhl, J. 1998. While the cat's asleep: the making of the "new" ESA. *Natural Resources and Environment* 12: 187–190.

Shannon, M. A. 1993. Community governance: an enduring institution of democracy. Pages 219–246 *in* U.S. Congress House of Representatives, Committee on Interior and Insular Affairs. *Multiple use and sustained yield: changing philosophies for federal land management.* Print Number 11. U.S. Government Printing Office, Washington, D.C., USA.

Sher, V. 1993. Travels with Strix: the spotted owl's journey through the federal courts. *Public Land Law Review* 14: 41–80.

Society of American Foresters. 1993. *Task force report on sustaining long-term forest health and productivity.* Society of American Foresters, Bethesda, Maryland, USA.

Thomas, J. W., and S. Huke. 1996. The Forest Service approach to healthy ecosystems. *Journal of Forestry* 94(8): 14–18.

United States Department of Agriculture (USDA) Forest Service, and United States Department of Interior (USDI) Bureau of Land Management (BLM). 1997. *An assessment of ecosystem components in the interior Columbia basin and portions of the Klamath and Great Basins.* Volumes I–IV. Pacific Northwest Research Station, Portland, Oregon, USA.

United States General Accounting Office (U. S. GAO). 1994. *Ecosystem management: additional actions needed to adequately test a promising approach.* GAO/RCED-94-111. U.S. General Accounting Office, Washington, D.C., U.S.A.

Weaver, T. 1997. Litigation and negotiation: the history of salmon in the Columbia river basin. *Ecology Law Quarterly* 24: 677–87.

Wilkinson, C. F. 1992. *Crossing the next meridian: land, water, and the future of the West.* Island Press, Washington, D.C., USA.

Wilkinson, C., and M. Anderson. 1985. Land and resource planning in the National Forests. *Oregon Law Review* 64: 1–373.

Yaffee, S., A. Phillips, I. Frentz, P. Hardy, S. Maleki, and B. Thorpe. 1996. *Ecosystem management in the United States.* Island Press, Washington, D.C., USA.

Yagerman, K. 1990. Protecting the critical habitat under the federal Endangered Species Act. *Environmental Law* 20: 811–856.

20

What Have We Learned about Forest Fragmentation in the Southern Rocky Mountains?

William H. Romme, Richard L. Knight, William L. Baker,
Frederick W. Smith, and Steven W. Buskirk

This book grew out of the symposium on forest fragmentation that was held at Colorado State University in Fort Collins in November, 1997. The goal of that symposium, and of this book, was to summarize the state of our knowledge about forest fragmentation in the Southern Rocky Mountain region, to identify threats to biodiversity and ecosystem integrity that may be caused by forest fragmentation, and to recommend the most urgent research and management priorities.

As Buskirk et al. point out in Chapter 1, forest fragmentation is a paradigm that originated in other landscapes that were characterized by nearly continuous forest cover prior to intensive land use by Euro-Americans. We need to be cautious about applying concepts developed in these other regions to the naturally heterogeneous landscapes of the Rocky Mountains. Even in the absence of human effects, these mountain forests would be patchy, as a result of pronounced gradients and discontinuities in environmental factors such as soil type and microclimate (Knight and Reiners, *this volume*) as well as chronic natural disturbances by fire, insects, and weather (Veblen, *this volume*). In fact, the pervasive natural patchiness of our region has led some to question whether forest fragmentation is really even a serious issue in the Southern Rocky Mountains. We conclude that it is, because superimposed upon this natural patchiness are new anthropogenic landscape patterns and processes created by logging, road-building, exurban development, and associated activities such as recreation and livestock grazing. It is with the causes and implications of these new kinds of fragmentation within an already patchy landscape that this book is primarily concerned.

We have learned much about some aspects of anthropogenic forest fragmentation in our region. We now have some excellent conceptual and computational tools for quantifying spatial patterns in landscapes (Baker, *this volume*), and we have begun to develop useful simulation models with which we can explore the likely consequences of alternative management strategies (Tinker and Baker, *this volume*). Quantitative analyses of landscape structure conducted to date suggest a general syndrome of forest fragmentation in our region, in which a landscape of relatively few large patches of old forest containing much interior area, is transformed into a landscape of many smaller and often younger patches containing little interior area and much edge (Baker, *this volume*). Simulation modeling suggests that, if the rates and practices of timber harvesting that characterized the last few decades are continued, this syndrome will be played out to the point where little of the original old, interior forest remains in at least some portions of the Southern Rocky Mountains (Tinker and Baker, *this volume*).

We also know something about how some organisms respond to forest landscape patterns, particularly birds, a few mammals, and some vascular plants (Beauvais, *this volume*; Hansen and Rotella, *this volume*; Baker and Dillon, *this volume*; Ruefenacht and Knight, *this volume*; Carter and Gillihan, *this volume*). We understand some of the principal causes of forest fragmentation in the Southern Rocky Mountains, including the conspicuous effects of logging, as well as the less obvious but significant effects of road-building, recreational activities, and exurban development (Baker and Knight, *this volume*; Smith, *this volume*; Knight, *this volume*; Theobald, *this volume*; Baker, *this volume*; Lowsky and Knight, *this volume*; Shinneman and Baker, *this volume*). We have learned that in some parts of our region (e.g., in some low-elevation forests) the trend during the last century actually has not been forest fragmentation so much as coalescence and homogenization of formerly patchy forests as a result of fire exclusion and early logging practices (Veblen, *this volume*; Smith, *this volume*; Romme et al., *this volume*).

However, there is still much that we do not know. Our book has no chapter on the effects of logging, road-building, exurban development, or recreation on the small creatures—soil fungi and bacteria, bryophytes, invertebrates, reptiles, and amphibians—that may play crucial roles in ecosystem function (Perry and Amaranthus 1997). The reason for our inadequate treatment of these taxa is simply the paucity of research to date on their ecological roles and responses to fragmentation. The limited research that has been conducted on the less conspicuous wildlife species indicates that some, such as land snails, are very vulnerable to adverse effects from logging, grazing, and road-building (Frest and Johannes 1993). Even for the larger species of wildlife, which have received far more attention than the smaller organisms, most previous research has been conducted without reference to the context or processes of anthropogenic change in these ecosystems. The chapters in this book on responses of plants and birds to fragmentation (Baker and Dillon, *this volume*; Ruefenacht and Knight, *this volume*) are among the first efforts to explicitly evaluate the effects of high-contrast edges (produced by roads and timber harvests) on the native organisms of our region.

It appears that no vertebrate or vascular plant species has yet been extirpated from the Southern Rocky Mountains by the effects of forest fragmentation, although the lynx is a possibility. However, we may not yet have seen the long-term effects of past land use activity in these ecosystems where short growing seasons and long life spans of dominant species combine to produce slow responses, as perceived by humans, to changes in landscape pattern (Baker and Dillon, *this volume*). Moreover, the nascent theory of meta-population dynamics teaches us that mere presence of a species in an area is no indication of long-term population viability (McCullough 1996, Hanski and Gilpin 1997). We know almost nothing about the spatial patterning of source and sink habitats for native species in the Southern Rocky Mountains, but the little we do know suggests that some of our most intensive land use activities (e.g., logging, outdoor recreation, exurban development, and road systems) may be concentrated in places (e.g., riparian areas and highly productive forests) that are critical for long-term viability of some wildlife species (Baker and Knight, *this volume*; Knight, *this volume*; Hansen and Rotella, *this volume* and *in press*).

We have much experience in manipulating forest ecosystems to meet short-term needs and desires, but the combination of craft and science that we need to manage Rocky Mountain ecosystems for long-term ecological integrity, is in its infancy. Plenty of good ideas are available to work with in this regard, based on principles of landscape design and an understanding of the natural disturbance processes that characterize our region (Knight and Reiners, *this volume*; Baker and Knight, *this volume*; Baker, *this volume*; Aplet, *this volume*; Romme et al., *this volume*; Armstrong, Epilogue). However, we need to acknowledge the uncertainties and the experimental nature of all forest management, and implement these new techniques in an explicit framework of adaptive management (Holling 1978, Walters 1986, Christensen et al. 1996). The need for adaptive management is especially pressing in the context of global climate change, which was not explicitly treated in this book, but which has the potential to greatly confound our attempts to understand and ameliorate the effects of anthropogenic fragmentation (Baron et al., *in preparation*).

There is an urgent need for research to document the effects of human land use—past, present, and future—on biodiversity and ecological integrity of Rocky Mountain forest ecosystems. But as we prepare to plunge into specific studies, we also need to step back and make sure that we are asking all of the important questions. Much of our thinking thus far about human impacts on Rocky Mountain forests has focused on the effects of logging, grazing, mining, and roads. Indeed, clearcutting is perhaps the most conspicuous form of forest fragmentation in our region, and timber production probably was (along with its associated road building) the most important fragmentation process in this region during the 1950s–1980s (Baker, *this volume*). However, the Mountain West is now undergoing profound changes in demography, economics, and social expectations, and this change has been especially rapid during the last decade (Knight 1997, Riebsame et al. 1997, Romme 1997). If current trends continue, the major anthropogenic stresses on Rocky Mountain forest ecosystems during the next half-century may be very different from those of the last half-century. Researchers, managers, and forest users need to make sure that we are not so preoccupied with the problems of the past that we fail to recognize the crucial new issues that are now erupting in the Mountain West.

The human population in the western states that encompass the Southern Rocky Mountains is now growing more rapidly than the populations in many third-world nations. And these people are moving not just to the cities. During the 1980s, the nonurban counties of the American West grew more rapidly than either the regional metropolitan areas or the nation as a whole (Knight 1997). One of the predominant forms of new housing development in the West today is the "ranchette"—a large home on a large lot far from the nearest town. The most popular sites for ranchettes are scenic locations near public lands. City dwellers also have increasing wealth and mobility with which to enjoy recreating in nearby (or even relatively distant) national forests and parks (Riebsame et al. 1997). The ecological impacts of these new land development patterns and recreational trends on wildland ecosystems of the Southern Rocky Mountains are virtually unexplored—but potentially enormous (Romme 1997, Knight and Clark 1998).

This is not to downplay the importance of continued research and development of new strategies to minimize the fragmenting effects of timber production and road construction in Rocky Mountain forests. There are good reasons to expect, or at least hope, that traditional economic activities will continue into the next century (Knight 1997). We need new management techniques and a new emphasis on landscape-scale ecological design to mitigate some of the undesirable effects of logging and grazing and to restore ecological structure and processes that have been lost due to past practices (Baker and Knight, *this volume*; Aplet, *this volume*; Romme et al., *this volume*; Kohm and Franklin 1997). The point is simply that the new land uses that are likely to dominate Rocky Mountain forest lands in the twenty-first century—particularly recreation and exurban development—have the potential to disrupt ecological function and native biodiversity as much or even more than the logging and grazing that dominated the twentieth century.

When we build expensive homes in fire-dependent forest ecosystems adjacent to or even within a national forest or park, we not only put human lives and private property at risk of loss to wildfire, we also place serious constraints on the public land manager's ability to implement an ecologically sound prescribed fire program (Knight and Clark 1998). Extensive road systems and homes along the boundary of a tract of public wildlands provide innumerable points of entry into that wildland area for humans, for their dogs and cats, and for the exotic plants and animals that accompany humans. Ever-increasing automobile traffic within and adjacent to public lands means more road-kills, road pollutants (e.g., salt, oil, gasoline), and disruption of traditional wildlife migration and dispersal routes (Baker and Knight, *this volume*). And the mere presence of humans, on roads, hiking trails, and off-trail, may disrupt native plants and wildlife far more significantly than was once thought (Knight, *this volume* and 1997).

So, to return to a question raised at the beginning of this chapter: is forest fragmentation a serious issue in the Southern Rocky Mountains? Yes, it is—but not just for the reasons that come immediately to mind. The fragmenting nature of timber-cutting and road-building are visually conspicuous, even if their long-term effects on biodiversity and ecological integrity are not yet well understood. In addition to this traditional concern, however, the residential developments, nonnative species, and year-round outdoor recreational activities that are springing up within and all around our treasured wildland areas are creating unprecedented landscape patterns that will be with us for a very long time. And this new transformation of the western landscape is occurring at breakneck speed. Researchers, managers, and forest users must not only deal with the traditional forms of forest fragmentation, but also must clearly acknowledge the potential impacts of these new stresses and develop forward-looking strategies to deal with them more effectively than we have so far.

Given our general lack of knowledge about the long-term effects of anthropogenic fragmentation of Rocky Mountain forests, and some of our past experiences, we urge managers to be conservative and cautious when they contemplate new, intensive land uses for the twenty-first century. As Paul Hirt (1994) points out, many of the forest management goals that we pursued so energetically during the second half of the twentieth century, such as liquidation of old-growth forests and development of efficient transportation systems within the forested landscapes of public lands, have been largely accomplished—but with unexpected and unwanted consequences for native biodiversity and ecological integrity. It is a great irony that just at the time that we have nearly achieved that earlier goal of converting our national forests into a network of "managed" stands, society has decided that timber production is no longer the best and highest use of our national forests. A high priority for the twenty-first century probably will be simply to preserve the ecological structure, diversity, and processes of those few remaining areas where Euro-American impact has so far been minimal, to provide benchmarks against which we can measure the effects of our extractive and recreational uses of the land. Another priority will be to restore ecological structure and diversity in those places where human impacts have been especially severe. Indeed, intensive manipulation and alteration of ecosystems and landscapes increasingly will be carried out with a goal of restoring lost ecological capacity rather than of bending a raw nature to our ends.

Aldo Leopold wrote that our most difficult task is learning to use the land without spoiling it (Meine 1995). The chapters in this book suggest that we have not yet learned to use the landscapes of the Southern Rocky Mountains in quite the ways that Leopold would recommend. Nevertheless, as the book's management-oriented chapters suggest, we have great potential to do a better job than we have done in the past. Moreover, our laws and institutional structures, while imperfect, nevertheless provide opportunities and even some mandates to better conserve native biodiversity and ecological integrity (Keiter, *this volume*). Let us hope that we are successful in our efforts to live gently within this very special region. The scenery, biota, history, and natural ecological processes of the Southern Rocky Mountains are unique and significant at a global scale. Hopefully, they will continue to be sources of wonder and spiritual refreshment, as well as utility, for many generations to come.

Literature Cited

Baron, J. S., D. Fagre, and F. R. Hauer, editors. *In preparation. Rocky Mountain futures: an ecological perspective.*

Christensen, N. L., A. M. Bartuska, J. H. Brown, S. Carpenter, C. D'Antonio, R. Francis, J. F. Franklin, J. A. MacMahon, R. F. Noss, D. J. Parsons, C. H. Peterson, M. G. Turner, and R. G. Woodmansee. 1996. The report of the Ecological Society of America committee on the scientific basis for ecosystem management. *Ecological Applications* 6: 665–691.

Frest, T. J., and E. J. Johannes. 1993. Land snail survey of the Black Hills National Forest, South Dakota and Wyoming. Final Report to U.S. Forest Service and U.S. Fish and Wildlife Service, Deixis Consultants, Seattle, Washington, USA.

Hansen, A., and J. Rotella. *In press.* Abiotic factors. *In* M. Hunter, editor. *Managing forests for biodiversity.* Cambridge University Press, Cambridge, UK.

Hanski, I. A., and M. E. Gilpin, editors. 1997. *Metapopulation biology: ecology, genetics, and evolution.* Academic Press, San Diego, California, USA.

Hirt, P. 1994. *A conspiracy of optimism: management of the national forests since World War Two.* University of Nebraska Press, Lincoln, Nebraska, USA.

Holling, C. S. 1978. *Adaptive environmental assessment and management.* John Wiley and Sons, New York, New York, USA.

Kohm, K. A., and J. F. Franklin, editors. 1997. *Creating a new forestry for the 21st century: the science of ecosystem management.* Island Press, Washington, D.C., USA.

Knight, R. L. 1997. Field report from the new American West. Pages 181–200 *in* C. Meine, editor. *Wallace Stegner and the continental vision: essays on literature, history, and landscape.* Island Press, Washington, D.C., USA.

Knight, R. L., and T. W. Clark. 1998. Boundaries between public and private lands: defining obstacles, finding solutions. Pages 175–191 *in* R. L. Knight and P. B. Landres, editors. *Stewardship across boundaries.* Island Press, Washington, D.C., USA.

McCullough, D. R., editor. 1996. *Metapopulations and wildlife conservation.* Island Press, Washington, D.C., USA.

Meine, C. 1995. The oldest task in human history. Pages 7–35 *in* R. L. Knight and S. F. Bates, editors. *A new century for natural resources management.* Island Press, Washington, D.C., USA.

Perry, D. A., and M. P. Amaranthus. 1997. Disturbance, recovery, and stability. Pages 31–56 *in* K. A. Kohm and J. F. Franklin, editors. *Creating a new forestry for the 21st century: the science of ecosystem management.* Island Press, Washington, D.C., USA.

Riebsame, W. E., H. Gosnell, and D. Theobald. 1997. *Atlas of the new West: portrait of a changing region.* W. W. Norton & Company, New York, New York, USA.

Romme, W. H. 1997. Creating pseudo-rural landscapes in the Mountain West. Pages 139–162 *in* J. Nassauer and D. Karasov, editors. *Placing nature: culture and landscape ecology.* Island Press, Washington, D. C., USA.

Walters, C. J. 1986. *Adaptive management of renewable resources.* Macmillan, New York, New York, USA.

21

Epilogue

Conservation of Wildlife in Rocky Mountain Forests: Process, Pattern, and Perspective

David M. Armstrong

Wander for a moment somewhere in the Rockies and think about connections—processes and patterns, antecedents and consequences. Wander on your own if you choose (for all landscapes have stories to tell), but I am thinking back to autumn and I am thinking of a forest, a forest that only last century would have been a woodland, its trees larger, fire-spaced.

In today's forest are stumps, some sawed, blue-stained, flat-topped; some roughly peaked, ax-cut; some charred and irregular. The flat-topped stumps are no larger around than salad plates; the peaked stumps are the size of dinner plates; the burned stumps are of various sizes but some once supported trees I could not have reached around (and we think we discovered memory).

As forests have changed, opportunities for wildlife have changed as well: more shade, more moisture, more understory, more long-tailed voles. But bright green clusters of needles beneath some remnant trees are proof-positive that Abert's squirrels still lurk nearby; and bare brown duff beneath other trees, uncluttered with green needles, labels them as unpalatable, protected, reflecting patterns of genetic heterogeneity and consequent patterns of monoterpenes.

In the forest is a meadow, cradled gently in the rugged granite elbow of a pine-clad ridge. Broad outlines of the topography must date at least to the Pleistocene, but what started the crack that made the gulch that captured the silt that slowed the drainage and allowed the meadow (and prime habitat for pocket gophers)? Perhaps a particularly dry Precambrian afternoon.

Off across the meadow is a curiously orderly line of currants, running straight downhill from a large old ponderosa, the bushes spaced at eight feet on center. Rectilinear is a surveyor's pattern, a farmer's pattern. Why plant currants, and why plant them here? Closer at hand are hints, as there usually are. Inside some of the shrubs are the stumps of pitch posts, their tops long since harvested for kindling. The master pine at the top of the line shows rusty, pinched scars of barbed wire loops long outgrown. Perhaps birds planted the bushes. The rancher a century ago merely planted the posts, changing the landscape mosaic, the mosaic of wildlife opportunity.

Another straight line, hard-edged, divides tough browning grass above from rank green grass below. A little probing tells a tale. A long-forgotten iron pipe has rusted through, and for the past few years or decades has drip-irrigated the ground downslope, etching a straight green line across a south-facing xeriscape, extending the range of meadow voles at the expense of deer mice. Once seen, such a line naturally draws the eye, this time upslope to a patch of rhubarb, shadows, a spring, and a homesteader's midden of rusty cans—tobacco and motor oil for sure, and maybe store-bought beans—the labels have been recycled.

Beans would do poorly here. The season is too cool on the shoulders and fairly short all told. But things do grow, and someone especially enterprising or hungry could clear some meadow, down in the draw where the moisture stays longest, and plant something substantial, like potatoes—plant them down there where the snowberry now grows so thick—and maybe, for awhile, make a go of a piece of land like this.

Earlier Americans would not have stayed here long and would have left little trace as they followed game up and back with the seasons. In a sylvan quiet broken only by a solitaire's song, pattern in forest and meadow summarizes expanding human influence and undue optimism. Trails of hunters and hunted millennia old were a logger's skidtrails in the 1860s, plowed over by Jeffersonian farmers in the 1890s, abandoned in the 1930s, grazed in the 1960s, and ripe for subdivision or conservation in the 1990s. This forest and this meadow have seen some change, and we have imagined only the surface, and only for a moment.

Landscape Ecology: The Eagle's-Eye View. Landscapes are spatially heterogeneous areas, characterized by structure, function, and change (Turner 1989). "Landscape ecology emphasizes broad spatial scales and ecological effects of the spatial patterning of ecosystems. Specifically, it considers (a) the development and dynamics of spatial heterogeneity, (b) interactions and exchanges across heterogeneous landscapes,

(c) the influences of spatial heterogeneity on biotic and abiotic processes, and (d) the management of spatial heterogeneity" (Turner, 1989).

Landscape ecology is the study of "the object spread out beneath an airplane window" (Forman 1995), the ecology "of a mosaic where a cluster of local ecosystems is repeated over a kilometers-wide area" (Forman 1995:39). This scale of view is critically important, but consider the metaphor. Whether pilot or passenger, the typical human, newcomer to an aerial view, may not quite see all there is to see, all that needs to be seen. Let us think of the landscape scale as the "eagle's-eye view." A pre-industrial image feels better, and more important, the eagle sees beyond and beneath the vegetation and keeps an eye on the rest of the wildlife.

Landscape ecology is not quite new (McHarg 1969; Turner 1987, 1989; Forman 1995; Lidicker 1995; Hansson 1995); its complex, multidisciplinary, and macroscopic vision dates back at least to the scientific foundations of wildlife biology (Leopold 1933). Like our visionary forebears, our aim as ecologists, conservation biologists, managers, and citizens should be to see the Southern Rockies whole. Duerksen et al. (1997) wisely observed that conservation biology is not rocket science; but the converse also is true: mere rocket science is not as complex as natural history and conservation biology. The naturalist's practiced eye—the mental macroscope—may be the only tool available to provide the requisite perspective. More than a large-scale view is needed. The useful understanding is multi-dimensional; it is about connections in space and time.

This volume is about fragmentation. Fortunately, in landscape ecology the technical term mostly preserves its common sense: the breaking up of a habitat, ecosystem, or land use type into smaller parcels (Forman 1995; also see Buskirk et al., *this volume*). Fragmentation is a dynamic process in space and time and a measurable feature of landscapes. Landscapes of the Southern Rockies are fragmented at whatever scale one cares to notice. They are heterogeneous on all interesting timeframes. They are heterogeneous naturally and fragmented unnaturally, and we should explore the differences.

What Is Wildlife? Often, the eagle's-eye view is green, a pattern dominated by autotrophs, but the landscape mosaic also is *animated*— it is populated by wildlife sensitive to (and influential in) the pattern. The regional landscape of the Southern Rockies is a mosaic with patches of forest and meadow and much more. "Forest" and "meadow" inspire mental images rich in color and complex dimensionality. Mention of "forest wildlife" should do the same.

When I say wildlife, I mean to say something integrated and complex, something considerably broader—and hopefully deeper—than "elk-deer-bighorn sheep . . . and by the way turkeys." I mean to challenge myself to see wildlife whole. I cannot do that, of course, but that does not mean that I should not cherish the challenge. The challenge of curiosity and remnant ignorance gets us into the field.

By wildlife I mean the sum of co-occurring animal populations, structured by their symbioses (*sensu* Odum 1971—negative, positive, neutral—competition, predation/parasitism, mutualism, etc.), the emergent sum of post-competitive niches of species populations in a place at a time. This view of wildlife is the zoological equivalent of "vegetation." "Vegetation" is a concept with a wealth of connotation. Zoologists should insist on something as rich for animals. Minimally, "vegetation" implies a floristic list, community structure (interaction), and physiognomy—the 3-dimensional geometry of the community. For animals, this construct has been explored only minimally, but its deep exploration would be worthwhile.

For practical reasons (including space and ignorance), having defined wildlife expansively, I will tend to speak mostly of a much more restrictive concept, the fauna, particularly the terrestrial fauna. And rather than saying much about the fauna whole—perhaps 10,000 to 100,000 species—I will tend to focus on a minute, and in many ways aberrant subset of the fauna, the mammals, with fewer than 100 species in the Southern Rockies today (Fitzgerald et al. 1994). As behaviorally complex endotherms, mammals are poor examples in many ways and they are difficult to study, so our ignorance is vast. But even mammals have lessons to share (Schaefer 1992).

Wildlife in the Landscape: Patterns in Space. Life is patterned at all scales of space (Table 21.1), from the invisibly small to the unimaginably large. At conveniently accessible scales, wildlife is not distributed at random. In the long term, and ultimately, species occur where they do because of geologic processes: forests are where they are because the Southern Rockies are where they are (athwart the prevailing Westerlies) because the crust was unstable there, on the western side of a mid-continental craton. On a geographic scale, populations occur where they do because (1) they evolved there (that is, they are autochthonous) or (2) they could get there (that is, their vagility was adequate) and they could stand it (their genetically influenced limits of homeostatic tolerance were such that they could survive and reproduce and thereby become established and eventually become native to the place).

Table 21.1. Scales of space (powers of 10 m) relevant to understanding wildlife in landscapes of the Southern Rocky Mountains.

$m \times 10^n$	Unit	Example (for approximate scale)
4×10^7		diameter of Earth
1.4×10^7		length of American Cordillera (Alaska to Tierra del Fuego)
6		
		extent of Southern Rocky Mountains
5		total canals, conduits, siphons, Colorado-Big Thompson Project
4		landscape scale: extent of eagle's-eye view
		elevation of Mount Elbert (14,433 ft. = 4399 m.)
3	kilometer	dispersal distance of Wyoming ground squirrel
2		flight distance of mule deer
		height of large, old ponderosa pine (unless lightning-struck)
1		
0	meter	length of lynx or wolverine
		length of pine marten, pine squirrel
−1		length of pygmy shrew
−2	centimeter	
		length of ponderosa pine bark beetle
−3	millimeter	breadth of Douglas-fir needle
−4		hairsbreadth; thickness of Colorado hairstreak's wing
−5		diameter of mammalian erythrocyte
−6	micrometer	breadth of virus particle
−7		
−8		breadth of glucose molecule
−9	nanometer	diameter of DNA double helix (2 nm)
−10	Ångstrom unit	diameter of carbon atom

Usually vegetation is the single best predictor of the presence or absence of a particular animal species in a locality ("locality" defined at about any scale). Vegetation provides consuming wildlife with food (directly or indirectly) and often with cover. Habitat selection in some groups of wildlife (ectothermic vertebrates, for example—see Hammerson 1982) is influenced more by physical substrate than by vegetation, but mostly it is vegetation that the naturalist sees: the rattle-snake dens under a sheltering boulder, in the patch of skunkbush at the edge of the ponderosa pine woodland.

Bioregions. Pattern is where we allow ourselves to see it. Bioregions are patterns in the ecosphere as viewed from space—the astronaut's view (Forman 1995). NASA's technological heroics have provided pictures of Earth round and whole and wonderfully patterned. What once was merely imagined now can be seen directly. In bioregional view, the Southern Rockies are an island, a forested fragment cut off from the rest of the western Cordillera and surrounded by a sea of shortgrass and shrub steppe (Bailey 1995).

The wildlife of a place and time is dynamic, not static, not a state but a process. Species populations come and go (the subject-matter of ecology and zoogeography), and species populations change in number (population ecology) and genetic composition (population genetics, evolution). Direct fossil and subfossil evidence of wildlife assemblages of the Southern Rockies is virtually nonexistent: a bit of tooth in a piedmont gravel bar or a piece of bone in a remnant glacier arc about all that is known, so zoogeographic inference may be valuable (Armstrong et al., *in press*).

Wildlife of mid and high elevations of the Southern Rockies represents a relict of the last (Pinedale) full glacial interval (Armstrong 1972; Armstrong et al., *in press*). Presently, many species of higher elevations of the Southern Rockies are "marooned" on a relatively mesic island of montane woodland, subalpine forest, and alpine tundra, surrounded by a "sea" of steppe environments (Armstrong et al., *in press*). Analysis of the distribution of mammals (Armstrong 1972) indicates that strongest faunal relationships of forested habitats are to the west and north, with the Middle Rocky Mountains of northern Utah and western Wyoming (rather than directly to the north along the Continental Divide in Wyoming). Comparable studies have not been done for most other components of wildlife, but there is every reason to imagine that other taxa would exhibit similar patterns (just as the flora does—see Weber 1965, for example).

Because forests and tundra today are islands and archipelagos, principles of island biogeography are useful in understanding and conserving their wildlife. Given the distance of the island from the "mainland" of the Central and Northern Rockies and the boreal forest beyond, however, extinction is likely in many groups, but colonization on time scales of mere centuries and millennia is unlikely for any but the most vagile kinds of wildlife. Therefore, this is nonequilibrium island biogeography (*sensu* Brown 1971).

The Southern Rockies are several mountain ranges, not one, built of different materials at different times, resulting from different geophysical processes and presenting different biotic opportunities (Benedict 1991). Mountain forests are naturally fragmented by passes, valleys, and tundra ridges. Topography influences the movements of animals and hence the flow of genes. The composition of the wildlife differs subtly from one range to another, and there is some reason to believe that there are genetic differences within species between ranges as well (Armstrong 1972, Hafner and Sullivan 1995, Lindsay 1987, Sullivan 1996).

Vertical Heterogeneity. In the Southern Rocky Mountains even the most casual observer has to be impressed by environmental pattern. The Eastern Slope of the Southern Rockies presents one of the most dramatic changes in topography in interior North America. From the Colorado Piedmont to the Divide one can traverse 2,400 m of elevation in less than 30 km, a 7–8% pitch. This is not a steady climb, of course. There is a steep rise to a wide landing about half-way up the slope, and then another steep step to the summits (steps highlighted as pattern in vegetation and consequent wildlife). Rivers heading in glacial cirques cut canyons through the metamorphic basement rock and then slice through the foothills. The inspiring scene has defeated many human intentions, but some cultural achievements have been perpetrated on scales grand enough to see in landscape or even bioregional view (Riebsame et al. 1997, Tyler 1992, Veblen and Lorenz 1991).

From the plains one can see an upper and a lower timberline, and it is easy to imagine the forests as a series of islands (topped with another archipelago of tundra). The present regional landscape was built over 60 million years, by processes as large as regional uplift, block faulting, volcanism, and glaciation; as widespread and recurrent as fire and wind and flood; as local as lichens and gophers and beavers, as germination in a neglected cone cache, or expansion with refreezing of a drop of snowmelt in some minute but critical corner of the fractal geometry of the situation.

Just how individual ecologists have dealt with vertical heterogeneity seems to depend on their taste in categories. Does one emphasize the exceptions or abstract a rule? Does one emphasize the ecophysiological individuality of species along gradients of physical conditions (Whittaker 1975) or categorize the recurring combinations (Merriam 1890; Cary 1911, 1917; Bailey 1932)? Does one see habitat "polygons" soft-edged, coalescent, and informal (Gregg 1964, Knight 1994) or hard-edged and categorical?

In panoramic view, it is not hard to imagine how early ecologists in the West invented a concept of life zones. Life zones are real enough, by inspection. Temperature relates roughly to elevation, and there is a

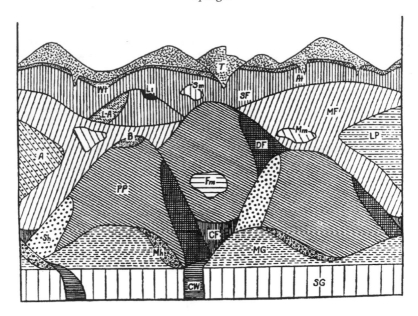

Fig. 21.1. Diagrammatic distribution of vegetation types in the mountains of the Front Range in Boulder County, Colorado. (SG = shortgrass prairie, CW = cottonwood-willow forest, MG = mixed grass prairie, PP = ponderosa pine forest, Sh = mixed shrubs, grass, and yucca, Mh = mountain mahogany brush, CF = canyon forest, Fm = foothills meadow, DF = Douglas fir forest, MF = mixed montane forest, A = aspen forest, LP = lodgepole pine forest, Mm = montane meadow, B = rocky bald, SF = spruce-fir forest, L-A = lodgepole pine-aspen forest, Li = limber pine forest, Sm = subalpine meadow, Wt = wind timber (krummholz), T = tundra, At = avalanche track—from Gregg 1964.)

strong similarity between the insular forests of the Southern Rockies and the "continental" Canadian taiga. Despite their reality at a certain level of abstraction, however, by mid–twentieth century most ecologists had taken a closer look, rejected Merriam's (1890) life zones as theory, and begun to deal with complexity. Sometimes emphasis was on the physical environment that helps to shape the vegetation (Marr 1961), and sometimes emphasis was on wildlife and the habitat patches that supported it. For example, Gregg (1964) sketched a remarkable, macroscopic view (Fig. 21.1) of the Front Range in Boulder County, a pattern of ants and vegetation overlaid on physiography.

Landscapes and Habitat Patches. Within bioregions are landscapes, the eagle's-eye view. Landscapes—at least patches of habitat within the mosaic that is the landscape—often are the mouse's-eye view as well (Armstrong 1977; Beauvais, *this volume*). Scales of space relevant to getting the mouse's-eye view would include points of observation (trapsites), the territory, a daily home range, the lifetime home range (perhaps in plural separate patches no more than a furtive nocturnal dash apart, the patches connected by mouse-scale corridors). Sum this complexity for all of the individual mice of a species and we have a geographic range. What do the mice have to say about the natural patchiness of landscapes in the Southern Rockies?

Consider a representative example. Rocky Mountain National Park, Colorado, is mostly forested, and it is a naturally heterogeneous landscape. Armstrong (1987) tabulated the extant native mammalian fauna of the park (a total of 66 species) across eight biotic community types. Only four species (coyote, long-tailed weasel, striped skunk, mule deer) were indicated (Armstrong 1987) as being typical of all eight community types. Different habitat types support different numbers of species, from 23 (in sagebrush) to 41 (in ponderosa pine woodland). No habitat type supports more than two-thirds of the fauna. The mosaic of patches is critical to the maintenance of the whole fauna. Some habitat types are more similar than others, but generally "it takes all kinds"—all kinds of patches to support all kinds of wildlife. Of course, niches and scale matter greatly. The herbivorous mouse's-eye view is not the carnivorous marten's-eye view (Bissonette and Broekhuizen 1995). A foraging marten may move farther (and through a greater diversity of vegetation) in a night than a lineage of red-backed voles moves in several generations.

Wildlife in the Landscape: Processes in Time. A deer mouse population, a patch of habitat, a landscape—any piece of the ecosphere at any point in time—is a progress report on evolutionary and ecological processes as old as Earth. Nothing in biology makes sense without attention to its history, on timescales from eyeblinks to eons. Time on the scales we need to know may take some imagination. We feel directly only a few of the relevant timescales. Seconds are counting time, the timescales of eye-blinks and heartbeats. My watch provides an analog for minutes, hours, and days, and it has a lifetime guarantee, but lifetimes are too much for most of us to imagine, so how can we know millennia without a metaphor?

Visualize three broadly overlapping brackets of time in the histories that make a difference in the way landscapes appear and operate: evolutionary, ecological, and physiological (Table 21.2). Almost 70 million years back, the crust rose up locally and exposed rocks as old as meiosis (a third the age of Earth), rocks that support last century's

Table 21.2. Some timescales of importance to understanding landscapes of the Southern Rocky Mountains (A = physiological time; B = ecological time; C = evolutionary time).

Timescale	Biological events/processes	Cultural events	Seconds	Years	A	B	C
milliseconds	cycle of echolocatory pulse of little brown bat		4×10^{-7}		—		
	wingbeat of hummingbird		10^{-2}		—		
	eyeblink; little brown bat captures moth		10^{-1}		—		
seconds	heartbeat		10^{0}		—		
minute			6×10^{1}		—		
hour	generation time: bacterium; mitotic cell cycle		3.6×10^{3}		—		
day	sleep cycle of Wyoming ground squirrel		8.6×10^{4}			—	
week	gestation period: deer mouse		6.0×10^{5}			—	
month	generation time: deer mouse		1.8×10^{6}			—	
year	generation time: mule deer; color cycle of ermine		3.15×10^{7}	1×10^{0}		—	
decade	generation time: human		3.15×10^{8}	8×10^{1}		—	
century	lifetime of some people, turtles	Euro-American settlement	3.15×10^{9}	1.4×10^{2}		—	—
millennium	duration of some habitat patches	Fremont Culture	3.15×10^{10}	1×10^{3}			—
	Holocene	human occupation	3.8×10^{11}	1.4×10^{4}			—
	Pleistocene ice ages			2×10^{6}			—
	origin of *Peromyscus*			5×10^{6}			—
	Laramide Orogeny			6×10^{7}			—
	K/T boundary		2×10^{15}	6.5×10^{7}			—
	meiosis/sex		4.7×10^{16}	1.5×10^{9}			—
	life, RNA		1.1×10^{17}	3.5×10^{9}			—
	planet		1.4×10^{17}	4.5×10^{9}			—
	solar system		3.15×10^{17}	1×10^{10}			—
	cosmos (Big Bang)		6.3×10^{17}	2×10^{10}			—

crop of pine trees and last year's crop of pine squirrels. In a view scarcely longer than ecological time, a mountain is a fleeting monument. Twenty thousand years ago, glaciers lay in the mid-elevation valleys of the Southern Rockies, their cirques concentrated around today's treeline. Pinedale glaciation gave general shape to the mountains; the whole of the Pleistocene carved the major canyons. More recent events and processes and lives have added the merest detail. The natural landscapes that we seek to understand and manage are only about 20,000 years old—700 human generations, perhaps 30,000 mouse generations. There are faint hints of migratory human occupation over millennia, but landscapes marked by perennial human influences—"modern" landscapes—are only about 150 years old, and they have been of significant extent for less than a century.

Wildlife as Agents in the Landscape. Wildlife is not simply shaped by the landscape. Rather wildlife species and communities rank along with geophysical and vegetational processes as shapers of the landscape. We can glimpse today a period a century and more past when beaver, over-exploited in the first third of the nineteenth century (Fitzgerald et al. 1994), were absent or negligible as agents in the subalpine landscape. We see this as flood channels a size too large for today's streams and gulches that once were headward-cutting but now are stabilized. Subalpine meadows of the Southern Rockies would not be same without pocket gophers (Armstrong et al., *in press*) and gophers would not be the same without badgers. Pine squirrels and Clark's nutcrackers cache and then forget seeds that germinate into patches of conifers that diversify the landscape mosaic and continue their food supply. The physical effects of ungulates (presently elk, mule deer, and bighorn sheep, but formerly bison as well) have been poorly studied, but surely they are (and have been) important. Trails along and across contours contribute to microrelief. Trampling of vegetation influences the persistence of individual plants and productivity and succession in communities.

Humans as Agents in the Landscape. Since their arrival in the Southern Rockies more than 10,000 years ago, humans have impacted patterns of distribution and abundance of wildlife and its habitat. Impacts have occurred in three broad (and grossly unequal) time-frames: (1) several millennia of subsistence hunting; (2) the nineteenth century, a time of market-exploitation; and (3) the twentieth century, an era of management of species and habitats for increasingly diverse wildlife values: recreational, commercial, scientific, educational, and esthetic (Fitzgerald et al. 1994). Table 21.3 is a chronology of some major events in the recent ecological history of the Southern Rockies. Note especially that the most recent episode—the brief century since the "closing of the frontier"—is less than 1% of the period of human occupation in the Southern Rocky Mountains, a piece of reality that might be dismissed as an aberration, "statistically insignificant."

Landscape heterogeneity is obvious on a wide spectrum of scales of space and time, a universal feature in landscapes of the Southern Rockies, but causes of heterogeneity differ. In simplest terms, some landscape heterogeneity is natural whereas some is anthropogenic.

The sophist would ask immediately, "how can humans, members of the wildlife of the Southern Rockies for over 10,000 years, be considered unnatural? After all, we people are as native to this place as pine martens and pine squirrels—and even some of the pines."

Human impact is easy enough to distinguish. As nature abhors a vacuum, so she shuns straight lines. The fastidious rectitude of roadcuts, powerlines, gaslines, and fencelines, concrete-lined canals, parcel boundaries, city limits, and county lines is unnatural, alien to natural landscapes at any scale larger than the mineralogic. Ecosystems, in their structure and rambunctious functional complexity, are inherently untidy affairs.

The Southern Rockies are fragmented politically and bureaucratically. The Southern Rockies are not quite Colorado's Rockies. There is a private West carved out of a federal West (Riebsame et al. 1997), which was superimposed on an aboriginal West, a seasonally occupied commons, a West once more fluid and curvilinear: Ute Country, Blue Sky Country, the Land of Shining Mountains.

Patterns of heterogeneity sometimes are artifacts of administration, ownership, or management. In the eagle's-eye view there is a difference between national parks and national forests. City limits and county lines sometimes are visible from space, reflecting zoning regulations and even the decisions of individual planners. Plenty of anecdotal evidence suggests that elk can read "No Hunting" signs, sometimes better than license holders. There is a wildland/suburban interface, where soft, curved edges give way to hard, rectilinear perimeters. A fenceline that a coyote can walk beneath might separate grazing regimes that produce habitat patches suitable for Wyoming ground squirrels at one extreme and habitat for montane voles at the other.

Human effects on wildlife have been direct and indirect (Table 21.3). At the level of landscapes (indirect effects), we readily list mining, transportation, forestry, watershed manipulation (storage, channelization, transmountain diversion), and recreational, residen-

Table 21.3. Major events in the recent history of the wildlife of the Southern Rockies (after Fitzgerald et al. 1994 and references cited therein).

Time (YBP*)	Event
$>1.5 \times 10^4$	Access to Southern Rockies by Cordilleran and Boreo-Cordilleran species, including tool-and fire-using subsistence-hunters: *Homo sapiens.*
1.5×10^4	Recession of Pinedale ice; human-influenced (?) extinction of Pleistocene megafauna.
1.9×10^2	Arrival of Euro-American occasional, itinerant, market-driven hunters; near-extirpation of beaver and perhaps other native species.
1.4×10^2	Pre-industrial permanent Euro-American settlement; establishment of extractive, market-driven exploitation of native species and substrates; creation of artificial habitat for bats and other cavernicolous species.
1.0×10^2	Permanent, industrial settlement; trans-mountain water diversion, export-market-driven, industrial-scale mining of substrates and overburden (forests = wildlife habitat); suppression of wildfire; deliberate eradication of keystone wildlife species (bison, grizzly bear, gray wolf); seasonal amenity-driven migration (summer visitors).
5×10^1	Re-invention of skiing; seasonal (summer and winter visitors) and year-around, amenity-driven settlement.

* Years before present

tial, and commercial development. Each has its impact and each takes its toll. Heterogeneity is native to landscapes. What is the fundamental difference between the islands in a block-cut forest and the meadows or the mountain-tops? Between a beaver pond high on the Williams Fork and the Williams Fork Reservoir downstream? Between a game trail and National Forest Trail 401? Between a riparian woodland corridor along a rushing stream and a riparian woodland corridor along a leaky diversion canal? Holes are holes; is there a fundamental distinction between the Roberts Tunnel and Groaning Cave? Between the Bobtail Mine and Cave of the Winds (before the lights came on— that is)?

Natural and cultural landscape change do not necessarily differ in scale. There must be far more land in avalanche tracks than in ski areas in the Southern Rockies. The 1997 Zirkel Ridge Blowdown in Colorado's Park Range leveled an area the size of Boulder. Scale is not the issue. Rather, the difference between natural and cultural change often is as simple (and as complex) as asking, "How old was the solar energy that powered the change?" The distinction is between contemporary solar flux (moving water or wind or stored in biomass living or dead for at most hundreds to a few thousands of years) and fossil solar energy, photons fixed by photosynthesizers tens to hundreds of millions of years ago.

If we glance at Table 21.2 and mentally fill in the blanks with details of places we know, it is obvious that—save for some Tertiary volcanism and some faulting here and there—landscape change for most of the time since the Laramide Revolution has been powered by contemporary solar flux. The gods were annoyed when Prometheus stole their fire, but all that Prometheus and his Paleolithic heirs burned for a half million years was the likes of forests, grasslands, and buffalo chips. Culturally kindled fire obviously set people apart from all other products of evolution, but in itself it was a modest enough step. The impact of people remained on a biological scale; our forebears were burning biomass accumulated across at most a few recent generations.

It was only a couple of hundred years ago—when fire was set to fossil carbon compounds—that we humans made the quantum leap to unnatural and undisputed dominance. With the exploitation of fossil fuels, we assumed dominion over landscapes on a geological scale. The Industrial Revolution arrived late in the Southern Rockies. The Union Pacific reached Cheyenne in 1866 and the Denver Pacific arrived in Denver in 1870. However, with the arrival of coal-fired transportation and excavation, people could do work on a new scale, a geological scale, no longer constrained by mere manpower, horsepower, water power, wind power, or other manifestations of contemporary solar energy. Fossil fuels changed the rules; they have produced a change in the kind of impact, not just in the degree. Fossil fuels are the unnatural act.

Fossil fuels are finite, of course. Environmental degradation powered by fossil fuels is a self-limiting process. But we can do better than simply wait for the inevitable thermodynamic end of the binge. We can choose. Fossil fuels give us power, freedom. Freedom implies responsibility. The power to destroy ecosystem processes implies a responsibility not to. "We find ourselves, for better or worse, business agents for the cosmic process of evolution" (Huxley 1953).

Scales of Conservation. The landscape scale not only helps us to define the problem; it helps us to visualize the solution. Because they are extensive enough to accommodate biotic diversity and processes of change, landscapes are the right scale for conservation (Forman 1995). A number of agencies and nongovernmental organizations are beginning to recognize this truth and to invest in it. We witness today new scales of conservation (see The Nature Conservancy 1997) and fund-raising (consider the Great Outdoors Colorado Trust Fund), and in the Southern Rockies and elsewhere in the West, we are beginning to move from success to significance. We are beginning to have a healing impact on the eagle's-eye view and even on the view from space. Intact, functioning landscapes representative of the diverse dynamic of bioregions may even provide the biota with a buffer against anthropogenic global climatic change (Wessman 1992, Tinus 1995, Pitelka et al. 1997). "Landscapes and regions are exactly the right scale for sustainability. . . . Large area is a surrogate for long term" (Forman 1995). We are not merely saving species, however important that might be. We are saving opportunities for the continued evolution of species and ecosystems, saving the ecological theater for the continuation of the evolutionary play (Hutchinson 1965).

Emerging Principles. To base conservation at the level of landscapes clearly is preferable to thinking about one species at a time. Species occur as symbiotic assemblages, guilds, and communities. Ecosystems are dynamic because physical conditions change and because the response of species surely is idiosyncratic, because their genetic information is unique.

The idea that ecology and conservation biology can be purely rational is perhaps untenable and probably harmful. Esthetics and ethics taint the logic of conservation science in productive ways. Preservation of long-term ecological and evolutionary opportunities at the expense of short-term economic gains is essentially a commitment to vision and values. That having been said, some rational principles of wildlife conservation for the Southern Rockies are emerging from landscape and ecosystem ecology and conservation ecology (e.g., Risser 1987, Lidicker 1995, Christiansen et al. 1996, Bowers 1997, Duerksen et al. 1997).

Where can management be effective? We are wise to target what we can control. The larger and smaller scales of time and space (Tables 21.1 and 21.3) are the most difficult to predict, and I can imagine practical souls being impatient with the nearly infinite and the nearly infinitesimal, supposing them to be negligibly large or small. But the very large and the very small are not mere decoration. We need them for perspective. The extremes of space and time bracket the essence and limits of things here on the Home Planet. Earth is round and therefore finite. Carbon forms covalent bonds, informed in living systems by genetic "know-how." Populations grow. Growth rates of the human population in the Southern Rockies are about the same as those in sub-Saharan Africa. Populations of bacteria cultured at mammalian body temperatures may double every 30 minutes; "minute" does not mean negligible (Hardin 1972). Simple geometry and simple physics lead inexorably to intractably complex biology. "It is time for biologists to face squarely the complexity of the natural world we attempt to interpret" (Johnson and Jehl 1993).

Next Steps. I am going to suppress an instinct to make gratuitous suggestions for further research. First, the list could be immense; most things about most biosystems are unknown (although our profound ignorance should not obscure the adequacy of our understanding). Also, I envision the obvious criticism of special pleading: researchers always list needs for further research, lists that represent job security. Further, there are plenty of wise lists of opportunities for research (e. g., Chew 1978, Billings 1979, Soulé and Kohm 1989, Forman 1995, Freemark et al. 1995, Lidicker 1995, Bowers 1997).

The most important reason to avoid listing research needs is the possibility that policy makers will use a list of suggestions for research not as opportunities for deeper understanding but as pretexts to do nothing, to wait for comprehensive right answers. These leaders must be reminded repeatedly of related fallacies: first, the fiction that time and research support can provide comprehensive knowledge; and second, the illusion that comprehensive knowledge is necessary for action. We are largely ignorant, to be sure, but we surely know more than enough to begin to do some things right. For one thing, we know that Hardin (1972) was right: we can't do nothing; because John Muir was right: everything *is* hitched to everything else. If we wait until we understand it, we will never get it saved. Not to act is a strong choice. We do not need more data to get started in the right direction; we need more vision and more resolve.

What does a landscape perspective tell us about conservation of wildlife in the Southern Rocky Mountains? That we need to understand the bioregion whole—the landscapes, the patches, the populations, the symbioses, the history. We are incompetent severally or collectively to do that. Fragmentation is not just pattern, but process. We three-dimensional organisms need to simplify multidimensional realities even to approach understanding. In our mere linear minds we must hold space constant to observe change over time. We must hold time constant to observe change over space. Given time's arrow, true experiments simply are not feasible. We had better be comfortable with uncertainty, ignorance, uncontrolled experiment, and successive approximation. The serious scientist may be annoyed by these insistent realities; the naturalist, however—perhaps inspired by the revealing re-photography of Johnson (1987) or Veblen and Lorenz (1991)— might well imagine the landscape into motion, run the mental macroscope ahead a few hundred years or so, begin to feel the dynamic and the complexity and raise the real questions, and then get on with the practical scientific and political jobs at hand.

LITERATURE CITED

Armstrong, D. M. 1972. Distribution of mammals in Colorado. *Monograph, University of Kansas Museum of Natural History* 3: 1–415.

Armstrong, D. M. 1977. Ecological distribution of small mammals in the Upper Williams Fork Basin, Grand County, Colorado. *Southwestern Naturalist* 22: 289–304.

Armstrong, D. M. 1987. *Rocky Mountain mammals, a handbook of mammals of Rocky Mountain National Park and vicinity, revised edition.* Colorado Associated University Press, Boulder, Colorado, USA.

Armstrong, D. M., J. C. Halfpenny, and C. H. Southwick. *In press.* Vertebrates of Niwot Ridge. *In* W. Bowman and T. Seastedt, editors. *Structure and function of an alpine ecosystem: Niwot Ridge.* Oxford University Press, New York, New York, USA.

Bailey, R. G. 1995. Map, 1:7,500,000 *in Description of the ecoregions of the United States,* 2nd edition revised. Miscellaneous Publications, USDA Forest Service 1391: 1–108.

Bailey, V. 1932. Mammals of New Mexico. *North American Fauna* 53: 1–412.

Benedict, A. D. 1991. *A Sierra Club naturalist's guide, the Southern Rockies.* Sierra Club Books, San Francisco, California, USA.

Billings, W. D. 1979. High mountain ecosystems, evolution, structure, operation, and maintenance. Pages 97–125 *in* P. J. Webber, editor. *High altitude geoecology.* Westview Press, Boulder, Colorado, USA.

Bissonette, J. A., and S. Broekhuizen. 1995. *Martes* populations as indicators of habitat spatial patterns: the need for a multi-scale approach. Pages 95–121 *in* W. Z. Lidicker, Jr., editor. *Landscape approaches in mammalian ecology and conservation.* University of Minnesota Press, Minneapolis, Minnesota, USA.

Bowers, M. A. 1997. Mammalian landscape ecology. *Journal of Mammalogy* 78: 997–998.

Brown, J. H. 1971. Mammals on mountaintops: nonequilibrium insular biogeography. *American Naturalist* 105: 467–478.

Cary, M. 1911. A biological survey of Colorado. *North American Fauna* 33: 1–256.

Cary, M. 1917. Life-zone investigations in Wyoming. *North American Fauna* 42: 1–95.

Chew, R. M. 1978. The impact of small mammals on ecosystem structure and function. Pages 167–180 *in* D. P. Snyder, editor. *Populations of small mammals under natural conditions.* Special Publications Series, Pymatuning Laboratory of Ecology, University of Pittsburgh, Pittsburgh, Pennsylvania, USA.

Christiansen, N. L., A. M. Bartuska, J. H. Brown, S. Carpenter, C. D'Antonio, R. Francis, J. F. Franklin, J. A. MacMahon, R. J. Noss, D. J. Parsons, C. H. Peterson, M. G. Turner, and R. G. Woodmansee. 1996. The report of the Ecological Society of America Committee on the scientific basis for ecosystem management. *Ecological Applications* 6: 665–691.

Duerksen, C. J., D. L. Elliott, N. T. Hobbs, E. Johnson, and J. R. Miller. 1997. Habitat protection planning: where the wild things are. Report, Planning Advisory Service, American Planning Association, 470/471: 1–82.

Fitzgerald, J. P., C. A. Meaney, and D. M. Armstrong. 1994. *Mammals of Colorado.* Denver Museum of Natural History, Denver, and University Press of Colorado, Niwot, Colorado, USA.

Forman, R.T.T. 1995. *Land mosaics, the ecology of landscapes and regions.* Cambridge University Press, Cambridge, UK.

Freemark, K. E., J. B. Dunning, S. J. Hejl, and J. R. Probst. 1995. A landscape ecology perspective for research, conservation, and management. Pages 381–427 *in* T. E. Martin and D. M. Finch, editors. *Ecology and management of neotropical migratory birds.* Oxford University Press, New York, New York, USA.

Gregg, R. E. 1964. Distribution of the ant genus *Formica* in the mountains of Colorado. Pages 59–69 *in* H. G. Rodeck, editor. *Natural history of the Boulder area.* Leaflet, University of Colorado Museum, 13: 1–100.

Hafner, D. J., and R. M. Sullivan. 1995. Historical and ecological biogeography of Nearctic pikas (Lagomorpha: Ochotonidae). *Journal of Mammalogy* 76: 302–321.

Hammerson, G. A. 1982. *Amphibians and reptiles of Colorado.* Colorado Division of Wildlife, Denver, Colorado, USA.

Hansson, L. 1995. Development and application of landscape approaches in mammalian ecology. Pages 20–39 *in* W. Z. Lidicker, Jr., editor. *Landscape approaches in mammalian ecology and conservation.* University of Minnesota Press, Minneapolis, Minnesota, USA.

Hardin, G. 1972. *Exploring new ethics for survival, the voyage of the spaceship Beagle.* Viking, New York, New York, USA.

Hutchinson, G. E. 1965. *The ecological theater and the evolutionary play.* Yale University Press, New Haven, Connecticut, USA.

Huxley, J. 1953. *Evolution in action.* Harper and Brothers, New York, New York, USA.

Johnson, K. L. Rangeland through time: a rephotographic study of vegetation change in Wyoming 1870–1986. Miscellaneous Publications, Wyoming Agricultural Experiment Station, 50: 1–188.

Johnson, N. K., and J. H. Jehl, Jr. 1993. A century of avifaunal change in western North America: overview. *Studies in Avian Biology* 15: 1–3.

Knight, D. H. 1994. *Mountains and plains, the ecology of Wyoming landscapes.* Yale University Press, New Haven, Connecticut, USA.

Leopold, A. S. 1933. *Game management.* Charles Scribners' Sons, New York, New York, USA.

Lidicker, W. Z., Jr. 1995. The landscape concept: something old, something new. Pages 3–19 *in* W. Z. Lidicker, Jr., editor. *Landscape approaches in mammalian ecology and conservation.* University of Minnesota Press, Minneapolis, Minnesota, USA.

Lindsay, S. J. 1987. Geographic size and non-size variation in Rocky Mountain *Tamiasciurus hudsonicus:* significance in relation to Allen's rule and vicariant biogeography. *Journal of Mammalogy* 68: 39–48.

Marr, J. W. 1961. Ecosystems of the east slope of the Front Range in Colorado. University of Colorado Studies, *Series in Biology* 8: 1–134.

McHarg, I. L. 1969. *Design with nature.* Doubleday/Natural History Press. Garden City, New York, USA.

Merriam, C. H. 1890. Results of a biological survey of the San Francisco Mountain region and Desert of the Little Colorado in Arizona, I. General results with special reference to the geographical and vertical distribution of species. *North American Fauna* 3: 5–34.

Odum, E. P. 1971. *Fundamentals of ecology,* 3rd edition. W. B. Saunders, Philadelphia, Pennsylvania, USA.

Pitelka, L. F., and the Plant Migration Workshop Group. 1997. Plant migration and climate change. *American Scientist* 85: 464–473.

Riebsame, W. E., H. Gosnell, and D. Theobald, editors. 1997. *Atlas of the new West, portrait of a changing region.* Norton, New York, New York, USA.

Risser, P. G. 1987. Landscape ecology: state of the art. Pages 3–13 *in* M. G. Turner, editor. *Landscape heterogeneity and disturbance.* Springer-Verlag, New York, New York, USA.

Schaefer, J. 1992. *Conversations with a pocket gopher and other outspoken neighbors.* Capra Press, Santa Barbara, California, USA.

Soulé, M. E., and K. A. Kohm. 1989. *Research priorities for conservation biology.* Island Press, Washington, D. C., USA.

Sullivan, R. M. 1996. Genetics, ecology, and conservation of montane populations of Colorado chipmunks (*Tamias quadrivittatus*). *Journal of Mammalogy* 77: 951–975.

The Nature Conservancy. 1997. Designing a geography of hope, guidelines for ecoregion-based conservation in The Nature Conservancy. Arlington, Virginia, USA.

Tinus, R. W., technical editor. 1995. Interior West Global Change Workshop, April 25–27, 1995, Fort Collins, Colorado. General Technical Report, USDA Forest Service RM-GTR–262.

Turner, M. G. 1987. *Landscape heterogeneity and disturbance.* Springer-Verlag, New York, New York, USA.

Turner, M. G. 1989. Landscape ecology: the effect of pattern on process. *Annual Review of Ecology and Systematics* 20: 171–198.

Tyler, D. 1992. *The last water hole in the West, the Colorado-Big Thompson Project and the Northern Colorado Water Conservancy District.* University Press of Colorado, Niwot, Colorado, USA.

Veblen, T. T., and D. C. Lorenz. 1991. *The Colorado Front Range, a century of ecological change.* University of Utah Press, Salt Lake City, Utah, USA.

Weber, W. A. 1965. Plant geography in the Southern Rocky Mountains. Pages 453–

468 *in* H. E. Wright, Jr., and D. G. Frey, editors. *The Quaternary of the United States*. Princeton University Press, Princeton, New Jersey, USA.

Wessman, C. A. 1992. Spatial scales and global change: bridging the gap from plots to GMC grid cells. *Annual Review of Ecology and Systematics* 23: 175–200.

Whittaker, R. H. 1975. *Communities and ecosystems*, 2nd edition. Macmillan, New York, New York, USA.

List of Scientific Names

Mammals

Abert's squirrel	*Sciurus aberti*
American badger	*Taxidea taxus*
American bison	*Bos bison*
American marten	*Martes americana*
American pika	*Ochotona princeps*
Big Horn Mountain least chipmunk	*Tamias minimus confinis*
Big Horn Mountain pika	*Ochotona princeps obscura*
Big Horn Mountain snowshoe hare	*Lepus americanus seclusus*
Bighorn sheep	*Ovis canadensis*
Black bear	*Ursus americanus*
Black Hills red squirrel	*Tamiasciurus hudsonicus dakotensis*
Black-tailed prairie dog	*Cynomys ludovicianus*
Bobcat	*Lynx rufus*
Brown bear	*Ursus arctos*
Canada lynx	*Lynx canadensis*
Common water shrew	*Sorex palustris*
Cougar	*Felis concolor*
Coyote	*Canis latrans*
Deer mouse	*Peromyscus maniculatus*
Dusky shrew	*Sorex monticolus*
Elk	*Cervus elaphus*
Fisher	*Martes pennanti*
Florida Panther	*Felis concolor*
Gray fox	*Urocyon cinereoargenteus*
Gray wolf	*Canis lupus*
Grizzly bear	*Ursus arctos*
Key deer	*Odocoileus virginianus*
Least chipmunk	*Tamias minimus*
Lemming	*Dicrostonyx* spp.
Long-tailed vole	*Microtus longicaudus*
Long-tailed weasel	*Mustela frenata*
Marmot	*Marmota* spp.
Masked shrew	*Sorex cinereus*
Meadow vole	*Microtus pennsylvanicus*
Montane vole	*Microtus montanus*
Moose	*Alces alces*

Mountain goat	*Oreamnos americanus*
Mountain lion	*Felis concolor*
Mule deer	*Odocoileus hemionus*
Muskox	*Ovibos moschatus*
Northern flying squirrel	*Glaucomys sabrinus*
Pine marten	*Martes americana*
Pine squirrel	*Tamiasciurus hudsonicus*
Pocket gopher	*Thomomys* spp.
Pronghorn	*Antilocapra americana*
Red fox	*Vulpes vulpes*
Red squirrel	*Tamiasciurus hudsonicus*
Rocky Mountain elk	*Cervus elaphus*
Silver-haired bat	*Lasionycteris noctivagans*
Snowshoe hare	*Lepus americanus*
Southern red-backed vole	*Clethrionomys gapperi*
Striped skunk	*Mephitis mephitis*
Vole	*Clethrionomys* spp.
Water vole	*Microtus rechardsoni*
Weasel	*Mustela* spp.
Western heather vole	*Phenacomys intermedius*
Western jumping mouse	*Zapus princeps*
White-tailed deer	*Odocoileus virginianus*
Wolverine	*Gulo gulo*
Wyoming ground squirrel	*Citellus richardsoni*
Yellow-bellied marmot	*Marmota flaviventris*

Birds

American crow	*Corvus brachyrhynchos*
American robin	*Turdus migratorius*
Black-backed woodpecker	*Picoides arcticus*
Blue jay	*Cyanocitta cristata*
Brewer's blackbird	*Euphagus cyanocephalus*
Broad-tailed hummingbird	*Selasphorus platycercus*
Brown creeper	*Certhia americana*
Brown-headed cowbird	*Molothrus ater*
Cassin's finch	*Carpodacus cassinii*
Chipping sparrow	*Spizella passerina*
Clark's nutcracker	*Nucifraga columbiana*
Common nighthawk	*Chordeiles minor*
Common raven	*Corvus corax*
Cordilleran flycatcher	*Empidonax occidentalis*
Dark-eyed junco	*Junco hyemalis*
Evening grosbeak	*Coccothraustes vespertinus*
Golden-crowned kinglet	*Regulus satrapa*
Gray jay	*Perisoreus canadensis*

Green-tailed towhee	*Pipilo chlorurus*
Hairy woodpecker	*Picoides villosus*
Hammond's flycatcher	*Empidonax hammondii*
Hermit thrush	*Catharus guttatus*
House wren	*Troglodytes aedon*
Japanese quail	*Coturnix coturnix*
Mexican spotted owl	*Strix occidentalis*
Mountain bluebird	*Sialia currucoides*
Mountain chickadee	*Parus gambeli*
Mourning dove	*Zenaida macroura*
Northern flicker	*Colaptes auratus*
Northern goshawk	*Accipiter gentilis*
Northern spotted owl	*Strix occidentalis*
Olive-sided flycatcher	*Contopus borealis*
Ovenbird	*Seiurus aurocapillus*
Pine grosbeak	*Pinicola enucleator*
Pine siskin	*Carduelis pinus*
Pygmy nuthatch	*Sitta pygmaea*
Red-breasted nuthatch	*Sitta canadensis*
Red crossbill	*Loxia curvirostra*
Ruby-crowned kinglet	*Regulus calendula*
Steller's jay	*Cyanocitta stelleri*
Swainson's thrush	*Catharus ustulatus*
Three-toed woodpecker	*Picoides tridactylus*
Townsend's solitaire	*Myadestes townsendi*
Tree swallow	*Tachycineta bicolor*
Veery	*Catharus fuscescens*
Vesper sparrow	*Pooecetes gramineus*
Violet-green swallow	*Tachycineta thalassina*
Warbling vireo	*Vireo gilvus*
Western tanager	*Piranga ludoviciana*
White-breasted nuthatch	*Sitta carolinensis*
White-crowned sparrow	*Zonotrichia leucophrys*
Williamson's sapsucker	*Sphyrapicus thyroideus*
Wilson's warbler	*Wilsonia pusilla*
Yellow-rumped warbler	*Dendroica coronata*

Reptiles

Rattlesnake	*Crotalus* spp.

Insects

Bark beetle	*Dendroctonus* spp.
Mountain pine beetle	*Dendroctonus ponderosae*
Spruce beetle	*Dendroctonus rufipennis*
Western spruce budworm	*Choristoneura occidentalis*
Douglas-fir bark beetle	*Dendroctonus pseudotsugae*

Vegetation

Alpine timothy	*Phleum alpinum*
Alsike clover	*Trifolium hybridum*
Annual bluegrass	*Poa annua*
Beardtongue	*Penstemon virens*
Bigflower cinquefoil	*Potentilla fissa*
Big sagebrush	*Artemisia tridentata*
Birch	*Betula* spp.
Bitterbrush	*Purshia tridentata*
Blue spruce	*Picea pungens*
Blue wildrye	*Elymus glaucus*
Bristlecone pine	*Pinus aristata*
Buffalo-berry	*Shepherdia canadensis*
Bur oak	*Quercus macrocarpa*
Canada bluegrass	*Poa compressa*
Common dandelion	*Taraxacum officianale*
Common juniper	*Juniperus communis*
Cottonwood	*Populus* spp.
Cristata	*Koeleria* spp.
Currant	*Ribes* spp.
Douglas-fir	*Pseudotsuga menziesii*
Drummond's rockcress	*Arabis drummondii*
Drummond's rush	*Juncus drummondii*
Dwarf huckleberry	*Vaccinium scoparium*
Dwarf mistle-toe	*Arceuthobium* spp.
Engelmann spruce	*Picea engelmannii*
Fescue	*Festuca* spp.
Gambel oak	*Quercus gambelii*
Geranium	*Geranium* spp.
Golden banner	*Thermopsis divaricarpa*
Groundsel	*Senecio* spp.
Heartleaf arnica	*Arnica cordifolia*
Juniper	*Juniperus* spp.
Kentucky bluegrass	*Poa pratense*
Kinnikinnik	*Arctostaphylos uva-ursi*
Limber pine	*Pinus flexilis*
Lodgepole pine	*Pinus contorta*
Mountain mahogany	*Cercocarpus montanus*
Orchardgrass	*Dactylis glomerata*
Oregon-grape	*Mahonia repens*
Paper birch	*Betula papyrifera*
Penstemon	*Penstemon* spp.
Pinon pine	*Pinus edulis*
Poa	*Poa* spp.
Ponderosa pine	*Pinus ponderosa*

Pussytoes	*Antennaria* spp.
Quaking aspen	*Populus tremuloides*
Red sandspurry	*Spergularia rubra*
Rhubarb	*Rheum rhaponticum*
Rocky Mountain juniper	*Juniperus scopulorum*
Rough bentgrass	*Agrostis scabra*
Ryegrass	*Lolium* spp.
Sagebrush	*Artemisia* spp.
Saskatoon serviceberry	*Amelanchier alnifolia*
Serviceberry	*Amelanchier* spp.
Shrubby cinquefoil	*Pentaphylloides* spp.
Skunkbrush	*Rhus trilobata*
Smooth brome	*Bromus inermis*
Snowberry	*Symphoricarpos occidentalis*
Spreading groundsmoke	*Gayophytum diffusum*
Stonecrop	*Sedum stenopetalum*
Subalpine fir	*Abies lasiocarpa*
Thinleaf alder	*Alnus incana*
Thistle	*Cirsium* spp.
Timothy	*Phleum pratense*
Trisetum	*Trisetum* spp.
Western pearlyeverlasting	*Anaphalis margaritacea*
White clover	*Trifolium repens*
White fir	*Abies concolor*
White spruce	*Picea glauca*
Willow	*Salix* spp.
Wood's rose	*Rosa woodsii*

REFERENCES

American Ornithologists' Union, Committee on Classification and Nomenclature. 1983. *Check-list of North American birds.* Sixth edition. American Ornithologists' Union, Allen Press, Inc., Lawrence, Kansas, USA.

Arnett, R. H. 1997. *American insects: a handbook of the insects of America north of Mexico.* The Sandhill Crane Press, Inc. Gainesville, Florida, USA.

Behler, J. L., and F. W. King. 1979. *The Audubon Society field guide to North American reptiles and amphibians.* Alfred A. Knopf, Inc., New York, New York, USA.

Burt, W. H., and R. P. Grossenheider. 1980. *A field guide to the mammals of North America north of Mexico.* Third edition. The Peterson Field Guide Series. Houghton Mifflin, Boston, Massachusetts, USA.

Fitzgerald, J. P., C. A. Meaney, and D. M. Armstrong. 1994. *Mammals of Colorado.* Denver Museum of Natural History and University Press of Colorado, Niwot, Colorado, USA.

Hall, E. R. 1981. *The mammals of North America.* Volume 1. Second edition. John Wiley and Sons, New York, New York, USA.

Jones, C., R. S. Hoffmann, D. W. Rice, M. D. Engstrom, R. D. Bradley, D. J. Schmidly, C. A. Jones, and R. J. Baker. 1997. Revised checklist of North American mammals north of Mexico, 1997. *Occasional Papers Museum Texas Tech University* 173: 1–19.

United States Department of Agriculture, Natural Resources Conservation Service (USDA, NRCS). 1997. The PLANTS database. (http://plants.usda.gov). National Plant Data Center, Baton Rouge, Louisiana, USA.

Weber, W. A. 1976. *Rocky Mountain Flora*. Colorado Associated University Press, Boulder, Colorado, USA.

Metric to English Conversions

When You Know	Multiply By	To Find Length
Length		
millimeters (mm)	0.04	inches
centimeters (cm)	0.40	inches
meters (m)	3.30	feet
meters (m)	1.10	yards
kilometers (km)	0.60	miles
Area		
square meters (m^2)	1.20	square yards (yd^2)
square kilometers (km^2)	0.40	square miles (mi^2)
hectares (ha)	2.50	acres
Temperature		
Celsius (C)	9/5 (C) + 32	Fahrenheit (F)

About the Contributors

GREGORY H. APLET is a forest ecologist in The Wilderness Society's Denver office, where he analyzes ecological aspects of federal land management policy. Most of his work has focused on ecosystem management and the conservation of biological diversity and forest ecosystem health. His research includes studies of the dynamics of Rocky Mountain and Hawaiian forests, the ecology of biological invasions, and the conservation of biological diversity.

DAVID M. ARMSTRONG is a professor of environmental, population, and organismic biology at the University of Colorado–Boulder, where he has taught since 1971. He is the author or co-author of several books and numerous articles on mammals and habitats of western interior North America.

WILLIAM L. BAKER is a professor of geography at the University of Wyoming, Laramie. His major research interest is in landscape ecology, particularly the spatial ecology of natural and human disturbances.

GARY P. BEAUVAIS received his Ph.D. in 1997 from the Department of Zoology and Physiology, University of Wyoming. Currently, he is the Heritage Zoologist for the Wyoming Natural Diversity Database, where he is continuing his research on the distribution and conservation of fauna in the Rocky Mountain West.

STEVEN W. BUSKIRK is a professor of zoology and physiology at the University of Wyoming where he teaches mammalogy and conservation biology. His research interests center on the ecology and conservation of mammals, especially carnivorans. He and his wife, Beth, and son, Reid, enjoy hiking, travel, and movies.

MICHAEL F. CARTER is the Executive Director of the Colorado Bird Observatory, a bird conservation organization he founded in 1988. His research interests generally tend toward topics that directly contribute to the conservation of birds and their habitats. He is a past chairperson of the West Working Group of Partners in Flight, past president of Colorado Field Ornithologists, and can't think of a better place to work.

GREGORY K. DILLON is a graduate student in the Department of Geography and Recreation at the University of Wyoming. He is studying edge effects associated with roads in Rocky Mountain forests.

M. LISA FLOYD studied botany at the University of Hawai'i and environmental biology at the University of Colorado. Her research interests include the ecology and fire history of the semi-arid Four Corners landscape. She is a professor of environmental studies at Prescott College, Prescott, Arizona.

SCOTT W. GILLIHAN is the Forested Ecosystems Program Coordinator for the Colorado Bird Observatory. His current research interests center on pattern and process in forested landscapes as they relate to the distribution and breeding success of birds and the composition of forest bird communities.

DAVID D. HANNA studied environmental education at Antioch University. He is a lecturer of environmental studies at Prescott College, Prescott, Arizona. His research includes applications of GIS and remote sensing to vegetation mapping, forest fragmentation, and fire studies on the Colorado Plateau.

ANDREW J. HANSEN is an associate professor in the Biology Department at Montana State University. His research focuses on the linkages between natural disturbance, landscape patterns, and vertebrate communities, with particular emphasis on landscape management. His current studies examine interactions between biodiversity and human land use in the Greater Yellowstone Ecosystem.

ROBERT B. KEITER is the Wallace Stegner Professor of Law and Director of the Wallace Stegner Center for Land, Resources, and the Environment at the University of Utah. His books include *The Greater Yellowstone Ecosystem: Redefining America's Wilderness Heritage, Reclaiming the Native Home of Hope: Community, Ecology, and the West,* and *Visions of the Grand Staircase–Escalante: Examining Utah's Newest National Monument.* He is also the author of numerous book chapters and journal articles on natural resources law and policy.

DENNIS H. KNIGHT is an ecologist with over 30 years of experience in the Rocky Mountain region, and is the author of *Mountains and Plains: The Ecology of Wyoming Landscapes.*

RICHARD L. KNIGHT is a professor of wildlife conservation at Colorado State University, Fort Collins, Colorado. His books include *A New Century for Natural Resources Management, Wildlife and Recreationists, Stewardship Across Boundaries,* and *The Essence of Aldo Leopold.* His research interests deal with land-use changes on public and private lands in the West.

JONATHAN F. LOWSKY is the wildlife biologist for Pitkin County, Colorado. He received a B.S. in Economics from Hobart College in 1985 and a M.S. in Wildlife Biology from Colorado State University in 1996. He is dedicated to landscape level protection of native biological diversity and is currently studying the effects of rural development on ecological communities.

JEFFERY S. REDDERS earned a B.S. in natural resources management at the University of Wisconsin in Madison. He is the ecologist for the San Juan National Forest in Durango, Colorado. His areas of expertise include rare plants, research natural areas, wetlands, riparian ecosystems, and soils.

WILLIAM A. REINERS is an ecosystem ecologist who uses remote sensing and GIS methods to understand cross-landscape interactions of ecological processes.

WILLIAM H. ROMME has a Ph.D. in botany from the University of Wyoming, and is a professor of biology at Fort Lewis College in Durango, Colorado. His research interests are in vegetation, fire, and landscape ecology of the Rocky Mountain region.

JAY J. ROTELLA is an associate professor in the Biology Department at Montana State University. His research focuses on the population ecology of birds, compares population dynamics in natural and human-disturbed settings, and emphasizes applications of findings to conservation. His current studies involve a variety of species and ecosystems in the Rocky Mountains and prairies.

BONNIE RUEFENACHT received her Ph.D. from Colorado State University in 1998 after completing her study of responses of forest bird communities to natural and forest clear-cut edge types. Her research interests involve landscape ecology and conservation biology. She currently lives in Salt Lake City, Utah.

DOUGLAS J. SHINNEMAN is a former graduate student of the Geography and Recreation Department at the University of Wyoming, Laramie. He is currently employed with the City of Boulder Division of Mountain Parks in Colorado.

FREDERICK W. SMITH is a professor of forest sciences at Colorado State University.

DAVID M. THEOBALD is a research associate at the Natural Resource Ecology Lab at Colorado State University. His research interests are in understanding patterns of landscape change, the consequences of development on wildlife habitat, and conservation planning in the Rocky Mountain West.

DANIEL B. TINKER is a Ph.D. student in the botany department at the University of Wyoming where he is studying the spatial dynamics of coarse woody debris in lodgepole pine ecosystems. His other research interests include disturbance and landscape ecology.

THOMAS T. VEBLEN received his Ph.D. in 1975 from the University of California at Berkeley, and he is currently a professor of geography at the University of Colorado in Boulder. Previously, he was on the faculty of the Forestry School of the Universidad Austral de Chile in Valdivia, Chile (1975–1979) and was a research scientist with the Forest Research Institute in Christchurch, New Zealand (1979–1981). He has conducted research on forest dynamics in Guatemala, Chile, New Zealand, Argentina, and the Colorado Rockies.

Index